THE KING'S SERVANTS

THE KING'S SERVANTS

The Civil Service
of Charles I

1625-1642

by

G. E. AYLMER

Routledge & Kegan Paul

LONDON

First published 1961
by Routledge & Kegan Paul Ltd.
Broadway House, Carter Lane, E.C.4.

Printed in Great Britain
by T. & A. Constable Ltd.
Hopetoun Street, Edinburgh

CONTENTS

v

CONTENTS

TABLES

TABLES

viii

ILLUSTRATIONS

ix

PREFACE

I HAVE tried to explain in the Introduction what my purpose has been in writing this book. I wish here to thank all those who have helped me in its preparation.

I am grateful to the Master and Fellows of Balliol College, Oxford, for having elected me to a Junior Research Fellowship, tenable for the years 1951-4, and particularly to my former Tutor, Mr Christopher Hill for having constantly stimulated and encouraged my interest in seventeenth-century history. I owe much to my former supervisor, Professor R. H. Tawney, who has given me a great deal of help and advice; I am also indebted to Professor Wallace Notestein for encouragement and several useful suggestions in the early stages of my research.

I am grateful to those who have helped me over sources and other points: including Professor L. W. Forster, Mr. G. Hammersley, Dr. G. L. Harriss, Professor E. Hughes, Canon J. S. Purvis, Mr. G. D. Squibb, Q.C., Mr. Lawrence Stone, Mr. A. F. Upton, Professor R. B. Wernham, Dr. Penry Williams, and Miss Jean S. Wilson, and to all the county archivists and others who have answered my queries about manuscripts in their custody.

I should also like to thank the staffs of all the libraries and record offices where I have worked while collecting material for this book: including the British Museum, the Public Record Office (especially Mr. H. N. Blakiston and Mr. E. K. Timings), the Literary Research department of Somerset House, the Institute of Historical Research, the Bodleian Library, Mr. V. Quinn of the Balliol College Library, the John Rylands Library, the Central Reference Library, and the University Arts Library in Manchester, the National Library of Wales, the County Record Offices of Bedfordshire, Berkshire (especially Mr. P. Walne), Buckinghamshire (especially Mr. E. J. Davis), Essex, Gloucestershire (especially Mr. I. E. Gray), Hampshire, Hertfordshire (especially Mr. J. R. L. Whitfield), Lancashire, Middlesex, and Northamptonshire (especially Mr. P. King), the Leeds and Sheffield City Libraries, the Dorchester Museum, the William Salt Library (Stafford), the Dagenham Borough Library, and the Minet Library (Brixton) and Miss W. D. Coates of the National Register of Archives.

I should like to thank the following for their hospitality, and for kindly allowing me to read and cite manuscripts in their custody

xi

and possession: Lord Brownlow, Mr. A. O. Elmhirst, Captain A. Fanshawe R.N. (retired), the late Major J. R. H. and Mr. C. Harley, Mr. H. B. Lenthall, and Mr. J. Salmon.

I am grateful to the Duke of Portland and the Trustees of the Chequers Trust for permission to reproduce pictures in their possession, and to the following for their help with the illustrations: Mrs. K. Hill, Mr. M. R. Holmes, Mr. Oliver Millar, Miss A. H. Scott Elliot, and the staff of the Print Room in the British Museum.

I am indebted to Mr. P. D. Marshall and Dr. E. B. Fryde for reading particular sections and making helpful comments. I am very deeply indebted to Mr. J. P. Cooper for reading chapters 2-7, and to Mr. D. H. Pennington for reading chapters 2-6; both suggested numerous improvements and saved me from many blunders.

I am of course entirely responsible for any mistakes which remain. I am especially aware that in parts of chapters 2 and 7 I have been discussing subjects on which I have no claim to expert knowledge; chapter 2 is intended chiefly for the non-specialist, to help to provide the background for chapters 3-6.

I wish to thank Miss M. Norquois and Mrs. J. Walmsley, who typed several of the chapters. I am immensely grateful to my wife for several readings of all the chapters, and a great deal of other help especially with the illustrations, the proofs, and the index.

Although its range may appear fairly narrow to some readers, this book covers a good deal of ground. And I have not included a bibliography, since to be comprehensive this would have to cover virtually the whole of English administrative history, as well as English history in general for the early and mid-seventeenth century, and I see no merit in 'select bibliographies'. I have however referred to a good many secondary authorities (as well as original sources), notably in chapters 2 and 7. Full titles are given the first time that any printed work or manuscript is cited, and after that abbreviated, but I hope recognizable ones. For printed books, place of publication is London, unless otherwise stated. After the first citation, Public Record Office documents are referred to only by the call-number of their class.

In quoting, I have tried to follow the original texts in all cases. But I have not preserved the original spelling, abbreviations, or punctuation, except where the sense or flavour of the quotation might otherwise be lost.

The 'Old Style' dating (that is the Julian Calendar) has been used throughout, except that the year has been taken to begin on the 1st January. In citing original sources, where the New Year is dated from the 25th March, I have used the form 1630/1 (i.e. to indicate the period 1 Jan. to 24 Mar. 1630 in contemporary usage, but 1 Jan. to 24 Mar. 1631 in ours).

G. E. AYLMER

February, 1960.

1

INTRODUCTION

SOME SUBJECTS in history suggest themselves for study, define their own scope and boundaries, and explain themselves. Others require definition and explanation. A biography of a great man or woman, the history of a nation, a dynasty, a war, or a revolution, belong in the first category. Many studies undertaken by historians today fall within the second; in these it is necessary for an author to say rather more about what he intends, and what he sees as the scope and purpose of his work, for there is no guarantee that either will be self-evident to the reader.

This book deals with the officials of the central government under King Charles I, from his accession in 1625 up to the eve of the Civil War in 1642. It is an attempt to describe the administration, and more particularly the men employed in it, in relation to the general character of Charles I's government, especially during the 1630's, and to the causes and significance of that government's overthrow; it also seeks to assess the place of that period in the evolution of bureaucracy and in the growth of the modern Civil Service. In pursuing these objectives, some account will first be given of the various institutions concerned, their structure, composition, and activities, and their relation to royal policy. An attempt will then be made to describe the men who staffed these institutions, by investigating their conditions of entry and service, their financial position, their social background and economic interests, and their political and religious affiliations.

A   1

This attempt to build up a composite portrait of a King's servant, or to be literal, several hundred portraits of King's servants, inevitably raises questions of historical method. The technique of collecting biographical information about large numbers of Members of Parliament in order to generalize about their characteristics is now well established, but the same has not been done for civil servants, at least not for any before the late nineteenth century. Many of King Charles I's servants, like the officials of any epoch, were quite obscure men, and were not of any historical importance as individuals. They are interesting, rather, because of their careers as officials and the part which they played in the administrative system. It must certainly be asked how far the collection of material about such men is likely to give a 'true' picture. The means by which they entered the King's service, the conditions under which they served, and the ways in which they were paid can be described with some confidence from the available evidence. But the social origins of the more obscure among them, and the attitude of almost all of them towards their work and towards the great issues of their time remain largely unknown. Thus there is an experimental aspect to this book; it may be that a method which has proved fruitful for the study of parliamentary history cannot profitably be applied to the study of administration, at least not in the seventeenth century.

However, the problem is not only a biographical one. The nature and purposes of government and of institutions constitute a subject for study in their own right. Indeed, there is a need for a fuller study of the actual workings of English government (as opposed to the men involved in it) than has been attempted here. Below the top level, the structure and operation of English administration have received little attention from students of seventeenth-century history. If anything new can be said about this, it may in turn contribute to a fuller understanding of English political history in the period leading up to the Revolution and the Civil Wars.

The choice of the years 1625-42 requires some explanation. It arose from an initial interest in the connexion between the Civil War and Interregnum (1642-60) and the development of English administration. The most cursory survey soon showed that this subject could only usefully be investigated after a study had been made of the administrative system and the men involved in it prior to these upheavals. To take 1625 as a starting point may seem to need more justification. The death of James I and the succession of his son

2

Charles I is not an event of great administrative significance. Indeed, considered in terms of institutional development, the whole period from the early years of Elizabeth I to the eve of the Civil War is a relatively static one. And it may well be that much of what is said here of Charles I's servants would be true of his father's, and even of Queen Elizabeth's. This, however, strengthens the case for taking a kind of cross-section at the end of the longer period (*c.* 1560-1640), partly to use it as a norm by which to measure the changes which followed. The years 1628 or 1629 to 1640 have more unity in political history, but for this very reason it is better not to choose dates which coincide with them; to do so might prejudice any conclusions as to the connexion between political and administrative changes. There is another elementary point, but one worth making. Whatever his faults, Charles I was no *roi fainéant*: the King's servants were his own, and not yet those of some institutional abstraction, the Crown or the State.

No similar study exists for comparative purposes. There is a wealth of fascinating material about the officials who served the thirteenth- and fourteenth-century kings in Tout's great book, *Chapters in the Administrative History of Mediaeval England*. But apart from a single lecture on 'The English Civil Service in the Fourteenth Century', Tout wrote nothing exclusively about the officials, as distinct from the institutions of government and the interplay between administration and politics. On the whole he was more concerned with the development of the central institutions than with the personnel of government.[1] And, although they include admirable biographical studies of individuals, the same is broadly true of both the recent books on English administration in the early and mid-Tudor period.[2] The two pioneering works on administration

---

[1] For one of the fullest and liveliest biographical sections see T. F. Tout, *Chapters* (Manchester, 1920-33), vol. V, ch. XVI, on the Clerks of the Privy Seal in the fourteenth century. This was probably one of the last things which Tout wrote before his death (*ibid.*, preface). See also Tout, *The Collected Papers*, vol. III (Manchester, 1934), 191-221, 'The English Civil Service in the Fourteenth Century'.

[2] W. C. Richardson, *Tudor Chamber Administration 1485-1547* (Baton Rouge, Louisiana, 1952); G. R. Elton, *The Tudor Revolution in Government* (Cambridge, 1953). See also Richardson, *Stephen Vaughan: Financial Agent of Henry VIII* (Baton Rouge, 1953), esp. ch. II.

in the early modern period, by Mrs. Higham and Professor Hughes,[1] also include much valuable biographical material, but neither is primarily a study of the officials themselves. A recent book on *The Development of the Treasury* in the later seventeenth century includes a study of its officials, chiefly from the institutional viewpoint and using almost exclusively the official records.[2] On the eighteenth century, despite the great amount of work which has been done on M.P.s, many of whom were also office-holders, only rather more specialized studies have been made of any administrative personnel who were not also M.P.s.[3]

The most comprehensive survey of English central government in the period 1558-1640 was written by an American historian, E. P. Cheyney, over forty years ago.[4] He gives an admirably clear picture of the work and structure of each department in the years 1588-1603; the outline survey in the second chapter of this book is certainly not intended to replace it. But Cheyney was not particularly concerned with the office-holders, their conditions of service, remuneration, social background, and role in politics. Dr. A. L. Rowse's study of the central government under Elizabeth I is less detailed than Cheyney's, but livelier and more accessible; it too does not deal directly with the officials.[5] Sir John Neale's lecture, 'The Elizabethan Political Scene', is the most suggestive work yet published on the realities of office-holding in the later sixteenth and earlier seventeenth centuries; but by its nature it is only an introduction to the subject.[6]

Many other books and articles, by historians dead and living, which bear on particular aspects of the subject, will be referred to in the chapters which follow. It must, however, be impossible for any

[1] F. M. G. Evans (Mrs. C. S. Higham), *The Principal Secretary of State . . . from 1558 to 1680* (Manchester, 1923); E. Hughes, *Studies in Administration and Finance 1558-1825: with special reference to the history of salt taxation in England* (Manchester, 1934).

[2] S. B. Baxter, *The Development of the Treasury 1660-1702* (1957), chs. 8-10.

[3] See particularly W. R. Ward, 'Some Eighteenth Century Civil Servants: the English Revenue Commissioners, 1754-98', *Eng. Hist. Rev.*, LXX (1955). 25-54.

[4] *A History of England from the Defeat of the Armada to the Death of Elizabeth*, vol. I (1914), chs. II-VIII.

[5] *The England of Elizabeth* (1950), esp. ch. VIII.

[6] J. E. Neale, 'The Elizabethan Political Scene', *Raleigh Lecture on History* (Brit. Acad., 1948).

student of history to acknowledge all his indebtedness. Historical study, it should not need to be said, is largely a collective endeavour; best of all can this be seen in the use historians make of the work of those who have gone before. If we manage to see further than our predecessors in any direction, it is indeed because we are pigmies standing upon the shoulders of giants. Among the living, it would be at once servile and presumptuous to particularize; but among the dead, it must be obvious that this book could never have been written but for the existence of S. R. Gardiner's *History of England*, covering the years 1603-42,[1] and Tout's *Chapters*.

The most that any historical writer can dare to hope is that his work will in turn be of some use to his successors as well as being a source of edification and entertainment for his contemporaries. In the eyes of posterity our attempts are destined, like those of earlier generations in our own eyes, to appear backward if not obsolete in technique, limited in sympathy and understanding, and—worst of all—either ineffably tedious or hopelessly prejudiced. Rare indeed is the historical wine which improves with keeping.

It is an accepted truism that the writings of all historians reflect in some measure the ideas and prejudices of their own times. And it is certainly difficult for a mid-twentieth-century Englishman to be confident of his own detachment when writing about government and society in seventeenth-century England. Consciously or unconsciously, his attitude towards present-day problems will affect his treatment of the subject in many different ways. For instance, an interest in administrative history is sometimes in itself regarded as evidence of a conservative bias. On such an assumption this book will probably appear no more than a justification of the established order projected back three hundred years. However, the author's intention is neither to defend nor to attack English government in the time of Charles I, but to try to explain some aspects of it rather more fully than has previously been done. To achieve this entails studying a relatively small number of people, most of whom were moderately well-to-do and some extremely wealthy. It does not involve detailed consideration of the majority of the population, the common people; but this does not indicate unawareness of their existence, their role in the economy, and the conditions under which they lived. Nor, because the author's purpose is explanatory and not polemical, does this imply disinterest in the constitutional, religious,

[1] All references are to the 10-vol. crown octavo edn.

5

and social conflicts of seventeenth-century England, or indifference towards their outcome.

The rise of bureaucracy, of professional, salaried Civil Services, is a prominent feature of modern European history. Even a fragmentary contribution to one chapter of this story may be of some help in understanding the place of bureaucracy in recent times and in the contemporary world. Bureaucracy is a common word today, its evils perhaps more often denounced than its nature and purposes understood. Further, the interpretation of its role in history occupies quite a central place in the ideological debate, by which historians, like the rest of mid-twentieth-century humanity, are divided.[1] Whatever the resolution of these debates, the evolution of bureaucracy needs to be better understood if we are to evaluate its present situation and its future prospects. One of the recurring themes of this book will be the consideration of how far and in what sense English government in the time of Charles I can be called bureaucratic; another will be the relation of this to political and social changes.

In the chapters which follow, these questions are approached from different angles: first by a general survey of the institutions of central government, intended mainly as a 'bird's eye view' for the non-specialist, and then by the four main chapters dealing with the royal officials from different aspects. In the concluding chapter the administrative system of Charles I's time is set in perspective against the long-run development of English government, and is compared with the systems in other European countries, particularly France. Finally, an attempt is made to assess the place of the officials and of office-holding in English seventeenth-century history.

Some of the subject-matter may seem abstruse, the details technical, obscure, and perhaps on the long view unimportant. But whatever may be true of some kinds of historical writing, a study like this does not allow of any short cuts. Little will be achieved without acquiring some grasp of detail, while at the same time keeping in mind the wider issues and implications. Nor need details be dull: they can often be more interesting than generalities, besides being less misleading.

[1] See Chapter 7, s. iii, pp. 453-63.

2

THE CENTRAL GOVERNMENT

i PROLOGUE

IT IS BOTH a paradox and a truism to say that early Stuart England was at one and the same time a 'much-governed' country and a country with very little government. It was an age, as every student knows, of detailed and widespread government controls over many aspects of social and economic life, yet there was no standing army, no proper police force, and by contemporary continental standards very little central bureaucracy. In the localities the will of the central government depended for its execution on the voluntary co-operation of a hierarchy of part-time, unpaid officials: Lord and Deputy Lieutenants, Sheriffs, Justices of the Peace, High and Petty Constables Overseers of the Poor, and Churchwardens.[1] Without their co-operation the central government was helpless: witness the failure in 1639-40 to collect Ship Money or to raise an efficient army against the Scots. Such is the traditional picture, and, although liable to be reduced to a caricature if too drastically over-simplified, it has stood up well to the rigours of modern research. Curiously enough, the resources of government at the centre seem more in need of re-appraisal than those in the country at large.

Behind the imposing façade of conciliar government—Privy Council, Star Chamber, High Commission, and the rest—again

[1] On local government see W. Notestein, *The English People on the Eve of Colonisation* (1954), chs. 17-20; W. B. Willcox, *Gloucestershire . . . 1590-1640* (New Haven, 1940), ch. 3.

7

familiar alike to the authors and the readers of the standard political and constitutional histories,[1] lay an obscure and little-known administrative structure. When this has been surveyed, it will be easier to keep in mind the resources at the disposal of the central government and to remember what institutions are being referred to when we discuss the officials in the chapters which follow.

The institutions which made up the government could be classified in a number of different ways. In this chapter they have been grouped as follows:

   (i) the Central Executive itself, comprising the individuals and departments concerned with administration proper: the King, the Secretaries of State, the Privy Council, and the subordinate officials responsible for in-coming and out-going communications, other than strictly judicial and financial ones, between Crown and people;

  (ii) the royal household, a whole family of departments, still in some respects not fully cut off from the rest of the central government (chronologically the household should come first, as the source from which all the other groups had originally developed);

 (iii) the revenue or finance departments, a well-defined group even though the biggest of them still had important non-financial duties;

 (iv) the other departments, concerned with defence, the coinage, and other aspects of the government's activity, not covered by those in the previous groups or in the next one;

  (v) lastly the law courts, of which some were also revenue departments, others—in effect—offshoots of the Central Executive, and one was a branch of the household.

Already two terms have been used which were unknown at the time, but this classification is chosen for our convenience and not because it is the way in which contemporaries would have seen the King's government. The name 'Central Executive' was not used then or subsequently, and is meant only as a convenient label for the controlling system inside the central government. The word 'department', later to become commonplace, is also in this sense an anachronism; it is used here of institutions other than courts of law.

[1] For example S. R. Gardiner, *History of England . . . 1603-42*, (1883-4, and 1884-90); D. L. Keir, *The Constitutional History of modern Britain 1485-1937* (3rd edn., 1948).

Contemporaries referred to an institution either as a 'court' or as a 'council', or, if neither of these designations fitted, simply as an 'office'; then, as now, an office could denote either a post held by a single individual or an institution.

At this stage it may also be well to try to explain what is meant by 'government' and 'administration'. This book is primarily a study of the administrators, the officers *below* the highest ranks. Privy Councillors and other great officers have been included because, as will become clear in the course of the inquiry, it would be artificial to leave them out altogether. But they will not be its primary concern. The famous names known to every reader of English history—Buckingham, Laud, Strafford, Pym, King Charles himself—will certainly come into the story, but they are not its central subject. Instead an attempt will be made to portray a large number of much obscurer men. The student of seventeenth-century history will find the names of other leading politicians—Manchester, Weston, Cottington, Vane, Secretary Coke, Windebank, and of other great magnates on the Council—the third and fourth Earls of Pembroke, Earl of Arundel and Surrey, the Marquis of Hamilton, the Duke of Lennox, the second Earl of Salisbury, the tenth Earl of Northumberland. Peers have not been excluded; but if they held office, with relatively few exceptions it was great office at the Privy Council level.

Administrators can be defined as officials below the level of those who helped to make policy, or at least of those who were meant to make it and were openly trying to do so, and above the menial levels of copying clerks, messengers, porters, and cleaners. At this stage it would be a mistake to try to be more specific. But whereas some distinction can be drawn between policy-makers and administrators, there was virtually no clear distinction between politicians and civil servants. All office-holders were the King's servants, and all were expected to support the Crown with equal fervour at all times. In practice there was often opposition to royal policy *within* the government, both at the ministerial level (in the Council), and at the administrative level (in the middling and lower ranks). As will be seen, apart from the Judges and Crown law officers remarkably few ministers or officials were ever dismissed for such opposition; indeed, as will be explained, many of them were all but irremovable.[1] Nor did contemporaries see anything unnatural in this. Only very

---

[1] See Chapter 3, s. iii.

gradually in the course of the eighteenth and earlier nineteenth centuries did the modern distinction emerge between 'non-political' offices which did not change hands with changes of ministry, and political ones which did. Since in Charles I's time there was not even a rudimentary distinction between 'political' and 'non-political' offices, it would not be surprising, on a modern analogy, to find quite sweeping purges of office-holders taking place when there was a major change of royal policy or when something like a new ministry was formed. So far from this happening, officials in seventeenth-century England on the whole enjoyed as much security of tenure as their 'non-political' descendants. The gradual emergence of the distinction between administrators and politicians is related to the evolution of 'ministries' in the modern sense, i.e. coherent groups of ministers with a common platform and policy who enter and leave office more or less as a group. It is also bound up with the struggle to exclude 'placemen', as a later generation came to describe permanent royal officials, from the House of Commons, and with the eventual disqualification of civil servants from taking any direct part in parliamentary politics. If pursued, these themes would lead far beyond the limits of this study.

For present purposes the distinction between politicians and administrators is therefore to be thought of more as a matter of seniority than of type. The contrast is between policy-makers, in the sense of the King's advisers in the Privy Council plus perhaps a few more like the Crown law officers and the senior Judges, and the executants of royal policy. Obviously there was an overlap: the Secretaries of State belong in both categories. The distinction may become clearer and more meaningful when it has been more fully illustrated.

The idea of 'policy' in the modern sense was scarcely recognized by the men of the early seventeenth century. The modern meaning of the word was not wholly unknown, but it was far from being the most usual.[1] This can be related to the fact that the King still ruled as well as reigned: not before the eighteenth century is it profitable to think of two (or more) distinct groups of politicians competing for royal and popular favour and parliamentary support, in order to win control of the government and to carry it on for agreed purposes. Until then the King chose his ministers on their individual merits and because of their usefulness to him. Except during the Interregnum,

[1] *Oxford English Dictionary.*

'policy' in our sense could only be changed by persuading the King to try new methods or take new advisers. And even in such cases policy should certainly not be thought of as being embodied in two or more sets of rival legislative programmes. In 1641 eight peers who had been amongst the leading critics of the Court and its policies the year before were made Privy Councillors, and two or three major offices were given to members of the same group.[1] But even then there was far from being a change of ministry. There remained no less than seventeen others whose membership of the Council dated from 1633 or earlier, and thus included the major part of the 'personal government'.

In practice, 'policies' in the modern sense are ascribed to individual statesmen and to groups of politicians in the seventeenth century. James I, Robert Cecil Earl of Salisbury, and Archbishop Bancroft are said to have tried to consolidate the monarchy, the nobility, and the church against the social and ideological forces which threatened them. Lionel Cranfield, who was active as a reformer from 1617 on, and was Lord Treasurer from 1621 to 1624, is described as having stood for a policy of peace and retrenchment. By contrast, Buckingham and Charles stood for a 'war' policy (1624-8); Lord Treasurer Weston stood for peace and retrenchment once more (1628-34). Laud and Strafford stood for 'Thorough', by which they meant more efficient government, and more effective central authority in church and state, alike in England, Ireland, and Scotland, even at the cost of trampling on men's customary and legal rights where these impeded the execution of their grand design. As regards their methods at least, Laud and Strafford were quite explicit in their letters to each other. Their ultimate objectives are less clear. They probably aimed at the reduction of parliament to servility rather than at its indefinite suppression; Laud probably did think in terms of some eventual compromise between the churches of England and Rome, but only—paradoxically—on terms which could never in fact have been acceptable to Rome. Finally the 'opposition' peers and the Commons' leaders of 1640-1—Pym, Hampden, Hyde, Falkland, and others—are spoken of as having stood for reforms in church and state, for

[1] New Councillors: Earls of Bedford, Bristol, Essex, Hertford, Warwick, Viscount Saye and Sele, Lords Mandeville, Savile; new office-holders: Saye and Sele, Master of the Wards; Oliver St. John, Solicitor-General; Essex, Lord Chamberlain as well as Captain-General; Bedford would probably have become Lord Treasurer but for his death in May 1641.

11

the overthrow of royal autocracy and of the Laudian church. Turning to more short-term considerations, the politicians of the 1620's and 1630's were often divided on questions of foreign policy; usually this meant a division into pro-French and pro-Spanish factions, though these were flexible and imprecise groupings.

Thus there may seem to be no lack of policies and policy-makers in early Stuart England. But the conscious purposes of statesmen cannot necessarily be inferred from the effects of their policies, as these appear either to their contemporaries or to posterity. This warning applies alike to James I and Salisbury and to Strafford and Laud.

Too much should not be read into the evidence. Seventeenth-century politicians, like other men of the time, were considerably less self-conscious or introspective than modern men. And they were even more pre-occupied than modern statesmen with the day-to-day management and manipulation of affairs, with the mechanics and the routine of politics. Some of the great peers probably took it almost for granted that they should hold high office and have a place in the Council; such men tended to follow the main stream of royal policy when they had the position and the influence which they felt to be their due, and to manœuvre and intrigue for them when they did not. This too may be helpful in trying to distinguish between politics and administration; for here was a powerful group in the government who were liable to be unenthusiastic or even hostile towards its policies. Yet its policies are the only features by which nowadays a government can be distinguished from a group (however admirable in themselves) of mere administrative caretakers. While it is obvious that the men of Charles I's time agreed and disagreed with passionate conviction on a whole range of great issues, it is thoroughly misleading to draw anything like the modern distinction between a political programme and its implementation, or to look for early Stuart counterparts of the Cabinet (and its parliamentary majority), and the permanent Civil Service. Nor was there any convention that officials ought not to share in decisions about policy; no doubt in practice few of them had the opportunity to do so, but no prohibitions either formal or tacit excluded them from what would nowadays be considered impermissible political partisanship.

ii THE CENTRAL EXECUTIVE[1]

This branch of the government was very largely concerned with receiving, sorting, and answering incoming communications (letters, reports, petitions, etc.) and with preparing and issuing outgoing ones (questionnaires, warrants, letters, writs, and charters). This process involved quite a complicated internal organization; its workings, necessarily in a much simplified form, can be illustrated by a diagram. Provided it is remembered that this is only a metaphor, the Council, the Secretaries of State, and the Seals can be thought of as constituting, below the King, the core or spine of the system.

It is quite correct to say that the King still ruled as well as reigned. But the means open to him for acting directly and personally as an executive agent of government need to be looked at more closely. The King could still receive incoming letters and petitions, consider the problems which they posed, and send out answers to them or other orders and instructions, without the *necessary and invariable* interposition either of the Council or of one of the Secretaries between him and the subject, or between him and the administrative machine. Even so, this power was less important than might at first appear. The four Masters of Requests, for example, who waited at Court on a monthly rota, could present petitions to the King without these first having to be submitted to the Council or one of the Secretaries. If a petition concerned 'any person of what degree soever', they were to keep any hint of it from that person until after it had been seen by the King. If, however, it concerned the proceedings of the Council, of any great officer of state, or of any other individual Councillor, they were to inform the Council or the person concerned,

... to the end [that] they may give timely and due information to his Majesty, of the ground of their proceedings, soe as his Majesty may not by surprisall, be induced in such public occasions, to give any direction, which upon due information, his Majesty shall have cause to Retract, or by which his own service or public Justice may suffer.[2]

Likewise in answer to petitions the King sometimes sent a letter under

[1] Full lists of the individual posts in the central government, arranged as in sections ii-vii, will be found in the Appendix, pp. 470-87.

[2] Public Record Office, Privy Council Registers, PC 2/47, p. 215; see also PC 2/41, pp. 439-40.

TABLE 1. THE CENTRAL EXECUTIVE

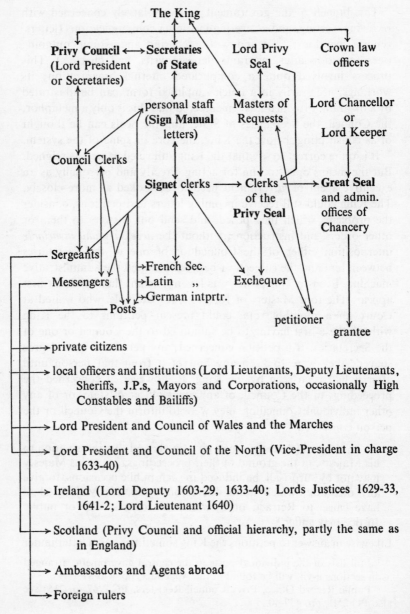

The King

Privy Council ⟷ Secretaries   Lord Privy   Crown law
(Lord President   of State   Seal   officers
or Secretaries)

       personal staff   Masters of   Lord Chancellor
       (Sign Manual   Requests   or
       letters)   Lord Keeper

Council Clerks

       Signet clerks ⟶ Clerks ⟵⟶ Great Seal
                   of the   and admin.
                   Privy Seal   offices of
                            Chancery

Sergeants

Messengers   →French Sec.

          →Latin   ,,   Exchequer

    Posts   →German intprtr.

                             petitioner

                                   grantee

→private citizens

→ local officers and institutions (Lord Lieutenants, Deputy Lieutenants, Sheriffs, J.P.s, Mayors and Corporations, occasionally High Constables and Bailiffs)

→Lord President and Council of Wales and the Marches

→ Lord President and Council of the North (Vice-President in charge 1633-40)

→Ireland (Lord Deputy 1603-29, 1633-40; Lords Justices 1629-33, 1641-2; Lord Lieutenant 1640)

→Scotland (Privy Council and official hierarchy, partly the same as in England)

→ Ambassadors and Agents abroad

→Foreign rulers

the Privy Seal, signed by its duty Clerk, without following the usual procedure (described below), which was bound to involve one of the Secretaries of State. In theory the Masters of Requests and the Clerks of the Privy Seal were subordinate to the Lord Privy Seal, but his administrative duties were in abeyance at the end of the fourth Earl of Worcester's tenure, in the years 1625-8. On one occasion Worcester took the seal away to his house in Wales, and the Council authorized the use of the Signet in its place; sometime later the Comptroller of the Household had charge of it.[1] But in any case the Masters and the Privy Seal Office did not form a separate hierarchy; they merely provided *a* channel for communications to and from the King.

Great as was his power, the King's personal freedom of action was very circumscribed. If the suits contained in them were acceptable, petitions to the King were either referred to the Council or granted straight away in the form of an instrument under the Privy or Great Seal. On receiving a petition the Council might reach a decision and make a positive recommendation to the King; or it might in turn refer the matter to the Attorney-General, if the Crown's legal or constitutional rights seemed to be involved, to the Lord Treasurer, the Chancellor of the Exchequer, or both, if it concerned finance, to one of its own standing committees, or even to a specially constituted *ad hoc* committee, which might be authorized to co-opt expert advisers from outside the Council. Depending upon the Council's final report, and on any additional influences which might have been brought to bear in the interval, the King then either refused the suit, let it go forward with modifications, or allowed it in its original form. If successful, it could by this time hardly avoid the normal machinery for the issue of outgoing directives. However, it usually followed the same route even if the King approved it straight off without reference to anybody: from Sign

[1] *Acts of the Privy Council of England* (1921-   ), *1625-6*, pp. 147-8, 193. Worcester was Lord Privy Seal from 1616 until his death in 1628 (*The Dictionary of National Biography* (Oxford, 1908-9), XVIII, 639-40); a distinction should be drawn between this office and the actual custody of the Privy Seal; this may explain why some authorities describe one of the Secretaries of State as keeper of the Privy Seal around this time (*Handbook of British Chronology*, ed. F. M. Powicke (1939), pp. 73-80). The office was vacant under Elizabeth, and from 1642 to 1661; except under the Republic the Seal was generally in the charge of one of the Secretaries.

Manual to Signet to Privy Seal to Great Seal, emerging in the end as a Letter Close or Patent according to its subject matter. A letter or writ of Privy Seal was normally valid as a final instrument only when the King was authorizing a money payment or some other financial transaction. Certain grants *could* be made under the Privy Seal, the Council's own seal, or the Exchequer seal, but most were only valid if passed under the Great Seal.

The most impersonal royal directive was a proclamation issued by the King in Council. This was the weightiest government pronouncement short of a parliamentary statute. Proclamations were issued under the Great or the Privy Seal; after April 1639 they had to pass the Great Seal before they could be printed.[1] An order sent out from the Council, drafted by one of its own Clerks, was more remote from the King, but not necessarily more formal or less personal than his communications under the Privy or Great Seal. A letter patent under the Great Seal was the most formal and public kind of missive from the King; letters close were not in the modern sense 'private', but they generally dealt with less public matters than letters patent.[2] Letters of Privy Seal were not necessarily less formal, certainly not than letters close, but tended to deal with rather different matters.

Communication between Crown and subject could take more personal forms. The King could send a letter via one of the Secretaries of State under the Signet Seal, or, as happened more and more often, one of the Secretaries could write under his own private seal on the King's behalf. Finally, the most personal and intimate form of all, the King could write a letter himself, or dictate it to one of the Secretaries' staff, sign it (the Sign Manual), and seal it if at all, with one of his small personal seals. In short, the King could do very little unless he was accompanied at least by one of the two Secretaries and some of their subordinates.

The Secretaries of State were administrative officers as well as having executive authority. They could deal with all but the most important matters of state on their own initiative, while at the same time their personal secretaries, clerks, and servants looked after most of the King's correspondence and drafted or copied his letters

[1] PC 2/50, p. 253.
[2] Letters close were folded and then sealed up, while letters patent were open with the seal hanging from the bottom; they also involved slightly different formal procedures in Chancery.

for the Sign Manual, on the threshold of the issuing and grant-making process. In addition, their subordinates, the Clerks of the Signet, managed the next stage of the process. Although senior to them in rank, the Secretaries did not have authority *ex officio* over the Masters of Requests or the Clerks of the Privy Seal, nor did they have such complete authority over the Clerks of the Council as they had over the Signet Clerks, the French and Latin Secretaries, and their own personal secretaries and clerks. However, after 1631 there was no Lord President of the Council,[1] and the Secretaries resumed their role as co-ordinators or liaison officers between the King and the Council; in practice they largely organized the Council's agenda, and supervised its subordinate staff.[2]

In addition to the Council, the Secretaries, and the Lord Privy Seal, and their respective staffs, many officers of Chancery were involved in the central administrative machinery. For an instrument to pass under the Great Seal an elaborate procedure had to be set in motion, involving much time, paper, and sealing-wax, and the payment of numerous fees. By the seventeenth century most of this had long ceased to be *bona fide* administration and become formalized bureaucratic ritual. The sole exception was the Lord Chancellor's or Lord Keeper's power to delay grants going through and even to stop them altogether; he had a genuine if rarely used suspensive veto over the actions of the Crown and Council, more particularly over those of his colleagues the Secretaries and the Lord Privy Seal, if he thought that they were giving the King bad advice or allowing royal bounty to be misdirected. The existence of this veto meant that the Lord Chancellor (or Keeper) was still a key figure in the whole machinery, although his department no longer exercised any initiative in administrative matters.[3]

It may be helpful to define what these various officials and departments could and could not do. The Council and its Clerks could

---

[1] This office had been vacant for many years before 1621 and it was not to be filled again until Charles II's ostensible reorganisation of the Privy Council in 1679.

[2] Higham, *Principal Secretary of State*; E. R. Turner, *The Privy Council of England 1603-1784* (2 vols., New York, 1927).

[3] G. W. Sanders, *Orders in Chancery*, vol. I (1845); H. C. Maxwell-Lyte, *Historical Notes on the use of the Great Seal of England* (1926); J. S. Wilson, 'The Administrative work of the Lord Chancellor in the early Seventeenth Century', London University Ph.D. Thesis (1927). For Chancery as a court of law see below, s. vi.

both initiate government actions and issue all but the most solemn
and binding instruments of final instance. The Secretaries and their
staffs initiated much business but did not normally issue final
instruments (as opposed to carrying on correspondence) except
to ambassadors and foreign rulers. A distinction should be drawn
here: the Signet Clerks conducted formal correspondence and
prepared documents for the Privy Seal; the Secretaries' personal
assistants conducted their masters' and the King's private and
informal correspondence, and prepared the first draft of formal
documents for the royal 'Sign Manual' (for which incidentally,
Charles I did not have a stamp, as he signed everything himself),
before these went on to the Signet. But this division was not rigid;
the Signet Clerks could still be called on by the King to deal with
less formal correspondence. Much of the time there was a Scottish
Secretary of State and a special under-Secretary for Ireland working
in Whitehall or at Court. Even so, the Secretaries kept up a far
wider correspondence than did the Council, let alone any of the
other great officers. The Privy Seal Office could not initiate action,
though the Masters of Requests could expedite business which might
possibly result in direct royal action; it could issue final instruments
(i) in answer to petitions to the King, (ii) for the payment of money,
when, as we shall see, the original initiative often came via the
Signet Office from the Exchequer itself. The Chancery, that is the
Great Seal, could never initiate action, but except in the cases
specified it had to pass all final instruments, with a suspensive or
negative veto on their issue.

The division of business between the Secretaries and the Council
appears in retrospect often to have been haphazard and arbitrary,
and at best inexact. It is a truism that far more depended on differences of personality then than now: no Caroline Secretary was as
important, as able to act independently, and in as close touch with the
sovereign as William Cecil (afterwards Lord Burghley) from 1558
to 1572, or his son Robert (later Earl of Salisbury) from 1596 to
1612. In theory, prerogative matters, that is religion, foreign affairs,
and dynastic questions, were the sovereign's personal business with
the Secretaries of State acting as the Crown's executive agent, while
matters involving jurisdiction, arbitration, the raising and spending
of extra revenue, and domestic affairs (other than religion) were in
the Council's sphere. Frequent exceptions could be found to this.
And even if contemporary witnesses could be called and cross-

examined, they would probably be hard put to it to define or explain the division of duties at all precisely. At least this would be so for the 1620's and 1630's. Later practices *may* have been more regular and have conformed more nearly to some general rule. Most surprising perhaps to the modern eye is the relatively large amount of time spent by sovereign and Council on private matters, often of a seemingly trivial nature, such as petty disputes between party and party. By contrast, a Secretary might for long periods exercise almost single-handed control over complicated negotiations which involved the gravest issues of national policy.[1] Buckingham's control over policy, *c.* 1623-8, was of a different nature, owing more to his personal dominance over two successive kings than to his offices as Lord Admiral and Master of the Horse, or his membership of the Council.

The nature of the Privy Council itself and its relations with the sovereign were liable to alteration. James I's Council was larger than Elizabeth I's had been, and Charles I's was if anything larger still; in addition, after Salisbury's death in 1612 there was no single minister who possessed both the authority and the intellectual capacity to carry on complicated high-level negotiations. Because of these two changes, by the 1620's a small inner ring of Councillors had emerged, selected by the King as his advisers mainly but not exclusively on foreign policy. Except in its capacity as the standing committee of the Council on foreign affairs, this body did not exist officially, and its wider role was not publicly admitted. But contemporary observers had no doubt of its importance; they sometimes referred to it as the 'cabinet council'. Much ink has been spilt, not on the whole to great effect, in debating whether or not this should be thought of as the ancestor of the later Cabinet. Whatever the future might hold, and for all the encroachments already made, at this time the Privy Council was still (under the King) the supreme executive body in the country. It is therefore important to be clear who its members were. (See Table 2 below.)

The proportion of Scots exceeded one-fifth only briefly in the mid-1630's, and then by the accidents of mortality more than by conscious design. The number of churchmen cannot be considered excessive, unless one agrees with those contemporary critics who believed that they should not have been there at all. The number of non-office-

---

[1] Turner, *Privy Council*, chs. V-VIII, and Higham, *Secretary of State*, *passim*, especially chs. X-XIII, broadly confirm this division of business between the Secretaries and the Council.

holders might be expected to vary more widely than other categories; for by appointing such extra Councillors the King could co-opt men of importance in the country into his government without giving them office. It was a way of winning friends and influencing people on the cheap; the only trouble was that Charles I tended to pick the

TABLE 2. COMPOSITION OF THE PRIVY COUNCIL[1]

Date	1625	1630	1635	1640
Total	30	42	32	35
Lay Peers	20	30	24	27
Commoners	7	8	6	5
Bishops	3	4	2	3
Office-holders	25	33	27	27
Non-office-holders	5	9	5	8
Peers	3	5	3	6
Bishops	2	4	2	2
Scots	4	6	7	6
Holders of Scottish Office	2	4	3	3

wrong men. Archbishop Laud once described one of them as 'a very thin tree in a storm', adding 'he will soon be wet that takes shelter there'.[2] The number of commoners in the Council is also of interest; for, as Professor Willson has shown, they constituted the potential Crown 'front bench' in the Commons if and when there was a parliament.[3] The fall in their number during the 1630's may have been a reflection, if only an unconscious one, of Charles's attempt to

[1] Turner, *Privy Council; Acts of the Privy Council, 1625-9* (printed register, 5 vols.); P.R.O., Privy Council Registers, PC 2/39-53 (MS. continuation 1629-42). The late Professor Turner may have relied too much on the lists of Councillors given at the beginning of most volumes of the MS. Register (the Registers are contemporary fair copies of originals which have not survived); these need to be checked with (i) actual attendance as recorded in the body of the registers, (ii) other primary sources, (iii) *D.N.B.*, G.E.C., *The Complete Peerage*, ed. V. Gibbs, H. A. Doubleday, G. H. White (1910-59), abbrev. as G.E.C., for dates of Councillors' deaths and for retirements, dismissals, etc.

[2] W. Laud, *Works*, ed. W. Scott and J. Bliss (Oxford, 1847-60), VII, 568, to Wentworth in May 1639, apropos the Earl of Berkshire.

[3] D. H. Willson, *Privy Councillors in the House of Commons* (Minneapolis, 1940).

do without parliament. Numerically more striking, though not necessarily so significant, is the number of additional office-holders who entered the Council in the late 1620's: between 1625 and 1630 the Lord Presidents of Wales and the North, the Chancellor of the Duchy of Lancaster, the Vice-Chamberlain, and the Captain of the Gentlemen Pensioners, none of whom had been members continuously in James's reign, were admitted. In addition, the post of Lord Great Chamberlain was revived in 1626, as those of Lord President and Earl Marshal had been in 1621.

In the seventeenth century it is not very clear which 'great officers' of state were indisputably *ex-officio* members of the Council. Under Charles I the list was probably as follows:

TABLE 3. *Ex-Officio* MEMBERS OF THE COUNCIL

Archbishop of Canterbury
Lord Chancellor, or Lord Keeper
Lord Treasurer
Lord President of the Council
Lord Privy Seal
Lord Admiral
Lord Steward
Lord Chamberlain
Lord Lieutenant, or Lord Deputy of Ireland
Chancellor of the Exchequer
2 Secretaries of State
Treasurer of the Household
Comptroller of the Household

Borderline cases:—
Lord Great Chamberlain
Earl Marshal
Queen's Lord Chamberlain
Lord Treasurer of Scotland

Members more often than not, but not apparently *ex-officio:*—
Archbishop of York
Master of the Horse
Chancellor of the Duchy
Master of the Wards
Master of the Rolls

As the Council got bigger, it developed a system of committees. Besides foreign affairs, under Charles I there were normally standing committees on Ireland, Trade, the Militia (and/or military preparations), and (from the mid-1630's) Plantations. There were also

21

numerous *ad hoc* committees, some of which had power to co-opt non-councillors; these mixed committees were in practice very like some of the Stuart royal commissions which included Privy Councillors, other officials, and non-office-holders.

Royal commissions served the early Stuarts as investigating and advisory bodies, and for sometimes dubious fiscal purposes. But besides the periodic putting of great offices of state 'into commission', like the Admiralty after the death of Buckingham, other uses of the royal commission can fairly be regarded as extensions of conciliar government. The High *Commission* ('for Causes Ecclesiastical') speaks for itself. The two regional instruments of prerogative rule— the Councils in the North and in the Marches of Wales—were also technically royal commissions under the Great Seal, which were reissued at the accession of a new monarch, on the appointment of a new Lord President, and if their composition, powers, or procedure were being substantially changed. 'The Council of War' was another standing commission with administrative as well as advisory duties. It consisted largely of experts, at least of men with some experience as naval or military commanders, and acted in co-operation with the defence departments (see below, s. v), and with the Privy Council itself, or its military committee.

To return to the machinery of the central executive, three types of officers were normally available to carry communications from the King, the Council, and the Secretaries to their intended recipients. This was true regardless of which seal was used or what sort of informal instrument. Foreign dispatches and diplomatic correspondence were usually carried by the staff of the royal postal service, occasionally by special emissaries from the central executive itself or from the royal household. Some domestic correspondence and most of that between the central government and Dublin, Edinburgh, York, and Ludlow[1] was carried by the home postal staff. A large proportion of all the mails carried were in some sense official, and private individuals only used the royal postal services by courtesy. For home mails there were also private enterprise carriers, but except for one or two of the great trading Companies the foreign mails were a royal monopoly, open to private users only as a special favour—almost in the way that some governments today permit foreign travel only as a reward for the chosen few.

[1] Normal seats of the Irish and Scottish administrations, and of the Councils of the North and the Marches of Wales respectively.

The 'Posts' were limited to the carriage and delivery of correspondence. When an important missive needed to be handed to a particular person, whether a Lord Lieutenant, a J.P., or a private citizen, and an immediate answer collected, or when a warrant was issued for someone's arrest or their appearance in London, the task was normally entrusted to one of the forty-odd Messengers of the Chamber. Of these, some attended at Court, at the call of the King and Queen, and the chief officers of the Household, a few were detached to wait on individual heads of departments (like the Lord Treasurer), on royal commissions, and on committees of the Council; the residue, probably a majority, attended on the Council itself and were also available for use by the Secretaries. If urgent orders were being sent simultaneously to all the counties of England and to the Lord President of Wales, forty was none too many, and by the later 1630's there were several Messengers extraordinary over and above these.

The Messengers often had to keep those whom they arrested in their charge until they were brought before the Council, so they had to be able to lodge men of quality, sometimes for weeks on end. Peers and perhaps also gentry were more often arrested by Sergeants-at-Arms than by Messengers; the Sergeants tended to be of higher social standing than the Messengers. Some of the Sergeants too were detailed to wait on various great officers and departments of state, but the majority were divided between the Court and the central executive, being available for the service of King, Council, and Secretaries. Whereas the Messengers had powers of arrest as well as being dispatch-riders, the Sergeants appear to have acted exclusively as policemen and not normally to have carried messages. Contrary to what their name may suggest in modern usage, the Pursuivants seem to have been strictly under-officers in the College of Arms without other administrative duties.

The Councils in the Marches of Wales and in the North, and to some extent the central governments of Ireland and even of Scotland, can be thought of as regional extensions of the English central executive. More will be said of the two former in discussing the courts (s. vi); each had a miniature hierarchy of secretary, attorney, clerks, messengers, etc., under its Lord President and the other

Councillors. In Dublin there was a smaller Council but a considerably larger official staff. Apart from the interval of rule by two Lord Justices from 1629 to 1633, the Lord Deputyship or Lord Lieutenancy of Ireland represented a more concentrated personal autocracy than did the limited delegacy of royal powers to either of the regional Lord Presidents; Wentworth was a far more absolute ruler in Ireland (1633-40) than he could be in the North (1628-33). Despite this, the dignity of being a Privy Councillor in Ireland, if inferior to that of being one in Scotland, was greater than that of being a Councillor in Wales or the North. The Irish Council simply seems to have been ineffectual as a check on a strong Lord Deputy. Under the Lord Deputy, the central executive in Ireland resembled that in England, reduced in scale, rather than the administration in Wales or the North, however much enlarged.

Scotland presents a very different picture. Two distinguished historians have recently cast light on Scottish politics and society at this time.[1] But neither of them is very explicit about the actual relations between the two governments after the union of the Crowns (and before the union of the Kingdoms); nor are the standard histories of Scotland any better in this respect. It is common knowledge that Charles I's non-parliamentary régime was finally broken on the rock of Scottish Calvinism, and that paradoxically the 'second Stuart despotism' of his sons was much more effective in Scotland than in the southern kingdom (1660-88). This is not the place to try to write the full history of Anglo-Scottish political and administrative relations even during the limited period 1625-40. Under Charles I, as under his father, the links were very close. There were from four to seven Scots in the English Privy Council. Between two and four of them were holders of Scottish offices; by the 1630's the Lord Treasurer of Scotland had almost achieved the status of an *ex-officio* member. Correspondingly from 1633 on there were between six and nine English councillors in the (much larger) Scottish Privy Council. But the exchange of office-holding, as opposed to Council membership, was a one-way process; no Englishman held a Scottish office, and it is doubtful if any of suitable calibre would have wanted to do so. In the 1630's the Scottish Secretary of State received a salary on the English establishment, was on many English royal commissions, and would seem, like the Lord Treasurer

---

[1] D. Mathew, *Scotland under Charles I* (1955); D. H. Willson, *James VI and I* (1956).

of Scotland, to have spent most of his time in the south.[1] Except for his visits in 1633 and, under very different circumstances, in 1641, Charles I never presided over the Scottish council, though at times there may almost have been a quorum of its members in the south. In so far as Scotland enjoyed 'home rule', the Council was in theory the seat of power; in practice, Scottish government was carried on by an inner circle of councillors, most of whom were also great officers, assisted by an administrative staff comparable to but quite distinct from its English counterpart. This inner group seems to have exercised little initiative and to have acted closely under the direction of the King in England. There was no English equivalent to another key institution, the 'Lords of the Articles', a largely nominated parliamentary standing committee, at this time more powerful than the Scottish parliament itself.[2]

Nominally, therefore, Scotland was an independent country which happened to share a common sovereign with England. Ireland, although also styled a 'Kingdom', was avowedly ruled as an English dependency. But Scottish independence was in large part illusory: from 1603 until the religious crisis of 1637-8 Scotland was ruled, although not administered, from the English court.

Ambassadors and other representatives of the English Crown abroad can also be thought of as members of the central executive. Under the King, diplomacy and foreign relations were in the charge of the two Secretaries of State, between whom a functional division into a 'northern' and a 'southern' department was already taking shape.[3] Despite the absence of any organized diplomatic service, a

[1] Turner, *Privy Council*; Mathew, *Scotland*; C. V. Wedgwood, 'Anglo-Scottish Relations, 1603-40', *Trans. Royal Hist. Soc.*, 4th ser., XXXII (1950); *Acts of the Privy Council, 1625-9*; PC 2/39-53; *Registers of the Privy Council of Scotland*, 2nd ser., I-VII (Edinburgh, 1899-1906). See *D.N.B.* and G.E.C. on William Alexander, Earl of Stirling, William Douglas, Earl of Moreton, and John Stewart, Earl of Traquair.

[2] Willson, *James VI and I*, p. 313; Mathew, *Scotland*, p. 31; see also P. Hume Brown, *History of Scotland* (Cambridge, 2nd edn. 1905), bk. VI, ch. II, 240-1, 276-8, ch. III, 284-95; and on the 'Lords of the Articles', C. S. Terry, *The Scottish Parliament 1603-1707* (Glasgow, 1905), pp. 103-113, 118-20; R. S. Rait, *The Parliaments of Scotland* (Glasgow, 1924), pp. 59-62, 367-74.

[3] Higham, *Secretary of State*, indexed under Secretary of State, *Division of duties*. The division was set out formally when the elder Sir Henry Vane succeeded Sir John Coke in January 1640 (*Calendar of State Papers Domestic, 1639-40*, pp. 332, 433).

distinction can be drawn between regular resident envoys, and ambassadors or agents extraordinary. There were five regular resident Ambassadors, accredited to the Crown of Spain, the Crown of France, the Emperor and the German Diet, the States-General and the Statholder of the United Provinces, and the Sultan of Turkey. There were about sixteen regular Agents (at Madrid, Paris, Vienna or Ratisbon, or jointly at both, The Hague, Brussels, Hamburg, Copenhagen, Stockholm, Danzig, Warsaw, Moscow, Venice, Turin, Genoa, Florence, and on the Barbary coast).

It is not always easy to disentangle resident Agents and minor envoys extraordinary, nor to distinguish resident from extraordinary Ambassadors. On occasions there might only be an Agent (who was then more or less the equivalent of a modern chargé d'affaires) in Paris or Madrid; equally there were sometimes Ambassadors with the Kings of Denmark, Sweden, and even Poland. The Ambassador in Germany may at this time always have been 'extraordinary' rather than resident, although the post was more often filled than vacant; the envoy to the Porte represented the Levant Company as well as the English Crown, and ranked well below the other resident Ambassadors. The hierarchy of diplomatic ranks was inexact; there were English Consuls in the main European ports and sometimes in those of North Africa and the Levant, but they were probably either British merchants resident there, or foreigners acting on behalf of the English Crown; it is hard to estimate their number, but there was certainly nothing resembling a regular consular service.[1]

iii THE ROYAL HOUSEHOLD

As long as the King ruled the country, his household was bound to be of some importance in its government. But the nature and extent of this importance were changing. In the early seventeenth century the household played a lesser part in politics and administration than it had done before the mid-sixteenth century. Yet although its importance was perhaps continuing to decline, its costs were rising steeply.

The term 'household' itself requires some further explanation. It consisted of the King's Household above stairs, more often known

[1] Mr. Garrett Mattingly in his brilliant study, *Renaissance Diplomacy* (1955), does not deal in detail with English diplomacy in the sixteenth and early seventeenth centuries, but much of what he says about the European powers in general applies equally well to England.

as the Chamber, and his Household below stairs, usually just called *the* Household. As well as all the sub-departments and offshoots of these two, the household in the wider sense could also be said to include (when they existed) the establishments of the Queen consort and of the royal children.

By the 1620's eighty or ninety years had passed since the Chamber had last rivalled the Exchequer as a national treasury. And the administrative importance of the household no longer extended to other branches of the central government, more and more of which had at various dates from the twelfth to sixteenth centuries in Tout's famous phrase 'gone out of court' and become quite separate from it.[1] Yet under Charles I, the household departments accounted for over 40 per cent. of all peacetime royal expenditure. Excluding officers extraordinary and the private servants of royal officials, their staff numbered over 1,800 people, of whom probably a third to a half were on duty at any one time.

This total was made up as follows:

TABLE 4. SIZE OF THE HOUSEHOLD DEPARTMENTS

Household below stairs . . .	305 (+ *c.* 195 servants' servants)
Royal Stables	263
Chamber and offshoots . . .	580-620
Great Wardrobe	*c.* 60
Gentlemen Pensioners . . .	55
Yeomen of the Guard . . .	210
Household and Chamber of the Prince and other royal children .	202 (in 1636-40; none in 1625-30)
Queen's Household and Chamber .	172

Total *c.* 1840-60 (minimum) plus an unknown number of officers' servants (say 400 as a minimum, quite possibly more like 700 to 800).[2]

However of the 305 officers in the Household below stairs there are only about 48, ranging from the Lord Steward down to the

[1] Tout, *Chapters*; F. C. Dietz, *English Government Finance 1485-1558* (Urbana, Ill., 1920), and *English Public Finance 1558-1641* (New York, 1932); Elton, *Revolution in Government*; Richardson, *Chamber Administration.*

[2] P.R.O., State Papers Domestic, Charles I, SP 16/154/75-7, 386/97, 474/3; Accounts Various, Queen's Household, E 101/438/7; Declared Accounts, Chamber, E 351/544-5, AO 1/393/66-395/76; Gentlemen Pensioners' Rolls, E 407/box 1/42-9; Lord Chamberlain's misc. records, LC 3/1; British Museum Harleian MS. 7623; Additional MS. 6418; National Library of Wales, Wynnstay MSS. 166, 168.

Clerks and Sergeants of the sub-departments,[1] with whom we shall be concerned in the chapters which follow. The Surveyors of the Long Carts, the Wine Porters, the Pages of the Scalding House, the Yeomen and Groom Cooks, and the Breadbearers of the Pantry, to mention only a random selection, are likely to remain mere names. It is not so much that they are uninteresting; it would be very well worth knowing how the lower ranks of the Household were staffed, and by what kinds of men. But with a very few exceptions, below a certain level there is simply not enough evidence to make it worthwhile trying to collect biographical material.

Similarly in the other branches of the household. Above stairs it might be possible to collect information about a rather larger proportion of the total number. The duties of Chamber officers tended to be less menial and more honorific, and so in general the Chamber attracted men of higher social standing than the Household below stairs. Those Chamber officers, who were unpaid and whose administrative duties consisted merely of attending at Court one month in four, like the Gentlemen of the Privy Chamber, have only been included if they held other offices, or were important recipients of royal favours—grants, pensions, etc. Only the Captain, Master, or other officers in charge have been included from such groups as the Bargemen and Watermen, the Messengers, the Musicians, the Huntsmen, Harriers, and Falconers, the King's Guard, and the Band of Pensioners. In the case of the two latter, because most of the Yeomen are too obscure and because it seems misleading to think of the Gentlemen Pensioners as royal officials—rather than as part-time attendants at court.[2] However, biographical information will be drawn on relating to the holders of about 120 posts in the Chamber and its offshoots.

In the Stables the administrative staff was small; most of the posts there were either honorific or menial. So the proportion of the officers who will be considered in later chapters is a good deal smaller.

On a reduced scale the Queen's and the Prince's households reproduced the same basic structure as the King's. As in his, so in theirs there are many minor royal servants with whom this study is

---

[1] For these, see Appendix, p. 472; also E. K. Chambers, *The Elizabethan Stage*, vol. I, (Oxford 1923), ch. I.

[2] Unlike the Gents of the Privy Chamber, they were each paid, £50 p.a. plus £50 'board wages' (for which see Chapter 4, s. i).

not concerned, at least not as individuals. The complete establishments of Queen Henrietta Maria and of Prince Charles and the other royal children were large and elaborate.[1]

Finally there is the Great Wardrobe, which was the supply department for furnishings and clothing, in large measure independent of both the Household and the Chamber. Apart from a small administrative staff, most of its members can be classified as artisans, some of whom may only have been employed on contract, and so fall outside the scope of this inquiry.

In general, it is correct to think of the Household as having had charge of supply and the Chamber of ceremonial and entertainment. But there are a few exceptions to this rule. Supply of food, drink, lighting, and fuel, of transport and lodgings when the court was on the move, and of some furniture and fittings was the Household's business. But the construction and maintenance of buildings pertained to the office of Works (a sub-department of the Chamber), permanent furniture, curtains, tapestries, carpets, and so on to the Great Wardrobe, royal clothing and officers' liveries and uniform jointly to the Great Wardrobe and the Robes (another sub-department of the Chamber). By this time the Household was more concerned than the Chamber with administration in the conventional sense; it provided most of the necessities of life, while the Chamber regulated the routine and ceremony of the Court. What the Household was responsible for providing, the Chamber saw was consumed with due pomp and elegance.

Below the Lord Chamberlain and Vice-Chamberlain the administrative staff of the Chamber consisted only of the Treasurer and his clerks. With an annual turn-over averaging more than £25,000 a year this was by no means a top-heavy bureaucracy. Otherwise in the above stairs departments only the Keeper of the Privy Purse, and the senior officers of the Band of Gentlemen Pensioners, the Robes, the Revels, the Tents and Toils, and the Works were involved in administration. As head of the Bedchamber, the Groom of the Stole enjoyed semi-autonomy, but financially the Bedchamber was an integral part of the Chamber itself. The other principal offshoots of the Chamber, unlike the sub-departments of the Household, did account direct to the Exchequer, and were financially independent of the parent department. This was not a matter of size: the Revels, the Tents, and even the Robes had a far smaller annual turnover

[1] See Appendix, pp. 474-5.

than the busier of the sub-departments below stairs. It was due rather to the historical evolution of the Chamber as a less unified structure than the Household, whose finances were all under the charge of the Cofferer and the Compting House.

Below stairs the administrative hierarchy was more elaborate. The Lord Steward presided; he, the Treasurer, and the Comptroller were known, from their badges of office, as the 'whitestaves'. The Treasurer, Comptroller, Cofferer (there were two Cofferers, 1625-30), the two Clerks of Greencloth, and the two Clerk Comptrollers constituted the Board of Greencloth, in direct charge of finance and organization. The function of the Compting House is obvious from its name; the size of its staff (fourteen) indicates the scale and complexity of the Household's financial activities. Discipline and order were the responsibility of the Master of the Household; the office being in abeyance after 1632, these duties were performed by the Board of Greencloth and by various subordinate officers. While financially the Household was highly centralized, it performed its duties through an elaborate system of devolution. Besides the Compting House, the most important of its twenty-three sub-departments were the Acatry (in charge of buying, especially of meat), Kitchen, Bakehouse, Poultry, Cellar, and Buttery.

Independence of both the Household and the Chamber was enjoyed, in varying degrees, by the Master of the Great Wardrobe, the Master of the Horse, the heads of the Queen's Household, and the Governor to the Prince. Oddly enough, the Stable was not financially independent; it received all its money and supplies from the Household or the Great Wardrobe, although the Master of the Horse took precedence above all household officers except the Lord Steward and Lord Chamberlain.

A fortuitous degree of unity resulted from the headship of Household and Chamber being exercised by the Herbert brothers in 1626-30, and then from the Lord Stewardship being left vacant for ten years. In the 1630's the Lord Chamberlain seems to have been recognized as the acting head of the whole household, above and below stairs; in 1638 the officers of Greencloth appealed to his authority when trying to resist the reform of their accounting system.[1]

---

[1] *D.N.B.* and G.E.C., William, third Earl of Pembroke, Lord Chamberlain 1615-26, Lord Steward 1626-30, and Philip, fourth Earl of Pembroke and first Earl of Montgomery, Lord Chamberlain 1626-41; P.R.O., Lord Steward's dept., misc. books, LS 13/169, pp. 313-16.

On the middle levels there is quite a marked contrast between the types of men in the Chamber and those in the rest of the household. Courtiers and royal favourites of noble or gentle birth, and peers or gentry with some Court connexions are more likely to be found in the Chamber; administrative careerists, some of landed, others of urban middle-class origin, are more likely to be found below stairs, or in such outlying departments as the Wardrobes and the Works.

While the whole central government was no longer dominated by the royal household as it had once been, there was still far from being a complete divorce between them. The two Secretaries of State and the Lord Privy Seal had tables and dined at Court. The Messengers, who carried the Crown's instructions into the localities, made arrests, and brought men before the Council, were technically officers of the Chamber and were paid by its Treasurer, as were some of the other subordinates of the Secretaries and the Council. An additional link arose from the greater household officers being ministers of state in their capacity as Privy Councillors. Four out of the fourteen *ex-officio* members of the Council were household officers (the Lord Steward, Lord Chamberlain, Treasurer, and Comptroller); from 1625 to 1640 between six and eleven household officers were councillors at any one time, in the 1630's never less than nine.[1]

Offices in the various branches of the household attracted men for different reasons. Some, especially in the Privy and Bed Chambers, were esteemed primarily for their nearness to the sovereign, and as stepping-stones to other offices, to grants, and to royal favours for their holders and for the holders' friends, relatives, and 'clients'. In all branches money wages were on the whole very small, but free board and lodging enormously increased the real value of many household offices.

Not only did the household cost a great deal. It was probably bound to be the major item of Crown expenditure in peacetime. But its glaring wastefulness, due to bad methods of catering and accounting, to redundancy and sinecurism, and to downright fraud, made it an obvious, though not for that reason necessarily an easy, target for financial and administrative reformers. This was true over a period of several centuries; the situation was only more acute than usual under the early Stuarts on account of the fall in the value of

[1] SP 16/8/78 p. 1, 1625; *Acts of the Privy Council, 1625-9*; Privy Council Register, PC 2/39-53; *D.N.B.;* G.E.C.

money since the early sixteenth century, the growing alienation of the bulk of the taxpaying classes from the Court, and the consequent parliamentary deadlock. Yet at the same time household reform affected royal prestige as well as royal solvency: the King must keep a fitting state, and must dispense his hospitality and his favours with a decent liberality. It is arguable that on this score James and Charles were more popular with some of their subjects than had been the frugal, not to say parsimonious, Elizabeth I.[1]

iv THE REVENUE DEPARTMENTS

The financial institutions of England had been under almost continuous overhaul from the later fifteenth century to the early years of Elizabeth I.[2] There had been relatively little change since then, except within the existing institutional framework. There were three 'national' financial departments: the Exchequer, the Court of Wards and Liveries, and the Duchy of Lancaster. None was simply and solely concerned with finance, and none, not even the Exchequer, had what would now be considered even the minimum qualifications required to constitute an effective treasury or finance ministry. Alone of the various revenue courts which had blossomed and withered under the earlier Tudors, the Court of Wards remained independent of the Exchequer. It did not come under the Lord Treasurer and Under-Treasurer (who combined this office in the lower Exchequer with that of Chancellor in the (upper) Exchequer, by which title he was already more often known). The Receiver-General of the Court of Wards did not have to render yearly accounts in the Exchequer; and payments out of its surplus revenue could be made either to the Exchequer or direct to the spending departments. However, in the years 1550-4, 1572-98, 1608-12, and 1621-3 the Lord Treasurer was also Master of the Wards, and from 1635 to 1641 Cottington combined this post with that of Chancellor of the Exchequer and Under-Treasurer.

'Wardship' derived from the rights of a feudal ruler over all holders of land who owed him military or other service instead of

---

[1] For further details on household reform see G. E. Aylmer, 'Attempts at Administrative Reform 1625-40', *Eng. Hist. Rev.*, lxxii (1957).

[2] Dietz, *Government Finance* and *Public Finance*; Richardson, *Chamber Administration*; and Elton, *Revolution in Government*; Mrs. M. D. George, 'Notes on the Origin of the Declared Account', *Eng. Hist. Rev.*, xxxi (1916).

Left to right: Chief Clerk of the Wardrobe, Chief Clerk of the
Kitchen, two Clerk Comptrollers, Clerk of the Greencloth, Master
of the Household.

Left to right: Deputy Clerk of the Market, two Cofferer's Clerks,
Diet Clerk, Master Cook, Clerk of the Pastry, Clerk of the Larder,
Clerk of the Scullery.

1. OFFICERS OF THE ROYAL HOUSEHOLD IN 1603.

2. CHARLES I DINING. (Painting by Houckgeest).

rent. It had developed into a royal fiscal right, to administer the entire estates of minors who inherited property any part of which was held of the King by knight service in chief, and such parts of the estates of other minor heirs as were held on any of the other feudal tenures (except socage). It included guardianship of the heir, or heiress's person, and the right to arrange their marriage at the appropriate time; it extended to the estates of idiots and lunatics (of any age), and to the remarriage of widows holding land by these tenures. 'Livery', in this context, derived from the King's right to approve all those who inherited land held direct from him, even if they were male and of age; it had developed into a fiscal right to mulct them when they inherited their property, or—if they were wards—when they came of age. Together livery and wardship constituted a small irregular tax on most landed families (anyway of gentry status), and a much heavier levy (more like a crude kind of death duty) on some of them. Whereas the incidence of both depended on the accidents of mortality, all families holding such property would from time to time have to pay livery, but all might hope—and some reasonably expect—to escape the far greater burden of wardship. Much of the Crown's supervisory and educational work, which wardship implied, was delegated to private persons, to whom wardships were frequently granted, or in effect sold. But, even so, the Court should not be thought of as having been entirely concerned with royal finance, to the exclusion of welfare and estate management.[1]

The Duchy of Lancaster administered royal estates all over England, though mainly in the north, and had its own jurisdiction in the County Palatine of Lancaster and over its scattered properties; it was partly concerned with estate management and partly with Crown finance. Representing institutionally the fusion of the Crown of England with the Dukedom of Lancaster (continuous since 1399), it too had survived the various sixteenth-century amalgamations and reshuffles more by accident than consciously planned design. In the county of Lancaster the Duchy exercised a separate 'palatine' jurisdiction, which falls outside a survey of the central government.

[1] H. E. Bell, *An Introduction to the History and Records of the Court of Wards and Liveries* (Cambridge, 1953); J. Hurstfield, 'Lord Burghley as Master of the Court of Wards', *Trans. Royal Hist. Soc.*, 4th ser., XXXI (1949), 95-114; 'The Revival of Feudalism in Early Tudor England', *History*, n.s., XXXVII (1952), 131-45; *The Queen's Wards: Wardship and Marriage under Elizabeth I* (1958).

In the capital, too, it was a court of law as well as an estate office and a revenue department; the Court of Duchy Chamber was thought of by contemporaries as a 'prerogative' court, to be bracketed with Star Chamber and the two regional councils.[1]

Besides being the third of the ancient common law courts,[2] the Exchequer was the principal financial institution of the kingdom. It was divided into two parts. The upper Exchequer, or Exchequer of Audit, was in charge of government accounts; the lower Exchequer, or Exchequer of Receipt (often known simply as 'the Receipt'), received and paid out money in cash and credit, and kept records of all in- and out-payments. All revenue accounts, except those of the Wards and the Duchy, and all spending accounts, except those of the Queen's Household, were audited in the upper Exchequer; in the years 1631-5 89·5 per cent. of the regular Crown revenues were audited there, the net surplus of Wards and Duchy together amounting to only 10·5 per cent. (this excludes capital items, like land sales, the greater part of which were also handled by the Exchequer).[3]

There were important differences of method inside both Exchequers. In the upper half there were three principal and various subsidiary methods of accounting in use, each involving different procedures and different sets of officials. This was because the Exchequer, first instituted in the early twelfth century, had been added to in the thirteenth and fourteenth centuries and again in the sixteenth century; different offices and methods co-existed like overlapping geological strata. The whole of the Pipe Office and some of the officials in the two Remembrancers' Offices audited a few of the revenue accounts in the traditional way, as evolved from the twelfth to fourteenth centuries. Perhaps 'audit' is a misleadingly modern term to describe this obscure and intricate process known to contemporaries as the 'ancient course' of the Exchequer. A larger group of accounts was dealt with by the seven Revenue Auditors, partly according to the methods adopted for auditing the Crown land revenues since Henry VII's time, and partly according to those

[1] R. Somerville, *The Duchy of Lancaster*, vol. I to 1603 (1953), 2nd volume in preparation; 'The Duchy of Lancaster Council and Court of Duchy Chamber', *Trans. Roy. Hist. Soc.*, 4th ser., XXIII (1941), 159-77.

[2] See s. vi of this Chapter.

[3] These and the percentages given below, are based on P.R.O., Treasury Misc. T 56/2, a balance of revenue and expenditure for the previous five years, made in December 1635, using corrected totals where the contemporary copyist has made obvious mistakes.

evolved in the Tudor Court of Augmentations (set up in 1536 and amalgamated with the Exchequer in 1554); apart from the slightly different way of auditing the land revenue accounts themselves, the system for this group is sometimes known as 'augmentation-wise'. All the remaining accounts (with negligible exceptions) were dealt with by the two Auditors of the Imprests, whose own posts had only been created in the early 1560's. Their method of audit differed only in detail from that of the Revenue Auditors; to make the distinction clear it is known as 'prest-wise'. A prest is an advance of money on an account not yet rendered by the payee; imprests are monies so advanced. The prest accounts are classified in the Public Record Office as the Declared Accounts, because they were 'declared', or heard orally, before the Lord Treasurer, the Chancellor of the Exchequer, or both of them, and were signed by them as well as by one or both of the Prest Auditors. The accounts handled by the Revenue Auditors were normally signed by one of them and by one of the Barons of the Exchequer. The early Stuart Household accounts seem to have been taken by a mixture of 'augmentation-' and 'prest-wise'; they were checked by the Revenue Auditors but declared before the Treasurer and Chancellor. The same was true of the Alienations' Accounts (this department is described later in this section).

By the 1630's accounts which between them covered 93 per cent. of all the incoming revenues audited in the Exchequer were handled by the two sets of Auditors. The two Prest Auditors alone had charge of accounts covering between 63 and 69 per cent.; only a paltry 4 per cent. was covered by the 'ancient course', and the other 3 per cent. odd was audited in ways which do not correspond to any of the principal methods. The accounts of virtually all the spending departments were audited in the newer ways, mainly 'prest-wise'. The Queen's Household accounts seem to have been declared before the members of her own Council and audited by her own Revenue Auditor, who happened also to be one of the seven Auditors of the (King's) revenues. Alone among paymasters of spending departments, the Keeper of the King's Privy Purse did not have to account at all anywhere.

At the Receipt the vital distinction was between in- and out-payments made in cash and transactions where only tallies changed hands. Taking the annual averages for 1631-5, 49·5 per cent. of the ordinary revenue was handled in cash and 50·5 per cent. by tallies or other credit instruments; for ordinary expenditure the corresponding figures were 49·8 per cent. and 50·2 per cent. The ratio of cash to credit payments at the Receipt, for any particular type of revenue or expenditure, had no connexion with the various ways in which different revenue and expenditure accounts were audited in the upper Exchequer.

Various links existed between the two Exchequers. There was the common headship of the Lord Treasurer and the Chancellor-cum-Under Treasurer, and there were two or three ways in which the officers of the upper Exchequer, who were involved in the auditing, could keep a check on the accountants who came before them, by means of information passed up from the officers of the Receipt. The traditional method was by the famous notched tallies which were split, half being given to the accountant and half being passed to the upper Exchequer; these were, or at least could be, rejoined when the accountant came in for his (normally annual) audit. This method may still have been effective for the ancient-course revenues, but it was largely nominal for most of the others. There are many manuscript and two or three printed descriptions of early Stuart Exchequer procedure, not all of which agree on all points; but almost all emphasize that tallies *ought* to be rejoined when accountants come to the upper Exchequer for auditing. According to one representative memorandum of *c.* 1638, 'this course of joining of tallies is now almost growne out of use'; modern research points to the same conclusion.[1] As an alternative, parchment certificates could be issued at the Receipt, as evidence that in- or out-payments had been made there; some officials disapproved of these because they were said to leave more room for fraud than the tally system. The use of these 'Constats' or 'Acquittances' as they were called, was complained of around 1600 and again in 1630.[2]

[1] On tallies see H. Jenkinson, 'Exchequer Tallies', *Archaeologia*, LXII (1911), 367-80, and 'Exchequer Tallies', *Procs. of the Soc. of Antiquaries*, 2nd ser., XXV (1912-13), 29-39; 'Mediaeval Tallies, Public and Private', *Archaeologia*, LXXIV (1925), 289-351, esp. 289-310; also Jenkinson, *A Manual of Archive Administration* (2nd edn. 1937), Appdx. V, pp. 228-30; SP 16/406/22.

[2] P.R.O., E 407/71, Exchequer of Receipt, misc. papers, mainly to do with an internal dispute between the officers; P.R.O., T 56/16, Treasury letters, report by the Attorney-General on the Exchequer's failure to observe the provisions of the Statute of Rutland (of 1284!); see *Statutes of the Realm* (1810-24), I, 69-70; P.R.O., Exchequer, Lord Treasurer's Remembrancer's misc. books, E 369/117, report by Clerk of the the the Pipe.

The newest method of liaison consisted simply of periodic statements, or lists of out-payments, sent up to the Auditors of the Prests by the Auditor of the Receipt. By the 1630's he was sending up certificates of all money paid out imprest from the Receipt, not only of money paid to those who would subsequently have to account to the Prest Auditors.[1] Since the use of certificates was never universal, the auditing staff and those who accounted to them might still have to fall back on tallies as a cross-check on *cash* in-payments and on *credit* out-payments (i.e. those made by talley, and recorded on the in-payments' side in the lower Exchequer). And tallies remained important credit instruments *out*side the Exchequer long after they had ceased to be vital to its internal workings, for example from the 1660's to the 1690's.

Among Exchequer officials there tended to be a division between prestige and responsibility. The central office-holders on whom the efficient operation of royal finance depended were the Auditor of the Receipt, the two Prest Auditors, and the seven Revenue Auditors. Yet the King's and Lord Treasurer's Remembrancers, the two Chamberlains, and the Clerk of the Pells all ranked above them, and some of these posts were also more lucrative. The Pipe and the King's Remembrancer's Offices were both among the 'trouble spots' of the administration; neither was any longer of much consequence except to those unfortunate accountants and litigants who still had to deal with them. However, these happened to include the High Sheriffs of counties, who were chosen annually, more often than not from amongst the greater gentry.[2] The trouble which Exchequer officials caused to the Crown, especially in the matter of fees and remuneration, could almost be said to have varied inversely with their usefulness in national finance!

Executive orders and instructions to the Exchequer and the other revenue departments most often came from the Privy Seal. Authorizations for out-payments almost invariably did so. But the original initiative usually came from the Lord Treasurer (and sometimes the Chancellor of the Exchequer), or from the Treasury Commissioners (of whom the Chancellor was always one, generally

---

[1] P.R.O., Exchequer of Receipt, E 403/2154-5, Prest books, Auditor's (described as being the Clerk of the Pells' books in M. S. Giuseppi, *A Guide to the Manuscripts preserved in the Public Record Office* (1923-4), I, 185: a rare slip); SP 16/377/2.

[2] Notestein, *English People*, ch. 17.

constituting the *quorum*). By virtue of having to pass through the Signet Office, before appearing as letters under the Privy Seal, these orders came within the orbit of the Secretaries and received the King's formal approval; they were issued to the Exchequer, or to one of the other revenue courts, as warrants under the Privy Seal. The theoretical sequence was thus: Crown (i.e. Sign Manual) to Signet, Signet to Privy Seal, Privy Seal to Lord Treasurer and Chancellor (*or* to Receiver-General of the Wards, or the Duchy), Treasurer and Chancellor to officers of the Receipt. Between 1625 and 1640 in practice the commonest sequence was: Lord Treasurer (and his secretary), *or* Treasury Commissioners (and their secretary) to Auditor of Receipt, Auditor to Signet, Signet to Privy Seal, Privy Seal to Treasurer and Chancellor, finally Treasurer (*or* Treasurer and Chancellor) or his secretary to Auditor (in some cases alone, in others jointly with other officers of the Receipt). The Treasurer's secretary sometimes dealt direct with the Signet, cutting out the Auditor the first time round. The following sequence can also be found: Treasurer's secretary to Signet, Signet to Privy Seal, Privy Seal to Receiver-General of the Wards or the Duchy.

Thus the Lord Treasurer (or the Treasury Commissioners) enjoyed the *de facto* power to give himself (or themselves) *de jure* authorization for the issue of money. In addition, the Treasurer and Chancellor (or the Commissioners) did have some control over the *external* relations of the Duchy and the Wards with the rest of the government, though not over their internal management.

Out of the very small staff of Treasurer's secretaries or clerks who handled the initial informal requests for formal authorizations, and who transmitted the Privy Seals to the Receipt, was to develop the modern Treasury. The traditional view, that the rule of Lords Commissioners rather than of a Lord Treasurer hastened the growth of the Treasury as a distinct department of state, does not seem to be wholly true of the commissions in 1612, 1618, and 1635, and may not even be valid for those of 1667 and later.[1] Under Charles I it is certainly wrong to think of the Treasury as a department distinct from the Exchequer. Nor did the Treasurer, unless

---

[1] Compare Baxter, *Development of the Treasury*, who plays down the importance of 1667, with F. S. Thomas, *The Ancient Exchequer of England* (1848), and other older authorities.

by indirect influence over the King, yet have the power to stop other departments from incurring expenditure, even though he controlled the payments to them for what they had spent. The Treasurer and Chancellor could not by themselves authorize major items of extraordinary expenditure or new methods of raising money. Such matters would have to be discussed by the King in Council, even if the original initiative had often come from the Treasurer and Chancellor or from the head of one of the spending departments. At the height of his power Buckingham (in his capacity as Lord Admiral) seems virtually to have been able to authorize the issue of money on his own initiative; but only because Ley, Earl of Marlborough (Lord Treasurer 1624-8) was content to be a mere 'rubber stamp'. Much always depended on the personalities of the men involved, and on their standing with the King; between 1612 and 1673 the Lord Treasurer can only properly be thought of as having been the King's principal or 'first' minister from the autumn of 1628 to sometime in 1634.[1]

The Customs service was the most important single branch of the revenue administration, and it was closely related to the Exchequer. The customs were largely farmed under Charles I, that is leased to business syndicates. These farmers, who were mostly great London merchants and financiers, are only of concern here because some of them were also regular paid officials. As a group the Customs farmers were doubly important in that they were largely identical with the Crown's principal creditors in the City, on whom the whole of royal finance depended so much. The Surveyors were the most important Customs officials in that they always remained answerable direct to the Lord Treasurer. When some customs were farmed and others not, the Collectors, Customers, and junior officials (Searchers, Waiters, etc.) presumably had a divided responsibility, in respect of some goods and duties to the Exchequer, of others to the farmers. The London customs staff were more important than those in all the other ports put together, because of the great concentration of the export and import trade through the capital. And they

---

[1] Robert Cecil, first Earl of Salisbury, d. 1612; Weston, later Earl of Portland, may be described as 'first minister' from 1628 until 1634, the year before his death, but he was very much *primus inter pares*. The Lord Treasurer was not to be first minister again until the time of Danby, 1673-9. The office was mainly in commission from 1667, and permanently from 1714.

can certainly be classified as members of the central government.[1]

The Alienations Office was the smallest revenue department to enjoy even semi-independence. It handled the revenues raised by fines and compositions paid when land held by feudal tenure from the Crown was bought and sold, but not when it was leased; the tax on alienations was one reason for the evolution of the 99, and even more of the 999, year lease (in terms of purchase price, and security of title, contemporaries virtually equated these leases with sales; avoidance of wardship might also be a motive with the buyer). The Lord Treasurer and Chancellor of the Exchequer had been responsible for this office since late in Elizabeth's reign, but they left its normal running to a subordinate staff.[2]

During Charles I's reign finance was continuously the central problem of royal government and policy. This was true even in the deceptively calm years 1630-7, between the restoration of external peace and the clash with the Scots. Ample evidence can be found in the general political histories of the times and in the standard history of public finance;[3] the effect of this on the administration is apparent. Very few governments in history have had as much money as they wanted, and few régimes have not had to cut their coat according to their cloth. But the constant awareness of imminent crisis, with the bogey of parliament and of 'redress before supply', must have been a dominating influence on almost every member of the English government in the 1630's.

---

[1] A. P. Newton, 'The Establishment of the Great Farm of the English Customs', *Trans. Roy. Hist. Soc.*, 4th ser., I (1918); W. P. Harper, 'The Significance of the Farmers of the Customs', *Economica*, IX (1929); F. C. Dietz, 'Elizabethan Customs Administration', *Eng. Hist. Rev.*, XLV (1930); Dietz, *Public Finance*, esp. chs. XIV-XVI; R. Ashton, 'Revenue Farming under the Early Stuarts', *Econ. Hist. Rev.*, 2nd ser., VIII, 3 (1956), 'Deficit Finance in the Reign of James I', *ibid.*, X, 1 (1957), 'The Disbursing Official under the Early Stuarts', *Bull. Inst. Hist. Res.*, XXX (1957). The list given in the Appendix is also based on primary sources for the 1620's and 1630's, and F. Peck, *Desiderata Curiosa* (1732), I, ii, 3-4; H. Hall, *History of Customs Revenue in England* (1885), II, 55; N. S. B. Gras, *Early English Customs System* (Cambridge, Mass., 1918), pp. 94-100; and E. E. Hoon, *The Organisation of the English Customs System, 1696-1786* (New York, 1938), chs. V and VI.

[2] Giuseppe, *Guide*, I, 258-9.

[3] e.g. Gardiner, *History*, vols. VI-IX; Dietz, *Public Finance*, chs. X-XII.

V OTHER DEPARTMENTS OF STATE

The household group was easily the largest and most expensive of the departments of state which were not constructed on the model of a council or a court of law, or built round the management and use of a seal. But others were more important for the future. Of these, some originated as offshoots of the household, others including the most important, were substantially of Tudor origin.

As the department responsible for the coinage of money, the Mint clearly was bound to be closely linked to the Exchequer, although it had remained 'in' the household long after the Exchequer had become a fully separate institution, 'out of court'. While its history is obviously of numismatic and economic interest, we need only consider the Mint as a department, or branch of the central government. Judged by the number of its staff and its scale of operations, it was one of the medium-sized departments, comparable say to the Great Wardrobe (though its head was not as senior in rank as the Master of that office).[1]

In the absence of any war office, or permanent military establishment, the Ordnance Office was relatively more important than it was to be later. At this time it also supplied the Navy with armaments and some other equipment. It was responsible for the ordering, purchase, storage, maintenance, issue, recovery, and repair of all munitions of war both by land and sea; manufacture was in private hands, but the suppliers of both cannon and gunpowder were paid under-officers in the department, as were those responsible for match, cordage, timber, and iron ware. The Ordnance was directly subordinate to the King and the Council; in the 1620's it also took orders from Buckingham, in his capacity as Lord Admiral.

The Armoury was a much smaller sub-department, in theory and to some extent in practice independent of the Ordnance. Its head, the Master, probably ranked below the second in command, the Lieutenant, of the Ordnance, but one holder of the office used it as a stepping-stone to much greater things.[2] Broadly speaking, the Armoury had charge of the older hand-to-hand weapons, the

---

[1] J. Craig, *The Mint* (Cambridge, 1953). For controversy concerning Mint offices, see below, Chapter 6, s. vi.

[2] William Legge, Master 1638-49, 1660-70, ancestor of the Earls of Dartmouth; after the Restoration he was also Lieut. of the Ordnance.

Ordnance of all fire-arms, and of tools and other equipment; but in wartime or other emergencies bulk orders for swords, pikes, etc., were often handled by the larger, more active department.

The Navy was a bigger and more important department than any of these. But if we exclude dockyard workmen its permanent shore staff was smaller than that of the Ordnance. It was already quite separate from the Court of Admiralty. Like the Ordnance, it was directly subordinate to the King and Privy Council. Even under Buckingham (Lord Admiral, 1619-28), although the Navy was almost an *imperium in imperio*, financial necessity compelled the discussion of its affairs in the Council; and the unmistakable evidence of mismanagement led to successive royal commissions of inquiry which tended to find everyone more or less at fault except the Lord Admiral himself. After his death the Admiralty Commissioners included the Lord Treasurer (except in 1635-6), the Chancellor of the Exchequer, and the two Secretaries of State, so in a sense the Navy was brought more directly under the control both of the Exchequer and of the central executive; the next Lord Admiral (Northumberland, 1638-42) neither enjoyed, nor aspired to, the position of Buckingham.[1]

Of all the branches of the government so far discussed, the Navy, the Ordnance, and the Wardrobes had the worst contemporary reputation for waste and fraud. However, it is doubtful if any of them were as flagrant as the Household below stairs, whose accounting officers were shown in 1638 to have been cheating the Crown of between £6,000 and £10,000 p.a. for the previous forty years.[2]

The garrisons of royal forts and castles, like the officers and crews of H.M. ships, do not belong in this survey, except in so far as some Captains of such garrisons were also courtiers or holders of central office. Out of over ninety royal castles, forts, 'bulwarks', and 'sconces', about thirty on the sea coasts from Essex to Cornwall were ostensibly

---

[1] M. Oppenheim, *The Administration of the Royal Navy . . . from 1509 to 1660* (1898) is a remarkably able book written by a medical practitioner. Oppenheim was not much concerned with individual officers and their problems, and he tended to contrast the corruption and ins efficiency under the early Stuarts too emphatically with the achievement of the Long Parliament and Commonwealth (for the latter point I am indebted to Mr. D. E. Kennedy of Trinity College, Cambridge, and Melbourne University).

[2] Aylmer, 'Attempts at Administrative Reform', *Eng. Hist. Rev.*, LXXII, 250-1, n. 7, and 255; and see below, Chapter 4, s. i.

kept in a state of defence. The officers of the Tower and of the other royal prisons in London (as of the royal hospitals there) can more properly be thought of as members of the central government.

The College of Arms, founded in 1483, still played a genuine part in government. Early seventeenth-century English society was at the same time intensely hierarchical and relatively fluid. Men rose in the social scale fairly rapidly and in quite large numbers, and more rarely they also fell. The exact definition of rank or social status mattered alike for people's own self-respect and for their standing in society. Genealogy and heraldry were far from being matters primarily of antiquarian or aesthetic concern. What was more, and certainly from the Crown's point of view equally important, there was money in them! Those magnificent 'Visitations' of the different counties carried out by the Kings of Arms and the Heralds, dating to the hundred years or so *c.* 1560-1640 and 1660-88, most of which have been published by the Harleian Society, were far from being the products of disinterested research. The Crown wanted to keep a check on the number of gentry in the country, indeed almost to take small-scale censuses of them county by county. And in particular to ensure that only those entitled to do so should use coat armour and style themselves Esquire. As readers of the contemporary dramatists will know, there was a comic and occasionally a seamy side to all this: pedigrees and coats of arms were sometimes for sale, ready concocted.

Although sinecurist and antiquarian elements are discernible, the heraldic staff can fairly be treated as a branch of the central government. And it would be pedantic to separate the Heralds from the Court of Chivalry, though strictly the latter should belong in the next section of this chapter.[1] And, although not technically in the same department, the regular officers of the Order of the Garter may conveniently be mentioned here. Their duties cannot have been heavy, though the preparations for the annual feasts and celebrations must have been quite elaborate to judge from their cost (£700-£750 on St. George's day). The Order of the Bath, the only other English order of chivalry with a sizeable but well-defined membership, does not seem to have had a comparable staff.

[1] A. R. Wagner, *Heralds and Heraldry* (2nd ed., Oxford, 1956), and *The Collections and Records of the College of Arms* (1951); *Burke's Landed Gentry* (1952 edn.), pp. cvii-xxi. I am grateful to Mr. G. D. Squibb and the late H. S. London for help with the officers of arms.

vi JUSTICE AND THE LAW COURTS

Provided it is accepted that the most basic functions of government are justice, finance, and administration, it is proper to consider the law courts as a part of the central government. This must be done without becoming involved in the history of English law in the seventeenth century.[1] The officers of the central law courts make up a sizeable proportion of all those whose duties and careers will be considered in the chapters which follow.

Several of the courts also functioned in other capacities, and so have already been mentioned. For simplicity's sake they can all be divided into four or five groups: the three ancient common law courts of King's Bench, Common Pleas, and Exchequer; the equity courts of Chancery and Requests; the 'prerogative' courts of the Privy Council functioning judicially, Star Chamber, the High Commission, the Councils of the North and in the Marches of Wales, the Court of Wards and Liveries, the Court of Duchy Chamber, the Court of the Stannaries, and the Court of Castle Chamber in Dublin; the central ecclesiastical courts of the Delegates, and the Arches, and the Prerogative Court of Canterbury; finally, in a category by itself, the Court of Admiralty, dispensing a mixture of Roman civil law and English law merchant. A very brief account will now be given of those which have not already been surveyed.

As its name implies, King's Bench was primarily the court where Crown actions were brought. Its role in the execution of criminal justice gave King's Bench its rather vague and ill-defined primacy among the law courts, and produced the feeling that it was still in some sense nearer to the Crown, less far 'out of Court', than the other common law and equity courts. On its private, or 'pleas', side procedural changes in the fifteenth and sixteenth centuries had won business away from Common Pleas, and had also redistributed it within King's Bench, to the loss of all but one of the Filazers and to the great gain of the Chief Clerk and the remaining Filazer. Thanks to its gains from Common Pleas, by the seventeenth century King's

[1] See W. Holdsworth, *A History of English Law* (1903-), esp. vols. V and VI. Even if it no longer satisfies the modern inquirer at all points, Holdsworth's *History* is unlikely to be superseded, except by specialist studies.

Bench was doing a thriving business in private actions of party versus party.[1]

The Marshalsea court and the court of the Verge, which were subordinate branches of the household, had originated as offshoots of King's Bench. Charles I set up a new and ostensibly more impressive Palace court, for all cases arising from offences committed within twelve miles of his Court (or person), but in practice it was only a reconstructed combined version of the Marshalsea and Verge courts, and its effective jurisdiction was narrower than might appear from its paper constitution.[2]

None of the common law courts had adapted themselves to meet changes in the conditions under which property was held, or in economic activities generally. All were intricate in procedure, dreadfully slow and expensive, and archaic, if not sometimes unpredictable and even arbitrary in judgment. In these respects King's Bench was only less unsatisfactory than Common Pleas. But, as so often in human affairs, the bad helped to stand in the way of the worse; the common law was undoubtedly a barrier of a sort against arbitrary government.

Common Pleas was *par excellence* the court for civil actions between private parties, especially for cases which involved property. Although it had lost business of different kinds to King's Bench, Exchequer, and Chancery, it was still, on the strictly legal side, the largest of the courts; its Chief Justiceship was a more lucrative and professionally more coveted post than the more honorific and politically more significant Lord Chief Justiceship of King's Bench.[3]

The third common law court, the Exchequer, has already been described. As a court of law in our sense it specialized in cases which involved the Crown's financial rights: disputes arising out of the

---

[1] Holdsworth, *History*, I (3rd edn.), 198-200, 219-22, appdx. XXV, pp. 672-3; Giuseppi, *Guide*, I, 219; M. Blatcher (Mrs. S. T. Bindoff), 'The working of the Court of King's Bench in the 15th Century', London Ph.D. Thesis (1936). See below, Chapter 4, s. iii, and Chapter 5, s. iii.

[2] Holdsworth, *History*, I, 208-9; *Foedera*, ed. T. Rymer, R. Sanderson (1704-35), XIX, 431, *Cal. S.P. Dom. 1629-31*, p. 281; SP 16/531/47, 125; Nat. Lib. Wales, Wynnstay MS. 160.

[3] M. Hastings, *The Court of Common Pleas in 15th Century England* (Ithaca, N.Y., 1947). This is the fullest modern account of any single court and its work for any period between the thirteenth and nineteenth centuries. For Common Pleas' loss of business to Exchequer, see Holdsworth, *History*, I, 236-7, 240.

collection of taxes, customs dues, fines, debts. Many commissions of inquiry of a semi-judicial, semi-administrative character were issued under the Exchequer seal, and some led to court actions. The officers of the Exchequer, like those of Common Pleas, King's Bench, and Chancery, had an *ex-officio* right to cite cases in which they were parties into their own court. The King's accountants, and up to a point his debtors, could also do so. Like the other Chief Justices and Judges, the Chief and Puisne Barons went on circuit twice yearly; it is impossible to say how much of their time at Westminster was spent on legal rather than financial business. Of the three, the Exchequer was the least-used common law court; it also functioned as an equity court, in which the Lord Treasurer and the Chancellor were judges as well as the Barons, the clerical work being in charge of the King's Remembrancer's Office. The equity side of the Exchequer handled only a fraction as much business as Chancery.[1]

Numerous officers of Chancery were involved in the passage of instruments under the Great Seal (see Table 56, p. 470). But even without them Chancery would have been one of the largest central institutions; nearly fifty of its officers come within the scope of this investigation, including those already mentioned as members of the central executive. Below them, as in other departments, there is probably seldom much to be discovered; no other court seems to have had as many petty under clerks as Chancery.[2]

The distinction between 'law', i.e. common law, and equity is not an easy one for the layman to grasp. However, there is no doubt that the equity business of Chancery had grown enormously in the course of the fifteenth and sixteenth centuries, and that this was in part a direct reflection on the inadequacy of the common law courts. In theory, a civil action which should have gone to Common Pleas or King's Bench could only be taken to Chancery for some specific reason, e.g. that the documentary evidence was lacking or that the witnesses were dead. The plaintiff had to argue that evident justice was on his side, but that by the letter of the common law he would

---

[1] Giuseppi, *Guide*, I, 75-6; Holdsworth, *History*, I, 236, 240-2.
[2] Wilson, Thesis, app. III, lists all Chancery personnel whose offices were valued for a commission of inquiry in *c.* 1630, not only those on the administrative side. Compare Holdsworth, *History*, I, app. XXVI, pp. 674-7, a list of the officers of Chancery in 1740; Maxwell-Lyte, *Great Seal*; Giuseppi, *Guide*, I, 6-9.

have no chance of a remedy. It is fair to guess that the officers of Chancery did not analyse this too closely; the officers of the other courts sometimes tried to recover business, but it is most unlikely that those of Chancery deliberately turned clients away. The situation reaches its most ironical when no less an officer than the Chief Prothonotary of Common Pleas is found requesting the Lord Keeper that he 'may be relieved . . . in Equitie', in a case between himself and his own colleague, the third Prothonotary, because 'at or by the strict rules of the Common Lawes of this Realme' he is remediless in his own court![1]

Although of pre-Tudor origin, the Court of Requests had been reorganized by Wolsey to deal specifically with 'poor men's causes'. It had had its own permanent judges, the Masters of Requests, from Edward VI's reign. Broadly speaking, this court was meant to handle cases too petty for Star Chamber, and to cater for litigants too poor or too impatient for Chancery. By the seventeenth century it would probably have been regarded as an 'equity' rather than a 'prerogative' court. Despite attacks on its jurisdiction by the common law courts in the 1590's and 1610's, under the active direction of Lord Privy Seal Manchester in the 1630's it seems to have been busy, reasonably prompt, and popular with those who used it. The smallness of its staff indicates the speediness and the relative informality of its procedure rather than lack of use; nor was there much money in it. That the upper classes, the property owners, and perhaps the lawyers disapproved of the Requests is shown by its jurisdiction having been greatly reduced, though not formally abolished, by the 'Star Chamber' Act of 1641. The Court sat until 1642; it did not function again after 1660, although the Masters continued to handle petitions to the Crown until the 1670's.[2]

Wide as were the differences in law and in procedure between the three common law courts and the equity courts of Chancery and Requests, the gulf which separated both these groups from the prerogative courts was still wider. The *ad hoc* decisions of Chancery or the court of Requests, based on an appraisal of the equitable

---

[1] P.R.O. Chancery Proceedings, 2nd ser., C 3/397/96, Brownlow *v.* Moyle, 1637.

[2] *Select Cases in the Court of Requests*, ed. I. S. Leadam (Selden Soc., XII, 1898), pp. ix-lii; Holdsworth, *History*, I, 412-16; Elton, *Revolution in Government*, pp. 35, 134-8, and *England under the Tudors* (1955), pp. 83, 414.

principles involved in a case, might seem to have more in common with the rough and ready 'amateur' justice dispensed by the Privy Council or Star Chamber than with the intricate and traditionalist case-law of the common law judges. Looking back across three centuries without the eye of a trained lawyer, this impression is almost irresistible. Yet in the historical context of the time, it was not so. Whatever men's doubts about the court of Requests, Chancery was accepted as an integral part of the legal system of the country. Star Chamber was not. The hostility shown to Chancery by some common lawyers seems to have died down after Lord Chancellor Ellesmere's victory over Chief Justice Coke in 1616. Most of the would-be law reformers under the Commonwealth attacked its slowness and costliness, and the corruption and inefficiency of its officers; but it was not felt, as Star Chamber had been in 1640-1, to be an instrument of despotism. And the more radical law reformers of the Interregnum attacked the common law courts just as much as Chancery, for being thinly disguised instruments of class domination; granted their premises, this was a perfectly valid conclusion.

Star Chamber was peculiar in having many judges (all the Privy Councillors and the two Chief Justices) but few permanent officials. The smallness of its staff does not necessarily indicate that its dispatch of business was more prompt, but does argue its relative cheapness for the litigant, compared especially with Common Pleas and Chancery.

Whatever its merits are admitted to have been under the Tudors, Star Chamber under the Stuarts is usually thought of almost exclusively as an instrument of royal despotism. That it *was* such an instrument is proved beyond doubt by the justly notorious cases of the 1630's. But the vast majority of the cases heard before it, on which the greater part of its time was spent, were in no sense political; they included both public and private actions, many of them involving physical violence, intimidation, fraud, and defamation, that is, crimes which tend to require summary treatment if they are to be kept in check. It would be small comfort to the injured party in such cases if it took years or even decades for justice to be done, as was quite liable to happen in the older courts. Nor do its records suggest that Star Chamber was declining in popularity with certain kinds of users; it was its political use by the Crown and its moral-*cum*-ideological use by the Bishops which were coming to be felt as intolerable grievances; also the legal profession was implacably hostile to it.[1]

The most surprising thing about Star Chamber, as about the Privy Council acting in its judicial capacity, is the apparent triviality of many matters on which it spent time. Considering the eminence of its membership, it is staggering that quite minor cases of party versus party had to be heard in Star Chamber and could not be dealt with adequately by one of the numerous other central courts. There is some evidence that this had become more marked, that under the earlier Tudors and perhaps into Elizabeth's reign, Council and Star Chamber had delegated more of their judicial work to commissions and sub-committees.[2] It may, however, be felt that it is a merit in sovereign bodies—be they executive, judicial, or legislative—to be ready to give time to minor issues affecting obscure individuals: 'question time' in the modern House of Commons comes to mind. But whatever the case for the present-day volume of parliamentary questions, it is surely a bad analogy. We should certainly think it odd if the Cabinet or the Appeal Court were found to be doing what should be the work of a Rural District Council or a bench of J.P.s.

Nor did Star Chamber and the Council act as appeal courts, at least not in our sense of that term. They did hear some cases because other courts had failed to settle them, but in general both were courts of 'first instance'. The concept of an appeal court, if not completely unknown, was at best very imperfectly understood. Errors, that is appeals theoretically due to mistakes in the formal record of the case, from Common Pleas were heard in King's Bench. The Lord Treasurer and Chancellor of the Exchequer, acting as judges in the court of Exchequer Chamber, heard errors from the common law side of the Exchequer. They and the Barons of the Exchequer also met there as judges for the equity side of the Exchequer (not errors from this). From 1585 the Justices of Common

---

[1] C. L. Scofield, *A Study of the Court of Star Chamber* (Chicago, 1900); H. E. I. Phillips, 'The Last Years of Star Chamber', *Trans. Roy. Hist. Soc.*, 4th ser., XXI (1939). See also A. F. Pollard, 'Council, Star Chamber, and Privy Council under the Tudors', *Eng. Hist Rev.*, XXXVII-XXXVIII (1922-3), and Elton, *Revolution in Government*, pp. 161, 343-4, and *England under the Tudors*, pp. 65, 82-3, 414-17.

[2] W. H. Dunham, jnr., 'Henry VIII's Whole Council and Its Parts', *Huntington Lib. Qly.*, VII (1943-4), 7-46. This contrast is not supported by the other authorities.

Pleas and the Barons of the Exchequer, also meeting in and as the court of Exchequer Chamber, heard errors from King's Bench other than those taken straight to parliament, which was in a sense *the* supreme court of appeal. On occasion the court of Exchequer Chamber could also consist of the twelve common law judges meeting to discuss and decide on particularly difficult cases in any of the three courts. By Charles I's time Exchequer Chamber kept its own records; but despite the four different capacities in which it could function, it was hardly a separate institution in the same sense as Star Chamber, let alone King's Bench.[1]

The Councils in the North and in the Marches of Wales exercised jurisdiction which overlapped with that of King's Bench, Common Pleas, Exchequer, Chancery, and Requests. But in their procedure they bore more resemblance to Star Chamber. The powers of the two regional Councils were not identical in every respect, but similar enough to be considered together here. Both had criminal and civil jurisdiction in addition to a wide range of administrative duties. In the rest of the country (apart from the royal palatinates of Chester and Lancaster and the Duchy of Cornwall) there was no intermediate level of administration between the Privy Council itself and local government at the county level and below. Nor was there any intermediate judicial level (other than the judges' half-yearly circuits) between the quarter sessions of J.P.s and the central courts at Westminster.

The legal and administrative staffs of the two Councils are not always easily distinguished, and some of their officers functioned in both capacities. At York most of the councillors did not attend regularly, though all were liable to be called on in exceptional cases. Normally the judges there consisted of the President, or Vice-President, and the four paid councillors, usually men of legal experience. In the years 1633-9 the Vice-President was effectively in charge since Wentworth, the Lord President, was away in Ireland almost all the time.[2]

The Council in the Marches had also come to rely on a few paid

[1] Holdsworth, *History*, I, 213-15, 242-6; Giuseppi, *Guide*, I, 76; *Select Cases in the Exchequer Chamber . . . 1377-1461*, ed. M. Hemmant (Selden Soc., LI, 1933), xi-lxxxiii, esp. p. xiii.

[2] R. R. Reid, *The King's Council in the North* (1921); F. W. Brooks, *The Council of the North* (Historical Association pamphlet, 1953); Leeds Public Library, Temple Newsam MSS., Council in the North

councillors. Three of them, together with the President and the Chief Justice of Chester, who was *ex-officio* Vice-President, normally acted as the judges. In addition to the Council there was for some purposes a separate administration for Wales, which did *not* (unlike the Council) extend to Monmouth or the four English 'border' counties (Salop, Herefordshire, Gloucestershire and Worcestershire); there was also a separate judicial hierarchy for Wales and Chester. The twelve Welsh counties were divided into four groups of three; each group had a 'chancery' and an 'exchequer' so-called, with a Chamberlain presiding over them. On the legal side there was a Prothonotary and Clerk of the Crown for each group, responsible to the two Justices of each of the four Welsh circuits, or Courts of Great Session (the paid councillors at Ludlow were often also judges of Great Session).[1]

There remains to consider the least tangible and formalized but by no means the least effective or unpopular of the prerogative courts. The Court of High Commission was a standing royal commission 'for causes ecclesiastical', which included the whole Privy Council, all the Judges, all the Bishops, Deans, and Archdeacons of the Province of Canterbury, several of the most eminent civil lawyers, and a number of other important peers and gentry some of whom were not central office-holders. It had been regularly constituted as a court since the 1580's. Until 1625 the commission (and court) was limited to the Province of Canterbury. There was another 'commission for causes ecclesiastical' for the northern Province including all the Bishops, Deans, and Archdeacons of the Province of York, plus civil lawyers, etc.

The High Commission is rightly bracketed with the 'prerogative courts'. The scope of its jurisdiction, extended to the Province of York at Charles's accession, was further enlarged to cover Scotland

[1] C. A. J. Skeel, *The Council in the Marches of Wales* (1904), and 'The Council of the Marches in the 17th Century', *Eng. Hist. Rev.*, XXX (1915); 'Wales under Henry VII', *Tudor Studies . . . presented . . . to A. F. Pollard*, ed. R. W. Seton-Watson (1924), 1-26; W. Rees, 'The Union of England and Wales', *Trans. Cymmorodorion Soc. session 1937* (1938), 27-100, esp. pp. 57-8, 64-5, 74-5, 88-9, 100; Hist. MSS. Comm. *4th Rept.*, House of Lords, p. 22; Penry Williams, *The Council in the Marches of Wales in the Reign of Elizabeth I* (Aberystwyth, 1958). See also *The Statutes of Wales*. ed. I. Bowen (1908), pp. 104-5, 110, 115-16; W. O. Williams, *Tudor Gwynedd* (Caernarvon Hist. Soc., 1958), pp. 33-5. I am grateful to Mr. Penry Williams for help with sources for Welsh government.

in the reissues of 1629 and 1633. R. G. Usher, its only modern historian, was convinced that Charles I and Laud meant to increase its power as well as to enlarge its scope. Yet to the last it remained a court only by virtue of a periodically renewed royal commission, and as a 'court of record' its statutory position was dubious. It had the same political significance as Star Chamber, but its work was concerned with sexual and ecclesiastical offences, and with clerical discipline. Its existence was a tacit acknowledgment that the post-Reformation church courts were not equal to the burdens which the Crown and the hierarchy wished to lay on them.[1]

The most senior of the ordinary ecclesiastical courts had been set up to fill the gap left by abolishing appeals to Rome. But the Court of Delegates, as it was called, in fact practically never functioned, at least not in the early seventeenth century. It was an extraordinary and not a standing body, which acted as the appeal court from the Admiralty as well as from the church courts; it consisted of the Privy Council together with certain of the bishops, some of the judges, and the most distinguished 'civilians', or civil lawyers of Doctors' Commons.[2] In practice the King in Council, the Court of High Commission, and even Star Chamber, could be said to have done much of what it had ostensibly been meant to do; in part the gap was simply filled by administrative action by the Crown, the Primate, and the bishops, to enforce uniformity and to decide other questions of ecclesiastical policy.

The other church courts had jurisdiction over only one Province. In the Province of Canterbury, which comprised nearly three-quarters of the Kingdom, including most of the richest and more populous areas, the next senior court was that of the Arches. The 'official principal', or Dean of the Arches, was normally a distinguished civilian; this was the most prized office for ecclesiastical administrators. Next was the Judge of the Court of Audience, the institution for enforcing the Archbishop's jurisdiction over the other bishops in his Province. Again it is not clear how much use was

[1] R. G. Usher, *The Rise and Fall of the High Commission* (Oxford, 1913), the standard, indeed the only authority, has virtually nothing on its officers; Holdsworth, *History*, I, 605-11; J. S. Purvis, *Tudor Parish Documents of the Diocese of York* (Cambridge, 1948), pp. xiv-xv, on the northern commission (I am grateful to Canon Purvis for further information about this body).

[2] Holdsworth, *History*, I, 604-5; *Report of the Commissioners on the Ecclesiastical Courts* (Command Paper 3760, 1883).

made of this court, as opposed to the much more effective administrative power of visitation. If any officials of the Court of Audience
existed during the years 1625-40, they have left very little trace. The
Prerogative Court of Canterbury, in charge of wills and probate,
was subordinate to the 'official principal', but also had its judge or
commissary. The Archbishop's Vicar-General also had a court, but
he too acted primarily by administrative rather than judicial means.
To some extent these courts, excluding the Court of Delegates, were
reproduced in the Province of York, but only the principal ones in
the southern and premier province can fairly be classified as central
institutions. There does not seem to have been any purely judicial
body in which the Primate (Canterbury) could assert his authority
over the junior Archbishop (York).[1]

The Court of Admiralty administered 'law merchant'. Owing to
the archaism and other limitations of the common law and of its
practitioners, civil lawyers were on the whole better qualified to deal
with the ever-increasing volume of litigation concerned with commerce and finance, especially foreign trade. Further to that, while
there was no shortage of common lawyers, indeed some contemporaries thought there were too many, civil lawyers of any ability
were at a premium. From 1624 to 1633 the same man was not only
Dean of the Arches and Judge of the Prerogative Court but also
Judge of the Admiralty Court. This was not mere pluralism and
jobbery, for there was an actual shortage of men with the right
qualifications. The compactness of this court, even if it included
under-officers so obscure that little trace of them remains, is in
striking contrast with the elaborate hierarchies of Common Pleas
and Chancery. In Charles I's reign the common lawyers attacked the
jurisdiction of the Admiralty more than they did that of Chancery.
There was a professional difference. Although there were separate
so-called 'Chancery Inns' in London, all who practised in Chancery
had also been to one of the Inns of Court and were trained in the
common law; by the seventeenth century the Chancery Inns were
definitely subordinate to the four great Inns, and did not train equity
lawyers in any independent system of law. By contrast, civil lawyers
were trained at universities, often abroad, or at Gresham's College
in the City, and resided in Doctors' Commons, near St. Paul's.
After the death of Buckingham the Admiralty may have been more

---

[1] Holdsworth, *History*, I, 599-603; *Report of the Commissioners*
(1883).

vulnerable to such attacks; whereas the Lord Admiral's own prestige and his income were involved in the jurisdiction of his court, it is not clear that the Admiralty Commissioners felt the same about it. However, a royal commission was appointed in 1631 to define the boundary between the jurisdiction of the Admiralty court and that of the common law courts, and in 1632/3 the judges of King's Bench passed a series of resolutions limiting the grounds on which cases might be transferred from the Court of Admiralty by the issue of 'prohibitions'—the same common law instrument which Coke had used against the High Commission in 1606-11.[1]

Besides the special jurisdictions of Wales and Chester and of Lancaster, one other regional institution should be mentioned here. The court of Stannaries had wide, if ill-defined, authority over all engaged in the tin-mining industry and over the districts where it was located in Devon and Cornwall. The Lord Warden of the Stannaries was technically appointed by the Duke of Cornwall, and in law, appeals lay from the Lord Warden to the Council of the Duchy. In 1632 the Privy Council in effect ruled that the whole county of Cornwall came under Stannary jurisdiction. But the Stannaries were not identical with the Duchy of Cornwall, which for administrative purposes was at this time little more than a sub-department of the land revenue side of the Exchequer. And in the autumn of 1633 the judges of King's Bench decided that the jurisdiction of the Lord Warden's Court 'is only for tinners and tinne matters' and that appeals lay from it to the courts at Westminster.[2]

Finally, one indisputably national institution of a judicial nature was not a central or regional court. The jurisdiction over royal forests, exercised by the two Justices in Eyre, north and south of Trent, had been important during the Middle Ages and became so again briefly in the 1630's, with Charles I's notorious policy of using the forest laws as a fiscal weapon. The whole system of forest courts and forest law had fallen into disuse by the end of the sixteenth century; under Charles I the two Justices did not in fact itinerate, and the effective jurisdiction, in the courts of Justice Seat of the southern Eyre, was exercised by certain of the judges acting as the Justice's deputies. If there was any regular staff of these courts, it

[1] Holdsworth, *History*, I, 544-68; see also *Foedera*, XIX, 279-81; G. Croke, *Reports of Cases* (1665), p. 781.

[2] Holdsworth, *History*, I, 151-65; G. R. Lewis, *The Stannaries* (Harvard Econ. Studies, III, 1908), pp. 100-13; Croke, *Reports* (1665), p. 795.

would seem to have been personal to each Justice; at least there is no record of any other Crown appointments.[1]

English law and the judicial authority of the Crown were imposed in Ireland through a legal hierarchy exactly modelled on that in England. The three common law courts and the Chancery court functioned in Dublin much as their counterparts did in Westminster, with very similar establishments and divisions of duties; the judges went on assize circuits, though how far they administered English as opposed to Irish 'Brehon' law over the whole country is unclear; above all, the court of Castle Chamber in Dublin was an exact and deliberate replica of Star Chamber. The Crown could cite cases from Castle to Star Chamber, and in cases of error appeal seems to have lain from the Irish to the English court of King's Bench.[2] By contrast, Scotland kept its own law: the Scottish courts were quite distinct from those in England, and in no way subordinate to them.

As well as the regular officers and clerks of the law courts, there were two or three categories of lawyers who can be considered as quasi-officials. The paid Councillors in the North and Wales have already been mentioned. In the courts at Westminster the position of the 'King's Sergeants' and the newer 'King's Counsel' was slightly different. 'K.C.' was not simply a mark of professional distinction like 'Q.C.' today, but it carried obligations with it. In 1635 about six lawyers were receiving retaining fees from the Crown as King's Sergeants or K.C.s. In general, the degree of Sergeant had been declining and that of King's counsel growing in importance, but the Sergeants retained their monopoly right as pleaders in Common Pleas. The K.C.s and King's Sergeants acted, in effect, as assistant legal advisers to the Crown, along with the Attorney- and Solicitor-Generals.[3]

Furthermore, there were Attorneys of some individual courts as well as the Attorney-General, principal legal adviser to the Crown.

[1] Holdsworth, *History*, I, 94-108.

[2] J. Davies, *Historical Tracts* (ed. G. Chalmers, 1786); *Analecta Hibernica*, I, 152, II, 93-291, esp. 114-16, 120-4; H. Wood, 'The Court of Castle Chamber or Star Chamber of Ireland', *Procs. Roy. Ir. Acad.*, XXXII. C. (1914-16), 152-70. I am grateful to Mr. Penry Williams for telling me of these sources.

[3] SP 16/301/9; twelve are listed, but six held other offices under the Crown. See also Holdsworth, *History*, II (4th edn., 1936), 487; V (1945 edn.), 340-1; VI (1937 edn.), bk. IV, pt. I, 457-81; and Hastings, *Common Pleas*, ch. V.

But the word was also used of those who had the exclusive privilege of managing certain types of business in particular courts. For instance, besides *the* Attorney of the Court of Wards and Liveries, there were also four attorneys there; it is said to have been his loss of place as *an* attorney in the Court of Wards (for political and religious opposition to royal policy) that caused John Winthrop to emigrate to Massachusetts.[1] He was not *the* Attorney of the Court of Wards. Similarly there were attorneys in Star Chamber who appear to have been closely related to the Examiners of that court. The attorneys of the Pipe Office in the Exchequer were not pleaders, nor were they royal officials, paid by the Crown and holding by patent. Between them they looked after, and took fees on, all the accounts and other items which passed through that Office. An attorney had originally been more or less what is now meant by a solicitor, as opposed to a barrister or pleader. By the seventeenth century some attorneys were acting as pleaders in some courts, while solicitors were emerging as lawyers of a separate type who carried on their work wholly outside the courts.[2]

In 1633 the Privy Council ordered a census to be taken of all attorneys qualified to practice in King's Bench and Common Pleas. The recent increase in their number was

> conceived to be a principall Cause of the stirring up and multiplying of Suites in all parts of the Kingdome where they reside, to the great damage and vexacion of his majesties subjects.

On the report being presented, the number was 'conceived to be exorbitante'; a fixed schedule of names was to be kept, and ways considered of reducing the number, as also that of 'Common Solicitors,' 'being both of them Sowers and ffomenters of suites'.[3]

For all this, and for all their attacks on the other law courts (e.g. Requests, Admiralty, Marches), it would be wrong to think of all common lawyers as enemies of the prerogative courts and so of absolute monarchy. Except where civil law was in use (Admiralty, Arches, etc.), legal practice in those courts was in the hands of

[1] A. P. Newton, *The Colonising Activities of the English Puritans* (New Haven, 1914), p. 45. C. M. Andrews (*The Colonial Period of American History*, I (New Haven, 1934), 387 n. 2) expressed doubts that Winthrop was actually deprived of his place. See *Winthrop Papers*, II (Massachusetts Hist. Soc., 1931), 94, 99-100.

[2] Holdsworth, *History*, VI (1937 edn.), 431-57.

[3] PC 2/43, pp. 115, 138, 278.

qualified common lawyers; the Inns of Chancery were supplementary to the Inns of Court, not an alternative or rival system, and there were no special institutions to train prerogative lawyers. The alliance between the common lawyers and the constitutional opposition to the early Stuarts was never complete. None of the Stuarts ever lacked for able lawyers to support their policies, even when these involved the use of prerogative courts or other methods of government derogatory to the dignity and interests of the common law courts, and of those who practised in them.

To the men of the seventeenth century the 'courts' which have been described in the second section of this chapter because they had executive functions, or in the fourth because they were primarily revenue departments, were just as much courts of law and record as the ones described in this section. Royal commissions were reissued periodically under the Great Seal, in theory renewing the authority of High Commission and the Councils in the North and the Marches of Wales, which had in practice achieved permanent status under the Tudors; the two latter were usually known as 'Councils', yet they had many of the characteristics of courts—more perhaps than the 'Court' of Requests. When constitutional historians speak of the Tudor and early Stuart reigns as the age of 'conciliar government', they have in mind the Privy and regional Councils as well as the 'prerogative courts'. The close connexion and intermixture of executive and judicial power gave this period part of its characteristic quality, by contrast with that which followed.

vii PARLIAMENT

So far in this survey one important branch of English central government, Parliament, has not been touched on at all. There are various reasons why it has been left out. It was an occasional and not a regular part of the government. Before the Civil War it had very little part in administration; its activities were advisory, inquisitorial, and to a lesser extent legislative and judicial. Members of Parliament and peers were not, as such, regular paid officials of the central government. Parliament actually sat for a total of about four and a quarter years from 1603 to 1629 (the reign of James I and the first four years of Charles I); it did not meet at all from then until the spring of 1640; it sat for three weeks in April-May, and then almost continuously from November 1640 on. Even if we consider the period from March 1625 to January 1642 (the accession of

Charles to his leaving London after the attempt on the 'Five Members'), parliament was only sitting for about one year and eight months out of sixteen years and nine months, or about a tenth of the time.

Before the evolution of Cabinet government there was a much clearer division between the legislature and the executive than is generally thought of as existing today. True, the Privy Councillors were either in the House of Lords, or else, if not peers, almost invariably sat in the Commons, as did the holders of a number of lesser offices, normally not less than about thirty from the central courts and departments. But there was nothing corresponding to a government and an opposition party as there came to be in the course of the eighteenth and nineteenth centuries.

The Crown was dependent on parliament for the legal grant of extraordinary supplies, which included virtually all *direct* taxation. To this extent its general policy had to commend itself to a majority in both Houses. But as is suggested by the famous slogan 'redress before supply', this did not so much involve the passage of a coherent government policy as a series of *ad hoc* bargains, whereby the executive undertook to remedy particular grievances, and then the legislature complied with a grant of taxation. By the 1620's, far more was involved than the settlement of grievances. In the parliaments of that decade there was a series of intense and sustained debates on general issues of policy: on religion and foreign affairs in 1621 and 1624; on religion in 1625; on the King's principal adviser and his conduct of the war in 1626; on the liberties of the subject in 1628; on religion and taxation in 1629. The old system of 'horse trading' between Crown and Commons had broken down; the clash was one of principles as well as interests. Between 1607 and 1641 taxes were granted by parliament only in 1621, 1624, and 1628. Even from a fiscal point of view it can hardly be argued that parliament was part of the regular machinery of government. But to go on to speak of a 'decline of parliamentary government' is surely exaggerated:[1] from 1604 to 1640 there was less legislation on agreed, constitutionally uncontroversial subjects than in the sixteenth century, not because of any parliamentary decline but precisely because the House of Commons was growing more powerful and was beginning increasingly to challenge the Crown's policies. Since the King made

[1] R. W. K. Hinton, 'The Decline of Parliamentary Government under Elizabeth I and the Early Stuarts', *Camb. Hist. Journ.*, XIII (1957), 116-32.

tactical use of adjournments, prorogations, and dissolutions in these struggles, many agreed as well as disputed bills were lost before they could become law.

Peers and M.P.s would not have thought of themselves as royal officials. The payment of members had virtually lapsed during the sixteenth century; in any case before that it had not been the Crown but their constituencies who had paid them. True, during sessions of the Lords, the peers present were given dinner at the expense of the Household; but, though some of their modern successors might be glad of the calories, this was a relic from the days when the whole Baronage was identified with the King's Great Council, the indirect ancestor alike of council and parliament. The Knights of the Order of the Bath (in both Houses) seem to have had a similar right, which may have already been falling into abeyance.

The permanent staff of both Houses, who did not go out of office when parliament was dissolved, can certainly be numbered among the officials. Being within the 'verge of Court', parliament's staff and buildings came under the authority of the household, which meant in practice that of the Lord Steward or Chamberlain.

Later, in considering the theme of 'Office and Politics' it will be necessary to ask how far the officers who were also M.P.s formed a coherent group. And it may then be possible to make some comparisons between the office-holders as a body and the M.P.s at least of the Long Parliament, about whom much information is now available.[1]

viii THE GOVERNMENT IN OPERATION

How well did this system of government work in practice? The early years of Charles I's reign are famous for the King's disputes with his first three parliaments (1625, 1626, and 1628-9), disputes which were almost as much religious as constitutional. On the administrative side there was general discontent at the misconduct of the wars against Spain (1625-30) and France (1626-9). The failure against Cadiz in 1625 revealed inadequacies in naval and military supplies, which reflected on the Navy and the Ordnance. The failures at the Isle of Rhé in 1627 and the consequent surrender of the French Huguenot rebels in la Rochelle (1628) was described by one con-

[1] M. F. Keeler, *The Long Parliament 1640-1641: A Biographical Study of its Members* (Philadelphia, 1954); D. Brunton and D. H. Pennington, *Members of the Long Parliament* (1954). See below, Chapter 6.

temporary as the worst defeat England had suffered since the loss of Calais, seventy years before. Apart from religious and constitutional suspicions of Charles and Buckingham, feeling in the country, as expressed through the House of Commons, was much exasperated by these disasters and by the incompetence of which they were symptomatic.

It may fairly be asked whether the administrative system as such can be held responsible for this inefficiency, and it is well to keep a sense of proportion. By twentieth-century standards all government in the sixteenth and seventeenth centuries was hopelessly inefficient. The naval and military exploits of Elizabeth I's reign took place in spite of constant administrative confusion. Breakdowns, shortages, and deficiencies were chronic in almost all kinds of munitions and supplies, in masts and cordage, in victuals and clothing, in powder and shot, in entrenching tools and swords, and above all in pay. The inefficiencies and corruption of 1625 and 1627 were different perhaps in degree, but certainly not in kind from those of 1596 or even 1588. From the Peloponnesian War to 1956, amphibious expeditions have been notoriously chancy. The attack on Cadiz and the relief of la Rochelle *might* well have achieved partial success given only slightly more foresight and resolution together with better luck. Because both were abject and disgraceful failures, an unusual amount of unwelcome attention was focused on what would now be called the planning and logistic sides. Meanwhile the government's financial plight was acute: this was both cause and effect of its bad relations with successive parliaments. Parliament mistrusted the King and his favourite, yet supported the war against Spain in the Protestant cause, and, with a good deal less enthusiasm, that on behalf of the French Protestants; hence they voted supplies, but not nearly enough to pay for the sort of operations which they wanted to see undertaken; yet the failure of such operations as were attempted led them to attack the Crown and its servants for corruption and incompetence, if not for downright treachery, and made them all the more reluctant to vote more money to the same executive.[1]

Apart from their attacks on the management of the Navy, and

[1] Gardiner, *History*, VI; Dietz, *Public Finance*, chs. X-XI. Interpretations slightly more favourable to the King may be found in Keir, *Constitutional History*, ch. IV, and K. Feiling, *England under the Tudors and Stuarts* (1927), ch. VII, or *A History of England* (1950), bk. IV, chs. VIII-IX.

the supply of victuals and munitions, parliamentary critics might well have remarked on some weaknesses in the central executive itself. In the summer of 1625, both Secretaries of State were men whose background was exclusively military and diplomatic, and who were almost wholly lacking experience of domestic affairs. On the death of the junior Secretary that autumn he was replaced inevitably by a Buckingham nominee, who happened to be a very conscientious administrator but not a man of any originality or much independence of mind. In 1628 the senior of them was succeeded by another man who had spent most of his adult life in embassies abroad.[1] Until July 1628 the Lord Treasurer was an ineffectual old man, incapable of serious efforts to raise more revenue or to reduce expenditure, while the Chancellor of the Exchequer seems to have been concerned only to trim his sails to the prevailing wind.[2]

In the Privy Council Buckingham's ascendancy had produced some odd results. Although the Herbert brothers, the Earls of Pembroke and Montgomery, contrived to maintain a sort of clandestine opposition from within the government, four other Councillors were dismissed or suspended from the board between 1624 and 1628.[3] How could the Council perform its primary duty, of advising the King honestly and objectively under these conditions? On the judicial side of government a Lord Chief Justice was dismissed in 1626—the second in eleven years.

Foreign policy and war apart, it is not easy to say how good a cause contemporaries had for criticizing the administration in Charles I's early years. Certainly, despite the 'economical' reforms carried out by Cranfield between 1618 and 1623, the cost of the spending departments had crept up again; the Chamber, Household, and Wardrobes in particular were costing much more than they should have been. Extraordinary and extra-legal sources apart, royal revenues had been increased, but no fundamental improvement had been achieved in the financial administration. Under Bucking-

[1] *D.N.B.*, Edward, first Lord Conway, Secretary 1623-8; Sir Albertus Moreton, Secretary 1625; Sir John Coke, Secretary 1625-40; Dudley Carleton, Viscount Dorchester, Secretary 1628-32.

[2] *D.N.B.*, James Ley, first Earl of Marlborough, Lord Treasurer 1624-8; Richard Weston, later first Earl of Portland, Chancellor of the Exchequer, 1621-8.

[3] Gardiner, *History*, V and VI; *D.N.B.* and G.E.C. for the Herberts, the Earl of Arundel and Surrey, and the Earl of Bristol; *D.N.B.*, Archbishop Abbott, and Bishop Williams.

ham the Crown was alive to the need for administrative reform, if only to help to make ends meet; a number of royal commissions and Council committees were appointed for such purposes, though very little was achieved.

There were no serious naval or military operations after 1628 and the country was officially at peace from 1630 on. Although King Charles more than once seemed to be on the point of concluding a firm alliance which would involve him in the Thirty Years War on one side or the other he drew back each time, probably realizing that this would mean a renewed recourse to parliament.

After 1628 it is possible to make some distinction, of which there had been scarcely a trace under Buckingham, between royal favour and political importance. For instance, James Hay, Earl of Carlisle (Groom of the Stole 1631-6), was generally agreed to be one of the most influential figures at Court and a close favourite of the King, but his political importance is doubtful. Conversely, Weston and Cottington did not always stand too well at Court, nor later did Laud and Wentworth. To some extent the Council came into its own again. The great magnates on it reasserted what they believed to be their natural and rightful influence; or rather they tried to do so, but they were to some extent thwarted first by Weston and his group, later by Laud and his.

The early and mid-1630's saw a series of attempts at administrative reform, few of which were carried through with sustained resolution. Promising starts were made with the Household below stairs, the Wardrobes, the Ordnance, and the Armoury around 1629. The Navy had already been tackled under Buckingham (in 1626), so notorious had been the scandal after Cadiz and the next year's fleet which had failed to get clear of the Channel. In 1627 an inquiry had been launched into the fee payments of officials in the law and revenue courts and in other branches of central and local government, partly to meet a popular grievance and partly in order to raise some extra money by fining the offenders; it was reinforced in 1630 when Wentworth joined in its proceedings. Postal reform was begun in 1632, and eventually completed in 1637. There were stirrings at the Mint. Royal commissions proliferated, many with an ostensibly reforming purpose. Wentworth breathed new life into the Council in the North and then into the government of Ireland. Laud attempted reform in the church—high church orthodoxy, and better pay for the clergy.

In 1635 the Treasury Commissioners, led by Laud, initiated the most thorough inquiries into the state of the royal finances undertaken since the time of Cranfield. Meanwhile the raising of non-parliamentary revenues went forward relentlessly and with considerable efficiency: fines for not taking up knighthood, and then Ship Money, being the two most important, if not the most oppressive. In 1637-8, due perhaps to the renewed demands of military expenditure, another attempt was made to reduce the cost of the Household, but with less success than in 1629-32. This phase of the reign may be said to have closed in the summer of 1638 with the decision to raise an army with which to compel the Scots to accept the new Prayer Book.

How much had been achieved? The middle years of peace, and perhaps it should be added of retrenchment and reform, have been variously judged by historians of different epochs, viewpoints, and temperaments. From the great Earl of Clarendon down to Professor Keith Feiling, Archbishop David Mathew, and Miss C. V. Wedgwood in our own time, royalist historians and those with a natural sympathy for King Charles and his court have found much to admire. Clarendon's remarks about the prosperity, tranquillity, and contentment of the nation are well known; it is perhaps not so well known that this is a selective quotation, and that the great Cavalier statesman and historian found plenty to criticize in the 1630's, both in the court and in the government of church and state.[1] Only the character of these years in English administrative history is in question here.

Even discounting our foreknowledge of its eventual failure and collapse, the achievement of the 'personal government' must be reckoned meagre. This should not be exaggerated. Attempts at reform were certainly made, and not all were total failures. The Postal Service seems to have been considerably improved, although personal and professional jealousies soon led to the dismissal of the man most responsible for this.[2] Little permanent economy was achieved in the spending departments, although the Crown may have got better value for its money in some cases.

---

[1] Edward Hyde, Earl of Clarendon, *History of the Rebellion and Civil Wars in England* (ed. W. D. Macray, Oxford, 1888), I, 93-5; see also *ibid.*, pp. 84-92, 96.

[2] J. C. Hemmeon, *The History of the British Post Office* (Cambridge, Mass., 1912); H. Robinson, *The British Post Office: A History* (Princeton, 1948); Higham, *Secretary of State*, ch. XII. See below, Chapter 6, s.v.

On the revenue side, achievement is harder to assess. Neglecting the possible effect of any further fall in the real value of money due to price increases, royal revenue rose considerably during the 1630's. But it would be very difficult to compare total revenue from all sources at the beginning and end of the decade. It is however possible to compare the annual averages for regular or 'ordinary' items during the two five-yearly periods 1631-5 inclusive and 1636-41. Leaving aside the question of how reliable the Exchequer officials' figures were, this is certainly better than nothing.

TABLE 5. INCREASES IN SELECTED ORDINARY REVENUES, 1631-41

Source of Revenue	Annual Averages	
	1631-5	1636-41
Great and Petty Customs Farms	£210,000	£245,000
'New Impositions' (Customs) .	53,091	119,583
Additional New Impositions .	9,500	60,092
Coal Duties and Farms . .	8,400	18,400
Payments from Soap-makers .	—	29,128
Forest of Dean . . .	—	17,951
The Mint	5,984	24,428
Court of Wards and Liveries .	53,866	75,088
Total of all ordinary revenues .	£618,376	£899,482

The striking increase in the Customs revenue may be ascribed to five factors: the raising of the rents paid by the farmers, the alteration of the rateable value of goods which were already dutiable, the extension of the range of dutiable goods, more honest and efficient administration, and some improvement in the general state of trade. The increase in the net surplus available from the Court of Wards and Liveries was also due in part to greater efficiency in the years 1635-9. The money raised from indirect taxation in the form of monopolies or 'projects', especially soap, also rose steeply. The Forest of Dean item represents mainly the Crown's profits from leasing the right to use timber as fuel in the ironworks there; the Mint item signifies profit on coinage and re-coinage operations.

By contrast, some branches of the revenue showed no appreciable increase. And contrary to what might have been expected the yield from Star Chamber actually fell: very few of the spectacular fines imposed were ever levied in full. Revenue from Crown lands also

3. PRESENTATION OF PRIVY COUNCILLORS TO MARY DE MEDICI, QUEEN
MOTHER OF FRANCE, IN 1638.

4 MEETING OF THE COUNCIL OF WAR, 1624 (A Contemporary Broadside.)

fell. This was due largely, and perhaps wholly, to the heavy land sales of the late 1620's, which continued until 1635 and then came to an abrupt halt until 1640. The yield per acre from the Crown's landed property was very probably rising, but not fast enough to offset the loss from sales.

It is more difficult to compare 'extraordinary' and non-recurrent receipts in the early and late 1630's. In the first ten years of the reign (1625-35) a contemporay calculation reckoned these to have *averaged* about £240,000 a year. But this figure covers the quite heavy direct taxes and forced loans collected in the years 1625-30, as well as exceptionally large alienations of capital (i.e. land sales). Extraordinary royal *income* in the stricter sense may well have averaged under £100,000 p.a. during the years 1631-5; the largest single item to be comprised under this heading, the fines and compositions for not taking up knighthood, apparently realized £173,537, most of it spread over about five years (1630-5). If extraordinary income was less in the years 1631-5 than in 1625-30, it was certainly rising again in 1636-40. Taking the whole six years when it was levied (1635-40 inclusive), Ship Money yielded an average of *c.* £107,000 p.a., far in excess of any previous direct tax in peacetime. And this average allows for the exceptional years 1639 and 1640, when 20 per cent. and 79 per cent. respectively of the amounts directed to be raised were not collected; taking only the three years 1636-8, the average yield was nearly £188,000 p.a.

It seems reasonable to think of total royal receipts from all sources, including alienations of capital, as rising from about £700-750,000 p.a. in 1631-5 to about £1,050-1,150,000 in 1636-40. But this is only a tentative estimate which may well need further revision.[1]

To judge by results, Charles I was able to keep going without recourse to parliament as long as he kept out of war. Broadly speaking, he managed this by a combination of several illegal or at

---

[1] F. C. Dietz, 'Receipts and Issues of the Exchequer during the reigns of James I and Charles I', *Smith Coll. Studies in History*, XIII (Northampton, Mass., 1928); Dietz, *Public Finance*, chs. XI-XVII; Bell, *Court of Wards*, pp. 49-50, 57-9, Table A (fcg. p. 192); M. D. Gordon, 'The Collection of Ship Money in the reign of Charles I', *Trans. Roy. Hist. Soc.*, 3rd ser., IV (1910); P.R.O., T56/2, T 35/1 (a continuation for 1636-8); SP 16/285/89 (extraordinary revenues 1625-35; see also B. M. Harleian MS. 3796, fols. 22, 36); Duchy of Lancaster accounts, DL 28/12/1-13; Shaftesbury Papers P.R.O. 30/24/463-4 (yearly averages of ordinary revenues and issues 1636-41).

least dubious and unpopular revivals and innovations, a small measure of economy in the spending departments, and some limited improvements in the ordinary and legal revenues. Despite Professor Dietz's argument, that the 'Bishops' Wars' of 1639 and 1640 against the Scots *were* in fact financed without parliament's help, it remains true that the King's means were quite inadequate for such a crisis and that these 'Wars' did make the calling of parliament a financial necessity.[1]

The institutions of government remained substantially what they had been in the 1630's until July 1641, about eight months after the meeting of the Long Parliament. But in terms of the connexion between administration and politics the whole four years from the autumn of 1638 until the outbreak of civil war in September 1642 can be thought of as a single protracted crisis with intermittent climaxes and interspersed pauses. How did the central administration and the men who manned it stand up to the demands of these extraordinary years? Again one must keep a sense of proportion. It would be a mistake to think of the England of Charles I as having been by seventeenth-century standards a particularly ill-governed country. Nor indeed, by any standards, did the administration show up too badly when the testing time came. The routine of central administration, justice, and finance was long and deeply established; with the exception of one or two brief intervals during the worst years of the fifteenth century, several of the major courts and departments had been functioning continuously for between 300 and 500 years. Such a system was not to be easily disrupted. There had been internal peace in the south of England since the 1550's, in the north since the 1570's, marred only by Essex's 'rebellion' in 1601 and the Gunpowder Plot of 1605. The settled habits of generations were the best guarantee against any sudden or light-hearted resort to extreme measures.

None the less, there were grave weaknesses in the administrative system, which inevitably accelerated the collapse which began in 1640. The failure of the military expeditions to the north in 1639 and 1640 is normally ascribed to the determination and high morale of the Scots, and to the half-heartedness and disillusion of the English, due to the Crown's failure to enlist support for its policy either from the upper classes or the mass of the people. This is correct. But the lack of efficient military preparations, after nine years of peace, was

[1] Dietz, *Public Finance*, pp. 285-7; compare Gardiner, *History*, VIII-IX.

certainly a contributory cause. The rearmament of 1635 to 1639, based on Ship Money, had affected only the Navy. The expedition of 1640 appears to have been better equipped and supplied than that of 1639, and in neither were the munitions and victuals as bad as in 1625 or 1627. But there were still serious shortcomings for which the Ordnance Office was partly responsible.

The basic failure in 1639-40 was one of sympathy and accord between Crown and country. And the very officers responsible for carrying the central government's directives to those who were supposed to execute them in the country may have contributed to this failure. In August 1640, at the climax of the second northern expedition, the Council in London ordered the dismissal of twelve out of forty of the regular Messengers for gross negligence and misconduct.

Nor was the financial situation as satisfactory as Professor Dietz implies. Leaving military needs aside, the ordinary level of spending had risen again since the early 1630's; although the yield from the ordinary revenues had been greatly increased, many of these were earmarked for years ahead. In January 1640, the alum and sugar revenues were mortgaged until 1645, the wine licence revenues until 1651! Scarcely any revenues were available before 1641; that is, the Crown was at least a year behind in balancing its budget. Contemporaries deplored the growth of what they called 'Assignment' or 'Anticipation' (see Chapter 4, s. ii). In July 1635 the King's debts had been reckoned at just under two years' gross ordinary revenue. Some revenues were promised for particular departments, or for royal pensioners and annuitants; a large part of them was mortgaged to the King's creditors, so that, in practice, the Crown had very little ready money for immediate needs.[1] Nor did it enjoy the compensatory advantages of a fully-fledged credit system, such as began to come into existence during the 1690's with the Bank of England and the National Debt. But these weaknesses only proved disastrous in conjunction with the refusal of the London magnates, for political and other reasons, to advance more money to the Crown in the summer of 1640.

Gravest weakness of all, in the central as in the local administration, the Crown did not get whole-hearted support from its own servants. Below the Privy Council, response to the royal demands for

[1] SP 16/443/10; B.M. Harl. MS. 3796, p. 28; P.R.O., T 56/2; See also Chapter 4, s. ii.

loans in 1639 to 1640 was patchy, some officers actually refusing to lend. Many of them must have been hostile to Strafford and Laud, and some to the whole tenor of royal policy since the 1620's and to the attempt to rule without parliament. From the King's point of view, except in the sphere of finance, the men were more at fault than the institutions. But, as will be seen, this arose from the nature of the system, and from the conditions under which officers served, more than from the failings of individuals.

It is easy to speak of 'the administrative system'. But after reading the earlier sections of this chapter it may pertinently be asked whether such a thing existed. It is far from clear how much the law courts had in common with the departments, or the institutions of Tudor origin with those of medieval ancestry. By studying officers' conditions of entry and service, and the ways in which they were paid, it may be possible to understand their common interests and problems better than by making more detailed comparisons between the structures or workings of the different institutions. The nature of service under the King, or participation in what has here been called the 'old administrative system', may itself have constituted a common factor, giving a measure of unity to this otherwise diverse collection of men and institutions which made up the King's government.

3

CONDITIONS OF ENTRY AND SERVICE

i APPOINTMENT AND PROMOTION

IN NO RESPECT were seventeenth-century officials further removed from modern civil servants than in the way they were appointed. Advertisement, examination, formal interview, and professional qualifications are today so much a part of the mechanism for filling posts in government service that it is hard to think back to the time when such methods were unknown.

How in those 'bad old days' did people enter royal service in the first place, and having entered gain promotion? We must begin by asking in whose hands appointments lay. All major offices, many in the middle ranks, and some minor posts were in the Crown's gift. Below the top level this sometimes involved an actual personal choice by the sovereign; but more often the Crown simply gave formal approval to a choice in practice already made by the head of the department concerned or by some other minister, and even in his personal choice the sovereign was often swayed by the importunities of suitors and Court favourites. Apart from this, many medium-ranking and a mass of minor offices and petty clerkships were not even nominally royal appointments. Just as one can think of a metaphorical 'pyramid' of tenants in the feudal system of land-holding, so what can be called 'subinfeudation' was firmly entrenched in most branches of the government. Greater officials had the right to appoint their subordinates, and so on down the scale. The boundaries of the Crown's right to appoint also varied considerably from one branch of the government to another.

Rights of appointment were often disputed, sometimes between two 'great officers' or ministers of state, sometimes between the Crown and the head of the department, or sub-department concerned. For example, in 1637 there was a quarrel between the Earl of Holland, recently appointed Groom of the Stole and First Gentleman of the Bedchamber, and the Earl of Pembroke and Montgomery, then Lord Chamberlain, about the disposal of places in the King's Bedchamber, the Galleries, the ante-Chamber, and certain other sub-departments of the Household above stairs. Pembroke claimed that all offices above stairs were in his gift; Holland denied this. The King ruled that Pembroke should keep the gift of places in the Bedchamber itself and that Holland should have the gift of the lesser contiguous offices.[1] The only doubt here was whether Holland or Pembroke should make these appointments: there was no question of the King doing so. Or, to take a case where the King's right to appoint was usually only nominal, there seems to have been some competition for regional patronage between the ministers and courtiers most immediately around the King, and the Lord Presidents of Wales and the North. In 1631 the King compromised, directing that

> no grant of place . . . in either of our Provincial Courts of Wales or York should pass our signet before themselves [the two Secretaries of State] or our Presidents there [in Wales and the North] for the time being might be made therewith acquainted, and humbly offer such advice as they should conceive to tend to the bettering of our service in such cases as do more properly and particularly fall within their knowledge and charge than any other of our Ministers.[2]

And in 1632, after Wentworth had been appointed Lord Deputy of Ireland, but before he went over to take up his new duties, the Masters of Requests were forbidden to move before the King any petitions concerning Irish business, posts in the Lord Deputy's gift, or new offices in Ireland. The King and the Privy Council confirmed the Lord Deputy's full rights of appointment, and guaranteed them against any encroachment.[3] Wentworth was presumably trying to secure his rear against courtly job-hunters and

---

[1] *The Earle of Strafforde's Letters and Dispatches*, ed. W. Knowler (1739), II, 130, a news-letter to Wentworth.

[2] SP 16/197/14-15, to Secretaries Dorchester and Coke.

[3] PC 2/41, pp. 439-40, an order from the King; Knowler, I, 65-6.

more serious enemies, in the same way in Ireland as he had already tried to do in the North.

The King's right to appoint was at its most limited in the older courts and departments. And there is some rather fragmentary evidence from the 1630's to suggest that the Crown was trying to extend its direct patronage, and to reduce the amount of official 'subinfeudation' which had grown up over the centuries. For example, the gift of offices in Chancery was shared by the King, the Lord Chancellor (or Lord Keeper of the Great Seal), and the Master of the Rolls. The Lord Chancellor disposed of the twelve Masterships, the twenty-four Cursitorships, and several miscellaneous posts; the Master of the Rolls had the gift of the Six Clerkships, the three Clerkships of the Petty Bag, the seven Clerkships of the Rolls Chapel, the two Examinerships, and the posts of Usher, Porter, Cryer, Garden-keeper, Chaplain, and Keeper of the Records in the Tower.[1] The King had less patronage than the Lord Chancellor or his second-in-command.

The very lucrative and not over-exacting Six Clerkships of Chancery provide an instance of the trouble which could arise from disputed rights of appointment. According to Clarendon, Sir Julius Caesar, Master of the Rolls since 1614, tried to secure a vacant Six Clerkship for his son Robert; but Weston, Lord Treasurer 1628-35, persuaded the King to stop this, and to compel Sir Julius to accept another candidate, who incidently paid £6,000 for the Clerkship; Weston, however, agreed that Robert Caesar should have the next vacancy, even if his father was by then no longer Master. Writing some years after the event, and of a time before his own entry into public life, it is not surprising that Clarendon muddled up the details of this appointment: he says that the office sought by Sir Julius for his son (in 1631) was instead sold to one Terne, when the buyer was in fact William Carne (a Nathaniel Terne was at this time a very junior clerk in the Navy Office, and later became Clerk of the Cheque at Deptford). Robert Caesar, who was already a Clerk of the Enrollments and of the Petty Bag, did not in fact obtain the next Six Clerkship to be vacant (in 1632), but the one after that (in 1635), and only, as will be seen, after more hard bargaining.[2]

[1] G. W. Sanders, *Orders in Chancery*, I (1845), 611-12; Wilson, Thesis, pp. 8, 19-22.
[2] Clarendon, *Hist. Reb.*, I, 64-7.

In 1635, as part of an elaborate agreement between the Six Clerks and the Crown, they were forgiven all their misdemeanours and were confirmed in their offices and their official privileges. In return they were to pay £2,500 or £3,000 apiece to the Crown. At the same time their places were resumed for ever into the King's gift. Not surprisingly Sir Julius Caesar objected to this. According to one letter writer:

> so long as the present Master of the Rolls lives, their [the Six Clerks'] patents from the King are not legal, unless the old man [Caesar] will surrender his patent and take a new grant, leaving out the dispositions of those six Clerks' places

This ambiguity also affected the reversions which had been granted to future vacancies:

> Mr. Burrowes has the King's hand and promise for the first six clerks' place that falls vacant after Sir Julius Caesar's death, and Mr. Robert Caesar has the grant of the first six Clerks' place that shall fall vacant after his father's death under the Great Seal.[1]

This difficulty was resolved. In the treaty Robert Caesar was confirmed as first reversioner, his father having presumably first been compelled to acknowledge its validity. And when one of the Six (George Evelyn, the future diarist's first cousin) died not long after, he was succeeded by Caesar fils.[2]

There was more trouble to come, over the reversions which had been granted *before* the Crown had resumed the right to appoint the Six Clerks. On Sir Julius Caesar's death in 1636, Sir Dudley Digges, a leader of the parliamentary opposition in the 1620's but holder of the reversion since 1630, had succeeded to the Rolls. In 1637 Robert Caesar died; Arthur Evelyn, second son of George, late Six Clerk, now petitioned the King for the vacant Six Clerkship, claiming that his father had paid the King £2,500 for the next vacancy after his death and that of Robert Caesar; in return, Arthur said he had been expected to pay off about £2,000 of his father's debts, which he said he had been trying to do since August 1635. He alleged that on Robert Caesar's death he had paid Digges another

---

[1] Hist. MSS. Comm. *Hastings*, II, 79, news-letter to the Earl of Huntingdon, 28 March 1635.

[2] SP 16/291/61, 293/36; PC 2/45, pp. 21-4; Knowler, I, 511. (There is a conflict in the sources as to the date of Evelyn's death.)

£3,000 to give to the King, and he hoped that the King would approve his admission; at £5,500 it was not cheap.[1]

The letter of the 1635 treaty took no account of reversioners other than Robert Caesar. But its spirit might well have been thought to include the sanctity of other existing reversions. George Evelyn had been a party to it; and he had presumably paid a 'composition' of between £2,500 and £3,000, like his five colleagues, in order to have his privileges fully confirmed, including presumably any reversion he might have secured. There may have been a muddle about whether or not this sum covered the reversion. Whatever the answer to this, his son Arthur did *not* in fact become a Six Clerk.

At the end of 1637 Digges tried to recover his lost patronage as Master of the Rolls. Although not formally a party to it, he had 'fully assented' to the treaty of July 1635. But he now argued that, while intended merely to transfer the gift of the Six Clerkships to the King, it had been used by the Clerks to secure a pardon from Star Chamber proceedings which were then pending against them for alleged extortions; they might thus appear to have secured his approval, which he now formally repudiated, for the right to take fees from the users of the court which were not properly theirs and some of which should even have been going to him or to other Chancery officers. It was a shrewd point. The King and the Council protested that the treaty had not in any way been meant to worsen the position of the Masters of the Rolls or to improve that of the Six. But, although the judges were directed to look into the matter and report back, the Master did not recover the gift of the Six Clerkships until after 1660.[2]

The surprisingly uneven extent of royal patronage in different departments is not always easy to explain. In the Ordnance Office such relatively humble officers as the Clerk of the Deliveries and the Master Gunner were nominally appointed by the King. In the Household below stairs this was true of scarcely anyone below the Clerk Comptrollers (the two junior members of the Board of Greencloth), by contrast with the Chamber where the proportion

[1] SP 16/340/5, 536/95, Arthur Evelyn's petitions, n.d., but after the death of Robert Caesar (and so wrongly calendared in *Cal. S.P. Dom.* as 1636 not 1637); Hist. MSS. Comm. *Gawdy*, p. 166, ref. in a news-letter to the recent death of Robert Caesar, Six Clerk, 3 November 1637; Sanders, *Orders in Chancery*, I, 200-1.

[2] PC 2/48, pp. 434-5; also *Cal. S.P. Dom. 1637-8*, p. 174, a counter-petition from the Six Clerks, 20 January 1638.

of posts in the royal gift was much higher. In the Central Executive all the positions of any consequence, except those of the personal assistants to the Secretaries of State, were in the King's gift. In the various revenue and law courts there was a much more even distribution of the right to appoint, between the King, the head of department, and other senior officers, as can be seen with offices in Chancery.

Granted that different people had the disposing of them, and that disputes often arose about this, let us return to our original question of how men went about getting offices. In the course of investigating this, we may also find that we have gone part of the way towards answering the obviously connected question of *why* they wanted to enter the King's service. But this is a wider issue and it inevitably involves the further question: *who were* the men who were seeking and obtaining office under the early Stuarts? This will be answered more fully in a later chapter when a social analysis of the officials is attempted. As to *how* men entered the King's service, the answer quite simply is: by knowing someone influential and by using their name when asking for an office, or by getting them to ask.

Initial appointment, involving entry to the King's service and not just to a particular office in it, naturally differed from later transfers or promotions. In May 1629 John Carleton wrote to his uncle, then Secretary of State, on behalf of a young man who wanted to become Feodary of his county. He explained that a previous request for a reversion had been rejected by the King on the grounds that the present holder had been ill but not dying; he was now dead, hence the renewal of the suit. Carleton sang his candidate's praises, adding 'besides the place is not of profit but rather an entrance or an introduction to his better fortunes'.[1] Since Feodaries were appointed by royal patent on the choice of the Master of the Wards, the Secretary's nephew presumably pinned his hopes either on his uncle's proximity to the King or on his friendship with the Master. Even a Secretary of State could hardly have secured such an appointment over the Master's head.

If minor offices were sometimes sought as the first step on the ladder, they were also valued as providing pensions for widows and dependants. The applicant's approach varied to some extent with his motive in applying. His health ruined by a fever caught on the

[1] SP 16/143/45.

Isle of Rhé expedition in 1627, and his credit hopelessly over-extended on the Crown's behalf, Sir Allen Apsley, the Victualler of the Navy, tried in 1628-9 to secure for himself and his eldest son, or the longer lived of them, a reversion to the office of Custos Brevium (Keepership of writs) in the Court of Common Pleas. After his death in 1630 this seems to have been extended to his heirs general, who sold it for £3,000 in 1634. Whether Sir Allen had himself bought the reversion is uncertain; between July 1628 and his death he made otherwise unexplained payments totalling £4,000 to the Lord Treasurer, but these may also have been intended to hasten the straightening out of his affairs as Naval Victualler, in which capacity he claimed to be owed great sums by the Crown.[1]

In August 1628 Sir Henry Hungate, who later enjoyed a monopoly in the export of butter, tried to get an existing reversion to half a Six Clerkship extended to his heirs and assigns, because of the dangers which he anticipated on the relief expedition for La Rochelle. Sometime in the next three years he obtained a rather vague promise from the King.[2] About 1635 Thomazin Lady Carew, widow of a minor Jacobean courtier, petitioned the King about the Prothonotaryship of Chancery. Her husband had held this office; after his death King James had confirmed it to her use during the lives of three other people, two of whom were now dead, while the third was elderly; she therefore sought a re-grant for the duration of two additional—and younger—lives, since the office provided the sole livelihood for herself and her children and enabled her to retain an honorific post in the Queen's household.[3]

When an office was not being sought as a stage in a young man's career but as a reward for past services or an endowment for someone's dependants, it was usual to make a personal appeal to royal generosity. Otherwise a man would rely on the patronage of one or

---

[1] For Apsley see *D.N.B.*, I, 523, and recollections by his daughter, in Lucy Hutchinson, *Memoirs of Colonel Hutchinson* (ed. C. H. Firth, 1906), pp. 6-12; also *Cal. S.P. Dom.*, *1628-9*, p. 183, *1629-31*, pp. 94, 127, 182, *1634-5*, pp. 97-8; PC 2/44, pp. 74-7; *State Papers collected by Edward, Earl of Clarendon* (ed. R. Scrope and T. Monkhouse, Oxford, 1767), I, 158-9; Knowler, I, 227.

[2] SP 16/114/59, memo on Hungate's request, 1628; *Cal. S.P. Dom.*, *1631-3*, p. 215, the King's answer, n.d., ascribed by the editor of the *Calendar* to 1631, but perhaps earlier.

[3] SP 16/309/15, Lady Carew's petition, *c.* 1635; for her husband, Sir George, see *D.N.B.*, III, 959-60.

more intermediaries; a normal applicant did not petition the King direct. Since the connexions between applicant, patron, and Crown were quite informal, there is little written evidence concerning what we can infer to have been the commonest mode of entry. We may learn more about this if we consider some of the implications of appointment by influence or patronage.

Appointment by patronage and other personal contacts was not incompatible with men rising on their merits. As with the unreformed House of Commons before 1832, the methods of entry into the old administrative system were more haphazard than those with which we are familiar today; it does not follow that they invariably produced worse results. The idea of appointment or promotion solely by merit and qualifications was not wholly unknown, but was usually only advocated by isolated authoritarians like Wentworth, or by disappointed critics from outside the system. Of the latter, Sir William Monson, retired Admiral and a ferocious critic of Jacobean and Caroline naval administration, is a fair example. For the principal executive officers of the Navy Office he wanted: (i) as Treasurer a merchant or marine man, who was an experienced ship-owner, and capable of raising money on his own credit, (ii) as co-Surveyors, for this office needed to be split into two, (a) a first-class Shipwright, and (b) a qualified and intelligent sea Captain, (iii) as Comptroller and Clerk, for these two offices should be combined into one, a reliable and experienced clerk.[1] Such explicitly functional requirements were most unusual.

But, if 'professional qualifications' in the modern sense were seldom required, it would be a mistake to think of a 'closed' system with no competitive element about it. Many offices required neither expert knowledge nor experience—except perhaps in the ways of the world—and only a minimum of honesty and intelligence. But when, in such cases, they were in addition financially profitable and also carried social prestige, the competition for them was liable to be fast and furious.

When the Household of Prince Charles, the future Charles II, was being enlarged on the eve of his eighth birthday in May 1638, there were said to be 300-400 candidates for the top twenty or so places. The names of those appointed show little evidence of careers

[1] *The Naval Tracts of Sir William Monson* (ed. M. Oppenheim, Navy Record Soc., 1902-14), III, 416-18, n.d., from internal evidence probably post-1628.

being open to talent rather than birth. The Earl of Newcastle, who for six years had been complaining to his friend Wentworth about his need to have a lucrative office if he were to stay at Court or to entertain royalty at his home, became Groom of the Stole, sole Gentleman of the Bedchamber, and Governor to the Prince; two out of four places as Gentlemen of the Privy Chamber went to friends of his, both already Knights; Thomas Jermyn junior, son of the King's, and brother of the Queen's Vice-Chamberlain, became a Groom of the Bedchamber, as did Henry Seymour, cadet member of another great family, and already Page to the Queen. The brother of a previous Vice-Chamberlain's widow and the younger son of one of the Secretaries of State became Ushers of the Privy Chamber. Another Gentleman of the Privy Chamber was of sufficient standing to be sheriff of Essex. As the price of his entry, the only middle-class appointee, a wealthy mercer's son, was to marry the niece of the wife of the Master of the Great Wardrobe, the Earl of Denbigh.[1] In terms of these honorific posts at Court the greater gentry and those with Court connexions should be thought of as bracketed with the peerage, and not with the gentry at large or with the urban and professional middle class, with whom they often acted politically, notably in parliament.

It is hard to imagine how anyone got appointed in the first instance without knowing an existing officer or courtier or some other influential person, or as a last resort without knowing somebody who knew such a person. At the lowest levels, of course, it need only have meant knowing, or knowing someone who knew, quite a junior officer. And once a man was in office in however humble a capacity there was obviously more scope for advancement on merit. But here too patronage was very important, the more so considering how often positions of trust and importance in the King's service were filled by the private secretaries and confidential servants of Court peers and great officers. For example Sir Thomas Aylesbury, Bart. (great-grandfather of Queens Mary and Anne), who was a Master of Requests (1625-42) and at the same time first the Surveyor of the Navy (1625-32) and then co-Master of the Mint (c. 1635-42), began as secretary and possibly mathematical expert to the Lord High Admiral, Howard of Effingham, later Earl of Nottingham; on Nottingham's retirement he became naval secretary to his successor

[1] Knowler, II, 166-8; for Newcastle's lament to Wentworth on his enforced withdrawal to Welbeck in 1633 see *ibid.*, I, 101-2.

the Duke of Buckingham.[1] He had about twenty-five years' administrative experience before he became technically a *royal* official. George Bingley, Auditor of the Prests, *c.* 1635-42, and principal Auditor for Parliament, *c.* 1642-50, first emerges as a servant of Sir Francis Gofton, Auditor; and on Gofton's death in 1628 he became Deputy to Sir Ralph Freeman, Auditor 1628-35. By contrast with Aylesbury, who although the younger son of a non-noble London family was educated at Westminster and Christ Church, Bingley had no family or educational advantages; he was only admitted to Gray's Inn after becoming Deputy Auditor.[2] Kenrick Edisbury, alias Wilkinson, of Denbighshire, rose from being a servant of Sir William Russell, Treasurer of the Navy 1618-27 and 1630-42, to become Surveyor of the Navy (1632-8). He was able to send his eldest son to the Queen's College, Oxford, and the Inner Temple, and later procured him a reversion to the Prothonotaryship and Clerkship of the Crown for Denbigh and Montgomeryshire. Edisbury too seems to have been of quite humble origin.[3] Thomas Meautys, who was descended from Henry VII's French Secretary, owed his Clerkship of the Privy Council, 1622-*c*.1642, not to his ancestry but to his having been confidential man of business to Sir Francis Bacon for ten years or more before entering the King's service.[4] To take two better known men: Edward Nicholas, Council Clerk 1635-41, Secretary of State 1641-6 and 1660-5, began in the service of Edward Lord Zouch, Warden of the Cinque Ports in the middle of James I's reign, and then transferred to the service of George Villiers (later Duke of Buckingham) when he succeeded

[1] *D.N.B.*, I, 749; G. E. Cockayne, *The Complete Baronetage* (Exeter, 1900-9), II, 11; A. Wood, *Fasti or annals* (ed. P. Bliss, Oxford, 1813-20), I, 305; *Biographica Britannica* (1747), I, 308-9.

[2] Somerset House, Prerogative Court of Canterbury, 93 Barrington, Gofton's will; PCC 53 Segar, will of Sir Richard Sutton, Auditor, d. 1634; Exchequer Records *c.* 1630-42, *passim*; P.R.O., Index to Patent Rolls, part 11 of 7 Charles I (grant of reversion to Auditorship, 7 March 1631/2); *The Register of Admission to Gray's Inn 1521-1889* (ed. J. Foster, 1889), p. 201; *Calendar of the Proceedings of the Committee for the Advancement of Money 1642-56* (ed. M. A. E. Green, 1888), p. 308; *Calendar of the Proceedings of the Committee for Compounding 1643-60* (ed. M. A. E. Green, 1889-92), p. 2269.

[3] *Cal. S.P. Dom., 1635*, p. 562; PCC 122 Lee (Edisbury's will); G. Ormerod and T. Helsby, *History of Cheshire*, III (1882), 896; J. Foster, *Alumni Oxonienses* (Oxford, 1891-2), I, 445a; *Foedera*, XX, 124.

[4] See Chapter 5, s. iii.

Zouch; Endymion Porter, Groom of the Bedchamber and personal favourite of King Charles and Queen Henrietta Maria, was successively in the service of the Spanish favourite and minister the Condé duc d'Olivares, of Buckingham's half-brother Sir Edward Villiers, of Buckingham himself, and then of Charles when he was Prince of Wales.

Returning to a more obscure level, the study of one man's career in more detail will help to illustrate the workings of patronage without connexions.

Edward Sherborne, whose name was also spelt Sherburne (1578-1641), is said to have come of a minor Lancashire gentry family. But his father, presumably a younger son, scarcely attained that status; he was employed as a groom by Corpus Christi College, Oxford, and had a small property near Folly Bridge. Mrs. Sherborne, so that snob Anthony Wood retails, 'sold ale in some of the skirts of the city'. But neither of their sons was kept down by these antecedents. The elder became private secretary to Sir Ralph Winwood (diplomat, 1599-1613, and Secretary of State, 1614-17), and then Escheator and Clerk of the Peace in the West Riding of Yorkshire.

The younger son, Edward, first appears in 1610 as a personal assistant to George Calvert, who was then a Clerk of the Council. Of his previous life, that is before he was about thirty-two, there seems to be no record. In January 1611/12 he was provisionally appointed Registrar, or chief under-clerk, to the Secretary of the Council in the North; but there was another candidate, appointed by a previous Secretary, and Sherborne failed to make good his claim. He did not *formally* enter royal service for another twenty-four years. Meanwhile, by some time early in 1612, he had transferred from Calvert's service to that of Lord Treasurer Salisbury, who may have been his backer for the post at York. It is not clear whether Sherborne returned to Calvert's service when Salisbury died in May of the same year. But in 1613 he was granted a reversion to the Clerkship of the Ordnance, evidence of some influence at least. In 1616 he re-emerges as manager, in England, of the affairs of Sir Dudley Carleton, Ambassador at The Hague. In 1617 Sherborne again transferred, this time to the service of the new Lord Chancellor, Francis Bacon; Carleton was somewhat aggrieved at this. Bacon's fall in 1621 left Sherborne in an awkward situation. There is no evidence how he spent the next two or three years, unless he returned to the service of his old patron, Calvert, by then Secretary of State.

By 1624 Sherborne was in the service of the East India Company. In 1625, despite brisk competition, he became their Secretary, a post which he occupied until his death sixteen years later. The importation of saltpetre and the manufacture of gunpowder brought the Company and the Ordnance Office together. Saltpetre collection was an unpopular minor royal prerogative and its use in powder-making was a royal monopoly then leased to the Evelyn family. The Company, which needed gunpowder for its ships, soon saw the chance of importing good-quality saltpetre cheaply from India, and of having it made into powder more cheaply and efficiently than by the royal patentee. After a tussle with the Evelyns and Lord Carew, then Master of the Ordnance, they got their way. And it was their powder-maker who won the Crown monopoly from the Evelyns in 1636-7. By the time Sherborne finally succeeded to the Ordnance Clerkship in 1636 he therefore had considerable experience of government business, and of the seventeenth-century equivalent of 'lobbying'. He appears to have had no difficulty in combining his two posts, and secured his son, also named Edward, a reversion to the Ordnance Clerkship in 1637/8. The younger Edward Sherborne, a poet and translator as well as an administrator, was an active royalist and was eventually knighted by Charles II; like Pepys, he was finally driven from office in 1689.

The elder Edward Sherborne's career is the more remarkable in that he, like his better known son, was a Roman Catholic, and so in theory should not have been in office at all. This certainly points to Calvert as his main backer. Even so, it is a mistake to look for complicated explanations when simple ones will do. To have been employed by Salisbury, Carleton, Bacon, and 'John Company' successively argues first and foremost that Sherborne was an exceedingly good secretary.[1]

[1] *D.N.B.*, XVIII, 72-3 (a short and not very accurate ref. in the article on his son); Hist. MSS. Comm. *Buccleugh*, I, 91; *Cal. S.P. Dom., 1611-18*, *passim; The Letters of John Chamberlain*, ed. N. E. McClure (Philadelphia, 1939), many refs. between I, 618 and II, 612; J. Spedding, *The Letters & Life of Francis Bacon* (1861-74), VI, 182, 200, 326, 336, VII, 83, 255-6, 259; *Cal. S.P. Colonial, E. Indies, 1625-35*, and *Cal. Court Minutes of the E. India Co., 1635-41*, *passim*; A. Wood, *Life & Times*, ed. A. Clark II, (Oxford, 1892), 349-50; C. D. Sherborn, *History of the Family of Sherborn* (privately, 1901), pp. 22, 81 (inaccurate on the E.I. Co. and the Ordnance); Leeds Public Library, Temple Newsam MSS., Council in the North, 68, 74.

Among officials of the second rank, transfer from private to royal service seems to have been the commonest single mode of entry. This does not apply to those who already had a foot inside the door simply by virtue of their birth and family connexions. The influence of family on office-holding might vary from an elaborate connexion like that built up by Buckingham in the years 1616-28, spreading across the household, wardrobes, Mint, Ordnance, Exchequer, and King's Bench, to a simple father-to-son succession such as existed in the following offices: those of King's Gunfounder and Powder-maker, the Clerkship of the Liveries, the co-Auditorship and the Surveyorship of the Court of Wards, the co-Victuallership of the Navy, the Clerkship of the Wardrobes, the Clerkship of the Duchy of Lancaster court, the Treasurership of the Chamber, the Postmaster Generalship, the Clerkship of the Pells, the Lord Treasurer's Remembrancership, and—longest span of all—the King's Remem-brancership.

We may distinguish 'lateral' and 'vertical' family connexions. By vertical is meant inheritance of one office by successive generations of the same family; by later, family control of several offices over a more limited period of time.

Some family connexions were a mixture of both types. To take an example of a mainly lateral connexion: Francis Slingsby, a Yorkshire gentleman, married Mary Percy, sister of the seventh and eighth Earls and aunt of the ninth Earl of Northumberland. Their eldest surviving son, Sir Henry, was Vice-President of the North in the 1620's, their second son, Sir William, a Carver to James I's Queen and a royal commissioner in the next reign, and their third son, Sir Guilford, Comptroller of the Navy (1625-31). In the next genera-tion, Sir William's daughter was the second wife of Buckingham's mad brother, John Villiers Viscount Purbeck, and his son a Master of the Mint in the 1660's. In the 1630's Sir Guilford's first son, also Guilford, was one of Wentworth's secretaries in Ireland, then Lieutenant of the Irish Ordnance, and finally Vice-President of Munster, and his second son, Sir Robert, eventually also became naval Comptroller (in 1660-1).[1] Since the Percies were in disgrace with the Crown almost continuously until the 1630's, it is not likely to have been this connexion which gave the Slingsbys their opening.

[1] *D.N.B.*, XVIII, 375-8; *The Diary of Sir Henry Slingsby* (ed. D. Parsons, 1836), pp. v-xx, 395-413 (the diarist was the Vice-President's son).

And the Villiers connexion, while doubtless helpful, can only have fortified an already established position.

The motives behind the building up of such a connexion are of more interest than the details of its composition. For the younger sons of such a strongly based landed family, with important regional connexions (and for *their* younger sons), civil office under the Crown might offer a more congenial alternative than the church, law, business, or military service abroad, to life as annuitants in the head of the family's household. In 1638 a wealthy Hampshire gentleman, Sir Henry Knollys, Clerk of Greencloth and Receiver of First Fruits and Tenths, bequeathed to his second son £1,200 to be 'laid out in purchasing and obtaining of some office'. Knollys was also in the process of selling the First Fruits Office for £2,000, but this money was for his eldest son, to be used as the heir thought best.[1] Over and above direct economic motives such families as the Slingsbys and the Knollyses may have felt, in some rather vague and undefined way, that however well established they were in their localities, it was desirable to have one of their members at the centre of affairs, in the King's service. This projection of family interest onto the national level was perhaps as near as most men had yet reached towards even an embryonic concept of public service. In most cases the over-riding motive was probably a mixture of personal ambition and family prestige; rare indeed was the 'lone wolf' who sought advancement for himself alone and not also for his family. The objects aimed at may have been power and status as much as direct material gains, but in practice this too is largely an artificial distinction.

It will be useful to distinguish family patronage from influence or 'connexion' in the wider sense. Family patronage is best referred to as 'patrimony', although strictly this term should be limited to direct father-to-son succession. Patrimony may be thought of as extending to sons, grandsons, and brothers, and sometimes to nephews, brothers-in-law, and sons-in-law. As the term is used here, patrimony probably did not often extend further, that is to cousins or to more remote 'in-laws', unless there was some special reason for its doing so. Therefore it does sometimes matter who was whose cousin, but not for this purpose so very often; and, as the recent historians of the *Members of the Long Parliament* decided when they

[1] PCC, 144 Lee; for a comparable instance see *The Knyvett Letters (1620-1644)*, ed. B. Schofield (1949), p. 25.

found that John Hampden and King Charles were distantly related,[1] a line has to be drawn somewhere!

The system of Patronage, or as Sir John Neale has termed it for the Elizabethan age, 'Clientage', did not necessarily involve either kinship (by blood or marriage) or service. It could be based on friendship, common interests, or merely that attachment by a lesser man to the following of a greater, which was still so characteristic a feature of English political and social life. Especially where the client was neither a close relative nor a regular servant of his master, patronage often secured entry to office in conjunction with purchase. Even sons following fathers, or secretaries transferring from private to royal employment, might have to pay for their offices; but where the relationship corresponded more to what Professor Neale means by clientage, purchase was more often also involved. For example, Sir William Uvedale's father had been Treasurer of the Chamber under Elizabeth I, but it was as the friend and perhaps the 'client' of King James's current favourite Robert Carr, Earl of Somerset, that the son approached the same office. In 1613 Lord Stanhope, the holder, sold the reversion for £2,000 to Somerset, who had apparently secured it for his then friend and confidant, the ill-fated politician and man of letters, Sir Thomas Overbury; two years later Overbury was dead, poisoned at the direct instigation of Lady Somerset, perhaps with her husband's tacit connivance; before Somerset's fall he got the reversion transferred to Uvedale, who duly succeeded Stanhope in 1618 and held office until 1642; his own son-in-law, Sir Edward Griffin, became reversioner in 1640, and succeeded to it in the 1660's. It would be interesting to know who raised the £2,000: Carr, Overbury, or Uvedale?

Some who aspired to office were too poor to buy, and too impatient or unsure of themselves to rely on a single patron. To take a somewhat tragi-comic example: a certain Rowland Woodward obtained a post in the Signet Office, thanks to the patronage of Francis Windebank, the future Secretary of State, who was then Clerk of the Signet. He committed an indiscretion or misdemeanour, for which he was expelled in June 1630. He wrote as follows to his patron:

> Sir I begin now a little to come to myself & recollect my spirits since the blow I received last week, which left me in a manner senseless and unmovable, as coming so suddenly upon me, that I

[1] D. Brunton and D. H. Pennington, *Members of the Long Parliament* (1954), p. 17.

could put on no armour of defence & stand upon my guard. And as all blows do stupify & astonish, and rather take away sense and motion, than cause pain immediately, so it is with me now that the stupefaction is over I feel a soreness and debility in all my parts, for which there is no better remedy than patience, and putting trust in Him that hath promised to ease all them that are heavily laden, and call upon Him for help, saying with Job: the Lord hath given & the Lord hath taken, blessed be the name of the Lord.

He had already appealed to the Bishop of London (Laud), and to Secretary Dorchester; so generous were their answers that 'truly I think it would be easier to obtain than to find out a good suit'. He appealed to Windebank for help in his restoration. Some five weeks later he reported that his grant of the Assistant Mastership of Ceremonies had passed the Signet Seal and was, he hoped, about to pass the Privy and Great Seals. He had by then also solicited help from the Lord Chamberlain and the Queen's Attorney. A week later he reported a delay at the Great Seal; if the Lord Keeper was involved, this would have to be overcome by asking Laud to get the Lord Treasurer's support for it. He was past shame, or doubt about approaching *any* potential patron, for, as he explained,

to confesse ingenuously to you, if I should stay longer here [i.e. London] my money would fall short (not with standing my boldness with you in detaining your Dividend [i.e. Windebank's monthly or quarterly share in the profits of the Signet Seal]) to defray me into the country.

Over four months later, he was about to petition the Lord Treasurer to ask for the quarterly payment of the fee due on his new office and for the enrolment of his name on the Exchequer's list of those receiving wages from the King. The Auditor of Receipt had advised this; it was apparently possible to be appointed to an office without the salary being properly authorized. The machinery was always slow and cumbrous except for the favoured few: unless he was simply a fraud, Woodward's trouble was that he could afford neither purchase nor patience, and that having once been safely in office he had been unwise or unlucky enough to get thrown out, and this made it harder to get back.[1]

[1] *Cal. S.P. Dom.*, *1627-8*, p. 548, *1629-31*, p. 555; SP 16/169/4, 171/23, 56, 177/13; *Foedera*, 22 July 1630. For Woodward's earlier career see J. W. Stoye, *English Travellers Abroad 1604-1667* (1952), p. 139; *Lincoln's Inn Admission Register*, p. 112; J. Nichols, *Progresses of James I* (1828), II, 247; *Chamberlain Letters*, I, 372.

The sale of offices will be examined in its economic aspects later, when their monetary value is considered. Here it is relevant simply as a mode of entry.

Were there enough evidence, it might appear that everyone who obtained a major Household or Chamber office did so by means of patrimony or patronage, sometimes combined with purchase. Entry into some branches of the royal household may occasionally have been achieved by purchase alone, but very seldom. Sir Allen Apsley, already mentioned in another connexion, made his entrance into the Chamber, so his daughter tells us 'by means of a relation at court', but he had also commuted a small annuity inherited from his father, for a lump sum, and perhaps he bought his first place.[1] A more prominent figure of the 1630's, the elder Sir Henry Vane, claimed at the end of his life to have begun his official career with just this mixture of patronage and purchase: 'I put myself into Court and bought a Carver's place, by means of friendship of Sir Thomas Overbury which cost me £5,000.' Vane also recorded that the net value of his estate was only £300 p.a. when he succeeded his father in 1611; in 1612 his wife brought him a jointure of £3,000, but the whole of this and another £250 was soon laid out on a third share of the Subpoena Office in Chancery. It is perhaps more significant that, despite his being quite a minor landowner, Vane had been knighted in 1611, and until Overbury quarrelled with the Carrs had in him a friend of considerable influence at Court. An outlay of £8,250 in under two years is colossal for a man in Vane's then financial position. He does not appear to have borrowed by bond; and, even if he could be shown to have mortgaged his entire property in order to raise this money, his story might still be suspected of having grown a little with the years. Whatever the accuracy of his figures, the investment paid off handsomely: by 1625 Vane was co-Cofferer of the King's Household; in 1630 he became Comptroller and a Privy Councillor; and by 1640-1 he must have been one of the richest commoners in the kingdom, with his great seat at Raby, contriving for a year and a half to hold both the Treasurership of the Household and a Secretaryship of State.

The story of Vane's two purchases illustrates very aptly two of the different ways of obtaining an office: the Subpoena post by purchase alone, and the Carvership by purchase plus influence or patronage. It also illustrates two of the different motives for acquiring

[1] Hutchinson, *Memoirs*, pp. 6-12.

office, quite apart from the means by which it was acquired. The Carvership, a Chamber post, was valuable primarily as a stepping-stone, affording its holder a strategic position near the King, from which he might hope to acquire a better paid and more important position, and to obtain and dispense favours. By contrast the third share in the Subpeona office, to which the King later added a free grant of the reversion to the other two-thirds, was not going to bring its holder any appreciable patronage, status, or other benefits beyond a fairly steady income. Vane's Chamber office may thus be thought of as having been entrepreneurial in character, as depending on what he made of it, with great possibilities but also with certain risks attaching to it. His Chancery office was more like an annuity, the secure investment of a rentier.[1]

Sir Marmaduke Darrell, co-Cofferer with Vane and sole Cofferer before and after that (in 1615-25 and 1630-2), was also involved in an episode which reveals different approaches to office. In 1615 the then Cofferer, Sir Robert Vernon, was aged, infirm, and scarcely able to execute his duties; his wife was a pushful woman many years his junior who thought that she knew what was best for her husband; Sir Arthur Ingram, son of a London merchant, was a highly success-ful business-man, and had already held office, first in the Customs and then as Secretary to the Council in the North, when he deter-mined to obtain a place of honour and profit at Court; apt inter-mediaries were at hand, to bring Sir Arthur and Lady Vernon to a meeting of minds. A bargain was struck, though not without some haggling: the Cofferership was to go to Ingram, for £2,000 down to Sir Robert and 100 golden guineas (£110) to his wife, plus a life annuity of £500 to Sir Robert and then after his death one of £200 p.a. to Lady Vernon, the whole secured by the conveyance to trustees of Ingram's Lincolnshire properties (his main estates were in York-shire), this in turn being secured by a bond from him for £4,000. It was later alleged that Sir Robert had only been brought to sign the deed of surrender when told that King James had demanded it, which was almost certainly untrue, although the King's *tacit* approval for the transfer may well have been secured in the early stages. Ingram became Cofferer at the end of February 1615, but he was

[1] *D.N.B.*, XX, 113-16; C. Dalton, *History of the Wrays of Glentworth* (Aberdeen, 1881), II, 113. The Carvership was probably worth *c.* £400-£500 p.a. including diet, and one-third of the Subpoena office *c.* £633 p.a. (see Chapter 4, s. iii).

forced out of the office again in April. According to the *Dictionary of National Biography* and such histories of the period as touch on the episode, King James was persuaded that his plebeian origins and mercantile background made Ingram unfit for such honourable employment. Doubtless this was urged against him, but more important, the King was reminded of his promise, made a few years earlier, that he would allow certain Household appointments to go in succession by seniority, as was said to have happened in earlier times. Starting from the bottom, the hierarchy was as follows: senior Clerks and Sergeants in charge of sub-departments, Clerk Comptrollers, Clerks of Greencloth, Master of the Household, Cofferer, Comptroller, Treasurer. After a complaint by Darrell, then Master of the Household, and by six others below him on the ladder, the matter was referred to the Lord Chancellor and the Lord Chief Justice, and as a result of this the King declared the office to be vacant, as it had been forfeited by both Vernon and Ingram for breaking a statute of Edward VI's reign against the sale of offices. Frequent lip service was paid to this Act, but it was never in fact invoked unless there was some ulterior reason for wanting to get rid of someone, or to bring them to justice; by and large, it was a dead letter for most of James's reign. On this occasion the effect of its invocation was as intended: Darrell became Cofferer and the other six Household officials each got a corresponding step up.

This was not quite the end of the story, which explains why so much is known about it. Ingram not having obtained his Coffererership, the Vernons might seem logically unable to claim the capital sums and annuities from him. Darrell and his six supporters felt so unsure of their position that they voluntarily raised £2,110 between them, and paid it to Sir Arthur, to cover his down payments to the Vernons; thus they had themselves *in effect* bought out Vernon! They had also been unwise enough to secure Ingram in respect of his £4,000 bond, by giving him a counter-bond against themselves for £6,000. Ingram and Lady Vernon were not two to let such a chance slip. A collusive action was brought against Ingram by the Vernons demanding the forfeit of his £4,000 bond; at the same time Ingram let it be known that if he lost this action, as it was later alleged he had every intention of deliberately doing, he would proceed to get the £6,000 bond honoured by Darrell and co. The case finally came before the Lord Chancellor in 1617, the Chief Justice of Common Pleas and a London jury (perhaps composed of tradesmen or other citizens sympathetic to Ingram) having failed to reach agreement. Eventually the only legal point at issue was whether or not there had been improper collusion between Ingram's and the Vernon's lawyers, but the wider issue of whether or not the office had been corruptly and illegally sold was also inevitably debated. As far as can be seen, neither bond had to be honoured, so the result could be called a draw in Darrell's favour. Ingram had suffered a serious rebuff, but no material loss.[1] Through the agency of his judges King James had been able once more to act his part as 'the English Solomon'.

Whatever had been true of the Household in earlier times, there was not very much automatic promotion by exact seniority in any part of the early Stuart administration. There is no sign that it was enforced as a fixed rule, though something which amounted to promotion by seniority often took place. To take some further changes in the Household: Vane was successively Cofferer, Comptroller and Treasurer; the Master again succeeded as Cofferer in 1632, but in 1639 the Vice-Chamberlain became Comptroller and he was in turn succeeded as Vice-Chamberlain by the Master of the Queen's Horse, whose place was filled by her Vice-Chamberlain. Ten years earlier the Queen's Vice-Chamberlain had also been promoted to be her Master of the Horse. The advancement of Household clerks and sergeants to the Clerk Comptrollerships and from these to Clerkships of Greencloth continued, but in the higher ranks this rather irregular promotion by seniority is hard to distinguish from what we may call the seventeenth-century equivalent of ministerial reshuffles. For example, in 1628, following the death of the Earl of Worcester, Lord Privy Seal, the Earl of Manchester was moved to that office, leaving the Lord Presidency of the Council for the Earl of Marlborough, who thereupon surrendered the Lord Treasurership to Richard, Lord Weston, who was in turn succeeded as Chancellor of the Exchequer by Edward Barret, Lord Newburgh, an ex-ambassador. The latter was soon found to have been a mistaken appointment. Barret was not Weston's choice, and no sooner had the new Lord Treasurer's position been strengthened by the assassination of his own erstwhile patron Buckingham, than a further sequence of changes began. Dudley Carleton, Lord Dorchester, was

---

[1] *D.N.B.*, X, 449; P.R.O. Chancery, C 2, James I, D 12/77, file of papers on the case, 1617 (I am grateful to Mr. G. Hammersley for drawing my attention to this source); the Ingram Papers (Temple Newsam MSS., Leeds P.L.) do not appear to contain anything on this episode.

moved from the Vice-Chamberlaincy to a Secretaryship of State; Lord Conway, the senior Secretary, succeeded Marlborough, the elderly and now ailing Lord President, who died early the following year almost immediately after his final retirement; meanwhile the Chancellor of the Duchy of Lancaster succeeded as Vice-Chamberlain (he too was to die within a year, leaving the way open for a further reshuffle), making way in turn for Barret, who was promptly replaced at the Exchequer by Weston's friend and protégé, Sir Francis Cottington. Sometimes the long way round was the *only* way home.

Below the top level interchanges of this kind were unusual. At the same time, systematic promotion, whether by seniority or merit, was made difficult, indeed all but impossible, by the operation of the three 'Ps': Patrimony, Patronage, and Purchase. Promotion in fact depended on much the same factors as initial appointment, but less exclusively so. There was more scope for industry and talent to receive their due reward; none the less granted two men of even approximately equal ability and diligence, the one without influence and connexions might well spend all his working life in the same post, while the one with effective patrons would be promoted once, twice, or even more times. But it is far from certain that everyone who obtained an office wanted to be promoted. In particular, some of those who purchased legal and other offices tenable for life probably wanted no more than the steadiest return on their outlay compatible with the minimum of risk and effort. Vane for instance wanted to keep the Subpoena office, not to be promoted in the Chancery hierarchy, for which incidentally he had no qualifications.

Two of the three 'Ps', or even all of them, might be involved in any given appointment or promotion. The marriage, either of the candidate himself, or alternatively of his sister or daughter, to someone of his patron's choice might supplement, or even replace, an outright cash payment as the price of office. Such a transaction itself probably implies some prior connexion between patron and client, and so should usually be distinguished from entry by purchase alone. Buckingham had a particular penchant for marrying off his female relatives to his official dependants.

The exact borderline between patrimony and patronage is bound to be rather arbitrary. This can be illustrated from a 'lateral' connexion, that of the Dorset men who were officers of the Exchequer between the late sixteenth and the mid-seventeenth centuries. Robert Freke, esquire, of Iwerne, near Blandford, was a Teller in the Receipt for some years before his death in *c.* 1592; his wife's sister (*née* Swayne—a Blandford family) married one John Pitt, also of Iwerne, who was or subsequently became a clerk in the Exchequer; their son, William Pitt, was a Deputy Teller by 1611; in 1618 he was knighted and appointed a commissioner to inquire into the state of the Navy; about ten years before Sir William's death in 1636 his son Edward became a Teller, an office which he held until his death in 1643; Sir William Pitt's son-in-law, Sir Robert Seymour of Handford, was also a Teller towards the end of James I's reign; another son-in-law, Clement Walker, one of the very few strictly hereditary office-holders, became Usher of the Receipt, apparently in succession to an uncle or cousin, and held this office throughout the 1630's and well into the 1640's; Seymour's sister was married to Arthur Squibb the elder, who was William Pitt's clerk by 1611, chief clerk to Seymour *c.* 1619-22 and a Teller himself *c.* 1625-49; Squibb was related to Pitt not only through the Seymours but also by a paternal aunt who was married to another William Pitt, uncle of the Exchequer Sir William. Another sister of Seymour married Arthur's first cousin, John Squibb; of their sons, the third, Lawrence, had a reversion to a Tellership in the 1630's, was a royalist in the Civil Wars, and became a Teller, *c.* 1661-74; the fourth, Arthur the second, was also a reversioner in the 1630's, but, like his first cousin once removed Arthur the elder, he was a parliamentarian, and he did not make good his claim to a Tellership in the 1660's. Apart from Clement Walker, who acquired the Ushership from a relative named Billesbie, or Billisby, this whole connexion is probably traceable to the original Freke-Swayne foothold in the Exchequer, although in Sir William Pitt's case, as he married a Wareham heiress, purchase may also have been involved. Nor can it definitely be ruled out in some of the other instances.[1]

In some of the law and revenue courts, offices may simply have been put up for sale, especially during James's reign. The well-known private money-lender, Hugh Audley, may not have been anyone's client, as opposed to their creditor; on hearing that a reversion to

[1] *The Dorset Visitation of 1623* (Harleian Soc., XX); H. H. London and G. D. Squibb, 'A Dorset King of Arms: Arthur Squibb, Clarenceux, 1646-1650', *Procs. Dorset Nat. Hist. & Arch. Soc.*, LXVIII, 54-65; Dorchester County Museum, items relating to Sir William Pitt; for Pitt pedigrees see A. von Ruville, *William Pitt* (1907), I, 17; *The Diary of William Hedges* (ed. H. Yule, Hakluyt Soc., LXXVIII), III, 28-9; T. Lever, *House of Pitt* (1947).

the co-Clerkship of the Court of Wards was available, he may merely have made the necessary preliminary contacts and have taken his £2,000 or 3,000 along at the right time and place.[1] George Mynne, clothier, ironmaster, and ex-deputy paymaster of the forces in Ireland, may or may not have been more easily able to buy the Clerkship of the Hanaper in Chancery because he was related by marriage to Secretary Calvert. Richard Brownlow, ancestor of the present Earls of Brownlow, may have begun his long and lucrative tenure of the Chief Prothonotaryship of Common Pleas as someone's client; his maternal grandmother was a Zouch, and possibly connected to the courtier family of that name, but this seems a little remote. Lionel Cranfield's first patron, the Earl of Northampton (of the Howard creation), may have helped him when he bought his first office, the Receiver-Generalship of Somerset and Dorset, but probably not. In all these cases, if patronage was involved, it was subsidiary to purchase. On the other hand, although in the 1630's he was reputed to be one of the most venal of all office-holders, Sir Henry Croke of Chequers, Bucks, acquired his initial half-share in the Clerkship of the Pipe at least as much through the influence of his father and his uncle who were both Judges, as by purchase. Patronage probably explains the appointments of Sir Sackville Crowe as Navy Treasurer (1627-9), Sir Henry Mervyn, an Anglo-Irishman, as Vice-Admiral of the Narrow Seas in the 1620's, and of Sir Henry Mildmay as Master of the Jewels (1618-42), though purchase also helped in Mervyn's case and quite possibly in those of the other two.

Appointments could also be affected by other elements obviously related to Patronage, but not identical with it: Favour and Merit. Merit speaks for itself; favour can best be distinguished from Patronage as more often representing a temporary attitude on the part of the King or someone of influence towards the recipient, than as a more or less stable relationship between them. A man could enjoy someone's favour without necessarily being their 'client' or being under their 'influence'. Favour could of course be a consequence of merit and not of mere amiability. Promotion as a reward for merit was seldom distinguishable from promotion as the result of favour; there could—all too easily—be promotion due to favour without merit, but not to merit alone, without favour, or any of the three 'Ps'.

[1] *D.N.B.*, I, 721; Bell, *Court of Wards*, pp. 28, 38.

A first appointment, or a promotion made as a reward for service, was likely to be both a mark of favour and a recognition of ability. Except in extreme cases, this was a matter of proportion one way or the other. There were some mere favourites, but fewer than is often supposed, even in the household departments: some of the Scots in James I's early years, in his middle years Carr Earl of Somerset, and spanning part of his and his son's reigns Buckingham, Herbert Earl of Montgomery, Rich Earl of Holland (these two were both the younger brothers of Earls and born of great Tudor families), and Hay Earl of Carlisle; coming on into Charles's reign, Sir James Fullarton, Sir David Cunningham, the Gorings of Sussex, and the Jermyns of Suffolk. Even Endymion Porter was useful as a diplomatic go-between because of his Spanish contacts and his mastery of that language.

Favour and merit could also be combined with purchase. In March 1640 a correspondent told the eminent diplomat Sir Thomas Roe that he could have the Comptrollership of the Household for £3,000, although Sir Peter Wyche, the Ambassador in Turkey, had offered £6,000 for it; in the event the holder, Sir Thomas Jermyn, kept it until August 1641; it was said that Wyche then paid £5,000 and that another £2,000 compensation was raised for Jermyn.[1]

Often, too, naval and military distinction and diplomatic service were rewarded with offices, for which the recipients were sometimes adequately suited, but perhaps equally often not. A recent study of English travellers abroad in the early and mid-seventeenth century shows how often foreign service was a gateway to office at home,[2] although such cases are often hard to distinguish from those of the private secretaries who entered royal service. The military men found their rewards in the Ordnance, the Armoury, Governorships and Captaincies of castles, forts, and blockhouses, and the Lieutenancy of the Tower; the only appointment to wonder at here is that of Sir Edward Conway to the Secretaryship of State in 1623. The central executive was perhaps *over*staffed with foreign experts of one kind and another; it has often been pointed out that the elder Dudley Carleton, later Viscount Dorchester, who had spent so much of his time abroad as an Agent and then as an Ambassador, was not a wise choice for the Secretaryship in 1628. In 1625 neither Secretary (Conway and Sir Albertus Moreton) had much domestic experience;

[1] *Cal. S.P. Dom.*, *1639-40*, p. 589, *1641-3*, pp. 73, 77.
[2] Stoye, *English Travellers*.

per contra after 1632 neither (Coke and Windebank) was a foreign expert. At the administrative rather than the political level, two out of the four ordinary Clerks of the Privy Council were foreign experts, or had begun as such, except briefly in 1635-6, when only one was; about three of the eight extraordinary Clerks of 1625-41 had the same general background; the French, and to a lesser extent the Latin, Secretaryships and the German Interpretership were obviously likely to be filled in the same way; on the other hand, few, if any, such types are found among the Clerks of the Signet and Privy Seal, or the Secretaries' personal assistants.

Because ability is so hard to isolate from patronage and favour, it does not follow that it was unimportant. In graduating from private to royal service and in promotions it could clearly count for much. It is less clear how seventeenth-century men measured what we should call administrative ability, or indeed whether they were even familiar with such a concept. They did not usually mean the same as we do now when they described someone as 'able'; often to them it meant simply that someone was thought to be suitable, or qualified for a particular post. Under Merit we may therefore include special skills and qualifications, as well as ability in the modern, more general sense.

In legal offices and others where expert knowledge and skill were important, professional distinction may *sometimes* have secured entry unaided. Financial experience and ability, then as now perhaps considered more recondite and mysterious than they really are, certainly helped into office men who would not otherwise have got there. Cranfield is the obvious case, but his career is hardly typical. As more 'typical' figures it would be better to cite: Ingram; Sir John Jacob, Customs officer and Council Clerk extraordinary; Hugh Audley; Sir Simon Harvey, the Elizabethan grocer who rose to be Clerk of Greencloth, *c.* 1624-8; Sir William Russell, a leading man in several of the great overseas trading companies before he became Navy Treasurer; and the gifted reforming Postmaster, Thomas Witherings, denounced by his courtly opponents as a mere business-man. We must not of course, assume that these men and others like them obtained their offices solely because of their business ability. Russell, for instance, may have been hoping for prestige and social advancement as well as for profit if it is true that he paid for the office twice what it was reckoned to be worth. He was knighted when he became naval Treasurer for the first time, and was created a baronet on his reappointment.[1] The more successful a business-man was, the more likely that he would be in a position to buy an office, and if necessary to pay more than someone who already had court or government connexions. Even if we ask why Russell was appointed, rather than why he wanted to be, his commercial experi-ence and distinction were decisive only in conjunction with his readiness to buy his way in.

The lawyers were much the largest group who often obtained their offices because of their professional qualifications. Even if we exclude the great officers of state, the Judges, and the Attorney- and Solicitor-Generals, an impressive number of lesser legal offices seem to have been filled by distinguished lawyers. This statement has to be qualified. Family connexions were certainly important *inside* the legal profession, both among lawyers in private practice and among legal officers; there were several great legal dynasties, like the Crokes, Finches, and Montagues, and numerous lesser family connexions. It was obviously easier for a lawyer with family influence to get to the top of his profession than it was for one without. Yet such influence was definitely neither a prerequisite nor a guarantee of success at the bar or in office under the Crown. John Bankes, later Lord Chief Justice, enjoyed no such advantages, but he had already made a name at the bar when he took up his first post, as Attorney to the Prince, in 1630. Sir Thomas Bedingfield belonged to a family with some legal connexions—of the second rank—but he was already quite an eminent pleader when he became Attorney to the Duchy in 1638. Sir Julius Caesar was the son of an Italian physician at the court of Elizabeth I, but he rose entirely on his talents as a civil lawyer. Sir John Finch, later Lord Keeper, came of a very well established legal family, but he was already an outstanding pleader when he became Attorney to the Queen in 1626; the same was true of the future Attorney-General, Edward Herbert, cadet member of a great aristocratic house, when he was made Steward of the Marshal-sea in 1630. Orlando Bridgeman, the eldest son of a bishop, future Chief Justice and then Lord Keeper, and reputedly the inventor of the 'strict settlement', was called to the bar six years before he ob-tained his first office, as Vice-Chamberlain of Chester, and eight

[1] *Chamberlain Letters*, II, 158, 161; G.E.C., *Btge.*, II, 65; for his fin-ancial importance see R. Ashton, 'The disbursing official under the early Stuarts: the cases of Sir William Russell and Philip Burlamachi', *Bull. Inst. Hist. Res.*, XXX (1957), 162-74.

years before he entered the central administration as Solicitor to the Prince.

A legal education at one of the Chancery Inns or Inns of Court was included in the upbringing of so many members of the upper and even middle classes that it is not always easy to distinguish professional lawyers among the officials from men with *some* legal training. Professionals, who had been called to the bar (or if they were civilians had obtained a doctorate), were normally appointed to all major offices on the legal side of Chancery, e.g. the Masterships, and less certainly the Six Clerkships. And the same was true of all posts in Common Pleas, except those of Custos Brevium, Marshal, and (sometimes) Chirographer, of all those in King's Bench, except the positions of Marshal, perhaps Clerk of the Crown, and (until 1629) Chief Clerk, and of all offices on the legal side of the Exchequer. This also applied to a smaller range of posts in the prerogative and ecclesiastical courts.

Whether such men bought their offices or acquired them solely on account of their professional eminence does not affect the argument. Unless he had married an heiress, Thomas Corie could only possibly have paid £10,000 for the Chief Prothonotaryship of Common Pleas in 1638 through success at the bar. Only by such success would otherwise quite obscure men have been able to pay the normal price of £6,000 for a Six Clerkship in Chancery. This argument may even be extended to cover the greater legal offices as well. A lawyer was unlikely to become important politically unless he was, or had been, successful professionally. Of course, he might be more formidable in the House of Commons or the Council, or as an administrator, than he had ever been in the Courts. And the reverse might be equally true: a man of great forensic talents, then as now, could turn out to be politically a 'dead duck', whether in parliament, council, or a department of state. Nor should one suppose that all the best lawyers necessarily became legal officers, or even Judges. Again it is scarcely for an outsider to the mysteries of the law to say whether or not success is the only or even the most important criterion of professional significance. Success due to talent is just as hard to distinguish from the effects of patronage and purchase among professional lawyers holding office, as it is in the rest of the Civil Service.

Early Stuart officials cannot all be neatly classified according to how they obtained their offices. In some cases one element appears to have been more important, in others another, and this normally bore some relation to social background. Those with aristocratic, Court, or administrative connexions, were likely to owe most to patrimony or patronage; members of gentry families without these connexions to patronage or purchase, or both, plus, often, some element of ability as well as ambition; business-men to purchase, plus patronage or ability, or a mixture of the two; lawyers, private secretaries, tutors, and confidential servants to patronage together with ability, often in the form of linguistic or other special skills.

ii REVERSION

As can be seen from the Six Clerks' case in the 1630's, the granting of reversions to offices was not always a straightforward matter. A reversion was normally a written grant of the succession to an office. It could also be a verbal promise of the succession, and this may have been more usual in the case of offices *not* in the Crown's gift. A reversion could also be a grant of the succession to any one of a group of individual posts, e.g. to any of the six Six Clerkships; there could be a queue of two or more reversioners either to a single position or to a group of posts. The reversion was almost invariably granted by whoever had the gift of appointment to the office concerned. In the case of Crown appointments, this again involves the problem of nominal and real appointing power; reversions to certain lesser offices in the King's gift were no doubt in practice normally awarded by the head of department, or after agreement between various senior officers, but as with the appointments themselves they were made in the King's name. And as with appointment, royal favour or the effective support of a powerful patron might lead to someone securing the grant who had not been chosen by the head or the other senior members of the department, someone perhaps whose eventual entry to the office they were positively against.

Chancery was not the only department where reversions were affected by changes in the rights of appointment. Next to Chancery no court or department, outside the royal household, offered a larger number of lucrative posts involving only work of such a routine nature that it could easily be done by a deputy or under-clerk, than the court of Common Pleas. Not unnaturally it was a happy hunting-ground for many besides successful lawyers.

Sir David Cunningham, a moderately prominent courtier with no legal pretensions, succeeded another Scot as Receiver-General of the revenues which Charles I had enjoyed as Prince. In 1641 he was to become first Cofferer and then Treasurer and Receiver-General to the then Prince, the future Charles II. In November 1635 he was granted a reversion to the office of Chirographer. The following May a Mr. Drake reported that Cunningham was now ready to resign and surrender his interest back to the King, so that it could be transferred to him, Drake; the Attorney-General was accordingly told to prepare a fresh grant. Nothing was said about payment, but it looks as if Cunningham had simply acquired the reversion as a speculation; if he had kept it and later become Chirographer, he would doubtless have performed by deputy.[1]

In the space of little more than a year even such minor posts as the Filazerships attracted a Crown creditor who had failed to obtain a Six Clerkship, the great Dr. William Harvey, and a prominent Jacobean courtier, Robert Carey Earl of Monmouth. Harvey was acting on behalf of a young relative, 'bred in the said office and fit for the execution thereof'. There were about thirteen Filazers, and in 1636-7 at least five reversioners.[2]

All reversions tended to limit the Crown's future freedom of appointment. But the significance of any particular reversion varied according to the ages of those concerned. In May 1636 three brothers petitioned the King for successive life grants to the Clerkship of the Warrants in the Common Pleas, that is for a life grant of the office with reversions for two further lives; they reported that the present holder and the two present reversioners, Thomas and Henry Jermyn (the sons of Sir Thomas, the Vice-Chamberlain and a Privy Councillor) were all ready to surrender. In approving the new grant, the King observed 'No great difference in years appearing between the petitioners and the patentees'. As in the case of the Chirographership, these applicants may have been buying the Clerkship; alternatively

---

[1] Bodleian Library, Bankes MS. 50/30, 46; P.R.O., Lord Steward's Dept., misc. books, LS 13/251, pp. 156, 170; *Cal. S.P. Dom.*, *1629-31*, p. 177; *Foedera*, XX, 516; G.E.C. *Btge.*, II, 153, 384; J. Summerson, *Architecture in Britain 1530-1830* (Harmondsworth, 1955) pp. 94, 337.

[2] Bodl. Bankes MSS. 41/20, 48, 51/8. For these offices in Common Pleas, see below, Appendix pp. 483-4.

they may have been the creditors of the existing holder or of the reversioners.[1]

The ages of those involved in such transfers were bound to affect the holders of other reversions as well as the Crown. Moving to another department, in 1637 the second reversioner to the Keepership of the Council Chamber complained that the first reversioner, aged seventy, had sold his place to a man of twenty—a catastrophic blow to the petitioner's hopes.[2] Returning to the court of Common Pleas, in 1638 another royal creditor claimed that he had been granted a reversion to a Filazership in return for having cancelled a £1,000 loan. There were already six reversions in existence, three of them for two lives each, so unless all nine of these 'lives' were elderly or unsound it was a remote prospect; he doubted if the market value of such a reversion was £100, and claimed to have spent more than that in suing for his £1,000 and in securing the passage of his reversion; now, as a last straw, the Lord Keeper had stopped his grant at the Great Seal. With the hyperbole characteristic of the age he alleged that he was poised on the brink of irretrievable ruin, and begged that the grant might go forward. The King referred his plea to the Lord Keeper and the Secretary of State for Scotland, directing that if his facts were correct the grant was to go through without delay.[3]

In July 1641 the House of Lords ruled that certain existing reversions to offices in the Common Pleas were invalid. The Chief Justice was to have the gift of these offices 'as in former times he had done'. This, as we shall see, was related to an earlier dispute about the three Prothonotaryships, which were amongst the most lucrative of all legal offices. But its most immediate impact was felt by John Cockshutt, Clerk of the Council in the Star Chamber. He was about to lose that post as a result of Star Chamber being abolished by the Long Parliament; shortly before this, when the then Exigenter of Common Pleas died, Chief Justice Bankes appointed in his place Cockshutt, who had begun his career in Bankes's service; certain clerks of the court had then complained and threatened to petition the House of Commons, on the grounds that Cockshutt had been admitted in his capacity as the holder of a reversion, which was invalid according to the Lords' recent ruling, and secondly because

[1] *Ibid.*, 50/34.
[2] *Cal. S.P. Dom., 1637*, p. 29.
[3] SP 16/323, book of petitions, fol. 321.

he had no proper training as a clerk in the court. Cockshutt asserted that he was perfectly competent, and that he had been admitted by the Chief Justice, and not *qua* reversioner; he also claimed that previous Chief Justices had appointed such of their own servants as happened to be law clerks to vacant Exigenterships; he had been in legal service for twenty years, notably under Bankes when he was Attorney-General (1634-41); he asked to be confirmed and continued in his office.[1]

A few years before this, John Gulston and Robert Moyle, the second and third Prothonotaries of Common Pleas, had been concerned about the succession to their respective offices, and the question of whose gift they were in. Some of Gulston's worries about the future took the form of a petition, which can be dated to the summer of 1636, just after he had obtained a pardon for any offences which he or his subordinates might have committed in his office; it was as follows:

Sheweth most Humbly that he hath submitted himself to your Majesty's Royal pleasure in the payment of moneys, and abatement of fees belonging unto your petitioner's office of second prothonotary. . . . And had no grant of the Reversion thereof, for that the same is in the dispose [gift] of your Majesty's Custos Brevium of the same Court, whereby many of your petitioner's children (being eleven in number) will be unprovided for in the case your Petitioner (being aged and sickly) should be taken from them. In regard whereof your Petitioner Humbly beseecheth your most Excellent Majesty for to grant unto John Smyth and John Stubbs and to the longest liver of them the next and immediate Reversion of the first Philazer's office of your Highness' Court of Common Pleas at Westminster, which shall first happen to be Void after several grants thereof already made by your Majesty to . . . [the names include those of the 1636-7 grantees as well as Lord Monmouth's still unnamed nominees]. . . . To the use of Edward Gulston, sixth son of your Petitioner, during his natural life, And if he shall die before he receive any fruit of this your Majesty's grant, then to the use of William Gulston, seventh son of your Petitioner, during his natural life, And that the said John Smyth and John Stubbs respectively being now clerks of the said Court, may execute such office, when it shall become void,

[1] SP 16/482/123; *Lords Journals*, IV, 139, 291, 322-3; Hist. MSS. Comm. *Fourth Report*, House of Lords Papers, p. 22. The Chief Justice recovered the gift of several offices including two Prothonotaryships.

by themselves or their deputies to the uses and purposes afore-said. . . .[1]

In June 1636 the Attorney-General was notified that an agreement had been reached in principle with Gulston's colleague, Prothonotary Moyle. But the full treaty between Moyle and the Crown, setting out the terms of his appointment, the fees he could take, and the future disposition of his office, was only finally ratified in March 1637, and must have followed some sort of agreement between the Crown and the Custos Brevium, recognizing the King's sole right to appoint Prothonotaries. The draft of Moyle's pardon was in the Attorney-General's office on 10 September 1636, and at the Great Seal on 8 November. Sometime before 24 May 1637 he had paid the Crown £2,200, the price of his own pardon and of royal approval for the future disposition of his office. The £1,500 which Gulston had paid for his pardon in June 1636 does not appear to have covered reversions; as we have seen these were not then in the King's gift, and he was after a reversion to a Filazership instead.

Moyle was given the right to transfer his office to any fit person within the next four years, 'whereby to enable himself for payment of his debts or provision for his children'. His successor was to be admitted for life, with a reversion to Moyle's eldest son, if he was still living and was of age, and, failing him, to the second son; Moyle's executors were to name trustees to hold the office for the benefit of either son should he succeed while still under age. The text of the final treaty referred to Moyle's appointment in 1627 as

[1] SP 16/154/25, n.d., ascribed by the editors of *Cal. S.P. Dom.* to 1629. My reasons for preferring 1636 are (i) the first sentence quoted almost certainly refers to Gulston's payment of £1,400 to the Privy Purse on 4 June 1636, and the pardon issued to him on 22 July (Bodl. Bankes MS. 37/39; Birmingham R.L., Coventry Papers, MS. 604085/97), (ii) the list of existing reversioners given in the petition dates it to 1636-7 or later, (iii) the implication that the Custos Brevium still had the gift of one Prothonotaryship suggests a date *after* 13 October 1635, when the Chief Justice abjured *his* claim to appoint them (Hist. MSS. Comm. *Fourth Rept.*, p. 22), but before the then Custos Brevium was required to give a bond for £8,000 as a pledge that he would allow the King to appoint them (SP 16/340/1, n.d., ascribed to 1636, but presumably before that November; by then the Custos had given up any claim: see the Crown's agreement with Gulston's colleague, Moyle, *Foedera*, XX, 76-92). I have not been able to find this bond entered either with those 'in the form of Statute Staple', or on the Close Rolls. (I am grateful to Mr. J. P. Cooper for the references here and below to the Coventry Papers in Birmingham.)

having been 'for the term of his life, *as his Freehold*' (my italics), but not to his having had to give the then Chief Justice a bond for £5,000 on taking up this appointment! Presumably this had either been as security for his good conduct in the office, or, if he was buying the office, as security for the purchase money, or perhaps to cover both; the bond was cancelled after three years. Moyle's final treaty named one Gilbert Yard, gent., Prothonotary's clerk, as the trustee should either son succeed as a minor; Moyle himself was also allowed to act by deputy on account of his age and ill-health. He was not given permission specifically to sell, as opposed merely to transferring the office, but a well-informed contemporary believed that when Moyle died in 1640 his successor paid £4,000 for it. As far as can be seen, neither of the younger Moyles nor Mr. Yard ever enjoyed the benefits of their reversion.[1]

The comprehensive agreements, or 'treaties', between the Crown and the Prothonotaries should warn us against treating any one aspect of office-holding in isolation from the rest. Questions of appointment, reversion, tenure, remuneration, and sale often interlocked with each other as in these cases. The Crown's resumption of the right to appoint the three Prothonotaries and the Six Clerks of Chancery suggests that there may almost have been a general policy to recover royal patronage and destroy bureaucratic 'sub-infeudation'. This would of course have involved reversions as well as direct appointments to offices.

Once it became known that the reversions to certain posts in Common Pleas were in the Crown's gift, others began to urge their claims. About 1636 Sir Robert Gordon, a Gentleman of the Privy Chamber, alleging that he was owed £4,450 by the Crown, asked for a reversion to Gulston's or Moyle's office; he promised to make over to the King whatever he might raise from the sale or the tenure of a Prothonotaryship, after his debt and the interest due on it had been paid off. The King seems to have approved of a grant but for

[1] Bodl. Bankes MS. 37/55; Birmingham R.L., MS. 604085/266; PC 2/47, pp. 277-8; P.R.O. Exchequer of Receipt, E 403/2591, pp. 48b-49; Lord Chamberlain's Dept., books of recognisances for debts, LC 4/200, p. 256; Gloucestershire R.O., Colchester Papers, Journals, I (on the back of other entries for 1638); *Foedera*, XX, 76-92; *Cal. S.P. Dom., 1637-8*, p. 76, *1640-1*, p. 266. For briefer treaties with the Chief and second Prothonotaries see *Foedera*, XX, 123-4; the former paid £4,000 for his pardon (Elmhirst (Pye) MSS., now at Worsborough Bridge, Yorks., Exchequer Papers (1), fol. 53; Birmingham R.L., MS. 604085/267).

Gordon's own lifetime only.[1] As with some of those who sought places as Filazers or as Chirographer, legal qualifications were not a prerequisite for these posts.

Reversions and the complications to which they could lead were far from being confined to the law courts. A few months before his death in 1611, the Comptroller of the Navy, Sir Henry Palmer, who had commanded a ship in the Armada campaign, secured a reversion to his office for his son Henry. The latter was probably too young to succeed, but in any case there were prior reversioners. Henry Palmer the second was knighted in 1618, commanded a ship on the Algiers expedition of 1620-1 against the north African pirates, acted as Vice-Admiral of a squadron in 1625-6, and was made co-Vice-Admiral of the Narrow Seas (that is joint commander of the Channel station) in 1628; but when there was a vacancy again in 1627-8 he was still not appointed Comptroller. He finally succeeded to this office in 1632, and by 1638-9 he was already arranging for a younger man to share it with him because of his age and infirmity. When his immediate predecessor had been ill in 1631, Palmer had ventured to remind Secretary Coke of his twenty-year-old reversion, but he had added that he would naturally far prefer to become Comptroller solely as a result of the King's favour. His qualifications were certainly better than those of many people who did not have to wait so long to take up their inheritance.[2]

Not all suitors for reversions, any more than for direct appointments, were successful. Some merely lacked the right connexions in the patronage system; others were intrinsically less deserving; those who had neither effective patrons nor qualifications to counterbalance this could hardly expect to be serious candidates. On a par with the Rowland Woodward mentioned in the last section was a Mr. Nicolls, who appealed to Secretary Windebank in 1639. For sixteen years he had been in the service of Windebank's predecessor, Lord Dorchester; he had been unwise enough to quarrel with Dorchester's widow over the sorting and disposal of her husband's papers, and he had found no alternative employment. Already in

---

[1] SP 16/310/14, n.d., ascribed to 1635, but probably 1636: see p. 100, n. 1.

[2] W. Shaw, *The Knights of England* (1906), II, 168; *Acts Privy Council 1625-6*, pp. 215, 461; *Cal. S.P. Dom. 1627-8*, p. 563, *1628-9*, p. 408, *1639-40*, pp. 147, 157, *1641-3*, p. 179; Hist. MSS. Comm. *Cowper*, I, 427; Clarendon, *Hist. Reb.*, II, 217, 221-2; *D.N.B.*, XV, 128.

Dorchester's lifetime Nicolls had been an unsuccessful suitor for the French Secretaryship and the Bailiffship, or Bailiwick, of Jersey, and since then for a Signet Clerkship and a Filazership of Common Pleas. In desperation he struck out wildly and begged for any

> of the sutes following. Either of the reversion of Mr. De Vic's place [the French Secretaryship] or of that of Assistant to the Master of the Ceremonies . . . lately bestowed on Sir Balthazer Gerbier [the painter and connoisseur]; and if of neither of these, then (unless it be too great presumption in me) of a Clerk's place of the Council.

Failing all these, he would settle for a lump sum of money, for an annual allowance to collect and collate foreign intelligence, or for the right to make a new baronet, that is in effect to sell a baronetcy.

> These particulars, though peradventure not very plausible, I am bold to offer to your Honour's consideration, to be either entertained or smothered according as best shall seem to your great wisdom.

As an afterthought he added one last hope: reversions to two or three Filazerships, or Exigenterships of Common Pleas, when they fell vacant, namely when all existing reversioners had succeeded to offices.[1] Whatever his other qualifications, Nicolls's sense of proportion was certainly at fault: a Clerkship of the Council was hardly for one who had failed to become Assistant Master of Ceremonies or Bailiff of Jersey. But, deserving or not, the man without effective patrons was in a sad way.

Allowance must be made for the extravagant language of the time. Even a man so well connected and relatively affluent as Balthazer Gerbier, a knight, who was both Woodward's successor in the Ceremonies Office and the King's Resident in Brussels, could write in mock pathetic tones to Windebank when he heard, in August 1640, that the Postmastership, of which he professed to have had some hopes, had been disposed elsewhere. He concluded: 'I shall humbly desire for the continuance of your favour towards me, for I do stand in extreme need to have somewhat that may serve to keep me floating.' The following year he became Master of Ceremonies, but not by then at Windebank's instance; this, and his

---

[1] SP 16/428/102; Higham, *Secretary of State*, pp. 188-9, and refs. given there.

103

failure to obtain the Post Office were only phases in a colourful and chequered career.[1]

Those who secured reversions by patronage or other means did not always live to enjoy them. Windebank's chief personal secretary, his nephew Robin Reade, first became reversioner to a Signet Clerkship as trustee for his cousin Thomas Windebank, and then in his own right to a Tellership in the Exchequer, and later also to a Signet Clerkship. In the autumn of 1640 he was a candidate for the forthcoming vacancy among the Clerks of the Privy Council, but he was forced to flee abroad with his uncle in December, and died still in exile after the restoration of Charles II.[2]

The respective ages of those concerned were especially important where there were multiple reversions to a group of offices. There were normally at least half a dozen reversioners to the thirteen Filazerships of Common Pleas; at one time there were four reversioners to the four Signet Clerkships. But the most complicated example relates to a single office, the Secretaryship of the Council in the North. In 1613 its holder was granted the right to name four reversioners who were to hold the office during the lifetime of either of two of his own sons; ten years later, three of these four reversioners being dead, the holder and the fourth reversioner asked for a re-grant to fresh nominees. This case might equally well be considered a curiosity of tenure as an example of a reversion; we shall meet the same office and its various holders again in this and subsequent chapters.[3]

Reversions involved men of all ranks and social degrees, at least among those who aspired to any office under the Crown. There may have been relatively more reversions to legal offices than to any others, but they were common throughout the central administration, in the royal household and in almost all the other departments. They were not obtainable for the 'great offices of state' or for the judgeships. There are a few exceptions to this. In 1628-9 the Chancellorship of the Exchequer was said to have a reversion attached to

[1] *D.N.B.*, VII, 1106-8; H. Ross Williamson, *Four Stuart Portraits* (1949), pp. 26-60, 143-50; SP 16/464/70.

[2] *D.N.B.*, XVI, 796; Foster, *Al. Ox.*, p. 1241a; Higham, *Secretary of State*, pp. 105-7, 163, etc.; *Cal. S.P. Dom.*, *1631-3*, p. 155, *1637-8*, p. 6, *1640-1*, pp. 205, 458, *1660-1*, pp. 304, 445; *Foedera*, XX, 203, 307; *Middlesex Pedigrees* (Harl. Soc., LXV), p. 123.

[3] Berkshire R.O., Trumbull Papers, misc., XIX, 83; Leeds P.L., Temple Newsam MSS., Council in the North, no. 111.

it, but this was most unusual; at different times in the 1620's and 30's the Chancellorship of the Duchy, and the Masterships of the Wards, the Rolls, and the Ordnance carried reversions. In the household departments the Treasurership of the Chamber, in effect the fourth senior post above stairs, was the only major office with a reversion.

In the middle ranks of the central government rather more than half the offices seem to have carried reversions at any given time. A new reversioner was by no means necessarily appointed every time a post changed hands. The attachment of more than one reversion to the same office was never the rule, and can only be found in a small minority of cases. Reversions to offices in the King's gift were normally recorded and enrolled in the same way as the actual appointments to these posts. There is no comparable evidence about reversions to offices in the gift of other people; appointments to these positions are only known from casual references and not from any regular record of them. But since offices not in the King's gift were quite often sold, reversions to them were probably obtainable. Private reversionary agreements would only have been legally binding if embodied in legal documents, such as indentures; some may have had penal bonds attached to them, putting a financial sanction on the fulfilment of the contract.

Exactly as with direct appointments which did not follow from reversions, influence of some sort was essential. Again this was normally obtained by close family ties, by patronage, or by money, or by some combination of these; again merit, ability, and special qualifications might sometimes obtain their reward, but seldom if ever could they do so alone and unaided.

Reversions, and the Crown's attitude to them, affected existing office-holders as well as aspirants to office. In 1615 King James had approved a memorandum condemning the excessive number of reversions to Keeperships and other posts in the royal parks and forests because it became difficult to reward the King's servants adequately if too many of these places were tied up for too far ahead.[1] It may seem strange that the same principle was not felt to apply with equal force in the central courts and departments, but these Keeperships were largely used as extra endowments for men who already had some position at court or in the administration, or who had already been serving the King in some other capacity.

---

[1] Hist. MSS. Comm. *Buccleugh* (*Montague*), I, 170.

There is no sign that fewer reversions were being granted at the end of James's reign than during its middle years. But they were not always easy to obtain. In 1621 Bishop Williams, then Lord Keeper of the Great Seal and thus, one would have supposed, ideally placed in such matters, lamented the King's refusal to let him issue a reversion to a friend; he gave three instances of men who had obtained two each. This was in a letter to Buckingham's personal secretary, through whose capable and no doubt well-greased hands the applications for these other grants had most probably passed, so it was more than a broad hint.[1] From about 1619 to 1628 reversions, like the rest of royal patronage, were largely funnelled through Buckingham and his entourage, but there is no clear evidence that his death had any immediate effect on their frequency one way or the other. Several years later, in March 1637, not long after the Crown's resumption of patronage in Chancery and Common Pleas, the Admiralty commissioners expressed their opposition to any further reversions for naval posts of all ranks, ashore and afloat.[2] This should be related to the various attempts which were made in the 1630's to recover or extend the Crown's rights of appointment, and to alter the tenure by which offices were held. Entry to office by way of reversion was closely bound up with the form of tenure enjoyed after entry had been secured.

iii TENURE

Although offices under the Crown were often treated like pieces of private property, and were sometimes even described as 'freeholds', they were not all held on the same tenure. Most offices of the middle rank in the central courts and departments and in the regional councils were held for life, but a few of these, together with most of the great offices of state and the judgeships of King's Bench and Common Pleas, were held during the King's pleasure, while the baronies of the Exchequer, the Crown law offices, and a few lesser posts were held during the good behaviour of the holders (*quam diu se bene gesserint*). A few major offices were held on life tenure: the Mastership of the Horse, the Treasurership and the Comptrollership of the Household, the Chancellorship of the Exchequer, the Master-

---

[1] *Fortescue Papers* ed. S. R. Gardiner (Camden Soc., 1871), pp. 166-7, 169.

[2] *Cal. S.P. Dom., 1636-7*, pp. 462-3.

ship of the Rolls, and the Mastership of the Ordnance. To explain exactly why these great offices were so held, or why the Barons of the Exchequer had a different tenure from the Justices of Common Pleas, would involve a detailed study of medieval government; no systematic survey is available of tenure in the Middle Ages. It is clear that all three basic forms of tenure were prevalent from the thirteenth to fifteenth centuries; there is also evidence of changes from one tenure to another at different dates.[1] Sometimes the tenure of an office in the seventeenth century can best be understood by looking back to its earlier history. For example, the Chancellor of the Exchequer held for life possibly because he was the descendant of a much humbler official, the Lord Chancellor's clerk; but this type of explanation would not fit the Master of the Horse.

Lengthy research into the history of earlier centuries would likewise be needed to explain why certain posts were heritable. Such, in the lower ranks, were those of the Usher of the Exchequer and the Marshal of Common Pleas (both held in the 1630's by Clement Walker, future Civil War pamphleteer). Near the top of the hierarchy, the Lord Great Chamberlaincy was secured by Lord Willoughby of Eresby, later the Earl of Lindsey, in 1626 after a dispute with the Veres, Earls of Oxford; the office of Earl Marshal was in practice, though not until 1672 statutorily, hereditary in the Howard family, whose head was at this time Earl of Arundel and Surrey. The medieval history of some of the greater heritable offices can be traced in J. H. Round's *The King's Sergeants* and in the Appendices to the latest edition of 'G. E. C.'s' *Complete Peerage*. The details are of little concern here since heritable offices were a rarity in the seventeenth century. More interesting is the way in which reversions were secured by successive holders of the same offices, and used to make some offices *in practice* hereditary in certain families.

Security of tenure was at its greatest in heritable offices, though it could not survive an attainder, as witness the restoration of Thomas Howard as Earl Marshal in 1621. Next in security came those held

---

[1] T. Madox, *The History and Antiquities of the Exchequer* (1769 edn.), I, 63 *et. seq.*, II, 33, 52, 56-7, 267, 270, 275, 281; *Calendar of Patent Rolls, 1436-41*, pp. 90-197 (I am grateful to Dr. G. L. Harriss for giving me these references); see also J. Fortescue, *The Governance of England*, ed. C. Plummer (Oxford, 1885), note to ch. XVII, pp. 326-37: Tout, *Chapters*, I, 185 and n.

for a life or for lives; on this scale tenure during good behaviour would rank above tenure during pleasure, since in the former case the officer had to be shown to have misconducted himself in his office before he could be turned out, but in the latter he had only to displease the King. Even the strongest King could more easily withdraw his own pleasure than he could prove misbehaviour in someone else.

A straightforward reversion to the holder's son was not the only way in which tenure could be made heritable. An office could be granted for the lives of A, B, and C, and then, when A died, for the lives of B, C, and D, etc.; alternatively, the holder might wait until A and B were both dead, and then obtain a new grant for the lives of C, D, and E. This kind of grant was not much favoured by the Crown except where some or all of the 'lives' were avowedly those of trustees for widows or minors, as with the Secretaryship of the Council in the North already mentioned. In 1640 the Surveyor-Generalship of the Customs in the Outports was granted to three members of the Dawes family on the surrender of an earlier grant to two of them; here C was simply added to A and B, near the end of A's life. In another case the Keeper of a royal park (an office of somewhat greater standing then than now), who was holding it for the term of someone else's life, asked leave to change it to his own life on this other person's death; he seems to have succeeded in doing so.[1]

The Crown law officers who themselves only held during good behaviour, the Lord Keeper who probably held during pleasure, and the Judges who certainly did so, may sometimes have tried to check these multiple grants, which the King's generosity was liable to lead him into making, and which might tie the royal hands for decades to come. The Lord Chancellor, or Lord Keeper, could delay, and sometimes in practice 'veto' a grant when it came to pass the great seal; the Attorney- or the Solicitor-General, or both, usually had an opportunity to report unfavourably on a proposed grant at an earlier stage; the Judges were not normally involved, unless some legal point was at issue which had led or might lead to a court action, although occasionally one of the Chief Justices was consulted about a proposed grant at the same time as one of the Crown law officers.

Probably the most important and certainly the most interesting questions about tenure relate to how often men were deprived of

[1] P.R.O., Treasury books misc., T 56/5 p. 59; *Cal. S.P. Dom.*, *1628-9*, pp. 272, 344.

their offices, and why. But we shall be better able to deal with security of tenure if we first consider a slightly different question, to which we shall have to return: the attitudes of the Crown and of contemporaries to the different types of tenure.

Various doubts and disputes, which arose in connexion with a particular office, namely the Secretaryship of the Council in the North, caused attempts to be made to formulate some general definitions. In the early 1620's, two distinguished lawyers, when asked for an opinion, affirmed that, although ordinary members of the Council in the North held during pleasure like other Judges, the Secretaryship, which was combined with the Keepership of the Council's seal, might be granted for life, as it had been in the case of the then holder, Sir Arthur Ingram senior. These two lawyers, plus two others of equal distinction, subsequently ruled that the existing life grant to Ingram was good at law; but as far as can be seen from Ingram's papers these were merely the opinions of counsel whom he had consulted. In January 1634, about ten months after the appointment of a new Secretary, Ingram having then become an ordinary Councillor, the King told the Vice-President of the Council that the new Secretary should have a vote like any other councillor, but that he should be guaranteed against any possible future charge or accusation that as a 'ministerial' officer he was involving himself in 'judicial' acts. There seems to be an implication here that judges or judicial officers were different from administrative officers (which is more or less what 'ministerial' appears to mean here, though it could also mean subordinate). This distinction between different kinds of responsibility may have been thought of in connexion with tenure. The ordinary Councillors at York could be got rid of much more easily than the Secretary; the King could issue a new commission at any time, and simply leave out the names of those who were not wanted.[1] It seems to have been tacitly assumed that 'judicial' officers were answerable in a special way for what they did and so should be the more easily removable, while 'ministerial' officers, being the Crown's executive agents, were less responsible for what they did, and so might properly hold for life: in part at least the reverse of modern ideas. A similar distinction between the

[1] Leeds P.L., Temple Newsam MSS., Council in the North, 108; Sheffield Central Library, Wentworth Woodhouse MSS., Strafford Papers 13c/157 (I am grateful to the Trustees of the Fitzwilliam Settled Estates for permission to use this collection); *Foedera*, XIX, 410-29.

two types of office was drawn by the judges of King's Bench in 1639, and was still current in the early eighteenth century.[1]

Occasionally an office was granted temporarily, pending a more formal grant for life or lives. Wentworth offered to grant the Clerkship of the Market in Ireland to an English courtier during pleasure; it was only in his power, he explained, to make a grant for a single life; the grant for two lives, which the applicant wanted and to which the Lord Deputy professed himself perfectly agreeable, must be obtained direct from the King.[2] But by and large under Charles I the tendency was the other way, towards briefer and less secure tenure.

Some offices which had only been granted during pleasure by Queen Elizabeth may have been granted for life by James I. If so, this may have been due to the generosity of the King, the carelessness of his advisers, or both these factors. John Coke, the future Secretary of State, implied that this had been happening when in 1618 he recommended to Buckingham, who was then about to become Lord Admiral, that all the under-officers of the Navy who had procured life grants should be reduced again to holding during pleasure.[3] For some years nothing came of this proposal.

It is difficult to generalize about security of tenure. Like the Chancellorship of the Exchequer, the Secretaryship of State (normally shared between two holders) had also only recently emerged as a major office of state:[4] unlike the Chancellor, the Secretaries held during pleasure.[5] A precarious pleasure it could be. In 1619 Lake was disgraced and stripped of his offices; in 1623 Naunton was forced to resign, even if with an immediate pension of £1,000 p.a. and the Mastership of the Wards soon to follow; in 1624-5 Calvert resigned on declaring himself to be a Catholic, although he was said to have been allowed to sell the office, and to have got £6,000 for it; in 1628 Conway was unceremoniously 'kicked upstairs' into the Lord Presidency of the Council; early in 1640 Sir John Coke was virtually dismissed, politer attempts to make him resign because of age and

[1] G. Croke, *Reports of Cases* (ed. H. Grimston, 1683), III, 555-7; G. Jacob, *A New Law Dictionary* (1729), 'Office'.

[2] Sheffield C.L., Strafford 8/49-50.

[3] Hist. MSS. Comm. *Cowper*, I, 99.

[4] See Elton, *Revolution in Government*, pp. 31-2, 56-9, 298-315, and Higham, *Secretary of State*, pp. 27, 30-1.

[5] On appointment Sir Albertus Moreton was granted £700 p.a. during pleasure for Intelligence and other expenses as Secretary, but a £500 p.a. pension for life (*Foedera*, 9 April 1625; E 403/2563, p. 1).

infirmity having failed; late in 1640 Windebank was forced to flee the country, and in 1641 Edward Nicholas was appointed in his place; at the end of 1641 the elder Vane was dismissed. Only Moreton (1625) and Dudley Carleton, Viscount Dorchester (1628-32), died in office. Taking the whole span from 1603 to 1642, five Secretaries died and seven were sacked or forced to resign.[1]

Among the other great offices, those of the Lord Treasurer, Lord Keeper, Lord Deputy, and Lord Chamberlain would seem in practice to have been appreciably less secure than those of the Lord President, Lord Privy Seal, Lord Steward, and Groom of the Stole. The insecurity of the first three arose directly, as with the Secretaryships, from their political importance.

Some offices changed hands more frequently than others because, apart from their tenure being more or less secure, they often acted as stepping-stones, or rungs on the ladder. There were certain 'natural', that is generally recognized and frequently followed, ladders of promotion. The Crown law officers and the Chief Justice of Common Pleas between them had a very good chance of filling the posts of Lord Chancellor or Lord Keeper, and Lord Chief Justice, though the Attorney- and Solicitor-Generals often rose to those heights via the Chief Justiceship. The Chancellor of the Exchequer was sometimes thought of as the heir apparent to the Lord Treasurership, but this particular promotion only took place once between 1603 and 1642, in which time seven Lord Treasurers were appointed. Only in the Household was there a regular and officially recognized ladder of promotion, through the ranks of Master, Cofferer, Comptroller, and Treasurer, though even this pattern was broken three times (in 1627, '39, and '41) with the Comptrollership, and once (in 1641) with the Treasurership.

A few cases of deprivation are worth examining more closely. In October 1629, after Chief Baron Walter, together with the two Chief Justices, had been called upon to validate the Crown's action against the leaders of the opposition in the recent parliament, he fell into such disfavour that his removal was attempted. According to Bulstrode Whitelocke, the memorialist, Walter was suspended in October 1628, when the judges and barons had been consulted about the refusal of Mr. Rolle, M.P., and others to pay customs duties not granted by parliament; but on this occasion he seems in fact to have supported the King. In 1629, if Whitelocke's account is

[1] Higham, *Secretary of State, passim*, esp. chs. IV, V.

correct, Walter did indeed give an evasive answer in the case of Eliot and the other M.P.s whom the King wished to bring to trial, namely 'That a Parliament-man for misdemeanour in the House, criminally, out of his office and duty, might be only imprisoned, and not further proceeded against. . . .' The King, says Whitelocke, charged the Chief Baron with 'dealing cautelously, and not plainly with him. . . .' Walter was formally charged with laxity in enforcing militia musters when he had been on circuit for the assizes, but Gardiner shows convincingly that this was only a subterfuge. Fighting back, Walter asserted in reply that it was up to the Crown to prove that he had misbehaved himself, and that a writ of *Scire Facias* had to be brought before he could be deprived. James Whitelocke, Bulstrode's father, was offered the Chief Barony but declined it; and, although Walter did not again sit as a judge in the Exchequer or go on circuit, no successor was appointed until his death in 1631.[1] So in this case 'during good behaviour' did prove to give some protection and not to be a mere form of words.

A few years later the distinction between this, and during pleasure appears in a rather different light. The dismissal of Chief Justice Heath in September 1634 was almost certainly connected with the issue of the first 'Ship Money' writs five weeks later; Gardiner was probably correct in adding that 'some thought his ecclesiastical tendencies were obnoxious to the Archbishop' (i.e. Laud), although he had no doubt that the Ship Money question was decisive. Charles I had adequate political and religious reasons for wanting to get rid of Heath, who in other minor respects had already shown himself to be a man of conservative views. He had defended the orthodox and old-fashioned procedure in the Exchequer, and also opposed the introduction of an inquisitorial new oath to be taken by witnesses before the commissioners on officers' fees.[2] It is clear that Heath's post was then in the broad sense a 'political' one. No attempt was made to impugn his professional competence as had been done with Walter; indeed he was made a King's Sergeant-at-Law in 1636 and a Judge of King's Bench in 1641. Three weeks after Heath's dismissal Richard Sheldon, or Shilton, the Solicitor-General, was sacked, or

---

[1] B. Whitelocke, *Memorials of the English Affairs* (1682), pp. 11, 16; Gardiner, *History*, VII, 88, 110-15. The *Liber Famelicus of James Whitelocke* (Camden Soc., 1858) does not mention this episode.

[2] Gardiner, *History*, VII, 361; *D.N.B.*, IX, 346-9; T 56/16, 10 February 1630; Exchequer, King's Remembrancer's misc., E 165/46 p. 58.

forced to resign. Gardiner says he was inefficient, but his having been a lame-duck in the parliament of 1628-9 is no proof that he was in other respects a bad legal adviser or a poor pleader, nor does it seem a good reason for getting rid of him over five years later, when no fresh parliament was contemplated. There seems to be no record of any ostensible grounds for his dismissal; a political motive, for example, that he may have been unsound on the legality of levying Ship Money in peacetime, seems the best guess. Sheldon had at one time been a client of Buckingham, but then in the 1620's this was almost a pre-condition of entry into royal service; otherwise his political affiliations are obscure. That he held during good behaviour and Heath during pleasure made little practical difference in this case.[1]

Other such dismissals and resignations concerned personalities more than political issues. Mention has already been made of the ministerial reshuffles in 1628 and 1629. Within three months of the appointment of Edward Barret, Lord Newburgh as Chancellor of the Exchequer, his own chief, Lord Treasurer Weston, was planning his removal. The difficulty of finding him another office as compensation has already been explained, but apparently there was a further obstacle. It was said that Newburgh had already sold the reversion to his office to Christopher Villiers, Earl of Anglesey, Buckingham's younger brother, for an annuity of £1,200 from land, and that, as he would have to restore this on giving up the Chancellorship, he would require a double compensation. He was next reported as having turned down an offer of the reversion to the Mastership of the Rolls with a grant of £600 p.a. until he succeeded to it. Three other transfers or promotions and one compulsory retirement were necessary before the Chancellorship of the Duchy became vacant, when Sir Humphrey May was persuaded to become Vice-Chamberlain of the household, with a reversion to the Rolls (ironically May died only a year later, whereas Newburgh outlived the then Master of the Rolls by eight years). Newburgh was then persuaded to accept the Duchy. It probably still ranked above the Exchequer in formal precedence, and may have been worth about the same to its holder; it undoubtedly involved less work. Life tenure of the Exchequer had certainly proved its value here.[2]

[1] D.N.B., XVIII, 43-4; Gardiner, *History*, VI, 240, 243, 268; VII, 44, 366·
[2] *The Court and Times of Charles I* (ed. T. Birch, 1848), I, 452; Hist. MSS. Comm. *Buccleugh*, III, 329-30; G.E.C., I, 431; D.N.B., XIII, 140-1.

A complicated case in 1635 involved several important men, and may have had political repercussions later. William Cecil, second Earl of Salisbury, was only twenty-one when his father died in 1612; he had already been married for four years, to a daughter of the Earl of Suffolk, a leader of the Howard faction in King James's government, in which Suffolk was to be the principal figure from 1614 to 1618. Robert Cecil had hoped that the match would heal the feud between the two families which had been proceeding intermittently since the 1560's. It does not seem to have done so. The second Earl of Salisbury did not impress contemporaries as a particularly pleasant young man, nor, any more than his uncle the first, and his cousin the second Earl of Exeter, did he have the ability of his father or grandfather. Clarendon describes him as both stupid and nasty, but the foremost of royalist historians is not at his most impartial in dealing with parliamentarian peers; it is not otherwise clear why Salisbury has been so severely judged by historians. It was a difficult if not uncommon situation: the failure of transcendent abilities in the third generation. Nor had Robert Cecil secured his son any major office or any firm reversion. Perhaps partly due to his father-in-law's increased influence, for Suffolk was not one to scruple at nepotism, but mainly to honour the King's obligations to help him meet his father's debts, Salisbury was granted a pension of £3,000 p.a. for twenty years from Christmas 1615, assigned on the duties on velvets, silks, and other rare imported fabrics. He soon reassigned £2,000 p.a. of this, probably to his father's creditors or to trustees for their use; in June 1625 the remaining £1,000 p.a. was three years in arrears; it was then taken off the Customs and reassigned to him on the Court of Wards. Meanwhile, also while his father-in-law was Lord Treasurer (1614-18) he had been promised the succession to the Mastership of the Court of Wards, an office which his grandfather and father between them had held for fifty years. New Masters of the Wards succeeded in 1619 and 1623, on the former occasion almost immediately after Lord Treasurer Suffolk's own downfall. After the appointment of ex-Secretary Naunton to the Mastership in 1623 there seems to have been a definite understanding that Salisbury was next in succession.

From 1631 on, Naunton's retirement—or even his death—was being talked of as imminent. Rumour also had it that the chronic and increasing ill-health of Salisbury's brother-in-law, the second Earl of Suffolk, would soon mean another vacancy in the Captaincy of the Band of Gentlemen Pensioners. But Suffolk, then the second senior member of the great office-holding Howard dynasty, had no intention of retiring. In December 1633 he was called on to surrender his office on the grounds that he was too lame to command the Pensioners effectively; in January 1634 he was reported to be taking this very badly; by various procrastinations and quite possibly with the help of his cousin the Earl Marshal, he was still in office at the beginning of 1635. In retrospect it is easy to see when the mistake had been made. In 1628, Suffolk had been given something for nothing when he was made Lord Warden of the Cinque Ports; then would have been the time to move him from the Captaincy. He was also sole, or co-Lord Lieutenant of about six counties, Vice-Admiral of four, Keeper of Greenwich Park, a Privy Councillor, and a Knight of the Garter. But the really urgent need to free the Captaincy for his brother-in-law, Salisbury only arose in 1633 or 1634. In January 1634 Cottington, the Chancellor of the Exchequer, was said to be advising Suffolk to surrender it with a good grace *as if* he held it during pleasure, even though his tenure was in fact for life. Suffolk, who was still under fifty, may genuinely have hoped to recover sufficiently to carry on; furthermore, Cottington was an interested party. He wanted to by-pass Salisbury and to succeed the ageing and incompetent Naunton as Master of the Wards; if Naunton's death or compelled retirement was to clear the way for Cottington, Salisbury would have to be compensated for the loss of his reversion. The Captaincy was the obvious answer. Cottington would seem to have inherited something of his master Weston's deviousness; the whole plan was reminiscent of the reshuffle in 1629 which had brought Cottington to the Exchequer. Whether or not Suffolk was intelligent enough to detect Cottington's motives, there is no doubt of his reluctance to take the proffered advice.

When it became clear that sooner or later he would have to quit the Captaincy, Suffolk placed his hopes on a reversion to the Chancellorship of the Duchy. Since the then Chancellor was to outlive him by four years, he lost nothing material by not getting this; as far as can be seen, his only compensation was the Governorship of Berwick and a personal assurance from the King that he could remain Lord Warden of the Cinque Ports undisturbed for the rest of his life. By contrast, Naunton was probably more concerned to ensure that, if he retired, his existing pension of £1,000 p.a. would be regularly and punctually paid. Also the Wards being far more valuable than the Captaincy, he stood to lose more in money, Suffolk more in prestige.

Naunton, too, did not resign without a struggle. By February 1635 the pressure on him was heavy, and it was an open secret that he was to be succeeded by Cottington and not by Salisbury. On 5 March he protested to the King that he was not so ill as people said; he begged for a term to be set for his recovery, after which he would retire if he was not better; he preferred this to the idea of being investigated by a royal commission, with which he was now threatened, for unlike Suffolk's his office was held during pleasure and not for life. Within eight or nine days of writing this letter he had resigned, apparently as an alternative to outright dismissal, and he died only another two weeks after that. It may be significant that Cottington's appointment as Master of the Wards was going through in March 1635 during the last and fatal illness of Lord Treasurer Weston, by then Earl of Portland. Cottington, who hoped to succeed as Lord Treasurer but was to be disappointed in this mainly, it is believed, on account of Archbishop Laud's opposition, apparently two or three days after Portland's death became Master of the Wards. Had Laud, and the other councillors near the King who did not want him as Lord Treasurer, persuaded Charles that Cottington must get the Wards instead as immediate compensation? One letter writer asserted plausibly enough that the dying Lord Treasurer was interested in Naunton's resignation for quite a different reason: to secure the Wards for his own son and heir! For '. . . he would not have been so violent to throw out Sir Robert Naunton for my Lord Cottington, or any friend else, but for that son'. So only Portland's death may have saved Cottington from being very neatly hoist with his own petard.

In February 1635 Salisbury had at last obtained a promise of the Captaincy, although he had informally renounced his reversion to the Wards several months earlier. And from March until May 1635 he had to be content with this, for Suffolk eventually resigned about two months after Naunton. The Captaincy was an honourable post at Court, well placed for the getting and giving of favours, and by no means valueless; but the Wards was one of the three or four most valuable offices in the country, as well as offering more scope for political ambition. There were certainly other reasons why Salisbury opposed the King in 1640 and was a parliamentarian during the Civil Wars, and perhaps also why Suffolk and then his son were to say the least rather tepid supporters of royal policy. But, although this exchange of offices in 1635 may well have made for greater efficiency as well as serving Cottington's personal greed and ambition, it may not have been without influence on these later events.

Here too the difference in tenure seems to have played only a minor part. Considering their respective tenures, during pleasure and for life, Naunton was treated with much more forbearance and Suffolk more peremptorily than might have been expected. Perhaps it was a personal difference; Naunton was rather pathetic and so the King was reluctant to sack him, as he could well have done, while Suffolk, illness apart, was merely tiresome, and was therefore pushed as hard as his securer tenure permitted.[1]

It is time to leave the realms of high politics and return to administrators of the middle rank. Here the Crown found it strikingly difficult to get rid of officers who held on life tenure.

This can be well illustrated from the career of George Mynne, which epitomizes several aspects of English history during these years. Mynne was a cadet member of a Shropshire family whose main branches had settled in Hertfordshire and Surrey; the head of the family belonged at best to the 'lesser gentry', and in his earlier years George probably did not even rank socially as a gentleman; he had few if any advantages of connexion, inherited wealth, or formal education; he was probably first in trade as a woollen draper, and in 1614, perhaps through the patronage of his relative by marriage George Calvert, he entered royal service as Deputy Paymaster of the forces in Ireland. In February 1620 he bought the Clerkship of the Hanaper, or Hamper in Chancery, for £2,400; his purpose in this was evidently twofold, to rise in the social scale and to make a quick profit on the purchase by increasing the annual value of the post. In August he petitioned for leave to charge higher fees of all those who used the office, that is virtually everyone who had any business at the Great Seal, including numerous other

[1] For Salisbury see G.E.C., XI, 404-6; *D.N.B.*, III, 1312; L. Stone, 'The Electoral Influence of the Earl of Salisbury, 1614-1665', *Eng. Hist. Rev.* LXXI (1956), 384-400; Brunton and Pennington, *Members*, pp. 105-6; Clarendon, *Hist. Reb.*, II, 542-3; Hist. MSS. Comm. *Denbigh*, p. 8; *Cal. S.P. Dom., 1634-5*, pp. 529-30; E 403/2563 p. 53. For the others see *D.N.B.*, IV, 1218-21, X, 61-2, XIV, 126-9; Bell, *Court of Wards*, pp. 19, 136; Birch, *Court & Times*, II, 228-9; Knowler, I, 167, 175, 388-9, 427; *Cal. S.P. Dom., 1634-5*, pp. 562, 607-8.

officials as well as litigants and grantees. The matter was referred to Bacon, then Lord Chancellor, though the King recommended him to allow some reasonable increase in the fees which Mynne could take from suitors for patents; this fitted in very well with what we know to have been Bacon's own views on raising fees *pari passu* with the rise in costs and prices, so we may safely assume that James had already taken his Chancellor's advice, and that the recommendation was a mere formality.[1] But whether due to the Chancellor's dilatoriness or to opposition from elsewhere, nothing had been done by the time of Bacon's own fall eight months later. In June 1621 Mynne again petitioned the King; this time his case was referred to the four commissioners for the Great Seal, who in turn consulted the Attorney- and Solicitor-Generals. Then, 'for that their Lordships conceived [that] the subject is then most exacted on when fees are uncertain and at the discretion of the officer . . .', they recommended that all Mynne's fees should be fixed with various minor increases. Before this was finally authorized by a Chancery court order of February 1622 it had also been referred by the King to the new Lord Keeper, Bishop Williams, who suggested some small reductions in the fees payable by ecclesiastical bodies and individual churchmen. A final proviso was added, that the Clerk of the Hanaper should not in any circumstances increase any fees which had been, or might be, fixed by parliament. This took account of the special interest which the 1621 House of Commons had shown in fees and other questions of administrative reform; it may also have been a small manifestation of that general attempt to conciliate parliamentary opinion which Williams was then urging on his patron, Buckingham.

Mynne had got part of what he wanted, but not enough to satisfy him. Some of his fees were raised; others remained as they had been fixed after the last major investigation of Chancery, in 1597-8, though no one really knew what some of them had been then. Not content with this, Mynne soon began to take larger fees than could be justified either by precedent or by the ruling of 1622. For several years all went well with him. Then in February 1630 King Charles I's commission to inquire into exacted fees, which had been appointed in 1627, got on to his trail. In April Sir John Finch, the future Chief Justice and Lord Keeper, and Wentworth's friend George Radcliffe, then Attorney to the Council in the North, were put in special charge of the case, but in June Mynne was discharged

[1] For Bacon's views on fees see Chapter 4, s. ii.

after being warned and probably censured by the commissioners. Nothing daunted, he was soon once more taking the larger and strictly illicit fees. Investigation of his case was resumed in 1634; this time the evidence of his exactions was unmistakable, and beyond hope of concealment or excuse. Thanks to his very considerable wealth—he was an iron-master and a land speculator as well as a draper and an official—Mynne was able to hire the best lawyers in London. To no avail. After three days' trial in Star Chamber he was found guilty of exaction and extortion of excessive fees and innovation of new ones. His judges were only divided on how severely to punish him. Most of the councillors and the other members of the Court favoured a fine of £3,000 and suspension from his office. Chief Justice Heath, the Earl of Manchester (who had been in turn Lord Chief Justice, Lord Treasurer, senior commissioner for the Great Seal, Lord President of the Council, and finally Lord Privy Seal), and Coventry the Lord Keeper (who like Heath had served as Solicitor- and then as Attorney-General) seem to have felt that this penalty was excessive; better than most of those present they knew the realities of being a legal officer in an inflationary age, knew perhaps its temptations too! Archbishop Laud by contrast felt that the sentence was not severe enough. As a compromise the court agreed on the punishment first suggested. The difference in attitude between the most eminent common lawyers present and the champion of 'Thorough' is probably no coincidence.

Among the records of this case are some interesting remarks made either by one of Mynne's judges or by prosecuting counsel:

> The person of Mr. Mynne: a gent; no disparagement nor stain to him to have been a woollen draper as long as he carries himself honestly and with integrity: if otherwise, a great many younger brothers descended of ancient gentry in ill condition. The stain of gentry is to commit base actions: and this it seems he did after he had the place that would otherwise have made him a gentleman.

The size of Mynne's fine may have borne some relation to his well-known wealth as well as to the enormity of his offence; it can also be argued that the fines imposed on delinquent officers were intended in some rather obscure way to be related to the value of their offices.[1] But it was a good deal smaller than the fine which Mynne had to pay for the wrongful felling of timber in the Forest of Dean,

[1] For the significance of these fines and compositions see Chapter 4, ss. ii-iii.

for use in his ironworks there. He and his partner Sir Basil Brooke were fined £12,000; this was later reduced, but even so Mynne paid £7,000, in return receiving a solemn pardon under the Great Seal for all offences committed by him and on his behalf in the Forest. He also shared with Brooke a later fine of £1,332 for misuse of timber in Pembrokeshire, also for an ironworks.

In spite of all this, on the eve of the Civil War his landed income was at least £982 p.a., a remarkable achievement for a man of his social rank and an amount which many of the 'greater gentry' probably could not exceed. As late as 1647, after many vicissitudes during the wars, the loans which he had made were estimated at over £22,000 net, and his gross income (without the Hanaper) at £2,468 p.a.

So much for the man and his story. What was involved in his suspension from office? Exactly who administered the Hanaper from June 1634 to December 1635, and on what tenure, is a minor mystery. In August 1634 Mynne's suspension was formally repeated, and Sir Richard Younge, bart., a Gentleman of the King's Privy Chamber, was granted the right to execute the office for the term of the suspension. In December, presumably both to protect the users of Chancery and to prevent Younge in turn from going wrong, the King appointed a small committee of senior Privy Councillors to fix the fees at the Hanaper; this would seem to imply that the scale of 1622 was again in the melting-pot. Perhaps because of the very seniority of these Councillors and hence their pre-occupation with greater questions, the new schedule of fees was only ready the following September, nine months later; it was embodied in a formal treaty, which also dealt with the tenure of the post, in December 1635. Meanwhile, for reasons which are unknown but do not affect the story, Mynne's existing reversioner was allowed to surrender his grant and have it transferred to one Robert Parkhurst, son of the Lord Mayor of London, a neighbour of Mynne in Surrey and a partner in some of his land transactions. From May to October 1636 an uneasy situation prevailed with Younge trying to obtain unqualified assurances that Mynne would not be allowed to resign in favour of Parkhurst. Finally it was agreed that Younge's tenure was to be for the term of Mynne's suspension, or for Mynne's life; in the event of Younge dying first, the Crown would have been free to appoint someone else on the same tenure. On Mynne's death Parkhurst was to succeed, but he was only to do so before that if the suspension was lifted. In 1636 Mynne was spoken of as being 'sequestered' from the Hanaper, and not just suspended, but the substantive difference is not clear; in June of that year he was confirmed in all his privileges and legal immunities as an officer of Chancery, which probably included special safeguards against being sued for debt; he was even given the right to inspect the Hanaper accounts, to make sure that the correct amounts were being paid in at the lower Exchequer. This curious state of half-deprivation seems to have persisted up to the Civil War, when Younge, as a royalist, lost control of the office. Mynne himself was a rather more equivocal supporter of the King, apparently being ready to do business with either side. But, so far from regaining control of the Hanaper, he was fined for his royalism all the more heavily in his capacity as an office-holder than he would have been otherwise, although he had not executed his office for about eight years before the war began! His shadow tenure of 1634-42 indeed reaped an ill reward.

Fined by the royal government in the 1630's for extorting fees and for felling timber in order to increase his output of iron, fined by the Long Parliament in the 1640's for supplying cannon and other iron materials to the King's armies and for holding an office which he had in fact long ceased to occupy, Mynne might seem to have had the worst of both worlds. Yet he was still a rich man when he died in 1651. A successful capitalist if anyone of his time was, his career fits ill with some conventional interpretations of the English Civil War, but it illustrates why and how men holding office on life tenure might be deprived of it, and what this 'loss' of office might amount to in practice.[1]

Other forms of tenure besides the three main types were rarities.

[1] P.R.O., Index of appointments, E 407/174; E 165/46 p. 59a; SP 16/269/66, 270/39-41, 375/32; PC 2/48 p. 628; Papers of the committee for the advancement of money, SP 19/90/45, 51-65, 69, 85-93; Bodl. Bankes MSS., 15/1, 16/30, 41/28, 55/4; Birmingham R.L., MS. 604085/95; Hertfordshire R.O., Cowper (Panshangar) MSS., C. 248, 252-9; B.M. Harleian MS. 4022, pp. 32-61; J. Rushworth, *Historical Collections* (1721 edn.), II, 267; *Foedera*, XIX, 710-16; Knowler, I, 266; Sanders, *Orders in Chancery*, I, 135-40, 196-7; Gardiner, *History*, VII, 364; Maxwell-Lyte, *Great Seal*, pp. 285, 336; see below Chapter 5, s. iii. For the Parkhursts see A. B. Beaven, *Aldermen of the City of London* (1908-13), I, 49, 183, II, 57; Shaw, *Knights*, II, 203, 205, 228; *Foedera*, XX, 125-6; Foster, *Al. Ox.*, p. 1117; Keeler, *Long Parliament*, pp. 296-7; and for Younge G.E.C., *Btge.*, II, 36; *Foedera*, 25 August 1634.

Inheritance has already been mentioned; in the middle ranks Clement Walker's was almost the only case. His post as Chief Usher of the Exchequer involved another unusual type; in the 1620's one Walter Sankey held it by lease from him. Another odd case concerned the Keepership of a royal garden, a grant for lives being equated with one for a term of years, as was then common in ordinary land leases; in March 1639 this Keepership was granted to two men for sixty years 'if they live so long'.[1]

There was an ambiguity about some grants for lives. A grant to A and B could be for as long as both of them were alive, or for as long as one of them was alive; the same alternatives held good for a three-life grant to A, B, and C. In the latter case the practical difference between the two tenures was of course much greater. Normally the grant of an office was made specifically for the lives of both the grantees *and* for the life of the longer lived of them. Where this was not specified, the grants were only for the briefer, and much less secure tenure of the grantees' joint lifetime.

Grants of office for a stated term of years were most unusual. In 1638 the Earl of Northumberland was made Lord Admiral until the twenty-second birthday of James, Duke of York, in 1655, the equivalent of a grant for seventeen years.[2] It is not clear what would have happened (the Civil War apart) if James had died before he was twenty-two, but theoretically the office would again have been at the King's free disposal. In 1640 the judges ruled that a grant for a specific term of years (of the Marshalship of King's Bench) was invalid. 'This', they resolved, 'being an Office of great trust and attendance in court, might not be granted for years, for that it might fall to persons insufficient, (of) whom the Court could not conveniently admit.' A sensible dictum; but one hard to reconcile with their decision two years before that an office might come to an infant by inheritance, or by reversion (as had happened in the case then at issue with the Registrarship of the diocese of Rochester). An infant could hold a 'ministerial' office, provided he appointed an adequate deputy, but a grantee for a term of years apparently could not.[3] All the examples which can be found of grants for years

---

[1] Bodl. Tanner MS. 318, fol. 81; *Cal. S. P. Dom.*, *1638-9*, p. 556.

[2] *D.N.B.*, XV, 830-5; Knowler, II, 54, 67, 154; *Cal. S.P. Dom.*, *1637-8*, pp. 321, 351 (the grant to Northumberland was made technically during pleasure).

[3] G. Croke, *Reports of Cases* (1683), III, 555-7, 587.

or on lease are insignificant compared to those for life or lives in the middle and lower ranks of the government, and those for life, during good behaviour, and during pleasure in the upper ranks. In cases where under-officers, clerks, and informal deputies were the personal employees of an official and not the servants of the King, they held for the tenure of that officer, be it his life or otherwise; his successor was normally at liberty to keep them on and quite often this happened. This did not apply to those whose appointment was not in the King's gift but who were none the less royal officials; they held in their own right on the usual tenures.

There is little evidence of any systematic attempt in Charles I's reign to alter officers' tenure, but there are traces of such a policy. Sometimes it arose over individual cases. As we shall see, there was trouble at the Mint in the early 1630's, so it is not surprising to find that in 1633 the grant of a subordinate post there, the Chief Gravership, was delayed while its tenure was changed from life to during pleasure. In another case whole departments were affected. The Admiralty Commissioners having declared against reversions in March 1637, issued a sweeping order the next year, expressing the King's will that henceforth no grants of Governorships and Captaincies of Ports, Castles, Forts, and Garrisons, nor any other appointments in the Navy or the Ordnance, were to be made for life, but only during pleasure. The Signet Clerks were warned to take special note of this in drafting grants of such offices, and for a time at least this order seems to have been observed. In so far as the Commissioners' successor, Northumberland, the new Lord Admiral, was still interested in naval reform by 1638, he presumably welcomed the change; but the fact that his secretary (and possibly Northumberland himself) took gratuities from those they appointed to naval posts may have made him less enthusiastic about it. The change of tenure may well have made such positions less sought after; in a private letter the Lord Admiral's secretary referred reluctantly to a grant being made during pleasure 'as all patents must run hereafter'.[1]

These changes of tenure had their wider political implications. If the supporters of 'Thorough' had gained a clear ascendancy over all the other factions at Court and in the government, and if they had had twenty, perhaps even ten years in which to turn England into a

[1] *Cal. S.P. Dom., 1633-4.* p. 361 (for the troubles at the Mint see below, Chapter 6, s. vi); SP 16/353, fol. 89, 442/33, 445/81; *Cal. S.P. Dom., 1638-9,* p. 22.

well-ordered autocracy, the tenure of all offices in the other departments of state, and perhaps in the law courts too, might well have been changed to during pleasure. In turn the treatment of offices under the Crown as pieces of quasi-private property might have declined in the mid-seventeenth instead of at the turn of the eighteenth to nineteenth centuries. Moreover, offices which were held during pleasure could of course still be bought and sold, as witness the Secretaryships of State. Nor does the history of seventeenth- and eighteenth-century France suggest that autocracy and the treatment of offices as pieces of property were necessarily incompatible. However, the loss of secure tenure and of freedom of disposition by means of reversions would have made many medium-ranking and junior posts financially less attractive. By and large, reversions and life tenure stood or fell together, and saleability was closely related to them. Among the greater offices it is very rare to find a reversion where the tenure was not for life.

The papers of Sir John Bankes, Attorney-General 1634-41 and then Chief Justice of Common Pleas, include the case of Sir Thomas Fanshawe, the King's Remembrancer, who was said to have wrongly admitted his personal clerks and assistants to practise as attorneys on the legal side of the Exchequer. Specific objections were brought against his actions, followed by a set of hypothetical but exceedingly pointed questions, all of which from their wording appear to expect the answer Yes. They include:

(i) If a law or revenue office is granted by the King to an unqualified person, is the grant automatically void?

(ii) Is even life tenure of an office conditional on its proper execution, and can such an office be forfeit for certain offences?

(iii) If a present is given, or brokerage paid, for an office in the King's gift, is the grant automatically void?

(iv) Are reversions also forfeited, in the case of (ii), if the reversioners are in fact trustees for the holder and his family?[1]

The points raised in this document touch on many aspects of office-holding besides tenure, and their implications are far-reaching. If it can be assumed that they represent the views of the King and his immediate advisers, then clearly the vested interests of many officials were seriously threatened on the eve of the Civil War, and this

[1] Bodl. Bankes MS. 5/64, 'charge against Sir Thomas Fanshawe', query 28 March 1641 (the date and title are almost illegible).

without any formal change of tenure. Furthermore, these questions can be related to a decision of King's Bench in 1637. The Customs Searcher at Sandwich was adjudged to have forfeited his office by voluntary absence from it, by crass neglect of his duties, and by the fraudulent conversion to his own use of goods seized in the King's name.[1] Like Fanshawe's, this case had explosive implications. Evidence has already been advanced of royal encroachment in matters concerning appointment and reversion; and it will be shown that there is further evidence of such encroachment concerning both tenure and the financial side of office-holding. All goes to show the key position of tenure, both as it affected the officers themselves and as an aspect of the whole administrative system.

iv DEPUTIES; PLURALISM; SINECURES

Performance of official duties by deputy, tenure of more than one office by the same man, and the existence of posts of value which involved their holders in little or no work are features of the administrative system which it is scarcely possible to treat in isolation from each other. Yet, as we shall see, they were three different things.

Even more than with the various kinds of tenure, it is hard to see that any general principles determined whether or not a particular office could be executed by deputy. Once a man taking up a post had managed to get a clause inserted in his patent allowing him to perform by sufficient, that is suitable deputy or deputies, which he might have done very much for personal reasons, then those responsible for drafting future grants of the same office would tend to include this clause automatically. Such is the way of bureaucracy. Wide as the range of posts was which could or might be executed by deputy, there were some which definitely could not be: deputies could *not* act for the great officers of state, the Crown law officers, or the Judges. The Mastership of the Ordnance, performed by deputy from 1629 to 1633 or 1634, is an exception, but it was only on the borderline of being a great office. An elderly and infirm Master was

---

[1] Croke, *Reports* (1665), p. 844 (1683), III, 491-2, the King versus Rookes; see also *Foedera*, XIX, 345, 765, XX, 202; *Cal. S.P. Dom.*, *1636-7*, pp. 206-7, *1638-9*, p. 258, *1639* p. 44, *Adds. 1625-49*, p. 521; Hist. MSS. Comm. *Fourth Rept.*, app., I, 109.

followed by one who was a general on active service in the Netherlands; the former's bastard son acted as deputy to each in turn.[1]
Then there were several senior administrative posts, at the top of
the second rank, where it is often hard to distinguish between an
officially sanctioned formal deputy and a private secretary or clerk,
who might in practice do everything that a deputy could do, except
to appear and act for his master on formal state occasions, or if
advice was wanted on a matter of royal policy.

Starting at the top, the great aristocratic pluralists must clearly
have had deputies for their lesser offices; but only for their lesser
offices. Even Buckingham, when from 1624 to 1628 he was simultaneously Lord High Admiral, Master of the Horse, Lord Warden
of the Cinque Ports, Chief Justice in Eyre south of Trent, Gentleman
of the King's Bedchamber, and Chief Clerk of King's Bench, would
not have dared to execute a major central office by deputy. He only
acted by deputy as Justice in Eyre and as an officer of King's Bench;
and when he was accused in his impeachment (1626) of having
engrossed several great offices, he argued that none of them was
full-time and that he could quite well attend adequately to them all.
Likewise William Herbert, third Earl of Pembroke, held several
regional and local posts which he may well have executed by deputy,
for example the Lord Wardenship of the Stannaries, the High
Stewardship of the Duchy of Cornwall, and the Captaincy of
Portsmouth castle; but he would not have thought of trying to
execute his principal post, first as Lord Chamberlain (1615-26) and
then as Lord Steward (1626-30), except in person. The same would
have been true of his brother, the fourth earl, who was both Lord
Chamberlain and Lord Warden of the Stannaries in the 1630's.
The case of Henry Rich, Earl of Holland, brother of the Puritan
Earl of Warwick, is slightly different; from 1629 to 1632 he did
combine two major central offices as Captain of the King's Guard and
High Steward of the Queen's Revenues, and from 1636 to 1641 he
combined the latter post with the Groomship of the Stole; he was
also Constable of Windsor, Governor and Captain of Harwich, and
from 1631 Chief Justice in Eyre south of Trent, in which capacity he
performed through deputies *de jure*, as did the Earl of Arundel and
Surrey who was Chief Justice in Eyre north of Trent (1634-42) as

[1] *D.N.B.*, III, 960-2, XVIII, 869-70, XX, 235-9; C. R. Markham, *The
Fighting Veres* (1888), pp. 421-53; *Cal. S.P. Dom.*, *1628-9*, p. 507, *1634-5*,
p. 197.

well as being Earl Marshal and in 1640-1 also Lord Steward.[1] Another court favourite, George Lord Goring, later Earl of Norwich, combined the Lieutenantcy of the Band of Gentleman Pensioners (1614-42) with the successive posts of Queen's Vice-Chamberlain (1626-8), Master of the Queen's Horse (1628-39), and Vice-Chamberlain (1639-42). But only the last of these was an office of the first rank, and the Lieutenantcy probably involved virtually no administrative duties and only periodic ceremonial appearances.

Below the top level, how extensive were absenteeism and performance by deputy? Thanks to the investigations of the commissioners on fees, we know more about Chancery than about any other court or department; probably over half the officers there had formal deputies around 1630.[2] In the absence of equally firm evidence elsewhere we cannot assume either that Chancery was typical or that it was *the* hunting-ground of would-be absentees. But the very fact of the Commission on Fees having spent so much time dealing with it is suggestive; in this it was rivalled only by the court of Common Pleas, and even that institution had fewer posts to attract this kind of applicant. In the law courts it is particularly difficult to distinguish formal deputies from under-clerks who were often deputies in all but name; as against this, not all officers whose patents allowed it did appoint deputies. Many Captaincies of forts and castles, Keeperships of houses, gardens, parks, chases, walks, and game, Stewardships of honours, courts, and royal manors, Vice-Admiralties, Lord Lieutenantcies, and other regional and local offices were held by men who spent most of the year in London or wherever the royal court might be; there may well have been more absenteeism in these posts than in the central government. In the fifteenth century Sir John Fortescue had actually commended this particular type of pluralism and performance by deputy.[3]

There were few if any official deputies in the royal household. Most offices in the Chamber involved very light duties, and the holders of many had only to be present for half or a quarter of the year, so there was little need for deputies. In the Household below stairs,

---

[1] For Holland see *Cal. S.P. Dom., 1637-8*, pp. 484-5, *1638-9*, p. 41, *1639-40*, p. 560, *1640*, p. 451; for Arundel *D.N.B.*, X, 73-6.

[2] Wilson, Thesis, app. III; *Cal. S.P. Dom., 1625-6*, p. 210, *1628-9*, pp. 555, 572; E 165/47 pp. 52, 81, 139.

[3] e.g. the Governorship of Jersey (*Cal. S.P. Dom., Adds. 1625-49*, p. 425), and the Water Bailiffship of Dover (*ibid., 1627-8*, pp. 539, 559). Fortescue, *Governance*, ch. XVII, pp. 150-3.

where there was more clerical drudgery and even manual labour, the proliferation of servants' servants, that is of the private employees of royal officials, was a standing complaint. In December 1628 the Lord Steward and the Board of Greencloth ordered 'that every yeoman, groom, and page shall wait in their places in person in their several weeks or waitings, and not by their servants in any wise'. Two nearly identical sets of household ordinances, dating to *c.* 1629-1630, show that censuses were to be taken and enrolled quarterly of everyone at Court, in order to check infiltration by unauthorized private servants, as well as to exclude other undesirables. These ordinances allowed none of the lowest categories of royal servants to employ their own servants; this covered the Porters, Scourers, Turnbroths, and Children, who worked mainly in the kitchens. But some scarcely more exalted auxiliary officers, such as Artificers, Laundresses, Horsewalkers, and Victuallers, who were not themselves on the regular paid establishment, could have their own servants, who were to be of civil and orderly conversation 'so near as may be'. When a fresh inquiry into the Household was begun by a strong committee of the Privy Council in December 1637, one of the most difficult problems was reckoned to be the multiplication at Court of officers' and other courtiers' private servants. The rank of Yeoman still constituted the borderline category between those officers who could and could not have servants, or in practice unofficial deputies; in January 1638 all Yeomen were at first forbidden to have their own servants, but a week later the committee relented and ruled that certain Yeomen in the Household could have them, but not the other Yeomen nor any one below that rank. There, in theory, the matter rested.[1]

On state occasions and at lesser Court functions it was quite literally their physical presence which was required of the Chamber officers. Their appearance was required in part just to put on a brave show, but largely because of their social distinction, nearly all being drawn from the peerage and the greater gentry. The prestige of the monarchy demanded that they should attend in person: substitutes would not do.

In the defence departments absenteeism was clearly felt to be undesirable. Several minor reforms were put through by Laud and

---

[1] LS 13/169 p. 48; LS 13/30, ordinances 6, 9, 10; B.M. Adds. MS. 6418, ordinances 6, 9; SP 16/378/16, 37, 92, notes taken by Edward Nicholas, 9 and 16 January 1638; Knowler, II, 140-1.

the other councillors remaining in London when the King and many of his courtiers were away in the north during the spring of 1639. Among these was an order, following up those against reversions and life tenure, that all Captains of forts and castles must be resident unless they had special permission from the King. If this was obtained, they were responsible for seeing that properly qualified Lieutenants and junior officers were resident.[1]

The employment of under clerks and private servants rather than official deputies must have made it all the harder to bring home responsibility for mistakes and abuses in the royal service. For example, the Six Clerks of Chancery, most of whose work was of a wholly routine nature, did not have individual deputies but each of them employed between eight and ten writing-clerks, sometimes known as the Sixty Clerks, and there were others again below these. In 1630 there were reckoned in all to be about 100 under-clerks in the Six Clerks' office. It is not clear whether the bottom forty-odd were employed by the Six or by the 'Sixty'.[2]

In 1630, at a meeting attended by Wentworth, the commissioners on fees decided that officers *were* responsible for excessive fees taken by their subordinates. This apparently included under-clerks and private servants as well as formal deputies, nor was it to be limited to the cases where the officers themselves could be proved to have benefited from the extortions. Here, though it may not have had the force of law, was an answer to one of the questions which were to be asked apropos of Sir Thomas Fanshawe in 1641.[3]

A dispute in the later 1630's about the Postmaster Generalship led to the enunciation of another general principle about deputies. This concerned the tendency for subordinate officers to multiply ('Parkinson's Law') and the resulting tendency for the ultimate responsibility for an office to be too remote from its daily execution. Lord Stanhope's objections to the Post Office being transferred to the charge of the Secretaries of State were being supported by his deputy, who was none other than Endymion Porter; but needless to

[1] PC 2/50 pp. 257-9, 10 April 1639; see also Aylmer, 'Attempts at Administrative Reform, 1625-40', *Eng. Hist Rev.*, LXXII (1957), esp. pp. 232-3.

[2] *Cal. S.P. Dom., 1640*, p. 88 (ref. to a servant of an under-clerk of the Six Clerks). There were reckoned to be three grades of under clerks: 40 getting £100 p.a. each, 20 £50 each, and 40 £30 each (Wilson, Thesis, app. III).

[3] E 165/46 p. 97b; see this Chapter, s. iii.

say Porter had not himself been performing in person. The same Attorney-General in whose papers the rhetorical questions about Fanshawe's office are found now reported, 'The Lord Stanhope hath power by his patent to make a deputy, but I conceive that such deputy can not make deputies'. And only one case has been found of someone described officially as a deputy's deputy (to the Receiver-General of the Duchy of Lancaster.)[1] The real problem was much more the employment of private clerks and servants.

In the central executive an interesting distinction emerges. Council Clerks, especially the Clerks extraordinary, were often absent, sometimes on government business, but they did not have deputies; the French and Latin Secretaries might be absentees and the former was abroad for most of the later 1630's, but at most, as in this case, they had acting deputies and not official ones holding by patent; the important but informal personal assistants to the Secretaries of State had no deputies. Coming nearer to those engaged on the formal business of passing documents under the Seals, but still considering men who also handled important diplomatic correspondence, the Signet Clerks did not normally have deputies. It was established that they could do so in 1627 when Sir Humphrey May, the Chancellor of the Duchy, apparently also held a Signet Clerkship for a short time. But this was exceptional. May had been granted the reversion in 1611, and then passed over for a less senior reversioner in 1623 on the grounds that a great officer of state, as he by then was, should not be trying to pick up lesser posts in this way and that the King could legally refuse to let him act by deputy in a position 'demanding personal service'.[2] When Francis Windebank was senior Signet Clerk, he had several assistants; that, even with Laud's support he could step straight from this to a Secretaryship of State, suggests that he might have been important and senior enough to have a deputy as Signet Clerk, but he did not. At the next and more formal stage in the administrative process, the Privy Seal, deputies were usual; in the early 1630's two deputies were each acting for two of the four Clerks of the Privy Seal; later in that decade the

[1] SP 16/351/35, rept. to the Council, 29 March 1637; Lancashire R.O. Molyneux Papers, DDM 13/2. For 'Parkinson's Law' see *The Economist*, CLXXVII, 635-8 (19 November 1955). On the Post Office see also *Verney Papers. Notes of Proceedings in the Long Parliament . . . by Sir Ralph Verney* (ed. J. Bruce, Camd. Soc., 1845), pp. 24-7, 4 March 1640/1.

[2] *Cal. S.P. Dom., 1619-23*, p. 591, *Adds. 1625-49*, p. 268, extract from the Signet books, February 1628; *D.N.B.*, XIII, 140-1.

same Clerks can be found acting in person and by deputy often within the space of a single year. As has already been explained, the final and most formal stage in the administrative process, the non-legal side of Chancery, was prolific in deputies and absentees. Even George Mynne, the notorious Clerk of the Hanaper, had a deputy, though we may be sure that this was because he was so busy with his other projects and not because he was leading a life of leisured ease. On the administrative, as opposed to the legal side of government, the prevalence of deputies does seem to have varied according to how stereotyped and formal the work was in different offices.

Inside the Exchequer there is a similar distinction, but it cannot be so clearly drawn. The officers with formal deputies tended to be those whose duties were the more concerned with formalities, or at least those whose work was most nearly a matter of well-established routine; those who played a more active and individual part in the control and supervision of public finance were more likely to have informal deputies, in the shape of their senior under-clerks or chief personal assistants. The two Chamberlains are the best example of the first type, performing by official Deputy Chamberlains in the upper Exchequer and by 'Under-Chamberlains', sometimes also called deputies in the lower Exchequer. The Auditor of the Receipt, whose chief under-clerk sometimes acted for him, is the best example of the second type. But this contrast is a little misleading: the King's Remembrancer and one of the co-Clerks of the Pipe had formal deputies, but the Lord Treasurer's Remembrancer appears not to have done so, although their duties were all about equally stereotyped. And from 1629 to 1633 there was an official deputy to one if not both of the Auditors of the Prests, although theirs were among the newest and least hide-bound posts in the whole of the Exchequer. Within certain broad limits, both in the Exchequer and elsewhere, who an officer was perhaps mattered more than exactly what office he held in determining whether or not he had a deputy. Other things being equal, aristocrats and courtiers were the most likely to have them, self-made careerists the least likely; but there are plenty of exceptions, and many officials do not fit neatly into either of these categories.

If much administrative work, like copying, engrossing, enrolling, and sealing, was formal and even tedious, it none the less had to be done. Offices which could be performed by deputy were not the same as sinecures. For example, the Clerkship of the Council in the Marches of Wales was held by Fulke Greville, later Lord Brooke, from 1583 until he was murdered by his valet in 1628. Then for sixteen months it was held by the late Prince Henry's ex-tutor, now Treasurer of the revenues enjoyed by Charles I when he had been Prince. In 1630, after a lawsuit with the new Lord Brooke, Fulke's Puritan cousin, about conflicting reversionary claims, it passed to the ubiquitous Lord Goring, also a chronic absentee.[1] Yet there is no question of this having been a sinecure, nor indeed would the work which this post entailed have been exclusively of a formal routine nature. To a lesser extent the same would have been true of the co-Clerkship of the Council in the court of Star Chamber, which was shared in the early 1630's by two courtiers and a Privy Councillor's widow. By 1635 one deputy was apparently acting for them all; three years later one of the absentees was replaced as Clerk by the deputy (who was the Attorney-General's own clerk).[2]

There were probably not many sinecures in the strict sense. But a number of posts in Chancery and Common Pleas, and some in King's Bench and the Exchequer entailed work which was by no means onerous or exacting. Such offices tended towards sinecurism, like those in the Chamber which involved only light ceremonial duties. At a guess, there may well have been more in the eighteenth century, when most of these same offices were still in existence, although they had been increasingly replaced in the real work of government; this was especially true in the Exchequer, due to the rise of the Treasury as a separate department. The formal duties required in most of these obsolescent offices put a premium on one special skill. Already by the early seventeenth century the continued use of the older medieval styles of handwriting in the three common law courts and in Chancery meant that specially trained writing-clerks were needed as deputies or informal under-officers.

If absenteeism and performance by deputy were not the same as sinecurism, in turn pluralism was not necessarily identical with either. If we exclude a few royal favourites, like Buckingham, the Herberts, Holland, Goring, and Porter, and if we also exclude the duplication of central and local posts, there were not many pluralist office-holders. Edward Nicholas, the future Secretary of State, was a Clerk of the Council extraordinary 1626-35 and ordinary 1635-41;

[1] *D.N.B.*, VIII, 248-51, 602-5, 606-7, XIV, 364; Deputy Keeper of the Public Records, *43rd Report*, App. p. 133; Croke, *Reports* (1683), III, 197-8.

[2] P.R.O., Signet Letters, SO 1/3/207-8.

at the same time he was Secretary to the Lord Admiral and then to the Admiralty commissioners, 1625-38, and Secretary of the royal commission for the advancement of the fisheries, sometimes known as the Fishing Association, c. 1630-40. This was not what is usually meant by pluralism, but a practical duplication of posts for the mutual benefit of Nicholas and the Crown. Just as 'Parkinson's Law' signifies the tendency of all bureaucracy to proliferate, so its opposite is the accumulation of more and more posts in fewer and fewer hands; from its most advanced, pathological stage this tendency may be called 'Pooh Bah-ism'. One would hardly for instance say that the great Duke of Wellington was a pluralist because he held several cabinet portfolios at once for a short time in 1834, but he clearly had the makings of a Pooh Bah. On a much smaller scale this is the way to think of Nicholas, and also of Georg Rudolph Weckherlin, the German poet who worked in the English secretariat for nearly thirty years. About 1624 Weckherlin became personal assistant to one of the Secretaries of State; he also acted as Latin Secretary, but without, it seems, ever being formally appointed, even as deputy; from 1631 he was also the official German Language Interpreter, and from 1636 he acted in addition as informal deputy to the French Secretary. In practice he was principal assistant for foreign affairs first to Secretary Coke and then, in 1640-1, to Secretary Vane.[1]

Nicholas held another office which was simply a means of rewarding him for his services. His patent to engross the land leases of recusant Catholics was not a sinecure in the strictest sense, but it entailed no work for him beyond employing one or two reliable clerks. Much the same could be said of Thomas Meautys, another Council Clerk (1622-c. 42), who was also Writer of processes to the Great Seal from the court of Star Chamber, and of the elder Sir Henry Vane in his capacity as holder of the Subpoena office in Chancery. On the other hand the senior Council Clerk was also *ex officio* Muster Master-General of England and Wales; as such he was supposed to act as the central co-ordinator of the work done under the Lords and Deputy Lieutenants in the counties, in keeping track of all men who were, or could be, mustered for service in the militia; the Muster Masters of individual counties had to pay him a share

[1] *D.N.B.*, XX, 1039-40; L. W. Forster, *Georg Rudolph Weckherlin* (Basel, 1944); Berks R.O., Trumbull Papers, loose bundles (Weckherlin MSS.).

of the fees which they received from defaulters and those who had been excused attendance at musters. Meautys was unable to make good his claim to the whole of this, and had to share it with Edward Nicholas, the Clerk who did most work for the Council on the military side. The Muster Master-Generalship thus represented in part a sensible combination of duties, in part a supplementary income for the senior or the most favoured Council Clerk.[1]

Where it did not involve offices which were in the process of becoming sinecures, or men who were special Court favourites, pluralism often served some functional purpose. The holding of subsidiary posts by quite important officials, to supplement their incomes, may be thought of as being on the borderline between practical duplication and sinecurism.

Outside this category, there are a few more instances of one man holding two or more offices at once. A man named Alexander Stafford was at the same time Clerk of the Revels and Clerk Comptroller of the Tents, Hales, and Pavilions; but the Tents and the Revels were both sub-departments of the Chamber with related duties—both for instance being involved in outdoor dramatics. So this could be called functional duplication. However, an Alexander Stafford was also Deputy Chamberlain or Joiner of Tallies, in the upper Exchequer, and someone of the same name was Clerk Remembrancer in the Court of Wards; it might have been useful administratively to have some men serving in both the Exchequer and the Wards, but there was no special reason for this particular combination. It cannot actually be proved that the same man did not hold all four of these offices, although this is unlikely just because he was an obscure individual.[2] Of comparable cases, the Auditor of the Mint was also co-Auditor of the Recusant Revenues. Windebank's servant, Edward Norgate, who became a Signet Clerk in 1638, was also Tuner of the King's musical instruments (at £60 p.a.) and Windsor Herald (at £26, 13s. 4d. p.a., plus fees); he had previously combined the posts of Tuner, Illuminator of the King's letters and patents, Bluemantle Pursuivant, and Signet Clerk extraordinary. Much more

---

[1] *Cal. S.P. Dom.*, *1627-8*, p. 472, *1639*, p. 19, *Adds. 1625-49*, p. 261; *Foedera*, 27 August 1626, 29 March 1636.

[2] P.R.O. Exchequer, declared accounts, Revels and Tents, E 351/2805, 2945-57; SP 16/301/9, 488/103, 105; *Cal. S.P. Dom.*, *1629-31*, pp. 56, 430; *Foedera*, 26 January 1630. For such problems of identification see also below, Chapter 5, s. i.

remarkable, Robert Henley was both a Six Clerk and the principal co-Chief Clerk of King's Bench from 1629 to 1632. The Six Clerkships were highly prized and much sought after, and the Clerkship of King's Bench was probably the most valuable post in the entire administration below the top half-dozen or so great offices. It is not clear either how Henley came to hold these two *in commendam*, or why he parted with the Chancery post after about three years. He was in addition co-manager of the farm of the sixpenny writs in Chancery, and this too he probably gave up in 1632.[1] After his appointment as a Six Clerk in 1631, William Carne transferred his office as a Teller of the Exchequer to his brother Edward, but he may have occupied both these places for a few months.

In the 1630's two out of the four Masters of Requests were technically pluralists. Sir Thomas Aylesbury (whose daughter was to marry Edward Hyde), was also firstly the Surveyor of the Navy and then co-Master of the Mint. His colleague Sir Ralph Freeman was also at first an Auditor of the Prests and then Aylesbury's partner at the Mint. Their cases may indicate a tacit acknowledgment by the Crown that Masterships of Requests were neither very arduous nor very well rewarded. Their respective posts in the Navy and the Exchequer were perfectly *bona fide* and involved plenty of work, but Aylesbury employed a confidential 'man of business' who in practice acted much like a deputy, and Freeman had an official Deputy Auditor; by contrast the Mastership of the Mint was almost a sinecure after 1635, for as far as can be seen the department was then being run by the two co-Wardens.[2] To take one other man of comparable standing: Sir William Russell, the Treasurer of the Navy, was also a customs farmer and Collector of the duties on silks and other imported fabrics, but to describe him as a pluralist would be pedantic and would have been quite meaningless to contemporaries.

Thus unqualified pluralism, like sinecurism in the strict sense, was exceptional. But complete or partial absenteeism, and performance by deputy were well established features of the administrative

---

[1] See Chapter 4, s. iii; on Henley see also Chapter 5, s. iii.

[2] Craig, *The Mint*, sheds little light on the effective division of duties between the Wardens and the Masters 1635-42. My interpretation is based on P.R.O. declared accounts, Mint, and scattered items in S.P.Dom., and *not* on the departmental records of the Mint itself, used by Sir John Craig. For Sir Robert Harley, Master before Aylesbury and Freeman, see Chapter 6, s. vi.

system. There are some signs that excessive absenteeism was thought to be undesirable; in the household and the defence departments there were attempts to limit the employment of formal deputies and of private servants acting as deputies. There do not seem to have been any official pronouncements against pluralism as such, although the House of Commons included it among the charges brought against Buckingham in 1626. The King's more intelligent and less rapacious advisers might have been expected to see that the royal bounty ought to be distributed as widely and evenly as possible, that office, like money in Bacon's famous simile, should be spread thin. Here Wentworth, the great exponent of 'Thorough', hardly set a good example by remaining Lord President of the North when he became Lord Deputy of Ireland. Perhaps, like Bacon before him, he found it easier to inculcate the principles of good government in others than to practise them himself.

v NEW OFFICES

The ninety years or so from the middle of Edward IV's reign to the early years of Elizabeth I's had seen many changes in the institutions of English central government. Not only individual posts, but whole courts and departments, and whole categories of officials had come and gone, been established, merged, transformed, re-established, abolished, often with bewildering rapidity. There had been practically no such changes since the early 1560's, and after another two or three generations a widespread prejudice seems to have arisen against the creation of any new offices and against any tampering with the established institutions. It is easy to see how this suited the vested interests of existing officers, but harder to understand why the prejudice became so powerful that the Crown's initiative was cramped, or indeed why the Crown itself seems to have come to regard the creation of new posts as *ipso facto* undesirable. First it is worth stopping to consider what is meant in speaking of the 'Crown' as opposed to the 'King'. Presumably the whole policy-making part of the government is intended: the King together with his ministers and advisers. If so, of the individuals who comprised this corporate entity, only the King himself, a very small minority of the Privy Councillors, a handful of other courtiers, and perhaps a bishop or two did not themselves hold civil office. Indeed, in the absence of any clear dividing line between politicians and civil servants, the 'Crown' merges, or shades off into the 'King's servants'.

Opposition by the holders of existing posts to the creation of new ones arose from a cardinal feature of the old administrative system. The payment of officers in fees, gratuities, and perquisites, rather than in salaries, tended to mean that a new post led to loss of income for the other existing officers in the same court or department, or for those who had previously done the work which the new officer was to do. This counter-weight to the mere proliferation of the bureaucracy ceased to operate in the nineteenth century when virtually all officials were put on to fixed salaries from the Crown. In the seventeenth century, in so far as its interests are separable from those of the office-holders, the Crown was less likely to be against new posts than against the multiplication of subordinate deputies, under-clerks, and private servants within the existing institutional framework. 'Parkinson's Law' thus turns out to need differentiating, as between the creation of new offices and 'subinfeudation' underneath existing ones.

Up to a point the Crown's attitude may only have signified a conscious or unconscious turning away from the innovations of the earlier Tudors, and a corresponding preference for settled established ways. But it was also a capitulation to existing office-holders, who were against new posts, but wanted to be allowed to have deputies and servants in their present ones.

The royal commission appointed in 1627 to inquire into the taking of excessive fees by officers was also ordered to find out what new offices had been instituted improperly since 1568-9. So much was this at first thought of as part of its main purpose that it became known as 'the Commission on Exacted Fees and Innovated Offices'. And the oath for witnesses who were called before the commissioners included provision for this:

> You shall well and truely inquire . . . and give true information . . . what offices and places were usually held, kept, and executed in the 11th year . . . of the late Queen . . . or at any time since then . . . And what offices and places have been since then . . . invented, innovated, designed, and ordained, or erected by any Judge or other Chief Officers in the said Court, and not granted or mentioned to be granted by letters Patents under the great seal. . . .[1]

---

[1] E 165/46, pp. 5, 12b; SP 16/150/115 (oath for Admiralty witnesses).

The Crown did not therefore admit to any general limitation on its prerogative right to create new posts through the proper machinery, but in practice it sometimes had to give way over particular cases[1]. The commissioners on fees did not spend much time investigating innovated offices. Either these turned out to be less numerous and obnoxious than had been expected, or else the inquiry into excessive fees was found to be much more complicated and far lengthier than had been anticipated; or most likely a bit of both. If anything, more fuss was made about new offices of the type which came outside the Commission's scope, namely those instituted by the Crown in the traditional way, for some of these were believed to threaten the status and income of existing officers. If a complete new court or department was being set up, or the duties of an existing one were being radically altered and extended, then the case for a particular new office might be irresistible. In 1583 the court of Exchequer Chamber was formally constituted, and recognized as what we should call an appeal court; it followed reasonably enough that it should have a Clerk to keep its records and to help arrange its business.[2] But few cases were as clear cut as this one.

The farming of the revenues, especially of the customs duties, sometimes caused new offices to be created or old ones to be revived. Thus in 1635 the Aulnagership of linen was resurrected after a long interval. One aspect of this, the farming of fines and forfeitures, achieved notoriety. Such was the grant of the fines arising from the re-discovery of fraudulently concealed Crown lands; or Endymion Porter's grant of the Collectorship of all fines levied in Star Chamber, which needless to say he performed by deputy. In 1630 a wider appointment, first made by James I and then confirmed by Charles, of two joint Collectors and Receivers of all fines and forfeitures under the penal laws against recusant Catholics, was ruled by the Judges to be contrary to law and unprofitable to the King. Despite a subsequent catalogue of abuses alleged in 1635 to have been committed by these same officers, they apparently survived this condemnation. Another small reorganization, probably well justified on grounds of efficiency, followed the separation of the ordinary standing taxes on recusants from the ancient revenues of the Pipe, which were accounted for by sheriffs of counties, royal bailiffs,

---

[1] B. M. Lansdowne MS. 163 fol. 92 (surrender by James I to the officers of Common Pleas); SP 16/377/178 (assertion of royal rights c. 1637).

[2] See *Cal. S.P. Dom.*, *1625-6*, p. 198, for ref. to the creation of this post.

mayors of towns, etc. Successfully opposed in 1627 by the Lord Treasurer, no doubt at the instigation of the Pipe and other 'ancient course' officers, two special Receivers of these taxes, to be responsible for the country north and south of Trent respectively, were however appointed in 1628. The northern Receivership went first to Sir John, later Lord Savile and then, in June 1629, to his successful rival among the Yorkshire gentry, Viscount Wentworth. The disposal of the southern Receivership reflected a compromise between rival patrons if not rival administrative interests; it was granted to George Fielding, a distant relative by marriage of Buckingham and confidential servant to the duchess, while the reversion went to Robert Long, the Lord Treasurer's personal secretary. Wentworth probably transferred his office to his brother at about the time of his own impeachment (1640-1), and Long succeeded Fielding in 1639. The appointment of separate Auditors of these accounts, which involved a protracted struggle, would have been harder to justify on grounds of efficiency alone; the existing Revenue and Prest Auditors of the upper Exchequer were in generally good repute and were definitely not open to the same criticisms as the officers of the 'ancient course'. The case for separate Auditors had been argued as early as 1630; a proposed grant was over-ridden by Lord Treasurer Juxon in 1636; the appointment was finally made in October 1639. Another revenue office, the Surveyor-Generalship of Crown lands, was revived in 1625; its first holder, Sir Thomas Fanshawe of Jenkins, Essex, was already Clerk of the Crown and Coroner in King's Bench, and his successor, Charles Harbord, was also an Auditor of the Duchy of Cornwall. These revivals and innovations have about them a slight flavour of the early Tudor approach: to create new posts such as those of Collector, Receiver, Surveyor, and Auditor to meet new needs.[1]

Were there many 'innovated offices' for the commissioners to discover? When the officers of the court of Common Pleas had to give an account of themselves to the commissioners in 1628, they

[1] *Cal. S.P. Dom., 1627-8*, p. 277, *1628-9*, pp. 199, 570, *1635-6*, pp. 4, 543-4, *1636-7*, p. 81-2; *Foedera*, 28 April 1625, 20 February 1630; XVIII, 988-9, XX, 380; Rushworth, *Hist. Colls.*, II, 58-9, 300-1; SP 16/488/103; T 56/4, p. 87, T 56/8, p. 196; Leeds P.L., Temple Newsam MSS., public offices misc. 31; Fanshawe MSS. (Bratton Fleming) vellum bound vol. on Exchequer misc., p. 103. (Note: in T 56/8, p. 196, a contemporary copyist by mistake makes Long succeed Fielding in the *northern* recusant Receivership.)

only admitted to the existence of one newly erected office; and they pleaded that this, the post of Superseder 'which (as we are informed) is granted by letters patent under the great seal . . .', was outside the commissioners' scope. By contrast it has been shown in a recent history that an unconcealed expansion took place in the court of Wards during the 1620's and 30's, both by the multiplication of semi-official under-clerks and by the creation of new posts, among these being the Clerk Remembrancership granted to the Alexander Stafford who has been cited as a possible pluralist. In the Wards greater efficiency was genuinely being aimed at: 'accounting became stricter and a stronger effort was made to bring in arrearages'. Since the Crown's revenue from wardship and livery rose considerably faster in these decades than did its total revenues, the extra clerks may fairly be said to have served their purpose.[1]

Further contrasts are provided by cases in other central and regional courts. In 1629 a new Clerkship of the Billets (bills or letters) was instituted for the Council in the Marches of Wales; after strong opposition from the other officers of the Council it was revoked the following year. It is not usual to find grants once made being formally revoked, and it may be relevant that this revocation coincided with a vacancy in the Lord Presidency of Wales, after the death of William Compton, first Earl of Northampton, and before the appointment of Thomas Egerton, first Earl of Bridgewater. Extra work requiring an additional officer can scarcely have been falling on the Council in the Marches at this date, and those who objected, whatever their personal motives, may very well have had the better case. Turning to the Exchequer, in 1635 the King's Remembrancer and his under-clerks petitioned successfully against the appointment of a new officer who was to have been in charge of all legal proceedings by English bill (that is, the equity side of the court's business); for them it was a bread-and-butter question, threatening serious loss of fees. A similar but more obscure case arose in King's Bench. In 1636 the case was argued in detail before the Privy Council, and then before a strong sub-committee of Council, in favour of a small new office, of Referee to count the number of days which elapsed in every case where a certain type of action was brought, between the defendant appearing to put in bail and the plantiff proceeding with the case; despite the welter of technicalities with which they sur-

---

[1] Bodl. Rawlinson MS. D 1123, fol. 1; Bell, *Court of Wards*, p. 31; see also *Cal. S.P. Dom., 1629-31*, p. 56.

rounded their arguments, the petitioners were unable to deny that the days had somehow been counted by someone in every such action since 1565-6 when the need had first arisen. The Council may have smelt a rat, for the grant did not go forward. On the legal side of the Exchequer unsuccessful application was made in 1637 for the appointment of a new Examiner; this may have been connected with the previous attempt to set up a separate office for English bills. In the central executive a proposal that a special officer should have charge of providing notebooks and loose paper for the Privy Council was opposed successfully—and sensibly—by the Clerks of the Council, on the grounds that such an officer would himself employ a deputy or servant, and that both would soon find their way onto the royal establishment. As Tout and other medieval historians have shown, a large part of the English central administration was built up much in the way objected to here; that the Council Clerks very likely wanted to keep the supply of stationery as a perquisite for their existing subordinates, does not invalidate their objection to the new office.[1]

Individual posts apart, no new central institution dates from the reign of Charles I. As has already been explained, the new 'Palace court', set up at Westminster in 1630 with its own small hierarchy of judges, clerks, and under-officers, does not constitute a true exception to this, representing merely a merger of the old Marshalsea and Verge courts. The Knight Marshal was the senior judge of the new court; Edward Herbert, future Solicitor- and Attorney-General, then a career lawyer in the process of going over to the 'Court', became its first Steward.[2] In 1635 a year of many administrative and financial surveys, a more important plan was proposed to the King, who referred it to the committee of the Council which dealt with matters of trade (and sometimes also finance); from this body it was sent on to the Treasury Commissioners. It was suggested that a commission should be issued and a new court subsequently erected, to collect and manage the revenues, and in general to provide for the household and other needs, of 'H.M.'s royal and blessed issue, being the props and stabiliments of all our future hopes'. This revenue department for Prince Charles and the other royal children was not to involve any payments to the Crown which affected private

---

[1] PC 2/46, pp. 5-6; *Cal. S.P. Dom., 1629-31*, pp. 254, 352, 527, *1635-6*, p. 56, *1636-7*, pp. 541-2, *1637*, p. 480.

[2] *Ibid., 1629-31*, p. 281. See above, Chapter 2, s. vi.

property rights; the practical implications of this proviso are not clear, but presumably it meant that such revenues should only be raised in constitutionally acceptable ways; nor was there to be any loss to the existing Crown land revenue departments; instead a policy was recommended of resumptions and discoveries of conceal-ments. While the means of raising the proposed revenue was thus left vague, the new staff were enumerated in detail; these were to include a Master, an Attorney, a Receiver, two Auditors, a Clerk, a Messenger, and an Usher. The annual accounts of the new court would be audited in the Exchequer, 'augmentation-wise', that is by the seven Revenue Auditors, as were the land revenue accounts. As had perhaps been the case with Henry VIII's experimental revenue courts, the central administrative structure of the Duchy of Lancaster seems to have provided a working model; but, unlike the Duchy, this new court was not to be independent of the Exchequer. The Treasury Commissioners evidently preferred to appoint a single financial officer for the Prince's Household, which was then in the process of being enlarged, and for this officer to be supplied with money partly from the Exchequer and partly by assignment direct from various incoming revenues. The plan which they rejected, again suggests what must surely have been a conscious resort to the precedents of an earlier epoch (c. 1470-1560).[1]

In 1634 Wentworth, as Lord Deputy of Ireland, professed reluc-tance in refusing a grant to Mr. George Kirke, Gentleman of the Robes and Groom of the Bedchamber. Concerning Kirke's plan to obtain the post of Gager, or Gauger, of thread, etc., in Ireland, he wrote: 'albeit I be against the erecting of a new office of Gager in this Country, yet I will do it so, as I trust shall be no prejudice to you, that are a Gentleman I love and respect with all my Heart.' In an earlier letter Kirke had implied that the office of Gauger was already in existence but had been combined with that of Weigher and Packer, and granted by Wentworth to one of his own servants. We should not necessarily expect to find 'Thorough' against all new offices; but even in this case, where the proposal was obviously a court racket, Wentworth felt obliged to offer compensation for his refusal, and promised to advance Kirke's other Irish projects.[2]

The natural corollary to the creation of new offices was the abolition of old ones. This too was difficult, if an office-holder

---

[1] SP 16/302/127, a proposition, November 1635.
[2] Sheffield C. L., Strafford MSS. 8/156-7, 13c/206a.

enjoyed tenure for life or during good behaviour, and especially if his patent included the grant of an annual Fee from the Crown. On a test case early in 1627 the twelve common law judges decided unanimously that the Keepership of a royal park terminated when the King 'dis-parked' the land in question, even though it was a grant for life. But by eleven to one they ruled that the ex-Keeper must continue to receive his Fee of £30 p.a.: a very qualified victory for the Crown.[1]

Neither the King and his immediate advisers, nor the main body of medium-ranking officials were likely to be consistent. Supporters of greater efficiency might favour some new offices and oppose others; existing office-holders would tend to oppose the creation of new, and the abolition of old posts and institutions, while often at the same time trying to increase the number of their own subordinates. Men's attitudes would vary according to who suggested a new office, or attacked an existing one, as well as according to the nature of the post itself; some of the innovations suggested were obvious sinecures and others were little more than extensions of existing monopoly patents. While the Crown still could and sometimes did create new posts, it had temporarily ceased to do so very widely, partly for its own reasons of state, and partly in deference to the administrative conservatism of existing officials. The latters' instincts for the most part reflected their own material interests; under the system of payment in fees and gratuities, if a new office meant a loss of business for existing ones, it would also entail a loss of income for their holders.

vi OATHS

Many royal officials had to take special oaths on first being admitted to their posts. It would be easy to say that in a more religious age than our own greater sanctity attached to the sworn word, and therefore that, where their texts have survived, these oaths provide an important body of evidence about the conditions of service. But it does not automatically follow that perjury and the failure of men to observe their sworn undertakings were relatively any less common then than now. We need to ask how seriously these oaths were regarded, and how men viewed the prospects of

[1] G. Croke, *Reports* (1683), III, 59-61. Curiously enough, Chief Baron Walter was the one who thought the Fee too should lapse.

being caught out and punished if they broke them. To do this we must consider how far oaths specify in detail the duties of particular officers, as opposed merely to repeating stereotyped generalities.

The general oaths of Supremacy and Allegiance seem to have become formalities by the 1620's and 30's, except when someone was suspected of being a secret Roman Catholic. These two oaths were designed to exclude all Roman Catholics from the royal service, unless they were in effect prepared to abjure papal authority; in theory they would also have debarred some extreme Puritans, for example Separatists, as well as Anabaptists and freethinkers. In practice only Catholics were likely to be candidates for office apart perhaps from the very occasional Puritan or Anabaptist fanatic at the lowest levels of the King's service amongst the porters and scullions, and the equally exceptional sophisticated sceptic at a much higher administrative and social level; the former was likely to be excluded, while the latter probably would not scruple to take the oaths if he were asked to do so. On occasions these oaths were tendered to suspected Catholics, who already held office, but this does not seem to have happened often. In 1638 two sons and a servant of one of the Tellers in the Exchequer had to take them; and in March 1642 a Council Clerk, who was also a J.P., certified that one of his late colleagues, a retired Clerk, had taken the oath of Allegiance.[1]

With obvious short-term regressions the position of Catholics in royal service gradually became easier during the first thirty years of the Stuart dynasty. It reached its most favourable under the plenitude of the 'personal government' (1633-9), and then suddenly deteriorated in 1640-1, to become if anything worse than it had been in 1603. The improvement, being gradual, is harder to date than the deterioration. George Calvert, later Lord Baltimore, may have resigned his Secretaryship of State in January 1625 because of conscientious scruples about concealing his conversion to Rome, or because at that date it would still have seemed unthinkable, to him and to others, that he should retain it, once he was suspected, or known in informed circles, to be a papist. Even in the 1630's there were gradations, from the avowed practising Catholic who either felt able to take the oaths or had contrived to avoid doing so, to the suspected sympathizer, the death-bed convert, and the various species of 'fellow traveller'. Few Catholics remained in office by the summer

[1] *Cal. S.P. Dom., 1637-8*, p. 301, *1641-3*, p. 298.

of 1641; yet in July the Long Parliament persuaded the King that all office-holders should be compelled to take the 'Protestation', which had been drafted in May during the crisis over the Army Plot and Strafford's attainder. This was to be taken first by the members of both Houses and eventually by everyone in the country; deriving from the Scottish national 'Covenant', but with notable Elizabethan precedents, it was in the form of an oath to defend Protestantism, parliamentary government, the peace of the realm, etc., against Popery and arbitrary government. Since no supporter of the King would have admitted to being against civil peace or government by King, Lords, and Commons, and since Roman Catholics should already have been excluded by the existing oaths (unless they had solemnly abjured papal authority), it is hard to see this as anything more than an exhortatory exercise.[1]

What can be said about the oaths which were framed for the holders of individual posts or the members of particular departments? In the autumn of 1635 the Privy Council ordered that all officers of the Navy and the Ordnance should take, or retake, the oaths of Allegiance and Supremacy, and also a third one 'for the due and faithful execution of their places and charge respectively'. This was probably connected with the successive royal commissions on the Ordnance Office (1629-34), which had found much amiss there, and with the scandal over the malversation of naval stores in 1634, involving several senior officials; nor is it fanciful to see this third oath as a prologue to the campaign against reversions, life tenure, and absenteeism in the defence departments, which was to follow in 1636-8.[2]

It is not clear how many individual posts had their own oaths which a new holder had to take on admission. Amongst those who might handle, or have access to, confidential documents, oath-taking extended some way down the administrative ladder. Besides the oath for all Privy Councillors, there was quite naturally one for the Council Clerks, and also one for the Keeper of its Chest and Records, and possibly even for the Keepers of the Council Chamber and the cleaning staff. When the Council Clerks objected to the appointment of a new officer to be in charge of stationery, they said that he *and his servant or deputy* would have to be sworn, and that this would help

---

[1] *Tudor and Stuart Proclamations, I, England and Wales*, ed. R. Steele (Oxford, 1910), pp. 225, 228.

[2] SP 16/302/1, 18 October 1635; also PC 2/45, p. 230.

to bring them both on to the permanent establishment.[1] Oaths were probably more important in the central executive than elsewhere. On 24 August 1638 the senior reversioner Edward Norgate succeeded to a Signet Clerkship on the death of an existing Clerk, but he was not formally confirmed in his new post until he had taken the oath two days later.[2]

Special oaths may occasionally have been devised to deal with special cases. When G. R. Weckherlin, who was known to be an ardent Lutheran, was appointed as German Interpreter in 1631, he had to swear 'upon the holy Evangelists' that he would bear allegiance to King Charles, keep secrets properly, and generally do his duty as he should, 'soe help you God'. Possibly allowance was being made for his religion, and he was not being asked to swear on the King James Bible, as was normal.[3]

In 1638 Laud refused to allow the new Clerk of Star Chamber to be sworn because there was only a Prayer Book and not a Bible available in the room. The archbishop was reported to have whispered that 'hee woulde maintaine the autority of the common prayer, yett he would not suffer any to be sworne upon it'. A Bible was duly fetched, and the ceremony proceeded.[4]

The oaths of Supremacy and Allegiance seem customarily to have been taken kneeling *on* the table of whatever council chamber or court room it might be. Oaths for entry to particular offices were taken either kneeling on the table, or standing at it.[5]

Small variations in the oaths which they took sometimes emphasize significant differences between the functions of different officers. Both the Masters of Requests and the Clerks of the Council were constantly handling confidential material, although the Masters more often dealt with matters concerning individuals than affairs of state. On admission a new Master swore to be a true councillor to

[1] *Cal. S.P. Dom., 1637-8*, pp. 41, 212; see also SP 16/301/9, declared accounts, Chamber, and *Cal. S.P. Dom., 1628-9*, p. 72 (the servant of the Keeper of the Chest and Records had £10 p.a. for attendance and for preparing quill pens).

[2] *Cal. S.P. Dom., 1637-8*, p. 603.

[3] Berks R. O., Trumbull Papers, unbound MSS.

[4] B.M. Hargrave MS. 404, p. 73.

[5] *The Lismore Papers*, ed. A. B. Grosart, 1st ser. (1886), III, 107-8, IV, 156; T. Barrett-Lennard, *An Account of the Families of Lennard and Barrett* (privately, 1908), p. 381; *Docquets of Letters Patent ... of Charles I at Oxford*, ed. W. H. Black (1837), p. 137.

the King, a new Clerk to be the King's true and faithful servant; this reflected the former's slightly superior status. Both swore that if they learnt of anything 'to be attempted, done, or spoken against his Majesty's person, honour, Crown, or dignity royal', they would hinder and oppose it with all their powers, and reveal it, or cause it to be revealed to the King or the Council. Both swore allegiance to the King, his heirs, and lawful successors (a successful usurper might become a lawful successor!), and to uphold all the King's 'Jurisdictions, pre-eminences, and authorities' belonging both to the King's person and to the Crown of England, against all foreign 'Princes, Persons, Prelates, or Potentates', that is, against the Pope as well as against secular powers. Both swore 'generally in all things' to do as they ought as councillor and servant respectively to the King, 'So help you God and by the contents of this Book'. But in the middle of the Clerk's oath was a passage which had no equivalent in the Master's:

> You shall keep secret all matters committed and revealed unto you, or that shall be treated of secretly in Council. And if any the said treaties or Counsels shall touch any of the Councillors, you shall not reveal the same unto him, but shall keep the same until such time as by the consent of his Majesty or of the Council publication shall be made thereof.

The Clerk's oath is very like the one for a Privy Councillor especially at this point, and both texts dated from at least *c.* 1570, when there was bitter factional strife in the Council, between William Cecil and his allies and the more aristocratic group, including at times Leicester. These texts may even date to the mid-sixteenth century when the Council had been the arena for the life-and-death struggles of the rival leaders in Edward VI's reign. The Masters of Requests' oath was if anything the more typical in *not* containing any detailed occupational provisions.[1] For instance, the oath for a member of the Council in the North, though lengthy, was couched in very general terms; it referred to good advice, secrecy, impartiality in counsel and justice, keeping matters which concerned them secret from other Councillors, etc. In practice, no more than in the Privy Council itself did such lofty declamations prevent faction and even

[1] PC 2/42, p. 3; PC 2/50, p. 4; *Select Statutes and other Constitutional Documents illustrative of the reigns of Elizabeth and James I*, ed. G. W. Prothero (Oxford, 1913), pp. 165-6.

disloyalty. Several of Wentworth's enemies remained on the Council during the 1630's, and contributed to his ruin in 1640-1.[1]

The oaths which appear more specific mostly turn out on examination to be largely tautologous. The Lieutenant of the Tower swore to serve the King faithfully in his office, to keep the Tower for the King, and his heirs and lawful successors, to advance the King's profits, to inform the King or the Council if he heard anything harmful to the King or to the Tower, etc. The general effect is well summed up in the penultimate sentence: 'In these and in all other things that to a Lieutenant of the Tower belongeth to do well and faithfully, you shall (according to your best power and knowledge) perform, fulfil, and keep'. There was only one passage with a slightly different implication: '. . . the rights and privileges of the Tower that to the same lawfully appertain you shall keep and preserve'. This may suggest that the head of a department, in this case the Tower, swore to preserve its departmental vested interests as well as to serve the King. What if the two were to clash? Taking the passage in its context the King's service obviously comes first, and too much should not be made of this provision.[2]

Some texts of oaths do tell us more about their holders' duties:

You shall swear that you shall well and truely after your learning and cunning exercise the office of the Register [Registrar] in the King's Court of Chancery. And that you shall justly and equally after your skill and knowledge without fraud or corruption take, draw up, and enter all such rules, orders, and decrees, and no other, as shall be hereafter made, pronounced or decreed in the said Court of Chancery, either by the Lord Chancellor, or by the Lord Keeper of the great seal of England for the time being, or by the Master of the Rolls, [or] by any other of his Majesty's commissioners appointed for that purpose, according to the true intent and effect of that which shall be pronounced and delivered. All which you shall truely perform without delay. So God you help.

Although several others can be found with a comparable amount of detail, oaths are likely to remain a minor source of information.[3] From most of the surviving ones little is learnt which is not

---

[1] Leeds P.L., Temple Newsam MSS., Council in the North, 87.

[2] PC 2/43, p. 7.

[3] B.M. Adds. MS. 34324, p. 286 (Chancery); see also B.M. Lans. MS. 168, fols. 272-3 (Exchequer of Receipt), 155, fols. 53b, 54b (Central Executive).

known, or could not safely be inferred from other sources. And it may be significant that more oaths were being devised all the time. This may seem to suggest a certain lack of trust on the part of the Crown, and later the Long Parliament, and perhaps also a lack of spontaneous loyalty on the part of the office-holders. It might be taken as evidence that oaths really were effective, or anyway that they were generally believed to be so. But equally this proliferation of oaths may imply the very reverse: the less effective they were, the more were devised. Despite the religiosity of the age, it is possible that taking an oath then had much the same significance as signing a contract has now. Contracts, it may be supposed, are more often kept than broken, but their character is far from sacred and they do not always reveal very much about the posts which they concern.

vii ROUTINE: WORK AND LEISURE

This chapter purports to deal with the 'conditions of service' of Charles I's officials. Some readers, especially any who may themselves have worked in a government department, will very likely by now be objecting that the most important things are being left out, that *Hamlet* is being played without the Prince. What we really want to know about is the officials' daily routine, what hours they kept, what holidays they had, where their offices were located and what these premises were like, where they lived and how they got to and from work, what the work itself was like, and how in practice they spent their working lives.

Curious as this may seem, the main difficulty is lack of evidence, especially of an intimate personal kind. *The Autobiography of Phineas Pett*,[1] Master Shipwright 1605-42, is a most entertaining work. It tells us much about his struggles with rival designers, and also how he built the *Sovereign of the Seas*, but less of his routine activities as an official. The diary of Richard Boyle, first and 'great' Earl of Cork, covers the years 1612-42, and is of great importance for Anglo-Irish history, especially for Boyle's relations with Wentworth. But Boyle was first and foremost a business-man, and his diary reflects this; its many references to his official career, and to office-holding in general, are almost all concerned with money to the exclusion of other aspects.

Apart from a few lawyers' commonplace-books, and scattered letters and notes, there is little else which can be called autobiographi-

[1] Ed. W. G. Perrin (Navy Record Society, 1918).

cal for any official before Samuel Pepys. Pepys's famous diary begins in January 1660, when he was privately employed as an under-clerk by one of the Tellers in the Exchequer; later in that year he became Clerk of the Acts, or Ships in the Navy Office, and, as is perhaps less well known, also Deputy Clerk of the Privy Seal, an office to which his patron Lord Montague held a reversion from before the Civil War. Pepys's career as a naval Clerk can be reconstructed from the Diary, supplemented by his letters and other printed sources.[1] From the Diary for August to December 1660 it can also be seen how he at first combined his naval work with his duties every fourth month in the Privy Seal Office. Thus we have ample evidence over a long period about Pepys as a naval official, and good but brief evidence about him as an under clerk in the Exchequer and as a Deputy at the Privy Seal. We need to ask how typical Pepys was of officials either in the 1660's or earlier, and how good his record of the 1660's is as evidence for the 1630's. By the very fact of his keeping such a diary he was a most exceptional man for the later seventeenth century; and by virtue of his achievements as a naval administrator, especially in the years 1672-8 and 1684-8, he was also exceptional (although Sir Arthur Bryant, in his enthusiasm for Pepys, is perhaps by implication rather less than fair to various other officials, including some previous naval administrators). These distinctions apart, there is no reason to suppose that he was untypical in all other aspects of his work and daily routine.

An attempt will be made in a later chapter, to discover *who*, socially, the office-holders were under Charles I. Meanwhile a little can be done to answer some of the questions which relate more particularly to the nature, hours, and place of work.

The various branches of the government were located as follows (moving approximately from east to west):

(i) In or near the Tower of London: the Armoury, the Ordnance, the Navy, the Jewels, the Records (of parliament, and some of the ancient records of the royal courts), the Customs, the Mint.

(ii) In the more westerly parts of the City: the Great Wardrobe

---

[1] *The Diary of Samuel Pepys* (ed. H. B. Wheatley, 1893-9); J. R. Tanner, *Samuel Pepys and the Royal Navy* (Cambridge, 1920); A. Bryant, *Samuel Pepys* (Cambridge, 1933-8). See also *The Life, Journals, & Correspondence of S. Pepys* (ed. J. Smith, 1841); *A Descriptive Catalogue of the naval MSS. in the Pepysian Library* (ed. Tanner), I (1903), general introduction; *Private Correspondence & Misc. Papers of S. Pepys* (ed. Tanner, 1926).

(quite near the present site of *The Times*), the court of the Arches, the Office of Arms (on its present site), the Fleet Prison.

(iii) In the Holborn-Chancery Lane-Fleet Street area: the main administrative offices of Chancery, and its records, and sub-departments of other courts (e.g. the Chief Clerk of King's Bench at one time had his office in Southampton Row); the Alienations Office.

(iv) At Charing Cross: the Stables.

(v) In Whitehall: the household departments, the Great Seal (normally wherever the Lord Keeper was), the Privy Seal office, the Signet office, the Privy Council, the Admiralty commissioners, the Gatehouse prison.

(vi) In Westminster: the courts of King's Bench, Common Pleas, Exchequer, Chancery, Wards, Requests and Star Chamber.

And finally, on the south bank, in Southwark:

(vii) The court of Admiralty, three other prisons.

Different parts of the same court or department were liable to be found in different places. In fact the 'office' might be where the individual officer lived or had his lodgings. The court of Wards sat at Westminster, but its Clerk's office was in the Inner Temple, and its two Auditors' offices in Holborn and the City respectively. As Mr. Bell observes, 'there were indeed offices all over London, where the individual officers transacted their business'. And, as can be seen, Chancery too functioned in at least three different places.[1]

Then there is the further distinction between those branches of the government which followed the royal Court from one palace to another and attended the King and Queen on their summer progresses, and those which normally stayed in the capital. A large part of the Household and the Chamber, and of their sub-departments, and contingents from the Wardrobes accompanied the royal family. The Privy and Great Seals might do so, according to what their respective Keepers did. One Secretary of State and at least one Signet Clerk were supposed to follow the King wherever he was, with perhaps at least a nucleus of Privy Councillors. The other

---

[1] J. Stow, *The Survey of London* (1633 edn.); W. Dugdale, *Origines Judiciales* (1666), pp. 146, 147, 150 (not necessarily evidence for the 1630's); Hutchinson, *Memoirs*, p. 12; Bell, *Court of Wards*, pp. 171-3; G. S. Dugdale, *Whitehall through the Centuries* (1950); R. Robinson, 'A Briefe Collection of the Queenes Majesties most high and most honourable Courtes of Recordes', ed. R. L. Rickard, *The Camden Miscellany*, XX (Camden Soc., 1953), dated 1592, but amended in 1602-3.

Secretary, a skeleton staff at the Signet, and an additional nucleus of Councillors were supposed always to remain in London, except sometimes when the plague was very bad; in practice, many of the Councillors who did not follow the King on his summer progress went home to their estates for at least part of the long vacation, and so usually did each of the two Secretaries in turn, though for shorter spells. The other departments and the law courts might be evacuated in a bad plague epidemic, but they no longer itinerated with the King. This was to be of political importance in 1642-3.

Most officials probably also lived in the Westminster district, in the City, or along the Strand and Fleet Street and the side-streets off them. Some lived further out, mainly to the west and south-west in the Kensington and Chelsea directions, but only the wealthier ones are likely to have done so, since this would have entailed having two horses, if not a coach as well.

While many household officers and some belonging to the central executive had to follow the royal court on its summer progresses, most of the King's servants had a holiday during the summer. In this respect officials can be divided into those whose attendance was on some kind of rota but covered the whole year, those who normally observed the law terms, and those who cannot be fitted into either of these categories. In the Navy, Ordnance, and Mint there was no formal provision for holidays either on a rotation basis or during the legal vacations, but most of their respective officers probably took time off during the summer. The personnel of the central executive and of the Chamber worked largely on a rota: one month on, two off; one month on, three off; five weeks on, eleven off (the Council Clerks); or three months on, nine off. The officers of the common law, equity, prerogative, and ecclesiastical courts all kept more or less the same law terms, though in theory Chancery was open all the year round. And skeleton administrative staffs of all the principal law courts were always available in Westminster or London. Like the legal branches of the courts to which they belonged, the finance departments (Exchequer, Wards, and Duchy) kept the law terms as far as possible. But there was a skeleton staff in the Exchequer of Receipt throughout the long vacation, with perhaps just a Deputy Chamberlain or his clerk in the Upper Exchequer to collect the tallies sent up from the Receipt. In 1635 the Auditors were probably kept at work most of the summer preparing the 'Balance' of revenues and expenditures since 1631. During the royal summer progresses, which approximately coincided with the long vacation, the palace of Whitehall and its outbuildings were emptied and cleaned out, and the same may have happened in the premises of the law courts down the road in Westminster.

By modern standards daily and weekly routine were irregular. In this matter Pepys' diary, especially for 1660-2, cannot be admitted as evidence; the routine of government departments is likely to have been somewhat more regular before 1640 than just before and after the Restoration. Different departments, and even sub-departments, probably fixed their own hours. Most officials seem to have worked a five-day week, starting very early in the morning at 7.0 a.m. or 7.30, or at daybreak, and often finishing for the day at dinner-time, which in the 1620's and 1630's was normally at 11.0 a.m., 11.30, or noon, and perhaps going on again in the afternoon only two or three times a week, to 4.0 p.m., 4.30 or—in winter—nightfall. But this is largely surmise, and exceptions would be easy to find. During their turns of duty, Household and Chamber officers worked a seven-day week, and some of them—in theory—a twenty-four-hour day. The Privy Council often met on Sunday; this involved at least one Council Clerk, a Chamber-Keeper, a Sergeant or two, and some of the Messengers and under-clerks. The duty Master of Requests was liable to receive petitions at any time, though a petitioner's chances of success would hardly have been improved by tactless intrusion. The Secretaries of State, like the King himself, were in a sense never off duty, but like the King in practice they were not always available for business. Generally speaking, hours of work, as well as the annual working year, are likely to have been shorter and more regular in the law courts and the revenue departments than in the central executive, some branches of the household, and the other (non-household) departments of state.

As for meals, the household provided dinner and supper. The Star Chamber, the court of Wards, and possibly other law courts provided dinner for the judges on full 'court' days. Some officers, e.g. of the Ordnance, drew a victualling allowance when out of town on duty. In general, meals were not provided for the staffs of most other offices; in practice many officers lived over their work, or worked at home.

It is obvious enough that, then at least as much as now, the kind of work done by administrators varied enormously. But this need not preclude any generalizations at all. If we take the middle level of administrators proper, that is leaving out artificers and menial servants, some similarities can be seen across a wide range of courts and departments. Keeping accounts, and auditing other people's accounts, taking inventories and checking other people's, drawing up, checking, and revising contracts, all this would be found in the revenue courts and the supply departments; preparing legal documents, grants, commissions, arbitrations, etc., much of this was common to all the law courts and to the Council; conducting correspondence with local and regional officers, with English diplomats abroad, with naval and military commanders, this was limited to the Council, the Secretaries, and their respective subordinates.

Next to the drafting of legal documents, letter-writing and the keeping of letter-books was probably the most time-consuming activity. For quite different reasons, Wentworth Earl of Strafford is no more typical than Pepys, but this does not mean that he was unique in every respect. To judge from the sheer bulk of his correspondence as Lord Deputy (now in the Sheffield Central Library), it must have made tremendous inroads on his own and his secretaries' time; much the same is true of Secretary Coke's correspondence (in the Foreign and Domestic State Papers and the Cowper Manuscripts)

Even quite senior and responsible officers in the law courts, in the upper and lower Exchequer, and at the various Seals must have spent a great deal of time making fair copies of accounts, issue and receipt books, legal instruments, warrants, orders, and letters. Once we come below the very top level, of men like Wentworth, documents of lasting historical interest seem to bear little or no relation to their contemporary administrative importance: for example, the fascinating but anonymous and undated plan to turn all officials into a salariat and to tax the sale of offices[1]; or Edward Nicholas's informal and perhaps private reflections on the problems involved in the collection of Ship Money[2]; or a letter from one Council Clerk to another in 1638 explaining why he thought that the attempt to achieve reform and economy in the royal household, on which they were then engaged, was almost bound to fail[3]; or the vivid series of letters written by one of the Signet Clerks, Edward Norgate, when he was with the King in the north during the first 'Bishops' War' of 1639, which reveal the almost paralysing divisions inside

[1] See Chapter 4, s. iv, and pp. 234-6, and 236, n. 1.
[2] *Cal. S.P. Dom., 1635-6*, p. 6.
[3] SP 16/390/115 (quoted in *Eng. Hist. Rev.*, LXXII, 256).

the central secretariat between the Coke and Windebank factions.[1] These are to be contrasted with the acres of parchment and paper covered with formal records, the historical interest of which is almost negligible, except where they lend themselves to treatment in bulk for statistical purposes. This is no peculiarity of seventeenth-century England; it is of the nature of bureaucracy. But it means that the student of administrative history is presented in its acutest form with a problem which most historians have to face in some measure: how far they are to concern themselves with matters to which contemporaries devoted their main energies and the main part of their working lives, and how far with those which seem in retrospect to be the most important. Sometimes the same things, and the same written records are important on both scores. Rank, status, and prestige probably mattered more to the men of the seventeenth century than they do to us; and this was of undoubted historical importance both then and later. By contrast there is sometimes a choice to be made. But, provided we are aware of this, there need be no conflict; different historians can have different purposes and be none the worse for it. The present study necessarily involves questions, and therefore source materials, of both kinds. To reconstruct the lives and work of Charles I's servants, we need to know what they thought was important and how they spent their time: not necessarily the same thing! To relate the administrative system and the office-holders to the general history of England in the seventeenth century and to the wider development of bureaucracy, it is also necessary to consider somewhat different questions, and so to deal with different kinds of evidence.

It is very hard to tell what contemporaries felt about routine paper work. The great bulk of formal records which have survived, not to mention the others which happily have not, may represent their real pre-occupations. One would for instance like to know what they thought about the successive stages by which a grant passed the Sign Manual, Signet, Privy, and Great Seals, being partially re-drafted, completely rewritten, docketed, summarized, and recorded *in extenso* at every stage. A concern with formal written records which may seem to us exaggerated was perhaps inevitable in a society where the typewriter and the duplicating machine were unknown, where the printing press was a good deal less used than it was to be

[1] SP 16/418/8, 52, 420/121, 421/34-5, 422/62, 423/15, 16 (summaries in *Cal. S.P. Dom., 1639*, pp. 59-60, 82, 144-6, 180-1, 242-3, 269-73).

even for eighteenth-century official documents, and not least where the law and lawyers played a relatively greater part in government and social life than they do today. As in estimating the importance of oaths, we can only conjecture that seventeenth-century men thought formal, and especially sealed, documents to be intrinsically more significant than most people would today. Forgery of official papers was easier and probably more widespread, and was certainly felt to be a more serious problem, than in the twentieth century.

Remembering once more that the early 1660's are not the 1620's or 1630's, Pepys took noticeably little interest in his work at the Privy Seal except as a way of making money. He was clearly aware that the passage of grants and letters there was entirely a matter of formal routine, but that as Clerk of the Acts in the Navy Office he was involved in problems of substance and might even influence decisions affecting national policy. These are not his words, but this is undoubtedly the sense of his reflections. Again there is no sure way of telling how many of his contemporaries, still less how many officials of a quarter of a century earlier, would have felt the same.

Some of these points can best be illustrated by taking a few individual officers selected from different branches of the central government. Thomas Meautys, a Clerk of the Council, can represent the central executive, John Packer, a Clerk of the Privy Seal, the more formal part of the administrative process, Cornelius Holland, a Clerk of the Counting House, the household, Edmund Sawyer, a Revenue Auditor, the more modern, and Christopher Vernon, Surveyor of Greenwax, the medieval machinery of the revenue system, Richard Colchester, a Six Clerk, the staff of the law courts, and Edward Sherborne, Clerk of the Ordnance, the departments outside the royal court. By the later 1630's only two of them did not have country properties which they would have wanted to visit at least once a year. To put it another way, five had other economic interests and commitments outside their official careers. All were married; three had sons or sons-in-law who were office-holders or reversioners to offices. In religion, Packer, Holland, and Vernon had 'low church' or Puritan leanings, and Sherborne was almost certainly a Catholic; the position of the other three is obscure, but it does not seem that any of them was an Arminian, or 'high church' Anglican. As for their politics, Meautys and Sherborne had been in Francis Bacon's service, and may have imbibed his ideas; Packer was a client of the Duke of Buckingham, and Holland of the elder Sir

Henry Vane; Sawyer was spoken of as a potential Chancellor of the Exchequer in 1628, but soon after this he was violently attacked by the House of Commons for his part in organizing and collecting customs duties which had not been sanctioned by parliament. When the Civil War broke out, Sherborne was already dead; of the rest, Holland became an active and extreme parliamentarian, Packer, Meautys, and Vernon passive supporters of parliament or neutrals inclined that way, and Sawyer a wavering and perhaps unwilling royalist; only Colchester was a straightforward royalist, and even he supported the King from the relative seclusion of his Gloucestershire estate and not at Oxford or in the field. How far these facts enable one to infer anything about their probable attitudes towards royal policy in the years before 1640-2 is a difficult question, which will be discussed in a later chapter.

All seven, except Colchester the Six Clerk, were at some time of some importance in helping to run the machine of government. Packer's Privy Seal duties were formal, and he alone of the seven acted by deputy; his active career had really come to an end with the assassination of Buckingham in 1628. The other six were all fairly hard working, and the work of all except Colchester was of more than routine consequence. The loss of any of the other five would have had to be made good with an experienced, industrious administrator, of above average ability, and reasonably uncorrupt by the standards of the time. It may be asked whether their importance went beyond this. Colchester and, after 1628, Packer dealt exclusively with matters of routine and were not concerned with the taking of decisions. But the way in which Sawyer and Vernon did their work was liable to affect the size of the royal revenue and more particularly the smoothness with which it was collected; Holland, and to a lesser extent Sherborne, were in a position to influence the level of Crown spending for better or worse, and Sherborne had a minor but significant responsibility for the state of its military preparedness; finally, Meautys may never have taken any important political decisions himself, but for twenty years he was at the ear and elbow of those who did. Before 1628, as Buckingham's patronage secretary, Packer was probably more influential than any of the others ever were. All in all, the outlook and beliefs of such men were clearly of some consequence.

It may be said that to select these seven out of the several hundred officials from the years 1625-42 is misleading, and makes such men seem more interesting and important than in fact they were. In part this is so. These seven could not, and are not meant to be a statistical sample; and it would be an odd proceeding for an author to offer his readers the dullest examples available! That these seven were untypical is a more difficult charge to answer. None of them, as far as is known, kept a diary, though Colchester kept what are described as 'Journals' but are actually account books with a few jottings on non-financial matters. An interesting account of Packer's life was written about the time of his death in 1648, probably by his son-in-law. A few personal letters of Thomas Meautys survive from the later 1620's, but almost all that can be discovered about him, Holland, Sawyer, Sherborne, and Vernon as individuals and not as mere units in the administrative system has to be pieced together from a variety of scattered sources. About the private lives and the thoughts of Colchester and Packer we know a very little, about those of the rest virtually nothing. In this they are all too typical; indeed, to have even a little biographical material for two or three out of seven suggests too favourable a picture; there is nothing like this proportion for the whole body of officials. Piecemeal as most of the records are, these seven are exceptional first and foremost in the amount which is known about them.[1]

No one would be more delighted than the author to learn that another 'Pepys' Diary' had been discovered for the 1630's, or even two or three additional sources of more limited value such as the 'Colchester Journals'. Meanwhile those who prefer the kind of historical fine writing which makes its bricks without straw, and in doing so trespasses freely on the territory of the historical novelist, will know where to go in search of it. If analysis sometimes seems to squeeze human interest out of these chapters, this arises solely from a prejudice against fabricating evidence, and in no way reflects a preference for desiccated, or 'de-humanized' history.

viii ENTRY AND SERVICE

To what extent is it possible, at this stage in our inquiry, to generalize about the administrative system and the men who comprised it? Until the payment of officers and the sale and value of

---

[1] Refs. for Sherborne will be found earlier in this chapter, p. 80, n. 1, and for the others in Chapters 5 and 6.

offices (Chapter 4), the social background and economic circumstances of office-holders (Chapter 5), and their political and religious affiliations (Chapter 6) have also been discussed, any generalizations are bound to be tentative and are likely to over-emphasize certain aspects of the subject. With this proviso, it is already reasonable to speak of an 'administrative system', not only in terms of 'the institutions comprising the government (Chapter 2), but even more by reason of the conditions of entry and service described in this chapter. The means of appointment (usually by patrimony, patronage purchase, or some combination of these), the creation of reversionary interests, the forms of tenure (particularly for life), pluralism and the performance of duties in absence (by official deputies or by under clerks and servants), were all in large measure interdependent. They characterized every branch of the central government, and every level within it except the highest (some of them were not unknown even there). Some other apparent features of the system, like sinecurism, turn out to have been less important than might have been expected, or else, like pluralism, to be easily misunderstood. And the oaths taken by officers are found to afford disappointingly little solid evidence about the nature of their duties or about the general character of the system; indeed oaths more often served ideological than administrative purposes, as they were to again in the years after 1649, 1673, and 1689. On the other hand, the creation of new offices appears as a definite source of friction between the Crown and the holders of existing posts; it was bound up with the problem of deputies and absenteeism, and with the tendencies understood by 'Parkinson's Law' and 'Pooh Bah-ism'. The Crown's freedom of action was limited by the opposition to new offices, as well as by reversions and life tenure. Restrictions on the Crown's right of appointment to already existing offices never went as far in England as it did in France, where many offices were in practice heritable. But the French Crown was more easily able to create new offices, as well as more eager to do so; in one sense this was a less urgent need in England precisely because existing offices were not generally heritable.

All the features of the administrative system which have been discussed in this chapter are in turn closely related to its financial aspects.

4

PAYMENT OF OFFICERS; SALE AND VALUE OF OFFICES

i FORMS OF PAYMENT

TO THE MODERN OBSERVER the number and variety of different ways in which officers were paid is likely to be one of the most bewildering features of the old administrative system. It is difficult to know how to classify them. The principal modes of remuneration were Fees, annuities, pensions, wages, diet or board wages, livery, and perquisites in kind from the Crown, and fees, gratuities, and presents from the subject (or from other officials). We need to examine each of these more closely.

Salaries or stipends, which we should expect to be the most important form of payment, were scarcely known under those names. But most officers received a (stipendiary) Fee from the Crown, either paid direct from the Exchequer or from the paymaster of their own court or department. Some officers received two such Fees, one from the Exchequer and another from their own department. These are best referred to as Fees, with a capital F, to distinguish them from fees paid by the subject.

Stipendiary Fees varied greatly in amount, but by no means necessarily in relation to the importance or seniority of the posts to which they were attached. They were seldom if ever, the recipient's sole source of income from his office, nor in the vast majority of cases was there any intention or pretence that they should be. At one extreme we have offices like the Surveyor-Generalship of the

160

Customs with a Fee of £367 a year, and the Remembrancership of Greencloth, in charge of purveyance compositions for the Household, at £401 p.a. At the other extreme a Clerkship of the Signet carried no Fee at all, and by this time the £5 p.a. Fee previously attached to Clerkships of the Privy Seal seems to have lapsed.[1]

Many officers, especially the more senior ones and those who enjoyed Court favour, had these Fees supplemented in various ways by the Crown itself. Some received pensions or annuities. These were paid from either the Exchequer, the Wards, or the Duchy, or else they were deducted at source from one of the incoming revenue accounts before reaching the Exchequer. Contemporaries often used the words pension and annuity interchangeably, but formally annuities were granted for life or for a term of years, whereas pensions were more varied and in some cases more easily revocable. In times of acute financial difficulty or crisis the payment of all pensions and annuities was liable to be stopped by the King and the Lord Treasurer, while even in more normal times the payment of these and of ordinary stipendiary Fees was often heavily in arrears. In July 1628 orders were given for the total stoppage of all out-payments until the relief expedition for La Rochelle 'be satisfied'. In June 1625, on £49,964 annuities granted by James I, £65,643 was owing, that is, payment was on average a year and three to four months in arrears, although this arrearage was very unevenly distributed. In November 1635, on £750 due yearly in Fees from the Exchequer to the officers of the Armoury, £2,147 was owing, and on £379 to the artificers of the Great Wardrobe £962; but, on the whole Fee payments were quite well up to date in 1635. By 1640, c. £1,227 was owing on the £590 p.a. due to the officers of the Ordnance, and although the Armoury was slightly less behind than in 1635, in general payments had fallen further into arrears.[2]

Pensions and annuities were also paid to a number of courtiers who did not hold office and to various other people who for different reasons had secured the King's bounty. Except for the Lord Treasurer, the Lord Keeper or Chancellor, the Secretaries of State, and a few other very senior officers, pensions and annuities were paid to individuals and not, in theory, *ex officio* to the holders of particular

---

[1] SP 16/301/9; T 56/5, p. 59; *Cal. S.P. Dom., Additional 1625-49*, p. 197; *Chamberlain Letters*, II, 363-4; Hist. MSS. Comm. *Montague of Beaulieu*, p. 58; Peck, *Desiderata Curiosa*, I, ii, 1.

[2] PC 2/38, p. 288; SP 16/3/117, 301/9, 474/2.

F

posts. In most cases, therefore, it is best not to think of them as a regular and certain method of supplementation. In 1630-1 about 83 out of 123 people to whom King Charles had so far granted pensions held offices of one kind or another. Annuities granted under the Privy Seal show a heavier preponderance of office-holders.[1] In practice, some pensions and particularly several of the annuities authorized by Privy Seal tended to be granted almost as a matter of course to the holders of certain offices; in all but name these might seem to be *ex officio* grants. None the less, this type of supplementation depended more on Court favour and on the effectiveness of an officer's patrons than on his seniority, ability, or devotion to the royal service. For example, the Grooms in ordinary of the King's Bedchamber, of whom there were normally about six, each had a pension of £500 p.a., more than almost anyone else except a few peers and great officers of state. But a man would only be a Groom by virtue of enjoying royal favour; the favour, not the office, explains these pensions.

Other forms of supplementation by the Crown were less direct. Those in favour with the King or Queen and other officers with sufficiently influential patrons might receive grants of Crown property, and have the opportunity of buying or leasing Crown lands and woods at favourable rates; they might become patentees or even monopolists, sometimes under the guise of being royal commissioners; alternatively they might become farmers of some branch of the royal revenues or of fines imposed for the breach of certain laws. All this can best be illustrated by examples.

Sir Robert Aitoun, a Scot who had come south with King James, was Principal Secretary and Sole Master of Requests to the Queen. As such his Fee was £100, later raised to £126, 13s. 4d. a year; in addition he had two annuities granted by King James, totalling £640, and he received a special payment of £200 a year from the Cofferer of the Household. So his total annual income from the Crown was not far short of £1,000, a handsome amount for the third son of a not very prominent or affluent Fifeshire gentleman.[2]

Others were less fortunate. In the intervals of being Ambassador to the King of Spain, at a nominal rate of £6 a day (or £2,190 for a

[1] SP 16/180/16, pp. 13-17b.
[2] *D.N.B.*, I, 772-3; SP 16/180/18, 474/3; E 101/438/7, 438/14, Queen's Household accounts; National Library of Wales, Wynnstay MSS. 166, 168, paybooks of the Queen's officers.

full year), Walter, Lord Aston, was glad to be made Keeper of the mulberry gardens and the silk worms at St James's, with a stipend of £60 p.a. According to his son, Aston's stipend and allowances as Ambassador were hopelessly in arrears when he died in 1639; in 1640 the Fee for the St. James's post was two and a half years over-due, and no successor had been appointed.[1] When he surrendered the Surveyorship of the Navy in 1632, Sir Thomas Aylesbury was compensated with a monopoly of the making and sale of weights and balances to test the coins in the Mint or anywhere else where they were to be tested in England, Wales, or Ireland, for which he paid a rent of £1 p.a. to the King; as a Master of Requests he already had a Fee of £100 a year. The weights and balances patent was probably not so much a *quid pro quo* for the Surveyorship as an interim reward for other services; in June 1631 he had been appointed chief com-missioner to investigate, and if possible settle, a dispute about various offices in the Mint. In July 1635, after this had been cleared up, he himself became co-Master at a Fee of £500 p.a.[2]

The exact arrangements were almost as numerous as the individual cases. Sir Thomas Fanshawe of Jenkins, Essex was Surveyor-General of Crown lands from 1625 to his death in 1631, as well as Clerk of the Crown in King's Bench. He appears to have used the former position to facilitate his purchase of the royal manor of Barking, on what were later alleged to have been scandalously favourable terms; at the least the price was somewhat reduced from its probable value on the open market.[3] Robert Kirkham, Signet Clerk, received £50 p.a. from the Crown as Surveyor of the salt-works at North and South Shields, while along with all the other Signet and Council Clerks he was on the royal commission to regu-late the brewing trade, a body which had power to compound with offenders against various laws and regulations. A few years earlier Kirkham had been reduced to asking for a patent to keep the die-stamps which were used for the marking of 'plate' when it was

---

[1] *D.N.B.*, I, 685; *Cal. S.P. Dom.*, *1628-9*, pp. 192, 324, *1634-5*, p. 403, *1637*, p. 520-1, *1638-9*, p. 60, *1639-40*, p. 252-3; SP 16/301/9, 474/2; *Cal. Clarendon State Papers*, vol. I, ed. O. Ogle, W. H. Bliss (Oxford, 1872), 69; Fanshawe MSS. (Bratton Fleming), notes on Ambassadors' pay.

[2] *D.N.B.*, I, 749; Craig, *Mint*, p. 146; *Cal. S.P. Dom.*, *1631-3*, pp. 46, 461-2, *1634-5*, pp. 7-8; SP 16/301/9; *Foedera*, XIX, 287-9, 390-3, XX, 200.

[3] Fanshawe MSS. (copies of documents in the P.R.O.).

tested for the proper silver content.[1] Although he held a small office in Chancery and was Receiver of Fines on tobacco licences as well as Muster Master-General of England, Thomas Meautys, Clerk of the Council, twice asked for a patent to oversee and enforce the clearing up of offal and other offensive remains by the London butchers, with power to take fees from them.[2] Christopher Vernon, First Secondary of the Pipe Office and Surveyor of Greenwax, made a speciality of discovering the titles to lost or concealed Crown lands; he was rewarded for this with lump-sum payments in 1628 and again in 1636, but his petition for the grant of some other debts which were owed to the Crown, as a reward for this unsolicited investigation of his own superior, Sir Henry Croke the Clerk of the Pipe, was less well received. In the end he got rather less than half what he had asked for.[3]

Apart from someone like Fanshawe, who was almost uniquely well placed by virtue of his office, favourable land sales and leases may more often have been made to courtiers and great officers than to these lesser administrators. They in consequence were more likely to be reduced to trying for patents or commissions, or—the last resort of all, greater and lesser, courtiers and officials, alike—for something in Ireland. While it should not be imagined as rigid, this contrast is quite marked. In 1630 Gillingham Forest, Dorset, and the surrounding land was granted to Sir James Fullarton, Groom of the Stole, and after an anti-enclosure riot there he was granted the forfeited bail bonds of those who had been bound over for taking part in it as well as the fines imposed on some of them in Star Chamber. At only £11 p.a. the rent which he owed for the Forest was derivisely low; for a further 2,400 acres of so-called waste he paid only £120 p.a. Over and above this and the very considerable emoluments of his office, Fullarton had a £300 a year pension from the Court of Wards.[4]

The higher up the ladder we look, the more such supplementation we find. When he was Chancellor of the Exchequer, Cottington bought a sizeable Crown property in Somerset on what appear to

---

[1] *Cal. S.P. Dom., 1631-3*, p. 217; *Foedera*, XX, 101, 125; T 56/3, p. 108.

[2] See Chapter 3, pp. 133-4; also *Cal. S.P. Dom., 1639*, p. 472, *Additional, 1625-49*, p. 619; T 56/1, p. 3b.

[3] *Cal. S.P. Dom., 1628-9*, p. 100, *1635*, p. 571, *1638-9*, pp. 72-3, 596; T 56/14, pp. 180-1; T 56/5, p. 33; E 403/2591, pp. 31, 38b-40, 68.

[4] *Cal. S.P. Dom., 1625-6*, p. 68, *1629-31*, p. 552; SP 16/180/17.

have been very favourable terms, and a large part of the purchase money for his main Wiltshire estate was deducted from his own loans to the Crown, again probably to his material advantage.[1] Buckingham, of course, provides the supreme example. But perhaps 'example' is the wrong word; it implies that recklessly extravagant grants to royal officers were typical. But even towards the top of the ladder this was not so. And the great majority of officials in the middle ranks had to be content at best with appointment to subsidiary offices, which as has been explained were not normally sinecures in the full sense, with membership of royal commissions, which were sometimes but by no means always profitable for their members, and less often with slightly preferential treatment concerning minor grants and leases.

The ceaseless quest by many office-holders for annuities, leases, grants, and so on must be related to the non-existence of any retirement pensions in the modern sense. A man who left office voluntarily before he died was more often than not reckoning to receive a lump sum, or an annuity, or both from his successor. Occasionally the Crown paid a lump sum to a retiring officer. Royal pensions were sometimes granted to an officer *and* his wife for as long as *either* of them was still alive, or to an officer *and* his son and to the longer lived of them. These acted in practice like pensions for widows and dependants, but they were far from usual, and were scarcely ever granted *ex officio*; more seem to have been granted to courtiers than to office-holders. In 1628 the dependants of two ex-Ordnance Surveyors received pensions; but at least one had been killed on active service overseas, besides his family had Villiers connexions.[2] This was not typical. Apart from those who were dismissed or bullied into resigning, most office-holders showed a marked reluctance to retire, and it was more usual for them to die in harness.

Some officers made up for inadequate Fees and pensions by becoming monopolists, patentees or members of those royal commissions which in practice were used as revenue-raising devices. But it would be wrong to identify patentees or monopolists with office-holders: there was an overlap between the two categories, no more. However, it may very well have seemed to those outside government circles that almost the entire administration was contaminated in this way. In fact, taking a sample of 118 officers (of all

[1] *Cal. S.P. Dom., 1631-3*, p. 173; E 403/2591 p. 34b.
[2] See *Cal. S.P. Dom., 1628-9*, pp. 163, 165.

ranks), on the widest definition only 18, or about 15 per cent., seem to have been involved in this aspect of the régime.

Some of the other ways in which officers were paid by the Crown appear simple and straightforward by contrast. A few of the departmental accountants were paid on a commission basis, known as Poundage, usually 3d. or 6d. in every £1 which they handled. The Lieutenant of the Ordnance, the Treasurer of the Navy, and the Queen's Treasurer and Receiver-General took poundage; the Lieutenant only on the ordinary (standing peacetime) allocation for the Ordnance, the other two on all the money they handled. This gave them a strong incentive to keep expenditure up; the other principal officers of the Navy were very bitter about the Treasurer's profits on poundage compared to the niggardliness of their own Fees and allowances. The collectors of some revenues, e.g. the 19 Receivers-General of the Crown land revenues, were allowed Portage, again a fixed percentage of all the money which they brought up to the Exchequer, in this case an incentive to efficiency, but perhaps also to over-rigorous exactions from the King's tenants and others.

Wentworth was involved in an interesting clash over poundage and portage. In 1633 he protested to the Lord Treasurer that 5 per cent. portage as Receiver of the northern recusant revenues would only come to about £500 for four years, and some months later he said that his portage fees since he had become Receiver in 1629 would amount to under £400. This was presumably calculated on the net yield of these revenues to the Exchequer; it is possible that he also received poundage, at a lower rate, on the money which he himself paid out.[1] It is therefore rather surprising to find that part of his attack on Lord Mountnorris, Vice-Treasurer and Treasurer-at-wars in Ireland, related to poundage, which Mountnorris had been taking at the rate of 6d. in the £1, or 2½ per cent. Wentworth, by then Lord Deputy of Ireland, told Secretary Coke that Mountnorris should be content with his 'very fair Fee' from the Crown, and that the Irish Admiralty officers were complaining of the loss of £25 out of every £1,000 on their estimate. Apart from the fact that he was taking it on a revenue instead of on a spending account, someone might well have objected to Wentworth's getting at least £50 in every £1,000 on the recusant money! Only after delay, and with some reluctance on the part of the King and the Privy Council, was he authorized to go ahead with his proceedings against Mount-

[1] Knowler, I, 89-90, 142-3; T 56/2.

norris. Meanwhile, not long before his breach with the Vice-Treasurer in 1634, Wentworth was authorized to take 2½ per cent. (6d. in the £) portage on the revenue from compositions paid in the north of England by those who had failed to get themselves knighted at King Charles's coronation. Out of this revenue he had already been granted £3,396, which was now said to have been solely for repairs to the Lord President's and the Council's premises at York, and not for his current expenses either as Lord President or as manager of the knighthood revenues. This new grant of portage would seem the less defensible in that he had been Lord President in absence since January 1633.[1]

Receivers had another more clandestine way of supplementing their income. This consisted of using the cash balances on their accounts for their own private purposes during the interval between collecting the revenue in question and paying it in to the Exchequer of Receipt (or, as the case might be, making direct out-payments). There was no need for an accountant to pay in his cash balance for a particular year to the Receipt until just before he was going to have his account for that year audited in the Upper Exchequer. Meanwhile, the money was his, to make what use of it he could. This practice does not seem to have been officially sanctioned, neither does much seem to have been done to prevent it. The time which elapsed between the collection of revenues and the passing of the accounts on which they were entered varied widely. It might be a matter of weeks, months, or years; but an interval within the range six months to two years was usual, and it was often even longer. Furthermore, the Receiver might enjoy up to another twelve months' start, depending on how early in the accounting year he could collect the money. In 1637 Wentworth reckoned that as Receiver of the northern recusant revenues he ought, if all was managed properly, to have the constant use of £4,000 to £5,000 in hand. This, he told one of his agents, 'was in Truth the chief Benefit of the Place'.

By contrast, some revenues were earmarked for out-payment every quarter. The opportunities for Receivers to make use of cash balances probably diminished according to the proportion of a given revenue which was 'assigned' in this way direct to spending departments, individual officers and pensioners, or royal creditors. As to the converse of these practices, in theory there was nothing to stop Treasurers of spending departments from using their cash

[1] Knowler, I, 250, 448; *Cal. S.P. Dom., Adds. 1625-49*, p. 476.

balances in the interval between receiving money and having to pay it out. But, although some of them were past masters at delaying payment even when they had the money, the general state of royal finance was such that this offered far less scope.

The Receivers-General of the Wards and the Duchy were in a special position. Their accounts were audited, but not in the Upper Exchequer, in addition they acted as their own Exchequer of Receipt, often (especially in the case of the Duchy) having money left in hand, after all out-payments were made, and their accounts passed. In part they combined the role of revenue receivers with that of treasurers responsible for expenditure. This must have offered unique opportunities for making use of balances in hand—and unique temptations to commit downright fraud.

The exact value of this form of supplementation cannot be worked out. But in an age of long-term inflation combined with a chronic scarcity of ready capital, its significance should not be underrated. However, like portage and poundage, only relatively few office-holders were able to take advantage of it.[1]

Many more officers had their Fees supplemented in kind or by money commutations of this. The most important of these forms of supplementation was 'Diet', or free board. It was the lavish provision of diet for courtiers and court officials which made the King's Household below stairs the costliest single department of government and in peacetime helped to keep the cost of all the household departments at around 40 per cent. of the total royal budget. What menus they were! The King, with his 24 meat-dishes twice daily, clearly fed his personal friends and also some of the Bedchamber officers from his own table. The Lord Steward, the Treasurer, and the Comptroller of the Household each with two tables of ten and six meat-dishes twice daily, the Groom of the Stole with two tables of seven dishes, the Lord Chamberlain with a ten-dish table, and the Cofferer and the Master of the Household each with a seven-dish table, must all have needed the help of their servants, under-officers, friends, relatives, suitors, and clients to face these groaning boards. Only when we get down to a three-dish diet, that is three meat-dishes twice daily, is there any conceivable prospect of one man, cast in however Gargantuan a mould, having done justice to them single

[1] See P.R.O., Exchequer, various and declared accounts; Duchy of Lancaster, Receiver-General's accounts; Wards, Receiver-General's accounts, etc., for the time lag in passing accounts; Knowler, II, 123.

handed. Tables, or diets, were also allocated to groups of officers. The nine officers of the Compting House (the central accounting bureau of the Household) shared a three-dish diet; the four Gentlemen Ushers of the Chamber had two five-dish diets, but various other Chamber officers, such as the Cupbearers, Carvers, Sewers, Esquires of the Body, and Gentlemen Ushers daily and quarter waiters, none of whom received diet of their own, may have reckoned to eat at their tables; and the six or eight Grooms of the Privy Chamber had one five-dish diet. Some officers who were not technically members of the Household had tables there: for instance the Secretaries of State and, sometimes, the Lord Privy Seal.

Most of the diets attached to the holders of individual offices were commutable into money payments, known as Board Wages. The initiative for this might come from the officer, if he expected to be absent from Court for any length of time; otherwise it came from the Crown in the interests of economy.[1] The value of diets, whether taken in kind or in cash, can be worked out from the Household accounts and other records, which in some cases show their cost as tables, in others the commutation rate; the lesser diets were reduced in value within five years of Charles's accession.

TABLE 6. VALUE OF DIETS[2]

Number of (meat) dishes in diet (other than on 'fish days') .	10	7	6	5	4	3	2
Value or commutation rate (p.a.) .	£1,095	c. £850	c. £750	£635	£440	£390	£230
The same before 1629-30 .	£1,095	c. £850	c. £750	£710	£490	£410	£250

As well as the officers who ate at Court, or else drew board wages from the Cofferer of the Household, diet or board allowances were enjoyed by *certain* officers of other courts and departments. Allowances for board, lodging, and transport were allowed to the principal officers of the Ordnance when they were out of town on official business. But below the level of great officers, diet was primarily an addition to the real value of household offices.

The figures given above for diets include estimates for the value

[1] On the last point see also G. E. Aylmer, 'Attempts at Administrative Reform, 1625-40', *Eng. Hist. Rev.*, LXXII (1957).

[2] SP 16/43/12, 178/6, 7, 339/3; LS 13/169.

of another payment in kind, 'Bouge' or 'bouche of court'. Bouge consisted of bread and ale (*N.B.* only the King's and Queen's diets included any provision for breakfast), firewood, and candles. Roughly speaking, the size of an officer's bouge depended on his diet, but quite a number of lesser Household and Chamber officers who got no diet of their own did get bouge. Bouge was not usually commutable; however, individual officers with two-dish diet and above could have it commuted at the low rate of £12, 3s. 4d. p.a., or 2d. a day. The biggest bouges consisted of three loaves, three gallons of ale, three torches, one lb. of wax, ten pieces of wood, and eight faggots a day; in 1526 the two top grades had been valued at £39, 13s. 3d. and £37, 12s. 0d. p.a. respectively, and by *c.* 1630 they must have been worth at least three times as much. Even the lowest grade, at half a loaf and half a gallon of ale, must have been worth all of 2d. a day by the 1630's.[1]

Bouge too was often allocated to a group of officers. At the lower end of the scale there were simply bloc allowances of so many loaves and gallons a day. The scale of these allowances, over and above the diets and bouges of individuals and groups of officers, can be seen in the amount of waste which was allowed. Both the sets of Household ordinances which date from 1627-30, when an economy campaign was supposed to be in force, set the *maximum* waste permissible daily at 200 loaves, 240 gallons of ale, twenty-four gallons of wine, and except on Fridays and Feast Days, eight sides of beef. This was in addition to sixty loaves and eighty gallons a day for the duty Yeomen of the Guard.

Diet, in short, was a very wasteful way of paying people. It is no wonder that from the King's own 48 dishes a day down to the scraps collected by the lowest porters and scullions the Household's average annual bill for diet in the early 1630's, on the whole a period of economy, was *c.* £47,000, or 6·5 per cent. of the Crown's total expenditure. Diet for the Queen and her household cost another £20,000 p.a., and by the mid-1630's that for the royal children and their establishments was running at £15,000, rising to over £20,000 p.a. By the end of the decade the total cost of diet for the King's and Queen's and their children's households was over £107,000 a

---

[1] B.M., Additional MS. 6418; LS 13/30; LS 13/279, p. 107b; *A Collection of Ordinances and Regulations for the Government of the Royal Household from Edward III to King William and Queen Mary* (Society of Antiquaries, 1790), pp. 162-4.

year. If it had been administratively and politically possible to limit diets in kind to what the royal family and their immediate attendants could themselves eat, £80,000 to £90,000 a year of this might have been available for raising stipendiary Fees or for the general purposes of government. But in the circumstances of the time there was no chance of this being done.

There were recognized perquisites in kind for certain officers in the Kitchens and other sub-departments below stairs. The Sergeant of the Cellar had a right to all empty wine-casks; other Cellar and Buttery officers had a joint right to four fingers at the bottom of every bottle that was opened; all fish heads and tails belonged to the Chief Kitchen Clerk and the Master Cooks; some of the skins, tallow, and heads of meat carcasses went to the Cooks; various officers of the Acatry (the principal buying department) got the heads, midriffs, paunches, belly, tails, and feet of all oxen, the heads of all muttons, the skins, heads, and feet of all calves.[1] With a little judicious mis-measuring and mis-cutting some of them may have been able to set up in business on their own account, reselling these bits and pieces.

A few Household officers also received special allowances on the annual accounts. Food and other supplies left over at the end of the accounting year, and the hides and tallow from most of the meat carcasses were sold by the Crown. Of the money raised from hides and tallows, two-thirds was supposed to go to the King, as an in-payment to the Cofferer of the Household, and one-third to the Cofferer and the heads of the sub-departments concerned, this being known as the 'Third Penny'. But until 1638 (and perhaps later) the unused supplies and these leavings were normally sold at cut rates to these very officers, or to their colleagues; they were then resold on the open market at considerable profit. To cap everything, from 1597 to 1638, by an almost incredibly brazen piece of juggling, the sales of unused supplies and the Third Penny sales were entered on *both* sides of the Cofferer's account, appearing as incomings and as outgoings. The Cofferer (or co-Cofferers) and the Sergeants and Clerks of the sub-departments pocketed the lot, value from 1625 to 1634 *c.* £10,500 p.a.![2] Except for the forty years' accounting fraud,

[1] LS 13/279.
[2] P.R.O., Exchequer, various and declared accounts, Household. (The Crown's average gain from the stopping of this fraud was £11,546 p.a., 1638-41.)

everything here was perfectly legal: as late as 1627 the third Earl of Pembroke, then Lord Steward, declared that the sales for such provisions

> as anciently have been allowed to the officers of his Majesty's house and others of his Majesty's servants be still continued at his Majesty's usual and accustomed prices as in former times, so the overplus of his Majesty's provisions will bear it.[1]

Only in 1638 was an order issued that all sales should be at the best (market) price obtainable. No sooner had this been done, and the ordinary and Third Penny sales taken off the out-payments' side of the Cofferer's account, than the cost of diet rose by over £10,000 a year. This sudden increase may be explained by visits from royal relatives, or by the northern expeditions of 1639 and 1640 (leading to heavier commitments and higher prices). But neither of these explanations is in fact convincing: the King's two nephews (the Palatinate Princes) cost the Household £8,576 in 1636-7, nothing in 1637-8, and £835 in 1638-9, the Queen Mother (Mary de Medicis) £3,393 in 1638-9, and £288 in 1640-1, the Prince of Nassau (before and after his marriage to the King's daughter, including the wedding) £3,690 in 1640-1, but none of these items were included in the cost of diet; the sudden increase of £10,648 came in the year ending Michaelmas 1638, before any northern expedition, and even if the first 'Bishops' War' does account for the further rise of £2,961 in 1638-9, the second saw a drop in the cost of diet (on the 1639-40 account) almost to the 1637-8 level. It therefore seems much more likely that the officers practised a further deliberate fraud in order to make good their losses from the detection of the previous one![2]

In various other departments there were legitimate perquisites for some of the officers. These too, such as the right of dockyard officials to dispose of wood chippings and other remains, were very open to abuse. The other widespread form of payment in kind, which like diet could sometimes be commuted, was less vulnerable. Many officers of all ranks received an issue of uniform or other clothing, or a money allowance to buy uniform, known as Livery. Some officers' liveries were charged on the accounts of their respective courts and departments, but the great majority were charged on the Great Wardrobe, the semi-autonomous department, whose

---

[1] LS 13/169, Lord Steward misc. warrant book, p. 2.
[2] Household accounts.

Master, like the Master of the Ordnance, was in the category of those who were just *not* 'great officers'. Some officers received individual outfits or payments direct from the issuing branch of the Great Wardrobe; for others, like the Yeomen of the Guard, their own departmental treasurer or paymaster received a block allocation. Individual livery payments totalled rather over £3,400 p.a. for the years 1626-37, but very few single ones exceeded £20-£30 p.a. Several thousands more were paid out for liveries to whole groups of officers.[1] As a form of payment, livery was not negligible, helping particularly the men at the lower end of the ladder, but in scale it resembled Bouge rather than Diet and Board Wages.

Another financial asset was negative rather than positive. Some office-holders enjoyed immunity from some forms of taxation and personal service. The Queen's French musicians did not have to pay subsidies and impositions; the officers of the Mint were for some reason exempt from contributing to Purveyance, whereby the royal household was supplied at below market rates; in 1641 they also claimed exemption from subsidies. There are indeed signs that the entire staff of the Household was seeking to establish immunity from all taxes. In December 1632 the Council specifically denied the existence of any such exemption and directed that this ruling should be made known to all concerned. James and Charles I did grant 'protections' against taxation to individual officers, like those which could be granted to debtors to guard them from their creditors (e.g. in 1633 to Inigo Jones). But under Charles I there is no sign of any general policy along these lines; and on the whole tax exemption was not a major attraction of office-holding in England.

There were other related immunities. In 1625 the court of Common Pleas ruled that none of its attorneys or clerks, quite apart from its officers, could be 'pressed' for military service, or 'elected' to any other office, e.g. in local government, *'sine voluntate sua'*; nine years later the judges of King's Bench decided that one of the attorneys in their court could not be compelled to serve as a Tithing-man, or Constable, in Taunton, on account of a particular house which he owned there. With these privileges can be associated the general right of all officers, attorneys, and clerks of any law court to sue and be sued in their own court. Such 'fringe benefits' as these lie on

[1] AO 1/2350/56, 2351/59, declared accounts, Great Wardrobe; E 351/ 3094-3102; LC 5/38, Lord Chamberlain's dept., Great Wardrobe, warrants; SP 16/178/10-11, 468/95.

173

the borderline between the financial advantages of office-holding and the conditions of service under the Crown.[1]

For many officers the most important single source of income was provided by fees, paid sometimes by other officials but more often by members of the public. They are described as fees with a small f, to distinguish them from stipendiary Fees paid by the Crown.

Such fees were paid at every stage in litigation and in all other legal proceedings, at every stage in the passing of all grants from the Crown, and on all audits in the upper, and all cash or credit transactions in the lower Exchequer, and correspondingly in the other revenue departments. Those most dependent on fees were therefore the officers and clerks of the Signet, Privy and Great Seals, the staffs of *all* the law courts—whether common law, equity, prerogative, or ecclesiastical—and the officers of the Exchequer, the Court of Wards and Liveries, and the Duchy of Lancaster. The royal prisons were also run on the fee system, and so, outside the central government, were parish churches, the London livery companies and similar mercantile bodies, town corporations, and other local institutions. By contrast, the Lord and Deputy Lieutenants and the J.P.s stand out as *not* having received fees, even though they had no stipendiary Fees from the Crown.

As with other aspects of the system (e.g. tenure), to explain how, when, and why exactly what fees had been fixed for what transactions would involve a prolonged and intensive study of the sources from the fourteenth, if not from the twelfth, to the sixteenth century. And at the end of it we should probably only have a fragmentary and unsatisfactory set of answers. Subject to correction by specialists on medieval administrative history, it seems unlikely that the full story of how this came about can ever be properly told. However, many fee payments in the law and revenue courts and at the Seals can be shown to have been established and officially recognized by the mid-fifteenth century. Then came the long series of institutional

[1] See E. F. Churchill, 'The Crown and its Servants', *Law Quarterly Rev.*, XLII (1926), 81-95, 212-29, 382-93, esp. pp. 94-5, which I think overrates the extent of tax immunities; also *Cal. S.P. Dom.*, *1627-8*, p. 475, *1628-9*, p. 454, *1638-9*, p. 33; Croke, *Reports* (1683), III, 11, 389; Aylmer, 'The Last Years of Purveyance 1610-60', *Econ. Hist. Rev.*, 2nd ser. X (1957) 89, n. 1; *The Journal of Sir Simonds D'Ewes*, ed. W. H. Coates (New Haven, 1942), p. 181; PC 2/42, p. 353; *Knyvett Letters*, p. 102; P.R.O., Index to Patent Rolls, 9 Charles I 4/22 (grant of tax exemption to Inigo Jones, 1633).

changes in the central government from *c.* 1470 to *c.* 1560, accompanied and followed by the gradual inflation of *c.* 1530 to *c.* 1630. It would be difficult to prove any close *direct* connexion between these two sequences of events, but happening as they did in conjunction, they had a great effect on the system of fee payments to officers, and on the problems to which this system gave rise in Elizabethan and early Stuart times. To take the institutional changes first, the marked growth of conciliar, other prerogative, and equity jurisdiction and the erection of new revenue courts and offices led to a relative, though not necessarily an absolute decline in the amount of business done by some officers in the common law courts and the Exchequer. The total volume of litigation may have been increasing so rapidly— for never it seems was there a more litigious age—that in the common law courts the loss was only relative, but in some branches of the upper Exchequer it was almost certainly absolute.

Now let us consider, on top of this, the effects of the 'price revolution'. Suppose that in the fifteenth century a given officer had received 2d. for every sheet of a given type of document which passed through his department, and that on average 300 such documents had gone through yearly, of average length three sheets each; his income from this source would have been $2 \times 300 \times 3 = 1,800$ pence or £7, 10s. 0d. p.a. And suppose for the sake of argument that the real value of money had fallen threefold between that date and the early seventeenth century; his successor in the same office would need to make £22, 10s. 0d. p.a. out of this type of document in order to enjoy the same real income from this source. To achieve this, he might devise, or help others so affected in devising, means to widen the range of cases or transactions in which documents of this type were required, and on which he could legitimately claim a fee. Failing this, or even despite it, he would be under constant temptation either to take more than 2d. a sheet, or to space out the writing so that the documents averaged more than three sheets each, or to encroach on the business of other officers and clerks so that more than 300 of these documents were drafted yearly. Often we find all these expedients in use at once; even so, a hypothetical increase to a fee of 3d., and to an average of 400 items a year, averaging four sheets each would still only mean a yield of £20 p.a., or less in real value than the yield of £7, 10s. 0d. in the fifteenth century. In the drive to keep up with inflation and with the changing pattern of legal and financial business, most of the office-holders who were affected relied primarily on taking larger fees. In the next section of this chapter we shall take one department, the Exchequer, and follow the story of increased, or as contemporaries often called them 'exacted', fees from the late sixteenth century to 1640. But we must remember that the same basic problem existed for all the many central and local, civil and ecclesiastical officers who were dependent on fees for a large part of their livelihood. The royal commissions of 1610-11, 1623-4, and 1627-40 on 'exacted fees' were only one by-product of this problem. In 1609 increased fees were authorized for the officers of the Council in the North, and were later challenged, independently it appears, of the fee commissioners. And in the 1630's it was proposed to pay the Masters in Chancery more because their posts had fallen in value.[1]

Unlike the other forms of direct payment which we have so far dealt with, the value of fees to particular officers can seldom be estimated with any accuracy. The size of the individual fee is often known, be it 2d. or 6s. 8d. or £5, but it is scarcely ever possible to find out how many times a year the officer in question would on average have received it. This in turn makes it almost impossible to assess the total annual value of many legal and financial posts. Where there is evidence, of varying degrees of reliability, for the *total* annual value of particular offices, it is easy, if we know how much to deduct for stipend, diet, etc., to arrive at residual totals. Unluckily it does not follow that these represent what the holders of the offices in question received in fees.

It is usually difficult and often impossible to distinguish fees from the most important unofficial, but *not* illegal, forms of payment— gratuities. To a great extent fees themselves had originated in this way, and had only been authorized by the Crown or by the heads of the respective departments after they had become stereotyped through customary usage. A fee differs only in degree from a gratuity: its amount is more strictly regulated and its warranty is more official. If a gratuity is taken, at a more or less standard rate, for the rendering of the same service over a long enough time, it can sometimes become a fee without anyone being aware of the transition, at least not until after it has happened. This, it appears, had been a constant process in the fifteenth and sixteenth centuries. Sometimes officers received gratuities in addition to fees for the same services rendered;

[1] Leeds P.L., Temple Newsam MSS., Council in the North, 6-7, 25-7, 35-7, 118; *Cal. S.P. Dom., 1635-6*, p. 422.

this was often so in the law and revenue courts and perhaps even more the rule at the Seals and in the central executive generally. But gratuities were also given in return for services, or in the course of transactions where no official fee payments took place; this was true of those received by the naval patronage secretary and by various officers in the greater spending departments—Household, Great Wardrobe, Navy, and Ordnance.

There is a further if even more obscure distinction to be drawn among the forms of payment, between gratuities and presents. To our way of thinking the concept of a gratuity, or tip, implies a customarily expected payment for a specific service and a tacitly accepted, if unofficial, tariff. A 'present' suggests more of a personal and less of a business connexion between giver and receiver, and perhaps also more of an *ad hoc* once-for-all occasion for the gift. At court however, the giving of presents was formalized. Vast quantities of silver plate changed hands in the form of New Year gifts; during the rest of the year money, jewelry, venison, and game were more usual presents. Apart from the Crown, it is hard to see who was the net gainer from all this. Some of these presents were genuine gifts made to personal friends, where calculations of profit and loss or political advantage did not enter, but in general the more senior an officer, and the more 'arrived' a courtier, then the more subordinates and clients, the fewer patrons and superiors he had, and the more he was likely to be enriched every New Year.

Presents given to courtiers or officials for specific services, as opposed to annual New Year gifts, differ, practically speaking, only in name from gratuities. Even so, a slight distinction should perhaps be drawn by the modern observer, as it probably was by contemporaries. Some idea of contemporary distinctions between fees, gratuities, and presents can be obtained from the printed papers of Richard Boyle, created Earl of Cork in 1620. In the summer of 1629 Cork sent Attorney-General Heath a total of £300 'for his favor & fees in passing my patents for my lands & yron'; on the occasion of his son being knighted in 1624 he had paid the Lord Deputy of Ireland's officers £40, 'their demands being' £37, 10s. 0d., that is for their fees. In both cases a gratuity is thrown in, over and above the exact fees which are due. Significantly it was 'my present of golde' (and *not* 'my gratuity') which Secretary Coke declined in 1629; some months earlier Cork had wooed sixteen of the leading men in the English court and government with New Year presents amounting to £216, 10s. 0d. worth of silver plate and a miscellany of presents in kind, most of which were 'white elephants' which had been given to him for this or some previous New Year. In February 1631/2 he sent a diamond ring as a present to Secretary Dorchester, then in principal charge of Irish business in England. In 1628 Mr. Noy, 'the great lawyer of Lincoln's Inn', returned eight out of ten 'pieces' (guineas) offered to him as a retaining fee; Cork retained the Attorney-General himself by fee in 1628 and his successor in 1637; at one stage in the 1630's he had eight lawyers on retainers of £2 a term and upwards. Like fees, gratuities could be once-for-all payments for specific services, such as the £10 given to Strafford's agent at court, Mr. William Railton, in February 1639/40, or recurrent, like the £40 p.a. which Cork, when he was co-Lord Justice of Ireland (1629-33), undertook to pay to Sir William Becher, secretary to the Irish committee of the Privy Council.[1]

Granted the rashness of generalizing from one source, something emerges from this. What were called fees would seem to have been paid to lawyers and law officers, and to the officials involved in passing grants, honours, and other patents; gratuities might be paid to the same people over and above these fees, but more typically they were given to under-officers and private servants, to 'my Lord Keeper's man' or to 'Mr. Secretary's secretary'; presents, apart from New Year largesse to underlings like the Porters, the Trumpeters and the Guard, were given or offered to great officers, important courtiers, peers. A fee was therefore the most formal and routine form of payment, and of the other two by and large a gratuity was given to an inferior (albeit sometimes a very influential one) and a present was offered to an equal or a superior.

The income of officers from gratuities and presents is naturally even harder to work out than that from fees. Apart from chance remarks in letters, there are virtually no sources which record these forms of payment. As with fees, in a few cases it is possible to deduct from the known total annual value of the offices the income from all other sources and to equate the residue with gratuities, etc.

If on one side presents and gratuities are often difficult to distinguish from fees, on the other they sometimes seem to merge with unofficial and illegal payments, namely bribes. This is partly a

[1] *The Lismore Papers*, 1st ser., II, 137, 264, 293-4, 335, 339, III, 70, 126-7, IV, 5-6, 91, 108-9, 146, V, 10, 120, 126, etc. Compare *Cal. Court Minutes East India Co.* 1640-3, p. 129.

matter of definition. Today tipping a public servant, other than someone like a railway porter, smacks of impropriety. But it would be a great mistake to equate tips with bribes in seventeenth-century England. At that time bribery implied an attempt to persuade an official to follow a course of action other than that which he knew he ought to have followed. It implied the acceptance of a present or gratuity by an official, knowing that its purpose was to influence his decision improperly. Nowadays a bribe does not even have to do this: if x, a contractor, offers a present to y, a civil servant, or to z, a politician, and if they accept it and give a contract to x's firm, then bribery has still taken place even if x's firm is the best in the world and the government has got the best possible terms.

This was not so in the seventeenth century. The distinction can be illustrated from Francis Bacon's case in 1621. As Lord Chancellor, Bacon had been accepting presents far in excess of the normal gratuities from parties to cases in Chancery; although he was able to show that his decisions had all been legally impeccable and had not been in any way affected by these gifts, it was clear that improper decisions were being sought by the donors. Because he had accepted such presents when he must have known this, he fell resoundingly from his great office and died a broken man five years later. Corruption of one kind or another was almost invariably alleged against a minister or great officer who was really being attacked for other, more important reasons. This was true of Cranfield in 1624, Buckingham in 1626, Strafford in 1640-1, Laud in 1640-4, Clarendon in 1667. Bacon's case was untypical in that his accusers' motives were genuinely more administrative than political: the parliament of 1621 was out to clean up the government. This was only a minor consideration in the other cases mentioned, except Cranfield's. During the debates in the Lords on the charges against him, a clear distinction was drawn between 'rewards', that is presents or gratuities, and 'bribes', which in his case were also said to be related to extortions, e.g. of excessive fees.[1]

It was not uncommon for charges of corruption to be brought against particular ministers or officials by individual litigants and even by their own colleagues. In 1634 there was an unsuccessful attack on Lord Treasurer Portland by his fellow-councillors, Archbishop Laud and Lord Keeper Coventry. The next year Coventry

[1] *Lords Debates in 1624 and 1626* (ed. S. R. Gardiner, Camden Soc., 1879), pp. 77-9.

himself was accused of corruption; the charges were found to be false, and, not being powerful enough to deflect his counter-attack, the Lord Keeper's accusers were found guilty and sentenced variously to fines, imprisonment, and the pillory. In 1638 a similar charge against him failed, and his accuser again suffered a penal fine. A more famous case, in which the judges of Star Chamber divided nine to nine (excluding the Lord Keeper's casting vote), was in effect a posthumous condemnation of Portland. The Lord Treasurer, through his personal control over all out-payments, and the Lord Keeper, as the senior *equity* judge, were perhaps uniquely exposed to these temptations. However, those who accused them had often tried to bribe them and failed, or else had been unable to distinguish between a bribe and a present or gratuity.[1] Arbitrary and unclear as the distinction may seem to us, contemporaries certainly tried to draw one.

The extent of bribery in the early seventeenth century is therefore partly a matter of definition. In the law courts corruption may have come to be the form most often assumed by those earlier evils, Embracery and Maintenance. We cannot consider here how far the proper course of justice could still be perverted by the corruption and intimidation of judges, jurors, witnesses, and court officials, or by the promotion of false and malicious suits. Until recently all this was believed to have been stamped out by the Tudors; the present tendency among historians is to suppose that a good deal went on until about the turn of the seventeenth to eighteenth centuries. Until the results of more research on this have been published, we can only say that *some* Embracery and *some* Maintenance, under whatever names, probably did persist through the Stuart period, and that royal officials may on occasions have profited thereby. But it would be a mistake to reckon bribes as a normal form of payment, despite the corruption of individual officers and even of whole departments, which was probably at its worst under James I, in the years *c.* 1613-21.

The payment of deputies and under-clerks is closely related to the

---

[1] Gardiner, *History*, VII, 355-6 (the attack by Laud and Coventry on Portland); Knowler, I, 426; *Cal. S.P. Dom., 1637-8*, p. 491; H. R. Plomer, 'The King's Printing House under the Stuarts', *The Library*, new series, II (1901), 353-75 (the various charges against Coventry); Gardiner, *History*, VIII, 89-91 (the often cited case of Pell, James I's one time Master of the Hawks, *versus* Bagg, his would-be broker with Portland).

distinction between fees, gratuities, and bribes. Officially recognized deputies sometimes had their own appointed fees in addition to those which they collected for their masters; so in certain offices had the chief under-clerks, who are often difficult to distinguish from informal deputies. Otherwise the deputy was paid a fixed annual salary out of the profits of the office, for which he accounted to its *de jure* holder; or failing this he was allowed a certain proportion out of all the fees collected there. Inflation, coming on top of legal and institutional changes, had much the same effect on deputies and under-clerks as on office-holders who were chiefly dependent on fees. At a meeting of the commission on fees, attended by Wentworth, in May 1630, Sir Henry Spelman, the famous antiquarian and one of its most active members, offered his solution. A strict limit should be set to the number of under-clerks allowed in every office; the proportion of every fee which was due to the subordinate should be fixed at a third, a quarter, or a fifth, as seemed best in each case; over and above this, all clerks and deputies should be paid a fixed allowance by the master of the office; no under-officer should ever accept a gratuity; all fees should be paid to the senior person present in the office and not to whichever under-clerk the payer happened to have been dealing with. The commission may not have had great faith in these remedies or have tried to enforce them, but they serve to illustrate the nature of the problem. Three weeks later the commissioners, again including Wentworth, laid it down that office-holders were always to be held responsible for the exaction of excessive fees by their deputies, under-clerks, and servants, even when they did not themselves profit from such extortions.[1] There are signs that an attempt was made to enforce this.

But vigorous as some of this may seem it still left the nettle ungrasped. Until officers were themselves adequately paid from one source or another, and until they were in turn compelled to pay their underlings a living wage, so long extortion and corruption were bound to go on.

Wentworth's special interest in the fee problem can also be illustrated from his career in Ireland. In June 1634, as Lord Deputy, he launched his own parallel but independent inquiry into alleged exactions by Irish office-holders. He directed a committee of three Irish councillors, including two of his most trusted friends, 'to begin

---

[1] E 165/47, pp. 29-31, 3 May 1630; E 165/46, p. 97b, 24 May 1630.

with such as are nearest in dependance on myself, to wit, with my own Secretaries'; he urged all speed with this,

> that thereupon I may not be delayed further than needs must, in my intended proceedings for a reformation through the whole kingdom. . . .

By the same autumn he was waiting impatiently for a table of the fees taken in the English Exchequer, which he hoped the King would agree should be applied in Ireland. Although only two weeks elapsed between the Lord Treasurer receiving Wentworth's first request for this table and his ordering the officers of the Receipt to provide a full list of their fees, Portland was soon sent a reminder of this and other outstanding points: the Lord Deputy was a hard man to please. Whether or not such urgency was justified, still less politic, Wentworth was now, as the ruler of an entire kingdom and the head of a sizeable administration, able to see the fee problem in its wider context. He explained to Secretary Coke

> As we are to study the Ease of the People, so we are to have Care to preserve for the Officer a Benefit moderate and competent, such as may encourage Men of Understanding and Parts to bestow themselves upon the Service of his Majesty and the Public, holding it . . . a great Prejudice in a Commonwealth, where the Magistrate and Ministeriall Officers are too much straitened or shortened in the Reward for their service. . . .[1]

The logical corollary of this was either for fees to be allowed to rise, or for the Crown to pay bigger salaries and allowances; but, if Wentworth saw this, he left it unsaid. As we shall see, higher fees had already been defended by two other men of an older generation, by one openly and by the other implicitly. But to all appearances theirs were voices crying in the wilderness.

ii EXACTIONS IN THE EXCHEQUER[2]

Criticism of the gratuities taken by Exchequer officers can be found as early as the beginning of the fifteenth century and perhaps

---

[1] *Clarendon S.P.*, I, 95; Knowler, I, 304, 333, 340; P.R.O., Exchequer of Receipt, original warrants, E 404/234, 10 November 1634.

[2] For part of the ground covered in this section see Jean S. Wilson, 'Sir Henry Spelman and the Royal Commission on Fees', in *Studies presented to Sir Hilary Jenkinson* (1957), pp. 456-70, and Aylmer, 'Charles I's Commission on Fees, 1627-40', *Bull. Inst. Hist. Res.*, XXXI (1958), 58-67.

before that. These tips were already hardening into regular fees, and after an ineffectual attempt to abolish most of them in 1455 they were codified in 1457-8.[1] Apart from minor changes, such as occasional authorizations of new or larger fees, this table was still the official basis of Exchequer fees in the seventeenth century.

In the course of the sixteenth century its inadequacy ought to have become increasingly obvious. By mid-Tudor times exaction of excessive fees and gratuities, trafficking in offices, and other forms of corruption were all being stimulated by the inadequacy of officers' stipendiary Fees from the Crown and of their authorized fees from members of the public who made use of their services. The reforming inquiry of 1552 apparently failed to face this issue.[2] For some time nothing more was done. In 1571, after being fully debated and amended in both Houses, a bill was passed against offences by various revenue officials; but the final version of this measure reflected the Crown's interest in efficiency rather than in the protection of the subject from exactions. In this same third parliament of Elizabeth I another bill was carried, first in the Lords and then in the Commons, 'touching the Limitation of fees for Counsellors [at law], and others towards the Law, as especially recommended from the Queen's Majesty'. Although it passed all three readings in the lower House and was presumably returned to the upper, this bill was somehow 'lost', and did not become law. By implication it would have affected lawyers in private practice and not officials in the law and revenue courts.[3] The increased influence of lawyers in the House of Commons can perhaps be illustrated if we compare this with what happened in another parliament, fifty years later.

Meanwhile criticism of lawyers, law officers, and other officials from outside the government was paralleled by disputes inside it of which fees were also the cause. In the Exchequer several separate, though often confusedly overlapping, quarrels of this type can be distinguished. From the 1560's to the 1600's the lower Exchequer of Receipt was divided by the struggle between the Auditor, or

[1] M. D. George, 'Verses on the Exchequer in the Fifteenth Century', *Eng. Hist. Rev.* XXXVI (1921), suggests that the semi-voluntary 'gifts' to Exchequer officials were the ancestors of later fees. *Stat. Realm*, II, 372-4; *Rotuli Parliamentorum*, V, 323b-324b; *Thys is a true copy of the ordynaunce made in the . . . reygne of King Henry the VI* (n.d., c. 1540).

[2] Elton, *Revolution in Government*, pp. 230-8; Richardson, *Chamber Administration*, pp. 393-4.

[3] *Commons Journals*, I, 84-93; *Stat. Realm*, IV, i, 535-7.

Writer of Tallies, and the Clerk of the Pells. This dispute was nominally, perhaps in fact, concerned first and foremost with whether the 'pell of issue' (the contemporary name for the issue roll, recording cash out-payments), which had been suspended in about 1480, should be kept again by the Clerk of the Pells; although it was recommended by a departmental committee as early as January 1584, Lord Burghley only authorized the restoration in 1597. The Clerk of the Pells thereby recovered quite a wide range of fees paid by those to whom money was issued; it is possible, but not very likely, that the Auditor of Receipt suffered some corresponding loss.[1]

The date 1597 is significant. A wider inquiry into fees was then in progress, leading in 1598 to a new codification of all fees taken in Chancery. And in the upper Exchequer from 1597 the 'prest' or 'declared' accounts (those heard orally before the Lord Treasurer and Chancellor of the Exchequer and audited by the Auditors of the Imprests) had to be deposited in the Pipe Office; thus the very accounts which were audited in the most modern and efficient way were now partially restored to the archaism of the 'ancient course', which had evolved between the twelfth and fourteenth centuries, but was by this time quite ossified. Almost certainly this change involved prest accountants paying extra fees to the Clerk of the Pipe and his underlings.[2] Thus these changes were not mere victories of ultra-conservative administrative formalism, but were related to the fall in the real value of fees. In 1598 certain changes were also ordered in the machinery and accounting methods *inside* the Pipe Office, concerning the accounts which were taken through the whole 'ancient course' and not dealt with by the Prest or Revenue Auditors. Again this probably meant that sheriffs, bailiffs, and others had to pay more fees, for instance to the Comptroller of the Pipe who was now to act as a check on the Clerk by duplicating most of his duties.[3] Later, as we shall see, there was rivalry between the Revenue Auditors and the champions of the ancient course, in which fees were inevitably involved.

[1] H. Jenkinson, *A Manual of Archive Administration* (2nd edn., London, 1937), app. V, esp. p. 229; Giuseppi, *Guide*, I, 179; B.M. Lansdowne MS. 164, p. 522; E 407/71, Exchequer of Receipt misc. (several items in this large uncatalogued bundle).

[2] M. D. George, 'Notes on the Origin of the Declared Account', *Eng. Hist. Rev.*, XXXI (1916); B.M. Cottonian MS. Titus, B IV, 359-60; Lansdowne MS. 171, p. 359; Additional MS. 38,008, p. 11b.

[3] B.M. Lansdowne MSS. 166, p. 110 *et seq.*, 167, p. 32.

Another parliamentary attack on excessive fees, in 1606, had an interesting result. A 'bill of sheets' was moved in the Commons, to limit the fees on all legal documents (that is, so much for each sheet, containing a specified number of words and lines). The bill was dropped after its second reading, but Francis Bacon, then an aspirant for high legal or political office, drafted a speech or a series of opinions on it. We do not know whether he spoke on the bill; he is not mentioned as having done so and he was not on the committee to which it was referred. In his paper he opposed the bill on many grounds. A similar one had been moved in 1592-3 but had obtained only 20 votes; precedent could be found for fixing the fees to be received by officers appointed to newly created posts, but not for reducing the fees due to the holders of existing ones; it would penalize the present holders by reducing the value of their offices; and then, a wider argument,

> it were more Justice to raise the fees than to abate them for we see Gentlemen have raised their rents, and the fines of their Tenants, and Merchants, Tradesmen, and farmers [the prices of] their commodities and wares, and this mightily within 100 years. But the fees of officers continue at one rate.

This was well said, and it needed saying. Bacon went on to deny that, because the number of legal cases had risen, fees should be reduced; the number of cases might fall again, and was indeed beginning to do so. He also attacked the bill as being inconsistent: it covered the Westminster courts, but not those in the Marches of Wales and the North, nor did it touch customs and municipal officials. Finally, most fees were of ancient provenance,

> and being mens' freehold, whereof they may have an Assize [i.e. may defend at Common Law], so as the Parliament may as well take any man's Lands, common, mines, etc. as these fees.

This was another shrewd blow, near to the bone in a parliament largely composed of landowners! Bacon conceded that some fees had been recently raised and could properly be investigated; but denied that they could all be treated in one category, while to fix so much per page, with a fixed number of lines per page and syllables per line was utterly unrealistic. The Commons committee which included the junior Secretary of State, the Solicitor-General, all four Masters of Requests, and the Auditor of the Receipt, may or may not have accepted these particular arguments; they simply recommended that the bill be dropped, declaring 'the fees not fit to be dealt with'.[1]

Bacon was himself an interested party. At the time of the inquiry into Chancery fees and their subsequent codification (1597-8) he had just obtained a reversion to the lucrative Clerkship of Star Chamber, an office technically under the jurisdiction of the Lord Chancellor or Lord Keeper. Hearing that some of its fees were about to be reduced, he wrote a supplicatory letter to Lord Keeper Ellesmere, but disclaimed any intention of intervening, the basis for such action being 'too watery for me or any other to stand upon'. In 1608, having succeeded to this Clerkship, which he almost certainly executed by Deputy, Bacon petitioned Ellesmere, by then Lord Chancellor, against any reductions in its fees. He regretted that whenever there was uncertainty about the correct fees the lowest figures were always accepted as the most ancient and therefore as the proper ones; fees, he argued, should not be classified as new if they were in fact old ones which had been slightly altered as a result of procedural changes; in any case new fees were not necessarily bad, for example if an officer was genuinely taking on new work. His tone was still respectful, but, now in the government as Solicitor-General, he obviously felt his case to be stronger than it had been ten years before. In theory, Bacon was ready enough to denounce exactions; in his ideal state every officer had 'salary sufficient of the state for his service', and any who accepted tips as well were referred to derisorily as 'twice-paid'. But in practice salaries were very far from sufficient, it was all but impossible to define 'exacted' fees satisfactorily, and men with the highest intentions were dragged down into the gutter.[2]

In October 1610 James I issued a commission to inquire into excessive fees taken in civil and church courts. Like the great revenue inquiry of 1552 it was probably intended to remedy popular as well as governmental dissatisfaction with officials; the Crown wanted better service, the public, especially the propertied classes, wanted fees and gratuities kept down. This commission consisted

[1] Bodl. Tanner MS. 169, fols. 42-3, printed, with comments, in Spedding, *Letters & Life*, III, 284-7. On the bill see also *Commons Journals*, I, 259, 261-2, 264, 268, 279; *The Parliamentary Diary of Robert Bowyer* (ed. D. H. Willson, Minneapolis, 1931), pp. 7, 12, 27, 38, 64, 140, 152.

[2] *The Egerton Papers* (ed. P. Collier, Camd. Soc., 1840), pp. 272, 429-32; Bacon, *Essays*, LVI, 'Of Judicature', and *The New Atlantis*.

of seven Privy Councillors plus the two Chief Justices and the Barons of the Exchequer. The fruits of its work, a series of depositions by witnesses, mainly concerning fees in the Exchequer, have survived in the papers of Sir Julius Caesar (then Chancellor of the Exchequer), but it does not follow that he was its most active member. An attempt was made to establish what fees were being taken, rather than to classify them by date of origin or degree of authenticity. There does not seem to be any evidence of when and why this commission lapsed; the dissolution of James's first parliament in 1611, or the death of Lord Treasurer Salisbury (1612) suggest possible explanations.[1]

Fees, notably of certain Exchequer officers, were again debated in the 'Addled' parliament of 1614. Exchequer fees were affected by a bill designed to alter the way in which debts on the Escheators' accounts were handled. One member protested on the officers' behalf, that 'These fees were all their Means of Living; and these fees ancient'; another introduced the standard argument that an office was a freehold, though not Bacon's additional point about prices having risen. The bill was returned to committee, the Chancellor meanwhile being directed to bring in lists of *all* Exchequer fees. Perhaps it was going to fail in any case, but this bill's fate was settled by the dissolution of parliament.[2]

During the seven years between this and the next parliament, fees once more became a source of controversy inside the Exchequer. In about 1616 a dispute developed which was to go on intermittently for the next twenty-six years. Originally there were three parties to it: Sir Henry Croke and Mr. Anthony Rouse, who had bought the Clerkship of the Pipe jointly in 1615; the attorneys or under-clerks in their office, later reinforced by the First Secondary of the Pipe, who was also Surveyor of Greenwax (joined in the 1630's by his son, the Comptroller of the Pipe); and Edmund Sawyer, originally a junior clerk in the Revenue Auditors' office, later a knight and the senior Auditor in the Upper Exchequer. It may well be asked why we need to concern ourselves with these petty and prolix wrangles, with these innumerable charges and counter-charges of venality and incompetence. It is because they illustrate so well how fees involved wider issues of good government, dividing the administration from

[1] Hist. MSS. Comm. *Sackville (Knole)*, I, 221-2; *Cal. S.P. Dom.*, *1603-10*, p. 637; B.M. Lansdowne MS. 168, fols. 77-135.

[2] *Commons Journals*, I, 490b.

within, and causing officials to believe (sometimes incorrectly) that one's gain must be another's loss, and *vice versa*.

Sawyer's original attack on the new Clerks of the Pipe was concerned mainly with the damage which the Crown suffered from abuses in the Pipe Office, in particular from the failures to collect debts owing to the King and to prosecute defaulting debtors. He contrasted the general hopelessness of the 'ancient course' with the superior system employed by the Auditors, which was even used for the accounts taken jointly by the 'ancient course' and the Auditors. Only when the under-clerks in the Pipe Office joined in the argument re fees mentioned. weThey of couers had no quarrel with the 'ancient course' as such, being themselves part and parcel of it; they charged Croke and Rouse with having deprived them of their due and proper fees and with having increased their own fees by disproportionate amounts. For example, the fee for certifying the discharge of a debt had been raised from 6s. 8d. to 33s. 4d., the consolidated fee levied on the sheriff of Cornwall when he entered his annual account from £2, 6s. 8d. to £8, and that on the Sheriff of Monmouth from 13s. 4d. to £2, 4s. 0d.; new or innovated fees on sheriffs' accounts included 3s. 4d. for the 'Quietus Est' (that is the final 'O.K.') and 1s. for every petition allowed, of which there were said sometimes to be as many as 300 (if true, this meant £15 p.a. more for Croke and Rouse from a single county). Ten years before, the excessive cost of having sheriffs accounts passed had been singled out for complaint in parliament.[1]

In 1621 M.P.s complained a great deal about abuses by office-holders. This parliament had to deal with the accumulated grievances of seven, indeed because of the shortness of the 1614 parliament, of ten years. Also, thanks to three American scholars, there is a magnificent modern edition of the journals and diaries kept by some of its members. It is therefore hard to know whether M.P.s were actually becoming more interested in officers and offices, or whether they simply had a bigger back-log of complaints, which have been more fully recorded than those ventilated in other parliaments.

---

[1] SP 14/88/34, 36, 37, (Sawyer's attacks) 93/102 (reply by Croke and Rouse), 94/97 (the under-clerk's charges); B.M. Lansdowne MS. 171, p. 315 (possibly on behalf of the Pipe, those attacked in it include the Auditors); E 369/118, p. 101, Lord Treasurers' Remembrancer, misc. books (ditto); B.M. Cottonian MS. Titus B IV, 4-18b (independent, criticizes the Clerks of the Pipe, and Auditors); *Bowyer's Parliamentary Diary*, p. 154 (expense in having sheriffs' accounts passed). For Croke see later in this section; for Sawyer see Chapter 6, s. iii.

The debate on fees and offices in 1621 cut across any divisions between government and opposition, or 'court' and 'country'. The Solicitor-General attacked excessive Exchequer fees, especially those taken on sheriffs' accounts. Soon a two-pronged campaign was launched: a general bill against increased fees and new offices, and a specific one to deal with exactions and procedural abuses in the Exchequer. The general bill set a deadline in the fortieth year of Queen Elizabeth (1598), when all fees in Chancery and some in the Exchequer had been regulated; none taken in excess of those were to be allowed. For new offices, the deadline was James's accession (1603); all posts created since then were to be abolished. The bill covered all the principal courts, including the regional ones, but *not* the Privy Council (in its judicial capacity), the Signet and Privy Seals, the court of Admiralty, the departments which were not courts of law, the organs of town and county local government. or the church courts. An interesting speech was made by Lionel Cranfield, the apprentice who became Lord Treasurer and Earl of Middlesex, and was then, as Master of the Wards, one of Buckingham's principal lieutenants in the Commons. He accepted suggestions from various county members that some pre-1603 offices should be abolished and that the correct fees of law courts should not be determined by the Judges of those courts; he evaded another demand that all church courts should be included; he recommended that parliament itself fix the fees of all the Westminster courts with reference to a 1558, not a 1598, deadline; he reminded them that Fees paid by the Crown were not in question, so the King could still create new offices, provided their holders were *not* to be paid by fees from the subject.

This was the session in which Bacon, with Buckingham's treacherous connivance, was overthrown for corruption. Was there no one to remind Cranfield, who of all those present should have known, that prices and costs had risen somewhat since Elizabeth's accession? Moral if not legal justice was perhaps done when the exaction of excessive fees was included in the charges on which he was in turn impeached in the next parliament.

For the moment there was no defence of higher fees. The Solicitor-General continued to press for the more realistic 1598 deadline: there was certainly no 'cabinet solidarity' in those days. A county member demanded the inclusion of town corporations. More to the point our friend, George Mynne, M.P. for Old Sarum, already a 'putrescent' borough, attacked the fees of ordinary, non-office-holding lawyers, 'who have most and do least'. William Noy, a future Attorney-General but at this time a leading critic of the government, related exactions to the sale of offices; either in ignorance of the Edward VI statute or knowing it to be largely a dead letter, he called for an act to prohibit this traffic. A further committee was thereupon appointed to consider this, in effect a third line of attack, and yet another bill was introduced, embodying Mynne's demand for a limit on ordinary lawyers' fees; it got little support, and was said to conflict with the general bill on officers' fees. Since in fact it was the obvious corollary of that bill, we may perhaps conclude that the lawyers succeeded in bamboozling their gentry allies, or anyway in directing attention back to 'official' abuses. The attack on church courts, for example, was renewed at about this time. Meanwhile a committee was at work on the Exchequer, and yet another specifically on sheriffs' accounts; at least two draft bills were produced. From the debates it is not always clear whether the general or the Exchequer fee bill was being discussed, and perhaps the members themselves were sometimes confused.

At a joint conference with the Lords, apparently on the narrower issue, Sir Edward Coke, the ex-Chief Justice now an 'opposition' leader, came nearer to an explicit defence of higher fees than anyone had done since Bacon in 1606. Those, he asserted, who chose to make use of the Westminster courts, when perfectly adequate justice could be had locally (from J.P.s, at the Assizes, or maybe both), could afford to pay reasonably heavy fees when they arrived there. He may have been referring to the fees received by the officers of these courts, those paid to counsel and solicitors, or both. But there is little sign of any common front developing between lawyers and officers: there was no English equivalent of the French *noblesse de la robe*.

Later in the same session the House resumed work on the Exchequer bill. The Solicitor-General promised to explain the Crown's intentions when one or other of the two fee bills was next debated; possibly an attempt was being made to amalgate the two measures. But nothing was to come of it. King James prorogued parliament before any more progress had been made. In its next session the House returned to the general bill on fees; it was now planned to tack one of the other bills onto this one, either that against lawyers' fees, or that dealing with the Exchequer. But more urgent matters caused the reading of the remodelled bill to be put off, and then parliament was dissolved. This was the last attempt at an agreed solution. Already Bacon's rational defence of higher fees had been washed away in the spate of criticism; henceforth officers who relied on fees fought underground, using camouflage and delaying tactics.[1]

Perhaps Buckingham realized, or was persuaded, that a hue and cry after exacted fees was a good red herring to divert attention from religion, foreign and dynastic policy, and defence. This may explain why a new commission was issued in March 1623. Its senior member, Viscount Mandeville, soon to be Earl of Manchester, had a wide experience of government, and should certainly have appreciated the problem.

After getting off to a slow start, this commission eventually began to collect information about the fees of local courts and officers and about those of the central institutions, mainly Exchequer, Wards, and Star Chamber. The commissioners did not stop at 1598 or even 1558, but went right back to the 1450's. The parliament roll of 33 Henry VI and the Exchequer memoranda roll of 36 Henry VI (by which the former had been amended) were freely cited to prove the unlawfulness of most of the fees which were being taken nearly 170 years later. No wonder that some striking increases were reported from the Pipe and other offices! An attempt was however made, probably by their old enemies, to lay more specific charges against Croke and Rouse. They were said to have raised the annual value of their office more than fivefold in about eight years, largely by increasing the existing fees and inventing new ones, to be paid by sheriffs, under-sheriffs, Crown debtors, and other 'ancient course' accountants; in particular there was the obnoxious shilling on each petition in a sheriff's account.

If any serious reform was intended, short of sweeping away the whole system, it was vitiated by the effects of an academic anti-quarianism on the part of the commissioners. Nor are the tables of fees which were collected for them of much use in working out officers' incomes, since they do not indicate the annual frequency of the various fees. But they do show one good reason why men were

---

[1] *Commons Debates, 1621*, ed. W. Notestein, F. H. Relf, H. Simpson (New Haven, 1935), II, 257, 267, 275, 341, 367-70, 482, III, 18, 149-51, 408, IV, 232, 255, 294-5, 374, V, 16, 136-7, 181, VI, 21, 98, 130-1, VII, 170-4, 211-13; B.M. Lansdowne MS. 151, fols. 17-19.

sometimes reluctant to be sheriffs, and why the Pipe Office in particular was so unpopular with the class from whom most sheriffs were drawn. In one year it cost the sheriff of Yorkshire *c*. £220 to have his account passed, in another year the sheriff of Derbyshire *c*. £48 and of Cornwall *c*. £83, in another the sheriff of Cornwall £131 and of Norfolk £84. The bulk of these fees, including all the most blatant exactions, were taken in the Pipe, which came out badly even according to the witnesses who stuck to the more realistic deadline of Elizabeth's thirtieth year (as appointed in the commission).

The commissioners of 1623-4 appear to have collected a weightier body of depositions than those of 1610-11, but this may only have been because their inquiry covered a wider range of officers and institutions. Their real innovations lay in calling outside, non-official witnesses, and in requiring subordinate clerks and attorneys to testify about their own superiors. Some of the under-officers in the Pipe needed no encouragement.[1]

In about March 1625, at much the same time as this commission formally lapsed on the death of King James, another dispute, involving fees, flared up inside the Exchequer. Someone, probably himself a participant in the 'ancient course', attacked the collection of the royal land revenues by the Receivers-General and the handling of their accounts in a new-fangled way by the Revenue Auditors. A return to the old, pre-Tudor ways was said to promise the subject a release from exactions and the King a great saving in expense. The interests of the officers in the Exchequer of Receipt were reflected in an additional demand that all royal revenues should be paid in there, and all out-payments be made from there in cash. This too was to be a recurring theme.[2]

In the parliaments of 1624-6 fees were a less prominent issue than they had been in 1621. In 1624 exactions and various forms of corruption were included in the charges against Cranfield, and in 1626 trafficking in offices was one of the principal charges brought

---

[1] *Cal. S.P. Dom., 1619-23*, pp. 515, 587, *1623-5*, p. 560; Bodl. Tanner MSS. 101, fols. 6b-7, 8b-9, 30-9, 44, and No. 51; 290, fols. 76-7; 318, fols. 46, 48, 51-2, 54-5, 65-6, 77, 93, 96-7, 110b-113, 123-45, 182-4, 188-98. (These items relate to the 1623-4 commission; the same volumes contain many items from Charles I's fee commission, 1627-40.)

[2] SP 16/14/27, anon., n.d., query 1625; E 369/118, p. 83, n.d., query 1623-4 (another attack on the Pipe, probably on behalf of the Auditors), p. 85 (rejoinder by Croke and Rouse, 1623-4).

Palatium Regis prope Londinum, *vulgo* White hall.

Ciuitatis Weſtmonaſterienſis pars.

Parliament House   the Hall   the Abby

Sala Regalis cum Curia Weſt-monaſtery, *vulgo* Weſtminſter hall.

5. VIEWS OF WHITEHALL AND WESTMINSTER FROM THE THAMES, AND OF WESTMINSTER HALL, IN 1647. (Drawings by W. Hollar.)

6. SIR HENRY CROKE, CLERK OF THE PIPE, 1616-59.
(Painting by Marc Gheeraerts, *c.* 1620)

against Buckingham by the Commons. But there is little evidence that any of these parliaments tried to deal with fees as such.[1]

A new commission was issued by Charles I within two years of his accession. It seems to have been heralded by a memorandum in which it was assumed that unparliamentary revenues would have to be raised; forced loans were indeed on foot. This paper outlined a plan to persuade 40 medium-ranking officials, ten of them in the Exchequer, to 'lend' the King £1,000 apiece; it was to be very like the 'compositions' which Henry VII had levied from officials whereby they were forgiven all offences past and present against both King and subject and confirmed in their posts and privileges. In this case the 'loan' was to be approximately related to the known wealth of those listed and to a recent general pardon confirming James's officers in their positions; 'otherwise the exacting unwarrantable fees from the subject might bring them to the danger of the Laws'. The author hinted that a commission or committee of inquiry would have no difficulty in adding the names of others who were comparable in wealth and equally guilty.[2]

This suggests that from the very start Charles I's commission on fees had a dual purpose. It was to redress, or at least to alleviate, the general grievance against exactions, and at the same time to raise money for the Crown by fining, or compounding with offenders. The new commission was to cover all courts—central, local, civil, and ecclesiastical, and a wide range of other officers going right down the scale to churchwardens. Only the central executive, the household, and the other spending departments were still excluded. Thus some Chamber officers received fees from newly created peers and knights; about the time of Charles I's coronation, when dubbings and ennoblements came thick and fast, the eight Gentlemen Ushers Quarter Waiters were authorized to double their creation fees; but this was never investigated.[3] The new commission had wide powers. Its task was to establish what fees had been taken and what offices had existed in Elizabeth I's eleventh year (1568-9). All fees

---

[1] See Aylmer, *Bull. Inst. Hist. Res.*, XXXI, 59. (There are no full modern editions of the parliamentary debates for 1624-8, and I may well have overlooked additional MS. evidence.)

[2] SP 16/52/61, anon., n.d., ascribed to January 1627, in the papers of Lord Conway, Secretary 1623-8.

[3] *Foedera*, 19 February 1626; Dep. Keeper Public Records, *43rd Rept.*, app. pp. 21, 115 (increase confirmed, September 1628).

larger than those, or of later date, were to be classed as exactions, all offices not then in existence as innovations; the commission was also required to suggest how to stop these evils, and how to prevent them from happening again. Why a different deadline was selected is unclear; it was less realistic than 1588 or 1598, more so than 1558, let alone 1458. The commission's real work began with the appointment, in December 1627, of an executive committee, dominated as in 1623-4 by gentry, antiquarians, and lawyers.

Perhaps because it had been investigated only three or four years before, the Exchequer was not one of the new commission's immediate targets. The commissioners turned first to Chancery and Common Pleas, in which there were probably exactions as glaring as any in the Exchequer. Not until 1630 did the commission (whose additional members now included Wentworth and two of his lieutenants) decide to tackle the Exchequer. Those who had been, or might be, sheriffs of Yorkshire had little cause to love the Pipe Office, which was soon called on to present a list of its fees. But, as with a solitary attack on Croke and Rouse by one of their own under-clerks in 1628, this move was not followed up. The commissioners were still pre-occupied with Chancery, and after 1630 also with prisons, parishes, the court of Wards and Liveries, and the Alienations Office. In 1631 orders were twice issued apparently renewing the investigation of the Pipe and of sheriffs' fees generally, but nothing came of these. In 1633 the commissioners switched their interest to the newer branches of the Upper Exchequer, and ordered all Receivers of Crown land revenues to disclose their fees, but this was still pending eight months later. Then, in the autumn of 1634 after the commission had been further remodelled and the 'court', or government, element in it again strengthened, the executive committee launched a rather more effective inquiry, 'touching the Officers of the Exchequer'. They directed

> that such persons as have been ancient and late Under Sheriffs, and others who are now in Town be warned to attend . . . for the discovery of the ancient and due fees and exactions paid by them or known to be paid to the said Officers for or concerning the passing of their Accounts, and such other matters as they can testify touching those officers.

Many witnesses were not only called but heard, or their written depositions collected. And several officers, past and present, handed in signed certificates of their fees. The commissioners concentrated on the Pipe Office and in particular on sheriffs' and escheators' accounts. One ex-deputy under-sheriff of London, an octogenarian, testified that fees had been much increased in 1596-7—long before the time of Croke and Rouse. Despite this and a few other 'scoops', progress was slow. In March 1635 the commissioners reverted to the land revenue Receivers, and in August they turned to the First Fruits Office and ecclesiastical revenues. Only after the final reissue of the commission in 1637 was anything more positive to be achieved with the Pipe. But before coming to this, we must go back to the other questions of financial administration relevant to the fee problem.[1]

Historians of English government finance have rightly seen the death of the Lord Treasurer, Richard Weston, Earl of Portland, in March 1635 as an important event. Almost at once, Laud and the four other Treasury commissioners, appointed in Portland's place, began a campaign of reform, including reform in financial administration. This can be illustrated from a number of papers dating from 1635-6, but we need only concern ourselves with those which show how fees were involved in such reforms. This connexion can be seen in an attack by the Auditor of the Receipt on 'assignation' and 'defalcation'. Occasional, or once-for-all payments, and standing charges could both be 'assigned'; they were authorized by tally from the lower Exchequer and recorded in its books and rolls of receipt (*not* those of issue). Only standing charges could be 'defalked', that is deducted at source from incoming revenues without the authority of a tally and without the lower Exchequer necessarily having any record of the deduction. Auditor Pye related these practices to the late Lord Treasurer's pernicious habit of personally authorizing out-payments direct from revenue officers, thus by-passing the Exchequer, and to the deplorable extent of 'anticipation', by which he meant the assignment of specified future revenues to specified items of expenditure or to the repayment of named royal

---

[1] *Cal. S.P. Dom., 1627-8*, pp. 168, 232, *1629-31*, pp. 179, 236-7; *Foedera*, XVIII, 844-7 (printed versions of the 1627 and 1630 commissions): E 165/46-49, the commissioners' fair copy minute books, 1627-30, 1630-2, 1632-4, 1634-6; E 215/773-6, 778-81, loose documents presented to the commissioners on Exchequer officers; SP 16/279/109; Bodl. Tanner MS. 318, fols. 33, 134, Bankes MS. 54/16.

creditors. He had made a very similar complaint against the previous Lord Treasurer some years earlier. The officers of the Receipt would undoubtedly have liked all revenues to be paid into their department, and all issues to be made from it. In all probability they sincerely believed that this would benefit both Crown and kingdom. Moreover, the fees payable at the Receipt for cash in- and out-payments were both larger and more numerous than for paper, or tally assignments, while none were payable on defalcations. In 1637 and 1639 the officers of the Receipt repeated these attacks. And the same demand, for all receipts and payments to be centralized in the Exchequer, was restated in a memorandum presented to the Earl of Bedford in the spring of 1641, when it was generally believed that he was about to be made Lord Treasurer.[1]

It is not clear whether Pye and the other critics genuinely identified assignment with anticipation, or whether they deliberately associated the former with the latter in order to discredit it. Anticipation of revenues, especially for more than one year ahead, reflected the weakness of royal finance; assignment, in so far as it merely involved the use of the Receipt as a registry of transactions and not as a cash treasury, in itself harmed no one except some of the officers there, who received less in fees than they might have otherwise. The same mixture of motives can perhaps be detected in one of the last pre-Civil War suggestions for financial reform. In 1642 Christopher Vernon, the First Secondary of the Pipe, proposed that the financial side of the Duchy of Lancaster should be amalgamated with the Exchequer: a step arguable on its own merits, but one which would undoubtedly have brought more fees to the officers of both Upper and Lower Exchequers.[2]

Meanwhile what had been happening to the Clerk of the Pipe and his exactions? In the mid- and late 1630's the Pipe Office was once again divided against itself. Vernon's son, the Comptroller, claimed that the Clerk (by now Croke was sole Clerk) had excluded him from his proper duties—and so presumably, though this was not

[1] B.M. Harleian MS. 3796, p. 7; Hist. MSS. Comm. *Cowper*, I, 229 (Harl. MS. 3796, p. 45, n.d., a fuller and more balanced paper by Pye, which is ascribed to 1635-6, is better dated to 1622-4. Its ref. to an impending windfall from the Prince's marriage is more likely to mean the future Charles I than the future Charles II, aged only five or six in 1635-6); SP 16/352/70, 431/70, 479/89 (fully summarized in *Cal. S.P. Dom., 1640-1*, pp. 565-7).

[2] C. Vernon, *Considerations for regulating the Exchequer* (1642), p. 58.

said, from the collection of his proper fees, the better to conceal his own depredations.[1] In 1635-6 there were numerous attacks on Sir Henry Croke. Christopher Vernon, his own Secondary, was probably behind most of them. Croke was charged with raising 1s. 8d. fees to 6s. 8d., and £1 ones to £5 and £10; his total extortions since taking office were given as £10,000.[2] Unless this was merely a convenient round sum, the implied gain of £500 p.a. was much more moderate than the earlier charge that the annual value of the Clerkship had been raised from £300 to £1,500 or £2,000. Considering the evidence for earlier fee increases in the 1590's, the smaller estimate for the post-1615 rise seems the more plausible.

In March 1636 Croke himself asked for official confirmation of his fees. He complained that the value of his office had fallen, as no doubt it would have if he had still only been taking the fees authorized in the mid-fifteenth century. This is the first sign that he was thinking of coming to terms with the commissioners, and not risking the same fate as George Mynne. In May 1637 the King was said to have agreed to his compounding for his errors and misdeeds, if these were conclusively proved. At this time the commissioners were busy collecting yet more evidence about Pipe Office and other Exchequer fees, and on 10 June Croke himself voluntarily presented another schedule of his own fees.

Although these proceedings failed to come to a head in 1636 or 1637, a decisive new twist had by then been given to the charges against Croke. The Pipe Office was not only under attack for alleged extortions. In July 1635 the Treasury commissioners had ordered the investigation of another long-standing charge against Croke, namely that he had consistently failed to collect the debts due from sheriffs to the Crown. For the time being he had managed to persuade the commissioners that he was doing his best with this, but a year or two later his fee exactions and his laxity over debt collection were shown by Vernon to be two sides of one and the same abuse.

. . . it is no ways probable or possible but that the Cry of Sheriffs and others from whom these great fees have been extorted, would have been much louder ere this, had they not received favour from the said Clerk of the Pipe by Posting and setting of the King's

[1] Bodl. Bankes MS. 60/9.
[2] See SP 16/536/83, 83i, (*Cal. S.P. Dom., Adds. 1625-49*, p. 543); SP 16/340/17; B.M. Harl. MS. 3796, p. 2b.

debts, which the said Sheriffs were to answer, and the like; in so much as in fine the King pays for the greatest part of this extortion.

Here was Croke's dilemma: if he met the charge of laxity by rigorous action against Sheriffs and under-sheriffs for the money which they owed to the King, these same men would come forward to testify against him before the commissioners on fees. Vernon incidentally was by way of being an expert on the real or alleged misdeeds of Sheriffs and their subordinates, as well as on the concealments of debts owed to the Crown.[1]

These attacks from inside the Exchequer and Croke's own fears for his future may well have done more to precipitate the denouement than any action by the commissioners on fees. In 'A Relation of the present state of Business upon the Commission of fees', dated 27 March 1638, the Pipe was listed with the departments of which investigation was least far advanced and furthest from legal action being taken against offenders. Chancery, Common Pleas, prisons, parishes, and London companies all retained their priority over the Exchequer. Besides the investigation of the Exchequer had been diffused, and so had lost momentum like a river changing from a narrow to a wide channel. Since the summer of 1637 almost as much information had been obtained about the fees of the revenue and prest Auditors as about those of the Pipe officers. In mid-April 1638 fresh summonses were issued to Escheators and under-sheriffs, to certify what fees they paid at the Pipe and elsewhere. If Vernon can be believed, these men were often as guilty of deliberately withholding from their accounts sums due to the Crown as Croke was of overlooking this and extorting excessive fees from them. Seventeen were summoned as witnesses on 26 June, but several had already been cited a fortnight before, and had neither appeared nor sent written certificates. There is little trace of any activity by the commissioners from the end of June to the beginning of November 1638 (their normal summer recess was from July to October).[2]

---

[1] T 56/1, p. 43; E 215/777, 782-812; SP 16/537/37; *Cal. S.P. Dom., 1635-6*, p. 433; Hist. MSS. Comm. *Eighth Rept.*, app. I, Bankes Papers, p. 211; B.M. Harl. MS. 3796, pp. 2b-3b, MS. 830, p. 227 (an attack on under-sheriffs). For Vernon see Chapter 3, s. vii, this chapter, s. i, and Chapter 5, s. iii.

[2] Bodl. Tanner MS. 318, No. 12; E 215/784-92; SP 16/537/131, 135-40. For other certificates, sent in April-November 1638, see E 215/795, 797, 800 (the worst case; 114 fees totalling £146, 14s. 8d. paid on the 1628 Essex shrieval account), 801, 807, 809.

Yet on the last day of June the King ordered the Attorney-General to prepare a pardon for Sir Henry Croke, from all the charges pending against him in Star Chamber, and for any other offences committed by him as Clerk of the Pipe. On 7 July Secretary Windebank told the Lord Keeper that the King wanted the pardon to be held up until further orders; this was due to the intervention of Sir Thomas Jermyn, the Vice-Chamberlain, who was not interested in the Clerkship of the Pipe as a reformer, but hoped to obtain it for his sons and may therefore have wanted to see Croke removed. On 9 September the King ordered the Lord Keeper to let the pardon proceed. Sometime in 1638 Croke paid the Crown a composition of £4,300 as the price of his pardon; and it appears that at least £1,500 of it had been received by 1 August. Nor is it clear whether his fees were reduced from their post-1617 level; the pardon does not specify fee reductions, but the Attorney-General was instructed to settle what Croke's fees should be. The following spring Jermyn's sons, Henry (the future Lord St. Albans, and alleged second husband of Henrietta Maria) and Thomas, were admitted as joint reversioners *after* a first reversion to Robert Croke, Sir Henry's son. Croke's return to favour is not only illustrated by this but by the payment of a special £80 reward to him in August 1639 for services connected with the northern recusant revenues; in June 1640 he even tried to encroach on the work of the Auditors of these revenues. Despite having paid the heaviest composition of any single office-holder in the 1630's, Croke had avoided the perils of a trial at law and the ignominy of public condemnation; he kept his office, chastened, and perhaps, as we shall see, embittered.[1]

No Exchequer official was actually tried and punished for taking excessive fees. The commissioners resumed their inquiry into Exchequer fees in the winter of 1638-9; for a time they proceeded parallel to, and to some extent in rivalry with, another investigation begun on the King's orders in October 1638. Sworn juries of junior officers and clerks were to be impanelled in all the main courts; these jurors were to produce written reports on oath of all the fees normally taken in their respective courts. Only the Exchequer jurors'

---

[1] Bodl. Bankes MS. 51/19; SP 16/395/25; SP 38/17, 6 August 1638; *Cal. S.P. Dom., 1637-8*, pp. 557, 587, *1639*, p. 1, *1640*, p. 367; Birmingham R.L., MS. 604085/301 (I am grateful to Mr. J. P. Cooper for this reference); T 56/5, p. 7; Elmhirst (Pye) MSS. Exchequer papers (1), fol. 53. P.R.O., E 405/176, Teller's roll, 1638. For Croke's career after 1640 see ref., in Chapter 6, s. vii. pp. 390-1.

report has been identified, and except in the case of Croke, who had already compounded, they made no attempt to distinguish old and permissible fees from exactions (that is increases on top of these) and innovations (completely new fees). Although this report shows what the fees were supposed to be, it came to very little. Nor did the last efforts of the commissioners: orders to send in certificates of Exchequer fees were issued at ten of their twenty-seven recorded meetings between November 1638 and December 1639, but to no visible effect.[1]

We are not concerned here with the success or failure of the commission on fees and of the special juries, but with the place of fee payments in the administrative system. In 1638, as in 1627, there seems to have been a close connexion between the inquiries into exacted fees and the Crown's financial needs. A paper ascribed to 1638, possibly prepared by Windebank, or under his orders, is headed 'Note of officers of ability in London and elsewhere'; and has on the back in another contemporary hand, 'exacted fees'; it contains a numerical table of all those who had held office at any time during the previous nine years, and the amounts of money which they could 'lend'. Including all central and local officers, the grand total is 5,150 and the total sum named is £1,150,000 (or more than one and a half times the Crown's ordinary annual revenue at the 1636-8 level). The 100 major officers of the Westminster courts were assessed at £1,000 each, as forty of them had been in 1627, and the 300 lesser officers and clerks there at £500 each. Virtually no office-holders were to be exempt except Lord and Deputy Lieutenants, J.P.s, and Constables. Whether these sums were thought of as loans or as compositions for exactions and other offences, such a scheme clearly went far beyond anything contemplated before and far beyond the scope of the commission on fees. Windebank had joined the commission in 1634; he is known to have associated at one stage with the Francophile court group centring on the Queen; there is other supporting evidence of French influences on English

---

[1] SP 16/400/17, 7 October 1638 (order to swear jurors), 376/43, n.d. (the commissioners' complaint to the King; should be dated *after* 400/17); Bodl. Tanner MS. 318, fol. 121, 11 December 1638 (the King's reply to SP 16/376/43); E 101/337/8 and T 64/297 (jurors' rept, on Exchequer fees; the copy in accounts various is dated 1639, and that in Treasury misc. 1638; the latter may mean down to 25 March 1638/9, but even so this seems commendably prompt); E 215/797-8, 808, 811; SP 16/538/109-38. See also Aylmer, *Bull. Inst. Hist. Res.*, XXXI, 65-6.

administrative ideas, including as we shall see a plan to institute a regular tax and a capital levy on office-holders. Another court official who had joined the commission on fees in 1637, Sir Henry Mildmay, Master of the Jewel House, wrote to Windebank in June 1639 asking him to persuade the Lord Treasurer (Bishop Juxon) to remind the King about exacted fees,

> . . . which will be an excellent way for money if he will put it in the right way to choose fitting commissioners and to give them power to reform as well as [to] compound, which will make it both profitable, and plausible to the people. . . .

Leaving aside fines and compositions from extortioners, the very considerable sums borrowed by the Crown from office-holders in 1639-40 were all genuine loans, though a few were made under duress. Their repayment was secured by 'anticipation', with tallies on future revenues; and in every case but two these loans were at the statutory maximum of 8 per cent. interest (Archbishop Laud and Attorney-General Bankes lent their money interest free). In January 1640 Windebank was hoping for £13,000 from three of the Barons and five other officers in the Exchequer, but any idea of a general levy on all office-holders seems to have been discarded. It was either thought too difficult to administer, or politically inadvisable.[1]

There is therefore plenty of evidence about the problems to which payment of officers in fees gave rise, especially at a time when the value of money was falling. It is not so clear either how far officers, such as those in the Exchequer, succeeded in raising their incomes from legitimate fees to meet this long-term inflation, or how far the Crown, through its commissions and juries, succeeded in stopping the exaction of unauthorized fees. In the Exchequer there had been many and large increases from the fifteenth-century level, and probably considerable ones over and above the fees which had been taken during most of the sixteenth century. But these increases were very unevenly distributed between different sub-departments and indeed among the individual posts inside them. Where the volume of business had fallen, the temptation to extort was at its most acute,

[1] SP 16/408/53 (the plan to raise £1,150,000), 423/67 (Mildmay's letter), 539/6 (loans anticipated from Exchequer officers). See also *Cal. S.P. Dom., 1639-40*, pp. 337, 567; Rushworth, *Hist. Colls.* II, ii, 912; T 56/5, pp. 65-103.

e.g. in the Pipe Office; where it had grown, this urge was correspondingly weaker, e.g. for the Prest Auditors. Apart from Sir Henry Croke, the only Exchequer officers to compound were two Escheators, who apparently took fright after a Feodary had been tried and convicted in Star Chamber for exactions and other offences. This is to be compared with nine or ten in Chancery, who were persuaded to compound or brought to trial and then fined, and three in the Common Pleas who compounded. In the Exchequer there may have been others just as guilty as Croke; some of his enemies were far from disinterested. Vernon, who was finally to portray the Clerk of the Pipe as *solely* responsible for *all* exactions, badgered the authorities for special rewards in recognition of his own services to such an extent that at one stage Lord Treasurer Juxon ordered him to be 'restrained from Medling'. Most later sixteenth- and early seventeenth-century officials were trying to push up their fees and other emoluments. Croke of the Pipe and Mynne of the Hanaper had succeeded all too well in this, but their exactions probably differed in degree rather than in kind from those of many others.[1]

Some officers were in a better position than others to insist on larger gratuities. It would have been impossible to define an 'exacted gratuity', indeed the concept is a contradiction in terms; and significantly no commission was ever appointed to deal with this problem. For the same reason that they were difficult to attack, there is little evidence about the increases in gratuities. The Council Clerks and other members of the central executive, as well as some courtiers and officers of the spending departments, may have coped with inflation in much the same way as those in the law and revenue courts who depended on fixed, authorized fees, only with less risk and more success.

Then there is the question of who paid. Where the increases in fees and gratuities fell on landowners, lawyers, and merchants who could well afford the extra burden, which was in any case often incurred as a result of their own litigiousness, we need not take too seriously all the propaganda against 'exactions'. Unfortunately poorer people, as well as members of the upper and middle classes on less flexible incomes, were also affected. Having a will proved, paying taxes and—on royal property—rents, manufacturing and

---

[1] *Cal. S.P. Dom., 1638-9*, pp. 72-3 (SP 16/400/90), 596; T 56/5, p. 33; T 56/14, pp. 180-1; E 403/2591, p. 68; Bodl. Bankes MS. 17/34; Vernon, *Considerations*, p. 76; see also Bell, *Court of Wards*, p. 44, n. 7.

selling cloth, even having a stall in a market, all involved the attention of officials and the payment of fees. Considered as a form of indirect taxation, fees and gratuities tended to fall most lightly on those best able, and most heavily on those least able to bear them. To remedy this was far beyond Stuart royal commissioners or any other reformers of the day.

iii ANNUAL AND CAPITAL VALUE OF OFFICES

It is always difficult and often impossible to work out the total income of a seventeenth-century official by adding up all the component items—Fee, fees, diet, etc. This can only occasionally be done with certainty, but contemporary estimates of the total annual values of various offices are also available. Of these, some can be checked against the totals arrived at by addition and shown to be reliable; others are mere gossip, not even approximately correct. For example, in 1620 the usually well-informed letter writer John Chamberlain estimated the Clerkship of the Crown in Chancery at £700-£800 p.a., but around 1630 it was reported to the commissioners on fees to yield £1,500 a year. Its value is most unlikely to have doubled in about a decade, and in other cases too the values certified to the commissioners are almost certainly too high; Chamberlain is therefore to be preferred, although an 'official' source is normally more reliable than a 'literary' one.[1]

Later in this section we shall consider the alternative ways of calculating the total annual value of offices, *other than* by adding up all the different items. The table which follows shows how some individual officers' incomes were made up, also the difficulties involved in such addition. In several cases there are figures for some of the component items, but totals can only be obtained by 'informed guesswork'. In other cases there are more or less reliable figures for the net or gross annual totals, but it is impossible to divide these into individual parts.

The paucity of the evidence and the difficulty of establishing reliable annual totals can best be seen by examining those about which we might expect to know most, the great offices of state. In the mid-1630's a Lord Treasurer who was watchful of his own interests but not technically corrupt was said to be able to make £7,000 a year.[2]

[1] *Chamberlain Letters*, II, 293; Wilson, Thesis, app. III.
[2] P. Heylin, *Cyprianus Anglicus* (Life of Laud), entry for 1635.

TABLE 7. INCOMES OF SELECTED OFFICERS[1]

Officer	Fee or Salary (£'s)	Pension, Annuity, Other Office (£'s)	Diet or Board Wages (£'s)	Gratuities and fees (£'s)	Total £ p.a.
Central Executive: Council Clerk, 1630's (William Boswell)	50	730 as Ambassador in the Netherlands. 81 as co-keeper of the records	6 a day as Ambassador +travel and Intelligence allowances	nil (permanently absent from Council duties)	£3,051 minimum (in theory)
ibid. (Edward Nicholas)	50	200 as naval secretary; c. 200 as engrosser of recusants' land leases	?	unknown but heavy as Council Clerk, and as Naval Secretary	(1,500 min. seems a fair guess)
ibid. (Thomas Meautys)	50	300 as clerk for letters from Star Chamber to Chancery	?	heavy as Council Clerk and from 1635 as Muster-Master-General	(say, 1,000-1,200) ?
Signet Clerk (Abraham Williams, 1630's)	nil	200 as Queen of Bohemia's Agent; 20 as a Game-Keeper; 300 on a lease of his London house for foreign diplomats	50 b.w.	c.250 as Senior Signet Clerk (plus gratuities and writing fees)[2]	c. 820 (min.)
ibid. (Robert Kirkham, 1625-38)	nil	50 as Surveyor of Salt Works	50 b.w.	c 90, plus ditto	c. 190 (min.)
ibid. (Philip Warwick, 1638-40)	nil	100 pension, query plus stipend from the Lord Treasurer as his Secretary	50 b.w.	c. 90, plus ditto, plus gratuities as Treasurer's Secretary	c. 240 (min.)

[1] Sources are not given for individual items unless contentious or of special interest. This table is based on: (1) Exchequer Fee and pension lists (SP 16/3/117, 180/16-18, 301/9, 474/2); (2) departmental records (mainly in accounts various and declared); (3) Household and Great Wardrobe records for diet and livery (as already cited); (4) misc. items in state papers domestic, privy council registers, records of fee commissioners, and other printed and MS. sources already cited; (5) certain secondary sources, such as Higham *Secretary of State*, Keeler, *Long Parliament*; (6) *Cal. Cttee. Compounding.*

[2] Higham, *Secretary*, pp. 206-11; SP 16/203/112, 214/96. (The evidence is fragmentary; by interpolation the senior Signet Clerk received *c.* £24 a month in sealing fees, 1631-2, and the three others about £7, 3s. 4d. each.

ibid. (Edward Norgate, 1638-40)	nil	50 as Tuner of musical instruments; 27 as Windsor Herald	50 b.w.	c. 90, plus ditto, plus Herald's fees	c. 277 (min.)
French Secretary	67	nil	diet at Secretary of State's table	query writing allowances	?
German Intrepreter, 1632-40	50	nil; also acting Latin Secretary (no Fee)	diet at Secretary of State's table	ditto, plus gratuities as chief assistant to senior Sec. of State	?
Secretary of State¹	100	700 for Intelligence	1,095 diet for senior + 390 diet for junior and their assistants or 577 b.w. each (1628)	2,800-4,000 (by interpolation)	c. 2,000 net. 4,800-6,000 gross. (The cost of running the dept. and the salaries of subordinates who were not paid in fees or by the Crown explain the big difference between the gross and net totals)
Household: Lord Steward (1626-30)	100	also Lord Warden of the Stannaries, Justice in Eyre, and Captain of Portsmouth	1,845 diet	brokerage on lesser Household offices	2,000+
Treasurer (1620-39)	124	750 c. 700 as Clerk of Crown in Chancery up to 1629	1,845 diet	query gratuities	3,419 later 2,719 (min.)
Comptroller (1630-8)	108	900 c. 1,000 on the Cofferer's annual account	1,845 diet	ditto	3,853 (min.)
Cofferer (1632-8)	144	c. 1,000 on his annual account	c. 850 diet	ditto; query other illicit profits	1,994 (min.)

¹ Higham, *Secretary*, pp. 211-21. (After 1629-30 the junior Secretary seems to have received a three-dish diet; Mrs. Higham implies that his table was abolished altogether: LS 13/30.)

TABLE 7 (*continued*)

Officer	Fee or Salary (£'s)	Pension, Annuity, Other Office (£'s)	Diet or Board Wages (£'s)	Gratuities and fees (£'s)	Total £ p.a.
Clerk of Greencloth (or a Clerk Comptroller)	44	—	c. 850 diet	query gratuities, etc.	894 (min.)
Chief Kitchen Clerk	44	—	c. 850 diet	perqs. in kind	894 (min.)
Sergeant of the Acatry	5-10-0	—	12 b.w.; bouge	ditto; profit on the accounts until 1638	?
Sergeant Porter	11	52 lodging allowance	160 b.w.	?	223 +
Knight Marshall	—	400; c. 182 extra allowances	21 b.w.	fees in Marshalsea Court	603 +
Chamber: Lord Chamberlain (1626-40)	100	3,600; also Lord Warden of Stanneries (1630-40). 67 Livery	1,095 diet	brokerage on minor offices	4,862 (min.)
Vice-Chamberlain (1630-9)	67	—; lesser offices in the same family	390 diet	query share in ditto	457 +
Treasurer	27 153	350-400 poundage	390 diet	query gratuities; query profit on his accounts	920-970 (min.)
Groom of the Stole	33	500 (1626-31); c. 2000 (1631-1636, plus c. 1,200 on Irish customs; 2,000 (1636-41), + c. 2,000 from Seal Office, also Justice in Eyre	c. 1,700 diet.	query brokerage on Bedchamber offices	1,600 (est. 1636-41), 2,500 (est. 1631) excluding pensions and other offices
Groom Porter	nil	nil	390 diet	?	?

206

Office			share in King's or Groom of Stole's diet	query gratuities	?
Groom of the Bedchamber	nil	500		ditto	
Page of the Bedchamber	10	47 livery —	55 b.w.		112+
Gentleman Usher	120	100	317 diet	?	537+
Carver	167	150 (3 out of 5 had this pension)	query share in King's diet. Bouge	?	317+
Groom of the Chamber	39	—	place at one of the tables	?	39+board
Groom of the Privy Chamber	20	1 at 133; 1 at 100; 4 at 60; 2 at 40 livery	c. 80 diet	?	4 at 200 min.
Gent of ditto	—	five out of 48 had pensions in 1630's, of av. value 345 each	board for quarter of the year	—	part board, otherwise nil
King's Barber	20	160 / 47 livery	49 b.w	expenses allowed	276+
Messenger	25	—	30 b.w.	expenses	55+
Master of the Revels	10	50 house rent / 73-10-0 allowance, later 90	—	c. 345 gratuities (by interpolation)	500 (possibly exaggerated)
Navy: Treasurer (1630-6)	221 or 271, includes allowances	200-653 poundage, ests. early 1630's; query 900-1,000 by 1637-40	—	gratuities min. 350 (by interpolation)	1,600 (1640)
Comptroller	155 (138 net)	av. 35 expenses; 120 from 1639	—	query gratuities	258+ (late 1630's)
Surveyor	145 (128 net)	av. 35 expenses; 100 from 1639	—	ditto	228+

TABLE 7 (continued)

Officer	Fee or Salary (£'s)	Pension, Annuity, Other Office (£'s)	Diet or Board Wages (£'s)	Gratuities and fees (£'s)	Total £ p.a.
Clerk	100 (92 net)	av. 32 expenses; 80 from 1639	—	ditto	172 + (salary and allowances raised from 180 to 350 in 1660) ?
Ordnance: Lieutenant (1627–40)	139	c. 122 poundage	—	query gratuities; 40 from Powder Contractors until mid-1630's	(261 min.) ?
Surveyor (1635–40)	92-10-0	c 117 allowances 243 as Surveyor of Forts and Castles	—	query gratuities	452-10-0 (min.)
Clerk (1625–36)	105	20 bonus, 37 stationery, c. 40 allowances, 40 on powder contract, c. 10 poundage in peacetime	—	ditto	252+
Exchequer: King's Remembrancer	56	46 5 livery, 289 (gross) for stationery	—	?	600 (1646; query under-estimate)
Lord Treasurer's Remembrancer	62	98 3 livery	—	?	?
Clerk of the Pipe	47	123 3 livery, 60 for work on recusant revenues	—	474 min.[1] (from fees which were taken a fixed no. of times p.a.; the frequency of others can not be calculated) 1638-9 probably over 1,000	c. 1,500
Comptroller of the Pipe	40	59	—	155 min. 1638-9 probably c. 300	c. 480 gross c. 273 net (1616-19)[2]

208

[1] T 64/297, pp. 6b-10b.
[2] P.R.O. Shaftesbury MSS. 2/12 (I am grateful to Mr. J. P. Cooper for this reference; the totals given here are based on my interpolations).

Office					
First Secondary of the Pipe	5	also Surveyor of Greenwax	—	542 min. 1638-9, to him and Second Secondary fees from accountants	c. 300+
Revenue Auditor	20	100(1); 20(1); nil (5) av. allowances =285 each	—		?
Prest Auditor	67	5 livery	—	c. 180 min. 1638-9	c. 270+
Receiver-General	10-20	av. allowances =140 each	—	c. 200, 1620's, falling to c. 100 av. 1630's	330-40[1] (Yorks, 1623) c. 190 (ib. est. in 1630's; sales of Crown lands, c. 1625-35, might explain this fall in value)
Auditor of the Receipt	260 or 317 (consolidated)	plus house	—	c. 610 min. 1638-9[2] by interpolation c. 1,200	1,500[3] (reliable)
Clerk of the Pells	172	129	—	c. 450 by interpolation	750
Teller	33	—	—	467 ditto	500 (perhaps too low for 1637-41)
Chancery: Lord Keeper	—	300 Exchequer annuity, 1,000 from Customs as a judge, 40 livery, 200 for Star Chamber attendance, 420 for diet plus 12 tuns of wine	—	100 on casual patents, 800+ from fines, gratuities, and brokerage on subordinate offices	c. 3,000 min., possibly twice or more times that. 3,000 in bribes from petititioners only, to the L.K. and his servants, 1621-5 (hostile critic)[4]

209

[1] Sheffield C.L., Wentworth Woodhouse MSS., Strafford 20c/231, 233-4; SP 16/274/67.

[2] E 101/337/8.

[3] Elmhirst (Pye) MSS., (1) fols. 61-4, values of posts in the Receipt, n.d. (presumably made during Sir Robert Pye's Auditorship, 1619-49, and 1660-2).

[4] Elmhirst (Pye) MSS. (8), n.d., possibly post-1660; Spedding, *Letters and Life*, VI, 327; *The Diary of John Manningham*, ed. J. Bruce (Camden Soc., 1868), p. 19, February 1602; B.M. Hargrave MS. 321, p. 643, n.d., temp. Eliz. I; see also A. Weldon, *The Court and Character of King James* (London, 1651), p. 130.

TABLE 7 (continued)

Officer	Fee or Salary (£'s)	Pension, Annuity, Other Office (£'s)	Diet or Board Wages (£'s)	Gratuities and fees (£'s)	Total £ p.a.
Six Clerk	—	—	—	entirely dependent on fees, which varied according to chance and seniority	2,000 c. 1630 (? hostile witness) 2,000 and upwards, 1650 (query uninformed) 1,413-1,476 av. 1608-30 (reliable) 864 net. 1635 (favourable witness); 860 net, 1638 (reliable) 770, 557, 525, 283 1639-42 (reliable but unclear)[1]
Common Pleas: Puisne Judge	188	—	—	1,194 for nothern circuit, 1627. 117 for one term in London, 1623. Share in profits of the Seal of C.P.s and King's Bench	? c. 2,000 min. (est. only)
Chief Prothonotary	—	—	—	estimated range of fees 1,500-3,000	6,000 (18th century tradition)[2]

[1] Wilson, Thesis, app. III (list of Chancery offices and their values, c. 1630); *Proposalls concerning the Chancery* (1650), B.M. E 593 (19); S. D'Ewes, *Autobiography & Correspondence* (ed. J. O. Halliwell, 1845), I, 177-8; E 165/49, p. 13; Glos. R.O. Colchester MSS. Journals, I, 326-290 (numbered from the back forwards). To reconcile £2,000 p.a. with £860 and £864 net, Six Clerkships must have varied greatly in value with the holder's seniority, or else their worth had declined steeply between the 1620's and the late 1630's; the £864 is £1,152 gross, and the Colchester figures depend partly on interpolation, partly on assuming that 'ff' in his accounts signifies fees.

[2] D. Barrington, *Observations on the most ancient statutes* (5th edn., 1796), pp. 508-9; this figure probably arose from a misreading of Richard Brownlow's account book for 1616/17-17 (Brownlow MSS., Belton) where the total annual outlay is £6,062, 10s. 1d., including capital transactions—a very different thing.

210

The last Lord Treasurer, Weston Earl of Portland had in fact made at least £7,000 a year from windfalls and capital gains alone, quite apart from regular day-to-day fees and gratuities. Portland had obtained the King's pardon, indeed his approval, for the £44,500 which he had thus received in his first six years and four months as Treasurer; but, although we may take it as axiomatic that he had made much more than he should have, that is well over £7,000 p.a. altogether, there is hardly enough evidence to assert that he actually made c. £14,000 a year from all sources. However, the disparity between the supposed net income of £3,000 a year (including fees) of the Lord Chancellor or Lord Keeper and the £4,160 made by Bacon in a single period of four months suggests that £14,000 is not utterly fantastic for a venal and unscrupulous Lord Treasurer. Of the others, gossip credited the Lord Admiral in peacetime with a slightly larger official income than the Lord Keeper, and in wartime (thanks to prize money and extra Admiralty jurisdiction) with a much larger one: a minimum therefore of £3,000-£4,000. The Earl Marshal probably received fees in his capacity as head of the College of Arms and of the Court of Chivalry, but his office was not of great money value; nor apparently were the posts of the Lord President of the Council or the Lord Keeper of the Privy Seal. The latter's headship of the Court of Requests was not very profitable, since from the litigant's point of view this was the best, that is the cheapest, of all the courts. The Lord Deputyship of Ireland was of variable but potentially very great value; one apparently sober estimate was £5,864, 8s. 11d. p.a. This show of accuracy is misleading, for the sum is made up of £10, 10s. 10d. a day from the Crown plus about £2,000 p.a. from produce in kind, the yield from land temporarily in the Deputy's hands, wine due at the customs, and brokerage on offices in his gift. The Lord Presidencies of Wales and the North are likely to have been worth a good deal less than this, but more than the Privy Seal or the Presidency of the Council. The value of the Chancellorship of the Duchy of Lancaster can be inferred from Lord Newburgh's agreement to transfer to it from the Chancellorship of the Exchequer in 1629; the reversion to it was also eagerly sought after. The Mastership of the Wards was among the half-dozen most valuable offices in the realm, but as with the Lord Treasurership the facts are obscure. In 1610 a letter writer had spoken of £20,000 a year compensation for the Master if the Court was abolished; this was surely a rumour which had grown in the telling. At the other extreme, when the Long Parliament did abolish Wardship in 1647 they only awarded compensation to the Master on a valuation of £1,400-£1,700 p.a. The Convention Parliament of 1660 was more generous, and spoke in terms of £5,000 p.a.; conceivably they had in mind the worth of the Mastership in the 1630's, while the Long Parliament had taken its greatly reduced value in the years 1642-6.[1]

Likewise we can only guess at the total incomes of most of the greater judicial officers. The Chief Justiceship of Common Pleas was reckoned the most lucrative judicial post, followed by the Lord Chief Justiceship (of King's Bench); in terms of money value it is not at all clear how we ought to rate the ordinary, or puisne, judgeships of these two courts and the Chief and puisne Baronies of the Exchequer. Nor is it easy to compare these with the Crown law offices proper, the Attorney- and Solicitor-Generalships. The Attorney-General was involved in the hearing of most petitions and in the passage of virtually all grants, so his income from fees, gratuities, and presents was princely. He could also accept private briefs, an advantage over the Judges. When Bacon told King James that the position was currently worth £6,000 a year to him in legitimate takings, he may or may not have been including his profits from private practice; since he was angling for promotion to the Great Seal and at the same time emphasizing how much he stood to lose financially by such a transfer, he may well have been exaggerating.

In this group the Mastership of the Rolls is almost unique in that there are quite reliable figures for it. The least sure rests on a seventeenth-century Chancery tradition, that in 1535 it was only worth £291 p.a. By the end of Elizabeth I's reign it was yielding between £1,100 and £1,500 a year, and in 1608-10, at its peak, an average of £2,048 p.a. Around 1614 it should have been worth c. £2,370 (gross) p.a., but from then until about 1630 its average yield was actually c. £1,600 p.a.; in the 1630's it was tending to fall back still further, to more like the Elizabethan level, that is nearer £1,100 than £1,500. It is not clear whether some of these totals refer to gross or to net income. Nor is it easy to see why the value of the Rolls should have

[1] *Clarendon S.P.*, I, 158-9; or *Cal. Clarendon S.P.*, I, 52 (for the Treasurership); Hist. MSS. Comm, *Leeds, Bridgewater, etc.* p. 290, Inner Temple Papers, n.d. but from context possibly 1634 (for the Deputyship); Spedding, *Letters and Life*, V, 242 (for Bacon); for the rest, sources already cited.

fallen so sharply after *c.* 1610 and again in the 1630's; conceivably this was due to the activities of the successive commissions on fees, but there may have been a slight decline in some kinds of Chancery business.[1]

Certain legal posts, not in themselves of major importance, ranked financially with all but the most lucrative of the great offices. The Seal Office of King's Bench and Common Pleas, known colloquially as 'the Green wax', was said to have been worth £2,000 a year in the 1630's. Under the Protectorate (1656-7) its gross yield was nearly £5,000; after deducting the standing charges payable to the Lord Protector, the Judges and subordinate officers, its value for the heirs, legatees, and creditors of the previous holder was £2,345, although by the time they had all been satisfied the present managers of the office were left with only £435 net profit. £2,000 p.a. for the 1630's presumably refers to net profit; but, as it was quoted by the Earl of Holland, at the best of times an untrustworthy character, when he was asking Parliament to compensate him for its loss, this figure is doubly suspect. However, even Holland is unlikely to have exaggerated wildly, if only to avoid getting caught out.[2]

The Keepership of writs in Common Pleas was in some respects comparable to the Seal Office. It was very valuable, and its holder, more often known by his Latin title of Custos Brevium, was usually a politician or courtier, not a professional lawyer. In 1547 it was apparently only worth *c.* £285 p.a. and in 1562 probably not very much more, but by 1603 its annual value was estimated at £1,500, and in the 1630's at £1,700-£2,000. By contrast, the other three most lucrative posts in Common Pleas, the Prothonotaryships, were normally filled by lawyers of some professional distinction.[3]

---

[1] E. Lodge, *Life of Sir Julius Caesar* (1827), pp. 30-1; Maxwell-Lyte, *Great Seal*, app. B (these figures are in Caesar's papers; he was Master 1614-36).

[2] *D.N.B.*, XVI, 997-1000; Paget MSS. (Plasnewydd), Correspondence, XII, 85 (I am grateful to Mr. J. P. Cooper for lending me his transcript of this document; the figure of £2,345 is based on my interpolation).

[3] Peck, *Desid. Cur.*, I, i, 8 (from William Cecil's MS. diary; the arithmetic is wrong, Peck giving £240 as the total value); *The Trevelyan Papers*, III (Camden Soc., 1872), 52-3; T. Barrett-Lennard, *An Account of the Families of Lennard and Barrett* (privately, 1908), pp. 15-18. SP 23/205, p. 207; Hatfield Private and Estate MSS., Accounts 46/9, 168/2 (I am grateful to Mr. L. Stone for these references). See also Hastings, *Common Pleas*, chs. VII-IX.

Easily the most valuable, and perhaps for that reason the most notorious office of this type was the Chief Clerkship of King's Bench. Since there is no adequate history of this court which goes much beyond the fifteenth century, it is impossible to tell the full story of how this office acquired its extraordinary value. Sometime between the later fifteenth and the later sixteenth century there had been a decisive shift of business, in civil cases, from Common Pleas to King's Bench, and inside King's Bench business had become more concentrated in the Chief Clerk's department at the expense of the Filazers. In all probability the same procedural change accounts for both these developments. In 1618, apparently prompted by Buckingham, the judges of King's Bench certified that it was proper for the court's business to be funnelled through the Chief Clerkship; a similar opinion was obtained from the Solicitor-General.

The curious story of the Chief Clerkship from the 1600's to the 1620's has already been commented on by historians. Something will be said in the next chapter of what happened to it in the 1630's and 1640's, but here only its value is in question. In the early years of the century this was put at £3,500 a year; Buckingham's followers valued it for him at £4,000 in 1619, £4,500 in 1623, and £3,800 in 1627; a less reliable source gives £4,000 in 1628. These were probably all *net* totals; another £1,700 should be added for standing deductions, making £5,500-£6,200 p.a. *gross*. In 1638 a hostile critic doubled this, quoting a figure of £12,000 a year to a special investigating commission of six privy councillors, appointed in October 1637 as if to admit that it was beyond the capacity of the commissioners on fees to deal with this office. Such a crude exaggeration suggests caution in accepting any evidence of annual values given to commissions of inquiry. How abnormal this office was can be judged from its having attracted in turn the attention of James I's two principal favourites, Somerset and Buckingham. At between £4,000 and £6,000 a year, it was worth considerably more than any other administrative or legal office of comparable seniority, with the possible exception of the Clerkship of the Court of Wards. Even this post, shared by two men in the 1620's and 1630's, probably came some way behind, followed by various offices in Chancery, Common Pleas, and the Exchequer, most of which have already been mentioned in one connexion or another. It is of course even more difficult to compare the value of these with that of posts in the Household

214

and Chamber or in the Navy and Ordnance, because the forms of remuneration involved were so different.[1]

There are other means of approach to the problem of valuing offices, when their annual yield from all sources and the value of the individual items comprising this yield are both unknown. At least three possible methods exist for trying to calculate or infer total annual values: from the securities which were often given on entry to office, from the fines and compositions imposed on proved or alleged delinquents, and from the capital value set on offices when they were sold. Each of these must be examined more closely.

The giving of security to the Crown, or to the head of department, before an officer entered upon his duties is perhaps best thought of as a condition of service, like the oaths which had to be taken and the tenure by which office was held. Even so, the size of the bonds given might be expected to bear some relation to the value of the office, but the point is its value to whom. These securities were meant to safeguard the Crown, or sometimes the head of department, where he enjoyed the gift of the office, against fraud or other gross misconduct. Bonds given to the Crown, therefore, seem more likely to be calculated on the value of the respective offices to the Crown rather than to their holders. They might be expected to have been based on some estimate of what the loss would be if the new holder turned out to be hopelessly incompetent or completely dishonest. Such a hypothesis is clearly contradicted by the case of a new Teller of the Receipt who gave bonds totalling only £3,000 in 1636 when he might well have been going to handle £60,000-£80,000 a year in cash, let alone in tallies. The security paid by new Receivers-General of Crown land revenues, usually about £5,000, took little account of the marked differences in the value of these posts, alike to the Crown and to their holders; however, the Crown's *average* annual receipts from each of the nineteen Receivers-General was £4,773 in

[1] Gardiner, *History*, III, 31-5; H. R. Trevor-Roper, *The Gentry 1540-1640* (Econ. Hist. Rev., Supplmts., I), pp. 10-11; Hist. MSS. Comm. *Cowper*, I, 104; Birch, *Court & Times of Charles I*, I, 408; J. Whitelocke, *Liber Famelicus* (Camd. Soc., 1858), p. 59; Chamberlain, *Letters*, II, 180-1; SP 14/149/91 (I am grateful to Mr. L. Stone for this ref.); SP 16/370/45; Bodl. Bankes MS. 24/1; Berks R.O., Packer MSS.1/20a, 107, 121; and other sources given above in Chapter 2, s. vi.

1631-5. The Receiver of First Fruits and Tenths gave £6,000 security; the First Fruits brought in between £5,000 and £7,000 a year, Clerical Tenths *c*. £12,500. The Receiver of the duties on imported beaver hats gave £1,000 security; he paid the King an annual rent of £500 and made what he could over and above this. On the basis of the figures which are available, it is impossible to offer any generalizations about securities and the value of offices.[1]

Are fines and compositions a more fruitful source for calculating the yield of offices? One important difference is that these were actually levied, whereas the bonds given as securities normally were not. On *a priori* grounds the fine or composition might be expected to bear some relation to the annual value of the office and to its importance for the Crown. But most of those who were fined or persuaded to compound were at least as guilty of offences against the subject as of crimes against the Crown. So these penalties and purchases of pardons might also be expected to depend in some measure upon the magnitude of the offence, the ease with which it was, or could have been, established at law, and lastly the privileges left to the officer (such as his continuing to take his existing fees, enjoy his previous tenure, and keep the right to dispose freely of the reversion or of the office itself). Since none of these factors would necessarily vary according to the value of the office, it follows that fines and compositions are unlikely to have borne a constant ratio to value; the table opposite will help to make this clear.

Fines naturally tended to be heavier than compositions; this is equally true whether they are considered in relation to the value of offices to the Crown or to their holders. But, as Croke's story should have made clear, in practice the distinction between a fine and a composition was sometimes quite artificial.

Calculation of the annual values of offices from their capital values is at once more promising and more complicated. The term 'capital value' includes the sale price, but is not synonymous with it. Valuations could be, and sometimes were, made of offices, as of other pieces of property, which differed radically from their purchase price either in private negotiations or on the open market. But the great majority of capital valuations which have survived refer to the

[1] T 35/1; T 56/2; T 56/3, pp. 22-4, 30, 124; T 56/7, pp. 29, 54, 198-9; T 56/8, pp. 36, 55, 60, 66, 70, 89, 166-7, 196, 207, 216; T 56/10, p. 85. LC 4/200, p. 256, recognizances for debts in the form of Statute Staple (bond given May 1627, cancelled November 1630).

price which was being asked or offered, or to the amount which was eventually paid. Scattered and unreliable as it is, considerably more evidence survives about the prices of offices than about their annual

TABLE 8. FINES AND COMPOSITIONS PAID BY OFFICERS[1]

Officer	Fine or Composition	Annual Value to the Crown	Annual value to the Holder
Clerk of the Hanaper	3,000 F	Average 1631-5 7,324	? 800
Assistant under-clerk of Hanaper	200 F	covered by value of Clerkship	? 1-200 (estimate only)
Clerk of the Pipe	4,300 C	average 1631-5 8,147 (cash value of accounts in his charge)	? 1,500 (see above)
Six Clerks	2,666-13-4 each C	not measurable in cash value	800-1,600 (? according to seniority)
Clerk of the Presentations, in Chancery	100 C	ditto	? 300 (possibly too high a figure)
Feodary of Leics.	1,000 F	?	
Feodary of West Riding	1,500 F	?	In 1660 the 18 Feodaries were compensated as if for an average income of £126, 13s. 4d. each
One Feodary and two Escheators	650 C (the three)	?	

values. The argument that the latter can be calculated from the former runs as follows: offices were bought and sold like other pieces of property, and generally regarded in the same way; freehold land with vacant possession normally sold at twenty years' purchase, i.e. at twenty times the annual yield; it only remains to arrive at the comparable figure for offices; this done, wherever the sale price is known it can then be divided to obtain the annual value. Professor Trevor-Roper has suggested that three and a half years' purchase

[1] T 56/2 and other sources already cited; T 56/14, pp. 150, 176; E 405/285; SP 16/250/24-5; Elmhirst (Pye) MS. (1) fol. 53.

was the norm for vacant possession of offices; if so, sale prices should normally be divided by 3·5, instead of 20 in the case of freehold land.

There is certainly some evidence that contemporaries regarded three to four years as a reasonable range within which to bargain for offices. In 1603 a courtier wrote that 'although it be at a very hard rate to give above 3 years value for any office', he would if necessary go to four. In 1634 Wentworth, acting as a broker or middleman, arranged for an Irish office to be disposed of at three and a half years, and he seems to have assumed that this was reasonable. In 1660 Pepys thought four years' purchase was about as much as he could reasonably ask when thinking of selling an office.[1]

At the same time there are logical and empirical difficulties in accepting three and a half as being in any statistical or exact sense a valid figure. The figure of twenty years for land is not only limited to freehold with vacant possession, but assumes that 'other things are equal', for instance that neither buyer nor seller is under exceptional pressure, that the property is not being auctioned between two or more keen rivals, etc. So with offices. If Dr. David Mathew was correct in supposing that reversions were normally sold rather than offices with vacant possession,[2] then other things never would have been equal; all would have depended on the age and health of the present holder, and of a prior reversioner—if any. Whether vacant possession or the reversion was in question, it is obvious that differences in the security of tenure would have affected the price. Offices held during good behaviour and during pleasure must be excluded altogether, or at the very least different figures for years' purchase must be expected to apply in their cases. There is a further difficulty, even with life tenure. As a general rule offices were not heritable; unless a purchaser also secured, or had a chance of securing, a reversion for his son without additional payment, he was buying the office for his own lifetime only. Would not the price which he was prepared to pay for a particular office depend in part on his own age and state of health, as well as on its annual value? It is hard to tell if such considerations entered into men's calculations. But if so, the other things which have to be equal must be assumed

[1] Trevor-Roper, *The Gentry*, p. 28; *Trevelyan Papers*, III, 57-8; Sheffield C.L., Wentworth Woodhouse MSS., Strafford 8/121; P.R.O., C 2, James I, F 8/2; *Pepys's Diary* (ed. Wheatley), I, 196.
[2] *The Jacobean Age* (1938), pp. 209 (and n. 1)-211.

to include that those who bought offices were (by seventeenth-century standards) in average health and in the prime of life, say between twenty-five and forty. It is perhaps more likely that the seller's, or would-be seller's, age and health would enter into his calculations of what price he would accept for his office. Only by arguing that over a sufficient number of cases these two factors cancel themselves out can both be disregarded.

Finally the price paid for offices may also have varied with other, less strictly economic factors. Under James and Charles I very few sales seem to have involved complete outsiders simply buying their way into the King's service by purchase alone. The buying of an office more often involved jockeying for position by one, two, or more candidates, and lobbying by their respective patrons; in part at least the outcome depended on the degree of favour enjoyed by a candidate with his patron and on the patron's influence at court or in the department concerned. The price thus tended to vary with the prospective buyer's professional and social qualifications, and with his own and his patron's political standing. The amount of competition obviously mattered: the more of an auction that a transaction became, the higher the price would be likely to go. It would also vary with the strength of the prospective buyer's non-economic motives for wanting the office. If he wanted it desperately to achieve political ambition or social advancement, he would be prepared to pay more than if he was buying it simply as a financial proposition. Since many offices of political consequence were held during the King's pleasure, or during good behaviour, they would in any case have been subject to a different convention about years' purchase. But in the middle ranks the social motive was probably more significant. Some of these considerations may indeed even apply to the purchase of land; so far from being backward in calculating a comparable figure (to the twenty years' purchase there) in the case of offices, historians have perhaps been too ready to assume that twenty years is applicable in all land transactions, to the possible neglect there too of non-financial considerations. Professor Trevor-Roper has himself asked, '. . . is it necessarily true that they [successful lawyers and business men] bought it [land] as a prudent economic investment . . .?' He goes on to ask: 'Why should we suppose that every purchase [of land] by a successful man is necessarily an investment for immediate profit?'[1] If this was true of land, it may have

[1] *The Gentry*, pp. 24-5.

been at least equally true of office, where the non-economic (or, to be more precise, the non-financial and non-actuarial) considerations are likely to have been at least as strong.

Even the cash value of the same office might vary with different holders. Those who held certain posts always received pensions from the Crown in addition to their stipendiary Fees. But just as these pensions were not technically *ex officio*, so they were not necessarily uniform. In the 1630's the eight Grooms of the Privy Chamber had yearly pensions of £133 (one), £100 (one), £60 (four), and £40 (two). Excluding such pensions, Grooms' places were worth *c.* £140 p.a. each, but with them the annual values ranged from *c.* £273 to *c.* £180. In such cases would three and a half years' apply to the value of the office alone, or to that plus such pension as the prospective purchaser hoped to obtain? The size of the pension would in turn depend partly on his backers' and on his own standing; a candidate with powerful patrons and strong family connexions might well expect to do better in this respect than a self-made man who was relying more on purchase as a mode of entry, and whose profits from the office were less likely to be swollen by a pension or annuity.

In some offices, mainly legal ones, the annual money yield was steady. Where in addition to this no appreciable prestige accrued to their holders, and no prospects existed of using them as stepping stones to better things, the holder's interest can be compared to that of an annuitant or rentier. Since most offices of this type carried life tenure, there may have been a conventional number of years purchase price, subject always to the special circumstances of individual bargains. Appointments with any political significance tended to be less secure, but in other respects more attractive; yet we can hardly assume that these two factors cancelled each other out and left such offices in the same category for years' purchase as those of a more annuitary character.

Even taking the whole of the later sixteenth and early seventeenth centuries, say the period 1558-1642, in very few instances are there reliable figures for both the annual and the capital value of the same office at approximately the same date. The list could certainly be lengthened by further research, especially in sixteenth-century manuscript sources, which have not been used here; even so, the evidence would probably not permit firm statistical conclusions. The table which follows consists mainly of materials from the years *c.* 1620-40, but includes a few from earlier in James's reign and some others where sources of a later date give what is probably the value before 1640-2.

TABLE 9. CAPITAL AND ANNUAL VALUES OF SELECTED OFFICES[1]

Officer	Price, or other est. of Capital Value	Annual Value	No. of Years' Purchase	Dates
Central Executive: Secretary of State	6,000 (conventional compensation) 10,000 (alleged offer)	2,000 net 4,000-6,000 gross	1-5 range (3 on net value)	*c.* 1618-28 1617
Household: Treasurer	5,000 6,000 (rumoured offer)	*c.* 2,000+	*c.* 2·5 *c.* 3	1616-17 1629
Comptroller	2,000 (compensation) 3,000 (for a favoured candidate) 5,000-6,000 (normal offers) 5,000-7,000 (offers)	*c.* 3,000 (? falling in 1638) to *c.* 2,000	0·67 1·5-3 or 1-2 1·67-2·33	1630 1641 1617-20
Cofferer	2,110+500 p.a. for seller's life (then sick and aged) and then 200 p.a. for his widow's life (much younger)	*c.* 2,000+	*c.*1+*c.* 25% p.a. falling to *c.* 10% p.a.	1615
Knight Marshal	3,000	600-1,000; pensions varied from £133 p.a. 1618-26 to £400 p.a. 1626-42	3-5	1618
Chamber: Treasurer	2,000 (for reversion realised four years later)	*c.* 1,000+	*c.* 2	1613
Groom of the Stole	6,000 (expected offer) 8,000 (rumoured offer)	2,500 (same source) 1,600 *c.* 1,800-2,000 (from Household records)	2·4 3·75-5 3-4 (according to 1630-1 offers)	1630-1 1636-41
Groom of the Privy Chamber	500-600	100-120	4·17-6	1603
Gentleman Pensioner	300-323 400 (incl. 50 brokerage fee)	*c.* 73 (Household records)	4·1-4·4 5·5	1603 1624
Exchequer: Lord Treasurer	20,000 plus a Viscountcy 15,000	*c.* 7,000-14,000	1-3	1621 1628

(*Note:* Lord Mandeville, who resigned in 1621, was middle-aged and healthy, and lived another 21 years; the Earl of Marlborough, who resigned in 1628, was elderly and ailing and died within a year of resignation.)

[1] Sources as already given for annual values, or officers' incomes; additional secondary sources, e.g. Gardiner's *History*, *D.N.B.*, Bell's *Court of Wards*; Leeds P.L., Temple Newsam MSS., for Council in the North.

TABLE 9 (*continued*)

Officer	Price, or other est. of Capital Value	Annual Value	No. of Years' Purchase	Dates
King's Remembrancer	8,000 (to be paid at rate of 1,143 p.a.; transfer to a brother)	600 (suspect) or c. 1,100-1,200	6·7-13·3	c. 1641
Clerk of the Pipe	3,600 (hostile witness)	300 (too low) c. 1,500 ('improved value')	12 c. 2·4	1616 1618-38
Receiver-General of Yorks	1,150	330-340, falling later to c. 200	3·4-c. 5	1628
Wards and Liveries: co-Auditor	500 (reversion) c. 1,100 (reversion) 3,000 (offer) 3,000 (compensation)	857 (by interpolation)	? c. 3·5 3·5	1624-5 1636 1634 1649
co-Clerk of Wards	1,500 (undervalued) 1,000 (reversion)	? 1,500 min. in 1630's		1660 1634
Alienations: Commissioner	1,300 (father to son)	c. 100 (probably too low)	c. 13	1642
Clerk	600 (transfer to a brother) 3,000 (compensation)	c. 400	1·5 ? 7·5	1636 1647
Customs: Surveyor-General	5,700 (alleged price) 600 (for ⅓ of it)	c. 1000	5·7 c. 1·8	1620's 1631
Waiter, London	630 (for wiping out of a debt)	60+	c. 10·5	? 1635
Navy: Admiral of the Narrow Seas	3,000 *or* 3,500	? 730	c. 4-4·75	c. 1620-5
Ordnance: Master	2,000	700 (suspect as too low)	2·86 or less	c. 1634
Mint: Master	3,000 (alleged offer)	500	6	early 1630's
Chancery: Lord Chancellor	30,000 (reported offer)	range 3,000+ to 12,000	2·5-10	1617
Master of the Rolls	5,000+5,000 for reversion (alleged offer) 15,000 (auction)	c. 1,600 c. 1,200-1,500	? 3·125 c. 10-12·5	1624 1639
Clerk of the Hanaper	2,400	c. 800	3	1620
Six Clerk	1,000 (reversion for the Master of the Rolls' son) 2,500 (ordinary father to son reversion) 3,000 (offer by reversioner) 6,000 (alleged normal price) 8,000-9,000 (offers)	range 800-1600	0·6-1·25 1·56-3·1 1·87-3·75 3·75-7·5 c. 5-11·25	c. 1624-8 c. 1634-6 1636 1620's 1637

TABLE 9 (continued)

Officer	Price, or other est. of Capital Value	Annual Value	No. of Years' Purchase	Dates
Writer to the Great Seal from Star Chamber	900 (promotion from second reversion)	300	3	c. 1630
Writer of the Sub-poenas	3,250 (reversion)	950	c. 3·4	c. 1614
Cursitor	1,300	300	4·3	c. 1620
Keeper of the Records in the Tower	1,000 (asked, and considered high)	160-200	5-6·25	1615-16
King's Bench: Clerk of the Errors	4,000 (loss estd. at)	500 (rent from deputy)	8	1631-42
Marshal	500-600 (reversion: holder an old man) 1,000 or more (immediate possession)	300-400	1·25-2 2·5-3·3	1603
Common Pleas: Custos Brevium	3,000 (reversion; holder aged 48; health fair)	c. 2,000	c. 1·5	1634
Filazer	1,100 (seventh reversion, three of the first six being for two lives each; about 14 Filazerships in possession)	120 upwards	? c. 4-9	1633-4
Seal Office	21,000 (query exaggerated)	c. 2,000 c. 4,500	net 4·67 gross 10·5	1630's and 1645
Council in the North: Secretary	2,000 (to add son's life to tenure of existing holder)	c. 800 (min.)	c. 2·5 or less	c. 1630
Clerk of the Bills and Letters	900 (alleged price)	514 falling to 480	1·75-2	1606, 1617-1618
Keeper of the Gaol and Castle at York	600-700 (unsuccessful bargain) 500+100 p.a. (agreed price)	c. 200	3-3·5 2·5+50% p.a.	c. 1603 post-1603

Some of these figures are more reliable than others, but they are enough to show the difficulty of generalizing with any great accuracy. One or two further examples, from sales of revenue farms, rents, and pensions, may throw more light on the problem of years' purchase.

James Hay, first Earl of Carlisle, a prominent courtier and a friend of both James and Charles I, had been granted the import duties on wines entering Ireland and the licensing of the sale of wine in that kingdom. Shortly after the Earl's death in 1636, Wentworth, in his capacity as Lord Deputy, explained to the widowed countess that she could not possibly hope to sell the customs grant at a rate equivalent to twenty-eight years' purchase: it was a prerogative grant, valid only for the present king's lifetime (Charles was then aged thirty-eight and in excellent health); in wartime its value dropped catastrophically, almost to nothing; ten years' was the most she would get even for heritable freehold land in Ireland. He recommended her to regard eight years' as an optimum figure. Indeed in May 1637 he told her brother, the Earl of Northumberland, that for such a grant even eight years' purchase 'holds no proportion in a Kingdom, where an inheritance of land is familiarly bought for 10 years' value', thereby implying that eight years' would have been reasonable in England, where freehold land sold at twenty years'. He appears to have equated these grants with a twenty-eight or thirty-one year land lease, for which the correct purchase price would be seven or more likely six years'. Eventually the Irish committee of the Privy Council was persuaded to agree on an offer of twelve years for the wine licences and about eight for the customs farm.[1]

There was also some traffic in pensions, which affords another comparison with offices. In 1623 Cranfield valued a life pension from the Crown at five years' purchase. In about 1630 Burlamachi the financier commuted his life pension, and the arrears owing on it, at twelve years': a fair bargain as it turned out for he died around 1643. On one occasion in James's reign a life annuity was sold at about eight years' purchase. As with offices, the age and health of those concerned were presumably involved in negotiations about life pensions. A retrospective denunciation made in the following decade credited Cranfield with having himself sold the Surveyor-Generalship of the Customs for the equivalent of 5·7 years' and the office for licensing the sale of wine by inns and taverns at about twelve years'. An individual of a very different stamp, the Marquis of Hamilton, was said in 1630 to be selling his pension in the customs at the equivalent of 4·8 years' in order to take a force of volunteers to Germany. In fact he does not seem to have parted with it, but at about the same time a pension on the silk duties held by assignment from another peer was commuted by the Crown at 5·25 years'.[2]

[1] Knowler, I, 525, II, 71, 76, 89, 102, 120, 175; *Cal. S.P. Dom.*, *1639-40*, p. 153; Sheffield C.L., Wentworth Woodhouse MSS., Strafford 8/69-71, 395-8, 10a/79-81, 85-7, 111-12, 301-2.

[2] *Cal. S.P. Dom.*, *1619-23*, p. 514, *1625-6*, p. 12, *1629-31*, pp. 188, 374-5; Hist. MSS. Comm. *Cowper*, II, 67; Birch, *Charles I*, II, 87-8; SP 16/180/17; E 403/2590, pp. 337-40; E 101/619/50; C 2, James I, D 3/58.

7. SIR THOMAS MEAUTYS, CLERK OF THE COUNCIL, 1622-41.
(Engraving by W. Greatbach after the painting by
P. van Somer, *c.* 1620).

8. RICHARD BROWNLOW, CHIEF PROTHONOTARY OF COMMON
PLEAS, 1590-1638. (Engraving after the portrait by T. Cross,
1638.)

When the Long Parliament considered the award of compensation for loss of office, it probably tended to err on the generous side, for only parliamentarian office-holders were normally eligible at all. Likewise when men such as the Earl of Holland or the Somerset courtier Edmund Windham reckoned up their losses in the Civil War due to permanent loss of office or temporary loss of income from it, they are likely either to have exaggerated its value, or to have over-rated the number of years' purchase, or both. Even so, awards of six to seven years' value would scarcely have been made, nor claims put in for at least eight years' compensation, if three and a half years' had been firmly accepted as the normal sale price. If the analogy with land is sound, the upheavals of the 1640's might be expected if anything to have depressed prices below their pre-war levels, and below their pre-war equivalents in years' purchase.

Offices of an annuitary character, such as has been defined above, provided conditions which were most nearly comparable to those obtaining in revenue farms and pensions. And they may have capitalized at a comparable rate. There is just enough evidence to support the further hypothesis that offices of this type fetched a higher price, in terms of years' purchase, than those of political and even those of administrative importance. There is little support, at least in the evidence used here, for a fixed rate of capitalization; non-financial factors and individual circumstances seem to have helped to determine the price of offices more often than not. Three and a half years' may sometimes have been regarded as an approximate starting point in negotiations, but unfortunately it is not safe to divide the sale prices of offices by 3·5 in order to calculate their annual values.

Nor finally was the extent of venality uniform in all branches of the government. This leads on to the subject of the next section, but the uneven extent of sales, due amongst other reasons to some of them being statutorily illegal, further helps to explain why a standard rate of purchase, analogous to twenty years' for freehold land, granted that it existed in some people's minds, was unlikely to operate unmodified in more than a minority of cases.

iv SALE OF OFFICES

Quite apart from its connexion with their annual values, the sale of offices is an important subject in its own right. It raises a number of questions, which little systematic attempt has so far been made to answer. Apart from a few pages in Holdsworth, the classical secondary authorities offer little guidance. Virtually the only treatments of the subject consist of a short chapter in a recent general study of the *Sale of offices in the Seventeenth Century*, by Dr. Swart, a Dutch historian, and some brief comments by Professor Trevor-Roper in his essay on *The Gentry 1540-1640*.[1] By comparison with Professor Mousnier's monumental study of the venal traffic in French offices,[2] Dr. Swart's account of English developments is necessarily slight. He connects the saleability of offices under the Crown with their having been regarded as pieces of quasi-private property and treated accordingly; this in turn he relates to legal and social factors:

> ... in England central government had come into existence earlier than elsewhere in Europe. In this period Feudal and Canonical Law were still dominant. The legal status of the civil servants in England was, therefore, often defined in terms borrowed from these legal systems . . . feudal sovereignty and ecclesiastical functions were generally considered as property to be bartered. These legal theories, however, could never have exerted such an influence if they had not been used by the aristocracy in their struggle for power.

Dr. Swart connects sale with the hostility of existing office-holders to the creation of new posts, and their consequent opposition to major administrative reorganizations. He considers that this extreme conservatism was common both to the supporters and to the opponents of royal absolutism, to Bacon and to Coke.[3] These theories are open to criticism in detail, and Dr. Swart is on safer ground when he contrasts England with France. He rightly emphasizes that the English Crown never became dependent on the sale of offices as a regular and official source of revenue, and that in England the profits of this traffic were principally important in helping to redistribute wealth inside the existing ruling class. More will be said about the last point later in this chapter and in the next.

---

[1] K. W. Swart, *Sale of Offices in the Seventeenth Century* (The Hague, 1949), ch. III 'England'; Trevor-Roper, *The Gentry*, esp. pp. 26-30; Holdsworth, *Hist. Eng. Law*, I (6th edn.) 246-62.

[2] R. Mousnier, *La Vénalité des Offices sous Henri IV et Louis XIII* (Rouen, [1945]).

[3] Swart, *Sale*, pp. 47-49.

First it is necessary to be clear what is meant by 'sale of office'. Purchase of a position in the royal service, or to be quite accurate payment made in order to obtain and take up such a position, might involve *as payee*:

1. The King;
2. some royal favourite or leading minister of state;
3. the head of the department, or of the sub-department concerned (depending on whose gift the office was in);
4. the existing holder;
5. his heirs, executors, or assigns;
6. any holder of a prior reversion who was being by-passed, or was surrendering his claim.

Often it involved a combination of two or more of these kinds of payment. A new Six Clerk in Chancery presumably paid his purchase price of £6,000, or whatever it was, jointly to the Master of the Rolls, who had the gift of these places, and to the outgoing Clerk, or, if (as was more likely) he was dead, to his widow and other dependants. But over and above this it was customary for him to give the Lord Chancellor, or Keeper, a *douceur*, or brokerage fee, of £500.[1]

In recording sales of offices, contemporary letter and memoir writers frequently fail to specify which type of payment was being made. When money raised in this way was paid to the Crown, it often seems to have gone into the Privy Purse or the secret service fund, of which no regular accounts were kept. In the 1630's, apart from the limited number of fines and compositions already mentioned very few entries in the Exchequer records look like the purchase money of incoming officers. And as with the destination so with the size of payments; like their estimates of the annual value of offices, the figures given by contemporary observers sometimes need to be handled with care.

Offices were sold under the early Tudors as they had been in the time of the Norman and Angevin kings.[2] Professor Richardson states that 'public positions were commonly sold', but does not specify who by. Dr. Elton observes 'signs that offices were sometimes sold'—by Henry VII. It seems possible that the first Tudor used this means of raising money to a greater extent than his son or his

---

[1] Sheffield C.L., Wentworth Woodhouse MSS., Strafford 8/214-19.
[2] See *Dialogus de Scaccario*, ed. C. Johnson (1950), pp. xv, xxv-vii.

grandchildren.[1] Traffic in offices may have increased during Henry VIII's last years and for most of Edward VI's reign; this was a time of financial crisis and general administrative corruption.[2] Before the end of Edward VI's short reign the sale of offices was felt to be a problem serious enough to merit legislation. A statute of 1552 forbade the buying and selling of any posts connected with royal property and revenue, justice, and defence. But it safeguarded the existing rights of the Chief Justices, and of all the judges when on assize, in presenting to subordinate positions; it recognized the validity of all recently concluded and pending bargains; and it made further exceptions for all hereditary positions, and for the Keeper-ships of royal parks, walks, gardens, houses, and game, and for other comparable semi-local offices.[3]

Perhaps partly as a result of this act but due also to a general improvement in administration, traffic in offices may well have been reduced under Mary I and for the first part of Elizabeth's reign. But despite Cecil's disapproval there is evidence that it was not stamped out. And by the 1590's it was again increasing, once more as an accompaniment of financial stringency and adminis-trative decline.[4] According to Dr. Swart there was a very marked increase in its volume under James I, and this could perhaps also be inferred from other historians—Professor Willson and Dr. Mathew. 'By the time of James I', Professor Trevor-Roper writes, 'almost every office was bought, either from the Crown, or from the favourites who made a market of the Crown's patronage, or from the previous holder . . .'[5] This may, however, have come about by stages, and perhaps only reached its peak in the middle years of James's reign.

[1] Richardson, *Chamber Administration*, p. 257 (see also p. 247); Elton, *England under the Tudors*, pp. 52-3 and 53 n. 1 (see also Elton, *Revolution in Government*, pp. 213 n. 4, 402 n. 4); J. D. Mackie, *The Earlier Tudors* (Oxford, 1952), p. 231 n. 1; Dietz, *English Government Finance*, p. 40 (figures for 1504-8).

[2] Richardson, *Chamber Administration*; Elton, *Revolution in Govern-ment*; J. R. Hurstfield, 'Corruption and Reform under Edward VI and Mary: the example of Wardship', *Eng. Hist. Rev.*, LVIII (1953), 22-36.

[3] *Stat. Realm*, IV, i, 151-2.

[4] *Cal. S.P. Dom., Adds. 1566-79*, p. 46, Armagil Waad to Cecil, n.d., query 1567; J. U. Nef, 'Richard Carmarden's "A Caveat for the Quene" (1570)', *Journ. Pol. Econ.*, XLI (1933), 46; Neale, *Raleigh Lecture*, pp. 7-9, 15-19 (but see also Rowse, *England of Elizabeth*, pp. 374-5).

[5] *The Gentry*, p. 28.

Every type of sale flourished under James I. There is no need to repeat the well-known descriptions of Buckingham as broker-in-chief. Some of the biggest payments to the Crown were disguised as loans. For the Lord Treasurership £20,000 was advanced in 1620 by Montague, who is said to have paid £15,000 to be made Lord Chief Justice less than four years before.[1] Incidentally, if it is safe to infer that he had already recouped himself on the earlier transaction, the minimum value of the Lord Chief Justiceship must have been £3,750 p.a.; but there are obviously too many unknowns in this kind of interpolation.

In the parliaments of the 1620's critics often linked the traffic in offices with the sale of honours—peerages and baronetcies. And in 1621, as has already been explained, it was also related to the exaction of excessive fees. The act of 1552 had either been forgotten or was so easily evaded as to be worthless. The sale of offices was specifically attacked in the second session of Charles I's first parliament; and in his second parliament (in 1626) it featured prominently in the Commons' attack on Buckingham. Pym, himself an office-holder, spoke on article ten of the intended impeachment. He took his opening stand on clause forty of Magna Carta, '*Nulli vendemus, nulli negabimus . . . justitiam*', and then enumerated the evils which must follow from the sale of judicial offices and other important posts:

1. The wrong type of men will buy entry, and then buy promotion, their wealth making up for their lack of merit;

2. litigation will increase because legal officers will want to increase the number of cases, in order to collect more fees;

3. ambitious men will devote themselves to raising the money needed for official advancement, rather than to their professional studies;

4. the richest men will always prevail over the most deserving [an 'auction' type of sale seems to be assumed here];

5. men who buy offices will aim both to maximize their annual value and to sell again for more than they gave; the broker-in-chief [Buckingham] will be bound to support them in this;

[1] *Diary of Walter Yonge*, ed. G. Roberts (Camd. Soc., 1848), pp. 29, 40; Hist. MSS. Comm. *Lonsdale*, p. 12; Rushworth, *Hist. Colls.*, I, 334-5, 387.

6. pretexts will be found to get rid of men who have been given office on their merits, in order to make room for those who are prepared to pay for it.[1]

Pym did not particularize further. But in many legal offices where technical training was essential purchase could still have been said to be limited largely to lawyers; to have made enough money in private law practice to be able to buy an office was itself some test of legal distinction, if this can be equated with professional success. So in this field purchase would not necessarily have operated against merit. A similar argument might have been developed with regard to the merchants, financiers, and other business-men who bought revenue or customs offices, but only to a limited extent; in any case this defence could not have been used for any other branch of government. Perhaps Pym over-simplified and exaggerated, but he was arguing a difficult case against a powerful and dangerous enemy.

While Buckingham survived this attack, there are signs of a new policy soon after his assassination in 1628. In March 1630 one Secretary of State wrote to the other, apropos of the Surveyorship of the Ordnance, 'H.M. doth persist in his good purpose not to permit in that or any other [place] belonging to his service buying and selling'.[2] Most of the legal and other offices which continued to be sold in the 1630's probably were not in the King's gift, so that he was less directly involved in their disposal. Too much should not be made of this distinction. The Six Clerkships, it will be remembered, came back into the King's gift by the treaty of July 1635, but this act of resumption does not seem to have stopped them being sold. However, there is less evidence of venality, and at the top markedly less, between about 1630 and 1638, than before and immediately after these dates. Its extent in the different branches of the central government cannot be measured with mathematical precision, but certain contrasts can be drawn. Under the 'personal government' there was little purchase in the central executive, or in the upper ranks of the armed forces and defence departments. It is true that in 1633 the elder George Goring bought Lord Vere's regiment and

---

[1] Rushworth, *Hist. Colls.*, I, 338 (wrongly cited as clause 29; it became successively clause 33, 36, and 32 in the 1216, 1217 and 1225 reissues of the Charter: W. Stubbs, *Select Charters*, ed. H. W. C. Davis (Oxford, 1921), pp. 297, 338, 343, 350).

[2] Hist. MSS. Comm. *Cowper*, I, 403.

troop of horse with the Netherlands army for £4,000 on behalf of his spendthrift son, but only in Ireland could other comparable instances be found.[1] Below the level of ministers and judges sale continued to be normal in the law and revenue courts, and perhaps in the household departments, though for these there is less evidence either way.

The reduction of the traffic in offices during the 1630's may have been connected with the attempts to alter their tenure and to reduce reversions. As indicated, the sale of offices could in itself make officers either more or less independent of the Crown, according to how it was operated. But the other changes, especially in tenure, were clearly meant to reduce their independence; considering the effects of venality in James's reign and under Buckingham, the campaign to reduce it may have had the same motive—and perhaps the same effect. It may possibly have been easier to dismiss Lord Chief Justice Heath in 1634 because, as far as is known, he had not bought his office in 1631, but had merely, according to current gossip, given the Lord Keeper a diamond ring worth £1,000, to present to the King on his behalf: a *douceur* rather than a purchase.[2]

In the upper ranks there were only isolated sales of offices during the 1630's. Sir Dudley Digges, an ex-leader of the parliamentary opposition, was said to have bought the reversion to the Rolls in the winter of 1630-1; he succeeded Caesar as Master in 1636. The Earl of Newport bought the Mastership of the Ordnance from Lord Vere of Tilbury in about 1634. By contrast, neither Windebank in 1632 nor Vane in 1640 seems to have paid to become Secretary of State; Juxon did not pay to become Lord Treasurer in 1636, nor Northumberland to become Lord Admiral in 1638 (in neither case was there an outgoing incumbent to be compensated); Cottington does not seem to have paid for the Chancellorship of the Exchequer in 1629 nor for the Mastership of the Wards in 1635; except in Ireland, no marked venality attaches to the common law judges appointed in the 1630's, and surprisingly little that can be traced even to the major household appointments. The Earl of Holland later claimed to have paid £21,000 for the Seal Office of King's Bench and Common Pleas in the mid-1630's, but although he was a councillor and in other capacities almost a 'great officer', this was not a great office. The notorious auctioning of the Rolls in 1639

---

[1] Sheffield C.L., Wentworth Woodhouse MSS, Strafford 13b/92.
[2] Birch, *Court and Times*, II, 137.

and the sale, again more or less to the highest respectable bidder, of the Comptrollership in 1641 reflect the Crown's desperate financial straits. The Rolls, it should also be said, was a valuable office, and one which conferred high rank and dignity on its possessor, but in practice it was not of great political importance.

Apart from the actual invocation of legal sanctions against those who trafficked in offices, there is weighty evidence of disapproval. In 1630 Sir Henry Mervyn, commander of the channel squadron, felt it necessary to write an unusually tortuous and circumlocutory letter to Nicholas, then secretary to the Admiralty commissioners, to check rumours that he was trying to sell his office without the Commissioners' approval; instead he emphasized his quest for the right influence at court to help secure his pay arrears, though his choice of the well-known virtuoso and dilettante Sir Kenelm Digby as a possible successor is perhaps surprising.[1] In the autumn of 1640 it became clear that Sir William Becher would not remain a regular Council Clerk much longer; not only was he ageing, but he seems to have wanted to retire in face of the coming storm; for if not a practising Roman Catholic, he was certainly a suspect. One candidate was Robin Reade, Windebank's factotum, another the courtier Sir John Berkeley. Reade, too, was to be swept away in the same cataclysm as his master, but before this Berkeley told him that:

> . . . it is true that being unprovided of any satisfactory course of life I had upon hard terms enough made an agreement with Sir William Beecher in case he could have leave to retire, which I meddled not with. . . .

This permission having been refused, he, Berkeley, had realized that his quest was hopeless and now wished Reade better luck in his. Reade had already implied that the King was more against the office being sold than against Becher parting with it. Reade had solicited one of the Jermyns, a favourite of the Queen, to help him, but apparently an explicit declaration of withdrawal was needed from Berkeley. Reade implied that he was a self-made careerist for whom this represented the chance of a lifetime, while Berkeley, as a well-born and well-connected court gentleman, would have plenty more opportunities. In an ironical sense this was true, but in February 1641 the Clerkship was granted to Richard Browne, royal agent in Paris. Suspicion of venality had delayed the transfer; perhaps also

---

[1] SP 16/173/6, fol. ib.

the Council was trying to keep a balance between foreign experts and others on its own staff, and to exclude mere courtiers like Berkeley from such positions.[1]

At least during the ten or eleven years after the death of Buckingham it does not seem to have been the case that 'almost every office was bought'. The question then arises, how much had the traffic declined from the level which Professor Trevor-Roper describes it as having attained under James I? There was more of a decline in the higher than in the middle and lower ranks of government, and more among central than among local appointments. Trade in Irish offices and in legal positions at home, to name but two categories, seems to have proceeded as briskly as before. Moreover, even in James's reign the evidence of well-nigh universal venality in all ranks is weighted towards the years c. 1615-23, and it may have been slightly less widespread before and after these dates. Thus in 1611 the judges of King's Bench resolved that the offices of Chancellor, Registrar, and Commissary in the church courts came within the scope of the Edward VI act, and gave a decision accordingly[2]: a sign that the law was not, at that date, a completely dead letter. Since, despite the continued predominance of Buckingham, there are also some signs of a slight slackening in the traffic after Charles's accession, it is possible to see both the change of dynasty in 1603 and the death of the favourite in 1628 as rather less dramatic breaches of continuity than they appear at first sight.

To offset this improvement in the 1630's, the commission on fees was being used, at first spasmodically but later systematically, to persuade or compel officers to compound with the Crown for their real or alleged abuses. In effect, a lump sum down was paid and the officer was allowed to keep his position on the same terms as before, or with minor changes, such as small reductions in some of his fees. Certain members of the government seem to have hoped for something altogether more grandiose, a systematic levy on all officers, comparable to the Paulette in France. In effect, there was a choice before the King and any would-be reformers: should royal policy be aimed at stamping out the traffic in offices, or at taking over and exploiting it as a regular, above-board, and potentially major contribution to the revenues?

Not unexpectedly the policies pursued under the early Stuarts show

[1] SP 16/470/84; Bodl. Tanner MS. 67, fol. 214; *Foedera*, XX, 447.
[2] Croke, *Reports* (1683), II, 269, Dr. Trevor's case.

traces of schizophrenia, particularly during the 'personal government' of Charles I. Wentworth disliked private revenue grants and farms, especially when they thwarted his own plans; Secretary Coke and Bishop Juxon, to take two of the more humdrum of Charles's ministers, both at different times expressed their opposition to 'projects' and farms.[1] Yet in the 1630's the customs were largely let to farmers, and there were many dubious and several disreputable 'projects'. The commission on fees itself came near to degenerating into a 'project', or revenue-raising device, and the honesty of its own employees was not above reproach. In these ways the Crown could be said to have become a partner in a miniature, or 'poor man's', imitation of the French system. Traffic in offices might have been put on a more organized basis, and operated to the Crown's advantage, as—at least in theory—it was in France. Failing this, although it can not be used as a kind of gauge or barometer to measure degrees of corruption and incompetence, it tended to fluctuate according to the Crown's financial needs and the outlook of the sovereign and his or her chief advisers.

At one point in the reign of James or of his son a far more radical and comprehensive plan was mooted. In its proposals for fees to be 'pooled' in each office or department, for a salaried Civil Service, and for the Crown to collect the surplus profits from government business, it was much more than just another plan to regulate fees and punish offending office-holders; indeed, it went far beyond anything that was even attempted before the end of the eighteenth and early nineteenth centuries. A contemporary copy of this proposal, which was apparently presented to the Council, has survived along with other papers which entered the national archives in the collection of Francis Hargrave, the eighteenth-century antiquary. Early in this century part of it was quoted by a German scholar, as if it belonged to the administrative reforms of Edward VI's reign. It is headed 'Concerning offices, officers, and fees, and a Commission to inquire after them', and opens with a recital of medieval precedents for royal action against administrative disorders, such as the great judicial purges of Edward I. The unknown author then came to his main suggestion.

It is therefore humbly submitted to your honourable consideration whether it will not suit as well with his Majestie's honour as proffit to resume all such offices, as shalbe forfeited into his royal

---

[1] Hist, MSS. Comm. *Cowper*, I, 129; *Cal. S.P. Dom., 1639-40*, p. 75.

hands, and to retain them by placing able Clerks as officers to execute the same, giving them competent allowances per annum out of the profits of the office; And all such officers so assigned to be bound in recognizances to keep a true book upon [*sic*] to be administered to them (when they enter these places) of all the particular businesses which shall pass in their several places per annum and to be true accomptants to his Majestie of the proffits thereof, deducting only their own yearly allowances and paying in the overplus half yearly to the Receipt of Exchequer, or to one to whom his Majestie shalbe pleased to make his Receiver-General of all moneys so arising; by which means his Majestie may know in one yeare what every office is worth per annum, and consequently the total of that yearely revenue, the greatness whereof may in some sorte be guessed at (though in a worse instance) by example of the Kinge of France. . . .

He then quoted the English translation of Botero to the effect that the French King made about seven million livres, or three million pounds sterling, yearly from the sale of offices, and went on

It is also humbly submitted to your Lordshipps' consideration whether it will not most advance the benefit and expedition of his Majestie's service of [*sic*. query: if] a Commission of Oyer and Terminer were granted to my Lord Treasurer, Lord Privy Seal, and others of eminent association, to punish those delinquents by ffynes & forfeiture of their offices into his Majestie's hands, whom the Commission of Inquirey shall discover, for it is doubtfull whether the Starr Chamber properly [may] censure most offences inquirable, whose cognizances are proper to a Commission of Oyer and Terminer; and the Starr Chamber will be too narrow for the numerous company of delinquents. . . .

Even such a special commission, he considered, would have to sit in the vacations as well as in term-time,

excepte a good rounde censure fall upon the first who shalbe there questioned, for a terror and example to bring the rest in by voluntary submission and Compositions.

The commissioners should be given powers to arrange compositions, and to certify the correct fees, 'That reformation may accompany the punishment'. Where officers had forfeited their posts, the new incumbents were to give bonds that they would only take the approved fees. The author emphasized (as did those of certain documents cited in the second section of this chapter) how the raising of extra revenue would thus be combined with the redress of popular grievances.

235

From this and from its mention of several parliamentary attempts to tackle the fee problem, the paper might have been an immediate prologue to the issue of any of the three commissions on fees, in 1610, 1623, or 1627. Nothing is specified about the commission of inquiry, which the author seems to distinguish from the recommended commission of oyer and terminer, nor does he do more than imply that such a commission was already in being. He could even have been addressing the commissioners on fees themselves, rather than the Council or a council committee; the senior commissioners, though hardly the so much more active sub-commissioners, would have properly been styled 'your Lordships'. From internal evidence the version of the plan which has survived cannot be earlier than 1616; granted this, its reference to the Lords Treasurer and Privy Seal points to 1616-18, 1620-4, or 1628-35. More accurately than this it cannot at present be dated.[1] In 1621-2, however, in his capacity

---

[1] B.M. Hargrave MS. 321, fols. 588-93, anon., n.d. (quoted in J. Hatschek, *Englisches Staatsrecht* (Tubingen, 1905-6), II, 574, n. 1.) The handwriting could conceivably be of any date from the mid-sixteenth to the late seventeenth century, but is very characteristic of the period *c*. 1610-40; the form of the MS. suggests the original draft of a petition. The following points are relevant to its date: (i) the previous item (fols. 581-7) is a petition dated 16 January 1632/3, and the next but one is a copy of a memo. dating to 1618-21 (fol. 612, ref. to Edward Wardour as a knight and Robert Pye as Mr.: Shaw, *Knights*, II, 169; *D.N.B.*, XVI, 514); the other items in this part of the MS. vol. are all in handwriting of the same period; (ii) the MS. (fol. 590) gives a page ref. to the 1616 edn. of Robert Johnson's translation of Botero, *Le Relationi Universali* (p. 109; published by Jaggard; *Short Title Cat.* no. 3403); this edition is dedicated to the Earl of Worcester, Lord Privy Seal; (iii) the ref. to the Lords Treasurer and Privy Seal as the best men to head the commission of oyer and terminer points to years when both these posts were filled by active and prominent ministers; the omission of the Lord Chancellor (or Lord Keeper) may also be significant. Except for (ii), Salisbury and North-ampton (1608-12) seem the likeliest combination. In view of (ii), the most plausible are Suffolk and Worcester (1616-18), or Mandeville and Worcester (1620-1, when the Great Seal was temporarily in commission after Bacon's fall). Cranfield and Worcester (1621-4) are plausible for the former, but the latter had by then become inactive, nor was either on the 1623-4 fee commission. Weston and Manchester (1628-35) seem more likely, since the latter was a fee commissioner in 1623-4 and 1627-40, but the omission of Lord Keeper Coventry is strange. To sum up: Johnson's dedication to Worcester suggests 1616-18, the Great Seal vacancy 1621, the implication that a fee commission was already in being 1623-4 or 1628-35.

as Lord Treasurer, Cranfield considered the possibility of a special levy, equivalent to one or two years' income, on all or some office-holders[1]; and there are obvious comparisons with the various plans for loans from officials in 1626-7 and 1638-9.

Little has so far been said in this chapter about the administrative importance of the sale of offices. We need to consider what difference it made to the King's service and to his servants; whether it tended to vary in extent with the level of honesty and efficiency in government; and whether it brought into office large numbers of ignorant parvenus who were totally unqualified to occupy the posts which they purchased, or *per contra* led to a healthy infusion of successful self-made men into an otherwise dangerously static bureaucracy. Attention has already been paid in the last chapter to some of these points. Sale, or rather purchase, was only *one* of several ways of entering office, and it seldom operated in isolation from any of the other factors: patronage, family connexion, special abilities and qualifications, reward for merit or service. Brokerage, involving the payment of a large gratuity to a middle man when an office changed hands, could of course occur when sale in the strict sense did not, and was thus more widespread; it often accompanied the methods of entry described as Patronage and Patrimony. When it was taken by the head of department or by whoever had the gift of the office (not excluding the Crown), a brokerage fee can also be likened to an entry fine or premium payable on a new lease. In so far as purchase can be considered in isolation as a way of entering office, there is little evidence either that it led to noticeably worse results than did patronage and patrimony, or that it brought into the government a high proportion of men who would not sooner or later have got in by some other means. There are of course men like Cranfield, Ingram, and Wyche, who might not have got as far as they did but for purchase, although, as already explained, Ingram over-reached himself badly and never fully recovered from this failure. Only in the customs and other revenue farms were such cases at all common.

This question can be left open until the social composition of the

---

[1] R. H. Tawney, *Business and Politics under James I: Lionel Cranfield as Merchant and Minister* (Cambridge, 1958), pp. 202 (and n. 4), 301; see also Chamberlain, *Letters*, II, 459-61 (esp. 460).

office-holding body has been more fully examined in the next chapter. Provisionally, it does not appear that many merchants or other business-men bought their way into the King's service with no previous contacts or official experience. Nor must we forget the varied purposes for which different men, and sometimes the same men, sought different offices. Offices which can be described as careerist and entrepreneurial were bought, so were annuitary or rentier ones; this has already been illustrated from the career of the elder Vane.

The staffs of Chancery, Common Pleas, and Exchequer, who had more often than not bought their offices, as well as paying brokerage on entry, were also those most criticized for extortion. Only the officers of the royal prisons were more severely attacked, and there payment in fees and gratuities gave unique scope for abuse. Not that the Navy, Ordnance, Household, and Wardrobes were well run; but in these cases the Crown, not the public, was cheated. Contractors and others who had dealings with these departments were often themselves parties to the deceits which were practised. In the law and revenue courts officers recovered their purchase money at the expense of accountants, litigants, and other members of the public. It is easy to see why, outside the government, more fuss was made, for instance, about Common Pleas than about the Household. And in so far as the staffs of the central executive and the other departments were at any stage less corrupt than those of the law and revenue courts, this may have been because they were more susceptible to short-term influences. Among these may be suggested the accession in 1625 of Charles I, more austere and less tarnished than his father, the changed political groupings and climate after 1628-9, and in the 1630's the presence of some men with altogether higher standards of public service at the top.

The third of these influences, the new men at the top, naturally suggests the names of Laud and Wentworth. In the field of administrative reform Wentworth is by far the more important of the two. In theory he would probably have liked to limit purchase to minor offices of routine importance only and to have excluded it wholly from all connected with justice, finance, administration, and defence; or at least only to admit purchasers who he and his allies felt sure would not use their positions in ways prejudicial to the royal interest. But unluckily the royal interest *could not* be well served, or only with great difficulty, by officers who depended on forms of payment like fees, gratuities, perquisites, and poundage. This problem Wentworth never seems to have faced, or, if he did, he gives the impression of having applied one law for himself and his friends and another for lesser breeds. Similarly, even if Laud's precept and practice were not actually inconsistent, his administrative ideals were at least tinctured with a dash of realism.

But for all that can be said to their discredit the two great protagonists of 'Thorough' did stand for cleaner as well as for more efficient and more absolute government. And up to a point they had the King with them. Others, perhaps Windebank in particular, were doubtless ready to argue the counter-attractions of the opposite policy, of extending and exploiting the sale of offices. Even Laud and Wentworth do not seem to have realized that the exaction of 'compositions' and 'loans' from officers, especially on the scale attempted in 1639-40, came very near to the French model. In France the Crown repeatedly mulcted the office-holders financially, and they correspondingly became an entrenched vested interest, able in some respects to inhibit royal freedom of action. Yet in Charles I's own mind, and in practice so far as he had personal control over royal policy, insular rectitude—or perhaps hypocrisy—apparently triumphed over cosmopolitan temptations.

This may give the impression that the sale of offices had no intrinsically bad effects, and that Pym's arguments of 1626 were misconceived or even deliberately falsified. That venality had some bad effects would not be denied by anyone who had studied English, let alone French government in the sixteenth to eighteenth centuries. For the most part, however, these abuses did not arise from the sale of offices alone, but from the general character of the administrative system, of which it was but one, though an important feature. Furthermore, it is artificial to isolate venality in government from its social and economic context; the old administrative system needs to be seen as a whole and in its proper historical setting.

V ECONOMIC IMPORTANCE OF FEES AND OFFICES

Two obvious and clear conclusions might appear to follow from what has so far been said about the economic significance of fees and offices: that the administrative system, of which the sale of offices was a part, did *not* provide the English Crown with a regular revenue of any great consequence, and that this system (again including the sale of offices) *was* a major factor in redistributing wealth *within* the propertied and governing classes. But both these propositions need to be examined more closely before they can be allowed to stand.

The least controvertible point is that the Crown did not derive any large direct income from the sale of offices. But this is not to say that it did not gain some, possibly indirect, economic or financial benefit from other aspects of the administrative system. The question is, in what ways and how much?

Scarcely more controversial is the hypothesis that in so far as the sale of offices and the payment of officers helped to bring about changes in the English social structure, this was primarily by enabling certain members of the upper classes (peers, gentry, lawyers, merchants) to prosper at the expense of their fellows and of those below them. The question here is how to measure the importance of this in relation to other factors which affected the structure of English society.

In following up these two lines of inquiry, it will be best to treat them together, as a single problem, and to try first to be more specific about the amounts of money involved in the administrative system. For when the traffic in offices and the gains of their holders were at their height the annual turnover of money must have been an appreciable fraction of the current national income. One way of trying to gauge the relative economic importance of office-holding would be by comparing the total earnings of government employees, as a proportion or percentage of national income, at different dates. Naturally the lack of statistical evidence makes an accurate comparison impossible between the twentieth and the seventeenth centuries; but if even the order of magnitude of the totals needed for such a comparison can be estimated, our inquiry will be set on an altogether sounder basis.

In this respect the payment of officers in fees and gratuities, rather than in wages and salaries, presents a special problem. Nowadays members of the public still have to pay fees if they make use of certain government services, but officials (as opposed to lawyers) who receive fees do not keep them in lieu of salaries from the Crown. And, apart from this, the total amount received annually in this way is negligible set beside the government's total income, let alone beside the entire national income. In the early seventeenth century this was not so. If all the fees and gratuities received by the staffs of the central courts and departments could have been added up, they would have been equal in amount to a very large fraction of the total royal revenues, and far from negligible as a proportion of the national income. Although accurate figures are out of the question, it is worth trying to make some provisional estimates. To take a modern comparison, in 1957 the national income of the United Kingdom is estimated to have been £17,604 millions, and the total of all personal incomes £17,987 millions; wages and salaries paid by central and local government (including the armed forces and the Post Office, but excluding the nationalized industries) were £2,458 millions, and total government expenditure £6,985 millions. Thus the pay of all (non-industrial) government employees constituted 13·7 per cent. of all personal income, 14 per cent. of national income, and 35·2 per cent. of all government expenditure.[1] Our problem here is to discover—very approximately—the corresponding percentages for the time of Charles I.

The evidence presented to the commissioners on fees includes the alleged annual values of most offices in Chancery. Since the stipendiary Fees paid by the Crown to the members of Chancery were in most cases very small or non-existent, and since in any case they almost all came out of the profits of the court (from fees and fines paid by its users to the Crown) no deduction need be made from these total annual values in order to calculate the non-stipendiary fees paid annually in Chancery. Values are not unfortunately assigned to the offices of the Lord Keeper, Master of the Rolls, Auditors, Comptroller of the Hanaper, Clerks of the Denizations and of the Pardons for Outlawry, Writers of Commissions of Appeal, and Cursitors' under-clerks. All of these, except perhaps the Auditors, must have received fees or gratuities. The total without them is c. £48,680.[2] The values of some offices, such as the Six Clerkships, may have been exaggerated by hostile witnesses; but as against what should be subtracted to allow for this there is the amount to be added on for those not included in the depositions; there is also the revenue of the Hanaper, in fees paid to the Great Seal and not remitted to individual officers, amounting in 1631-5 to another

---

[1] Central Statistical Office, *National Income and Expenditure, 1958* (1958), Tables 1, 2, 4, 12, 49, and 51, and pp. 79-80 (notes to Table 51).

[2] Wilson, Thesis, app. III. (The total given is based on my addition.)

£3,811 p.a.[1] Unless the evidence presented to the commissioners was systematically and grossly exaggerated, £55,000-£60,000 seems to be about the mark. Even if we assume an average over-estimate or exaggeration of 25 per cent. in all the items making up the £48,680, and so reduce this to *c.* £36,500, the final total would still be within the range £45,000-£50,000. For reasons that have already been suggested the officers of Chancery are likely to have had a larger collective income from fees than those of any other central court or department, for which a comparable estimate is needed.

For the court of Wards and Liveries a rather more speculative total can be worked out. A table was drawn up when the court was finally abolished in December 1660, on which was to be based the compensation for its officers, other than the unrepentant parliamentarians and those who had failed to make their peace with the restored royal government. Some of the items in this table differ markedly both from the 1647 valuations at six or seven years' compensation and from the 1649 ones at three and a half years'. In 1647 the maximum value to be set on the Mastership is £1,667 p.a., but in 1660 it was reckoned at £5,000 p.a. The Usher was rated at £1,000 p.a. in 1649 and £300 in 1660, but in the Messenger's case the discrepancy there is only between £343 and £350 p.a. Although the 1660 list is not complete, it is the fullest and the only one which gives annual values and does not leave these to be worked out. Taking it as a basis, supplemented where necessary by the 1647 and 1649 figures, and subtracting the £1,070 paid to the officers of the court in Fees and diet, the total received by them in fees is *c.* £21,680 p.a.[2]

So there is evidence about Chancery because of the commission on fees, and about the court of Wards because it was abolished. No

---

[1] T 56/2 (Total Hanaper revenues, 1631-5 = £7,324 av. p.a., less £2,933 received from the Alienations Office and £580 already counted, because it was paid out in Fees).

[2] Bell, *Court of Wards*, pp. 160-1, and Table A, fcg. p. 192; *Commons Journals*, VIII, 219-20. The two attorneys have been left out (see ch. 2 for explanation of this), also the second Clerk of the Liveries (presumably a reversioner) and the Clerk of the Wards in reversion; by subtracting the value given for half the Clerkship from that of the reversion to the whole, a value can be obtained for the other co-Clerkship, which is not on any of the lists; the 1647 figures have been used for the Surveyor and the Auditor, and for the junior co-Auditor the 1649 figure; the 1660 list of Feodaries covers only 23 of the English and Welsh counties, and interpolation must be used for the others.

such figures are available covering as large a proportion of the posts anywhere else.

There are reliable valuations of some offices in the lower Exchequer. In the upper Exchequer a *minimum* value can be worked out for the fees paid annually by certain accountants, but not for the actual amounts received there. Luckily independent sources give contemporary valuations, of varying reliability, for a few posts. This presents another difficulty, in that the totals for fees paid are not the same as either the gross or the net values of such offices: Fees, pensions, allowances, diet, etc., must all be deducted from the gross value, unless they came out of the court's own profits from fees and fines; and such overheads as officers had to spend on the wages of under-clerks and cleaners, stationery (not always provided), and in some cases heating, lighting, and maintenance, are excluded from the net value. With these cautions in mind, a figure within the range £38,000-£45,000 p.a. is reached for the Exchequer, made up as follows:

TABLE 10.   FEE PAYMENTS IN THE EXCHEQUER

Lord Treasurer	£7,000-9,000
Chancellor of the Exchequer . . .	2,000-3,000
Chief Baron, 3 Puisne Barons, and Cursitor Baron	7,500-9,000
King's Remembrancer	1,400
Lord Treasurer's Remembrancer . .	1,200
Clerk of the Pipe	1,500
Revenue and Prest Auditors . . .	3,000-3,500
Other officers of the upper Exchequer .	3,000-3,500
Receiver-Generals	2,000-2,500
Under-clerks in the upper Exchequer .	3,000-3,500
Officers of the lower Exchequer . .	5,000
Under-clerks there	1,500
Totals	£38,100 min. £44,600 max.

With the other common law courts our case is even worse. In King's Bench there are figures for the Chief Clerkship, and the range within which to put certain other offices can be gauged. This is not always easy. Thomas Fanshawe of Jenkins, Essex, was to assert that the Clerkship of the Crown was only worth £200 p.a., but since he compounded for a total income of only £650, while Lady Fanshawe believed that his father's estate was worth nearly £2,000 a year, his figure for this office should not perhaps be taken too seriously.[1] For the whole court £15,000-£20,000 p.a. is plausible. In Common Pleas no single office was worth as much as the top one in King's Bench, but the three Prothonotaries and the Custos Brevium all came in the next group, and there were probably more under-officers with largely formal duties than in King's Bench, if fewer than in Chancery or Exchequer. Then there was the Seal Office of the two benches (*alias* the Greenwax) of *gross* value £4,000-£5,000 p.a. All this is without taking into account the Judges themselves, though deductions must be made from their total incomes for what they received from the Greenwax and from the Crown. If £15,000-£20,000 p.a. seems reasonable for each of these courts without the Greenwax and the Judges, the final total for the two of them must be within the range £55,000-£65,000.

None of the other central courts compared in value with these five. But their members were of course far from unique in their dependence on fees. In the central executive, each Secretary of State must have received a minimum of £2,000 a year in fees and gratuities; this can be seen by subtracting the known emoluments of all other kinds from the commonly accepted *gross* value of a Secretaryship. The Privy Seal, Signet and Council Clerks, ordinary and extraordinary, and their deputies and underlings must have been particularly reliant on this form of payment. There is no suggestion that these posts compared financially with the great legal clerkships; even so, *c.* £15,000-£25,000 p.a. does not seem too much for the central executive. At least £5,000 and possibly nearer £7,000-£8,000 must be added for the Attorney- and Solicitor-General (excluding their gains from private law practice).

The other central courts and offices in which fees were paid include Star Chamber, of which the Clerkship was reckoned at £1,600 p.a. in the 1600's and £2,000 in the 1630's. The Clerkship of the Duchy of Lancaster court was rated at £600 p.a., yet the total annual revenue of the Duchy was under £11,000 (average) in the 1630's. Although Star Chamber was investigated by the fee commissioners in 1623-4, and again in Charles's reign, neither it nor the Duchy court had a bad reputation for excessive fees; nor, compared with the institutions for which totals have already been suggested, did the courts of Admiralty and Requests, the Alienations Office, the

[1] *Memoirs of [Anne] Lady Fanshawe*, (1905 edn.), p. 41; *Cal. Cttee. Compdg.*, p. 1661; Fanshawe MSS. (Bratton Fleming).

two regional councils, and the central ecclesiastical courts. There is no evidence in any of these institutions of a whole range of officers with fee incomes of over £1,000 a year. The following totals seem reasonable: Councils in Wales and the North £15,000-£20,000, Star Chamber and Requests £12,000, Duchy of Lancaster and the Stannaries £7,500-£10,000, Alienations (excluding the Clerk, included in Chancery figures) £3,000, Admiralty £5,000, central church courts £10,000. For this whole group the range seems to be £52,500-£60,000 p.a.

Two principal groups of institutions, or branches of government remain. The customs, most of the other revenue farms, and some of the monopoly patents and commissions involved fee or licence payments. From the volume of complaints in 1640-1 the patents and commissions might be thought to have imposed one of the heaviest burdens, but fees and gratuities paid to officials must be distinguished from the profits of middlemen (farmers, contractors, etc.) and from possible price increases born by the consumer as a result of monopolies. Industrial and licensing monopolies were probably more burdensome in raising costs and prices and in their actual restrictiveness than because of the fee and gratuity payments which they involved. Fees to customs officials, on the other hand, were obviously very considerable. Beyond the retrospective allegation that the Surveyor-General had been making c. £500 p.a. in fees around 1620, and inferences from one or two sale prices of customs posts there is remarkably little evidence. Several customs officials had their stipendiary Fees from the Crown supplemented by allowances deducted at source from the customs' revenues; this may imply that some of them were not making a great deal from legitimate fees, in proportion to their pains and responsibilities. For this whole group informed guesswork suggests a total of about £30,000 a year.

Then there are the spending departments, to be subdivided approximately into the household group and the defence group. Many officers in both these groups certainly received gratuities, but very few were authorized to take fees. The probable totals of these gratuities are just as relevant but even more obscure than the estimated fee totals. Perquisites, bribes, and frauds must be excluded: the first and last because at least in the first instance they were at the expense of the Crown rather than the subject, and the second because, unlike gratuities, they were, or were liable to be, recognized as abnormal and even culpable. For the gross annual gratuities of all officers in the spending departments the range is bound to be very wide: say a minimum of £20,000 and a maximum of £50,000.

It is therefore possible to work out estimated minimum and maximum grand totals.

TABLE 11. TOTAL FEE AND GRATUITY PAYMENTS IN
THE CENTRAL GOVERNMENT

Departments	Minimum	Maximum
Chancery	£45,000	£60,000
Wards	22,000	25,000
Exchequer	38,000	45,000
King's Bench and Common Pleas . . .	55,000	65,000
Central Executive	15,000	25,000
Law Officers	5,000	8,000
Other central and regional courts . . .	52,000	60,000
Customs, revenue farms, monopolies . .	25,000	35,000
Spending departments	20,000	50,000
Totals	£277,000	£373,000

Despite this ostensibly wide range, it would be foolish to assert that fees and gratuities definitely fell within these limits in the 1620's and 1630's. Bearing in mind the lack of firm evidence it seems safer to say that they are unlikely to have totalled less than £250,000 a year, or much more than £400,000. But what matters in this context is the order of magnitude.

This sum can be thought of in two ways, in relation to the royal government and to the structure of society. For the first, it represents the payment of royal officers other than by the Crown, and it can therefore be treated as a part of the monetary burden laid by the state on society at large, in short as a substitute for taxation or even as a special kind of indirect tax. The late W. R. Scott, biographer of Adam Smith and historian of the early joint stock companies, saw two aspects of this. For a group of traders or other entrepreneurs to obtain a charter,

> involved the bribing of prominent courtiers, and in this way trade was subject to a high indirect taxation, since those who obtained such grants were forced to re-coup themselves for the preliminary outlay.

246

This referred specifically to the Merchant Adventurers, whose new charter in 1617-18 was said to have cost them £70,000. At a humbler level Scott wrote of a lighthouse patent in the same period:

> . . . an altogether disproportionate amount was paid for the obtaining of this patent. This was where the real grievance lay; since in this, as in other cases, the sums payable to influential persons at Court by those who sought for grants, constituted a great drain on industry.

His other way of considering the problem is epitomized in Scott's next chapter heading, 'The Delegation of Indirect Taxation by the Crown to Monopolistic Companies, 1630-40'. Here he dealt in particular with the coal, salt, soap, and starch monopolies, from which he estimated the Crown made *c.* £80,000 p.a. at a cost to the consumer of £200,000-£300,000 p.a.; and he stigmatized this aspect of Stuart policy as 'indirect taxation of commodities . . . in a most wasteful manner'.[1] The Cambridge economist, Mr. Maurice Dobb, relates the cost of obtaining such grants and charters (in fees, gratuities, and bribes) to the social tension preceding the Civil War. He points out that, 'influence at Court determined the distribution of economic rights of way', and that 'the system . . . from its nature . . . was heavily weighted against the man of humble social origins, against the provincial by contrast with the Londoner, and against the *parvenu*'. The only reference which he gives is, however, to Scott's citation of the lighthouse patent.[2]

Most of the fees and gratuities of which our total is made up constituted a slightly different kind of indirect tax. Later in the seventeenth century Sir William Petty, one of the 'fathers' of political economy, was to liken offices which were supported by fees to monopolies; but he made this a comparison, not an identification. Fee taxation he in turn related to the sale of offices, and continued

> these are the Offices that are properly saleable, viz. where the fees are large, as appointed when the number of them was few, and also numerous, as multiplying upon the increase of business, and where the business is onely the labour of the meanest men: length of time having made all the work so easie, and found out

---

[1] W. R. Scott, *The Constitution and Finance of English, Scottish, and Irish Joint-Stock Companies to 1720* (Cambridge, 1910-12), I, 170, 176, ch. XI, 214, 216.

[2] M. Dobb, *Studies in the Development of Capitalism* (London, 1946), p. 166.

security against all the frauds, breaches of trust and male-administrations, whereunto the infancies of those places were obnoxious. *These Offices are therefore Taxes upon such as can or will not avoid the passing through them. . . . This therefore of Offices is a voluntary Tax upon contentious men,* as Excize upon Drink is, to good Fellows to [*sic.* query: who] love it.[1]

Total royal revenue, omitting extraordinary taxation and capital gains, averaged only *c.* £618,000 a year in the early 1630's. An indirect tax on top of this, amounting to between £250,000 and £400,000 p.a., thus emerges in its true perspective, as a major part of the whole fiscal, and indeed political, system. It was larger than any other single source of revenue; the Great Farm of the Customs came next at £150,000 p.a., rising in the late 1630's to £172,500. It was of comparable size to the principal *group* of revenues, for in 1631-5 all the customs including the 'New Impositions' amounted only to *c.* £313,000 (average) p.a. At its minimum of £250,000 a year, fee taxation represented an addition of another 40 per cent. to the total royal revenue of 1631-5; if it is added in, to obtain a new grand total of *c.* £870,000 p.a., fee taxation still amounts to nearly 29 per cent.

Taxation in fees can also be included in the proportion of total royal expenditure which went to the payment and maintenance of the King's servants. In calculating this proportion, there must be added to the minimum of £250,000 a year (which was probably in fact at least £300,000) fee taxation, the amount received by royal officers in the form of Fees, wages, pensions, allowances, diets, and liveries. (See Table 12 opposite.)

In 1631-5 total royal expenditure averaged £636,000 a year (not taking fee taxation into account); with fee taxation it amounted to *c.* £890,000 p.a. minimum, and probably at least £940,000. Of this, the remuneration of office-holders—in all its various forms—accounted for at least £590,000 and probably over £660,000, that is certainly for 66 per cent. and perhaps for 70 per cent.

The money which changed hands every year in fees and gratuities can also be looked at in another way. It represented a transfer of wealth from a large and mixed number of people to a relatively small number of politicians, courtiers, administrators, legal officials, and clerks. It was a net loss of £250,000-£400,000 p.a. to the heterogeneous many and, subject to the deductions for certain overheads, a

---

[1] *The Economic Writings of Sir William Petty,* ed. C. H. Hull (Cambridge, 1899), I, 75-7. My italics, and my small 'f' in fees.

net gain to the homogeneous few. Indirectly the £350,000 or so spent yearly by the Crown on its servants can also be thought of as part of this transfer; it was raised in the form of customs duties, land

TABLE 12. PAYMENTS BY THE CROWN TO OFFICE-HOLDERS (INCLUDING DIET), MID-1630's

	Amounts to nearest £100
Annuities and pensions	£131,100 p.a.
Perpetuities	5,300
Fees	41,600
Defalcations (deducted at source from various revenues)	53,900
(*Note.*—Not all defalcations, or all pensions, etc., went to office-holders; at least £10,000 should be deducted.)	
King's Household (diet, other than the King's and Queen's own at *c.* £16,200, plus Fees and wages)	*c.* 37,000
Queen's Household and Chamber . .	9,300
Prince's Household	7,100 (rising by 1640 to *c.* £13,000)
Chamber	17,300
Gentlemen Pensioners . . .	6,000
Great Wardrobe (liveries, plus its own wage bill)	*c.* 6,000
Works	1,100
Robes	500
Navy (excluding sea-going officers and ships' crews)	*c.* 1,000
Ordnance	*c.* 1,300
Forts and Castles (officers only) . . .	*c.* 1,900
Ambassadors and Agents	*c.* 20,000
Extra diets of regional Lord Presidents, Star Chamber, and others	*c.* 7,100
Keepers of Houses, Parks, Gardens, etc. .	5,000
Total (within the range) . . .	£340,000-£360,000 p.a.

rents, feudal dues, and taxes from the people at large—landowners, merchants, tenant farmers, clergymen, craftsmen, and others, who in different ways made a contribution to the royal revenues. To transfer wealth from society in general to the servants of the state is neither the sole function, nor even the principal purpose of government. That it is *one* of its inevitable effects is undeniable.

To assess how important an influence office-holding was in the social structure of seventeenth-century England involves asking who were concerned in this transfer of wealth, and how it compared in quantity with other forms of wealth, and with other parts of the national income. A detailed analysis of the likenesses and differences between the payers and the receivers in this process would anticipate the subject of the next chapter, in which an attempt is made to describe who the officers were. But it will already be evident that many of them were men of similar social and family backgrounds, members of the same class, as those who paid the greater part of the fees and a large part of the taxes by which they were supported. Sometimes, of course, the same individuals paid taxes, dues, and fees as in other capacities received Fees, diets, fees, and gratuities. This is most applicable in the upper and middle ranks of the administration, where many of those receiving salaries, fees, and other benefits of office either already were, or were in the course of becoming, members of the propertied armigerous class—in short, gentry. The gentry paid a considerable share of the rents, dues, taxes, etc., composing the Crown's revenues, but above all they were involved in the payment of fees and gratuities. There were several reasons for this: the extraordinary litigiousness of the age, especially it appears of the educated and propertied classes; the confused complexities of the law, notably as it concerned the inheritance and disposal of land; their prominence in local government and tax collection; and their unavoidable involvement in the passage of royal grants, the securing of titles to property, and the registration of transactions.

It is scarcely possible to calculate how much of the £250,000-£400,000 which changed hands annually in fees and gratuities was paid by members of different social classes. In so far as the gentry included many of those who were involved in trading, financial, industrial, and mining activities, they paid fees in these capacities too, when obtaining, or seeking to obtain, charters, licences, and exemptions, when complying with regulations and controls, and, above all, if they took an active part in foreign trade, to the customs officers in London or the outports. But most fees, of the type discussed by W. R. Scott and Mr. Dobb, were paid by middle-class merchants and business-men, members of a class with relatively few representatives in the administration. It could indeed be argued that office-holding—in its financial aspect—was a means whereby wealth was transferred to the gentry from other social groups, directly in fees, indirectly via taxation and then in salaries, diet, etc. It seems likely that a larger proportion of the £590,000-£660,000 or more p.a. involved in the transfer was received by members of the gentry than was paid by them. But it would be hard to prove that this was so, and the net transfer of wealth between classes due to office-holding may in general have been less important than the transfer within classes.

The place of the lawyers in this transfer process needs to be made clearer. Lawyers belonged, or did not belong, to the gentry by virtue more of their social status than according to whether or not they held office. Those in private practice, as opposed to the holders of legal posts under the Crown, were not involved in the transfer of wealth under discussion, except perhaps to a modest extent as fee payers and tax payers. They did however receive fees, amounting in the aggregate to an annual total, which cannot be measured but may well have been comparable to that paid in fees to office-holders. This too represented a transfer of wealth from a larger to a smaller number of people; again some of the recipients already were, and others were on their way to becoming gentry, while the largest share of the payment was probably made by the landed classes, of whom the greater part were gentry, with the business community in second place. Despite their quarrels with the Prerogative and in many cases their alignment with the parliamentary and religious opposition to the Crown, even the Common lawyers seem tacitly to have recognized that they occupied a privileged position in the relations then existing between state and society. As was to be seen between 1642 and 1660 (especially in the years 1646-53 and 1659), any radical attack on the established order was almost bound to involve the legal system, and so the wealth and influence of the lawyers. The great masque which was staged for the King and Queen in 1633 and was said to have cost over £21,000 may be taken to symbolize their recognition of this.[1] Yet so little did men forsee the course of events, that many of those who took part in this masque were to join in the attack on royal power in 1640-1, while only a minority of them can have been active royalists during the Civil War.

Lawyers' fees can be considered as a form of taxation in so far as the legal system is regarded as a part or extension of royal government. The concept of government will, however, begin to lose precise meaning if it is stretched too far; and it therefore seems

[1] Whitelocke, *Memorials*, p. 21.

better to keep lawyers' fees out of these reckonings. They can be considered as constituting a distinct but parallel and perhaps equally formidable transfer of wealth between, and within, various social groups; but unlike officials' fees, they did not constitute a concealed form of indirect taxation.

The importance of fees and gratuities in the fiscal system only needs labouring because historians have for the most part overlooked it.[1] The significance of office-holding in relation to the national economy and the social structure of the country remains more controversial. We may be better able to assess it after having examined the composition of the office-holding body and attempted to classify its members according to their social rank and economic circumstances.

[1] See J. Hurstfield, 'The Profits of Fiscal Feudalism, 1541-1602', *Econ. Hist. Rev.*, 2nd ser., VIII (1955), pp. 58-9 and *The Queen's Wards: Wardship and Marriage under Elizabeth I* (1958), esp. pp. 345-9; also G. E. Aylmer, 'Studies in the Institutions and Personnel of English Central Administration, 1625-42', (Thesis for D.Phil., Oxford, 1954), ch. IX, part ii. Since the Crown's 'ordinary' revenues (excluding its indirect gains from fees and gratuities) increased by no less than 45 per cent. between 1631 and 1640, the relative importance of fee taxation was declining. Even so it remained considerable, still representing at least an extra 33 per cent. on top of the ordinary revenue, and 25 per cent. of the gross total, including fee taxation (T 56/2; P.R.O. 30/24/463-4).

5

WHO THE KING'S SERVANTS WERE: A CHAPTER OF SOCIAL HISTORY

---

i IDENTITY

IN STUDYING ANY GROUP of people, the first and most obvious but not necessarily the easiest step is to define its membership. This is accepted as a commonplace by social as well as natural scientists, but not yet by all historians.

The group with whom we are concerned here is much the same body of men as that already discussed from other points of view in the last three chapters. But since this chapter is an attempt to identify them socially, such a definition is not precise enough. As before, the group is limited to those who held regular paid office at court and in central or regional government between the end of March 1625 and the beginning of January 1641/2, that is from the accession of Charles to his departure from London after the attempt on the 'Five Members'. But for present purposes it excludes some of those who have previously been mentioned, namely all those *below* the level of under-officers or chief under-clerks, such as menial servants, porters, labourers, guards, subordinate copying-clerks. There are some unavoidable borderline cases arising both from the dates chosen and from the definition adopted for office-holders. Should the famous Lord Falkland, who had hardly taken up his duties as Secretary of State before the King left London, be included? What about 'officers' who were in no sense 'administrators', such as contractors? In some cases the ruling is bound to be arbitrary.

Falkland and the others appointed around New Year 1641/2 have been left out; contractors and technical officers have been included if they were on the royal payroll and held by patent from the Crown, or were in any way involved in administration. The gunfounders, powder-makers, ironsmiths and rope-makers who supplied the armed forces therefore qualify; apart from the Purveyors, those who supplied the royal household do not. The two leading ship-designers of the reign, Burrell and Pett, took part in naval administration and were not simply technical experts, so they are included, but not the other Master Shipwrights. The Surveyor of the Armoury, the Master Gunner of England, and the Chief Engineer are included, but not the 30-40 Armourers, the 150-odd Gunners, or the other half-dozen Engineers. In the army and navy only officers of field and flag rank are included, unless they were connected with the central administration. In the household departments, those below the rank of Clerks, Sergeants, and Yeomen-in-charge of sub-departments have been excluded. In the law courts and in the central executive subordinate under-clerks have only been included if they seem to have played a greater part in the administration than was typical for men of their rank; except for their officers and central clerical staffs, the Gentlemen Pensioners, Yeomen of the Guard, Footmen, Watermen, and Messengers have been excluded. The Gentlemen of the Privy Chamber do not qualify, unless they held other positions, because they were both part-time and unpaid. In the Chamber only officers 'in Ordinary' have been included, but this rule has not been followed in the central executive where some of the Clerks 'extraordinary' of the Privy Council were very active administrators. A difficult case is presented by officers of the central courts, whose work, except perhaps for an annual visit to have their accounts passed, lay exclusively in the localities. Receiver-Generals of Crown land revenues, Escheators, and Feodaries have been excluded unless they held another office or seem to have been unusually much concerned in the central direction of their respective departments.

Despite these apparently narrow limits, and a time-span of just under seventeen years, or considerably less than that reckoned for a 'generation', the group under discussion in this chapter is still over 900 strong. Its members vary from well-known historical figures, with published biographies and many columns of print in the *Dictionary of National Biography*, to men of extreme obscurity who are virtually unidentifiable. An example or two will illustrate the problem of identification. Around 1630 there was a Cursitor of Chancery named Richard Smyth, *alias* Smith. In 1638 there were ten Richard Smiths in a census of London householders and another 38 Smiths and four Smyths unidentified by Christian names[1]; it is just as difficult to identify Cursitor Smyth in genealogical sources or from the Inns of Court admissions' registers. Thomas Jones esquire, Master of the Hales, Pavilions, and Tents, and of the Toils was a more prominent man. But was he the same Tom Jones as the Clerk of the custody of wardships and *post mortems* in Chancery, *c.* 1630, or the soap monopolist who was attacked by the Long Parliament, or the London 'girdler' who accompanied the King to Oxford in the Civil War and sought to compound in 1647, or the 'citizen and painter-stainer' of London whose will was proved in 1654? Jones and Smyth may seem rather defeatist cases to take. But a less usual name does not always mean an easier identification, particularly since Christian names tended to run in families. Out of at least four contemporaneous Simon Thelwalls of Denbighshire, one (identified by Mrs. Keeler) was a parliamentarian M.P. in the 1640's, one (so far unidentified) was Clerk of the Revels.

Given greater skill and patience than the present author possesses, additional information could certainly be collected about some of these men, especially from genealogical sources. A few more identifications could probably have been made. But the evidence is so scattered and its whereabouts so uncertain, even in print let alone in manuscript, that eventually a law of diminishing returns begins to operate. Nor, even if more relevant material could be collected, does it follow that the general picture of the group would be appreciably altered.

To obtain a more manageable group for sample purposes, only those whose surnames began with the letters A-C have been used in compiling the tables given in the next section of this chapter. Office-holding peers are included or not according to their surnames, not their titles. Out of about 240 officers whose names began with A, B, or C, 194, or just over 80 per cent., have been identified. These constitute the sample. Since the least-known men, biographically speaking, are also by and large the most junior officials, allowance will have to be made for an artificial 'weightage' towards seniority in rank, as well as in social status. When discussing the significance of

[1] *The Inhabitants of London in 1638*, ed. T. C. Dale (Soc. of Genealogists, 1931), vol. II, index.

the information which is presented in the next section, account will have to be taken of such ignorance about the obscurer men. The biographical studies in the third section of this chapter, like the general discussion of office-holding and the social system in the last section, are not confined to this A-C sample but are drawn from the whole group regardless of surnames.

ii SOCIAL ANALYSIS [1]

After having defined the membership of a group, the next step is to decide what kind of evidence to collect and how to analyse it. In a historical survey it is sensible to begin with people's dates, and to follow this with information about their families; and then to try to discover where they came from, what kind of upbringing and education they had, how they made their way in the world, and how they ended their careers—where they were living, and with what property, family, or other interests. All this is a fairly standard pattern. Few of the men in this group are interesting and important enough as individuals, or sufficiently well documented, to justify making a biographical dictionary of them.[2] Therefore, although not all the evidence about them is of a type easily represented in the form of tables, it has been grouped under the following headings:

1. Facts relating to age, date of birth, the number holding office at different times.
2. Numbers of only or elder, and younger sons.

[1] In s. ii of this chapter some use has been made of most of the sources used in the rest of the book. The following are among those on which it is mainly based: The Harleian Soc., *Visitations* (by the Officers of Arms), *Registers* (of marriages and burials); Inns of Court, *Admission Registers*; Forster, *Alumni Oxonienses*; J. Venn, *Alumni Cantabrigienses* (Cambridge, 1922-7); *Victoria County Histories*; older county histories where the V.C.H. is incomplete or non-existent; 'G.E.C.', *Complete Peerage* (latest edn. up to T); G.E.C., *Baronetage*; Shaw, *Knights of England*; Burke, *Commoners* and *Landed Gentry*; proceedings and transactions of county and other archaeological and historical societies; family and local histories.

[2] See M. F. Keeler, *The Long Parliament* (Sub-title: *A Biographical Study of its Members*), pp. 81-404. Many more of Mrs. Keeler's men are also in the *D.N.B.* than of those with whom we are concerned.

3. Fathers' social status (where possible *before* the sons entered office); own status at death or retirement (even if this is after 1642).
4. County or city of origin, and of own final residence and/or principal property.
5. Education and training.
6. Method of entry to first office.
7. Number and causes of promotions, transfers, etc.
8. Classification *other than* by social status or by offices held.
9. Other information.

It should be made clear that this is not a sample of those who were members of the administration at any one given time between 1625 and 1642. For instance, at the exact mid-point of the sixteen and three-quarter year span, in August 1633, 110 out of 194 were definitely in office, and up to 16 more may have been; only 33 were definitely in office, not necessarily in the same post, throughout the period, though 18 others may also have been. An alternative procedure would have been to take a particular date, e.g. 1 January 1629/30, and limit the sample to men holding office on that date, but it has seemed better, on common-sense grounds, to keep to the same time-span as in the other chapters, and to include those who held office at any time during those years.

Out of those whose year of birth is known, or can be estimated, 81·5 per cent. were born before 1600 (137 out of 168). Among them are almost all those in office in 1625 whose date of birth is known, and of these over half were still in office in 1633, while they include about two-thirds of those who lasted the whole way to 1642. Thus not only did Charles I, as might have been expected, to a large degree inherit his father's servants, but many of them were still with him on the eve of the Civil War. Despite the eloquent complaint to the contrary by Robert Carey, Earl of Monmouth, in the Chamber and other branches of the household some of James I's servants *were* replaced by those who had been in Charles's service as Prince of Wales.[1] But scarcely anyone was dismissed without some compensation, in the form of a grant, annuity, or pension.

King Charles succeeded to the throne in his twenty-sixth year, a second but only surviving son. In this respect it may be interesting to compare him with his servants.

---

[1] R. Carey, *Memoirs* (ed. W. Scott, 1808), p. 159.

Among the 115 whose age on entry to royal service can be calculated with reasonable accuracy, it varied between nineteen and sixty-five. Entry in men's thirties was the commonest, but the distribution is wide and entry at over fifty was not unusual.

TABLE 13. AGE ON ENTRY TO OFFICE

Age	under 20	20-29	30-39	40-49	50-59	over 60	unknown	Total
Number	1	30	42	23	16	3	79	194

The lawyers who became King's Sergeants or Judges straight from private practice often did so quite late in life; they account for a high proportion of the fifties' and sixties' group. The courtiers, especially those who enjoyed royal favour or other unusually effective patronage, might be expected to have entered office young. This was not altogether so. Relatively few families excepted, royal favour was not enjoyed consistently over several generations. This affected both would-be entrants to office and their potential patrons. When in the course of the years 1615-19 George Villiers rose to power and secured almost complete control over royal patronage, although he was in his mid-twenties, by no means all his relatives were so young, still less all those who attached themselves to him as clients, servants, and 'hangers-on'.

Some further contrasts can be drawn. Offices which in practice descended by patrimony from father to son were likely, taking into account the relatively low expectation of life, to be filled mainly by men in their twenties and thirties. Those who acquired posts at court tended to do so earlier than the general average; legal office tended to be entered later. It could also be argued that men of relatively humble social origins were more likely to be found in the lower ranks of the administration, and that they were also less likely than their social superiors to have been to a university or one of the legal Inns, let alone to have travelled abroad. On this score, if they entered the King's service before making a name in law or business, they might tend to do so younger than the average. Of course, if they had already pursued a successful career elsewhere before becoming officials, the reverse was likely to be true. Finally, junior officials were perhaps more likely to die of plague or other epidemics than their administrative and social superiors, though some striking

258

instances of continuity in office can be found in the lower ranks; tenure certainly was least secure at the top of the official ladder. For the rest, the diversity of age at entry is perhaps not surprising in an era when relatively few men made full-time professional careers in royal service, in any manner comparable to those of modern civil servants.

The ratio of only and eldest to younger sons may be expected to show more positive results. The figures are:

TABLE 14.   FIRST AND YOUNGER SONS

Only, first, and first surviving sons	76
Younger sons	57
Doubtful or unknown	61

Taking the 133 known cases only, the ratio is about 57 per cent. to 43 per cent. As will shortly be seen, these figures assume a rather different significance when subdivided according to fathers' social status. But the totals as they stand deserve some comment. The average seventeenth-century family almost certainly contained more than one son who reached the age of about thirty-five (the peak age for entry into office). But the average (for sons per family surviving to their mid-thirties) may well have been less than two; that is more only sons, eldest sons, and eldest surviving sons than younger sons probably attained that age. Hence on an absolutely unbiased distribution of offices a slight preponderance of elder over younger sons might be expected. To offset this, according to the traditional view, the influence of primogeniture on English social and political development might lead us to expect a larger proportion of younger sons. But, whatever else can be inferred from them, the figures certainly disprove any notion of a royal bureaucracy staffed predominantly by younger sons. This is quite compatible with striking individual instances, some of which will be cited later in this chapter, of younger brothers, or cousins of a 'cadet' branch of a family entering the King's service, and subsequently overtaking in wealth and status their elders, or cousins in the senior male line.

It is a truism that his father's status or 'degree' counted for much more in a man's social background, and in the making of his career, three hundred years ago than it does today. But, having said this much, what follows? The social rank of seventeenth-century men

259

has the advantage of being, within limits, quite easy to define and to classify, especially by comparison with such concepts as their economic interest or their 'class'. Not that trying to define our sample officials in terms of their fathers' rank in society does not have its own problems. The father may have risen in the social scale between the time of the son's birth or his admission to a university or an Inn of Court and his entry into royal service. It has been difficult to take full account of this, but where possible the father's rank at the time of the son's entry to office has been taken as being the most relevant. Taking the gradations of the social pyramid from the top downwards, it has not seemed worthwhile subdividing the peerage into its five degrees. Inheritances, promotions (including translations from the Scottish or Irish to the English peerage), and new creations have however been considered separately in comparing the ranks attained by office-holders themselves with those of their fathers. The rank of Baronet, instituted in 1611, is counted separately, followed by those of Knight, Esquire, and Gentleman. Apart from the dubious knighthoods conferred by the second Earl of Essex in Ireland and elsewhere, and the very rare surviving use of 'Sir' for clergymen, where we should say The Reverend, definition is fairly easy down to and including knights. None of these titles could be enjoyed unless they had been bestowed, or in the case of peerages and baronetcies inherited. But the significance of ranks and titles matters as well as their definition.

The lay peerage was more than doubled in the first quarter-century of Stuart rule; baronetcies were only invented in 1611, theoretically to fill the gap in rank between the peerage and the knightage. The profuse granting of titles, especially under James I, or as Mr. Stone well describes it 'The Inflation of Honours', tended to lower the value which men set upon them.[1] Thus there seems to have been little consistency among the greater gentry as to who was and was not a knight; this was particularly so when the lavish creations and even sales of knighthoods under James were followed by Charles I's enforcement of the ancient statute whereby all gentry with landed incomes of over £40 p.a. who had *not* come up to be knighted at the coronation in 1626 were fined or forced to pay compositions (1630-5). By 1640 the title of knight had been considerably debased, and some prominent gentry apparently preferred to be without it.

[1] See L. Stone, 'The Inflation of Honours 1558-1641', *Past and Present*, XIV (1958), 45-70, esp. pp. 48-52, and 67.

With the two lowest armigerous ranks there are difficulties of definition and in assessing their significance. Technically no one could style himself Esquire (or *Armiger* in Latin documents) unless he was the eldest son of a family entitled to wear coat armour, and had received permission to do so from the Office of Arms. According to two heraldic authorities of Charles II's reign, the title was properly limited to: (1) the heirs male, and descendants of the heirs male, of noblemen's younger sons; (2) the heirs male of Knights; (3) certain *ex officio* categories including sheriffs, J.P.s, some central office-holders, and (by courtesy only) barristers. On ceasing to hold the office which had qualified him, a man with no other claim was supposed to revert to his previous rank. One of these sources also admits: (4) those whose direct male ancestors had been so styled by long prescription. This is obviously a more flexible category, offering more scope for the faking of pedigrees and coats of arms. However, as early as about 1600 Thomas Wilson described Esquires as 'gentlemen whose ancestors are or have bin Knights, or else they are the heyres and eldest of their houses *and of some competent quantity of revenue fitt to be called to office and authority* in their Country where they live'. His latter category is not the same as that of Esquires *ex officio*, because provided a man is a gentleman and an eldest son all he needs is sufficient wealth to make him suitable for office, etc.— a very different thing. And we can safely assume that Wilson's criteria were the more realistic.[1] However, anyone who styled himself Esquire or Gentleman without satisfying the proper conditions was still liable to be publicly proclaimed for having done so, formally dis-rated, and in the case of a repeated offence even fined and brought to trial in the Earl Marshal's court. It would be unwise to take at its face value the commission, issued on Christmas Day 1633, directing the Kings of Arms to visit their respective provinces, in which they were authorized 'to convent and call before them . . . all manner of persons that do or pretend to bear Arms, or are styled Esquires or Gentlemen'. By the 1620's and 1630's (if not earlier) men were styling themselves Esquire who had no technical right to do so, and were often getting away with it. None the less they did not always manage to do so, and this title was still meaningful, even if it was

---

[1] See A. R. Wagner, *Heralds and Heraldry* (2nd edn., Oxford, 1956), pp. 3-5 and app. E, pp. 147-9; T. Wilson, 'The State of England' (ed. F. J. Fisher, *Camden Miscellany*, XVI, 1936), p. 23 (my italics).

becoming a test of 'reputation' (that is, of status, wealth and way of life) as well as of ancestry.[1]

The case of Gentleman (normally shortened by contemporaries to 'Gent.') is rather less satisfactory. As far as can be seen, it was meant to be limited to the younger sons and brothers of Esquires and to *their* heirs male: in practice it was assumed by anyone who felt himself to be a member of the gentry or wanted to pass as one. There were also permitted exceptions for members of the learned professions; just as M.D.s and D.D.s ranked as Esquires, so M.A.s seem to have been reckoned as honorary Gents. In any social classification the category of Gent. is unavoidable. But, although men were still being 'dis-claimed' for the wrongful use of this title, many of those so styled in town and country alike, and above all in London, did not come of armigerous families.

'Merchant' was another official description of social status often used in legal documents. But by no means all those who actually were merchants, or otherwise engaged in industry, commerce, and finance, would have been known by this title. The most prominent London magnates were often Knights, and many others of the business élite called themselves Esquires or Gents. For those with London connexions, 'Citizen' followed by the designation proper to the City Company to which the man belonged was probably preferred to 'Merchant': e.g. 'Citizen and Cordwainer', or 'Citizen and Mercer'. By this time company membership had long ceased to be a safe guide to a man's actual occupation, but 'Citizen' and 'Merchant' are not likely to have been used wrongly, even if men who graduated to higher things such as Esquires were often still in business and still citizens of London.

Below this, for the countryside there were the ranks of Yeoman, and then below that Husbandman, but in London and the towns no equivalent can be distinguished. In the University and Inns of Court records all those below the rank of Gent. are often simply styled 'plebeian'. Since there was no standardized contemporary usage, we can hardly hope to avoid inconsistencies, but as will be

[1] G. D. Squibb, *The High Court of Chivalry* (Oxford, 1959), pp. 170-7; Hist. MSS. Comm. *Middleton*, pp. 178-9, list of gentlemen disclaimed in Notts, 1614 (I am grateful to Mr. Cooper for this ref.); Harl. Soc., *Visn. Berks.*, II, 1-4, *Visn. Cheshire 1613*, pp. 1-4, *Visn. Cornwall 1620*, pp. 294-5, *Visn Kent 1663-8*, p. xi. *Visn. Oxford 1634*, pp. 333-7 (other notes of persons disclaimed); see also royal commission to the Kings of Arms, 25 December 1633 (*Foedera*, XIX, 498-500).

seen the broad contrasts are between: (1) Esquire and above; (2) the border zone of Gent.; and (3) all other categories. With these provisos, the fathers of the A-C sample have been classified as follows:

TABLE 15. FATHERS' STATUS

Peers (of whom 'new' peers 3, and bishops 1)	9
Baronets	—
Knights	32
Esquires and equivalent (courtesy Esquires, etc.)	48
Esquire-Gent. borderline	9
Gents.	29
Citizens, Merchants, Sea Captains, Yeomen, plebeians, others below Gent., and foreigners living abroad	32
Unknown	35

Esquires and above therefore total 89, or 45·9 per cent. of the whole sample, and 56 per cent. of the known cases. It is certainly reasonable to assume that most of the fathers of unknown rank were below Esquires, if not below Gents., simply by virtue of being harder to trace. But even if three-quarters of them are added to the non-armigerous groups, these still only amount to 68, or 35 per cent. of the total. Counting *none* of the unknown cases, fathers of gentry, or would-be gentry rank and above (Gents. and upward) number altogether 127, or 65·5 per cent. of the total, and almost 80 per cent. of the known cases. This upper-class preponderance is not surprising; in the seventeenth, as in the sixteenth century, individuals not of gentle birth can be found in the highest ranks of government: Cranfield and Laud, Wolsey and Thomas Cromwell. But numerically such men were exceptions under Charles I, and in all probability under his great-great-uncle Henry VIII. Unless a very marked change had occurred between 1603 and 1625, it can only be maintained that Tudor bureaucracy was staffed by men of predominantly middle-class origin if the gentry are classified with 'the middle classes'. Most early Stuart administrators, especially those in the more senior positions, were born of armigerous families, or at least of those on the way to becoming armigerous. How they should be classified in terms of their occupations (other than their official duties), or their economic interests is another question, to be considered later.

Having classified the sample according to fathers' status, the division into elder (or only) and younger sons may now appear more significant. It may be of interest to correlate office-holders' positions as sons with their fathers' social position, and both these with whether or not the fathers were themselves office-holders (as defined in this chapter, but not necessarily under Charles I).

TABLE 16. PLACE IN THE FAMILY RELATED TO FATHERS' STATUS AND SERVICE IN OFFICE

Fathers	Elder and Only Sons	Younger Sons	Son's Position Unknown	Total
Peers	6	3	—	9
Of whom office holders .	3	2	—	5
Knights	16	15	1	32
Of whom office holders .	9	8	—	17
Esquires or equivalent .	26	15	7	48
Of whom office holders .	6	1	—	7
Esquire-Gent. borderline .	1	4	4	9
Of whom office holders .	—	1	1	2
Gents.	11	9	9	29
Of whom office holders .	1	1	—	2
Others	11	5	16	32
Of whom office holders .	2	—	—	2
Unknown	5	6	24	35
Of whom office holders .	—	—	—	—
Total sons	76	57	61	194
Total sons of office-holding fathers	21	13	1	35

Where father's status and son's place in the family are both known, the knightly fathers have the largest proportion of office-holding younger sons, and the Gent. fathers the next largest. The proportion of younger sons is at its lowest for the noble and the non-armigerous fathers, and next lowest for the Esquires. However, eldest sons may simply be easier to trace, especially for the middling and lesser gentry, in genealogical and legal sources, and so the unknowns are likely to include a higher proportion of younger sons than do the known cases; this is most relevant for the seven unknown sons of Esquires, most of whom may be unknown precisely because they were in fact younger sons. Furthermore, the Esquire-Gent. borderline is of course an artificial category, and most or all of the four fathers (of younger sons) may in fact belong on the upper side of the line; likewise with the four Esquire or Gent. fathers of unknown sons, who might also swell the Esquire-younger son figure were more information available. Certainly, as the table stands, the sons of Esquires are strikingly out of step with those of the Knights above and the Gents. below them.

The figures for office-holding fathers confirm what has already been suggested. The total for the whole group is 18 per cent., and leaving out the fathers of unknown rank 22 per cent. The striking difference here is between the sons of Peers and Knights (22 out of 41, or 53·7 per cent.) and the sons of Esquires and below, that is of all other known ranks (13 out of 118, or 11 per cent.). A few junior office-holders (under Elizabeth I and James I) among the fathers have probably been overlooked, and these are likely to have been Esquires or below. Even so, there would still be a marked contrast in the figures, which illustrate three features of the administrative system: the upper-class background of most officials; the acquisition by many of them of knighthoods if not peerages; and the role of patrimony in helping to secure entry into the King's service.

The test of 'style' or social status can also be applied to the members of the sample themselves at the end of their lives. As might have been expected, many rose above their fathers' ranks. Of course, this may not have been due solely to their official careers; it cannot be proved that but for having been office-holders some of the same men would not have risen in the social scale for other reasons. The final ranks achieved are as follows:

TABLE 17. STATUS ACHIEVED

Peers, of whom new	.	.	.	.	. 19
promoted	.	.	.	. 2	
inherited	.	.	.	. 3	
				—	24*
Baronets (all new) .	.	.	.	.	. 9
Knights	.	.	.	.	. 64
Esquires	.	.	.	.	. 51
Esquires or Gents.	.	.	.	.	. 18
Gents. .	.	.	.	.	. 14
Others .	.	.	.	.	. 5
Unknown	.	.	.	.	. 9

* *Note*—One eldest son of a peer was illegitimate, and did not inherit his father's title but was given a new peerage.

Thus 148, or 76·3 per cent. of the total ended their days as Esquires or better. Even this does not do full justice to the remarkable rise in social status. Two of the 'others' were Monsieurs and probably equivalent to Esquires, and several of the unknowns may well have been Gents. if not Esquires by the end of their careers; the inclusive total of gentry rank and above should probably be at least 185, or over 95 per cent. Whatever the exact connexion between office-holding and economic advancement, office clearly did everything short of conferring gentility automatically, and frequently it even did that. Above the menial level, if petty officials did not always at once acquire a pedigree and a coat of arms, they were usually able to style themselves Gent. without being challenged, while many of no great distinction rose to be Esquires. The frequency with which official service was rewarded by a knighthood, and indeed at some levels entailed being knighted almost automatically, must naturally be related to the general rate at which Knights were being created. The steep rise under James was followed by a fall under Charles; and Mr. Stone's figures show that the rate in the years 1631-40 was actually lower than in the last 19 years of Tudor rule. However, several of our Knights were not dubbed until after 1642, and some not until after 1660, by which time political allegiances may have had more to do with who was or was not knighted.

The extent to which officers rose to a higher station than that occupied by their fathers at the time when the sons entered office, was naturally uneven.

TABLE 18.   EXTENT OF RISE IN SOCIAL DEGREE

Rose by three degrees or more . . .	19
Rose by two degrees	27
Rose by one degree	43
Remained stationary	47
Declined from father's rank . . .	13
Total of known cases	149
Unknown	45

Note—The baronetage is *not* counted as a degree where a man rose from knight to peer; but gradations in the peerage *are* counted.

Thus 59·7 per cent. of the known cases rose by one degree or more, and 30·9 per cent. by two or more; a combined total of 40·3 per cent. remained stationary or fell. But the general improvement in status is more striking than may at first appear, taking into account that knighthoods were not heritable by any, even eldest sons, and that no social rank, except perhaps that of Gent., was heritable by younger sons. The cases of apparent social decline can almost all be accounted for by younger sons in general, and by first and younger sons of Knights, though many even in these categories rose to their fathers' rank or above.

Geographically the sample officers can be classified according to where they came from and where they ended their days. Both these ways of describing them need a little more explanation. The counties in which they had their main estates and their principal residences are likely to be known for wealthy or distinguished fathers. But for those with more obscure fathers there are only brief references, for instance at the time of entrance to university or Inn of Court, or in some official document. Such references can be misleading: a man's family may have lived in two or more different places, or it may have moved once or more times between the date of the reference and that of his entry to office. Therefore it has seemed best to have a unit for each important property and place of residence: thus one man can be counted for say London and two counties, but this duplication is noted in the table.

TABLE 19. GEOGRAPHICAL ORIGINS AND DESTINATION

County, etc.	Of origin	Also had estates or residences elsewhere	Of own final residence or main estate	Also elsewhere
Bedfordshire	2	1	3	2
Berkshire	4	1	8	6
Buckinghamshire	4	1	9	7
Cambridgeshire	1	–	1	–
Cheshire	6	1	1	1
Cornwall	2	–	2	1
Cumberland	1	–	–	–
Derbyshire	4	–	3	–
Devon	3	1	3	3
Dorset	4	2	3	1
Durham	–	–	–	–

TABLE 19 (*continued*)

County, etc.	Of origin	Also had estates or residences elsewhere	Of own final residence or main estate	Also elsewhere
Essex . . .	7	3	14	8
Gloucestershire .	6	1	3	3
Hampshire . .	3	–	4	3
Herefordshire . .	1	–	1	1
Hertfordshire . .	8	4	9	6
Huntingdon . .	1	–	3	3
Kent . . .	10	2	14	11
Lancashire . .	4	2	1	1
Leicestershire . .	2	1	–	–
Lincolnshire . .	2	–	4	1
Middlesex . .	4	4	6	5
Monmouth . .	–	–	–	–
Norfolk . . .	7	3	8	8
Northamptonshire .	4	3	4	4
Northumberland .	1	–	–	–
Nottinghamshire –	3	1	1	1
Oxfordshire . .	8	3	8	6
Rutland . . .	–	–	–	–
Shropshire . .	2	1	1	1
Somerset . .	3	1	–	–
Staffordshire . .	4	1	1	–
Suffolk . . .	9	2	6	4
Surrey . . .	6	3	17	11
Sussex . . .	7	2	6	4
Warwickshire .	7	5	4	3
Westmoreland .	–	–	–	–
Wiltshire . .	2	–	1	1
Worcestershire .	8	2	3	1
Yorkshire . .	3	1	4	2
London and West- minster . .	33	13	83	47
Scotland . .	12	–	7	5
Ireland . . .	1	–	11	6
Wales . . .	2	–	1	–
The Channel Islands	1	–	1	1
Foreign countries .	3	–	1	–
Unknown . .	22	–	24	–
Total of known cases	205	65	260	168
Total of actual indi- viduals known .	172	–	170	–

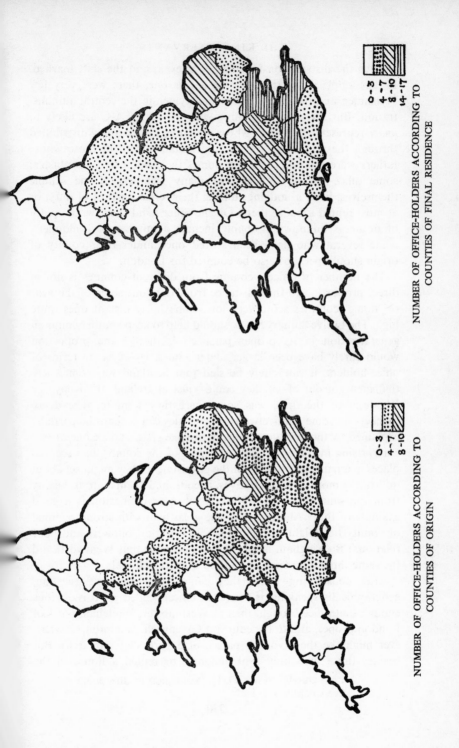

NUMBER OF OFFICE-HOLDERS ACCORDING TO
COUNTIES OF FINAL RESIDENCE

0-3
4-7
8-10
14-17

NUMBER OF OFFICE-HOLDERS ACCORDING TO
COUNTIES OF ORIGIN

0-3
4-7
8-10

Thus the distribution is wide but uneven, and the shift marked. If the sample is for this purpose a true one, there were very few Welshmen and not many north-countrymen in the central administration. But surnames beginning with the letters A-C are likely to *under*-represent the Welsh, whose surnames are unevenly distributed through the alphabet.[1] As for the capital, not all of those whose fathers were office-holders had homes in London or Westminster; some office-holding fathers, like many members of the sample themselves, lived in lodgings during their terms, or turn of duty, or at most rented a house there. On the other hand those whose place of origin is unknown probably include a number of Londoners, while several who have been scored once under their county of origin should perhaps also be counted for London.

The number of officers coming from different counties is not in direct proportion to their distance from London: some of the near or 'home' counties score very low, some fairly distant ones quite high. The twelve 'hungry Scots' should help to keep another common generalization in its proper perspective, though the proportion would surely have been larger under James. However, in terms of office-holders, it can safely be said that Scotland was somewhere that men got out of—if they could—just as Ireland, the Kenya or Rhodesia of the time, was somewhere they went to. The dense 'pockets' in some relatively distant counties can perhaps be partially explained by the workings of the patronage system: once one or two enterprising men from a particular part of the country had secured places in a particular branch of the government, they might set about infiltrating more of their relatives, friends, and clients into it, largely from the same area. The Dorset Exchequer connexion is a good example of this.[2] Alternatively, one great man with strong regional or county ties might bring in a whole troop of followers and poor relations: Buckingham is the supreme example, but Wentworth did the same thing on a smaller and more restrained scale.

After considering where they came from, the next question, geographically speaking, is where the officers ended up. It is obvious enough that office brought men to Westminster, Whitehall, parts of London proper, and to the court (at Greenwich, Hampton, or whatever might be the favourite palace of a particular monarch). But besides those who only took lodgings or rented a house in the

---

[1] I am grateful to Mr. D. H. Pennington for this point.
[2] See Chapter 3, s. i.

capital a number of great officers and many lesser ones in the household departments had lodging, if not in the palace, at least within the boundaries of the court; certain other posts of medium rank carried a house with them *ex officio*, e.g. the Auditorship of the Receipt. Moreover, the properties which office-holders themselves acquired were on the whole nearer to London than their homes had been. Some Londoners may have moved out into the country, generally into the home counties, as a result of rising by means of office into the gentry class, but in general office-holding can be related to migration from the more distant parts of the kingdom both to the capital and to the counties round it. As can be seen from the map and the preceding table, apart from London and West-minster, and Ireland, the shift was most marked *to* Surrey, Essex, Bucks, and Berks. Apart from Scotland, the shift was heaviest *away from* Cheshire and Worcs, while Glos, Suffolk, and Warwicks were also among the losers. The gains of Herts, Kent, and Middlesex, and the losses of Sussex are not sufficiently marked to be significant. In fact when it is subdivided like this under so many different possible headings, the sample is probably too small to be a safe guide to anything beyond a general trend.

Changes of county need to be related to the proportion of eldest sons, or heirs, to younger sons, or those who were not heirs. An heir might of course buy, or be granted, additional property in his own county besides what he inherited; such gains cannot be taken into account in the previous table or on the maps. Alternatively, he might sell his inheritance and move to another estate, possibly in the same, possibly in a different county. Again men might inherit property other than from their fathers, or childless elder brothers, say from grandparents, uncles, or more distant relatives, sometimes in quite different counties from those of their own origin. All of these cases are to be distinguished from those of younger sons who had not inherited estates, but who had instead acquired them from scratch. either by grant or purchase. Not, of course, that younger sons never inherited property: to judge from the wills of many officials and the family papers of a smaller number, in the years *c.* 1630-*c.* 1670, where there was landed property to be disposed of, more often than not the younger son or sons did inherit some of it.[1] However, only in the wealthiest families was such secondary inheritance by a

[1] For a similar opinion in relation to the peerage and other great landowners, see J. P. Cooper, *Econ. Hist. Rev.*, n.s., VIII (1956), 381.

younger son likely to maintain him unaided in any great state or comfort. And if a younger son made a successful career in law, trade, the armed forces, government or even the church, he was more likely than his elder brother to acquire additional property in a new county. This can be strikingly illustrated even if the total number of known cases is small.

TABLE 20. EXTENT OF GEOGRAPHICAL MOBILITY

Sons	Known to have moved from place of origin to another county, etc.	Proportions in the whole sample group
Eldest . . .	14=27·45%	39·2%
Younger . .	22=43·14%	29·4%
Unknown . .	15=29·41%	31·4%
Total . . .	51	(194)

In this instance even if the operation of primogeniture was far less extreme than has sometimes been supposed, its effects speak for themselves.

Generally speaking, the proportion of officers in the sample who had been to a university or had some legal training reflects the upper-class preponderance among them. But not entirely so, as the table on the opposite page makes clear.

Thus among those who are known to have been to a university 55·1 per cent. are known to have been the sons of Esquires and above, compared with 45·9 per cent. of the whole sample whose fathers were Esquires and above. For the Inns of Court and the other institutions for legal education the corresponding figure is 47·05 per cent., or very nearly the same proportion as in the whole sample. The significance of these figures becomes even clearer by taking the sons of men known to have been below the rank of Esquire; these constitute 31·4 per cent. of the whole sample, 30·8 per cent. of those who received university education, but 36·8 per cent. of those who received some legal training.

These figures do not in themselves prove that legal training offered

TABLE 21. EDUCATION, TRAINING, AND SOCIAL STATUS

Fathers	University Education			
	Oxford	Cambridge	Other	Total going to University
Above Esquire . .	13	10	1	24
Esquires . . .	9 (1)	9 (1)	3 (1)	19
Below Esquires . .	16 (1)	9 (1)	—	24
Unknown . . .	6	4	1	11
Total for universities .	44	32	5	78

Note.—The figures in brackets indicate those who also went to other institutions listed in the same table; they are counted each time under the totals of the institutions, but only once under the totals of men going to them.

Fathers	Legal Education[1]					
	Gray's Inn	Lincoln's Inn	Inner Temple	Middle Temple	Other	Total receiving Legal Educn.
Above Esquire .	8 (1)	1	9	1	1 (1)	19
Esquires . .	9	1	1 (1)	2 (1)	1	13
Below Esquires .	9 (1)	2 (1)	8	6	2 (2)	25
Unknown .	4 (1)	—	4 (2)	2 (1)	3	11
Total for places of legal education	30	4	22	11	7	68

[1] Records for admissions in the early seventeenth century have only survived for Doctors Commons and the Inns of Court; if the records of the other Inns were available, the Inns of Court would still retain their preponderance. In 1586 the Inns of Court had an average of 239 students each, seven of the Chancery Inns an average of 91 each (E. Williams, *Staple Inn* (1906), p. 105).

greater equality of opportunity than university education. But if this was *not* so, and if boys, presumably of above average ability, from non-armigerous families were as easily able to enter the universities as the Inns, then it follows that those who went to the Inns were markedly more likely to enter royal service. These two conclusions are not mutually exclusive: the Inns may have been slightly less of an upper-class preserve than the universities, and boys from other classes who went to the Inns may have been relatively somewhat more likely to become officials. Presumably a large proportion of the cleverer boys from non-gentry homes who went to the universities became clergymen, though this is unlikely to provide the sole explanation.

As has already been explained, it is seldom possible to give a single reason why a particular man obtained a particular office.[1] The unaided force of Patrimony, Patronage, or Purchase, or more often some combination of these factors, may offer an explanation of *how* he did so. But the motives of the applicant, the appointer, and the other parties concerned can never be fully known; only the outward, or apparent factors which seem to have operated in different cases can be suggested. In calculating how many people owed their entry to which causes, some men have been rated more than once, scoring a half under each heading. For example, Edward Bromley, Baron of the Exchequer 1610-27, was the son of a Judge of Chester and the nephew of Sir Thomas Bromley, the Lord Chancellor (died 1587), but it would be foolish to ascribe his advancement solely to these connexions; it is more reasonable for him to score $\frac{1}{2}$ under Patrimony and $\frac{1}{2}$ under qualifications and ability. Likewise the notorious Sir Henry Croke had very powerful family connexions but he still apparently had to buy his original half share in the Clerkship of the Pipe, so he is best rated as Patrimony $\frac{1}{2}$, Purchase $\frac{1}{2}$. This method is obviously liable to become dangerously mechanical when applied to individual cases; such enumeration can take little account of the complexities of human motivation, of envy, ambition, and the other emotions to which men are subject. It does not, however, follow that this approach is unsuitable for the study of a group of men in the aggregate. If this is less colourful, and to some

[1] See Chapter 3, s. i.

people less interesting, than a series of individual case histories, it is an equally valid way of looking at the subject.

TABLE 22.   FACTORS IN ENTRY TO OFFICE

	Whole Instances	'Half' or Part Instances
Patrimony	26	17
Patronage	32	35
Purchase	6	4
Special qualifications and professional (including administrative) ability .	11	31
Reward for services, and direct royal favour	5	7
Totals	80	94
Total no. of known cases (corrected for 'halves')	127 (65·5% of the whole sample)	

Some borderline cases are unavoidable, e.g. between Patrimony and Patronage, and between Qualifications and Reward. The unknown cases would certainly increase the Patronage and Purchase totals more than the others, by adding whole as well as half instances. As has already been explained, there tends to be positive evidence for Purchase less often than for other modes of entry to office, owing to the clandestine character of many such transactions.

Like the ways of entering office, the extent of mobility in the King's service has already been discussed. This too can be illustrated quantitatively in the same way. Reappointment (mainly in 1660) to the same office after interruption has not been counted, but promotions after 1642 (other than military commands in the Civil War) have been. Subsidiary posts held *in commendam* with principal ones have not been counted, and local offices, such as Escheator-, Feodary-, and Receiverships, only when their holders later obtained central offices.

TABLE 23.   TRANSFERS AND PROMOTIONS

Transferred or promoted once	49
Transferred or promoted more than once	37
Apparently remained in the same post throughout . .	108
Total known to have been transferred or promoted . .	86
This total in relation to the whole sample group . . .	44·3%

Therefore, up to 55·7 per cent. stayed put, and only 19·1 per cent. secured two or more transfers or promotions. By modern standards the degree of immobility is strikingly high; this is partly to be explained by the very limited extent to which royal service was then a 'career' in the modern sense. Although there is not enough evidence to prove it conclusively, men who entered office young were more likely to be promoted or transferred than older entrants; and promotion was likely to come fairly soon after entry or else not at all. As is to be expected, it can also be related to improvement in social status. Of those promoted or transferred more than once, about thirty were knighted, raised to the baronetage, or ennobled, and seventeen became Privy Councillors. Fifteen of them seem to have enjoyed direct royal favour or (equally effective) the patronage of Buckingham, while several, most of them lawyers, would have made their mark under any form of civilized government, being men of quite uncommon abilities or professional accomplishments. The categories of those enjoying royal favour or Villiers backing and of the uncommonly able were by no means mutually exclusive. Here at least uncommon ability was on the whole uncommonly well rewarded and sometimes, as perhaps in Cottington's case, too well.

The causes of promotion are more varied and harder to assess than those of entry. Diligence, aptitude, and the capacity for getting on with people would obviously count for more in promotion than entry, but their force can seldom be estimated. With this caution, the same system of scoring can be used; it gives a rather different picture.

TABLE 24. FACTORS IN TRANSFER AND PROMOTION

	Whole Instances	'Half' or Part Instances
Patrimony	1	0
Patronage	11	28
Purchase	4	4
Qualifications and ability (also seniority)	12	23
Reward and favour	10	13
Totals	38	68

Total of known cases (corrected for 'halves'). . . . . . 72 (83·7% of all those transferred or promoted)

Both Patronage and Ability become exceedingly hard to distinguish from the capacity to make a good impression on superiors. But in so far as the same categories are applicable in both cases, a comparison can be made between the causes of Transfer or Promotion, and Entry.

TABLE 25. COMPARISON OF ENTRY AND PROMOTION

Total known cases in Entry . . . 127
Total known cases in Promotion . . . 72

Factor or Cause	No. of Promotions to be expected if they were in the same proportions as entries	Actual Cases of Transfer or Promotion
Patrimony . .	19·6	1
Patronage . . .	28	25
Purchase . . .	4·5	6
Qualifications and ability	15	23·5
Reward and favour .	4·8	16·5

Therefore, once men were in office, Patrimony counted for very little, Reward and Favour for much, Qualifications and Ability for considerably more; in the latter case seniority of course operated as an entirely new factor. Patronage appears to have been slightly less important, Purchase slightly more. The same caution applies as with entry: the unknown cases would almost certainly divide differently from the known ones.

Granted that rank and social status counted for much more in the seventeenth century than they do today, there are other quite different ways in which the men of that time can be classified. The way in which they made their living and the occupation or *métier* which they followed are far from being self-evident from their style and station. Not quite all Esquires and above were landowners, and by no means all were only or even primarily landowners in terms of their economic position and their interests. A number of Esquires and some Knights also had some business interests other than in agriculture, or were practising lawyers. Some of those still styled Merchant or Citizen also owned land. No single social rank corresponds to membership of the legal profession.

277

A classification according to occupations, or anything of that kind, is bound to be more arbitrary than one according to ranks and titles; it is bound to leave awkward borderline cases, and perhaps to draw artificial distinctions. Such an analysis is none the less in some ways more interesting, and more informative, than the preciser classification by rank. The first and fundamental distinction to try to draw is between those who did and did not own land, but this is not enough. As far as possible the members of the sample have been classified in two ways: (i) according to whether or not they owned land, and when (but not for the moment how) they obtained it. A single piece of London house property is not reckoned to have made a man a landowner, although a considerable number of such properties would do so if this was known; (ii) according to their occupation or profession, or their special position in relation to their office. In Table 26 (see opposite), the second figure under each entry represents 'halves', or mixed classifications. Thus a man who was both a soldier and a professional administrator, or one who was both a lawyer and a financier, is rated under both headings.

The preponderance of known landowners (68 per cent.) could probably have been anticipated from the table (p. 265) showing social status attained. Since some landowners have certainly not been traced, the final total of those who did not own land would be below 30 per cent. Unless landed gentry are to be included in the 'middle class', any lingering preconception of royal reliance on middle-class officials must be finally dispelled. Even if the whole non-landed category except the Courtiers are added together under the latter heading, 46 plus 14 'halves' (= 53, or 27·3 per cent.) does not make a very impressive total, especially since *by and large* the non-landed officials were the junior and less important ones. Again it would be very interesting to know whether an analysis of Tudor office-holders would show similar results. The importance of the lawyers (42 plus 3 'halves' = 43·5, or 22·4 per cent.) could not have been inferred from the analysis of social status, although their general prominence in seventeenth-century England is a historical commonplace. Considering how much larger a proportion of the central government the law courts and their administrative bureaux then formed than they have come to do in more recent times, and remembering that the modern distinction between law and administration only existed in embryonic form, it would not have been surprising if the lawyers

278

had been even more prominent. It is worth noting how few of them were 'mere' lawyers: that is only 12 or 13 did not own landed property and of these 6 or 7 were law clerks, not qualified barristers or advocates.

TABLE 26. OCCUPATIONS, AND OWNERSHIP OF LAND

Description	Landowners			Apparently not Landowners	Total
	On entry to office	After entry	Date unknown in relation to entry		
Courtiers . .	14+3	3+3	11+1	7+3	35+10
Absentee office holders . .	5+1	– –	1 –	– –	6+1
Common (including Chancery) lawyers	5 –	4 –	12 –	1 –	22 –
Civil lawyers . .	– –	2 1	2 –	5 –	9+1
Law Clerks . .	2 –	2 –	2 –	5 2	11+2
(all lawyers . .	7 –	8 1	16 –	11 2	42+3)
Merchants, financiers industrialists, etc. .	2+1	1+1	3+3	13+4	19+9
Naval and military men	3+2	1+1	3 –	4+1	11+4
Foreign experts .	– 1	2+1	1 –	2+1	5+3
Medical doctors (incl. surgeons) . .	1 –	1 –	– –	2+1	4+1
Heraldic and anti-quarian experts .	2 –	1 –	2 –	1 –	6 –
Miscellaneous .	– –	1 –	– –	1 –	2 –
Professional adminis-trators . .	1 –	6+1	5+2	5+6	17+9
Unknown . .	5 –	1 –	14 –	7 –	27 –
Totals . . .	40+8	25+8	56+6	53+18	174+40
Corrected Totals .	44	29	59	62	
		132			194

A difficult but important question involves the threefold connexion between office, landownership, and occupation or profession. Some distinction should be drawn between the landowners and those who had previously been following a trade or profession: medicine, law, teaching (including tutoring young men on the 'grand tour'), naval and military service, commerce, finance, industry, etc. Many of those who had depended for their livelihoods on such professional skills ceased to make use of these once they were in office; sometimes they ceased to even when such qualifications had helped to secure their entry to the King's service. For the landowners this question did not arise. They were not normally office-holders because of any professional expertise as landowners but rather thanks to the social position (influence, connexions, etc.) which tended to go with landownership and with membership of a major landed family. Furthermore, by letting estates to tenant farmers, by entrusting the demesne or home farm to a capable steward or bailiff, and by visiting the property in the summer and perhaps briefly at other times of the year, landownership was easy to combine with regular employment under the Crown. Thus the 5 unclassified men who were landowners on entering office, and about 4 of the 14 unclassified ones whose dates of entering office and of becoming landowners cannot be correlated, might well be redistributed. They could be described as 'Landowners with office as a subsidiary means of support', and pictured as somewhere midway between absentees and professional careerists. With merchants and lawyers the case was usually different. The Attorney- and Solicitor-General could remain in private practice, but the holders of most legal offices, as opposed to attorneyships, apparently did not do so. A Collector of Customs duties could remain in business: even a Comptroller of Customs might do so. But once a merchant or financier left the Customs for some other branch of the administration he usually abandoned an active entrepreneurial role, although exceptions can be found, such as Ingram (Council in the North) and John Jacob (Council Clerk extraordinary).

Because a man became a landowner after he became an office-holder it does not follow that the one was a result of the other, at least not in any direct financial sense. It is difficult to estimate how often the profits of office provided the immediate means of acquiring property, and how often obtaining office signified rather a consolidation of advances already made in wealth and status. There are too few cases where enough is known for further analysis under occupational headings, but some evidence exists as to *how*, as well as when, office-holders acquired landed property.

TABLE 27. DATE AND MEANS OF ACQUIRING PROPERTY

Property acquired or substantially enlarged, *after* entry to office	
(i) by inheritance	2
(ii) by inheritance plus marriage (which may in turn have been partly due to official position) . .	3
(iii) presumably by the profits of office . . .	13
(iv) by some combination of (iii) with (i) or (ii), or with other forms of income	21
Date of acquiring, or enlarging, property unknown in relation to date of entering office, but profits of office probably a factor in such acquisition	23
Apparently not property owners at all	62
Property inherited before entry and not appreciably enlarged after	38
No connexion traced between office-holding and property ownership	32
All those for whom office was probably a positive factor in acquiring property	57-60
These in relation to the total sample	29·4-30·9%

Going outside the sample, a survey of 700 or so officials with names beginning D-Z confirms the same general impression. A great many office-holders acquired new estates or added substantially to their existing properties, but at the same time there were many others of whom neither description would be true.

One of the most debatable classifications is that of professional or 'careerist' administrators. But it is obviously central to the whole question of how far Charles I's servants formed a 'bureaucracy'. The professionals *might* be taken to include any or all of the following groups: (1) those who owned no landed property; (2) those who only acquired landed property after entering office and possibly as a result of this; (3) those who forsook private law practice for legal office, or abandoned some comparable career, e.g. in trade, soldiering or medicine, at a fairly early age; (4) those who had no visible advantages of birth or wealth, and no special technical qualifications. But these are not very satisfactory tests. Most courtiers and all absentees can obviously be excluded, likewise the majority of lawyers and business-men, and of those in the smaller occupation groups. But landownership should not in itself disqualify a man from being classed as a professional administrator: it would be misleading to describe Sir John Coke, Secretary of State 1625-40, in any other terms simply because he became a substantial landowner. The best tests to apply are rather: (i) the exercise of unspecialized administrative ability, as opposed to technical skill, after entry to office; (ii) (as far as it can be gauged) a serious 'full-time' approach to the duties of office; (iii) a 'careerist' attitude towards it, that is a heavy, though not necessarily an exclusive dependence on office for advancement in status and wealth. The total of 17-26 could easily be increased if the category was less exclusive. Some of the foreign experts were professionals in diplomacy or foreign languages; the special skill and interests of the heralds coincided with their official duties, though not all of them were full-time; some of the legal office-holders became administrative careerists. Even courtiers are not always easy to distinguish from professionals, especially in the Household below stairs and the Wardrobes, while some of those who did hold posts in the central executive, and other departments of state were in practice more like courtiers than professional administrators. In order to estimate the number of full-time careerists, as opposed to the narrower category of professional administrators, in the sample group, about a quarter of the lawyers (say 11) should be added, and probably about the same proportion of those in the business and other special occupation groups (say 12). This would mean a total of 40-49, or up to a quarter of the whole group.

From the Privy Council downwards the country was to a considerable extent governed by part-time officials, by men who were essentially 'amateurs' even if they were paid. Government by amateurs, in the seventeenth century as today, is sometimes thought to consist of the services of unpaid J.P.s and of others in local government who do not have fees, or remuneration from the Crown. But if amateur is to be equated with 'part-time' or with 'non-professional', it can be argued that this is too narrow a definition. If Charles I can be said to have had a bureaucracy at all, about three-quarters of its members were amateurs according to the definitions used here.

It would be interesting to know how far the professional administrators correspond to those of any particular rank or social status. Although little can be demonstrated quantitatively, they seem to have included a fairly large proportion of self-made men, that is of those whose fathers ranked as Gents. or below, and who themselves rose by two degrees or more in the social scale. As is to be expected, there is some correlation between those who acquired landed property in the course of their official careers and those who attained the title of Esquire or upward.

If it were available for enough members of the sample, there is much other information which would be of use in presenting a composite social portrait. As was suggested at the end of Chapter 3, all too little is known about the officials' daily lives, what company they kept out of office hours, what preachers they listened to, what their interests and recreations were, and so on. It does not take us very far to say that about 20 are known to have travelled abroad, and 18 to have seen some active naval or military service; although most of the others had probably not had either of these experiences, many of them must remain classified, under both these headings, as unknown. Still, apart from what they heard or read, insularity might tentatively be suggested as a group characteristic. The same limitations in the evidence apply to there being only 11 who are definitely known to have had interests in Ireland, and a mere 4 with colonial connexions. Other additional information of one kind and another, beyond that already used for compiling the tables in this section, is available for about 100, including facts concerning their properties and their family relationships. But for most of these 100 it is very sparse indeed. And it is simply not possible, as the author had at one time hoped, to treat quantitatively all the property transactions in which members of the sample were involved. Readers whose primary interest is in economic history may regret that the attempt has not been made, but it seems unlikely that sufficient evidence exists for such a survey to be worth undertaking.

The studies of families and individuals in the next section of this chapter are not necessarily representative examples, either of the A-C group or of the whole body of office-holders. They are to be thought of rather as case histories; where possible, some indication will be given whether or not they are likely to have been typical of many other cases.

iii OFFICE AND WEALTH: FAMILIES AND INDIVIDUALS

Families in Orbit. A decisive and lasting rise in the fortunes and social standing of a whole family can sometimes be directly related to one or more of its members having held office. Absolutely clear and unambiguous examples of this are not easy to find: the Fanshawes and Osbornes of the upper Exchequer, the Ropers of King's Bench, and a few others. Of these families it can be said that, even if they *might* hypothetically have risen by other means (law, trade, etc.), in fact they did so almost solely by holding office during successive generations. In other cases, to be distinguished from these, one member of a family who held office laid the foundations of his descendants' fortunes, but their prudence, skill, and good luck counted for as much as his pioneering achievement. To this, witness the Brownlows of Belton and the Henleys of Hampshire and Somerset.

Sometimes a change in family fortunes owed more to the indirect than the direct profits of office. A financially gainful marriage, itself perhaps due in part to the enjoyment of court favour, was probably at least as responsible for the recovery of the Sussex Ashburnhams between 1620 and 1642 as direct royal bounty, in the form of grants and pensions.[1]

Families whose wealth was due to their having held a Crown contract for more than one generation can be classified either as office-holders or as successful business-men. Such were the Evelyns of Godstone and Long Ditton, Surrey. The diarist's grandfather, uncle, and cousin were all in the somewhat unsavoury business of collecting and processing saltpetre for the royal gunpowder contract, which they enjoyed from Elizabeth's reign until 1636. The same uncle and another cousin held, in succession, one of the Six Clerkships of Chancery (1590-1606 and 1606-35), while in the 1630's yet another cousin was Foreign Apposer of the upper Exchequer. The family's fortunes seem to have been well and truly laid by the diarist's grandfather; George Evelyn (1526-1603) was successful both as a landowner and as a contractor, and plain lucky in that he inherited Long Ditton through his mother. Thereafter contracts and offices affected the position of individual branches, but the family's wealth rested primarily on land; the diarist believed his father, himself a younger son, to have had a landed income, before the Civil War,

[1] For Charles I's favourite, 'Jack' Ashburnham, see *D.N.B.*, I, 634-5; Keeler, *Long Parliament*, p. 89; *The Ashburnham Archives: A Catalogue*, ed. F. W. Steer (Lewes, 1958), esp. pp. x-xiii, 19; *Sussex Arch. Colls.*, XXXII, 19-22, XLIII, fig. 60; sources already given for Chamber officials 1625-41 (in *none* of these does he seem to be listed as a Groom of the Bedchamber; if he did hold this post in 1628, it may only have been for a short time).

of £4,000 a year.[1] That the sensitive and slightly prudish John Evelyn should have been the end-product of so much and such successful grubbing for excrement and distillation of urine provides an excellent illustration of Henry James's dictum that it takes a great deal of history to make a little literature.

A comparable case is that of the Darrells of Fulmer, Bucks, and Horkstow, Lincs, a cadet branch of the Coleshill family, prominent in the fifteenth and notorious in the sixteenth century. These Darrells were Victuallers of the Navy on and off from the 1580's to 1635. The principal architect of their fortunes was Sir Marmaduke (*c.* 1560-1632), fourth son of a third son of a second son. He combined his Victuallership with service in the Household, rising ultimately to be Cofferer; in 1604 he also became one of the four farmers of the export duty on sea coal. He acquired Fulmer, the principal of several Buckinghamshire properties, in 1607, and was succeeded there by his eldest son, Sir Sampson (1594-1635), who was assistant Navy Victualler to Sir Allen Apsley in the later 1620's and sole Victualler 1630-5, as well as co-Farmer of the coal duties. Horkstow, bought by Sir Marmaduke in 1620, passed to the second son, also Marmaduke.

To this branch at least of the Darrell family fortune proved but a fickle friend. Sir Sampson's son sold Fulmer in 1678, having parted with a succession of other properties in the preceding twenty-five years; Marmaduke the second's son sold Horkstow to a distant relative in 1685, and it finally passed out of the family in 1723.[2] One of Sir Marmaduke's daughters married James Harrington. Had he lived long enough and kept his eyes open, the author of *Oceana* might have learnt something about the mutability of fortune, even of landed wealth, from the history of his own in-laws.

The Harringtons themselves have recently been the subject of

---

[1] *D.N.B.*; Brunton and Pennington, *Members of the Long Parliament*; Keeler, *Long Parliament*; E. S. de Beer (ed.), *The Diary of John Evelyn* (Oxford, 1955), I, 136-41; *Cal. S. P. Dom.*, *passim* to *1636-7*, for the powder contract; sources as already cited for the Six Clerks of Chancery and for lists of Exchequer officers.

[2] V.C.H. *Bucks.*, II, 349, III, 164, 171-3, 176, 276-80, 296, 315; J.U. Nef, *The Rise of the British Coal Industry* (1932), II, 270, 307 n.; H. Hall, *Society in the Elizabethan Age* (London, 1886); Harl. Soc., *Lincs Pedigrees, Visn. Bucks*; *Cal. S.P. Dom.; Acts Privy Council;* PC 2/39-52; T 56/1; PCC 29 Audley, 84 Sadler; *Cal. Cttee. Compdg.*, pp. 2260-4; LC 4/200-2; sources as already cited for the Coffership of the Household.

controversy concerning the connexions between office, land, and wealth. The Rutland and Leicestershire Harringtons had unmistakably risen to be major landowners and 'greater gentry' in the course of the sixteenth century; this was partly, but, as Mr. Grimble their latest historian has shown, only partly, due to the profits of office. Soon after acquiring a title (the barony of Exton, in 1603), they began to decline. Why? Excessive mortality in the male line; tenure of the Governorship of the King's daughter, Princess Elizabeth, which was the very reverse of lucrative, in fact disastrously costly; spendthrift or unlucky heirs, succeeding to thrifty or fortunate ancestors. So much for the senior, or Exton, branch. There were two other lines: the two younger sons of Sir James Harrington (d. 1592), that is the younger brothers of the first Baron, were by no means ill provided for by their father. Sir Henry, the next brother, pursued a rather unsuccessful career as an adventurer in Ireland, but despite heavy indebtedness he retained some of his Leicestershire inheritance and some Irish acquisitions. Here also excessive male mortality contributed to decline: he died in 1612; his first son had predeceased him and his second died in 1614. The youngest brother of the first Lord Harrington, Sir James of Ridlington and Sapcotes, also died in 1614, but his sons both survived to enjoy their respective inheritances, and to leave as their male heirs respectively Sir James, the technical regicide, and James Harrington esquire, the political philosopher.

Dispute has centred on the third son of Sir Henry, that is the surviving heir of the middle, or Elmesthorpe and Bagworth branch, Sir William Harrington (1588-1627). According to Professor Tawney, Sir William was buying Crown lands in 1626-7 and may therefore have helped to provide evidence for his cousin's theory of the rising gentry. According to Professor Trevor-Roper he had no estate, and, if he did buy a little land at the end of his life, he 'was not a mere gentleman . . . but Lieut.-General of the Ordnance'. According to Mr. Grimble, there were two Sir Williams, Sir Henry's son who died in 1613 or 1614 and Sir William 'of Bagworth', whose relationship to the real Elmesthorpe-Bagworth branch Mr. Grimble wisely avoids making clear. In fact, there was only one Sir William; he did indeed inherit Bagworth, Leics, and properties in county Wicklow, but sold the former by 1616 and the latter by 1623-4. As far as this particular Harrington is concerned, Professor Trevor-Roper has the best of it.

His account of Sir William requires two qualifications. Firstly, although he was granted a reversion in 1621, Sir William did not become Lieutenant of the Ordnance until November 1625, succeeding his brother-in-law Sir Richard Moryson; Harrington was Moryson's executor, but before he had time to act in this capacity his sister, Moryson's widow, was acting as his own executrix; he had ceased to be Lieutenant by 17 April if not by 31 March 1626, and he died sometime during February or March 1627. Sir William's tenure therefore having lasted at most five and maybe under four months, it is misleading to describe him without qualification as Lieut.-General of the Ordnance and not a mere gentleman. His sister was indeed allowed up to £350 owed to the Crown on his account as Lieutenant, but this was in return for the commutation of a £109, 10s. 0d. p.a. life pension formerly granted to one of his Moryson in-laws. If any land was bought by him or his immediate heirs in 1626-7, the purchase money may well have included this £350.

The last point concerns precisely Sir William's heirs. In recounting the unfortunate marriage of his nephew, John Frescheville to Sarah Harrington, gambler and termagent, Gervase Holles, the memoir writer, described her as the daughter of Sir William of Bagworth. But it seems more likely that he made a mistake and that she was in fact the daughter of Sir William's half-brother, Sir John (d. 1614-15); Sir William had only one surviving daughter, Lucy, who married a man called Dinley. Without further probing of the genealogical sources, Holles's remark that Sarah would have been Sir William's heir 'if there had been any inheritance' is not therefore acceptable evidence that Sir William left no estate. But he certainly died in debt, and probably did leave none—or very little. What might have happened to this middle branch of the Exton Harringtons if Sir William had lived long enough to swallow and digest the fruits of office, instead of only tasting them in the last year of his life, is a matter for speculation rather than historical research.[1]

[1] See Tawney, 'The Rise of the Gentry', *Econ. Hist. Rev.*, XI (1941), 35 n. 3; Trevor-Roper, *The Gentry*, pp. 22-4; I. Grimble, *The Harington Family* (1957), esp. chs. V, X-XII, and for his identification of *two* Sir Williams pp. 143, 165, 169-70, 182, 203, 252. Sources other than those cited by these three authors: P.R.O. Close Roll indexes 1620-1, 1622-3; E 351/2654; WO 54/11, 55/454; SP 16/155/41; *Cal. S.P. Dom.*, *1619-23, 1625-6*; *Cal. S.P. Irish, 1611-32 passim; Visitation of Rutland 1618-19* (Harl. Soc., 1870), p. 39; Maddison, *Lincolnshire Pedigrees* (Harl. Soc. vol. 51) pp. 693-4; *Notes and Queries*, 10th ser., XII, 332-3; Burke, *Extinct Peerage* 'Frescheville'; G.E.C., V, 579; PCC 34 Skynner.

The history of another family connected with the same department confirms the difficulty of arguing that, because one member of a rising family held a particular office, therefore this was the cause of the family's rise. Having obtained a reversion to the Surveyorship of the Ordnance in 1627, Sir Paul Harris (1595-1644) acted largely by deputy from his entry to the office in 1628, and exclusively so from about 1632 until his final retirement in 1635.

When he asked for permission to resell the office, Sir Paul emphasized his poverty and his inability to afford living in London. Yet he was chosen Sheriff of Shropshire only a few years after this, and in the 1640's his son and heir compounded for a landed income of over £500 a year. At first sight Sir Paul looks a bit of a fraud.

Office had little to do with the rise of the Harris family. Sir Paul's great-grandfather was a yeoman farmer, and his grandfather a Shrewsbury draper trading in light-weight woollen goods. His father, a lawyer and business-man, who married an alderman's daughter, had become Esquire by 1614, bought a country estate in 1617 and went on to acquire a Baronetcy in 1624. So rapid was the family's rise in the social scale that he was actually charged in the Court of Chivalry with being of too base blood to support the title of baronet. But the case failed and Sir Paul, knighted in 1625, succeeded him as second baronet in 1629. Before his own death fifteen years later, Sir Paul had helped to raise his county for the King as a commissioner of Array (1642-3). To return to Harris's eagerness to part with his office, in view of the cost of coming to live in London, there may have been some truth in his claim that he had paid more than it was worth. But in any case his career as Surveyor cannot be given a large place in the story of his family's fortunes.[1]

Harris's first deputy as Ordnance Surveyor belonged to another family whose wealth rested on a combination of land, business, and revenue farming: the Bludders of Reigate. Sir Thomas senior (d. 1618), like the elder Darrell, was a naval victualler and a co-farmer of the coal duties; he also had interests in tin mining and the alum industry. The career of his son, Sir Thomas junior (c. 1597-1655), has been fully noted by Mrs. Keeler. He was a Gentleman of the

---

[1] G.E.C., *Baronetage*; WO 49/59, 54/12-13; B.M. Harleian MS. 429 Ordnance Order and Warrt. Bk.; SP 16/155/42, 301/9, 474/2; PC 2/39, pp. 304, 314; *Cal. Cttee. Compdg.*, p. 2027; T. D. Dukes, *Antiquities of Shropshire* (Shrewsbury, 1844), pp. 211, 275, 296; T. C. Mendenhall, *The Shrewsbury Drapers and Welsh Wool Trade* (Oxford, 1953), p. 90.

Privy Chamber, an unpaid post, as well as deputy or acting Surveyor under Harris, c. 1627-31, coal farmer, landed proprietor, part-time industrialist, and subsequently royalist M.P. His wife, a Brett, was related by marriage to Buckingham, Cranfield, and to Sir Paul Harris. Bludder, but *not* Harris, was already married when he entered office, and he may have done so partly as a remote member of the great Villiers 'connexion'. But office, as opposed to revenue farming and contracting, played a very small part in the Bludders' economy; even the knighthoods of the two Sir Thomases preceded their respective entries to central office and court circles.[1]

A family whose official ties were also with the Ordnance Office provides a more complicated but also more revealing example of the connexion between office, status, and wealth. The Heydons of Bacons-thorpe had been a great Norfolk family. Professor Trevor-Roper has given a vivid description of their rise, due largely to legal eminence and partly to office-holding, and of their catastrophic decline, due to their loss of royal favour and hence of office, culminating with involvement in the Essex rebellion of 1601. The next stage in the Heydons' story, if less dramatic, is equally instructive. The long climb back to favour and respectability was begun, in a humble way at first, by the two sons of that Sir Christopher whose career along with his brother Sir John's brought the family name and fortune so low. In 1613 John, the younger son, became Storekeeper of Sandown Castle, Deal, possibly through the patronage of Henry Howard, Earl of Northampton, then Lord Warden of the Cinque Ports. Meanwhile William, the elder son, had entered Prince Henry's service as a junior paymaster by 1611-12; later in James's reign he was paymaster to the royal commission on defective titles (in effect a fiscal body); by 1620 he was in the Prince of Wales' service. He was knighted, and became Paymaster, first of the 'volunteers' sent to the Palatinate and then of the English regiments in the Nether-lands. In 1623 he succeeded to what was left of the once great Norfolk estates; in March 1625 he became a Gentleman Usher of the new King's Privy Chamber and a year later Lieutenant of the Ordnance, in succession to Sir William Harrington.

[1] WO 55/1777, p. 10; *Acts Privy Council, 1627-8; Cal. S.P. Dom.;* Nef, *Coal Industry*; Brunton and Pennington, *Members*, p. 55; Keeler, *Long Parliament*; V.C.H., *Surrey*, III, 237, 297, 313; *Cal. Cttee. Compdg.*, p. 1498; O. Manning and W. Bray, *History and Antiquities of Surrey* (1804-14), I, 291, 305-6; LC 4/200-1.

John Heydon had apparently also been abroad and won some claim to mathematical and military distinction, presumably as a gunner. He also became Paymaster of the Posts. By contrast with his brother, who enjoyed a modest degree of favour with Prince, later King Charles, John Heydon relied on the patronage of successive Lord Wardens (Zouch, 1615-24, and Buckingham, 1624-8); he was knighted in 1629. Meanwhile doubtless by virtue of his already being Lieutenant of the Ordnance, William was made Lieutenant-General of Artillery on the isle of Rhé expedition in 1627, and was killed in action. John then succeeded him both as owner of the family estates and at the Ordnance Office, where he remained until 1642, when he was promoted to be Lieut-General of the King's artillery in the field, and later a privy councillor. It took him some years to restore the Lieutenants' authority after 1627. Thanks to the rapid turn over of Lieutenants and Surveyors, Francis Morrice, Sherborne's predecessor as Clerk, had virtually gained control of the office. The rights and wrongs of the matter are obscure, but according to Heydon, Morrice was caught burning incriminating documents on Good Friday 1628 after having said that he was going to set the day aside for prayer and devotions. Successive Masters of the Ordnance played little part in the everyday running of the office, and Heydon was responsible for supplying the fleets of 1635-9 and the armies of 1639-40. He thus combined the headship of a middling landed family with the management of a major department of state.

Sir John's royalism cost him dear, not only financially. But there is very little evidence before that of his having used his fifteen-year tenure of major office to restore the Heydon estates. In 1648 the Committee for Compounding, who had no reason to be tender with him, assessed his landed income at only £147, 5s. 0d. p.a.; although his lands had been confiscated since 1642-3, they were not in the war zone and should not have depreciated seriously in value. Sir John was in truth a rather pathetic figure. When, finding himself as he put it 'much oppressed with the Colique', he came to make his will about five years after compounding, he was burdened with debts and lawsuits, deserted by his wife, and unable to provide for his five children. There were only two manors and two parsonages left to meet his liabilities. Ironically he failed to name an executor and this task devolved upon his wife, whose alimony was another of his complaints. No doubt Sir John would have made a partial recovery if he had lived to 1660; but if his and William Heydon's tenure of office temporarily halted, it certainly did not reverse the decline in their family's fortunes.[1]

It is easy to find individual office-holders who rose decisively in status and wealth, and whose descendants appear to have made good this advance. It is far less easy to be sure that the best-documented cases are either the most representative or the most significant. Certain patterns do however seem to repeat themselves.

The Perfect Secretary. One such is that of the private secretary turned royal official. The career of Edward Sherborne, the classic example of this, has already been traced in discussing how men without wealth or family connexions entered the King's service. But despite his own and his son's evident ability, and the latter's knighthood, the Sherbornes failed, partly on account of their religion, to establish themselves for even one generation in the landed upper class. The elder Sherborne, servant of George Calvert, Robert Cecil, Dudley Carleton, Francis Bacon, the East India Company, and finally Charles I, epitomizes the administrative careerist of humble origins for whom entry to royal service was only another rung on the clientage ladder.

The connexions between royal and private service and social and economic aggrandizement can also be illustrated from the career of another Baconian. Thomas Meautys, alias Mewtis (*c.* 1590-1649), was descended from Henry VII's French secretary, who had come over from France in 1485. His great-, or great-great-grandfather was Henry VIII's Ambassador in France and acquired monastic property at West Ham, some of which was inherited by Thomas's father, the eldest son of a second son. He, Thomas's father, was also Thomas, as was his first cousin once removed, a professional soldier who served much overseas and was knighted in 1611. Our Thomas Meautys, himself a younger son, was in Bacon's service by 1616; he was later to marry his patron's niece, daughter of Bacon's half-brother Sir Nathaniel, and he may already have been related to him

[1] *D.N.B.; Cal. S.P. Dom., 1601-40; Acts Privy Council; Foedera,* XVII, 388-93, 407-10; PC 2/40 pp. 379, 387-8; T 56/1, 7-8, 13; WO 54/12-15; SP 16/230/42; Rushworth, *Hist. Colls.,* II, ii, 914; F. Blomefield, *Topographical History of Norfolk* (1805-10), esp. vol. VI; PCC 344 Alchin; *Cal. Cttee. Compdg.,* pp. 1500-1; C 54/2772/102; Trevor-Roper, *The Gentry,* p. 19. Shaw, *Knights,* and W. C. Metcalfe, *A Book of Knights* (1885), wrongly say John not William Heydon was knighted in 1620.

indirectly through the marriage of another cousin, his own future mother-in-law, to Sir Nathaniel Bacon. It is clear even from Bacon's printed papers that Meautys was on much more intimate terms with their master than Sherborne ever was. According to a will made by Bacon in 1621, Meautys was to receive a £500 legacy, and even the final version left him £50 in jewelry plus a horse, and a direction in its codicil that the executors were to repay his loan to Bacon before satisfying any other creditors. As we shall see, the last of these provisions had important consequences for Meautys. Meanwhile he had wisely reinsured himself by obtaining a reversion to a Clerkship of the Council, while in the course of acting as Bacon's go-between with Buckingham he so commended himself to the favourite that he was in no wise the loser by his patron's disgrace. In 1622 he succeeded to the Council Clerkship, and also secured a reversion to the Writership of Star Chamber to the Great Seal, which he held in plurality with his Clerkship from 1626 to 1631.

Bacon's executors found his finances too much for them and refused to act. The will remained unexecuted for fifteen months, then Meautys, perhaps in his capacity as priority creditor, and Sir Robert Rich, one of the executors, accepted letters of administration. In his capacity as administrator, and perhaps on the pretext of recovering his loan, Meautys established himself as the holder, or tenant, of various long leases and as the effective manager of other parts of the estate, on behalf of Bacon's other creditors. The manuscript records of these transactions are incomplete, and it may be that everything he did was entirely honest and legal. But, considering the hopelessness of Bacon's financial heritage, it is remarkable how well Meautys seems to have done out of it. In 1629 he paid £1,821 for a Crown manor in Hertfordshire, previously held by Bacon; in 1632 he arranged to pay £530 p.a. to Bacon's widow and her second husband for eighty years or for as long as the estate was in the hands of Bacon's creditors; in 1634 he sued out a general livery on behalf of Bacon's residual heir male, his cousin Thomas Bacon of Hessett, Suffolk. Why this obscure individual should have been Bacon's heir male, and not one of his nephews, does not appear from such of the Bacon estate papers as concern Meautys.[1] Perhaps he was a 'man of straw' deliberately put in because the estate's finances were known to be in a mess. Certainly since Thomas Bacon

[1] I have only consulted the Gorhambury MSS. which relate to Meautys. *No* heir male is mentioned in the wills printed by Spedding.

had in 1630 conveyed his entire interest in the estate to Meautys and other trustees, this livery was a legal fiction. And in the later 1630's and 1640's neither the heir male nor the widow but Meautys was making leases with the tenants and acting generally as manager of the Bacon estate. As earlier, it is difficult to distinguish his activities in this capacity from those as a property-owner in his own right. In 1641 he pledged the land which he had bought in 1629 as security for the raising of £1,510 as portions for his four maternal first cousins, the daughters of Thomas Coningsby. Later in that year this and other lands were given as pledges that after his death his heirs would settle land worth £500 p.a. on his wife (who was his own second cousin, Ann Bacon). In the course of building up his estate Meautys does not appear to have had to borrow money. He may have done so, but all the bonds which he entered into seem to represent security for the fulfilment of obligations connected with his property transactions, rather than loans.

All this time, down to 1641 at least, Meautys had been actively employed as a Council Clerk. His duties involved at least five weeks' attendance out of every sixteen, or four months a year altogether. He had also served on several royal commissions, had acted for a time as Receiver of fines on tobacco licences, and from 1636, in his capacity as senior Council Clerk, was also Muster Master-General, which involved him in the military preparations of 1638-40. He had sat in four of the five parliaments of the 1620's; and the influence of Lord Keeper Finch, steward of the borough of Cambridge, again secured him a seat there in the Short Parliament (April-May 1640), but he was defeated by Oliver Cromwell and another 'opposition' candidate in the autumn elections for the Long Parliament. None the less he was knighted in February 1640-1 and his career seemed far from ended. But in January 1641/2 Meautys was so seriously ill that rumour reported him dying. Although he recovered and apparently survived for another seven years, he retired completely from public affairs, and lived mainly in his old master's house at Gorhambury, as a kind of glorified caretaker. The parliamentary taxation officers let him off very lightly in 1645. But this may well have been due to good contacts with the county committee, or sympathy with their cause, and not to any decline in his fortunes. Within three years of his own death, his only daughter and sole heiress had died a minor, to be succeeded in her heritage, including the interest in the Bacon estate, by her uncle, Meautys's brother

Henry. The latter speedily liquidated his entire interest in both the Thomas Meautys and the Bacon estates, selling to the second husband of his brother's widow, the future Speaker and Master of the Rolls, Sir Harbottle Grimston, in two lots totalling £12,760. Since none of these interests were freehold they must presumably have fetched less than twenty years' purchase, and it can therefore be inferred that the landed inheritance which had come to Henry Meautys from his brother, via his niece, was worth not less than *c*. £700 p.a.; as no rentals survive, this rests on interpolation.

How much money Meautys made as Council Clerk, Muster Master, Receiver of fines, and Star Chamber Writer, and how much as co-administrator and then sole manager of the Bacon estate, can only be conjectured. An estimate of total annual value is only available for the Star Chamber office: £300. A total income of over £1,000 p.a. from office would seem plausible. Meautys's career illustrates the difficulty of isolating office as a factor in a man's financial circumstances. Although he did not succeed in founding a landed family, his purchase in 1629, his heavy pledges in the 1630's and early 1640's, and the posthumous value of his assets in land suggest that office under the Crown and the spoils of Gorhambury had alike been turned to good advantage.[1]

Esau's Pottage. At first glance Richard Colchester (*c*. 1600-43) appears a typical representative of the lesser gentry. His father, a small Worcestershire landowner, styled himself Gent., but apparently did not possess a coat of arms. His mother, Alice Roberts, came of another minor landowning family in the Worcestershire-Gloucestershire-Oxfordshire area, but his maternal uncle Nicholas Roberts (1572-1637) held the office of an Examiner in Chancery for most of James I's reign. Colchester had no university or legal education, and although he was the eldest son, he seems to have sought his

---

[1] Herts R.O., Gorhambury MSS., I, A, 18-43, B, 2-3, 25, 40, E, 31, H, 5-6, L, 1-2, II, A, 3-19, III, B, 45, IX, D, 21-32, and Pedigree; Spedding, *Letters & Life of Bacon*, II, 3, VII, 229, 292, 323-6, 342, 354-5, 390-1, 542, 545, 551; *The Private Correspondence of Jane, Lady Cornwallis* (1842); *Cal. S.P. Dom.*, *1623-41; Acts Privy Council; PC* 2/40-52; T 56/1, 3; *Foedera*, XX, 101, 125; P. Morant, *History & Antiquities of Essex* (1768), I, ii, 19; Chamberlain, *Letters*, II, 216; W. C. Abbott, *The Writings and Speeches of Oliver Cromwell* (Cambridge, Mass., 1937-47), I, 109, 114; Keeler, *Long Parlt.*, p. 36; *Cal. Cttee. Advcmt. Money*, p. 481; LC 4/197-201, esp. 201, fols. 22, 141; PCC, Admin. bk. 1649, fol. 165; Dep. Kpr. Pub. Recds., *43rd Rept.*, p. 181; C 54/3074/84, 3225/48.

fortune, very probably under his uncle's patronage, as an under-clerk in Chancery. By the mid-1620's he was clerk to Richard Chettle, another Worcestershire man, possibly a family friend, who in 1624 succeeded Nicholas Roberts as Examiner. In 1625 or 1626 Colchester obtained one of the twenty-four Cursitorships in Chancery: he now held a minor royal office and was no longer a mere under-clerk. He was already lending money to his less thrifty relatives; in 1626 he acquired a coat of arms; in 1627 he was admitted to Gray's Inn, rather as today an extra-mural student might come to the University some years older than the normal intake.

In 1632 he became a Six Clerk in Chancery. While no positive evidence affirms it, there is no good reason to doubt his having paid the normal purchase price of £5,000-£6,000. He might have raised part of this sum from the profits of the Cursitorship (worth perhaps *c.* £300 p.a.), which he had then held for about seven years, and some conceivably from the portion (at most a few hundred pounds) due on his own first marriage in the late 1620's. But it could hardly have come from the profits of landed wealth, for his father was not only still alive but had remarried since the death of Richard's mother. And he may even have raised part of the money by borrowing on the security of the office itself. However, his only recorded recognizance (a bond for £1,500 to Nicholas Hampson, the Clerk of the Statutes, in 1629[1]) may well represent security given for his good behaviour in office; alternatively, if it was a genuinely penal bond, it may have been a pledge for his uncle's debts (of which more anon).

In 1635 Colchester became liable for his share of the Six Clerks' £16,000 composition with the Crown. It is not therefore surprising that when the curtain goes up on his finances in January 1637/8, his gross debts totalled £2,345, or £1,184 more than was owing to him. Even so, he was able to minute with satisfaction that twelve months earlier his net indebtedness had been £2,377, i.e. if his own loans had been £1,161 (as they were in January 1638), his own debts must have been £3,538. Colchester's records of his financial progress have survived for the last five complete years of his life, 1638-42 inclusive. They reveal a spectacular progress.

By the beginning of 1640 Colchester reckoned that his loans easily exceeded his debts, and thereupon noted in his account book

[1] LC 4/200, fol. 411.

'Deo gratias in aeternum'.[1] 1639 was not only a key year for Colchester in seeing his debts cleared off. His first wife died in April, leaving him an eldest son and heir (Duncombe Colchester, 1630-94), a younger son (d. 1641), and one daughter. Almost at once, as if

TABLE 28. OUTLINE OF RICHARD COLCHESTER'S FINANCES, 1638-42

Year	Ordinary Expenditure	Outgoings of all kinds	Fees (? net) from Six Clerkship	Gross Receipts	Balance of Debts (owed by, and to him)
	£	£	£	£	£
1637	—	—	—	—	−1,184[1]
1638	336	1,895	860	2,244	−565
1639	449[2]	3,340	770	4,050[3]	+2,220
1640	367	4,868	750 or 557	4,900	+2,880
1641	334	2,124	525	2,123	+3,040[4]
1642	337	4,137[5]	283	3,942[6]	+250[7]

Notes (all figures are given to the nearest £)
1. £875 still owing on his composition as a Six Clerk.
2. Includes funeral of first wife, courtship and marriage of second.
3. Includes £100 left by first wife (died April 1639), and £400 out of the £1,500 portion obtained with second (married August 1639).
4. Calculated just before his biggest land purchase took effect.
5. Includes land purchase and its legal costs: £2,715.
6. Rents and entry fines on estate now reckoned at £1,286 for their first full year.
7. After his sale of £100 worth of plate, November and December 1642, but before his assessment for the twentieth at £600 (i.e. for an estate of capital value £12,000), January 1643.

prompted by this reminder of the shortness and uncertainty of life, he settled the Six Clerkship on his eldest son; in name he was to be succeeded by one of his own clients or servants who was to hold office as trustee for his son's life. The chosen reversioner was to hold the Clerkship until Duncombe Colchester was twenty-two, at the pleasure of Richard's executors; he was to receive an allowance from the profits of the office, the residue being allocated to the

[1] For similar pious ejaculations, see the journals of that great office-holding entrepreneur, Richard Boyle, first Earl of Cork (*Lismore Papers*, 1st ser., *passim*).

payment of Colchester's own debts and his children's education and maintenance.

About two months after being widowed, Colchester was courting again, and within five months he was remarried, to Elizabeth, daughter of Sir Hugh Hamersley. When she in turn was left a widow in 1643, his second wife proved herself a worthy scion of the London mercantile aristocracy. Prepared for possible charges that she was favouring herself and her own children (two sons and one daughter survived from Colchester's second marriage) at the expense of her step-children, she showed herself equally resolute in the face of enemies at law, blackmail by her late husband's half-brother, another Richard Colchester (who threatened to inform the authorities that young Duncombe had been in arms against Parliament during the second Civil War, of 1648),[1] and the machinations of the parliamentary Compounding Committee. Most relevant for us, she continued her husband's careful accounts and rendered up her stewardship when Duncombe came of age. She held the inheritance together during years when in less capable hands it would almost certainly have disintegrated.

By the end of the 1630's Richard Colchester had in economic terms become primarily a money-lender. He had presumably achieved this by frugality and by having made good use of the profits of office. Unfortunately his income, from fees, interest, and rent, cannot be distinguished from his capital gains and repayments; it is easier to analyse the out-payments side of his finances, but even this can only be done with any completeness for the first of the five years covered by his accounts.

TABLE 29.   COLCHESTER'S OUT-PAYMENTS IN 1638[2]

Share of Six Clerk's composition	£300
Capital repayment of debts	866
Interest paid on debts	154
Ordinary expenditure	336
Unaccounted for (i.e. extraordinary expenditure and new loans)	239

Just as Colchester's out-goings include repayments of money which

[1] Glos. R.O., Colchester MSS., F 18.

[2] *Ibid.*, Journal (1), pp. 1-59, monthly expenditure (ordinary), 326-290 (from the other end of this vol.), debts and accts.

he had borrowed, as well as payments of interest and new loans which he made, so his in-comings totals include capital as well as interest payments by people to whom he had lent money. With this proviso, in 1638 the direct gains of office constituted 38·3 per cent. of his gross receipts, in 1639 19 per cent., and in 1640 15·3 per cent. Thereafter the volume of business in Chancery was too much affected by the political situation for the comparison to be meaningful. Of course, his office was probably of indirect as well as direct financial advantage to Colchester, making it easier for him to borrow money on the best terms when he had to, and putting him in the way of sound potential borrowers. At his death, his widow reckoned that he was owed £3,403 in good or hopeful debts and £570 in desperate ones: no bad proportion considering the confusion of the times.

The date of Colchester's death was unfortunate in two respects financially. He died at the height of the Civil War, and very soon after completing the transaction which turned him from an office-holding money-lender into an office-holding landed gentleman. He had time neither to secure his legal titles against all possible attacks, nor to recuperate financially from his great outlay. Although some of Mrs. Colchester's figures are suspect, for she wanted them to prove too much, she may have reported correctly that her husband died with debts of £8,460, an increase of c. £5,700 in the nine months January to September 1643. And this apparently takes no account of £961 which he was posthumously accused of having sent to the King at Oxford, but of which no mention can be found in the papers of this prudent couple.

How Colchester obtained the estate by virtue of which he became a landed gentleman is another story. His uncle, Examiner Roberts, had acquired various properties in the counties of Gloucester, Hereford, and Oxford, and a rent charge in Lincolnshire. But having resigned from his office (presumably selling it), he failed to prosper as a landowner; his legal titles were challenged; he became involved in costly lawsuits, and fell heavily into debt. In 1637 he was succeeded by his son Cesar, who was apparently deaf and dumb, or for some other reason incapable of managing his own affairs; Cesar died without issue in 1641, and, his brothers having predeceased him, the estate then passed to his paternal uncle Giles Roberts, a very obscure lesser gentleman from Worcestershire. In 1641-2 Giles sold the greater part of the Roberts estate to Colchester; why he did so, and on what terms is not clear. According to the later heirs and claimants on the Roberts' side:

> Richard Colchester being Nephewe to Nicholas Roberts and well acquainted with the value of his estate and debts by him oweinge, of all which Giles Roberts was altogeather ignorant, Richard Colchester, intendinge to make a prey to himselfe of the estate, first gott the deeds into his hands upon pretence hee would keepe them for Giles Roberts his Uncles use, And pretended that the said Mannors Lands and premisses were charged or chargeable with divers debts statutes etc. amountinge to 9000¹ or 10000¹, and did perswade the said Giles that the said debts would bee his undoeinge and did propose to his said Uncle Giles Roberts that hee the said Rich: Colchester would undertake the dischargeinge of all the said debts if he might have the said Lands and premisses conveyed to him and such other persons as hee should nominate, and would alsoe pay to the said Giles 1200¹ upon the sealeinge and executeinge of the assurances, whereas the debts truely and justly chargeable upon all or any the premisses, did not amount to above 800¹ or therabouts.[1]

As told from Colchester's side, the story is rather different; and there is some evidence to support his claim that he had become liable for many of the Robertses' debts. A joint bond for £600 with Nicholas Roberts given in 1628/9 had been cancelled in 1631, but in 1634 Colchester advanced £1,500 to clear a 1628 mortgage off part of the Roberts estate; and in 1638/9 Cesar Roberts gave Colchester a bond for £2,400 and they became jointly bound in £1,200 to observe a Chancery court order. More of Colchester's own heavy indebtedness in 1638-9 probably represents obligations incurred as security for the Roberts family.[2] When the inheritance passed to the 'altogether ignorant' Giles Roberts, it may have been encumbered with debts exceeding its own total value. And Giles Roberts may therefore have been pleased to sell out to his nephew, even though at a much lower price than the property would have fetched if unencumbered, since the buyer now became responsible for all the bonds and mortgages. But as well as the creditors, this left other unsatisfied parties: William, son and heir of Giles Roberts, and more particularly Nicholas Roberts's widow and her second husband. Legal proceed-

---

[1] *Ibid.*, H 73.
[2] C 54/2732/132, 3186/25, 28; Colchester MSS., H 27, P 24, Journals (1) and table already given in the text.

ings, aimed at dislodging the Colchesters, were in progress on and off from 1641 until about 1660.

Perhaps Richard Colchester behaved badly in taking advantage of the improvidence and gullibility of his mother's relatives. Having agreed to pay his uncle £1,320, or possibly only £1,200 for the final transfer of the estate, he seems in fact to have paid him £875, the remaining £1,870 of his total outlay going to creditors, claimants, and (since it was 1641) royal tax-collectors. Colchester himself valued the estate at £8,650 net or £11,450 gross, the debts and other claims on it at between £10,167 and £18,608. According to surveys made in 1628 and 1636, its gross *annual* value should have been over £1,700, and it yielded Colchester nearly £1,300 in his first full year as owner.[1] Doubtless Colchester had persuaded himself that he was acting in the Robertses' own best interests in taking the estate off their hands. We may be sure that he never wavered in the conviction of his own rectitude, and gave sincere thanks to God at every crucial step. In its own modest way Colchester's entry to the landed class was an achievement worthy of the age which had produced a Baptist Hicks, a Hugh Audley, and an Arthur Ingram.

Thanks to his widow's tenacity, and to his son also marrying well (*his* wife's portion was £2,500) and having at least moderate aptitude for business, Colchester's foundations stood firm. Despite one or two defeats at law, and the usual vicissitudes of royalist landowners, his acquisitions in four counties survived without major loss. His son Duncombe was later knighted; he and his successors continued to enlarge the estate, with purchases totalling over £10,000, until well into the eighteenth century.[2]

In Richard Colchester's case, office merely provided part of the means by which financial talent found expression. Whatever career he had followed, such a man would surely have prospered. Still, at one stage office was probably the decisive factor in making his fortune.

[1] Colchester MSS., Journals (6), p. 329, (8), pp. 267, 284-5, H 59, G 2 (note: the largest possible total for Roberts's debts is arrived at by interpolation, since the figures in this paper of Colchester's do not appear to be internally consistent); S 18 (Apley, Lincs, £100, Mitchel Dean £636, other Glos. property £601, property partly in Glos. and partly in Herefordshire £375; total £1,712 p.a. A property at Stanton Harcourt apparently remained with the Robertses; the residue of an 81-year lease of another Oxon property had already been sold by them, for £168 p.a. or £2,520).

[2] *Ibid.*, Journals (2)-(3), (9), A 1, 3, B 8-38, F 4 (2), 17, 19, G 1.

Some account has already been given of George Mynne's career in discussing officers' tenure. Superficially he presents one of the clearest instances of wealth from office being used to buy out the office-holder's own relatives, and establish a new landed branch of the family. To avoid retreading familiar ground, it must be remembered, however, that Mynne was at no time solely, and probably never primarily, dependent on office for his wealth. Much more than in Colchester's early career, office was only one of several factors in the making of a single fortune.

Mynne may conceivably have been descended from John, Master of the Woods to Henry VIII. His father and grandfather do not seem to have been men of much substance in their native Shropshire, but a great-uncle and an uncle had come south and prospered at least sufficiently for the latter's heir, George's cousin Robert (1578-1630's), to have inherited a medium-sized property in Hertfordshire, which he added to early in the seventeenth century. Another probably more distant cousin, John, was also established as a landowner, in Surrey. There were two other Mynnes in Charles I's service: Sir Henry, Receiver and Paymaster of the Gentleman Pensioners (d. 1633), and his brother Captain Thomas, Knight Harbinger (d. 1639-1640). They came from Norfolk, but were offshoots of the Surrey line, and so presumably remote relatives of George. They were probably both Roman Catholics, but there is no clear evidence that he was.

Mynne's relatives seem to have been about as incompetent, or naïve as Colchester's. Robert Mynne had mortgaged part of his property in 1611; in that year one John Slany, citizen and merchant-tailor of London, coming to live near by, and seeing, according to George Mynne, that Robert lived beyond his means, offered to redeem the mortgage and lend him £500. This done, Slany asked neither for interest nor to have the principal paid back for six or seven years, and then suddenly confronted Robert Mynne with a large bill. George Mynne came into the picture in 1618 when he gave his credit to help Robert meet Slany's demands. By 1626 he thought that he had bought Slany out for payments totalling £980, though it took a legal action and a court order three years later to remove him finally. Meanwhile, whether for cash down or in return for having the rest of his debts taken over, in 1625 Robert made over most of his property to George for twenty-one years: the land was apparently all let to tenants and the rents due on it totalled £219 p.a.

In 1627, for an unknown sum Mynne took over more of Hertingford-bury from the Trustees of the lands held by Charles I before his accession, for the ninety-one-year remainder of a ninety-nine-year term; on payment of another £500 this lease was settled on Mynne's trustees or assigns. Finally on 23 July 1631 for £1,000 Mynne took over the seventeen-year remainder of a 1617 thirty-one-year lease of some Duchy of Lancaster property there, and for £2,550 he bought outright from Robert the big house and the main property (leased to him since 1625).

Concurrently with these operations Mynne was establishing himself on a considerably larger scale in Surrey. Although the details are unclear, by May 1628 he had bought property from his other cousin John Mynne, for which he had made payments and undertaken to cover debts together totalling £11,849, 14s. 4d. By the early 1630's his principal seat was at Woodcote near Epsom; Hertfordshire definitely dropped into second place.

Like Colchester, Mynne was a large-scale money-lender. Unlike Colchester, Mynne does seem to have paid a fair price to the relatives whom he replaced. He was also unlike Colchester in failing to found a landed family. His only son died without issue in 1652; his properties were divided between his two daughters, and eventually swelled the estates of several other families including the Calverts and the Evelyns.[1]

This aspect of office-holding can be more simply illustrated from a less complicated and so perhaps more typical case than Mynne's. Robert Wolseley (c. 1587-1646) was a younger son of a minor Staffordshire gentry family, and although his father was a first son, the grandfather, himself a second son, had neither inherited nor permanently acquired a landed estate. Robert's elder brother became a soldier and went to seek his fortune in Ireland. Robert's own early

---

[1] Richardon, *Chamber Admin.*, p. 366; Shaw, *Knights*, II, 148; Rushworth, *Hist. Colls.*, I, 395; sources already cited for other Chamber and Household officers (for Sir Henry and Captain Thomas); *Catholic Rec. Soc.*, XIV, fig. 314; G. A. Carthew, *Hundred of Launditch* (Norwich, 1877-9), II, 481-91; *Visn. Rutland*, p. 5; Herts. R.O., Cowper MSS., C 244-92, 322-6; PCC 107 Bowyer (will of Mynne's only son, 1651-1/2); V.C.H., *Surrey*, III, 274-6; sources already given in Chapter 3, s. iii (for Mynne's official career and subsequent troubles); LC 4/200, fols. 133, 206; 201, fols. 26, 346; 202, fols. 25, 54, 110, 131, 136, 205, 224, 233, 250, 266, 271, 312, 332, 341, 344; P.R.O., State Papers Supplementary (uncalendared), SP 46/78, fols. 97-114.

years are obscure. He succeeded to his father's small property sometime after 1614; but sometime between his growing up (*c.* 1607) and the 1620's he must have gone to London. Despite his lack of any formal legal training (or university education) he obtained an under-clerkship in the office of one of the Six Clerks. By 1618-20 he was in a position to act as a surety, if not as creditor, to his second cousin, head of the senior line, Sir Thomas Wolseley of Wolseley, whose fortunes were unmistakably in decline. By 1623 Sir Thomas had apparently mortgaged his estate, and by 1625-6 it can safely be inferred that his finances were in an almost hopeless state.

Meanwhile in 1625 Robert Wolseley obtained, whether by purchase or other means, a half-share in the clerkship of the Patents in Chancery, worth about £500 p.a. This office had only been created in 1618, but it was being investigated by the commissioners on fees in 1627/8. In 1630-1 the commissioners examined details of Wolseley's alleged exactions: he was charged with having received altogether £4, 12s. 0d. for one gunner's patent on which the basic fee was only 13s. 4d. Although he was not brought to trial, Wolseley was reduced to petitioning the King in 1637-8, and the commissioners were ordered to keep his case before them.

From the surviving Wolseley papers it is only possible to give a tentative account of Sir Robert's financial affairs, but the general outline is clear enough. In 1626 he raised about £550 on bond and £500 by mortgaging his own modest landed inheritance. In the same year he seems to have made some agreement with Sir Thomas whereby the profits of his office were offered as security, possibly for his making Sir Thomas and his family a series of payments. In 1627 Sir Thomas made over his properties to his wife and children, retaining only a life interest, and mortgaged the most valuable of them to Robert Wolseley for £2,500. In 1628-9 Robert apparently bought or redeemed a mortgage on two-thirds of another of Sir Thomas's properties for payments totalling £1,679. In 1629 Robert was himself mortgaging this and also another property, lately Sir Thomas's; by this time he was owed £3,700 by his improvident cousin. In 1629, too, Wolseley married the daughter of a Wiltshire knight with whom he received a portion of £2,000. In 1630 Sir Thomas died, and Wolseley, raising two further mortgages of £300 and £840 on properties, which he already controlled if he did not yet own, made absolute his acquisition of the main family estate at

Wolseley, Staffs, by increasing his payments to a final gross total of £6,800 (i.e. another £3,000 or so on top of what he was already owed in loans and interest). In 1633 for £475 he bought, or redeemed a mortgage on, the other one-third of the estate, two-thirds of which he had acquired in 1628.

Robert Wolseley's social progress was if anything even more rapid. In 1626 he was still styled Gent.; by 1627/8, whether by virtue of his office or for other reasons, he had blossomed into Esquire, and in November 1628 he became a Baronet, getting off all but £95 in fees of the full cost (£1,095 under James I). Considering that baronets were meant to enjoy a status part way between the knightage and the peerage, corresponding to that of medieval bannerets, this was good going.

Another peculiarity in Wolseley's career is the frequency with which he negotiated surrenders, pardons, and re-grants of, and in connexion with, his office. In 1625/6 he and his partner surrendered it back to Coventry, the new Lord Keeper (they having been appointed by Bishop Williams); in 1629/30 they obtained both a full pardon for any offences which they might have committed in office and a re-grant of the office and of their official privileges. In 1631 Sir Robert acquired a new co-clerk, possibly only a nominal partner, in the person of Sir Thomas's younger son; perhaps this was part of the purchase price of the Wolseley estate. In 1632 Sir Robert was granted the whole office with the name of a trustee for his infant son added to his own for extra security of tenure. In 1634 he secured yet another pardon and protection for anything done in his office; even so, sometime in 1637 he offered to compound with the Crown in the matter of his fees. Perhaps Wolseley's Clerkship was particularly vulnerable to attacks by the Commissioners on Exacted Fees and Innovated Offices, simply because it was a new office. In 1641 he was accused of fraud in his official capacity, but by then this charge may have had a political motive.

Whether or not because he had cause to be grateful to the Crown, Sir Robert was a firm royalist, and became a Colonel in the King's army. As a result his son and heir, Sir Charles (1630-1714), had to pay £2,500 to get the sequestration taken off the estates. This was paid in 1646-7; ironically, in 1648 the young man married the youngest daughter of the well-known parliamentarian peer, Viscount Saye and Sele. Her portion totalled £3,000, a nice illustration of penal taxation sometimes being as broad as it was long when members of the two 'sides' intermarried. We need not follow Sir Charles's later political career here: economically the family's fortunes seem to have remained very stable through the later seventeenth and earlier eighteenth centuries. The present Baronet still lives at Wolseley, thanks in part at least to the office held by his ancestor the Clerk of the Patents.[1]

Roper's Office without Roper—or Buckingham. We have already seen that the Chief Clerkship of King's Bench was an office of exceptional value, the object of aristocratic and court rivalries. Robert Henley, who succeeded to this office in 1629, was considerably less of a self-made man than some of the others whose careers we have been investigating. His grandfathers and his father ranked as Esquires; his paternal grandfather and an uncle were Sheriffs of Somerset; his father, apparently the second son, was at one time Mayor of Taunton. Robert Henley (1591-1656) was educated at Oxford and the Middle Temple. He qualified as a barrister in 1615/16. But in under three years he bought a Six Clerkship in Chancery, reputedly for £6,000. How he raised this sum is a mystery. He does not appear to have borrowed on bond; he had at this time little or no real property to mortgage, his father being still alive (not that *he* had much, having been left only £700 by *his* father in 1614); Henley's own inheritance from his grandfather, who had founded fifteen almshouses, had only been £100! And however promising a start he was making at the bar, he cannot have earned a great deal in so short a time. From then on, however, he had an assured income which varied (according to his seniority among the Six Clerks and the volume of business) between about £800 and £1,600 p.a.

Before his father died, Henley had acquired the notorious King's Bench office. Since 1621 this had been executed no doubt by deputy, by Sir Robert Heath (Solicitor-, then Attorney-General, then Chief Justice) and Sir George Paul (Registrar of the Court of High Commission) as trustees for Buckingham. In 1626/7 these two became trustees jointly for Buckingham and four of his principal creditors,

[1] *D.N.B.*, XXI, 791, and G.E.C., *Btge.*, II, 62 (brief ref. to Sir Robert in the notices on his son, Sir Charles Wolseley); the William Salt Library, Stafford, unnumbered Wolseley MSS., boxes 2A, 2B, 2C, 2F, numbered MSS. D 1781/44-6, 69, 71, 75, 75A, 85-93, 110, 174, 199, 200, Pedigree (1); PCC., 135 Twiss; other references in *Cal. S.P. Dom., Foedera*, P.R.O., LC 4/199-201, Wilson, Thesis, *loc. cit.*; P.R.O., E 165/46, pp. 18, 32, 72, 128b; E 165/47, pp. 76-8; SP 16/323, fols. 103-4, 135-6, 376/60, 537/37; Bodl. MS. Tanner 318, fols. 114, 116, 119.

London magnates who were also customs farmers. In 1628 Buckingham was killed; Heath and Paul then became trustees jointly for his
seven executors or trustees, his administrator, and these four
creditors. In July 1629, by a quadripartite agreement with the
executors and the administrator, the three surviving creditors, and
the two previous trustees, Henley and his younger brother, a London
merchant, were assigned the office. Once the transfer arrangements
were completed, they were to have sole and full disposal of its
profits, except for £1,000 p.a. reserved to Spencer, Lord Compton,
for his life (he succeeded his father as Earl of Northampton in 1630
and was killed in 1643). A few months later Henley and his clerk
Samuel Wightwick were granted the office for their lives (and the life
of the longer lived of them). Had Henley merely taken on the Chief
Clerkship for the Buckingham estate and its creditors, this would
have signified that he was ready to do so for a small share in its
annual profits, and was thought a more suitable trustee than Heath
(too distinguished) or Paul (too old). But in fact he acquired it
outright. Considering that he was able to obtain it on a term of *two*
lives, he can hardly have paid less than two and a half years' purchase
and he may have paid anything up to six or seven: taking £3,500 as
its annual value to him, anything between £8,750 and £24,500, or, if
the multiple of three and a half years was used, £10,750. Henley
must have lived very frugally indeed to have saved that much after
ten years as a Six Clerk, especially considering the setback suffered
by the Six in December 1621 when their house in Chancery Lane
was burnt down. According to Simonds D'Ewes, this fire cost his
father (a Six Clerk, 1607-31) £5,000, or including his own office next
door £6,000; Henley's share in the value of the property, and of the
credit notes and other records there was probably smaller.[1] When
his father died in the 1630's Henley came into the Somerset property;
again he may have had this settled on him in the 1620's and have
mortgaged it to raise the purchase money for the office. Alternatively,
Henley may have been helped by his marriages. His first wife died
without issue; his second, to whom he was married by 1621, was the
daughter of a Suffolk landowner. The portions which they brought
may conceivably have helped Henley to make his start.

The later stages of his career are more easily explicable. In 1632
he resigned his Six Clerkship, probably for the usual £5,000-£6,000,

---

[1] S. D'Ewes, *Autobiography and Correspondence*, ed. Halliwell, I,
177-8, 207; Chamberlain, *Letters*, II, 416-17.

in favour of Richard Colchester. But in 1635 he obtained a retrospective pardon for any offences committed *qua* Six Clerk between three and sixteen years earlier, and may have contributed to the composition which was paid by the existing Six. As has already been explained, the King's Bench office was investigated in 1637-8; it was apparently reckoned to be beyond the powers of the commissioners on fees to cleanse so Augean a stable. A special commission or committee was appointed, consisting of the Lord Treasurer, Earl Marshal, Chancellor of the Exchequer, senior Secretary of State, and two other Privy Councillors; but they did not bring Henley to book. In 1639 he bought a Hampshire estate for £9,500; in 1640 he lent the King £3,000; in 1640-3 he bought an additional property in west Dorset for £1,800. From 1642 his office was executed by Wightwick, who kept one-twelfth of its profits and remitted the other eleven-twelfths to Henley, who withdrew from London, showing a rather tepid preference for the King. He compounded for total payments of £9,000. Despite this and having in 1649/50 settled lands worth at least £1,000 p.a. on his son and heir's wife (whose portion was £4,000), he was able to leave his own wife £200 rising after his debts and legacies were paid to £400 p.a., plus £800 down, and £10,000 each to his two younger sons; he had two houses in London, one in Hampshire, and one in Somerset. Unlike his grandfather, he left nothing to charity. Henley's two elder sons both became baronets at the Restoration, but the senior, Hampshire line, through improvidence or other causes, fell very heavily into debt. Lands previously valued at £25,500 were sold in 1700 for £21,500. In 1745 the debts of the Hampshire Henleys totalled £28,690; however, they were still substantial landowners and had even regained ground by the time they came to support the dignity of a peerage (1760). The Somerset branch descended from his second son, and must be distinguished from Henley's uncles' descendants, who also lived in Somerset and some of whom had the same names; their fortunes varied less until they died out in the male line in 1740. The family had some share in the King's Bench office as late as 1675, but its tenure was not to rival that of the earlier Roper dynasty (1494-1616).

For Robert Henley the possession of one valuable and another exceptionally lucrative office clearly explains his own and his family's later prosperity. The mystery concerns his beginnings and how he acquired these offices. In this, office-holding does not seem to have had any direct share; he can only have become an officer on the profits of land or law, or else by borrowing on the security of posts which he had not yet obtained.[1]

Officers as Clients. If Henley's fortunes were advanced partly as a by-product of Buckingham's career and its aftermath, others owed their advance directly to the favourite's influence. The story of the brothers Pye provides a perfect illustration of Villiers patronage in operation.

Roger Pye of the Mynde, Herefordshire, a small landowner who ranked as a Gent. but married an Esquire's daughter, was one of a large clan of small and middling gentry in the western marches. His first son Walter (1571-1635) went to Oxford and then to a full legal training at one of the smaller Chancery Inns, then at New Inn, and finally the Middle Temple; he qualified as a barrister in 1597 and presumably began to practice. Robert (1584/5-1662), Roger's second surviving son, did not go to a university but entered the Middle Temple in 1607; he does not seem to have stayed for the full course and have qualified. The earlier years of both brothers are obscure, though we know something of what Walter was doing in the early years of the century. They emerge on the scene of public affairs as clients and servants of Buckingham in 1616: how they had first attached or commended themselves to him is not clear. In view of Walter's qualifications and Robert's later career, it can be inferred that the former acted as a legal adviser, the latter as a financial manager in the Villiers entourage.

By 1616 Walter Pye was already a lawyer of some distinction. He was an associate bencher of the Middle Temple and reader elect for the following year, when in February 1616/17 Buckingham's influence secured his appointment as Judge on circuit for the sessions in South Wales, over the head of the generally expected choice; he retained this post, which seems to have been an annual appointment, on and off until he became Chief Justice of Session for S.

---

[1] Dorchester Museum, MSS. 9781-7, 9877-9, 9897-9901; Hants R.O. MSS. 43M48/49/20-1, 74, 87, 90, 94, 52/7, 13M50/57; Middlesex R.O., MS. Acc. 58/15; Northants R.O., Henley MSS. bundle 33, wills; PCC 129 Berkeley; Foster, *Al. Ox.*, p. 693a; *Middle Temple Admissn. Regtr.*, I, 91; G.E.C., *Btge.*, III, 69-70; Beaven, *Aldermen*, I, 117, 149; *Cal. Cttee. Compdg.*, pp. 927, 966; *Cal. Cttee. Advcmt. Money*, pp. 113, 271-2; V.C.H. *Hants*, III, 395-6, IV, 36; J. Collinson, *History and Antiquities of Somerset* (Bath, 1791), I, xxxviii, II, 174, 369-70, 393, III, 24, 226; Chamberlain, *Letters*, II, 193; Harl. Soc., *Visn. London, 1633-5*, I, 375; P.R.O., E 403/2591, p. 84b; SP 38/16, docquets 1635; PC 2/49, pp. 294, 302-4; other refs. in *Cal. S.P. Dom.* and as given in Chapter 4, s. iii.

Wales in 1631 and again in 1633. During the winter of 1620-20/1 Buckingham obtained for him the important and lucrative Attorneyship of the Court of Wards and Liveries; just before his patent was formally completed, he was introduced to the King by his patron and knighted. He retained this office until his death nearly fifteen years later. Its value is not known, but £1,500 p.a. would seem likely as a *minimum*; he apparently farmed out the judicial profits in S. Wales at £200 p.a. Despite Buckingham's death in 1628, followed by an attack in 1632-3 on his own probity as a principal officer in the Court of Wards, Walter Pye was well established.

The surprising things about Walter Pye are firstly the amount he spent on land purchases, improvements, and building, *before* he attained major office, secondly the sheer rate at which he continued to buy and spend for his entire career of which record survives. His purchases began in 1602-3; his only incoming capital item in these early years was the £300 portion with his first wife, received in 1606. In addition his father died sometime before 1611 and he inherited a modest landed fortune of £100 or £126, 13s. 4d. *per annum*. By 1620 he had spent about £7,600 on land purchases, buildings, and other improvements (including £120 to arrange the lease of the judicial seal in S. Wales). This included the purchase of Kilpeck for over £1,000 in 1610 and £330 or more for renovations and a new water supply at his country seat, The Mynde. In his account book Pye noted the reasons which prompted him to spend money on The Mynde and not choose somewhere more fertile and sheltered: he had been born there; it had come to him through a long hereditary descent; he liked the situation (and, as we should say, the outlook); there was an easy water supply (it cost him £90); there was plenty of good fuel within easy access; there was good ground for hay and pastures in the vicinity, even if it was barren immediately round the house. Written for his own satisfaction and perhaps to justify himself to his heirs and successors, this tells us a little about the contemporary mind, most elusive of all historical abstractions. Here was the obverse to the busy, crowded, and vicious court of James I: an intense attachment to locality, which distinguished the man with roots from the 'mere' courtier or office-holder. This is not of course quite the same as the more tenuous distinction between new men and members of old-established families.

There is an apparent break in Walter Pye's accounts from 1620 to 1626. In the late 1620's his gross income from land varied between

£440 and £660 p.a.; in 1633-4 it rose to about £800; shortly after his death, when his many 'improvements' and new leases had begun to take effect, the landed income of his eldest son alone rose to over £1,500; in 1640 it reached an actual £2,009 and a possible £2,532 p.a., representing the full benefit of all these. From 1626 to 1637, by which year various purchases set in train by Walter Pye before his death had been completed by his son Sir Walter ii, between £23,400 and £25,400 was spent on capital outgoings, not less than £19,700 of it on land, buildings and improvements. With sisters' portions to be completed, £2,000 to find for his father's funeral, and exceptionally heavy purchases just completed or still pending, no wonder that Walter Pye ii got into difficulties. He sold some lands and timber for £2,350 in 1637 and more land for £2,410 in 1639. His father had provided quite well for Walter ii's mother and three brothers (as well as leaving £4 for the poor!); nor did Walter ii hold any paid office himself. Even so, he was able to lend the King £2,000 in 1640, and to raise troops for him in 1642-3. And in 1646 he compounded as if for an annual income of £1,350, which was probably less than he was really worth, and certainly well below his income before the Civil War.

Clearly the first Sir Walter Pye's rate of capital reinvestment must have been very high, even if his total income from office was over £2,000 p.a. The family's minimum *net* investment, in land, buildings, and improvements, from 1626 to 1639 was £14,940, or £1,149 a year (average); looked at another way, from 1626 to 1635 inclusive, at least £4,015 was paid out in portions, and at least £15,448 (or an average of over £1,500 p.a.) invested in property. Sometime after 1625 Sir Walter i was married for the second time, to the widow of a London magnate; the size of her portion being unknown, its place in his financial history is problematical but may have been of crucial importance. His outlay before 1621 can only be explained by a combination of success at the bar, extreme frugality, and great financial aptitude, and perhaps latterly by some 'pickings' as a Villiers client.[1]

[1] *D.N.B.*, XVI, 514, reference only; Whitelocke, *Liber Famelicus*; Bell, *Court of Wards and Liveries*, and other sources given by him for Court of Wards officers; Elmhirst (Pye) MSS. (5) Sir Walter Pye's account book; PCC 125 Sadler; *Cal. S.P. Dom., 1603-35, passim*; T 56/5, p. 82; *Cal. C.C.*, p. 1482; Chamberlain, *Letters*; Knowler, *Strafford Letters*; *Original Letters*, ed. H. Ellis, 3rd ser., IV (1846), 170-3; Berks R.O., Packer MSS. O 1/176, 280; Sheffield C. Lib., Strafford MSS. 8/51-2.

Sir Robert Pye, in some ways a more prominent and interesting figure, is in others a more elusive one. Apart from his entry to the Middle Temple in 1607, his career before 1616 is a complete mystery. It can be proved that he was not, as some writers have suggested, the Robert Pye of the Inner Temple who in 1602-3 was tried in Star Chamber and heavily punished for plotting against a fellow law student.[1] He may have been living on a very small property in Gloucestershire in 1614-15, and raising money by recognizance, or this too may have been one of his cousins of the same name. What indeed was the lot of younger sons who did not obtain office, take up a profession, or enter trade? Relatively generously as they were provided for, by means of rent charges, annuities, capital bequests or even divisions of their fathers' estates, life must still have been bleak for all except those from the richest families. Such men, living perhaps in part of someone else's house, or else in a glorified cottage or farm house, were the social, if not the lineal, ancestors of those twentieth-century 'gentlemen small-holders', who eke out a precarious living from chickens or fruit or a few cows, supplemented by increasingly inadequate pensions or dividends, and are often exceedingly tenacious of their gentility.

Once established as a Villiers client, Robert Pye rose rapidly from this trough of obscurity. In March 1616/17 he succeeded Cranfield as manager or farmer, on the favourite's behalf, of the 3d. in the pound Duty on the goods of merchant strangers entering the realm; in April 1618 he was appointed to a half share in the new Clerkship of the Patents (later Wolseley's office); the following July, when Buckingham overthrew the Howards and thereby gained control of royal finance, Pye replaced the notorious Sir John Bingley as acting Auditor of the lower Exchequer and Scriptor Talliorum, though his appointment was not confirmed until January 1619/20 when Bingley's patent was formally cancelled. From 1618 to 1624 Pye worked with Cranfield on many commissions and in the day-to-day management of finance; but in 1624 he followed Buckingham, and joined in the attack on the Lord Treasurer, giving crucial

---

[1] The existence of two different Robert Pyes can be established from the following sources: F. A. Inderwick (ed.), *Cal. of Inner Temple Records* (1896), I, xcii, 443, 473-6; *Visitation of Berks* (Harl. Soc., LVI); *Misc. Genealogica et Heraldica*, 5th ser., VIII, 252; *Middle Temple Admn. Regtr.*, I, 89. Even Professor McClure, the very scholarly editor of John Chamberlain's *Letters*, has been misled (I, 146 n.) into supposing them to be on and the same person.

evidence against him on an important charge in his impeachment. Meanwhile, in a way typical of the age, but certainly strange by modern standards, he remained in charge of Buckingham's private finances, although he was now a major royal official. He continued to act as an executor and financial adviser to the Villiers family all through the 1630's, '40's, and '50's, for over twenty years after his patron's death.

Although he began as a favourite's favourite, a lesser flea upon the back of a greater, Pye did not develop in an altogether likely or obvious way. Within the limits of the existing system he became a conscientious administrator, collaborating closely with successive Lord Treasurers and Treasury Commissioners from 1618 to 1642, in an attempt to set government finance on a sounder basis. In the later 1620's he even seems to have felt a sense of conflict between Buckingham's policies and what we should call the public interest; in short, he developed a sense of responsibility arising from his position at the centre of the financial administration. However, in the later 1630's he incurred the disapproval of Laud and Wentworth by standing up for the Villiers' interests to the detriment—as they believed—of the King's.

Socially he was advanced to a knighthood, also in 1621. Economically his career is far worse documented than his brother's. In 1622-3 he completed the purchase of a fine property, including the castle, at Faringdon in Berkshire, for £4,200, or just over two years' value of the two offices which he then held (the Auditorship £1,500 p.a.; the co-Clerkship of the Patents c. £500). He also acquired property in Derbyshire and Staffordshire, but he does not seem to have been such a persistent buyer and improver as Sir Walter. Perhaps the very fact of establishing himself as a landowner and the lord of a handsome manor meant more to him. Or possibly he was more absorbed in his work: both brothers must have maintained establishments in London as well as in the country, but whereas Walter may only have had rooms (he certainly left no town house in his will), Robert had a house in St. Stephen's Court, Westminster. This he occupied *ex officio* from 1618 to 1662, except for the years 1655-60 when he was temporarily displaced as Auditor of the Receipt. Sir Robert raised £2,000 for the Scottish expedition of 1640 and £1,000 for King and Parliament to suppress the Irish rebels in 1642; being a parliamentarian, however moderate and lukewarm a one, he did not lose too heavily during the Interregnum, though his land was fought over and his castle besieged (after being captured by the royalists). He died in 1662 a wealthy but not an immensely rich man. He left his Berkshire estate to his eldest son, and his northern properties to his second son, the founder of a baronetcy. The third son had been set up in business as a merchant in the Levant, but he died in 1660; after their father's death in 1662, the elder sons reckoned that over £3,000 had been invested in their brother's career since 1651. Sir Robert's bequests, totalling £145 in legacies, plus £20 p.a. and £100 to the poor, were more generous than Sir Walter's, but his family were by then off his hands, their portions long since paid, settlements drawn up and passed, etc., so the comparison is perhaps an unfair one. The role of matrimony in the finances of Sir Robert and his immediate family is unclear. He was himself married only once, and then to a lady of no great wealth who cannot have brought him much, and he had to raise portions for three, if not four, daughters. His eldest son, on the other hand, married John Hampden's daughter, and her £2,000 portion must have helped Sir Robert to meet the costs of marrying off his own daughters; this connexion certainly helped him at one or two awkward moments when his allegiance to the parliamentary cause in the Civil War was under grave suspicion.

Sir Robert's official career, unlike Sir Walter's, was interrupted by the political events of the Interregnum. Any comparison of the careers and achievements of the two brothers is bound to be rather artificial. The most striking difference is that the sources which have survived make it possible to gain some impression of Sir Walter's private life and affairs, while for Sir Robert they relate almost exclusively to his public career.[1]

It should not be assumed that spectacular economic, as well as social advance was the rule for most office-holders. The number who amassed major fortunes was limited, the number who founded

[1] *D.N.B.*, XVI, 514-15, (ref. only); Keeler, *Long Parliament*, p. 317; *Cal. S.P. Dom.*, vols. for *1611-62*, *passim*; Exchequer of Receipt records, 1618-62; *Foedera*, XVII-XX, *passim*; other printed sources for the period *c.* 1620-60 (Whitelocke, Knowler, *C.J.*, etc.); V.C.H., *Berks*, IV, 490-3; Berks R.O., MSS. D/EEl 1, T 1, 22, E 3/1-3; Elmhirst (Pye) MSS., D 1, 21, (6), (8); PCC 70 Laud; LC 4/198, fols. 56, 162; *Wills from Doctors Commons* (Camd. Soc., 1862), pp. 104-5.

landed dynasties still smaller. Naturally any figures that can be given depend on what bottom limit is taken to constitute a fortune, and what test of duration a dynasty. And the evidence, it need hardly be said, is very inadequate. But among the A-C groups examined in the last section under forty seem to have acquired landed property worth £1,000 a year and upward, or to have increased their landed income by £1,000 a year or more; and not all of these transmitted their estates intact to even one generation of male heirs.

Survival of a family in the male line or at least survival of the descent of an estate intact, as well as the sheer fact of worldly success in a man's own lifetime, have a good deal to do with the survival of documentary evidence, especially of family papers. Therefore records relating to the materially successful and the biologically fittest are more likely to have survived. So the twenty or thirty 'possibles' from which the individual sketches in this section have been selected are almost certainly not a fair sample of the whole office-holding body. Most of the documents relating to the land transactions of George Mynne, for example, have only survived because part of his property came (via his co-heiresses) by sale to the Earls Cowper, and then to one of their eventual co-heiresses, the late Lady Desborough, whose heir has allowed them to remain on deposit in the Hertfordshire Record Office.

Below the great officers of state, economic success on the scale achieved by Henley, the Pyes, or Mynne, while not unique was definitely untypical. And in order to give a more balanced picture, it may be well to close this section on a more subdued note, returning to a more humdrum level of achievement.

Croke's Worst Enemy. Christopher Vernon (*c.* 1583-1652) achieved a minor contemporary notoriety as a party to the disputes which divided the officers of the Upper Exchequer during the generation before the Civil War. Otherwise he left few traces; and historically his name is probably only known to specialists in financial history. He was a direct descendant, mainly through younger sons, of Sir William Vernon, Treasurer of Calais, who died in 1467. But little more than his pedigree and county of origin can be told of Christopher Vernon's early years. His father was a Gent., and lived in Huntingdonshire. Christopher obviously went to London to seek his fortune, but it is not clear how or when he entered royal service; by 1611 he was a very junior Exchequer clerk in the Pipe Office, but he had already, probably by 1608-9, married into a minor Exchequer family, the Darnells, his father-in-law being a Secondary (one of the two chief under clerks) in the Pipe. We can only guess which came first: marriage into the bureaucracy, or Vernon's own entry to office.

In the course of the next twenty years he rose among the Pipe Office clerks by seniority alone, becoming eventually First Secondary. Before this, however, he had made himself an expert in ferreting out concealed land revenues and in recovering lost titles for the Crown. In 1623 he was acting as Solicitor in such cases for the Prince of Wales; he was at this time reputed to be a client of Lord Brooke (Chancellor of the Exchequer, 1614-21), but in the following year he was said to have transferred his loyalties, other than those commanded by the Crown, to Sir Edward Conway (Secretary of State, 1623-8). At the end of King James's reign, presumably as part of some attempted reform of the 'ancient course' revenues, Vernon was appointed joint Surveyor and Receiver of the Greenwax; by the 1630's he was sole Surveyor. He held this office in combination with his ordinary clerkship in the Pipe. His work in connexion with the Prince of Wales's land revenues presumably lapsed in 1625, there being no Prince at all until 1630, and no separate Prince's establishment until 1635. But Vernon's specialized knowledge and abilities were soon put to use again in the late 1620's, under the commissioners for the sale and lease of Crown lands. Meanwhile, undoubtedly using his influence with the trustees of the land which the King had held as Prince, he began to acquire an interest in land at Hertingfordbury, which was to make him a near neighbour of George Mynne. By 1629 Vernon seems to have paid altogether £1,050, to secure his title to this and another nearby property, for the remainder of a 99-year lease made by the Duchy of Lancaster to the Prince's trustees in 1618, and in lieu of the claims of various other people including the widow of a Jacobean Lieutenant of the Ordnance, to certain parts of it.

Although he was granted £1,430 by the Crown in 1635-6 and £793 in 1639, as rewards for discovering concealed revenues and lost titles, Vernon bought no more land in Hertfordshire after 1630. Indeed in the mid- and late 1630's he sold his interest in a rabbit warren and another small plot of land to Mynne, notwithstanding the shatteringly heavy fines which had been imposed on Mynne for his offences as Clerk of the Hanaper and as an ironmaster.

Vernon's family commitments may help to explain the halt in his land buying, apart from one or two very small holdings on the western outskirts of London. He had four daughters to provide for: two married lawyers, and two lesser officials in his own department. His eldest son was sent to Cambridge, as a gentleman pensioner, and then to the Inner Temple, qualifying as a barrister in 1634, by which time he had already been appointed Comptroller of the Pipe, an office in theory senior to his father's; in 1638/9 he married the daughter of the co-Auditor of Chancery. When Vernon died in 1652 his eldest son seems to have retired to the country and the family's interest in the Pipe, inevitably dormant during the Exchequer's suspension from 1649 to 1654, was taken over by the second son. Despite the £2,000 portion brought by Vernon's senior daughter-in-law, quarrels with more senior Exchequer officials and their actual or suspected neutralism in the Civil War led the Vernons into economic difficulties in the 1640's and 1650's; by the mid-1680's Christopher Vernon's grandson had sold or mortgaged most of the estate.

Too little evidence survives to explain exactly why Christopher Vernon did as well as he did and no better. The violence of his attacks on the head of his office, Sir Henry Croke, Clerk of the Pipe, may well reflect Croke's success in engrossing fees and gratuities, which might, and in Vernon's view should, have gone to the First Secondary, to the Surveyor of Greenwax, or perhaps to the Comptroller of the Pipe. And to judge from the length of the negotiations about them, the special rewards, amounting in all to £2,223, which were granted to Vernon, may have been on 'dud' tallies, worth nothing or at best only a fraction of their face value. Alternatively he may have set up as a Gentleman in London and Hertfordshire, have lived in style, and have married off his sons and daughters appropriately, but have had little left for further capital investment after 1629 or 1630. Considering his starting point, in economic terms Vernon's career can be accounted a success, but a much more qualified one than that of some officers whose histories it is possible to reconstruct.[1]

[1] Herts R.O., Cowper (Panshanger) MSS., 268-9, 324, 329, 497, 641-4, 715, 719, 833-41, 869-81, 887, 891-2, 904-6, 915-25, Pym MS. 19128, Cashiobury and Gape MS. 8341; *Visitation of Herts* (Harl. Soc., XXII); V.C.H., *Herts*, III, 272-3; R. Clutterbuck, *History & Antiquities of Herts*, (1821), II, 200-1; PCC 144 Bowyer; B.M. Lansdowne MS. 168, p. 90; Bodl. Tanner MS. 101, No. 40; *Cal. S.P. Dom., 1623-43 passim*; Dep. Kpr., *43rd Rept.*, pp. 8, 64; *Cal. Cttee. Advcmt. Money*, p. 288. See also Chapter 4, ss. i-ii, pp. 164, 197-8, 202.

The Officer as a Failure. If the sources set a premium on success, can anything be said about those who failed? Social as opposed to economic decline was very much the exception, but it did happen, usually to those men whose fathers' titles were not heritable or who were younger sons failing to rise: for example, a knight's son remaining an esquire, an esquire's younger son remaining a gentleman. Leaving aside the extraordinary changes of fortune due to the upheavals of 1640 to 1660, a little can be discovered about some officeholders who were unsuccessful, at least in economic and financial terms.

Unlike most of the Scots who came south with James I, Sir James Fullarton (d. 1630/1) attained his greatest prominence under Charles I. In 1616 he was appointed Groom of the Stole to the Prince, on whose accession in 1625 he became Groom of the Stole and First Gentleman of the King's Bedchamber, a post reputedly worth between £1,600 and £2,500 a year. Fullarton seems to have been an ordinary courtier of the second rank; in a sense it is surprising that he reached such a senior position, the holder of which was usually of some political importance (e.g. Carlisle 1631-6, and Holland 1636-41).

Besides lesser trifles, Fullarton had been granted a long lease of a large royal property in north Dorset and Wiltshire on ludicrously favourable terms. None the less he was in a state of grave financial embarrassment when he made his will in December 1630. He settled two-thirds of this leasehold estate on his step-son Lord Bruce, apparently as trustee for his wife (Bruce's mother), and one-third on George Kirke, his colleague in the Bedchamber, conditional on Kirke paying £1,000 to Bruce and settling other debts of £467; Kirke seems already to have paid out over £3,000 on Fullarton's behalf, and this was to count towards the purchase price for his third share. The remainder of Fullarton's debts were to be paid by his wife, Lady Bruce, out of her income from the two-thirds of the estate (and from all of it until Kirke had completed the purchase of his one-third). In January 1631/2 the 41-year lease of two-thirds of Gillingham manor, park, and forest, totalling 1,760-1,800 acres, was granted in perpetuity to Lord Bruce, for an annual rent to the Crown of only £108. Even so, perhaps still burdened with his step-father's debts, in 1634 Bruce, now Earl of Elgin, mortgaged it to Edward Nicholas, then Admiralty Secretary and Council Clerk extraordinary.

He guaranteed to pay Nicholas £350 a year, and this arrangement apparently lasted for the next 27 years. In 1660-60/1 Nicholas, by then Secretary of State, finally bought the property outright for £21,500. This price argues that with proper management the Gillingham estate should have yielded at least £1,000 a year, and even then it was presumably only two-thirds of the original leasehold grant.

Fullarton left nothing else to his wife and daughter. But he appealed to the King for the payment of £8,000 which he claimed was still owed him by the Crown, out of £10,000 originally due. He may have spent so heavily while manœuvring for office that he achieved a well-rewarded position too late to recover; he may simply have been unlucky, or inept. But Fullarton's career is a reminder that a man could hold an office only just short of the first rank and still end his days relatively impoverished.[1]

The Carnes of Nash in Glamorganshire held two lucrative offices but still went downhill. William Carne (1599-1650's) and his brother Edward (c. 1600-36) were well connected and started life with several advantages. Their mother was a knight's daughter, one of the large and influential Mansel family; a great-uncle had been Sheriff, and a great-great-uncle and second cousin on their father's side knights: their father was Receiver-General for South Wales and probably held a reversion to a Tellership in the Exchequer. In 1625 William, the elder brother, became a Teller; as such his income would have been at least £500 p.a.; in 1631 he bought a Six Clerkship in Chancery (worth between £800 and £1,600 p.a.), made vacant by the death of Simonds D'Ewes's father, for £6,000, over the head of Robert Caesar and, according to Clarendon, with the backing of Weston, the Lord Treasurer.[2] At the same time, possibly again through the Lord Treasurer's favour, he appears to have transferred the Tellership to his younger brother Edward who was also made

---

[1] See Chapter 4, s. i; Cary, *Memoirs*, p. 154; *Cal. S.P. Dom.*, *1625-31*, *passim*; A. Collins, *Sidney State Papers* (1746), II, 358-9, 364; *Scots Peerage*, III, 476; Dorchester Museum, MSS. 4780, 5774; PCC 15 St. John and refs. in wills of Hierome Cocke (d. 1630), Joshua Downinge (d. 1630), Chief Baron Walter (d. 1630); D. Nicholas, *Mr. Secretary Nicholas* (1955), pp. 84, 188-9, 302.

[2] See Chapter 3, s. i, for this episode.

Receiver of the compositions for knighthood. In 1634 the brothers were made joint Receivers for tobacco licences.

What went wrong with the Carnes' finances? The only bonds to which they were parties seem to have been connected with marriages or family settlements, rather than evidence of outright indebtedness. The genealogical sources are confusing, but as far as can be seen their father had three daughters and two sons and William himself had three and seven. The raising of excessive portions in order to make good marriages is therefore one possible cause of William's difficulties. He also had to pay his share of the £16,000 composition levied from the Six Clerks in 1635-8. Edward apparently died in 1636, and by early 1640 William had parted with the Tobacco Receivership and the Six Clerkship. Assuming that the latter was sold for the normal price of £5,000-£6,000, he left about two-thirds of this (£3,800) in the hands of his colleague Richard Colchester, and either went abroad or into hiding in the country to escape his creditors leaving Colchester to contend with them! William Carne reappears as a militant parliamentarian acting as Lieutenant-Governor of the Isle of Wight in 1643-7, in which capacity, according to a royalist observer, he made £2,000 p.a. He was also rather grudgingly acknowledged as residual heir by his cousin, Edward Carne of Ewenny. This Edward was an active royalist; on one calculation he was worth over £700, and according to a casual observer £1,000 from land, but perhaps because of William's influence he was only fined as if for a landed income of £285.

The Carnes of Nash did not go under altogether. Their descendants continued as members of the Welsh gentry. But, considering their opportunities, and the fact that neither of them seems to have been dispossessed from office against his will, they can be accounted failures as an office-holding family.[1]

Other officers died impoverished, or more often embarrassed by

[1] Sources as for other Chancery and Exchequer officers; G. T. Clark, *Morganiae et Glamorganiae* (1886), pp. 374-6; *The Maunsell Family*, I (1917), 496-7; *Stemmata Chicheleana* (Oxford, 1765), p. 67; Glos. R.O., Colchester Journals (1); *Cal. Cttee. Compdg.*, p. 1369; PCC 173 Pembroke; P.R.O. C 54/3074/90, LC 4/200-1; J. Oglander, *A Royalist's Notebook*, ed. F. Bamford (1936), p. 111; R. Symonds, *Diary of the Marches of the Royalist Army* (Camd. Soc., 1859), p. 216; *Glamorganshire Pedigrees*; T. 34/1, p. 14.

heavy debts. Most of the extreme cases turn out on closer scrutiny to be due in one way or another to the Civil War. But among the holders of major office who died before 1642, the following left estates of distinctly less net value (after the settlement of their debts) than might have been anticipated, considering the positions which they had held:

Lord Conway (Secretary of State 1623-8, President of the Council 1628-31).

Lord Dorchester (Secretary 1628-32).

Earl of Carlisle (Groom of the Stole 1631-6).

Earl of Stirling (Secretary of State for Scotland 1626-40; who actually died a bankrupt, and so should have left nothing at all!)

Earl of Marlborough (Lord Treasurer 1624-8, Lord President 1628).

Lord Falkland (Lord Deputy of Ireland 1623-9).

Sir Robert Naunton (Secretary of State 1618-23, Master of the Wards 1623-35).

Viscount Savage (Queen's Chancellor 1628-35).

By including those whose careers ended later than 1640 or 1642, the list could be considerably lengthened. Lord Goring, Earl of Norwich (Lieutenant of the Pensioners 1614-42, Queen's Vice-Chamberlain 1639-44, Captain of the King's Guard 1660-62) is the clearest instance of a major office-holder who was ruined not by his loyalty to the Crown, but by his own and his family's reckless extravagance. Others who died after 1640 and whose financial embarrassments were not primarily due to their political allegiance include Sir Thomas Jermyn (Vice-Chamberlain 1629-39, Comptroller of the Household 1639-41), Sir David Cunningham (Receiver of the King's revenues when Prince of Wales 1630-5, Prince's Cofferer 1641, Prince's Treasurer and Receiver-General 1641-6), Sir Abraham Williams (Signet Clerk and Paymaster to the Queen of Bohemia), and Sir Edward Wardour (Clerk of the Pells 1618-46).

Some officers died poor or heavily in debt through their own improvidence, normally by overspending of one kind or another, and some through being left in the lurch by their employer, namely the Crown. In the second respect ambassadors and commanders of armed forces overseas were notoriously badly treated. Lord Vere of Tilbury (colonel and then commander in the Netherlands 1604-20, commander in Germany 1620-3, Master of the Ordnance 1629-34) is a good example of the military men who were left unpaid, the Earl of Leicester (Ambassador in Paris 1636-41) of the diplomats: the Sidneys could take this in their stride, the Veres could not. Those whose financial relations with the Crown depended on contracts were also very unsure of getting paid. The Navy Victuallers (Apsley, d. 1630; Darrell, d. 1635) and the Esquire Saddlers (William and Thomas Smithesbie) may be cited as evidence of this.

More cases could certainly be instanced on the other side, of officers who did prosper and found, or augment landed fortunes. But enough did not do so for it to be misleading to identify office with wealth or prosperity. Certain further reservations need to be made. As with other sixteenth- and seventeenth-century landowners, so with office-holding ones, much depended on the kind of family a man had, notably on the number of his daughters (to be married off and provided with portions), and of his sons (the short-term advantages accruing from daughter-in-laws' portions being offset in the long run by having to provide, at the expense of the eldest son, for younger sons, their widows, and descendants). For Charles I's servants much too depended on when a man died in relation to the dates 1642 and 1660, and to the age and situation of his heir at those dates. Not only their politics but also the geographical location of their estates affected men's fortunes. But most important of all was the personal ability in money matters of some men, and the carelessness, improvidence, or ineptitude of others. Thus the provident royalists mostly recovered from the tribulations of 1642 to 1660: such were Southampton, Nicholas, Sir Philip Warwick, the Fanshawes, the Osbornes, Sir Charles Harbord and Sir Robert Long.

It is reasonable to ask whether a higher proportion of officeholders prospered than of non-office-holders, selected at random from an equivalent social background. They well may have, but clearly this question cannot be settled from a study of office-holders alone. Besides this, two other points need to be considered. First, it cannot be assumed that all those who prospered in their capacity as officers would not have done so if they had not held office; some would surely have made money and amassed property whatever their *métier*. Conversely, the same is true of those who floundered or fell by the wayside; some of them would have got into difficulties

L   321

in any case, but being office-holders they were more likely to indulge in certain kinds of overspending, and could sometimes obtain credit more easily. The second point arises from this. Just as different posts offered varying opportunities for enrichment, so they required, or at least were likely to stimulate, different levels of expenditure. The fantastic amounts spent on building, interior decoration, and works of art, on confinements, marriages, funerals, and funeral monuments, and on jewelry, clothing, feasting, and gambling seem to be particularly associated with courtiers, great officers of state, holders of posts in the household departments, and aspirants for these positions. The holders of most legal, financial, and other administrative offices might not make as much money as the royal favourites and the leading ministers of state, but on the whole they lived at a more sober level. In general therefore their rate of capital investment may have been higher, though this would be very difficult to prove.

iv OFFICE AND SOCIAL STRUCTURE

Some means is needed whereby to measure the effect of office-holding on the social structure of early Stuart England, and more particularly its effect on social and economic mobility. For this purpose the estimated totals of fees and other payments to officials, put forward at the end of the last chapter, must be related to the social composition of the office-holding body which has been discussed in this chapter.

There are two fairly obvious ways of approaching the problem, both of which it is to be feared will appear crude and unsatisfactory compared with what can be done in studying twentieth- or even nineteenth-century society. The numbers of officials belonging to different social ranks and classes can be related to the probable total membership of these ranks and classes in the whole population. And the amount of money which changed hands annually via office can be related either to the whole national income, or to the total incomes of particular classes.

Since there are no reliable population figures for seventeenth-century England, it may seem unpromising to investigate the importance of office through the numbers of men involved. And were we primarily concerned with the population at large this would be so. For it can only be said that few historians or demographers would wish to assert that the population of England and Wales was less than three and a half or more than five and a half millions in the years 1620-70. But figures of a kind can be given for the higher ranks of society, which are the most relevant here. The number of peers is known; the approximate number of baronets can be worked out; the number of knights can be estimated; esquires are considerably, and gentlemen much more difficult, but even with them there is a little to go on.

Care must be taken to compare like with like. Thus either all those who held office at any time in the years 1625-42 must be compared with all those who were peers, knights, esquires, etc., at any time in the same period; or those holding office at a specific date must be compared with the total numbers of peers, knights, etc., at that same date. To make this difference quite clear: at any given time there were up to twenty-six bishops in England and Wales (often through vacancies there were one or two less), but in the years (March) 1625 to (January) 1642 fifty-three different men held bishoprics; altogether two bishops held central office during this time, one in 1625 and one in 1636-41. It would therefore be misleading to say that office-holding affected two out of twenty-six bishops, but reasonable to say that it affected *either* two out of fifty-three throughout the period, *or* one out of twenty-six for part, and none for the rest of the time. Since this book is a study of those who held office at any date within the years 1625-42, it seems more sensible to keep the wider definition here too, and not to limit ourselves to numbers at a particular date.

But this of course affects the way the totals are to be calculated. Allowance has to be made for the degree of heritability in the different ranks. At the extremes this is easy: peerages and baronetcies were heritable, bishoprics and knighthoods were not. But the two lowest armigerous ranks are more difficult: the ranks of esquire and gentleman were in theory only heritable if they had been inherited, or a right to them proved on grounds of descent, and not if they were only enjoyed *ex officio*, as for instance by an M.D. or an M.A. Allowance has also to be made for the younger sons of existing families tending to swell the numbers of those below them, as well as for new entries and creations. And all these factors must in turn be related to the length of time being treated. Inevitably in the lower ranks the figures become very

323

approximate. With these provisos, the following table can be constructed:

TABLE 30. NUMERICAL RELATION OF CLASS AND OFFICE, 1625-42[1]

Rank or Status	Held Office 1625-42	Total (as defined) 1625-42	Office-holders as a percentage of the total
English lay peers . .	52	206	25·2
Eldest sons of English lay peers, who were of age but had not succeeded their fathers by Jan. 1641/2 . . .	2	c. 15	13·3
Bishops . . .	2	53	3·8
Englishmen holding Scottish and Irish peerages	14	65	21·5
Baronets (including baronets of Scotland and Ireland if of English origin) . . .	29	472	6·1
Knights . . .	244	2,000-2,400	12·2-10·2
Esquires . . .	c. 750	10,000-14,000	7·5-5·4
Gentlemen . . .	c. 300	16,000-22,000	1·9-1·4
Total	c. 1,400	c. 26,000-c. 40,000	5·4-3·5

[1] The following have been used in working out the totals for the different social classes—general: T. Wilson, 'State of England' (ed. Fisher), pp. 16-26; E. Chamberlayne, *Angliae Notitia* (1st edn., 1669), pp. 28, 440-87; G. King, 'Natural and Political Observations and Conclusions', in G. Chalmers, *Estimate of the Comparative Strength of Great Britain* (1804), app. pp. 29-73; C. Clark, *National Income and Outlay* (1937), ch. X, esp. pp. 210-26; L. Stone, 'The Inflation of Honours', *Past & Present*, XIV (note: I have unfortunately not been able to use Mr. Stone's figures as an exact check on my own, since in all cases we are measuring slightly different things; however, as a general check, in trying to gauge the right order of magnitude, they have been very useful); peers: G.E.C., *Complete Peerage*; J. P. Cooper, app. to 'The Counting of Manors', *Econ. Hist. Rev.*, n.s., VIII, 389; C. R. Mayes, 'The Sale of Peerages in Early Stuart England', *Journ. Mod. Hist.*, XXIX (1957), 'The Early Stuarts and the Irish Peerage', *Eng. Hist. Rev.*, LXXIII (1958); Berks. R.O., Trumbull MSS., vol. XXXV (list of peers, 1626); bishops: *Handbook of British Chronology*, ed. F. M. Powicke (1939), pp. 132-206; baronets: G.E.C., *Baronetage;* knights: Shaw, *Knights;* Metcalfe,

In general, therefore, office-holding affected people in direct proportion to their seniority in the social hierarchy. One exception to this is striking enough to deserve comment. Proportionately fewer baronets than knights were office-holders; indeed, the proportion among baronets may well have been below that among esquires. Two explanations can be offered, though there may be others: knighthoods were very common rewards for senior officials, baronetcies (even relative to the total size of the two orders) appreciably less so; and proportionately more baronets than knights or esquires were probably the heads of well established landed families, who may on average have tended to be less interested in office-holding than the gentry at large.

Subject to possible errors in the preceding table, office-holding may be said to have affected one in every four English peers, about one in every five Englishmen with Scottish and Irish peerages, about one in every eight or ten knights, about one in every sixteen esquires, and say one in every fifty-three to seventy-three gentlemen. And it probably affected between one in every nineteen and one in every twenty-nine of the entire adult male armigerous population between 1625 and 1642. Numerically it must have been of almost negligible importance for the non-armigerous, though conceivably not for certain specific groups among them. Indeed, some non-gentry rose spectacularly by means of office. Enough has already been said of that, but there is perhaps a temptation to cite such men as Lionel Cranfield or Richard Boyle as examples of some general tendency; the more typical self-made office-holder was nearer to the modest level of an Edward Sherborne or a Christopher Vernon, although numerically careerists even as successful as them formed only a very small group. Therefore, if there was a fairly high degree of social mobility in early seventeenth-century England, office-holding can only have been responsible for a small part of it, except among the gentry and above. And if the upper and middling gentry themselves were growing appreciably in numbers, other than by natural

Knights; gentry in particular counties: A. J. & R. H. Tawney, 'An Occupational Census', Econ. Hist. Rev., V (1934), 25-64 (Glos); M. Campbell, The English Yeoman under Elizabeth and the Early Stuarts (New Haven, 1942), pp. 358-9 (Bedfs); W. G. Hoskins, 'The Estates of the Caroline Gentry', in Hoskins and H. P. R. Finberg, Devonshire Studies (1952), pp. 334-65; A. H. Dodd, Studies in Stuart Wales (Cardiff, 1952), pp. 2, 14, 179-81; A. M. Everitt, County Committee of Kent in the Civil War (Leicester, 1957), p. 8.

population growth, the influx of lesser landowners (in rank, gents., yeomen, or below), of lawyers, and of business-men must surely have been greater than that of office-holders. And this must be much more true for the lesser gentry (approximately corresponding in rank to the gentlemen). Admittedly, by including as central office-holders all those who held any position in the royal household (even if it was extraordinary and unpaid) the grand total is considerably increased, probably to over two thousand. If those holding paid posts only are included, the main change in the proportions shown would be among the gents., who might rise to 500, and so to one in every 32-44 of all the gents. in the country. Paid or unpaid, however, such posts as Gentleman of the Privy Chamber, Gentleman Pensioner, and Yeoman of the Guard, like many local Stewardships and Keeperships, might contribute to men's social or economic advancement, but can hardly provide the primary explanation of such promotion or prosperity.

Granted that many of the armigerous population were involved in office-holding, the next question to ask is how important it was to them financially, in relation to their other sources of wealth. According to the estimate made at the end of the previous chapter, between £590,000 and £760,000 may have changed hands annually through the medium of office (excluding capital gains and losses through venality). This sum must now be compared with the probable total incomes of the various classes involved; and since this means dealing with income *per annum*, the figures must be related to one particular year. It would probably not make a great deal of difference which year was chosen between 1625 and 1642, but for the sake of argument it seems best to take the exact middle twelve months of the period, February 1632/3 to February 1633/4.

None of the contemporary estimates for the wealth of the landed classes in the seventeenth century is very satisfactory. But something must be said about each of them before putting forward any alternative figures.

TABLE 31.   THOMAS WILSON'S ESTIMATES, *c.* 1600

	Total
61 lay peers, at an average income of £3,606 p.a. each	£220,000
500 knights, at an average income of £1,500 p.a. each	£750,000
16,000 esquires, at an average income of £750 p.a. each	£12,000,000

Note.—Wilson's average for the peers is almost certainly an under-estimate, possibly due to the late sixteenth century having seen a marked rise in landed income, especially from rents, which he failed to take into account. Nor is it easy to believe that the fifty-one counties of England and Wales each contained an average of over 300 landed gentry with an average income of £750 a head (in fairness to Wilson, he does say between £500 and £1,000; and it may be misleading to take an average of £750 p.a. each). His figure of 16,000 must surely include Gents., when these were landowners, properly armigerous, and heads of households; Professor F. J. Fisher has recently stated that 'according to contemporary estimates' there were 16,000 gentry families in England around 1600, and this presumably means separate households including those presided over by gentlemen as well as by esquires.[1]

TABLE 32. EDWARD CHAMBERLAYNE'S ESTIMATES, 1669

	Total
148 lay peers, average income £10,000 p.a. each	£1,480,000
700 baronets, average income £1,200 p.a. each	£840,000
1,400 knights, average income £800 p.a. each	£1,120,000
6,000 esquires and gents., average income £400 p.a. each	£2,400,000
16,000 younger brothers (no figures given)	—
Total for landed classes	£5,840,000
Total 'revenue' of England (approx.) p.a.	£14,000,000

Note.—Chamberlayne's figures are inconsistent on the number of peers and the totals for the gentry. Nor does his way of working out the population of the whole country (of which Wilson gives no estimate) inspire confidence; he simply takes the total number of parishes (9,725, which is also Wilson's figure), and multiplies it by 560 (that is he assumes an average parish of eighty families, consisting on average of seven persons each). However, the admirable Gregory King arrives at a very similar final total by what is only a more refined and elaborate version of the same calculation, so it would be foolish to cavil too much at Chamber-layne. More serious, it is not clear that he meant by 'revenue' what is now meant by 'national income'; this becomes evident if his table is compared with King's. Comparing his figures with Wilson's a very marked process of stratification was believed to have occurred: over about seventy years the peers had apprently grown vastly richer, while the gentry were believed to have grown very considerably poorer. It would be a mistake to take either set of figures too seriously, though they may possibly indicate, even if they greatly exaggerate, some kind of general trend. And if so, this would signify that the peers weathered the storms

[1] In *The Listener*, 5 September 1957, p. 345.

of 1640-60 better than the gentry, and perhaps that some of the factors described by Professor Habakkuk as having favoured the greater, partially at the expense of the lesser landowners in the years *c.* 1680-1740 were already at work in the mid-seventeenth century.[1]

TABLE 33. GREGORY KING'S ESTIMATES, 1688-96

	Total
160 lay peers, average income £2,800 p.a. each	£448,000
800 baronets, average income £880 p.a. each	£704,000
600 knights, average income £650 p.a. each	£390,000
3,000 esquires, average income £400 p.a. each	£1,200,000
12,000 gents., average income £240 p.a. each	£2,880,000
Total for these classes	£5,622,000
Total national income	£43,500,000

Note. Mr. Colin Clark observes that 'King's definition of National Income seems to have been almost identical with that now used', except for the omission of domestic (household) servants, for whom he suggests by interpolation the addition of another £5·7 millions. Thus we have:

Corrected total national income £49,200,000

Rapidly as the wealth of England was undoubtedly increasing in the later seventeenth century, a three and a half fold increase during the twenty years or so between Chamberlayne and King is of course preposterous; even in the twentieth century this would represent a staggering rate of growth. One less important point, but interesting for the present inquiry: King alone gives separate figures for office-holders:

5,000 'persons in offices', average income £240 p.a. each . £1,200,000
5,000 'persons in offices', average income £120 p.a. each . £600,000

It is not clear from the normal published text of his work whether the non-landed incomes of office-holding peers and gentry are included under the totals for these classes, or under those for the persons in offices. In any case, his total number of persons must include all local officials, and those at all levels in the government and royal service (except possibly menials). His total may be compared with that of 30,000 for all legal office-holders, and all barristers, attorneys, solicitors, and law clerks, suggested by William Cole in 1659. Cole suggested an average income of £250 a year each for all lawyers and law officers, making a total of

---

[1] H. J. Habakkuk, 'English Landownership 1680-1740', *Econ. Hist. Rev.*, VIII (1938); see also his 'Marriage Settlements in the Eighteenth Century', *Trans. Roy. Hist. Soc.*, 4th ser., XXXII (1950).

£7·5 millions. To reconcile these two sets of figures is difficult, since King allowed only £1·4 millions *per annum* for lawyers, or £3·2 millions for all officials and lawyers together.[1]

In general, there seems no good reason to suppose that King over-estimated. Indeed, his figure for the peers is fantastically low, and that for the greater gentry somewhat niggardly, unless he can be assumed to mean *net* income, after the payment of all standing charges (such as annuities to relatives, and interest on mortgages). And the same may be true for the middling and lesser landowners, unless they had been suffering a very marked decline. Mr. Clark also notes that in Thorold Rogers's view King's average of £400 p.a. each was too little for the 2,000 'merchants by sea'. But even allowing for an error of up to 20 per cent. either way in his corrected grand total, and for a 50 per cent. increase since the 1630's, the national income cannot then have been less than about £25 millions a year, and may well have been over £30 millions.

One other set of figures deserves mention. In 1660 Charles II was urged to found a new order of knighthood, the 'order of the Royal Oak', to commemorate his happy restoration. It was to be composed of gentry who were impeccably loyal and orthodox, and at the same time socially respectable and of sufficient wealth to support such a dignity. The list of suggested candidates for this new honour names them by counties, and gives an estimate of their annual incomes from land. Only five of the proposed new knights were already baronets, and about eighty already knights; the rest were all esquires, or holders of military rank presumably such as to make them equivalent to esquires; some of the army officers and the others listed under London and Middlesex were almost certainly not of armigerous ancestry.

There is no reason to regard the author of this paper (possibly someone in the Office of Arms) as particularly accurate. But his estimate is the more interesting for excluding many of those who may be supposed to have done well out of the Interregnum, and for including many who had presumably done badly out of it. (See Table 34 on the next page.)

After this lengthy but unavoidable digression, provisional figures can be offered for 1632/3-33/4. But certain reservations must be made concerning the numbers and wealth of the different ranks among the gentry. By 1633 the knightage must have been shrinking again, because those created by James I were probably by then dying off faster than Charles I was creating new ones; the extra knights and the entirely new order of baronets, created by James and Charles, had been mainly recruited from among the better off esquires, thus affecting the total number and the probable average income in that rank. At the bottom of the armigerous class there is the further

---

[1] W. Cole, *A Rod for the Lawyers* (1659), BM, E 989 (15), p. 8 (I am grateful to Mr. Cooper for lending me his transcript of this passage).

TABLE 34. ANONYMOUS ESTIMATES, 1660[1]

Knights recommended to be created in:

		Total Income p.a.
Cornwall	16	£22,500
Cheshire	13	£21,200
Devon	14	£18,700
Herefordshire	12	£24,000
Lancashire	20	£23,200
Norfolk	20	£24,600
Oxfordshire	16	£26,400
Somerset	15	£22,600
Surrey	32	£30,600
Worcestershire	16	£20,200
Yorkshire	20	£20,400
London and Middlesex	111	£134,700
The other 26 English counties	295	£321,600
Wales and Monmouth	75	£79,300
Total number of knights recommended	675	£790,000

Average income for each knight recommended £1,170 *per annum*

problem of how many of the gentlemen are likely to have been landowners. Virtually all the esquires, except perhaps a few of the *ex officio* ones, were landed gentry, many of the gentlemen probably were not, although the majority of them are likely to have drawn some income from land—if only as tenants, or stewards. These, and many other factors both economic and demographic are relevant to the problem; again, only provisional estimates can be given.

[1] J. Burke, *The Commoners of Great Britain and Ireland* (1833-8), I, app., pp. 688-94 (from the Le Neve MSS.); see Keeler, *Long Parlt.*, pp. 22-3, n. 112. Compare the figures given for gentry incomes in some counties in R. Symonds, *Diary of the Marches of the Royal Army* (Camd. Soc., 1859), and works by Professor Dodd and Dr. Hoskins cited above; also M. E. Finch, *The Wealth of Five Northamptonshire Families, 1540-1640* (Northants. Rec. Soc., XIX, 1956), an admirable study of four 'rising', or 'risen', and one 'declining', and later extinct, gentry families. Among the most difficult problems is how far the royalist composition papers (*Cal. Cttee. Compdg.* and SP 23/) and the assessments for the parliamentary taxes of the 1/5 and the 1/20 (*Cal. Cttee. Advcmt. Money* and SP 19/) are reliable guides to the wealth of those concerned. But calculations of income from fines in *Cal. Cttee. Compdg.* can only relate to net income, after all allowable deductions. (I am grateful to Mr. B. S. Manning for this point.)

TABLE 35.   SUGGESTED INCOME FIGURES, *c.* 1633[1]

	Total
122 English peers, average income £6,000 p.a. each .	£732,000
26 bishops, average income *c.* 950 p.a. each (gross: before tax)	£25,000
305-10 eldest sons of English peers (of age), Englishmen with Scottish and Irish peerages, and baronets, average income £1,500	*c.* £460,000
1,500-1,800 knights, average income £800 p.a. each . to	£1,200,000 £1,440,000
7,000-9,000 esquires, average income £500 p.a. each . to	£3,500,000 £4,500,000
10,000-14,000 gents., average income £150 p.a. each . to	£1,500,000 £2,100,000

Total income from land of these classes: within the range £7·4 millions to £9·3 millions p.a.
Total national income (suggested range): £25-30 millions

On the basis of these figures, the £590,000-£760,000 which is esti- mated to have changed hands annually through the medium of office-holding is equal to between 6·3 and 10·3 per cent. of the total annual income of the armigerous landed classes, and between 2 and 3 per cent. of the total national income. For what the comparison is worth, King reckoned office-holders to have been receiving the equivalent of 3·7 per cent. of his (corrected) total national income. By contrast, it will be remembered that in 1957 wages and salaries paid by government constituted about 14 per cent. of the national income of the United Kingdom.[2]

These provisional findings can now be tentatively related to the questions of social structure and mobility, and in particular to the 'rise of the gentry'. If this concept is to be reformulated as 'the rise *within* the gentry of certain families', it should now be possible to assess the proposition 'that office rather than land was the basis of many undoubtedly "rising" families'.[3] Clearly enough this was true

---

[1] In addition to the sources already cited, see L. Haward, *The Charges issuing forth of the Crown Revenue of England and dominion of Wales* (10 February 1646/7), BM, E 375 (8), pp. 52-5; and J. P. Cooper, a letter in *Encounter*, XI, 3 (1958), 73-4.

[2] *National Income and Expenditure, 1958*; see above, Chapter 4, s. v, p. 241, n. 1.

[3] H. R. Trevor-Roper, *The Gentry*, pp. 9, 26 (his italics).

of some families: the question is how many. Of those who rose into, within, and through the ranks of the gentry, the ones who did so primarily, if not solely thanks to office-holding, may be understood to have constituted anything from a smallish fraction to an absolute majority. Professor Trevor-Roper's meaning becomes clearer when he continues:

> Instead of the distinction between 'old' and 'new' landlords, between peers and gentry, I would suggest as the significant distinction of Tudor and Stuart *landed* society, the distinction between 'court' and 'country', between the office-holders and the mere landlords. And by the words 'court' and 'office' I do not mean only the immediate members of the royal circle or the holders of political office: I use the words in the widest sense to cover all offices of profit under the crown—offices in the household, the administration, and above all—for it was the most lucrative of all—the law; local office as well as central office, county lawyers as well as London lawyers, deputy sheriffs as well as ministers, 'an auditor or a vice-admiral in his county' as well as a Teller of the Exchequer or a Warden of the Cinque Ports.[1]

Since this study of Charles I's servants does not attempt to cover either the holders of local offices or the practising lawyers (as opposed to legal officers), it is not possible to make direct a comparison with Professor Trevor-Roper's conclusions. Beyond doubt he has been right to add the category of office-holders to that of lawyers (which had already been included by Professor Tawney in *his* definition of the rising gentry[2]), and in so doing he has greatly enriched our understanding of the period.

The actual number of families who owed their elevation into the 'risen' gentry primarily to office is another matter. If an élite, of ministers of state, court favourites, and holders of a few exceptionally lucrative lesser posts, is compared with the seventy-two new peers created from 1603 to 1629, or with the builders of some seventy great houses under Elizabeth and James I, Professor Trevor-Roper can claim striking confirmation for his analysis.[3] But if all the holders of central office are seen in relation to the whole body of the gentry, or even of the upper and middling gentry, it is less easy to agree with him.

---

[1] *Ibid.*, pp. 26-7 (my italics).
[2] *Econ. Hist. Rev.*, XI (1941), 4, 18.
[3] *The Gentry*, pp. 10-13, 15-16.

The total annual income of office-holders was very unevenly distributed. Very large incomes were enjoyed by the great officers of state, the royal favourites (whether peers or commoners), and those who held a few richly remunerated posts in various of the law courts and departments. If we compare what is likely to have been left over, for all the other members of the household and the central government, with the landed, business, and professional incomes of the same men, still more with the total income of the classes from which they were drawn, then office begins to assume a more modest economic significance. Out of *c.* £590,000-760,000 changing hands yearly through office-holding, between £150,000 and £200,000 presumably went to members of the peerage and of the non-armigerous classes; this leaves an amount between £440,000 and £560,000 for the gentry, but probably not much over £500,000. At any given time this income was distributed among rather under a thousand, or at most about one in every seventeen of all the gentry. The total landed income of the entire gentry class (here including baronets, but excluding all peers) was probably about £6·5 millions a year; so, on this calculation, office represented approximately a thirteenth, or 7·7 per cent. of their total income. Thus, while office was of crucial economic importance for some gentry, as it was for some peers and for some non-armigers, many other office-holding gentry must have enjoyed larger incomes from land, some from legal practice, and a few from business enterprise, than they did from their posts in the royal service.

On the basis of the evidence which has been used here, it is impossible to identify the rising with the office-holding gentry. As has already been explained, there is an obvious but important correlation between economic success, biological survival, and the availability of documentary evidence. Even so, examples of failures in economic and financial terms have not been far to seek. Nor, leaving biological and demographic factors out of account, does lasting material enrichment depend only on income. Expenditure, savings, and investment must also be studied if such permanent gains are to be understood. Some office-holders lived frugally, and ploughed their gains back into land purchases, improvements, and other capital investments; but by and large they probably lived more expensively than their country cousins, and this may be one reason why only a minority of them were able to build up substantial landed estates solely out of the profits of office. This is not to exclude certain *indirect* economic gains from office-holding: influence with other officials might secure preferential treatment in tax assessments of various kinds, sometimes even in litigation, and certainly in some types of development projects. These assets are not the less important because they are quite impossible to measure; but they are very hard to distinguish from satisfaction of the non-economic motives which men had for seeking office—ambition, prestige, and ideological conviction.

It is also necessary to remind ourselves of where the money came from, which made up officials' incomes. Some of it came from the Crown, in the form of Fees, diets, etc., and the rest direct from private individuals in fees and gratuities. But most of this wealth originated in the profits of land and business enterprise, while only a fraction of it simply circulated among the staffs of the law courts and central departments. Wealth changed hands via office under the Crown, but office did not create wealth.

If the precise connexion between office-holding and the fortunes of the gentry must remain an open question, the findings of this and the previous chapter are much further from suggesting that the English state in the early seventeenth century was controlled by a single economic class. Except of course that if the Crown and all the greater landowners (peers, greater and middling gentry, and upper clergy) are all comprehended within a single 'upper', or governing class, the proposition is unexceptionable but something of a platitude. The Marxian interpretation of English sixteenth- and seventeenth-century history involves classifying all landowners, at least all those above the yeomanry, as reactionary alias 'feudal', or progressive alias 'bourgeois', alias capitalist; and it involves identifying the pre-1640 state with the interests of the feudal ones. For this to be acceptable, it would not be necessary to prove that *all* Charles I's administrators were themselves economically backward, or feudal landlords. But it would have to be shown that most of the senior ones were, and that the government carried out measures designed to benefit such feudal landowners. Some of this can be more easily discussed in retrospect, looking back at the King's servants of 1625-1642 from the Civil Wars and Interregnum; and the connexion between office and politics forms the subject of the next chapter. But the findings of this chapter alone, however tentative some of them may be, make it impossible to identify Charles I's officials with any single economic class (other than that comprising all the greater landowners). Sherborne, Croke, Meautys, Mynne, Colchester Wolseley, Henley, the Pyes, Vernon: it is only necessary to name some of those whose careers have been discussed to see the difficulties in supposing them to belong to a feudal, or economically unprogressive class. Even setting our sights at a higher level, among those who rose to the very top only a few court favourites have the look of mere parasites, or of backward landowners. Such a description hardly fits the Cecils, the Russells, the Herberts, the Montagues, the Finches, Cranfield, Boyle, Cottington, or Coventry. There are no reliable printed sources from which the Howard and Villiers families can be assessed one way or other in their capacity as landowners. The Gorings, the Jermyns, and Endymion Porter were undoubtedly royal favourites, and also notorious 'projectors'; and they may have been unprogressive landowners, despite being interested in enclosure and land drainage. But in any case, three or even half a dozen families is hardly enough to identify the central government and its policy with the unprogressive landlords.

Some landowners obviously were more go ahead and more businesslike than others, and such differences are also to be found among those of them who held office under the Crown. But any attempt to classify all landowners as feudal or capitalist is best abandoned; still less does it seem profitable to think of the English state as having been, before 1640, the instrument of the feudal, to the exclusion of the capitalist peers and gentry.

There are other genuine and interesting differences of economic interest and outlook among the office-holders themselves. In their attitudes towards office, some men thought in terms of exploitable property, the value of which could, and should be maximised: this 'entrepreneurial' attitude can be seen at its clearest, perhaps we might say at its grossest, in Mynne's tenure of the Hanaper, and in Croke's career as Clerk of the Pipe, but several others exemplify it in a less lurid light. Other men held offices, usually unexacting ones, or such as could be executed by deputy, with the expectation of a safe and steady yield: this type of office-holder was more like an annuitant, or a rentier. Then there were those for whom economic motives were subordinate, who sought office, and used it primarily to satisfy their social aspirations, to relieve their personal frustrations, and in a far smaller number of cases, to advance their political ambitions. There were the professionals and 'full-timers', the amateurs or 'part-timers', and the absentees. All these types can to some extent be distinguished. Classification becomes a hindrance rather than a help to understanding only when it is based on assumptions which remain unproved hypotheses, like the identification of the pre-1640 government and its members with a feudal or reactionary ruling class, or *per contra* the identification of the office-holders with the rising and risen gentry.

One other distinction may be suggested, though its significance is hard to gauge. That is between those who were wholly, or overwhelmingly dependent on office for their social position and their livelihood, and those who could in the last resort make do without it, if they were prepared to curb their expenditure and their ambitions. Whatever may be said about the decisive divisions within the landed classes, one perhaps useful distinction inside the office-holding body might be that between the 'mere' officials, and those who had substantial landed property and other non-official interests and means of support.

Note.—Further references, in recent publications, for the number of gentry in particular counties, may be found in A. G. Dickens, *Lollards and Protestants in the Diocese of York, 1509-1558* (1959), p. 6 (for Yorks); and J. E. Mousley, 'The Fortunes of Some Gentry Families of Elizabethan Sussex', *Econ. Hist. Rev.*, 2nd ser., XI (1959), 467-83.

6

OFFICE AND POLITICS

i LOYALTY AND ALLEGIANCE

AS HAS ALREADY BEEN EXPLAINED, the idea of a 'non-political' civil service was wholly unknown in the England of Charles I. Nor was there any clear distinction between politicians and administrators. In the lower ranks of the central government there were, however, numbers of men who were socially too obscure to play an effective part in national politics, either at court or in parliament. And several of the office-holders who did become prominent in local or national affairs did not do so solely, or even primarily in their capacity as officer-holders, but rather on account of their social standing, wealth, and individual abilities.

National politics did not always and necessarily mean parliamentary politics. Even when there was a parliament in being, to some extent even while it was sitting, the royal court was also a political arena; this was obviously all the more true during the long intervals between parliaments, in 1614-21 and 1629-40. National politics, if these are defined as matters affecting more than local or family interests, as questions of public policy, might also be discussed in other places: in the Guildhall and the halls of the great livery and trading companies, at the Inns of Court, and in the country houses of great factional leaders. But ultimately, if anything was to be done, the Crown, that is to say the King, had to be influenced. This meant exerting pressure or influence through parliament, or in the court and the administration.

All officials, except those who were employed by more senior ones, were appointed and expected to conduct themselves as the King's servants. Technically the Queen's household officers and other servants owed obedience and loyalty to her, and the Prince's to him. But after about 1626-8 the royal family was united in affection and, except for religion, in outlook, so this made very little practical difference; in any case, as had been seen with Ann Boleyn and Catherine Howard, men's obligations to a Queen consort could not absolve them from their primary allegiance to the King.

Even in routine matters the duties and obligations of office-holders were based on loyalty to their sovereign. Yet is it absurdly artificial to abstract one facet or aspect of men's lives and analyse it in isolation. The mere fact of holding office, of being in the King's service, did not stop the peers, gentry, lawyers, and others who staffed the central administration from trying to advance causes and interests which they had at heart. Sometimes this involved using their official positions to influence royal policy. Sir Robert Pye provides one of the clearest examples in his brush with Laud and Wentworth, when in the later 1630's he was evidently using his position as Auditor of the Receipt in the interests of the Villiers family and thus preventing Wentworth's reorganization of the Irish revenues. If such victories of private over public interests were more usual and more blatant in Ireland, they were far from unknown at home. At a time when many landowners were smarting under Laud's use of the commissions on depopulation and enclosure, his own friend and lieutenant, Lord Treasurer Juxon, was authorizing the enclosure of a common in Flintshire by the King's Bedchamberman and confidant, Endymion Porter.[1] Again, royal policy in handing fen drainage over to wealthy syndicates of peers, courtiers, and entrepreneurs, whether or not it was economically sound, conflicted with the prescriptive rights of small men, which Charles and Laud are often said to have had at heart.

Sometimes there was not a clash but a mixture or confusion of royal and private interests. This can be seen in the use of royal commissions and patents partly for purposes of investigation, control, or reform, partly to provide a joint source of profit for the Crown and the commissioners or patentees. In the later 1630's the commissions on cottages and on usurers were among the most notorious. But that for the control and regulation of malting and

[1] P.R.O., Treasury misc. bks., T 56/8, p. 27, 11 July 1638.

338

brewing was in one respect more shocking: its members included several more men who might have been expected to know better and their names read like a roll call of the central executive.[1] By contrast the commission to enforce the statute of 1589, requiring every cottage to have not less than four acres attached to it and not more than one family resident in it, included those inveterate patentees the Earl of Dorset and Lord Goring; it was perhaps the more unpopular for including at least five prominent Scots, among them the Scottish Secretary of State, the Keeper of the Privy Purse, and the ex-Lord Treasurer of Scotland, now Captain of the Guard.[2]

The clash of private and public interests can also be seen in the Crown's attitude towards reversions, life tenure of offices, absenteeism, and the sale of offices. All of these were in theory disapproved of during the 1630's, but all continued to exist. In Ireland even Wentworth was not above accepting brokerage fees of £1,000 for the Chief Justiceship and £400 for an Exchequer Barony.[3] Sir Thomas Jermyn was a Privy Councillor throughout the 1630's. The reversions held by his young sons inhibited the King's freedom of appointment to the Clerkship of the Pipe, the Clerkship of writs and enrolments in King's Bench (Henley's, *alias* 'Roper's' office), the Attorneyship and Coronership of King's Bench, the Keepership of books and orders in Chancery, the Surveyorship of the Petty Customs of London, the Governorship of Jersey, and the Keepership of Hampton Court park.

All officials used their positions as a matter of course to advance their own personal interests. So much so that it is very tempting simply to deny outright that any distinction was recognized between public and private interests. This would be a mistake. The idea of

---

[1] All four ordinary Council Clerks, one reversioner to a Council Clerkship, four out of the six or seven Council Clerks extraordinary (of whom one was also an Ambassador, and another a Customs officer and farmer), three out of four Signet Clerks, and three reversioners, the French Secretary, the Lord Treasurer's Secretary, and a co-Warden of the Mint.

[2] For the membership of commissions see *Cal. S.P. Dom.*, *Foedera*, and the P.R.O. MS. indexes to the patent rolls. For their ambivalent place in early Stuart government see also G. E. Aylmer, 'Attempts at Administrative Reform, 1625-40', *Eng. Hist. Rev.*, LXXII (1957), 231-3. For the suggested reforms of the malting and brewing trades see P.R.O., Signet Office, SO 1/3/48 (I am grateful to Mr. Cooper for lending me his notes of this); *Foedera*, XX, 101-3.

[3] *Lismore Papers*, 1st ser., III, 220, IV, 25.

such a distinction was certainly ill developed, but there is abundant evidence of its existence, while some men were even aware of the potential conflict between public and private interests. In assessing administrative standards of morality, an occasional *cause célèbre*, like the fall of Bacon, and the activities of a few 'mere' favourites, like Villiers, Hay, or Goring, are less significant than the steady erosion of Crown revenues and the gradual undermining of royal policies by the main body of average, respectable office-holders. As has been explained, much of this, especially the financial wastage, can be directly related to the ways in which officers were paid, above all to the inadequacy of their salaries. But it has also been shown that bribery and extortion were recognized as wrong, and were sometimes brought to book; in short that there was a standard of loyalty and conduct which excluded these practices. Those who took gratuities or brokerage fees were by no means necessarily disloyal to their immediate superiors or to the King, but those who accepted bribes or extorted 'exacted' fees were. On the other hand, a concept of loyalty to the 'public interest' or even to the Crown, as distinct from the King, was scarcely comprehended by anyone. The absence of this later distinction is of course reflected in the parliamentarians' claim to be fighting *for* the King in the Civil War. It was the common form of the age to protest loyalty to the Crown, nor in most cases was it insincere; the monarch was a symbol of national solidarity as well as the head of the government.

But to say that before 1640-2 royal officers were, with a very few exceptions, loyal to the King and by their own standards served him reasonably well is only to restate the problem. Men differed widely in their ideas of how the country should be governed and what policies the King should follow. There was no lack of issues on which office-holders might have views and seek to exert influence: King Charles had many momentous alternatives before him, though in what sense he had a free choice between them is another matter.

The King could choose his friends and his advisers from as wide a circle as he pleased, or he might rely mainly on the existing peerage. Within broad limits he was free to summon and dissolve parliament when he thought fit; he controlled the frequency and the duration of parliamentary sessions. And he had to determine his attitude towards parliamentary privilege, especially in view of the Commons' tendency to identify privilege claims with their wider demands for statutory and other restrictions on the royal prerogative. In general, the King might tend to share the direction of affairs with the peers and the leaders of the Commons; alternatively he might model his rule more and more on that of the great continental absolutisms of Spain and France. In religion he might try to maintain the *via media* of Queen Elizabeth, to complete the Reformation as the Puritans wished, or to emphasize the Catholic nature of the English church with a possible view to eventual reunion with Rome. In foreign affairs he could come to the aid of his brother-in-law, and later of his nephew, the dispossessed Electors Palatine, by joining in the general European war; or he might try to hold the balance between the Habsburgs and their satellites on one side and the French, the Dutch, the Swedes, and the lesser Protestant princes on the other. He had to decide whether he could avoid committing England either to France, or to Spain, and whether it was desirable that he should do so. In commercial matters he might try to restrict overseas trade to the existing companies or encourage the so-called 'interlopers'. In fiscal policy, he might manage the customs and other duties direct through his officers or lease them on contract to Farmers. Apart from this, there was the vexed question of whether or not he could levy Tonnage and Poundage without consent of parliament, and raise additional duties other than by act of parliament. In social and economic questions he might seek to preserve medieval and Tudor controls over the location, organization, and processes of industry, or let these regulations lapse. Was he to enforce the laws against depopulation and enclosure, and to maintain the Elizabethan attitude towards vagrancy and unemployment? On a narrower front, he had to decide about the restrictions on urban and rural building, on the primary iron industry, and on usury, likewise concerning the royal and corporate monopolies in the alum, glass, tapestry, gunpowder and cannon-making industries.[1] Finally the King had some degree of choice between taking a personal interest in all these matters, and leaving them to his favourites and ministers in order

---

[1] For John Browne's monopoly in iron cannon see *Cal. S.P. Dom.*, *1637-8*, pp. 30-1; *1639*, p. 531; PC 2/50, p. 651; PC 2/51-2, pp. 86-7; T 56/6, pp. 18-19; T 56/8, pp. 174-5; E 403/2567, pp. 76-7; E 403/2590, pp. 428-33. It is not among those usually cited (e.g. in W. Hyde Price, *The English Patents of Monopoly* (Cambridge, Mass., 1906)); but Browne's contract was eventually extended to the sole manufacture as well as the sole export of iron ordnance, and at one stage even covered iron pots, kettles, and fire-backs; it was attacked as a monopoly in 1640 (J. Nicholl, *The Ironmongers' Company* (1851), p. 247).

to lead a more carefree private life. The amount of work which he did depended to some extent on his own inclinations.

All this is part of the general history of England and does not properly belong in a study of administration and administrators. But it is well to remind ourselves that loyalty to the Crown was compatible with a multitude of conflicting interests, policies, and ideals, as well as with personal and family ambitions. It would be wholly unreal to study the government and the office-holders under Charles I, *as if* England's political, religious, social, and economic development was going steadily forward along a well-marked course.

The officials of 1625-40 could not of course foresee or foresuffer the events of 1640-60. But it would be absurd to set those events aside as if they were irrelevant. By seeing what happened to those of the 1625-40 officials who survived into the Civil Wars and after, we may be better able to understand both the nature of Charles I's government and the causes of its fall. One way of doing this is to investigate the allegiance of these men in 1642 and after. Our concern therefore is not with the remoter causes of the Civil War but with the definitions of allegiance, or the devising of ways to conceal allegiance or to evade the issue, from the time when the outbreak of war seemed probable, in the late spring or summer of 1642, and after it began that autumn.

It is never possible, either in history or in contemporary life, to give a complete and irrefutable explanation of why an individual takes the political decisions he does, not even when he himself tells us why. And to arrive at even partial explanations of political behaviour, it is therefore all the more necessary to discover what else those who took much the same decisions in much the same circumstances had in common besides this.

For the time being it will be best to beg the question of loyalty to the King since this was professed by parliamentarians as well as by royalists. Some men made up their minds on the issues of constitutional or religious principle; some were actuated by the more limited concerns of their social class, their economic interest, their region, their county, even their district; some were swayed by loyalty to their patron or leader, be he peer or commoner; some by family ties —and antipathies. Nor should more general psychological explanations be overlooked, such as the forces of envy, fear, and pride acting on the minds and circumstances of some men, the sheer inertia of custom and habit on those of others. In most, perhaps in all, cases motives were mixed, and consciously held opinions were mingled with unconscious prejudices and emotions.

Is 'office' *as such* to be added to the ways of explaining how and why men took sides in 1642? It would be perfectly reasonable to argue, on *a priori* grounds, that office-holders would be likely to have reacted to this great crisis in a way which conformed to the general pattern of their interests and outlook as office-holders. But the evidence does not suggest that this was so, as can be seen by taking the years 1642-8 and defining all those concerned as (1) active royalists, (2) passive supporters of either side, neutrals, and 'trimmers' or side-changers, (3) active parliamentarians. 'Neutral' has been used to cover men who contrived to avoid taking any active part in the war, although many of them undoubtedly preferred one side to the other. The Earl of Arundel and Surrey, for example, was a royalist, not a parliamentarian, but he went abroad in February 1642 and stayed on the continent, like a kind of high-grade remittance man, until his death in 1646. The sympathies of the Earl of Huntingdon may have been more evenly divided, but after appearing to commit himself to the King's cause in the summer of 1642 he seems to have lived at home relatively undisturbed until his death in 1643. 'Trimmers' include those who fought on both sides at different times: the Hamiltons, and the Earls of Holland and Newport were obviously very different characters from some of the neutrals, but it seems just as misleading to classify them as either royalists or parliamentarians. Those who only changed over in 1646 or after, such as Presbyterians who became royalists in 1647-8, have *not* been included in this category.

Three groups have been examined with these definitions in mind: first the office-holding privy councillors and all other peers who held central office in the years 1625-41 (those only appointed in 1641 are excluded unless they held some other office before that), and who were alive at the outbreak of the Civil War, can be classified as follows:

royalists	neutrals, doubtful, etc.	parliamentarians
29	19	6

Then a survey of 200 men who held offices of medium rank (in England only) between 1625 and 1641 and whose attitude is reasonably clear or can safely be inferred: they divide into

royalists	neutrals, etc.	parliamentarians
96	62	42

Finally, in the group used in Chapter 5, of all those with surnames beginning with the letters A-C, those known still to have been alive in September 1642 can be classified as

royalists	neutrals, etc.	parliamentarians
50	43	16

Office-holding cannot therefore be identified with active support for the King, still less with any other single allegiance or evasion of allegiance. If the very fact of holding office was a decisive influence with all those concerned, it must have operated very differently in different cases.[1]

ii POLITICAL BACKGROUND: PEERS AND GREAT OFFICERS

To make sense of officers' allegiances in 1642 and after, it is necessary to relate the main phases of political history since 1603 to the workings of the patronage system, the ways in which officers were appointed, and the forms of their tenure.

In its early years James I's government had represented a fairly high degree of continuity with Elizabeth's in her last years, with Scottish courtiers and favourites and the Howards perhaps playing a relatively larger part, and the Cecils (despite Salisbury's vast burden of official duties) a relatively smaller one in the exercise of royal and ministerial patronage. There was so far no appearance of a major breach between Crown and Parliament, no outward commitment of the Crown to a High Church, an Anglo-Catholic rather than a Protestant Episcopalian, religious policy. Then came the middle years, of rival favourites at court and rival factions in the Council, with Rochester (c. 1612-15), then the Howards (c. 1615-1616), then Villiers (c. 1616-18) in the ascendant; these years saw a definite attempt to meet Parliament only on the King's terms (as in 1614) or to do without it (as from 1614 to 1621). The third and last phase of James's reign can be dated from 1618-19: Buckingham's victory over the Howards and his complete ascendancy over the King, also the outbreak of the Bohemian War and the beginning of the general European conflict. This phase really spans the change of monarch in 1625 and ends with the assassination of Buckingham

---

[1] For further explanation about the membership of these three groups see s. viii of this chapter.

(August 1628) and the dissolution of Charles I's third Parliament (March 1628/9): during these eleven years England sent money, arms, and 'volunteers' to help her European allies, and oscillated between the extremes of a projected Spanish marriage alliance (1623) and war with Spain (1625-30), and between an actual French marriage alliance (1625) and war with France (1626-9). These were the years of the five parliaments in which the initiative passed decisively to the Commons. Throughout this period, until his death, patronage was highly centralized in Buckingham's hands. When the great office of Lord Steward fell vacant just before the old King's death, Bishop Williams (then Lord Keeper) advised the Duke either to take it himself, and give up one of his other offices, or else to keep it unfilled. With due allowance for flattery, Williams seems to have assumed that Buckingham had an absolutely free choice in the matter: an astonishing position for any subject to have reached, and one almost without parallel in our history. Some months after Charles's accession, a correspondent observed to the Earl of Leicester: 'My Lord Duke's creatures are the Men that rise, the King's servants having little Hope of Preferment.'[1] Yet despite his having been criticized in the 1625 parliament, impeached in 1626, and again violently attacked in June 1628, there is no evidence that the favourite persuaded, or tried to persuade, James or Charles to adopt an anti-parliamentary policy. Indeed, by 1628 he was almost certainly ready to go further in trying to conciliate parliament than Charles himself. Still less, despite the rise of William Laud and the Arminian party, can Buckingham be identified with a high-Church policy or with systematic hostility to Puritanism. His influence should therefore be thought of as having been ubiquitous but *not* 'monolithic'. However, at court and in the central administration only the Herbert brothers (the Earls of Pembroke and Montgomery), and perhaps at intervals Thomas Howard, Earl of Arundel and Surrey, seem to have enjoyed any effective patronage independent of his.

Although the fact was only beginning to dawn on contemporaries by about the mid-1630's, in retrospect 1628-9 can be seen to represent a genuine political divide. In ecclesiastical matters the break may not be so easy to date, but Laud's promotion to London (July) and Archbishop Abbott's failure to recover full authority despite his readmission to the court (December 1628) may be taken as pointers.

[1] *Original Letters,* ed. Ellis, 3rd ser., IV, 191-5; Collins, *Sidney State Papers,* II, 366.

By 1630 the Laud-Wentworth partnership was taking shape, and the two predominant court groupings centred respectively on Lord Treasurer Weston and the Queen were becoming defined.

But there was no corresponding change in the administration. Apart from the ordinary effects of mortality and the removal of a very few individuals for specific offences, the same men remained in office to administer the policies of Charles, Portland, and Laud as had served under the very different conditions of 1618-28, or even in some cases those of a still earlier epoch. Nor, after 1628-9, were all officials invariably selected on account of their adherence to the particular policies then being followed in church and state. This was accentuated by the failure of any one favourite or faction to establish complete predominance at court or in the council; at no stage between 1629 and 1640 was there anything approaching a monopoly of royal or ministerial patronage. The threefold rivalry between Weston (Portland), Laud, and the Queen's circle was succeeded by the dual rivalry of Laud and Wentworth, versus Cottington, Windebank, and the Earl of Holland, while the two great families of Howard and Herbert continued to exercise some influence, as it were on the flank of these rivalries. This multiplicity of faction and influence made it all the more likely that some of those appointed to office would disapprove of certain royal policies; the likelihood of this was further increased by the lack of unity and consistency in these policies.

There is some evidence of tension and ill feeling between the two great exponents of 'Thorough' and certain officials. Wentworth's views on fees and the payment of officers have already been quoted. As well as playing an active part in the commission on fees in 1630-1, he launched a full inquiry concerning fees taken by Irish officeholders in 1634. Contrary to repeated complaints, he considered that the officers of the Navy were overpaid rather than underpaid; having been reduced to buying arms from the Netherlands to equip the Irish army in 1635, he reflected severely on the Ordnance Office to Secretary Coke, and continued:

> Indeed it is the Fortune of the Crown of England, I think, to be still so served by the Officers of the Navy, Wardrobe, Ordnance, and it may be in other Offices too; yet that some pretense or other shall be found out by the Parties themselves that receive the Benefit, which must serve the Turn to Keep Things still in the wonted Condition without Amendment.

346

His own inconsistency concerning Poundage and Porterage has already been pointed out. Irish offices were another source of misunderstanding. In January 1633/4 he sent George Kirke, Gent. of the Robes, a stiff lecture on his temerity in asking for the Clerkship of the Market, self-righteously contrasting his own virtues:

> It being my full resolution that neither my Selfe or any of mine, shall ever make benefitt here by thinges of that Nature.

How 'thinges of that Nature' were defined may well have puzzled the Lord Deputy's contemporaries: like the Queen of Hearts in *Alice*, he was quite capable of altering the rules as the game went on. And from an important paper presented to him by a Yorkshire friend in 1631 it is abundantly clear that *one* of his own motives in seeking to transfer from York to Dublin was to increase his personal fortune. Colleagues and subordinates with whom he quarrelled in Ireland included the Lord Chancellor, Lord Treasurer, Treasurer-at-Wars, Customs Farmers, and First Remembrancer of the Exchequer. The Master of the Wards was also sufficiently alienated to join in the attack on him in 1640-1. The number of English courtiers and officials seeking Irish favours whom, like Kirke, he felt obliged to disoblige was legion. The attitude of the more candid among them was perfectly summed up by the retiring Keeper of the Privy Purse, the Earl of Ancrum, in 1638. The King, he explained to the Lord Deputy, had every intention of rewarding him, but since their royal master was too busy to attend to all such matters, 'it becometh us to help ourselves with the least hinder to His Majestyes Affaires that may be'.[1]

Laud too found fault with more than one aspect of the administrative system in England and Ireland. Reluctantly he told the Bishop of Kilmore that it was unpractical, though eminently desirable, to try to change the tenure of Bishops' Chancellors from life to during pleasure. He agreed that,

> there arises a great deal of hurt to ourselves, and scandal to our calling, by the courses which our under officers take in our [i.e. the ecclesiastical] courts, and the harrowing of the poor people there.

[1] For Wentworth's own views and interests, and various appeals to him see Knowler, I, 89-90, 143, 247, 250, 304, 333, 340, 391, 448; *Cal. S.P. Dom.*, *Adds. 1625-49*, p. 476; P.R.O., E 403/2591, pp. 12b-13, E 165/46, p. 97b, E 165/47, pp. 29-31; Bodl. Tanner MSS. 287, fols. 37-44, 318 No. 26, 319 fol. 14; Sheffield C.L., Strafford MSS., 8/49-50, 10a/163, 21b/79; *Clar. S. P.*, I, 95. See also J. P. Cooper, 'The Fortune of Thomas Wentworth, Earl of Strafford, *Econ. Hist. Rev.* 2nd ser. XI (1958), 227-48; H. F. Kearney, *Strafford in Ireland 1633-41* (Manchester, 1959), ch. 12.

Laud's visitation records show similar pre-occupations. And the famous Canons of 1640 include several measures designed to improve ecclesiastical administration—to the annoyance, so we are told by the Archbishop's chaplain and biographer, of the civil lawyers who staffed this administration. Laud's attack on Lord Treasurer Portland in 1634 and his attitude towards Buckingham's one-time factotum, Sir James ('bottomless') Bagg, indicate divergent standards of administrative probity at the highest level. Laud's most direct experience of the central administration came in his year as senior Treasury commissioner 1635-6. He was driven to the conclusion that Cottington, as Chancellor of the Exchequer, and the lesser Exchequer officials actually did not want the King to have accurate and comprehensive figures of his own financial position. Supported we may surmise by Coventry, Manchester, and Secretary Coke, he got his way, but at the cost of deepening hostility from Cottington and Windebank. The latter had their revenge first over the well-known affair of the rival soap companies, secondly by being readier to fall in with the King's desire to 'empark' Richmond, which involved paying compensation to local property-owners.[1]

Bishop Juxon's appointment as Lord Treasurer in March 1636 has rightly been seen as a victory for 'Thorough' over its rivals in the government. Yet with one exception Juxon had to go on working with exactly the same officials as before; only his own secretary, young Philip Warwick, was new, replacing the Treasury Commissioners' secretary, Sir William Becher, a Council Clerk. Juxon tried to exercise closer control over the Customs officers, in part perhaps as a check on the honesty of the Customs Farmers, and declared his opposition to further revenue farms. But at the end of the 1630's the various customs and other revenue farmers were more essential than ever to Crown finance. And inside the Exchequer, though Juxon was industrious and conscientious, there is little evidence of positive reforms being achieved.[2]

[1] W. Laud, *Works* (ed. Scott and Bliss, Oxford, 1847-60), III, 223-4, VI, 281-8, VII, 97, 121, 143-5, 162, 177; E. Cardwell, *Synodalia* (1842), 409-10; P. Heylyn, *Cyprianus Anglicus* (Dublin, 1719), II, 123. For the soap business and Richmond Park see Gardiner, *History*, VIII, 71-6, 87-9.

[2] P.R.O., T 56/10, p. 10b (Juxon to the Customs officers of the outports, ordering them to send their books in for audit promptly and regularly, 28 February 1636/7); *Cal. S.P. Dom.*, 1640, p. 149 (unlike Laud's, Juxon's loan to the King in 1639-40 was apparently at 8 per cent. and not interest-free).

If the story of 'Thorough' and its adherents suggests that the road to Hell is indeed paved with good intentions, the same can hardly be said of all Charles I's other councillors. The meticulous priggishness of Laud and the rather more sinister 'double-think' of Wentworth are in striking contrast to the candid exploitation of high office for private gain by Portland and Cottington. And after Portland's death, Laud and Wentworth may well have had Cottington and Windebank principally in mind, rather than the general spirit of procrastination at court and in the government, when they referred in their letters to 'the Lady Mora'.[1] But on the whole these two acted as a negative dead-weight rather than as a positive opposition. The hostility of certain other councillors deserves more attention than it has usually received; and with this hostility there went perhaps a further contrast in administrative approach.

Philip Herbert, Earl of Pembroke and Montgomery, Lord Chamberlain 1626-41 and head of the whole household 1630-40, appears to have resented any outside interference. His opposition has already been noted to the Groom of the Stole's claim to control Bedchamber patronage. More serious, as early as 1626 the size and cost of the Chamber were shown to have risen out of all proportion since 1603, and a plan was put forward to save the King many thousands of pounds a year. Yet scarcely any economy was achieved and there was no further investigation of the Chamber before the Civil War. The Lord Chamberlain was also affected by inquiries into the Great Wardrobe and the Wardrobe of Robes. When in 1634 the reforming commissioners were reconsidering an earlier ruling that the Clerk of the Wardrobes should sign all demands for materials supplied from the Great Wardrobe to the Chamber, Secretary Coke noted that 'the Lord Chamberlain taketh exception to this as an inovation to his prejudice to have a Clerck joyned with his Lordship in his warrants'; in 1637 Pembroke was said to be once more deliberately flouting this order.[2] His position in the household apart, he enjoyed an unknown income as Lord Warden of the Stannaries, and received a £3,000 p.a. pension on the silk duties and another of £400 from the Exchequer.

Wentworth's most dangerous enemy, Henry Rich Earl of Holland,

---

[1] For differing interpretations of 'the Lady Mora' compare Trevor-Roper, *Archbishop Laud*, p. 212 and other refs., with Mathew, *Age of Charles I*, pp. 88-9.

[2] Hist. MSS. Comm., *Cowper*, I, 291-3; SP 16/259/26, 260/114, 375/6.

had even deeper vested interests in keeping the administrative system unreformed. From 1636 he had charge of the King's Bedchamber, of the Queen's revenues (being second in command of her whole establishment), and of royal forest jurisdiction south of Trent. He was also sole commissioner to control the movement of bullion, and the use of gold and silver thread, co-farmer of the new duties on sea-coals, and sole farmer of the seal office of King's Bench and Common Pleas. Over and above this he had a pension of £2,000 a year from the Exchequer.

The wealth and prestige of other aristocratic councillors were bound up with the existing conditions in various departments of state, or branches of the revenue. As Master of the Horse, the Marquis of Hamilton would be affected by any reorganization or retrenchment in the Stable; he was also dependent on a pension from the Customs and a large share in the profits from control over the retail wine trade. The Duke of Lennox had pensions from the Exchequer and the Court of Wards, but relied chiefly on his farm of the Aulnage duties on manufactured cloth. The Earl of Denbigh, not a Privy Councillor but as Master of the Great Wardrobe enjoying fairly easy access to the King, was almost certainly guilty of dishonest accounting, and stood to lose heavily from any genuine reform of royal finance. Thomas Howard, Earl of Arundel and Surrey, heir to the dormant dukedom of Norfolk, was more powerful but politically less 'committed'. As well as enjoying a share in the currant farm, a pension from the Alienations office, and authority over forest jurisdiction north of Trent, he was head of the Office of Arms and the Court of Chivalry. In 1639 he was forced to suspend Norroy King of Arms and Somerset Herald for corrupt practices (extortion, and forced sales of arms and pedigrees), but after a year he had them reinstated without further penalty. This can be paralleled by the two days which two officers of the Ordnance spent in jail for disposing improperly of the King's gunpowder in June 1629, and by the scandal about naval stores in 1634, which involved the Comptroller, Surveyor, and Store Keeper of the Navy and several subordinate officers.[1] The leniency shown in all these cases can be contrasted with Wentworth's treatment of Irish officers, and with the heavy compositions exacted from some of those in Chancery, Common Pleas, and Exchequer.

[1] For Norroy and Somerset see SP 16/417/3; *Cal. S.P. Dom., 1640*, p. 9; for the Ordnance, PC 2/39, pp. 304, 314; for the Navy, SP 16/260/88.

This is far from being a full list of the councillors and other major office-holders whose administrative activities alone suggest that they probably felt no sympathy for 'Thorough'. To be complete, it should also take account of the Earl of Dorset (the Queen's Lord Chamberlain), the Earl of Newport (Master of the Ordnance), Lord Goring, and Sir Thomas Jermyn.

Last but not least, the elder Vane was another councillor and great officer with a personal interest in preventing proper investigation of his own department. Whatever the exact degree of his guilt as Cofferer and then Comptroller of the Household, he certainly behaved very suspiciously during the last campaign for household reform in 1638. He was also later accused of having had a corrupt interest in the collection of saltpetre for making gunpowder; Sam Cordwell, who replaced the Evelyns as royal powder contractor, was a client of Vane's and had previously been on his staff in the Household. Sir Henry's antipathy to Wentworth, and less directly to Laud, may have sprung in part from such differences in attitude.

All of these men, except Hamilton, Lennox, and Newport, had been councillors, or in senior office, or both *before* the political climacteric of 1628-9 and the emergence of 'Thorough'.[1]

iii OFFICERS IN THE 1620's

It is relatively easy to plot the political and factional groupings amongst the councillors and great officers. Not so with the administrators of the middle ranks. Indeed, except by inference it is almost impossible to say what their attitude was towards the royal policies of the time, or after Buckingham's death towards the rival groups in the Council. There is, however, enough evidence concerning those of them who were members of parliament in the 1620's to suggest that like their aristocratic patrons and colleagues they were sometimes out of sympathy with royal policy and did not always conceal the fact.

The argument that loss of office was of crucial importance in alienating men from the court and the Crown finds classic expression

[1] For Pembroke and Montgomery, Holland, Hamilton, Lennox, Denbigh, Arundel and Surrey, Dorset, Newport, Goring, Jermyn, and Vane, see *D.N.B.*, or G.E.C. or both, and other sources already cited such as fee and pension lists: SP 16/180/16-18, T 35/1, etc.; and for Vane also J. Lilburne, *The Resolved Man's Resolution* (1647), pp. 14-15.

in the career of the great common lawyer Sir Edward Coke. But Coke's transformation, from Chief Justice (1606-16) to 'opposition' leader in the Commons (1621, 1624, 1625, 1628), was unique. Sir Ranulphe Crewe, dismissed from his Chief Justiceship for opposing the forced loan of 1626, did not take an active part against the court; indeed, like Coke himself up to 1621, for a few years after his fall he seems to have hoped for restoration to favour. Slightly different was the case of William Hackwill (1574-1655), whose post as Solicitor to the Queen automatically lapsed on the death of Anne of Denmark in 1618. He was not found a place in Henrietta Maria's establishment (set up in 1625, and reorganized in 1626 and 1628), although he was a commissioner on fees in the late 1620's and on the rebuilding of St. Pauls in the early 1630's. Hackwill had presumably been out of favour *before* he held central office, for in the 'addled' parliament of 1614 he had queried the Crown's right to impose extra customs duties. Yet he was sufficiently forgiven to be made a Crown law officer three years later. Ten years after his loss of office, in the session of 1629, he professed himself converted by William Noy (future Attorney-General and deviser of Ship Money!) to the opposition view that full parliamentary privilege was in force while parliament was prorogued.[1]

That subordinate officers who criticized royal policy or attacked the King's ministers could overstep the mark and as a result suffer loss of office is illustrated by the careers of the great Sir John Eliot and his friend William Coryton. Eliot's loss of office, as Vice-Admiral of South Devon, was permanent, but Coryton recovered his position as Vice-Warden of the Stannaries in 1630, having submitted and begged the King's pardon for his offences in the 1629 session of parliament.[2]

Parliamentary 'opposition', even to the Crown's entire policy, did not always lead to deprivation. John Pym was Receiver-General of crown revenues in Hampshire, Wiltshire, and Gloucestershire from 1613 to 1638; he was imprisoned in 1622 for his part in the parliament of 1621, and played a leading part in the impeachment of Buckingham in 1626. Despite the additional protection afforded by his term of office being for life, it is still remarkable that no

---

[1] For Coke, Crewe, and Hackwill see *D.N.B.* and Gardiner, *History*, for Hackwill also P.R.O., E 165/46; *Commons Debates for 1629*, ed. W. Notestein and F. H. Relf (Minneapolis, 1921), pp. 92-3, 233.

[2] See *D.N.B.* and H. Hulme, *Life of Sir John Eliot* (1957).

attempt seems to have been made to deprive him. Similarly James Whitelocke, a future judge of King's Bench, had pointed out the unconstitutional nature of James I's extra customs duties, in 1610 and again in 1614. He was imprisoned in 1613, ostensibly for oppos- ing—in legal cases where he was counsel—the jurisdictions of the Earl Marshal's court and of the royal commission to investigate abuses in the Navy. In 1616, it is true, he was forced to surrender his half-share in the trusteeship of 'Roper's office', as part of the circuitous campaign by which its revenues were annexed for Bucking- ham. But he kept his recordership of Woodstock; he was appointed to lesser legal offices and then to a Justiceship in Wales and to the Chief Justiceship of Chester in 1620.[1]

The idea of government solidarity either in or outside parliament was almost unknown. True, when Sir Henry Marten, who was Judge of the Admiralty court as well as Dean of the Arches and Judge of the Prerogative Court of Canterbury, found himself totally opposed to Buckingham as Lord Admiral, over the case of 'the *St. Peter*' (a French prize) in 1627, he did offer to resign. But in every other respect he had proved himself a competent and obliging servant, and his offer was not taken up.[2] More characteristic was the way in which the Solicitor-General (Sir Robert Heath) and the Master of the Wards (Cranfield) joined in the attack on fee exactions and abuses committed by officers of the courts in the parliament of 1621; the principal hue and cry at the moment happened to be against the Exchequer, but it could easily have involved the court of Wards or the Crown law officers.[3]

Several officers who supported royal policy in general spoke out against the favour shown to high churchmen or Arminians, and against the Crown's alleged leniency towards Catholics. In 1621 the Clerks of the Pells (Sir Edward Wardour, a future royalist) called for the flogging and imprisonment of the luckless Catholic propa- gandist Floyd: this was less than some members wanted done to Floyd, but more than the Crown would have done left to itself.[4] In 1625 the Master of the Jewels (Sir Henry Mildmay), the Receiver

[1] See *D.N.B.*, E. Foss, *The Judges of England* (1848-64), and Whitelocke, *Liber Famelicus*.

[2] *D.N.B.*; *Cal. S.P. Dom., 1627-8*, pp. 184, 208.

[3] *Commons Debates 1621*, ed. W. Notestein, F. H. Relf, and H. Simpson (New Haven, 1935), III, 149-51, V, 16.

[4] *ibid.*, III, 123-8.

of the Court of Wards (Sir Miles Fleetwood), the Surveyor-General of Crown lands and Clerk of the Crown in King's Bench (Sir Thomas Fanshawe of Jenkins), and one of the Council Clerks extraordinary (Laurence Whitaker) can all be found attacking the Arminians, or at least indicating that their own views were *more Protestant* than contemporary royal policy. In 1629 Mildmay, Fleetwood, and Whitaker again spoke out against Arminianism and were joined in this by the Surveyor of the Wards (Sir Benjamin Rudyerd) and the Master of the Mint (Sir Robert Harley).[1]

Fleetwood's share in the attack on the Earl of Middlesex (Cranfield), his own colleague and superior in the court of Wards, during the 1624 parliament is in two respects different. He did not join in the attack until it was clear that it was approved of by Buckingham and Prince Charles, and he had a personal motive in that Cranfield had apparently accused him of official malpractices three years earlier. However, unlike the others, he did on at least one occasion, in the Oxford session of the 1625 parliament, speak against an immediate vote of supply and in favour of first setting up a general committee of grievances; by contrast Rudyerd, who generally acted as a spokesman in the Commons for his patrons the Herberts, and Mildmay tended to support royal policy in these parliaments, other than on religious questions. None of this group joined in the attack on Buckingham in 1626; and Fleetwood, like Rudyerd and Harley, spoke in favour of some kind of compromise on the constitutional-cum-privilege issue over the customs in 1629.[2] Of these men, only Harley was evicted from office in the 1630's.

In the 1620's Vane, who has already been referred to among the councillors and great officers, stood out above Fleetwood and co. less on account of his official position than by virtue of being more of a courtier, nearer to royal favour. His political position is at first sight more puzzling, but explicable in terms of his having become a firm supporter of royal policy from 1625 on. In 1621, when he was

[1] *Commons Debates 1625*, ed. S. R. Gardiner (Camden Soc., 1873), pp. 6, 26, 52, 136-7, 140-1; *Commons Debates 1629*, pp. 114, 116, 140, 176, 219-20.

[2] *Lords Debates 1624 and 1626*, ed. S. R. Gardiner (Camden Soc., 1879), p. 61; *Commons Debates 1625*, pp. 9, 30, 90, 114; *The Parliamentary History of England*, ed. W. Cobbett (1806-20), I, 1394, II, 101, 234-5, 272-3, 334-6, 419; *Commons Debates 1629*, pp. 108, 167, 189, 232, 235. For references to Cranfield's attack on Fleetwood in 1620-1 see Berks R.O., Packer MSS., O/1/151, 234, letters from Fleetwood to Buckingham.

Cofferer to the Prince, he had spoken up for the liberties of parliament, though in such a general way that it would have been unlikely to cause offence at court. He may have disapproved of the Prince's trip to Spain in 1623, engineered by Buckingham; various awkward and even contradictory orders were issued to him as head of the supply side of the Prince's household. The quarrel or coolness between him and Buckingham in 1624-5, reported by letter writers and thought worthy of mention by Clarendon, may have arisen from the 1623 fiasco. However, by mid-April 1625 Vane was said to have made it up with the Duke and to stand well with him, the King, and others at court; in June he was appointed co-Cofferer of the King's Household, after an uneasy interval of two and a half months, from the King's accession, without office. Thereafter, if Vane had doubts about royal policy, he kept them to himself. In the 1630's and early 1640's his political attitude again appears obscure, but is not altogether inexplicable.[1]

The difficulties which some officers experienced in supporting policies which as M.P.s they felt bound to criticize is well exemplified by Sir Robert Pye's speech to the 1625 parliament. As to his sincerity, opinions may differ: candidly insincere would be one description of it.

> The diseases of the state are not incurable, yet to be redresd by no meanes but by this House; wherein he doubted not but to acquaynte the House with some things which should be usefull, and was afrayd of none, or did so much care for his office as to neglect his duty to the publicke. He confest he had been raised by him that [was] now at the helme [i.e. Buckingham], yet he would not but these things had bene spoken, hopeinge that lorde will make a good use of them, and become an instrument of much good hearafter. And when tyme serves for a reformation he would speak as boldly as any man, and bee as forward himselfe to be an instrument of it. For the present hee wisheth we should give the Kinge contentment [i.e. by voting supply] that we may not open a way to the enemyes of the State to make up their own fortune by hurting the publicke.

However, like Fleetwood, in 1624 he had dutifully joined in the attack on his own chief (Cranfield, the Lord Treasurer), and in 1626 he was to stand firmly by Buckingham when he in turn faced impeach-

[1] Gardiner, *History*, IV, 257; *Commons Journals*, I, 665; *Cal. S.P. Dom.*, *1619-23*, pp. 503-14, 523, 550, 560-4, *1625-6*, pp. 10, 66; Clarendon, *Hist. Reb.*, II, 548-9.

ment. After his patron's death his concern for financial solvency led him, in the face of a very Hostile House, to oppose the third of the famous resolutions of 2 March 1629, namely the one condemning merchants who paid of their free will the extra customs duties not voted by parliament. As against this, in October 1627 Pye had written privately to Buckingham, to tell him that the government's financial position simply did not permit of the war being carried on.[1]

It would be wrong to picture medium-ranking office-holders always in opposition to, or expressing doubts about, royal policy. Many supported it, some vocally. A few indeed appear on occasions to have been *plus royaliste que le roi*.

The part played by Edmund Sawyer, the Revenue Auditor, in the Exchequer fee disputes has already been discussed. This was only one aspect of his career. Like Christopher Vernon he was an expert at discovering 'concealed' Crown lands and at spotting flaws in titles to property. Unlike Vernon he entered briefly on the stage of national politics. He was knighted in 1624/5, and created a Master of Requests extraordinary in May 1628; on 11 June a letter writer mentioned him as a possible successor to Weston as Chancellor of the Exchequer. But his very diligence, in preparing the new 'book of rates' for the customs, which had commended him to the Crown, proved his undoing in the Commons. Presumably forewarned of their impending attack he absented himself from the House; ironically it was the future Attorney-General and royalist Chief Justice, John Bankes, then himself without government connexions, who reported from the committee on Tonnage and Poundage that Sawyer (a future royalist of a most passive if not neutralist character), was deserving of punishment by the House. Accordingly on 21 June he was not only deprived of his seat but barred from ever being an M.P. again, and was ordered to be committed to the Tower during the pleasure of the Commons. Luckily for Sawyer, parliament was adjourned on the 26th, and he was released two days later. Perhaps he had learnt his lesson, for there is no sign of his ever having played a political role again.[2]

---

[1] *Commons Debates 1625*, p. 113; *Lords Debates 1624 and 1626*, pp. 61, 66-7, 226-7; Hist. MSS. Comm., *Lonsdale* (*Lowther*), p. 13; *Commons Debates 1629*, p. 171; *Cal. S.P. Dom., 1627-8*, p. 353.

[2] *Cal. S.P. Dom., 1611-40, passim*; D.K. *39th, 43rd Rpts.*; Hist. MSS. Comm., *Cowper*, I, 354, 356; *Commons Journals*, I, 899-900, 916-17; *Acts Privy Council, 1627-8*, p. 473; Birch, *Court and Times*, I, 378; *Cal. Cttee. Advcmt. Money*, p. 181; *Cal. Cttee. Compdg.*, pp. 2939-40.

iv THE 1630's

After 1629 the intermission of parliaments makes it necessary to look elsewhere for evidence. It is however clear that lack of support for royal policy persisted, and in some cases became more marked. As before, differences of religion are the easiest to determine. It would be going too far to say that the main division *inside* Charles I's government corresponded to that between Catholics and Protestants. Even so, a list of the open, secret, and 'death-bed' papists, and the probable fellow-travellers with Rome, indicates the reality of this division: the Lord Treasurer 1628-35 (Portland), the Chancellor of the Exchequer 1629-42 (Cottington), one of the Secretaries of State 1632-40 (Windebank), the Queen's Chancellor 1628-35 (Lord Savage), the Receiver-General of the Duchy of Lancaster 1620-36 (Lord Molyneux), the Queen's Secretary 1638-41 (Sir John Wynter), one of the four Council Clerks in ordinary 1623-41 (Sir William Becher), the Paymaster of the Gentlemen Pensioners 1626-33 (Sir Henry Mynne), a Groom of the Bedchamber (Endymion Porter), the Surveyor of the Works (Inigo Jones), and the Clerk of the Ordnance 1636-41 (Sherborne). In secular matters the Catholics were not always united. For instance, Cottington and Porter were Hispanophile and would almost certainly have liked to see a firmer pro-Spanish policy pursued in the 1630's, while Windebank's preference seems to have oscillated between a Bourbon and a Habsburg alignment. The Catholics in the administration and at Court were important primarily because of the psychological effect which their presence had on the more militant, Puritan-inclined Protestants.

Unless their own religious convictions and sympathies had changed, those who had objected to the progress of Arminianism in the 1620's were bound to disapprove even more strongly of the Laudian church in the 1630's. That this was true of Fleetwood, Mildmay, and Whitaker can only be inferred. Rudyerd is found as a member of the Providence Island Company, whose role as an 'opposition' group was first noticed by A. P. Newton and has since been elaborated by Professor J. H. Hexter. Besides Receiver-General Pym, who was the company's Treasurer, the Clerk of the Duchy of Lancaster court (Sir Gilbert Gerrard) and the Clerk of the Checque (or paymaster) of the Messengers of the Chamber (John Graunt) were also members.[1]

It is hard to distinguish those who disapproved of Laudianism at home from those who felt that the Stuart Kings were betraying the Protestant cause abroad, particularly by not helping the Calvinists of the Palatinate. Nor indeed is it more than a convenience to separate these two aspects of Caroline policy.

From 1615 to 1628 John Packer had enjoyed considerable political influence, and a sizeable income from fees and gratuities, as Buckingham's secretary. But after his master's death, not only was he left merely with what he could make as a Clerk of the Privy Seal, but he must have had to swallow his disapproval of the Crown's religious and foreign policies. His benefactions to continental refugees, and his other good works have an unmistakably Puritan flavour.[2] As a champion in prose and verse, in three languages, of international Protestant (though basically Lutheran) solidarity, the acting Latin Secretary 1624-42, and German Language Interpreter 1631-42, Georg Rudolph Weckherlin cannot but have disapproved both of Laud and of Charles I's foreign policy. Indeed, the confused and indecisive nature of this policy was due partly to the chronic disagreements and incompatibilities between the two Secretaries of State, Coke and Windebank, and their respective assistants, Weckherlin and the crypto-Catholic Reade. René Augier, English Agent in Paris c. 1629-49, should almost certainly be included in the Coke axis; he probably had Huguenot leanings, though he is a more obscure figure than Weckherlin.[3]

[1] See A. P. Newton, *The Colonising Activities of the English Puritans* (New Haven, 1914), esp. chs. II, X; J. H. Hexter, *The Reign of King Pym* (Cambridge, Mass., 1941), ch. IV.

[2] *D.N.B.*, XV, 31-2; Hist. MSS. Comm., *Abergavenny, Braye, etc.*, Braye MSS., p. 174, Packer's 'Life and Character', possibly by his son-in-law John Browne, Clerk of the Parliament; *The Fortescue Papers*, ed. S. R. Gardiner (Camden Soc., 1871); Berks R.O., Packer MSS. (political and personal items additional to Braye and Fortescue printed collections).

[3] *D.N.B.*, XX, 1039-40; L. W. Forster, 'G. R. Weckherlin in England', *German Life and Letters*, III (1938-9), 107-16; Forster, *Georg Rudolph Weckherlin*; Forster, 'Sources for G. R. Weckherlin's Life in England: the correspondence', *The Modern Languages Review*, XLI (1946), 186-95. Berks R.O., Trumbull MSS., vols. XX, parts of XIX, and XXXV, and several loose bundles are in fact Weckherlin Papers (Weckherlin's daughter married William Trumbull the second, son of the English Agent

Disapproval of Charles I's foreign policy for not being militantly Protestant was by no means limited to foreigners and refugees in his service. Sir Francis Nethersole (Agent to the Queen of Bohemia, 1623-34) got into trouble in 1633 for trying to raise a loan for the liberation of the Palatinate without royal approval.[1] The distinguished diplomat and traveller Sir Thomas Roe (Ambassador to the Mogul Empire 1615-18, Ambassador to Turkey 1621-8, special envoy to Sweden and Poland 1629-30, Chancellor of the Order of the Garter 1637-42, Ambassador extraordinary to Hamburg, Ratisbon, and Vienna 1638-40) was for ever demanding a more positive, anti-Catholic and anti-Habsburg foreign and colonial policy. And it appears from the evidence that Laud may have been less than wholly honest with him in 1632, when Roe was hoping to succeed Lord Dorchester as Secretary of State and Laud avoided making clear that he was committed to helping Windebank, the successful candidate. It was however the Earl of Holland, the nominal head of the Providence Island Company, to whom Roe sent a long discourse on foreign affairs; as the history of the Commonwealth and Protectorate shows, it was scarcely easier for England to have a 'Protestant' foreign policy in the mid-seventeenth century than it was for the Labour government to pursue a 'Socialist' foreign policy from 1945 to 1951. After an attempt had been made to conciliate Roe by restoring him to office in 1637-8, he again seems to have had the illusion that Laud might favour his candidature, to succeed Coke as Secretary early in 1640; again he was disillusioned.[2]

There were other officers whose Protestant sympathies may have been equally strong, but were less openly avowed. What did Christopher Vernon, Secondary of the Pipe, think of the régime in the1630's?

in Brussels and Council Clerk who died in 1635). For Reade see Chapter 3, s. ii; Higham, *Secretary of State*, p. 155; *Cal. S.P. Dom., 1631-40, passim*; *Foedera*, XX, 409-13. For Augier see C. H. Firth and S. C. Lomas, *Notes on the diplomatic relations of England and France 1603-88* (Oxford, 1906) and sources given there; the *Huguenot Record Soc.* volumes contain refs. to several other seventeenth-century Augiers, but not, as far as can be seen, to this one.

[1] *D.N.B.*, XIV, 229-31.

[2] *D.N.B.*, XVII, 89-93; see esp. *Cal. S.P. Dom., 1631-3*, pp. 211-12, 350, 367, 401, *1637*, pp. 336, 429-30, 456, 529, 554, *1637-8*, p. 29, *1639-40*, pp. 525-6; *Cal. S.P. Col. 1574-1660*, p. 257. The formation of a West India Co. was one of Roe's favourite projects. Excellent as is the *D.N.B.* article, Roe still awaits his biographer; he deserves a good one.

The books which he named in his will as being among his most cherished possessions were not only Coke on Littleton but also the ultra-Protestant sixteenth-century biblical commentaries of Beza and Tremellius.[1] What too of Sir Theodore Turquet de Mayerne, Physician-in-chief to the King and Queen of England, and Physician extraordinary to Louis XIII of France? Having succeeded in winning complete tax exemption in this country, he went on to complain to the Secretary of State about the excessive price of passports! More to the point, Mayerne, a godson of Calvin's right-hand man Beza, left money in his will for an isolation hospital in Geneva and for refugee congregations in London.[2]

The direct effects of patronage on the political and religious sympathies of office-holders can be seen clearly in the Navy. The appointment of the Earl of Northumberland as Admiral of the Fleet in 1636-7 and Lord Admiral in 1638 meant that by 1640 the co-Treasurer, Surveyor, and patronage Secretary were all Puritans of one kind or another, while the Clerk of the Acts may have had eanings the same way.[3]

Everyone agrees with the truism that religion had a much wider and more vital influence over men's lives and thoughts in the England of Charles I than it does today. But there is very much less agreement about the explanations of seventeenth-century religious differences and their connexion with peoples' material interests. Without becoming involved in a general debate about why different people adhered to different religious positions, it may be enough to say here that the motives for such adherence seem sometimes, but not always or necessarily, to have been complementary to material ones.

Nor is the nature of the connexion between men's material circumstances and their political attitudes always self-evident. It

---

[1] Sources as given in Chapter 5, s. iii, esp. PCC 144 Bowyer.

[2] *D.N.B.*, XIII, 150-2; Dep. Kpr., *43rd Rept.*, app., p. 18; *Cal. S.P. Dom., 1636-7*, p. 21; PCC 115 Aylett.

[3] The younger Vane; William Batten, 'furious in the new fancies of religion' (Clarendon, *Hist. Reb.*, II, 225); Thomas Smith, 'highly infected with Presbyterian principles' (P. Warwick, *Memoires of the reigne of King Charles I* (1701), p. 120); Thomas Barlow (see refs. in Pepys's *Diary* for 1660-5).

could be argued that Sir Robert Pye's brush with Laud and Wentworth in 1637-8 angered and frightened him. And that this plus his son's marriage to Hampden's daughter had far more to do with his political attitude than any high-flown ideas of the public interest. A more obscure case concerns Sir Miles Fleetwood. In 1634-6 he was involved in a complicated and apparently inconclusive dispute with Sir Francis Crane (Chancellor of the Order of the Garter 1626-35, and chief manager of the Mortlake tapestry works 1619-35) and then with Crane's executor's. It involved Grafton Park, Northants, of which Crane was keeper; he had apparently obtained the mortgage on some of the land there recently alienated by the Crown, and by this means he was allegedly in the process of acquiring the whole of the ex-Crown property at far below its true value. £18,000 was said to be at stake, and Fleetwood may have been standing up for the King's interests against those of a courtly monopolist. It is perhaps also symptomatic that Crane was a commissioner for the emparking of Richmond, to which reference has already been made. In addition he was Auditor of the revenues which the King had had as Prince, at a Fee of £100 a year, an annuitant on the Duchy of Cornwall, and co-patentee for the issue of farthings. He was a client of the Howards, and it was this which led to his being involved in the farthings project.[1]

Nor can it be proved whether Sir Benjamin Rudyerd's attitude was more influenced by his previous reliance on the patronage of the Herberts and of Hay (later Earl of Carlisle) or by Protestant and constitutional principles, even supposing the two can be distinguished. The fourth Earl of Pembroke's attitude towards 'Thorough' has already been discussed. In his capacity as an ex-client of Carlisle, Rudyerd may also have been influenced by his widow, Lucy Hay (née Percy), and so indirectly by her brother, the Earl of Northumberland; but there is no evidence of this.

Likewise Sir Gilbert Gerrard's membership of the Providence Island Company may merely have reflected his friendship with the

---

[1] For Crane see *D.N.B.*, V, 9-10; *Foedera*, XVIII-XX, and *Cal. S.P. Dom. 1618-35*, *passim*; T 56/1, pp. 39b-40; M. F. S. Hervey, *The Life, Correspondence, and Collections of Thomas Howard, Earl of Arundel* (Cambridge, 1921), pp. 246-7. For the Grafton case see *Foedera*, XIX, 526; Dep. Kpr., *39th Rept.*, app., pp. 412, 420, 443-4; Knowler, I, 336, 524.

Rich family (the Earls of Warwick and Holland) and with Pym, rather than any strong interests or convictions of his own. There is a little evidence to suggest that this was not so. For nearly twenty years he was involved in a series of quarrels with his Middlesex neighbours the Pitts of Sudbury, principally with George Pitt, the Usher of Chancery. Their quarrel originally arose out of a dispute about a rabbit warren and other property questions on the boundary of the two estates; it soon spread to a dispute about the use of the chancel in Harrow church; it was a long drawn out battle, and Gerrard's descendants were still at law with Pitt's successors (the Rush-outs) in the 1680's! At one stage Pitt minuted for his Star Chamber counsel 'he causeth me to be unjustlie taxed [for Purveyance probably], he stirreth my tenants against me, he doth not pay ship money'. The last charge at least can be substantiated, for in October 1636 Sir Gilbert was £12 behind with his assessment, and the Council Clerk responsible was strongly advised to make an example of him. In the event it was Pitt who trimmed: his temporary reconciliation with Gerrard in 1644-5 signified his own submission to the one-time non-payers of Ship Money rather than pliability on the part of Gerrard, friend of Pym and in-law of the Barringtons. In the mid-1630's Pitt had his own troubles with the Crown. He was granted a royal pardon for all offences committed in his office, and at the same time his fees were fixed and authorized; it seems more than likely that he paid a heavy composition for this, although no official record of it has been found.[1]

Another future parliamentarian whose position in the 1630's may have been, to say the least, equivocal was Sir Richard Wynne, Receiver-General to the Queen 1629-49. As Mrs. Keeler rightly points out, Wynne's father had been out of favour at the beginning of Richard's career; he owed his advancement to a skilful blend of Howard and Herbert patronage. Mrs. Keeler also refers to Bishop Williams (Lord Keeper 1621-5) as having been a family friend; but in so far as Wynne was a friend of Williams, who was his own cousin,

---

[1] G.E.C., *Btge.*, I, 142; Keeler, *Long Parlt.*, pp. 185-6; Newton, *Colonising Activities*, p. 68; *Cal. S.P. Dom., 1636-7*, p. 155; Middlesex R.O., MSS. 76/779-845, 864, 1175, 1181. For Pitt see Chancery sources already cited; Bodl. Bankes MS. 43/4; Hist. MSS. Comm., *Hastings*, II, 77 (apparent ref. in a news letter to Pitt compounding, at the same date as his pardon); Middlesex R.O., MSS. 76/777, 848; *Cal. Cttee. Advcmt. Money*, p. 170; D. Lysons, *Environs of London* (1795-6), II, 563.

his father's god-son, and his sister-in-law's uncle, this might surely have led him to disapprove much more strongly of 'Thorough', in the person of Laud, than would these other connexions. In the middle and later 1630's Laud conducted what can only be called a vendetta against the moderate and worldly Bishop of Lincoln. Wynne's narrative of Prince Charles's Spanish trip in 1623 also suggests a certain insularity as well as a fairly robust Protestantism. And, apart from commending himself to a French Princess by his unimpeachable Hispanophobia, he seems an altogether odd choice as the holder of Henrietta Maria's purse-strings.[1]

The coolness of some medium-ranking officials towards the Crown may well have been due to their having been passed over for promotion, and in a few cases actually demoted or even deprived of office. The two Sir Arthur Ingrams, father and son, were dropped from the Secretaryship to the Council in the North in 1632/3; and in 1634 Wentworth accused the elder Sir Arthur of double dealing over the northern Recusant revenues. In 1634 Nethersole was dismissed by the King for insolence and disobedience when he refused to apologize for his blunder over the loan for the King's sister, Elizabeth of Bohemia and the Palatinate; even Secretary Coke, in general no enemy to the Electoral cause, questioned the propriety of the same man receiving two stipends, as her Secretary in England and as the King's Agent with the German Princes. Then there was Roe, out of office and, to judge from his complaints, out of pocket too, 1630-7. In 1633 Sir Henry Marten, who died in September 1641 but whose son was the first avowed republican in the Long Parliament, was replaced at the court of the Arches by Sir John Lambe, who was apparently reckoned a more pliant tool by the new Archbishop. In 1635-6, as Mrs. Keeler points out, Laurence Whitaker was passed over for promotion from an extraordinary to an ordinary Council Clerkship. And Weckherlin appears to have considered

[1] Keeler, *Long Parliament*, pp. 402-3; *Cal. Wynn Papers* (Aberystwyth, 1926); J. F. Rees, *Studies in Welsh History* (Cardiff, 1947), ch. IV; A. H. Dodd, *Studies in Stuart Wales* (Cardiff, 1952), pp. 130, 179-80, etc.; National Library of Wales, Wynnstay MSS. (some items on Sir Richard not in the Wynn Papers); *Autobiography and Correspondence of S. D'Ewes*, II, 415-58, 'Account of the Journey of the Prince's Servants into Spain A.D. 1623 by Sir Richard Wynne'. For Bishop Williams see J. Hacket, *Scrinia Reserata* (1693); *D.N.B.*; B. D. Roberts, *Mitre and Musket* (1938); and H. R. Trevor-Roper, *Archbishop Laud* (1940).

himself to have been ill rewarded for his services and deserving of
better pay if not also a more senior post.[1]

V THE POLITICS OF ANGRY MEN

It is tempting to equate most if not all of the senior and medium-
ranking officers who did not positively support the King during the
Civil War with those who had grievances of this kind. Deprivation,
demotion, failure to be promoted, punishment with fines or compositions (for offences like taking excessive fees, which the Crown's
meanness, combined with the inflation, all but forced upon them)—
these factors may surely afford sufficient explanations without drag-
ging in dubious arguments, based on admittedly tenuous evidence,
about men's attitudes and beliefs. But because such evidence inevitably is almost always tenuous, it does not follow that men's thoughts
are an unimportant influence on their political actions. It is of course
possible to agree with this, and still to argue that such ideological
alienation as did exist among office-holders was merely the effect of
previous losses in wealth, status, prestige, and self-respect. Imperfect
as it is, the evidence can be tested a little further.

What may for convenience be called the 'In-Out' hypothesis of
officers' political behaviour seems at first sight to fit best at the highest
level, among the peers and privy councillors. The Earl of Cork and
Lords Loftus and Mountnorris were all dismissed or suspended
from their positions in Ireland by Wentworth; none could be
described as a royalist, though Cork died in 1643 and Loftus was
more or less of a neutral. The Earl of Salisbury had been cheated of
his reversion to the Mastership of the Wards in 1635, and fobbed off
instead with the Captaincy of the Pensioners. The Earl of Leicester
had not been properly paid as Ambassador in Paris and had also
been one of the disappointed candidates for the Secretaryship of
State in 1639-40. The Earl of Northumberland had wanted to be

[1] Besides *D.N.B.* for the Ingrams see *Foedera*, XIX, 410-16; Sheffield
C.L., Wentworth Woodhouse MSS., Str. 8/136-9, 12d/309, 13a/56,
13c/233; for Nethersole *Cal. S.P. Dom., 1633-4*, p. 86 *et seq.*, *1634-5*, p. 48;
Knowler, I, 225; for Roe see p. 359, n. 2, above, and *Cal. S.P. Dom.,
1631-40, passim*; for Marten *ibid.*, *1631-3*, p. 388, *1633-4*, pp. 330, 401;
for Whitaker, Keeler, *Long Parlt.*, pp. 388-9; for Weckherlin p. 358, n. 3,
above, and *Cal. S.P. Dom., 1629-31*, pp. 514, 557, *1639-40*, p. 434; P.R.O.,
T 56/7, p. 226; T 56/14, p. 21.

made Lord Admiral for life since 1636 or 1637, but in 1638 was instead given this post on a seventeen-year tenure (or less if the Duke of York died as a minor). The Earl of Holland was a hard man to please, considering all that he did achieve. He was disappointed when he was not made Admiral of the Fleet in 1636; and, according to Clarendon, he was even upset in 1640 when Northumberland and Conway were appointed respectively General and General of the Horse for the second northern expedition, although he had been against the whole undertaking. Secretary Coke, after being compulsorily retired in January 1640, withdrew to Derbyshire; at the age of 79 or 80 his neutrality in 1642 was reasonable, but he did not *voluntarily* subscribe money to either side. Bishop Williams, out of office and favour from the end of 1625 to the winter of 1640-1, followed a tortuous path thereafter, but can best be described as a trimmer, or side-changer with a royalist bias. Lord Stanhope, who was forced to surrender his patent as Postmaster-General in 1637, and had received none of his promised compensation five years later, played no part in public affairs for the next twenty years, except to plead his poverty to successive governments, and finally squeezed £4,000 compensation out of Charles II.[1]

It remains to be considered how many of these peers and councillors had been disobliged because they were *already* out of sympathy with the régime. Otherwise the 'In-Out' theory may lead to a confusion of cause and effect. Thus, considering his connexions and his own behaviour, the surprising thing about Holland is not that the King disobliged him, but that he was so much obliged. And up to a point the same could be said of Leicester, and even Pembroke. Indeed, if Clarendon can be believed, Charles I himself felt that only Northumberland had really bitten the hand that had fed him.[2]

But since it appears to explain several cases of non-royalism among the great officers and office-holding peers, the 'In-Out' hypothesis clearly deserves to be tested more fully. It can of course only account for the royalism, neutralism, or parliamentarianism of past and present office-holders. It cannot, by definition, prove anything about the allegiance of those who had never held any position in the central government.

---

[1] See *D.N.B.*, or G.E.C., or both; for Stanhope see sources on the Post Office, Chapter 2, s. ii; for Holland and the army commands in 1640 see Clarendon, *Hist. Reb.*, I, 185.

[2] Clarendon, *The Life of . . . by himself* (Oxford, 1761), I, 153.

At the most obscure level it is unusual even to know enough about those concerned to say whether or not they were passed over or had any similar reason to be disgruntled. Even when their allegiance in the Civil War is known, or can be inferred, there is seldom enough other evidence to speculate about the *individual* motives of junior officials. It is not therefore profitable to apply this test to the A-C group used in Chapter 5, which includes representatives of all ranks.

At the middle level, the 'In-Out' hypothesis can certainly be tested on the 200 men in the second group. Several of those to whom it can reasonably be applied have already been mentioned as having been opposed to, or out of sympathy with, royal policy in the 1620's and 1630's. But there are others.

Sir William Balfour was compelled to resign from the Lieutenantcy of the Tower in December 1641, having held this post of special trust for over ten years. But this was far from being the sole cause of his later accepting a command in the parliamentary horse; he was removed from the Tower because he was already believed to be unreliable. In 1637 he had at last been paid part of the arrears owed him from military operations in Friesland nine years before, the rest remaining unpaid. Sympathy for his Scottish compatriots may be indicated by his having advanced only £30 for the 1639 expedition, and nothing in 1640.[1]

By contrast, Sir William Becher resigned his Council clerkship in January 1641 because he was obnoxious, not to the King but to the House of Commons, being suspected *inter alia* of Romanism. He spent most of the next ten years abroad and in the wars gave the King little, if any, financial help. Although he was probably in his sixties, if Becher had been kept on in office he might well have been a more active royalist. William Carne has already been mentioned as an office-holder who went down-hill financially. His exit from office in 1640 was due to his own exigencies rather than to royal action, and therefore can only be very indirectly related to his subsequent parliamentarianism. Sir Ranulphe Crewe, whose dismissal from the bench has already been discussed, is a neutral who seems at first to fit the 'In-Out' hypothesis. If his views had been moderate and his sympathies evenly balanced, then his deprivation sixteen years earlier and his subsequent absence from public life might well

[1] *D.N.B.*, I, 979; *Cal. S.P. Dom., 1641-3*, p. 210; *D'Ewes's Journal*, ed. Coates, pp. 330-1. A Constable of the Tower had been appointed over his head in 1640.

have decided him not to support the King, especially as he was in his seventies. But since Crewe had disapproved so strongly of the forced loan in 1626 he must surely have been all the more shocked by the financial proceedings of the 1630's, and in recording his death an observer in Crewe's native county had no doubt that he was a firm friend to the Parliament. To treat loss of office in isolation from such a man's evident opinions is quite misleading, unless it is to be argued that by staying in office he would have changed his views and supported Ship Money, etc.[1]

Sir Sackville Crowe had been removed from the Treasurership of the Navy in 1629. He was provisionally appointed Ambassador to Turkey in 1633, but only appears to have taken up this post in 1638 or 1639. He also acted as co-farmer of the Forest of Dean Ironworks from 1636 to 1640, but whether to his advantage or not is unclear. His royalism could be said to illustrate the sequence 'In-Out-In', though there is no evidence whatever that Crowe would have been other than a royalist if he had not re-entered office before 1642.[2]

Sir John Evelyn of Godstone lost the royal gunpowder contract in 1636 after it had been in his family for three generations. Presumably it was thought that Sam Cordwell, who already supplied the East India Company and had a useful patron in Sir Henry Vane, would give the Crown better value for money. Sir John's nephew, another John Evelyn, was also a parliamentarian M.P. He was a son of George the Six Clerk who had died in 1635 and a brother of Arthur who had failed to secure an alleged reversion to his place in 1636-7. No other reason is offered by Mr. de Beer or Mrs. Keeler why these two relatives of the diarist should have been parliamentarians; loss of contract and failure to succeed to office may well have been decisive in their respective cases.[3]

---

[1] For Becher see Stoye, *Travellers*, part one, chs. I-II; *Cal. S.P. Dom., 1640-1*, p. 433; *Cal. Cttee. Advcmt. Money*, pp. 1059-60. For Crewe see *D.N.B.*, Foss, *Judges*, and *Cal. Cttee. Advcmt. Money*; T. Malbon, *Memorials of the Civil War in Cheshire* (ed. J. Hall, Lancs & Ches Rec. Soc., XIX, 1889), pp. 193-4.

[2] For Crowe see *Cal. S.P. Dom., 1625-47, passim*; A. C. Wood, *A History of the Levant Company* (Oxford, 1935); H. R. Schubert, 'The King's Ironworks in the Forest of Dean', *Journ. of the Iron & Steel Inst.* vol. 173 (1953).

[3] *Cal. S.P. Dom., 1636-7, passim*; Keeler, *Long Parlt.*, pp. 168-70; de Beer, *Evelyn's Diary*, I, 6-7, II, 553-4 n. 7. For Cordwell see Household sources, Vane's will (PCC 159 Aylett), and V.C.H. *Surrey*, ii, 310, 319-21.

Sir Thomas Hatton (1583-1658), cousin of Queen Elizabeth's Lord Chancellor and uncle of the first Lord Hatton, Comptroller to Charles I at Oxford (1643-6), is another ex-office-holder whose support for the King was, to say the least, tepid. In the 1630's he was the Queen's Surveyor-General; in 1639 or 1640 he was replaced by Mr. Robert Long, future Secretary to Charles II when Prince of Wales. It may conceivably also be relevant here that Hatton's wife was a daughter of the Sir Giles Alington who was so heavily fined for marrying his own niece; perhaps more significant, she was a niece of the second Earl of Exeter (Sir Edward Coke's brother-in-law) and a first cousin of the third Earl—one of the twelve peers who petitioned the King to call a parliament and make peace with the Scots in August 1640.[1]

Cornelius Holland (c. 1600-1660's) did not rise from such obscurity as Edward Sherborne, but he can fairly be classified as a middle-class careerist who rose socially and prospered by means of office. He came of a London trading family and was educated at Merchant Taylors' School and then at Cambridge. By 1626 he was a clerk in the Cofferer's office under Sir Henry Vane; in 1629 he became Clerk of the Acatry, the sub-department responsible for buying the Household's supplies of meat; in 1635 he became Clerk Comptroller of the newly established Household of the Prince; in 1638 he was promoted to be Paymaster and sole Clerk of Greencloth to the Prince. As long as the star of his patron Vane continued in the ascendant Holland might expect another promotion at each successive enlargement of the Prince's establishment; he might expect to become Cofferer to the Prince (as Vane had been to the Prince's father), and then perhaps a Knight and who could tell what besides. What went wrong? Did Holland desert the King and become a leading member of the Rump simply in imitation of the Vanes? It is worth trying to establish whether his being passed over and his moving into opposition preceded or followed their alienation from the court. The Vanes were in disgrace from April 1641 and lost office at the end of the year. In January 1641 Sir David Cunningham, a Scottish courtier already referred to as a reversion hunter, was created Cofferer to the Prince over Holland's head; in April Cunningham took over from him the management of the wine composition

[1] G.E.C., *Btge.*, II, 97; *Cal. Cttee. Advcmt. Money*, p. 322; E 101/438/7; N.L.W., Wynnstay MSS. 166, 168. For Alington see Gardiner, *History*, VII, 251-2; for the Earls of Exeter see G.E.C.

in the out-ports (a form of Purveyance by which the Household was supplied at less than market rates); to complete the rebuff, in August 1641 Cunningham, who at least was a baronet and a minor court favourite, was succeeded as Cofferer by a mere Esquire of origins as humble and obscure as Holland's own. By October Holland had become a spokesman of the anti-court, anti-episcopal party, and from then on he was committed to the extremist wing of the parliamentary cause. Therefore it is not possible to relate the chronology of his defection exactly to the Vanes' position. There is however some evidence that Holland's disappointments in 1641 followed rather than preceded the first signs of his unreliability as a royal supporter: in 1639 he refused to subscribe to the loan for the first 'Bishops' War' and was apparently not even called upon in 1640. Too much cannot be made of this because some future royalists were also non-subscribers, but, unlike Sir John Heydon and perhaps others of them, Holland was in no financial difficulties; in the spring of 1642, no longer an office-holder, he subscribed £600 to parliament's loan for the reconquest of Ireland.[1]

Along with his patron, Secretary Coke, Thomas Witherings (c. 1596-1651) was responsible for one of the few authentic improvements achieved under the early Stuarts: the reorganization of the postal system. Witherings had joint charge of the foreign posts from 1632 to 1635 and sole charge of them from 1635 to 1637; he was also acting manager of the home posts from 1634 or 1635 to 1637; and from then until 1640 he was sole manager of the whole system under the Secretaries of State as Postmaster-Generals *ex officio*. The Coke-Witherings reforms aimed at making the mails quicker and surer, but also more profitable to the Crown. A crucial element of Witherings' plan was the transformation of the subordinate 'Posts' and carriers into salaried public servants, and the annexation of the fees and charges to the Crown. Needless to say, the reformers encountered furious opposition, from Lord Stanhope, Postmaster-General until 1637, from Mathew de Quester, manager of the foreign posts until 1632, and his heir Joco, from Martin Frizell, co-manager of these with Witherings in 1632-5, from Frizell's patrons, the Earl of Arundel and Surrey (for whom he was a picture buyer on the continent) and Secretary Windebank, from Stanhope's deputy,

---

[1] *D.N.B.*; Keeler, *Long Parlt.*, pp. 218-19; P.R.O., E 101/438/1, LS 13/251, pp. 28, 30, 83, 100, 117, 156, 160, 170, 172; *D'Ewes's Journal*, ed. Coates, p. 30; Rushworth, *Hist. Colls.*, II, ii, 914, III, i, 564.

Endymion Porter, and from most of the subordinate 'Posts', who resented encroachments on their traditional methods and forms of remuneration. Naturally Witherings was attacked for not practising what he preached, for having bought his own office and for selling subordinate places at exorbitant rates. True or false, that was to be expected.

He was also attacked on 'class' grounds. Windebank found it outrageous that 'a broken mercer' could, by misuse of the King's bounty, have grown to be worth £800 a year from land alone, while Frizell cast doubts on the technical qualifications of 'a home-bred shop-keeper without languadges'. This is not the only sign that when men of non-armigerous origin were accused of crimes and misdemeanours committed in office, they tended to be judged more severely than their gentle-born colleagues. The Star Chamber judgment on George Mynne has already been quoted. And when another extortioner (Goodhand, the Feodary of the West Riding) was condemned in the same court a year or two later, he was said to have been

> a goldsmith first, and then a sollicitor of causes in the court of wardes, and then he becam a feodary. After he was a feodary he continued a sollicitor of causes in the court of wardes.

At a much higher level, in 1624 Bishop Williams attacked the great Lionel Cranfield as 'a man *plebeius*, creeping into soe many offices, where there are soe many worthy and learned noblemen'. And, when demanding economy in the royal household, Sir Edward Coke said that it

> must be reform'd otherwise than by such men as leape from the shopp to the green clothe; by occasion wherof hee named Sir Lionell Cranfield, and Sir Symon Harvey.

This attitude, of what can only be called jealousy on the part of the upper class, is also displayed in James I's abortive order to the Judges,

> that none be from henceforth admitted into the Society of any House [i.e. Inn] of Court, that is not a Gentleman by descent.[1]

[1] See Chapter 3, s. iii; SP 16/313/33; *Lords Debates in 1624 and 1626* (ed. S. R. Gardiner, Camd. Soc., 1879), p. 83; *Commons Debates in 1625* (ed. Gardiner, Camd. Soc., 1873), p. 86; W. Dugdale, *Origines Judiciales* (1666), p. 316.

The political effect of such social snobbery is hard to gauge. Some self-made office-holders may, as a result of it, have been led to adopt protective camouflage by identifying themselves all the more closely with the Court and the upper class; others, including perhaps most of those who were openly attacked on these class grounds, may have been further alienated from a régime which was ready to exploit their abilities without concealing its contempt for their persons.

It is perhaps not surprising that Witherings only survived the retirement of his patron, Coke, by a few months. He was soon declared guilty of almost every conceivable form of extortion, corruption, dishonesty, and incompetence. In his place Windebank and Vane appointed the suave bankrupt international financier Philip Burlamachi, who was living in London protected by the Crown from his creditors. The Long Parliament tried to have Witherings restored in 1641-2, but without success; claimants to the office multiplied and his hopes faded. Apparently a neutral in the Civil War, Witherings was twice acquitted on being accused of secret royalist leanings. He died a wronged man, but not one who had in fact done any better out of the Long Parliament than out of Charles I.[1]

Several of the parliamentarians and neutrals who had previously been passed over for promotion or deprived of office therefore had other grounds for not supporting the King. Their rebuffs before 1642 and their attitude after that may alike have been the effects of their already having had particular beliefs, sympathies, and interests. Balfour, Crewe, Cornelius Holland, Nethersole, Whitaker, and Witherings may all already have held low church (or Puritan) convictions, or constitutionalist political views, or both. Among the peers and councillors, this may have been true in varying degrees of the Earls of Cork, Leicester, and Northumberland, of Sir John Coke, Sir Thomas Roe, and Bishop Williams. At the top, only Lords Loftus, Mountnorris and Stanhope, and on the middle level only the Evelyns and the Ingrams seem to provide unmistakable support for the 'In-Out' hypothesis.

Those who were alienated from the Crown in these ways can be

---

[1] Sources on Post Office as for Lord Stanhope; see also Bodl. Bankes MSS. 5/63, 51/39; SP 16/375/20, 535/36; Essex R.O., Sage MS. 556; *Visitation of London, 1633-5* (Harl. Soc.), II, 340; *Cal. Ctee. Advcmt. Money*, p. 1052; *Cal. Cttee. Compdg.*, pp. 2297-8; PCC 251 Grey.

thought of as the converse of those previous opponents of the Court who were won over to its cause: Digges, Noy, Bankes, Edward Herbert—and greatest of them all Wentworth. But with them too it cannot be assumed that their new-found support for royal policy was due entirely to their being given office, important as this obviously was, and with some of them decisively so.

vi SIR ROBERT HARLEY: A CASE HISTORY

The history of Sir Robert Harley can profitably be considered in detail in order to test this theory of the connexion between office-holding and political allegiance.

The organization of the Mint has already been briefly described, with its rather curious dual control under a Master or Co-Masters, and a Warden or co-Wardens.[1] In 1625 the Wardens were Buckingham's half-brother, Sir Edward Villiers, and an obscure ex-diplomat with Kent and Surrey connexions, Sir William Parkhurst. From August 1625 to his death a year later Villiers was in Ireland as President of Munster. During his lifetime Parkhurst, though not a deputy, was probably in practice a salaried *locum tenens*; not long after Villiers' death Anthony St. Legar, alias Leger, also of Kent, became co-Warden. He and Parkhurst only come into the story of Harley and the Mint incidentally, but their existence must not be forgotten.

In July 1623 Sir Randall Cranfield, brother of the Lord Treasurer, became Master. He was described by Chamberlain the letter writer as 'a meane merchant'; as with his brother, with Witherings and others, class jealousy may have aggravated disapproval of his conduct in office. Sir Randall was suspended in July 1624 ostensibly for corruption and incompetence; 'the office', wrote Chamberlain, 'hath ben as gainful a place to him for the time as to any man within our memorie'. The suspension can also be interpreted as a consequence of the campaign against his brother, which had brought Buckingham and the Commons into such convenient temporary agreement.

In April 1625 Parkhurst and three subordinate officers of the Mint, to whom Villiers was subsequently added, were appointed to collect the profits of the Mastership. Later that year Cranfield was

---

[1] In Chapter 2, s. iv. See also below, Appendix, p. 479.

formally sequestered from the office, though technically this still did not amount to total deprivation. This was the situation when Harley became involved.

Sir Robert Harley, K.B., grandfather of Queen Anne's Tory prime minister, was a country gentleman in his late forties. His family had considerable properties in the north-west of Herefordshire and across the border in Radnorshire. Sir Robert had sat in James's first and last parliaments, and was a prominent figure in his county. The evidence does not enable the history of his finances to be told at all fully, but some of the outlines are reasonably clear. In 1616 he had apparently been in financial difficulties, but had managed to tide this over without selling any of his estate. In 1623 his third wife Brilliana, daughter of Sir Edward Conway (then Secretary of State and himself a client of Buckingham), brought him a portion of £1,600. And in 1627 he completed a successful speculation in church property (making a capital gain of 37 per cent. in eight years), and paid off his last outstanding major debt. More to the point, however, his aged father Thomas Harley retained a life interest in the estate, and probably had first call on the greater part of it until his death in 1631. From then on, although Sir Robert can be found borrowing again in 1633, his landed income, which was between £1,600 and £1,750 p.a. gross in the late 1640's, cannot have been less than c. £1,000-£1,200 p.a. net. There is no evidence that he was in any serious financial difficulties in the later 1620's, in the 1630's, or indeed until the very different circumstances of 1649-55.[1]

Harley's desire for office can therefore be explained without picturing him as any kind of backwoodsman in desperate economic straits. In view of the *de facto* vacancy, his father-in-law set about acquiring the Mastership of the Mint for him, and in August 1626, pressed him to come up to London, not only to see the grant through safely and to kiss the King's hand, 'but for the satisfaction of your real duty in a place of honour and trust, without which the prejudice

[1] Harley MSS. (at Brampton Bryan), esp. bdls. 2, 22, 50, 61, and 84; LC 4/197, p. 220; 199, p. 449; 202, p. 213; *The Letters of Lady Brilliana Harley* (ed. T. T. Lewis, Camd. Soc. 1854), pp. vi-vii, x-xi, xlii, 218-19, 229-30; Hist. MSS. Comm., *Portland*, III (Harley Papers), 187-8, 248; *Montgomeryshire Collections*, XX (1886), 88, from the Herbert MSS. at Powys (I owe this ref. to Mrs. Keeler's article on Harley: *Long Parlt.*, p. 203); W. H. Howse, 'Contest for a Radnorshire Rectory in the seventeenth century', *Journ. of the Hist. Soc. of the Church in Wales*, VII (1957), 69-79.

of the King may be much, and the expectation of your integrity unsatisfied'. In short, he must at least initially perform in person, not by deputy. At about this time Parkhurst and the other trustees were ordered to make up their accounts before handing over financial responsibility to Harley, who was formally appointed Master for life with a yearly Fee of £500 by November 1626.

In February 1627 he complained that Randall Cranfield was trying to keep him out of the office, literally by hanging on to the key of the Master's premises, metaphorically by giving out that his own patent was uncancelled and Harley's therefore a usurpation. Harley also wanted to be paid on a commission basis, taking a proportion of the Mint's profits, as he said Sir Edward Villiers had done: either he had got his facts wrong or the Master's and Warden's duties were in part interchangeable with respect to financial control. As an alternative to all this he suggested a trial at law between the two patents as Master, his own and Cranfield's. The Council ordered Sir Randall to hand over the keys and the test coins (used for the trial of the pyx), but evaded the wider issue. Harley failed to obtain a grant of such fees and profits as had previously been enjoyed by Villiers, either in addition to, or instead of, his £500 p.a. He also came up against the ubiquitous Earl of Holland, whose patent as sole exchanger and comptroller of foreign bullion was seen by all the Mint officers as a threat to their interests. Harley acted as their spokesman and a compromise was reached in March 1628. However, he was told that he would have to be content with his £500 a year and no more; another £3,000 a year was said to be at stake, and the fact that all the profits had not been accounted for from Cranfield's tenure made the King, in Conway's words, 'more jealous now upon this occasion'. Meanwhile Harley continued to spend a good part of his time in Herefordshire instead of at his place of duty, and Cranfield continued to press for his own prior rights to be recognized.

So it went on until 1631. Early in that year Conway died, and as far as can be seen Harley was left without any friend or patron in high places. In June a special commission was appointed under Sir Thomas Aylesbury to investigate the rival claims. Why after five or six years was attention suddenly paid to Cranfield's complaints? There are several possible explanations. By the letter of the law his case was quite strong, and even in equity and common sense it could not be dismissed out of hand. Probably only Conway's influence had

374

prevented it from being heard sooner. Harley had also drawn attention to himself by his diatribes against high churchmen during the 1629 session of parliament, which had not been counter-balanced by his moderation on the constitutional and fiscal questions in the same session. Then there was Holland's grievance against him, dating from 1627-8, while Weston and Cottington may well have wanted to pay out a Puritan and at the same time to make an example of a recalcitrant office-holder and perhaps to bring his department more closely under Exchequer (or Treasury) control.

The commissioners heard Cranfield and Harley, and their respective counsel, and Attorney-General Heath for the Crown. They found that the 1623 grant had been to Randall Cranfield and his son Vincent for the life of the longer lived of them, and that the sequestration in 1624-5 had been 'not from the execution of the office but from the receiving the proffitts of the same'. Parkhurst and co. had simply been commissioned to collect these profits, not to execute a vacant post. The Aylesbury commission did not, however, accept Cranfield's contention that Harley, having agreed to help secure his reappointment, or rather re-entry to office, and then to buy him out, had broken off the bargain after even the price had been agreed upon. Legally there was one crucial point, and only one: had Cranfield's offences when in office been such as to cause his grant to be *automatically* voided, without its being formally and legally cancelled? These offences sounded less heinous in 1631 than they had six or seven years before. Furthermore, Buckingham was dead, there was no parliament either sitting or in prospect, and Cranfield's brother had been half pardoned and part of his fine remitted. The commissioners reported that 'howsoever it were, sir Robert Harley's Graunt Came somewhat hastilie and unusually before the other Patent was Legally avoided'. Their findings were the more cogent for being reasoned and moderate.

In the circumstances, the report was fatal to Harley. He remained Master until 1633, but Aylesbury's commission was transformed from an examining into an executive body with *de facto* control of the Mint, like Parkhurst's in 1625-6. Until September 1633 the commissioners continued to remit Harley his due profits, up to an average of £500 a year. Harley then accounted for his six years and ten months as Master, showing that the sums he had received annually varied between £151 (in 1627-8) and £865 (in 1629-30), but that the total was £28 short of what it would have been on a flat rate of £500 p.a., i.e. his average annual receipts were £496. Since Harley is unlikely to have made his case worse by falsifying figures which could easily be checked, this can reasonably be accepted as correct. Soon after presenting his account he was offered £3,000 for the Mastership, but a new appointment was felt to be incompatible with the position of Aylesbury, now joined as chief commissioner by his fellow Master of Requests, Sir Ralph Freeman. In the spring of 1634 Harley asked either to be readmitted or to be compensated for loss of office if the Cranfield patent was held still to be valid.

In 1635 the Treasury commissioners resolved 'To call Sir Rob: Harlow to accompt for the Mynte. Mr Attor: directed to send our processe for the officers of the mynte accompt.' The new plan was to make Aylesbury and Freeman joint Masters, for 'They pretend to have compounded with Cranfield for his patent, which is the best estate that any hath'. Proceedings hung fire. Randall Cranfield died on Christmas Day 1635, and his son Vincent then became the principal claimant. Shortly after this, Cottington received an anonymous letter, almost certainly from Freeman, reporting that 'I have lately agreed with him [Vincent Cranfield] for his interest, and he is willing to surrender his patent to my use'. The writer asked to be joined with Aylesbury, than whom 'there is noebody fitter for he is very intelligent in the business'; he also claimed to have had the late Lord Treasurer Portland's permission to buy out Harley's interest, but explained that the victory of the Cranfield claim made this unnecessary. From then until the Civil War the Mint was administered by Aylesbury and Freeman, with Wardens Parkhurst and St. Leger continuing to account in the Exchequer on the basis of Harley's indenture with the Crown made at his appointment in 1626.

Though in many respects an admirable work, the recent standard history of the Mint throws little light on these transactions. From a recent article, dealing explicitly with the economic and monetary, and not the administrative, aspects, it appears the years 1628-33 were about the least profitable to the Crown of any comparable period between 1603 and 1642. This could, however, have been due to strictly monetary causes and not to inefficiency or corruption on the part of the Master or Wardens.

Harley was restored in 1643, but left the Mint again in 1649, this time voluntarily because he refused to recognize the Republic. So much for the Mint. How much did his loss of office in 1631-5 have to do with Harley's allegiance in 1640-8?[1]

His Puritan sympathies antedated his eviction from the Mint. Besides his outbursts in 1629, there is his marriage to Brilliana; her militant Calvinism can scarcely be ascribed to the Mint episode, although exclusion from the social life of London and the court may have helped to harden her heart, as when she wrote of the Bishops in 1639 'I beleefe that herarchy must downe, and I hope now'. In 1615 Sir Robert had defended the Brampton Bryan parson against the charge that he was a non-conformist in the matter of ceremonies. He was involved in a long drawn dispute over the advowson of Presteigne rectory in Radnorshire, again supporting ministers of low church views against the Bishop and his candidate. Before his third marriage he engaged in a theological debate by letter with Sir Edward Herbert, the future Lord Herbert of Cherbury, who concluded by warning him against the snares alike of Jesuits and Puritans. Of his violently Puritan views in the 1640's the evidence is woefully abundant, for from 1641 to 1648 he had charge of the Long Parliament's official programme of iconoclasm, and so was responsible for the destruction of much fine medieval sculpture, glass, etc. This outlook was no recent growth; and, if Harley did become a more extreme Puritan in the course of the 1630's, this may have been a reaction, in which he was by no means alone, against the policy of Charles I and Laud.

Harley also had a brush with the Council in the Marches of Wales. He was at odds with its Attorney in 1630; two years later he and his wife were both cited before it in another action. The Council's jurisdiction over the English border counties had always been controversial and was attacked in more than one parliament.

Back in 1604-5 Harley had quarrelled with Sir Thomas, head of the influential county family of Coningsby, over a broken marriage treaty. And although in 1641 he tried to defend Sir Thomas's son, Fitzwilliam, his fellow member for Herefordshire, from being condemned (and expelled from the House) as a monopolist, Mrs.

---

[1] The Mint story may be traced in *Cal. S.P. Dom., 1623-35, Acts Privy Council 1625-8, Foedera*, XVIII-XIX, all *passim*; Hist. MSS. Comm., *4th Rpt.*, app. I, p. 17; and *Portland*, III, 21-33, 110. See also *D.N.B.*, VIII, 1282-3, XX, 324-5; Craig, *Mint*, ch. VIII; and J. D. Gould, 'The Royal Mint in the early Seventeenth Century', *Econ. Hist. Rev.*, 2nd ser., V (1952), 240-8.

Keeler, who does not mention the earlier quarrel, probably goes too far in describing them as friends. More significant, in 1632 Harley and his wife were both at law before the Council in the Marches against the even greater county figure, Sir William Croft of Croft Castle. Mr. Eure, the Attorney of the Council in the Marches, the Coningsbys, and the Crofts were all royalists. Another neighbour, with whom Harley had disputes about Sunday observance and irrigation works may have been one too. It is arguable that Harley's parliamentarianism was simply a reflection at the national level of these local and family issues. But there is a logical difficulty here. Granted that the Harleys were enemies of the Coningsbys, the Crofts, and Eure, did this compel them to take opposite sides in 1642? There must surely have been many private enemies who sank their differences in 1642 as well as many previous friends who came to a parting of the ways. And, even granted that the Harleys were parliamentarians because their local enemies were royalists, why were the latter royalists, other than because the Harleys were parliamentarians? Any attempt to provide a complete explanation along these lines is likely to end in a tautology. This method, of seeking to explain the origins and nature of the Civil War primarily in terms of local rivalries, may be designated the 'Grass Roots' hypothesis. It does not of course relate exclusively or even primarily to officers and ex-officers; indeed, in so far as they were more likely to be involved in some degree with national issues at the centre of affairs, it would seem less applicable to them than to men whose horizon was more completely bounded by their district or province.

Besides their undoubted Puritanism, there is also scattered evidence that the Harleys were agricultural improvers. Too much should not be made of this in isolation. But in general it may plausibly be argued that, given the kind of people Sir Robert and Lady Brilliana were, it was thoroughly 'in character' that they should have got into trouble with the Bishop, and with the Council in the Marches. That they should have been found on one side and the Coningsbys, Sir William Croft, and Sampson Eure on the other may well have been characteristic of the Civil War as a whole, and not just of a little corner of the west country.

The 'In-Out' hypothesis needs more careful consideration. It can never be proved what Harley would have done in 1642 if he had not been deprived of his Mastership. However, other men of a broadly similar background who kept their offices still failed to support their royal master when the war came. Nor can it be proved that Harley's militant Puritanism was caused by his deprivation. He already had strong Puritan sympathies before his eviction from the Mint, which roughly coincided with the beginning of Laud's archbishopric (1633); in so far as many low churchmen became more extreme in opposition after the early 1630's, it is impossible to distinguish the effect on Harley of two such simultaneous influences as Arminianism triumphant and loss of place. As to how loss of office affected his financial position, the facts are not absolutely clear, but there is nothing to suggest that it made any decisive difference. The £500, or to be exact £496, a year from the Mint must obviously have been important to him, especially before his father's death in 1631, and he had originally hoped to make a good deal more out of it. But, granted this, office cannot plausibly be said to have determined whether Harley was a member of the rising, or of the 'mere' and declining gentry.

Because a hypothesis is unacceptable in one, perhaps extreme, form, it does not follow that it should be discarded altogether. The trouble is that if hypotheses are watered down too much, or hedged about with too many qualifications, they begin to look like platitudes. Thus, by comparison with his attitude in the 1620's, the vigour and firmness of Harley's opposition to the Crown from 1640 to 1647 or 1648 can safely be ascribed in large part to what had happened in the intervening period, not least to his eviction from the Mint.[1]

vii THE EARLY 1640's

Some historical truisms are more often cited than pondered upon. One such is the fact that nearly two years elapsed between the meeting of the Long Parliament and the outbreak of Civil War. The issues at stake and the lines along which men divided on them changed vastly during that time. Something has already been said about the relative position of parliament in early seventeenth-century government. Granted that the almost continuous sitting of the Commons introduced a special factor into the political situation from November

[1] Hist. MSS. Comm., *Portland,* III. esp. pp. 1-9, 28, 31, 86-99, 132-4, 187-8; *Letters of Lady Brilliana Harley*, esp. pp. 62, 111; *Parliamentary Debates 1610* (ed. Gardiner, Camd. Soc., 1862), p. 138; *Commons Debates 1629*, pp. 108, 116, 232; B. Whitelocke, *Memorials of the English Affairs* (1682), pp. 45, 388; Keeler, *Long Parlt.*, pp. 139, 203.

1640 on, can anything useful be said about its effect on the office-holders? It might reasonably be asked whether or not royal officials acted, in and out of parliament, as a united bloc or a kind of pressure group, even to the extent that the higher bureaucracy did in France during the Fronde period. To this the answer is No. But it would be misleading to leave it at that.

Individual office-holders were prominent at different junctures. Sir Robert Pye was of special importance when the Commons wanted to understand the true state of Crown finances, so that, setting aside the unconstitutional taxes and exactions, they should know what supplies to vote. But, like his colleague Sir Edward Wardour, the Clerk of the Pells, who was called into the House from outside for the same purpose, Pye seems only to have provided the information on the basis of which other men shaped parliament's financial policy.

Mention has already been made of the loans raised from councillors, officials, and other selected individuals in 1639 and 1640, and of that raised jointly by King and Parliament early in 1642. The fact of having subscribed, having refused to subscribe to these loans, or of not having been asked, is not an adequate touchstone of allegiance. But once such loans had been made, the lenders might well have had a bias towards the kind of political solutions which seemed likeliest to safeguard their repayment. A complete breakdown of relations between Crown and Parliament, and the polarization of forces at the religious and political extremes, would tend to endanger their money, along with public credit generally. Pye lent £2,000 in 1639-40 and £1,000 in 1642. There are indications that he did act as a member of a fluid and ill-defined but by no means negligible middle group in the Long Parliament who were hostile to Strafford and yet hoped for a general settlement with give and take on both sides. Professor W. H. Coates in his edition of D'Ewes's *Journal* of the Long Parliament, and Mrs. Keeler have followed the author of the article in the *D.N.B.* on Pye's son in describing Sir Robert as a crypto-royalist from the start, or as one who merely swam with the parliamentary tide while secretly adhering to the King's interests. This is to underrate his reasons, alike as an office-holder and a Crown creditor for wishing to see a 'middle of the road' solution, also to neglect his continuing loyalty to the house of Villiers, of which Professor Coates himself prints an excellent example. And it is wholly to ignore the possibility of his having had

exceedingly moderate but perfectly sincere parliamentarian convictions. In January 1642/3 Pye was caught corresponding with
Edward Nicholas in the King's camp; he was only forgiven such an
act of treachery and retained in office through the influence of his
son-in-law, Hampden. But this is scarcely proof that he had all along
been a secret supporter of the King. Like many other sensible men
he probably detested the state of armed conflict and wanted a
compromise peace; it might be more meaningful to describe him as
a mild parliamentarian with neutralist or 'trimming' inclinations.
The same might easily have been true of Sir Miles Fleetwood had
he lived longer, for to the last he continued to breathe fire and
brimstone in matters of religion but to coo like a dove of peace on
political questions.

Sir Benjamin Rudyerd is another moderate, or neutrally inclined,
parliamentarian office-holder of whom the worst has perhaps been
too readily assumed. The facts of his having to be ordered to attend
the House twice in 1643 but finally retaining his seat until 1648, and
his known dependence on the Earl of Pembroke, do not suggest
independence of mind or high principles. But to offset this, there is
the magnificent speech which he delivered on 9 July 1642. After
reflecting on the awful gulf between King and Parliament, which
'makes the whole Kingdom stand amazed', he suggested that the
best immediate remedy 'is to make a fair way for the King's return
hither'. He continued:

> Mr Speaker, That we may the better consider the Condition we
> are now in, let us set our selves three Years back: If any Man then
> could have credibly told us, that within three Years the Queen
> shall be gone out of England into the Low Countries . . .; the
> King shall remove from his Parliament, from London to York,
> declaring himselfe not to be safe here; that there shall be a total
> Rebellion in Ireland, such Discords and Distempers in Church and
> State here, as now we find, certainly we should have trembled at
> the thought of it. . . . On the other side; If any Man then could
> have credibly told us, that within three Yeares we shall have a
> Parliament, it would have been good News; that Ship money should
> be taken away by Act of Parliament, the Reasons and Grounds of
> it so rooted out, as that neither it nor anything like it, can ever
> grow up again; that Monopolies, the High-Commission Court,
> the Star-Chamber, the Bishops' votes [in the Lords] shall be taken
> away, the Council-Table regulated and restrained, the Forests
> bounded and limited; that we should have Trienniall Parliaments;

and more than that a perpetual Parliament which none shall have Power to dissolve without your selves; we should have thought this a Dream of Happiness: yet now we are in the real Possession of it, we do not enjoy it.... We stand chiefly upon future Security; whereas the very having of these Things is a convenient fair Security.... There is more security offered, even in this last Answer of the King's ...; besides what else may be enlarged and improved by a select Committee of both Houses.... let us beware we do not contend for such a hazardous unsafe Security, as may endanger the loss of what we have already. Let us not think we have *nothing*, because we have not *all* we desire; and tho we had, yet we cannot make a Mathematical Security, all humane [human] Caution is susceptible of Corruption and Failing; ...

His peroration was the veritable *cri de coeur* of a man of peace, almost indeed of a pacifist in the modern sense.

Mr Speaker, It now behoves us to call up all the Wisdom we have about us, for we are at the very brink of Combustion and Confusion: If Blood begins once to touch Blood, we shall presently fall into a certain Misery, and must attend an uncertain Success ... every Man here is bound in Conscience to employ his uttermost Endeavours to prevent the effusion of Blood ... let us save our Liberties, and our Estates, as [in such a way that] we may save our Souls too. Now I have clearly delivered my own Conscience, I leave every Man freely to his.[1]

But in view of the King's counter-preparations, the orthodox maxim of *Si vis pacem, para bellum* carried the day and was followed by its usual consequences.

Whether or not Rudyerd was typical in his sincerity, his statesman-like moderation was far from being shared by all office-holders. Dr. Thomas Eden, Gerrard, Cornelius Holland, the Trevors of Enfield and Trevalyn, both Vanes, Whitaker, and after some initial wavering Mildmay and Wynne, were none of them moderate parliamentarians.[2]

[1] See *D.N.B.*, Keeler, *Long Parlt.*, Brunton and Pennington, *Members*, and other previous refs.; the text of the speech is from Rushworth, *Hist. Colls.*, III, i (vol. 4), 753-4.

[2] Eden (1580-1645) was a Master in Chancery and ecclesiastical administrator (*D.N.B.*, Keeler, *Long Parlt.*, p. 163). Sir John Trevor (1596-1673) was a coal farmer and Auditor of the Duchy; Sir Thomas (*c.* 1612-75 or 76), his cousin was Auditor (*D.N.B.*, *G.E.C.*, *Btge*, Keeler, *Long Parlt.*, Brunton and Pennington, *Members*; Venn, *Al. Cant.*; Nef, *Coal*, II, 270, 295; Enid Sophia Jones, *The Trevors of Trevalyn and their descendants* (privately, 1955), esp. chs. IV, VI, and VII).

Nor were all the office-holders in the Long Parliament who sub-sequently supported the King moderate in their royalism. Within a year or so of November 1640 several had been disqualified from sitting, as monopolists, for electoral malpractices, or for allegedly being involved in the various projected military coups. And even of those who were expelled, or disqualified in 1642 or later, only Orlando Bridgeman, if Clarendon's account of his attitude in 1643 can be trusted, was among those who favoured major concessions by the King in order to obtain peace.[1]

Sir Edmund Verney's reluctant royalism was of a rather different character. This is shown by Clarendon's well-known description of his attitude in 1642: 'for my part', said the Knight Marshal and King's Standard-bearer,

> 'I do not like the Quarrel, and do heartily wish that the King would yield and consent to what they [the Parliament] desire; so that my Conscience is only concerned in Honour and in Gratitude to follow my Master. I have eaten his bread and served him near thirty Years, and will not do so base a Thing, as to forsake him. . . . I have no Reverence for the Bishops, for whom this Quarrel subsists.'

While this feeling of direct personal loyalty to the King might be expected to have been strongest among the inner circle of Chamber and Household officers, it is not clear just how universal it was even among them. However, as will be seen, the proportion of positive royalists was larger in the Household departments than in the remainder of the central government.[2]

Just as some officers probably failed to support the King because they opposed his religious policy, others may have been royalists not primarily because they were office-holders but because they were convinced Anglicans. Such may well have been true of Edward Norgate, Signet Clerk, Windsor Herald, and Tuner of the King's musical instruments. In his will he referred affectionately to the late King 'of blessed memory', but gave thanks chiefly for having been bred up in the Church of England, which he believed to be 'truelie Catholique, Orthodoxe and Apostolique', and second to no church in the world either in doctrine or discipline. In the dark days of 1649 this is testimony indeed. Rather different is the case of Hugh Audley, the money-lending Clerk of the Wards. He left £400 to any forty

---

[1] *D.N.B.*; Clarendon, *Life*, I, 176.

[2] For Verney see *D.N.B.*, and Clarendon, *Life*, I, 135-6.

sufficiently virtuous and deserving *Protestant* maid servants, *provided that* they were known to believe in the government of the church by Bishops, and not to be Presbyterians, Quakers, or members of any other sect. Yet Audley had preserved his neutrality during the wars and the Interregnum, and it may be suspected that his Anglicanism was a somewhat forced growth in the entirely changed conditions of 1660-2.[1]

Some officers appear to have been moved by loyalty to their sovereign, some by loyalty to their church, and others by opposing constitutional principles or religious beliefs. But it would be naïve to neglect less exalted motives. Clarendon is at his most severe and his least reliable in dealing with councillors or other office-holders who did not support the King; none the less, he makes one or two shrewd points about some of them. He suggests that the Earl of Holland, Mildmay, and Whitaker were particularly influenced by the fear of being brought to book by parliament for their respective parts in the arbitrary and illegal proceedings of the 1630's: Holland because of his conduct as Justice in Eyre concerning the forest laws, Mildmay as the promoter of the gold and silver thread monopoly, and Whitaker for his activities as a royal commissioner and projector. The two latter should have been expelled from the Commons along with the other monopolists, and only saved themselves from this, in his view, by becoming identified with the extremist party. Taking this at its face value, together with the facts of his having voted against Strafford's attainder and then having gone over to the other side, and finally the charges of fraud made against him after the Restoration in his capacity as Master of the Jewels, the recent historians of the Long Parliament describe Mildmay as 'the worst type of rapacious scoundrel'. His Low Church leanings in the 1620's have already been illustrated; also Mildmay came of an eminent Puritan family, his grandfather having founded that seminary of sedition, Emmanuel College. While in the early phases of the Long Parliament he was still trimming on political issues, Mildmay's religious position was considerably less equivocal. Nor is it clear wherein the depravity lay in favouring a reprieve for Strafford and then having been a parliamentarian. If this was the course followed by Mildmay, Wynne, and Robert Scawen (Pym's successor as Receiver-General of Hants, Wilts, and Glos), so it was also by the great Selden. Nor is the truth at all clear about Mildmay's illicit profits from the Jewel House.

[1] PCC 9 Grey, 134 Laud.

9(*a*). SIR ROBERT HARLEY, MASTER
OF THE MINT, 1626-35 and 1643-9.
(Miniature by P. Oliver.)

9(*b*). SIR BENJAMIN RUDYERD,
SURVEYOR OF THE COURT OF
WARDS, 1618-47. (Engraving
after the portrait by W.
Hollar.)

S: Beniamin Rudyerd Surveyor
of his Ma.:ser Court of Wardes and Li
ueries.

The Court of High Commission abolished by Statute.

Secretary of State Windebank, Lord Keeper Finch, and
others pictured in flight, to avoid impeachment.

10. THE HOUR OF RETRIBUTION.
(Pamphlet illustrations, 1640-1.)

This is not to deny that a Puritan could be rapacious and even a scoundrel. But when in doubt judgment should be reserved, or justice tempered with mercy.

As for Whitaker, grounds have already been given for dissenting from Mrs. Keeler's suggestion that his Puritan sympathies may only have dated from his second marriage in 1638. He did in fact spend a week in the Tower during July 1641, but the Commons put him there for work done in his capacity as a Council Clerk extraordinary in 1629 rather than as a patentee. Reasons have already been explained for supposing that the Earl of Holland's motives were very mixed; even a combination of the 'In-Out' hypothesis and the fear of Parliamentary retribution seems unlikely to account altogether for his extraordinarily erratic course.

There is also the opinion of Manchester (then Lord Mandeville) that Hamilton made a pact with the opposition in 1640, to avoid being attacked, and that Cottington surrendered the Mastership of the Wards in 1641 with the same object in view.[1] The relative immunity which both enjoyed in the first years of the Long Parliament is certainly remarkable. But here again too much must not be proved. Although, like Holland, Hamilton was eventually executed for his part in the Second Civil War of 1648, in 1643-5 he was actually imprisoned by the King, and in the First Civil War he can only be classified as a trimmer, whereas from 1643 on Cottington seems to have been a steady if sometimes a factious royalist.

Fear of being brought to book for what they had done in the 1630's can fairly be added to the motives influencing office-holders in 1640-1; but it is less plausible as an explanation of what they did from 1642 on. Mildmay and Whitaker became extreme parliamentarians, the Earl of Holland a trimmer or 'side-changer', while such a notorious patentee as the glass monopolist (and Lieutenant of the Navy), Sir Robert Mansell, was apparently a neutral. Several others, who were at least equally vulnerable, were firm royalists: the Earls of Dorset and Ancrum, the elder Goring, the Jermyns, Endymion Porter, and Edmund Windham (Clerk of the Errors, and royal commissioner on soap, depopulations, wine casks, etc.). In general, leaving aside Hamilton and Holland, it might more plausibly be argued that such men were likely to favour an extreme solution one way or the other. A moderate outcome to the crisis, with King

[1] B.M., Add. MS. 15,567, fols. 30-1 (I am grateful to Mr. Cooper for this ref.).

and Parliament acting in partnership, would mean, as in 1640-1, the sacrifice of scapegoats for the sins of the 1630's: Strafford on the block, Laud in the Tower, Finch and Windebank in exile, time-serving judges impeached, monopolists purged.

It is worth remembering how many of the King's servants were proceeded against in one way or another, as well as how variously they reacted to this in terms of their political allegiance. Of the ecclesiastical officials, Sir John Lambe was accused in parliament and Dr. Thomas Eden threatened; Sir Nathaniel Brent and Dr. Arthur Duck may also have felt themselves to be in danger. But whatever the importance of this factor, Brent and Eden became parliamentarians, Duck and Lambe royalists. Of the common law judges, Sir Robert Berkeley was the most violently attacked, suffering impeachment and being very heavily fined; yet the Long Parliament was not unequivocally hostile to him, and when he was later living in retirement in the country his royalism had a passive or even neutral flavour to it. Chief Justice Bramston was impeached, but not finally condemned or punished, and his subsequent neutrality has an almost parliamentarian quality. Much the same could be said of Chief Baron Davenport except that his neutrality inclined, if at all, in the royalist direction. Justice Robert Foster was outwardly a straightforward royalist, but in 1643 parliament asked the King to continue him in office; he can hardly have been regarded as incorrigible. Sir Thomas Trevor, a Baron of the Exchequer since 1625, was impeached, and then fined and imprisoned, yet he resumed his seat on the bench and continued to sit, under Parliament's auspices, until 1648 or 1649. While only one judge, Justice Reeve, was an outright parliamentarian, only four or five out of twelve were positive and unequivocal royalists: Chief Justice Bankes (though even he tried to act as a mediator in 1642), Justices Crawley (who was impeached and punished), Heath, and Malet, and Baron Weston (who was impeached but not tried). Baron Henden's position is obscure; he was probably an inactive royalist.[1] With their passion for duly constituted authority, the Judges are not perhaps a good illustration of office-holders' reactions to the situation in 1640-1 or in 1642 and after. If in early Stuart theory they were meant to be 'lions under the throne', when the day of reckoning came the Judges turned out to be a somewhat mangy collection.

[1] For all these see *D.N.B.*, or Foss, *Judges*, or both; for extra material on some see *Cal. Cttee. Advcmt. Money.*

Pursuit or fear of pursuit by Parliament is therefore likely to have affected the attitude of many officials in 1640-1, but it certainly did not have the same effect on all of them in the very changed circumstances of 1642-3. This is the kind of historical explanation which does not fall down because it is bad in logic, but because on closer investigation it turns out to be an over-simplification, supported by some of the facts but contradicted by others.

It is naturally harder to discover the political attitudes of lesser office-holders. For them the particular motive just discussed can hardly have had much force. Officials of medium and junior rank who were not M.P.s and who were not singled out for investigation or attack in parliament offer as varied a picture as their more prominent superiors, when their allegiance is examined. But the influences to which they were subject, let alone the mental processes which they went through, in the course of reaching their final positions are almost unfailingly obscure.

Why did Arthur Squibb, Teller of the Exchequer, become a parliamentarian and at least two of his three colleagues, including his own first cousin once removed, royalists? The Squibbs have already been mentioned as a Dorset-Wiltshire family, but Arthur had become a landowner nearer London, by acquiring the manor and park of Henley, at Ashe in Surrey. In September 1641 he was appointed a commissioner on the boundaries of Windsor Forest, and in January 1642 he and the other commissioners presented their findings which were unfavourable to the King's interests. But this seems more likely to have been a symptom than a cause of Squibb's Civil War allegiance. Perhaps more indicative of his attitude, in 1633 his eldest daughter married the future parliamentarian lawyer, John Glyn, through whose influence he was later to be appointed Clarenceux King of Arms; and in the later 1640's a younger daughter married Griffiths Bodurda, an active minor politician under the Protectorate. The Arthur Squibb junior who had a reversion to a Tellership, took an active part on the Committee for Compounding, and was one of the radical leaders in the 'Barebones' Parliament of 1653, was not this Arthur's son, but probably the brother of Lawrence the royalist Teller. A third Arthur Squibb, our Arthur's son, was a merchant of unknown religious and political affiliations. Since there were at least four Arthur Squibbs between 1640 and 1680, identification is not easy. If it was the Teller and King of Arms, and not his fanatical namesake, who was an Elder or Overseer of the

387

Godalming presbyterian 'classis' in 1647, this may indicate some Puritan leanings, but it could equally be evidence of mere time-serving or swimming with the tide. Among the other survivors of the Dorset Exchequer connexion, Edward Pitt, whose father Sir William had moved to Hampshire, was a royalist; Clement Walker the pamphleteer, of a Somerset-Dorset family, was a very moderate, and subsequently disillusioned, parliamentarian. It would be equally pertinent to ask why Lawrence Squibb, brother of the Barebones Arthur, was a royalist, although apparently at first a concealed one. One answer to this would be that in the 1630's Lawrence had shared in the unpopular patent for dice and playing cards, whereas his cousin Arthur the elder had not been involved in any such projects. But on the 'skin-saving' theory this might have made Lawrence curry favour with Parliament at least in 1640-1, unless his royalism (like for example that of Endymion Porter) was so unequivocal that this would never have occurred to him. There may of course have been an element of family reinsurance about all this. Heads, the Squibbs win: Tails, the Squibbs do not lose! But it is just as likely that issues of theology and constitutional principle genuinely divided brother against brother, cousin against cousin.[1]

It may be futile to try to analyse the motives of individuals below the 'upper middle' range of officials. And, if so, a quantitative approach may be more fruitful, by establishing what other characteristics evident among office-holders can be related to the various forms of allegiance. Suppose, for the sake of argument, a thousand people, of whom one hundred were found to be left-handed and one hundred to be red-headed; in a random distribution, the expected overlap, or number of left-handed red-heads, would be about ten. And if in fact fifty were found to have both these characteristics, it would be correct to infer that there was some marked connexion between them; but it would not be correct to assume that either was necessarily a cause or an effect of the other, for it would be equally logical (and in this particular case more sensible) to suppose that both were the products of some common, if as yet unexplained, set

[1] For the Squibbs see Chapter 3, s. i; also *Cal. Cttee. Compdg.*, p. 1558; PCC 363, 378 Alchin, 148 Bunce, 50 Bath; Manning and Bray, *Surrey*, I, xiii, III, 681. For the 'Barebones' Arthur see H. R. Trevor-Roper, 'Cromwell and his Parliaments', in *Essays presented to Sir Lewis Namier*, ed. R. Pares and A. J. P. Taylor (1956), pp. 25-7.

of causes. This may prove to be the best method of investigating office-holders' allegiances during the Civil War.

An attempt must first be made to clear up a likely objection to the analysis of allegiances which has been adopted in this chapter. Granted that a threefold classification, into (1) royalists, (2) neutrals, trimmers, and side-changers, and (3) parliamentarians, makes better sense than the conventional dual one, into (1) and (3), it may still be objected that the so-called neutrals largely correspond to the elderly and infirm, to those who were unable to take an active part on either side. Many of the Judges are therefore classified as neutrals, etc., simply because they were in their sixties and seventies and retired to their homes in 1642-3. No attempt will be made to deny that the middle category includes more of the older office-holders than the other two. But there were plenty of men just as old and decrepit as most of the Judges who did become active supporters of one side or other, if not on the field of battle at least in their general attitude and by financial contributions. Nor would it be correct to think of anything like all the members of the middle category as too old to support either side.

Sir Dudley Carleton (1599-1654), nephew of Lord Dorchester (Secretary of State, 1628-32), himself a Council Clerk in ordinary since 1636, had been in the King's service for about twenty years in 1642. Yet he withdrew to his property in the Netherlands in 1643; although the parliamentary taxation committee regarded him as being against them rather than for them, Carleton avoided taking any active part for the King; before the end of his life he had accepted the Republic at least sufficiently to return to London. Carleton had spent much time in the Netherlands between the ages of eighteen and thirty-six, and Dutch influence may have helped to form his political outlook. Be that as it may, it must have been by deliberate choice that he did not rally to the King in 1642-3.[1] Then there were the diplomats who stayed at their posts, perhaps thereby hoping to remain out of harm's way and so to make good with whoever was victorious at home. Sir William Boswell (1580's-1650), Council Clerk extraordinary and Ambassador to the United Provinces, appears to have failed in this, in that Parliament came to regard him

[1] *Cal. S.P. Dom., 1641-3*, p. 463; *Cal. Cttee. Advcmt. Money*, p. 482; PCC 341 Alchin.

as a supporter of the King.[1] But Sir Arthur Hopton (c. 1588-1650), Agent and then Ambassador in Spain, did better. Unlike Boswell, whose early patrons included the future trimmers Lord Herbert of Cherbury and Bishop Williams, Hopton had begun in the service of no less a pillar of royal authority than Lord Cottington, through whose influence he had obtained the Madrid post. Although Charles I's grant of a peerage to Sir Arthur's nephew the royalist general included a remainder to him if Sir Ralph died without male heirs, Hopton managed to keep off Parliament's black list. In 1649 he came home via France, where he passed the time in a friendly way with the royalist exiles, and died peacefully the year after, his property unsequestered and without having had to compound.[2]

Some of the neutrals and trimmers in the Exchequer have already been mentioned in previous chapters. It is not surprising that Christopher Vernon was one, perhaps with parliamentarian leanings. Less expected is the case of Justinian Povey, maternal grandfather of William III's favourite administrator, William Blathwayt. Povey had been Auditor of the Queen's revenues from 1611 to 1618 and again (unlike Hackwill, being reappointed to the same post under Henrietta as he had held under Anne) from 1625; he was also one of the seven Revenue Auditors, so he was in a sense both a household and an Exchequer official. He was old, but scarcely too old to make the journey from London to Oxford when the King sent a formal summons to the Auditors in February 1643. When Povey drew up his will under the Commonwealth, he referred to 'these evill tymes' but there is little evidence that his royalist sympathies had ever gone much further than this.[3]

Another old friend who keeps turning up, perhaps like the proverbial bad penny, is Sir Henry Croke. Not only did he retain the Clerkship of the Pipe under Long Parliament, Commonwealth, and Protectorate, but on being assessed for parliamentary taxation in 1644 he pleaded that he had not got £100 to his name—and was let off! His son and heir was an active royalist; even so he seems to have had his reversion to the Pipe honoured when Sir Henry died in 1659, and his tenure was of course not disturbed in 1660. If the owner of Chequers had been an M.P. in 1640-2 he might not have been so

[1] D.N.B.; Cal. Cttee. Compdg., p. 2595-6.

[2] D.N.B.; Clarendon, Life, I, 201.

[3] G. A. Jacobsen, William Blathwayt (New Haven, 1932), pp. 35, 37-9, 40; Cal. Cttee. Advcmt. Money, p. 170; PCC 40, 51 Bowyer.

easily able to equivocate or conceal his sympathies; in that case, for him as for Sir Robert Pye the scales might well have tipped, however narrowly, in Parliament's favour.[1]

An instructive case is provided by that semi-independent offshoot of the Exchequer and of Chancery, the Alienations Office. By the time he came to write his memoirs, well after the Restoration, Sir George Courthorpe (1616-85) of Wyleigh, Sussex, had firmly persuaded himself that he had been a strong royalist all along. True he obtained special permission, or approval, from ex-Lord Treasurer Juxon in 1642, and from the emigré royal council in 1654 to carry on executing his office as Deputy Commissioner for alienations; true he was at one time accused of sending money to Charles II in exile; true though elected to the second Protectorate Parliament he was prevented from sitting. Even so, except for an involuntary interval in 1653-4 when the office was temporarily abolished, Courthorpe carried on without a break from 1642 to 1660. His reinsurance policy worked well. He was made a Gentleman Pensioner in 1660 and knighted in 1661, and he was able to transfer the Alienations post to a younger son, so keeping it in the family for a third generation. If he did *at the time* regard himself as a crypto-royalist in the 1640's, the layers of camouflage were so thick that for our purposes he belongs better in the middle category.[2]

Finally, what is to be made of Sir William Uvedale (*c.* 1585-1652), Treasurer of the Chamber since 1618 and Treasurer-at-Wars since 1639? He was one of four messengers from the King to Parliament in August 1642, by which date he had already been secluded from his seat in the Commons for joining the King at York. But instead of returning with his fellow envoys, Uvedale simply stayed in the Parliament's quarters. Clarendon says that when the King sent him off he gave Uvedale 'leave under that pretence to intend the business of his own fortune'. This may refer either to his estate having been in Hampshire, in 1642 a parliamentarian-dominated county, or to his having been since December 1640 Parliament's

---

[1] See Chapter 4, s. ii; also Keeler, *Long Parlt.*, pp. 147-8 (for the son); A. Croke, *The Croke Family originally named Le Blount* (Oxford, 1823), esp. II, ch. IV, s. iii; *Cal. S.P. Dom., 1640-60, passim; Cal. Cttee. Advcmt. Money*, p. 340.

[2] 'Courthorpe Memorials', *Camden Miscellany*, XI (Camd. Soc., 1907); *Al. Ox.*, I, 336; *Al. Cant.*, I, 405; P.R.O., accts. various, Alienations, E 101/1/7, 2/1, 2/5, 531/3-4, 605/1.

appointee as Army Treasurer and so dependent on them for the payment of money still owing on his account. Certainly Uvedale's correspondence with his Deputy Treasurer back in the winter of 1640-1 shows that he was determined to make as much profit as possible out of this office, and was not too scrupulous about the means used in doing so. In 1643 both sides were testing, or bidding for his allegiance: the King by appointing him a commissioner to assess and levy Hampshire's contribution to the cost of the royal armies, Parliament by naming him to sit on their committee for that county. Firmer evidence that he had made good with Parliament after his switch in 1642 is afforded by his readmission to the Commons in October 1644. He continued to sit until Pride's Purge, and was actually on the Assessment (taxation) committee for his county under the Commonwealth in 1649-50. His son-in-law, reversioner to the Treasurership of the Chamber since January 1640, like Croke's son, stood by the King and succeeded to the office in 1660.[1] Again there are grounds for suspecting an element of family reinsurance, but it cannot be proved that this was the intention rather than the effect of such divided allegiance. There is also the contrary possibility, namely that these divisions may sometimes have resulted from family feuds, or filial rebellions against parental authority. But this can hardly apply where reasonably good personal relations seem to have been kept up across the divisions of war.

Nor is the fact of neutralism and trimming the same as the explanation of its causes. Old age and infirmity apart, those classified in the middle category no doubt had just as mixed and various motives as the cavaliers and roundheads. Political and religious convictions which led them to favour a compromise settlement must often have been inextricably confused with personal and family interests, with a desire to keep on sufficiently good terms with both sides in order to stay in office and to preserve their property from major depredations.

[1] Keeler, *Long Parlt.*, pp. 196-7, 369-70; *Cal. S.P. Dom.*, *1640-1*, pp. 414, 424-5, 431-2, etc.; Clarendon, *Hist. Reb.*, II, 301, 304; Whitelocke, *Memorials*, p. 105; *The Acts and Ordinances of the Interregnum*, ed. C. H. Firth and R. S. Rait (1911), I, 335, 540, 696, 974, 1092, II, 42, 308, 477; W. H. Black, *Docquets of Letters Patent . . . of Charles I at Oxford* (1837), p. 68. I am grateful to Mr. Pennington for help with Uvedale.

viii EXPLANATIONS OF ALLEGIANCE[1]

All Ranks, Surnames A-C. The first group to be considered here is more or less the same as the one used in the second section of Chapter 5: officials of all ranks whose names began with the letters A-C, who were still alive in the autumn of 1642, and about whom enough is known for their allegiance to be examined in this way.

Following the striking discovery made a few years ago by Brunton and Pennington about the age differences between the supporters of the two sides in the Long Parliament itself, allegiance will first be related to date of birth.

TABLE 36. AGE AND ALLEGIANCE (i)

	R	NR	N & SC	NP	N or P	all N	P	Total
Born 16th century . .	27 (29·8)	5	12 (10·7)	5	3	25 (25·6)	13 (9·5)	65
Born 17th century . .	14 (11·5)	1	4	1 (2·3)	4	10 (9·9)	1 (3·7)	25
Unknown . . .	9 (8·7)	–	2	4	2	8 (7·5)	2 (2·8)	19
Total	50	6	18	10	9	43	16	109
Percentage . . .	45·9	5·5	16·5	9·2	8·3	39·45	14·6	–

Note. R=positive royalists; NR=passive, or neutrally inclined royalists; N & SC=neutrals, trimmers, and side-changers; NP=passive, or neutrally inclined parliamentarians; N or P=neutrals or parliamentarians; all N=all neutral, trimming, and passive categories; P=positive parliamentarians.

The figures given in brackets are those which might have been expected if the distribution in a particular category was the same as that in the group as a whole: thus passive or neutrally inclined parliamentarians numbered 10 out of 109, and those born after 1600 numbered 25, so that if there was no positive or negative bias in the distribution $\frac{10 \times 25}{109}$ =2·3 would be the expected number in the NP category also born in the seventeenth century, whereas actually there was only one. But where the totals involved are very small, a mistake about only one or two men can make such a big difference either way that the comparison between the expected and the actual distributions ceases to be worth making.

[1] Much the same sources have been used for this section as for the A-C group in Chapter 5, s. ii. Except for wills and some private papers, mainly printed sources have been used for the period after 1642; these include: *Cal. S.P. Dom* (covering the years 1642-62); *Cal. Cttee. Advcmt. Money; Cal. Cttee. Compdg.; Commons Journals; Lords Journals; Parlty. Hist.;* Firth and Rait, *Acts and Ordinances*; general county histories (V.C.H. and older ones); histories of the Civil War in individual counties; E. Peacock, *Lists of Cavalier and Roundhead Officers* (1863); Steele, *Proclamations*; Rushworth, *Hist. Colls.*; Black, *Docquets of Letters Patent; Cal. Clarendon S.P.; Nicholas Papers* (Camd. Soc.); *Thurloe State Papers*; T. Burton, *Parliamentary Diary*, ed. J. T. Rutt (1828); Hist. MSS. Comm., esp. House of Lords Papers in *3rd-7th Repts.*

I regret that I have not been able to make fuller use of contemporary

Thus the royalists were slightly more likely than the others to be aged 42 or under at the outbreak of war; the neutrals and trimmers were very slightly, and the parliamentarians appreciably more likely to be older than this. It will be seen that the unknowns are reasonably evenly distributed among the different categories of allegiance, but it is unfortunately not possible to assume that they would be distributed between the two age categories in the same proportions as the known cases. As has already been explained (in Chapter 5, s. ii) lack of information is weighted towards the lower end of the social hierarchy and towards the more junior officials. Therefore if there was also any correlation between social status, or official rank and allegiance, and between status, or rank and age, it would affect the distribution (age-wise) of the unknowns here. This caution, about concealed 'weightage' among the unknowns applies to several of the other tables in this section.

As has been suggested earlier in this chapter, several office-holders who were unenthusiastic about royal policy in the 1630's and failed to support the Crown in the early 1640's, had been appointed before the political 'climacteric' of 1628-9. It is therefore worth seeing whether there is any quantitative evidence for relating allegiance to date of appointment.

TABLE 37. DATE OF ENTRY TO OFFICE AND ALLEGIANCE (i)

	R	NR	N & SC	NP	N or P	all N	P	Total
Apptd. before 1628-9 .	25 (25·7)	6	11	6	3	26 (22·1)	5 (8·2)	56
Apptd. after 1628-9 .	25 (22·9)	–	7	2	5	14 (19·7)	11 (7·3)	50
Doubtful . . .	–	–	–	2	1	3	–	3

This shows only a slight correlation between royalism and entry to office after 1628-9; neutrals, trimmers, and passive supporters of both sides were appreciably more likely to have been appointed earlier. More surprising, positive parliamentarians were definitely more likely to have been appointed later; in so far as this group can be said to constitute a sample, the Civil Service does not seem to have been growing progressively more likely to support the royal cause.

pamphlet literature. But I do not think that this source would yield much new material on the allegiance of individuals, or that it would be likely to affect the general conclusions reached in this chapter.

In the previous chapter stress was laid on status, or social degree, as a means of classifying men in early Stuart England. And it is pertinent to ask whether their status (in or around 1642) offers any clue to the allegiance of office-holders.

TABLE 38. SOCIAL STATUS AND ALLEGIANCE (i)

	R	NR	N & SC	NP	N or P	all N	P	Total
Peers	7 (5)	–	2	–	–	2	2	11
Baronets and Knights .	20 (17)	4	5	2	1	12 (14·6)	5 (5·4)	37
Esquires and equivalent .	16 (17·9)	2	6	5	4	17 (15·4)	6 (5·7)	39
Foreigners . . .	1	–	1	–	–	1	1	3
Esq.-Gent. borderline .	2	–	2	–	–	2	1	5
Gent. and equivalent .	3	–	2	3	2	7	1	11
Below Gent. . . .	1	–	–	–	2	2	–	3
All below Esquire . .	7 (10·1)	–	5	3	4	12 (8·7)	3 (3·2)	22

Thus peers and baronets and knights were slightly more likely to be royalists, and slightly less likely to be neutrals or trimmers than might have been expected in an unbiased distribution. With esquires there is an even smaller difference the other way. Those below esquire show a rather more marked falling off from active royalism, and an inclination to neutralism of one kind or another; but this may simply be because, being obscurer and in general less wealthy, they had a better chance of concealing their allegiance, or avoiding commitment. Certainly nothing like a class struggle can be said to emerge inside the administration, but this would hardly be the place to look for it.

The connexion between allegiance and the location of office-holders' property is a more complicated question. Location is not easy to classify. If the whole of a man's estate was in Suffolk, which remained in the Parliament's quarters throughout the Civil War, or in Wales (other than Pembrokeshire), which was for practical purposes entirely in the King's quarters until 1645, there is no difficulty. But many office-holders had property of comparable extent in two or more distinct parts of England, and sometimes also in Ireland or Scotland. It is equally difficult to classify those whose estates straddled the main lines of division between the combatants, or lay in disputed areas which changed hands once or more often before Parliament's victory in 1645-6. To meet these objections, men with property in two areas which are classified differently have been rated at a half for each; and a category of 'doubtful and disputed territory' has been included. In defining the King's and the Parliament's quarters, the approximate lines of division of September 1642 to May 1643 have been followed; divided and disputed areas thus include Gloucestershire, Dorset, the mid-Thames basin, the central midlands, and Lancashire. This is still not wholly satisfactory: for a man who made his choice in 1642, Hampshire, and indeed a large part of the south-western counties as far as the Tamar, might have appeared firmly parliamentarian; yet for another who postponed committing himself until the summer of 1643 this area would have presented a very different picture—divided but predominantly under the King's power. The situation as regards Ireland and Scotland is even trickier, and no attempt has been made to subdivide them. London and Westminster in a sense 'over-weight' Parliament's quarters, but only men who had substantial property or whose main residence was there have been counted under that heading. With these cautions allegiance can be plotted against location.

TABLE 39. LOCATION OF PROPERTY AND ALLEGIANCE (i)

	R	NR	N & SC	NP	N or P	all N	P	Total
King's qtrs. . . .	7·5 (4·6)	1	–	0·5	–	1·5	1	10
Doubtful and disputed .	13 (12·8)	2·5	7 (4·6)	0·5	3	13 (11)	2 (4·1)	28
Ireland	2	–	0·5	0·5	–	1	0·5	3·5
Scotland . . .	3	–	0·5	–	–	0·5	–	3·5
Parlt.'s qtrs. . . .	23·5 (27·1)	2·5	10	8·5	6	27 (23·3)	8·5 (8·7)	59
Unknown or presumed none	1	–	–	–	–	–	4 (0·7)	5
Totals	50	6	18	10	9	43	16	109

Positive royalists were considerably more likely to have had their estates in the King's quarters, and less likely to have had them in the Parliament's than the other members of the group. As might have been anticipated, the various categories of neutrals and trimmers were a little more likely to have had theirs in disputed areas; less expectedly they were also more likely to have had them in Parliament's quarters, although this is not true of the active parliamentarians, who may however (on negative evidence) have been more likely not to have owned any appreciable property anywhere. About twenty active royalists seem to have had property exclusively in London and the counties wholly under parliamentarian control. This simply reflects the fact that all office-holders tended to live in or near the capital and to have their estates in the counties round it. But it is also a reminder that many of those who took the King's side had to abandon their homes, and leave their estates open to spoliation and confiscation. At least among these 109 the same did not apply to any appreciable extent the other way round, for parliamentarian supporters.

Medium-Ranking Officials, Surnames A-Z. This group comprises 200 men who held posts in the middle ranks of the government between 1625 and 1641. As well as Privy Councillors and great officers of state, all peers have been excluded even when they held minor offices. So have the twelve common law judges and the Master of the Rolls, but not the Masters in Chancery or the Masters of Requests. Foreigners have been excluded unless they seem to have been more or less permanently domiciled in England, and so have members of the Irish and Scottish (though not of the Welsh) administrations. The exact boundaries of such a group are bound to be arbitrary, and in some degree arguable. The span of seniority is wide, stretching from the Cofferer of the Household to the Clerk of the Acatry, from the Treasurer of the Chamber and the Vice-President of the North to the Deputy Chamberlains of the Receipt. If anything, the group has a bias towards those actively involved in administration (though sinecurists have not been excluded on principle), and away from the holders of honorific posts in the Household above stairs. Some measure of homogeneity may reasonably be claimed for its membership. And there is enough additional information about enough of them for this group to be classified under more headings than the first one.

TABLE 40. AGE AND ALLEGIANCE (ii)

	R	NR	N & SC	NP	N or P	all N	P	Total
Born 16th century . .	54 (64·3)	13	24 (17·4)	9	3	49 (41·5)	31 (28·1)	134
Born 17th century . .	30 (19·2)	2	1	1	2	6 (12·4)	4 (8·4)	40
Unknown . . .	12 (12·5)	2	1	2	2	7 (8·1)	7 (5·5)	26
Total	96	17	26	12	7	62	42	200
Percentages . . .	48	8·5	13	6	3·5	31	21	100

Those born before 1600 were considerably less likely to be royalists, and considerably more likely to be neutrals, etc., but only very slightly more likely to be parliamentarians than might have been expected from the divisions in the whole group. Conversely, those born from 1600 on were much more likely to be royalists and less likely to be parliamentarians or neutrals of any description. The age differences are a good deal more marked here than in the previous (A-C) group.

TABLE 41. DATE OF ENTRY TO OFFICE AND ALLEGIANCE (ii)

	R	NR	N & SC	NP	N or P	all N	P	Total
Apptd. before 1628-9 .	49 (56·6)	12	23 (15·3)	8	3	46 (36·6)	23 (24·8)	118
Apptd. after 1628-9 .	47 (38·9)	5	3 (10·5)	4	4	16 (25·1)	18 (17)	81
Doubtful . . .	–	–	–	–	–	–	1	1

Those appointed before 1628-9 were appreciably less likely to be positive royalists; they were much more likely to be neutrals, trimmers, or side-changers, and considerably more likely to be neutrals or passive supporters of either side. Those appointed after the political climacteric were correspondingly more likely to be active royalists, and very much less likely to be neutrals, trimmers, etc., than might have been expected taking the group as a whole. With the active parliamentarians date of entry to office seems to have made very little difference either way. Compared with the A-C group, the weightage of active parliamentarians appointed after 1628-9 has disappeared, and at this level the King can be said to have been acquiring a Civil Service more disposed to support him in the extremity of Civil War.

TABLE 42. SOCIAL STATUS AND ALLEGIANCE (ii)

	R	NR	N & SC	NP	N or P	all N	P	Total
Baronets . . .	9 (7·7)	1	3	–	–	4	3	16
Knights . . .	40	8	10	1 (7·3)	1	20	17	77
Esquires and equivalents .	42	8	10	8 (8·4)	4	30	17	89
Esq.-Gent. borderline .	1	–	2	3	2	7	2	10
Gents. and equivalent .	3	–	–	–	–	–	3	6
Probably below Gent. .	1	–	1	–	–	1	–	2

Little of interest can be seen here. Having excluded peers at one end of the scale, and very junior officers (copying clerks, menials, etc.) at the other, the preponderance of knights and esquires is overwhelming: 166 out of 200. And among them only one significant difference can be seen, passive or neutrally inclined parliamentarians, and other non-royalists (i.e. neutrals *or* parliamentarians) showing a bias away from knights and towards esquires. This approach might have more interesting results if more was known about a large enough number of under-officers.

TABLE 43. LOCATION OF PROPERTY AND ALLEGIANCE (ii)

	R	NR	N & SC	NP	N or P	all N	P	Total
King's qtrs. . . .	12 (8·9)	1	0·5	1	–	2·5	4	18·5
Doubtful, disputed . .	31·5 (31·4)	7	11·5 (8·5)	2·5	0·5	21·5 (20·3)	12·5 (13·7)	65·5
Scotland . . .	1	2	0·5	–	–	2·5	1	4·5
Parlt.'s qtrs. . .	43·5 (47·3)	5	13·5 (12·8)	8·5	6·5 (9·4)	33·5	21·5 (20·7)	98·5
Unknown or presumed none	8 (6·2)	2	–	–	–	2	3	13

Active royalists were a little more likely to have their property in the King's quarters, and a little less likely to have it in the Parliament's, compared with the distribution in the whole group. But it is difficult to see any other significant correlations, negative or positive, except that the neutral-parliamentarian and the neutral or parliamentarian categories show a bias towards having their property in the Parliament's quarters. Again it must be remembered that most office-holders had their landed estates in the south and south-east of England, quite apart from living and having property in London. More of them may have been drawn to parliamentarianism, or at any rate away from active royalism, than would have been if the King's power had extended deeper into these areas. And if he had been able to dispute for mastery over the capital itself, let alone if he had held it, the proportion of royalist office-holders might well have been much larger.

One of the ways in which the A-C office-holders were classified in the previous chapter was according to whether they were eldest, eldest surviving, and only, or younger sons. In the whole of that group the proportions were: first sons 76; younger 57; and unknown

61. But the 109 members of that group alive and identifiable in 1642, whose allegiance has been examined earlier in this section, include too many unknowns for this approach to be useful. It can however be attempted for the present, A-Z group.

TABLE 44. PLACE IN THE FAMILY AND ALLEGIANCE (i)

	R	NR	N & SC	NP	N or P	all N	P	Total
First	43 (36·5)	3	8	6	1	18 (23·6)	15 (16)	76
Younger . . .	22 (28·3)	7	10	5	2	24 (18·3)	13 (12·4)	59
Unknown . . .	31 (31·2)	7	8	1	4	20 (20·1)	14 (13·6)	65

The unknown cases are almost exactly evenly divided (compared with the group as a whole) among the different categories of allegiance. But, as has already been explained, it cannot be assumed that they would also be distributed in the same proportions as the known cases between the first and younger son categories; younger sons as such probably tend to be rather harder to identify, but even this can only be a conjecture.

Limiting ourselves to the known cases, first sons were more likely to be positive royalists, and less likely to be passive supporters of either side or neutrals of any kind. Younger sons were less likely to be royalists, and more likely to be neutral or inactive. This may be explicable by younger sons having been less likely to be landowners, and so less liable to taxation, forced loans, and confiscation. They might therefore have found it easier to conceal, or slur over their allegiance, if they did not want to commit themselves strongly one way or the other. For the same reason, however, they might have felt that they had less to lose, and therefore less incentive to hold back. Since most of those in this group, including the younger sons, held some property somewhere, even if they had not inherited it, too much weight should not be given to this factor whichever way it might be thought to have worked.

If the same kind of division could be shown to have existed among other comparable social groups (e.g. the sons of peers, baronets and knights, M.P.s, J.P.s, barristers), more could be made of this trend among office-holders. The Civil War might then appear if not as an uprising of younger brothers against their elders, at least as a struggle in which heads of families and heirs apparent were relatively more likely than younger sons to give positive support to the King. Among the Long Parliament M.P.s for the six south-western counties, on the other hand, the younger sons included relatively more royalists and fewer parliamentarians than would have been expected taking all the members from this region.[1] But among administrators of the middle rank the heads of gentry families were more likely to be active supporters of the King, while he was less likely to get such support from the slightly more 'self-made' younger sons of gentry families. It would be foolish to press this conclusion further on the basis of 135 men in a total group of 200.

Many of those in this group had at one time or other sat in the House of Commons, or were members of the Long Parliament itself. And some of them had sat in several parliaments before 1640. Incidentally, Mrs. Keeler gives a table of office-holding M.P.s in the first year or so of the Long Parliament (November 1640 to January 1641/2), but her figures cannot be used here. Some of the M.P.s counted by her are excluded from the present group of 200 because they were Privy Councillors or great officers of state, and others because their offices were not among those selected for

TABLE 45. MEMBERSHIP OF PARLIAMENT AND ALLEGIANCE

	R	NR	N & SC	NP	N or P	all N	P	Total
Too young to have sat before 1640 . . .	8	–	–	–	1	1	2	11
Totals corrected to allow for this . . .	88	17	26	12	6	61	40	189
Sat in any parlt. before 1640	34 (31·7)	7	9	2	–	18 (21·9)	16 (14·4)	68
The same, plus future peers, P.C.s, and judges . .	50	10	16	2	1	29	19	98
Short Parlt. . . .	19 (18·2)	1	4	1	–	6 (11·8)	13 (8)	38
With P.C.s etc. . .	22	1	5	1	–	7	14	43
Long Parlt., 1640-2 .	19 (19·2)	2	1	2	–	5 (12·4)	16 (8·4)	40
With P.C.s etc. . .	21	2	2	2	–	6	17	44

[1] I am grateful to Mr. Pennington for this information. Mrs. Keeler gives numbers of first and younger sons, but does not relate this to political allegiance.

inclusion in this group.[1] The information provided by other recent writers on early Stuart parliaments has been very useful in compiling this table, but in no case provides an actual cross-check on it. In order to see whether the exclusion of peers, councillors, and judges from the present group has led to a distortion of the proportions among M.P.s, an additional count has been made including them. Incidentally, the inclusion in the preceding table of those who were excluded from the 200 group because they were peers, councillors, or judges in 1642 does not materially affect the proportions in the main categories of allegiance.

Office-holders who had sat in the Commons before the 1630's were slightly more likely to be active royalists or active parliamentarians, and slightly less likely to be passive supporters, neutrals, or trimmers, than if they had followed the divisions among the whole 200 in the group. The Short Parliament (of April-May 1640) and even more the Long Parliament itself present a different picture. In both, the proportions of active royalists are almost exactly what might have been expected from the whole group, but the proportions of neutrals, etc., and of active parliamentarians are dramatically reversed. M.P.s may, of their own free and conscious choice, have been less likely than other office-holders to follow an inactive, neutral, trimming, or side-changing course, and more likely to be positive, committed parliamentarian supporters. Alternatively, they may have had poorer opportunities for hedging, for concealing their allegiance and deferring their decisions, than their official colleagues who were not in the Commons. As will be seen later in this section, such a factor does not seem to have operated with members of the House of Lords.

If the office-holding M.P.s are contrasted, not with the 200 office-holders but with the 550 or so members of the Long Parliament, the result is entirely different. The two analyses of the M.P.s of 1640-2 made by Brunton and Pennington and by Mrs. Keeler, do not employ identical categories for classification, and are not based on exactly the same totals. But their general conclusions are much the same; and whichever is adopted for comparison, the proportion of royalists to parliamentarians among office-holding M.P.s is almost the reverse of the ratio among the whole body of members.

[1] *Long Parlt.*, p. 18, Table 3. I do not agree with Mrs. Keeler that Sir William Uvedale was a Privy Councillor in 1640, as distinct from being on the Council of War (*ibid.*, pp. 18, 369); hence my total of Councillors who were M.P.s is one less than hers.

TABLE 46. OFFICE-HOLDERS IN THE LONG PARLIAMENT

	R	'Unclassi-fied'	'Straddlers etc.'	all N	P	Total
Brunton and Pennington totals .	236	14	–	–	302	552
Expected ratios from these totals	19·2	1·1	–	–	24·6	
Keeler totals .	226	5	6	–	310	547
Expected ratios .	18·6	0·4	0·5	–	25·5	
Actual office-holders	22	–	–	6	17	45

Note. In this Table — signifies that no such category was used.

As might have been expected, officials who were also parliamentary politicians did to a limited extent help to form the nucleus of a royal party in the Commons. However, only about five of the twenty or so of the future royalist office-holding members who were still in the House (a few had already been disabled) voted against Strafford's attainder on 21 April 1641.

Those who had been deprived of office, whose posts had lapsed, or who had been passed over for promotion were much less likely to be royalists, and correspondingly more likely to be either neutrals, etc., or parliamentarians than those who had not suffered in these ways. Those who had lost office and then been restored to it again were more likely to be royalists, as also were those whose offices were abolished, or severely curtailed in scope by Parliament in 1641.

TABLE 47. OFFICE AS A GRIEVANCE

	R	all N	P	Total
Deprived and dismissed . .	1	5	4	10
Passed over or demoted . .	–	1	3	4
Lapsed, or retired, and not re-employed	2	2	2	6
Removed and later restored . .	3	–	–	3
Attacked by Parliament, 1640-1 .	12	1	1	14

Note. The following are counted in the bottom line and also in one of the others: (i) Laurence Whitaker (already discussed in an earlier section of this chapter); (ii) William Coryton (who was deprived in 1626 but restored in 1630, and whose department—the Stannaries—had its powers reduced in 1641).

The contrast between the top and bottom parts of this table speaks for itself. Office-holders, and ex-office-holders apparently knew who their friends, or more often their enemies, were, and acted accordingly. But only 35 men are covered by this analysis, or $17\frac{1}{2}$ per cent. of the whole group. Convincing as the 'In-Out' hypothesis undoubtedly is when applied with reasonable caution to some individuals, it cannot conceivably serve as an explanation for the allegiance of office-holders in general.

For a different reason, much the same is true of religion. The difficulty here is lack of evidence. In so far as they are known, or can safely be inferred, religious leanings and affiliations do show marked correlations with allegiance in the Civil War.

TABLE 48.   RELIGION AND ALLEGIANCE (i)

	R	all N	P	Total
Roman Catholics . . .	4	1	–	5
High Church Anglicans . .	1	–	–	1
Low Churchmen and Puritans .	1	2	14	17

As far as $8\frac{1}{2}$ per cent. of the group is concerned, Gardiner's view of the Civil War as a 'Puritan Revolution' is therefore confirmed. But these figures of course beg the question of whether Puritanism was the cause or effect of parliamentarianism, or whether both were symptoms of some prior set of interests or psychological predispositions. The same could be said of the correlation between royalism and Romanism, with the added proviso that Parliament treated all papists as *ipso facto* royalists even though some of them would for choice almost certainly have remained neutrals! The more serious difficulty is how to classify the strong Protestants who were also strong Episcopalians; such middle-of-the-road Anglicans presumably constituted the back-bone of the royalists' strength, both in numbers and morale. If more information were available, a large proportion of the 200 might turn out to belong under this heading, including most of the 96 positive royalists. As it is, the correlation of religion with allegiance is clear at the extremes but remains non-proven for the group as a whole.

Finally, the allegiances of these 200 can be considered according to the particular institutions, or branches of the government in which they held office. It can then be seen how far the lines of division varied among the different departments.

TABLE 49. ALLEGIANCE IN DIFFERENT BRANCHES OF THE GOVERNMENT (i)

	R	NR	N & SC	NP	N or P	all N	P	Total
Expected ratios in every 10	4·8	·85	1·3	·6	·35	3·1	2·1	10
All Household depts.	24 (19·2)	5 or 6	8	—	—	13 or 14 (12·4)	3 (8·4)	40 or 41
Office of Arms and Court of Chivalry	4 or 6	—	—	—	—	—	—	4 or 6
Ordnance and Armoury	6	—	—	1	—	1	2	9
Other military	2	—	—	—	—	—	2	4
Mint	2 or 4	—	—	1	—	1	1	4 or 6
Customs	5	—	2	0 or 1	3	3 or 4	—	8 or 9
Law officers	4	—	—	—	—	2	1	7
Star Chamber	2 or 3	1	0 or 1	1	—	1 or 2	—	3 or 5
Council in the North	2	—	—	—	—	2	—	4
Council in the Marches (and other Welsh posts)	3	—	—	1	—	1	—	4
Navy	4 or 5 (4·8)	—	2	1	—	3 (3·1)	3 (2·1)	10 or 11
Exchequer	11 or 12 (13)	3	4	3	1	10 (8·4)	6 or 7 (5·7)	27 or 29
Common Pleas	1 or 2	—	—	3	2	5	—	6 or 7
Central Executive and diplomatic	7 or 9 (10·1)	4	4	—	—	8 (6·5)	6 (4·4)	21 or 23
Chancery	8 (10)	1	3	—	2	6 (6·5)	7 (4·4)	21
Wards and Liveries	1	—	1	1	—	2	3	6
Duchy of Lancaster	2	—	—	—	—	2	5	7
Requests	2	1	1	—	—	2	—	4
Kings' Bench	1	1	—	—	—	1	1	4
Stannaries	—	—	—	—	—	1	—	1
Alienations	1	1	—	—	—	—	—	2
Admiralty	—	—	—	—	—	—	—	1
Ecclesiastical	2 or 3	—	—	—	—	—	1 or 2	3 or 5

405

Note. The alternative figures given under some of the headings in this table include those who held subsidiary posts in the department in question, but who are also counted for a main post held elsewhere; the expected figures given in brackets exclude them.

In terms of allegiance, these institutions and groups of officers can be divided into five categories.

In the royal household there was a markedly heavier royalist predominance than in the central government as a whole. But this was at the expense of parliamentarianism, not neutralism or trimming. The Office of Arms (including the Court of Chivalry), the Ordnance, the Mint, the Customs, and the Crown law officers were also more positively royalist than the group as a whole. The total numbers involved in these branches are too small for much to be said about the other forms of allegiance. Although only senior customs officials who held by patent from the Crown have been included, the five active royalists among them had all at some time also been involved in customs farming (customs farmers, as such, are not within the scope of this study); if they were excluded, and lesser customs officials put in to fill their places, the picture would be rather different.

The Exchequer, the central executive (including the diplomatic service), and the Navy are divided in almost exactly the same proportions as the whole group. In the Navy, however, the royalists include one voluntarily retired officer, and another who had practically been superannuated; the key men ashore were mainly parliamentarians, as were the majority of the sea-going captains. So the apparent evenness of distribution there is somewhat deceptive.

Common Pleas is unique in having a preponderance of neutrals or passive parliamentarians. Indeed, they constitute an absolute as well as a relative majority there.

In Chancery and the Court of Wards and Liveries there is a relative preponderance of parliamentarians, while royalists are in a clear minority. In the Duchy of Lancaster there is an absolute parliamentarian majority; there and in the Wards the numbers involved are too small for much to be inferred about the proportions in the other categories.

Nothing much can profitably be said about any of the other branches. Where so few men are classified under each heading, the expected distribution involves calculating small fractions of men; the results of small mistakes in research then become disproportionately large. It would be foolish to build conclusions on less than half an office-holder one way or the other!

It must also be emphasized that the numbers taken from each branch of the government are in no way 'samples' of the allegiances of the whole staff in these branches. 'Middling rank', the basis of this group, is inevitably a slightly arbitrary notion; some branches of the government had many more such posts, relative to their total strength, than did others. Nor did the under-officers in a department necessarily divide in even approximately the same proportions as these relatively more senior ones.

Leaving aside lapsed or evicted officers, the Council in the North shows a strong royalist bias. Small as are the total numbers involved, it and Star Chamber should perhaps both be added to the royalist dominated group. The figures already given for officials whose posts had been attacked by the Long Parliament point the same way. They are also relevant for the Court of Chivalry, the Stannaries, and the ecclesiastical officials. Clarendon illustrates this point very well by telling how in 1642 he found himself to be a most unwelcome lodger in a house at York; he was puzzled as to the cause of his host's attitude until he learnt that

> the Man of the House had been an Attorney in the Court of the President and Council of the North, in great Reputation, and Practice there; and thereby got a very good Livelihood with which He had lived in Splendour; and Mr. Hyde had sat in the Chair of that Committee, and had carried up the Votes of the Commons against that Court, to the House of Peers, upon which it was dissolved:

He had sympathized, and found new lodgings.[1]

Some contrast in attitude may be suggested between those who had already lost their offices, or had the scope of them restricted through the Long Parliament's activities, and those who feared that they might be among the next victims of its reforming zeal. Wardship and Livery were regarded as acute grievances by most armigerous landowners, and so by most M.P.s. The reform, if not the outright abolition of the Court of Wards, was in the air during 1641; indeed, but for the intensified political crisis in the autumn of that year and the sequence of events which followed, it might well have been abolished by act of parliament, passed by King, Lords, and Commons, in 1642 or 1643, instead of by ordinance (passed by Lords and Commons only) in 1646. The Duchy of Lancaster was less unpopular, but its jurisdiction too was associated with the exercise of royal prerogative; and, as with the Wards, it was also argued that greater efficiency would be achieved by centralizing all royal revenues in the Exchequer, and doing away with both these other independent

---

[1] *Life,* I, 128.

revenue institutions. The Duchy's prerogative jurisdiction was in fact removed by the 'Star Chamber Act' of 1641, but its financial independence survived until 1686.[1] The Alienations was another threatened office. Its *raison d'être* depended largely on the maintenance of the feudal land tenures and on the Crown's ability to use them for fiscal purposes. As well as the Clerk who is included among the parliamentarians in this group, its other principal and at least one secondary official seem to have been neutrals of some kind; and no officer or clerk in the Alienations appears to have been an active royalist. Although it was not abolished in 1646 or in 1660, the Alienations ceased to be an effective part of the revenue machinery when the feudal tenures were abolished; it survived through the eighteenth century only as a rather ineffectual registry office for land transactions and as the home of a few sinecurists.[2] The Courts of Chivalry and of the Stannaries, on the other hand, had already been attacked by Parliament in 1641; and for this purpose their staffs should rather be classified with those of the Council in the Marches of Wales and of the departments which had succumbed altogether to reforming legislation.

The political attitudes of the officers in the Court of Wards and Liveries, and perhaps in other threatened departments, may have arisen partly from the need to keep on the winning side, in order to be compensated if and when their posts were abolished. The compensation schedule of 1647 only catered for the parliamentarian officers and clerks of the Wards; likewise in 1660-2 only the royalists, and perhaps some of the more discreet neutrals among the underofficers, had their claims considered.

It is hard to see any coherent pattern in some of the other departments. Why did the officers of the Mint and the Ordnance mainly go for the King, while by comparison those of the Navy did not? Northumberland's patronage as Admiral of the Fleet, 1636-7, and then as Lord Admiral, 1638-42, has already been suggested as a partial explanation for the latter case. And, although most of the senior men in the Mint and Ordnance were royalists, a number of their subordinates appear to have stayed in London, continuing with their normal duties, as passive or neutral supporters of Parliament, even if not in most cases as active parliamentarians.

[1] S. B. Baxter, *The Development of the Treasury 1660-1702* (1957), p. 55.
[2] Giuseppi, *Guide*, I, 258-9; see also J. E. D. Binney, *British Public Finance and Administration 1774-92* (Oxford, 1958), p. 76.

The King's failure to command decisive support among the judges has already been commented on. It may be partly ascribed in some cases to fear of further retribution at Parliament's hands, but genuine constitutional convictions should not be discounted. For all that had happened in the 1630's, the political implications of Coke's judicial ideals had perhaps not been wholly replaced by those of Ellesmere, Bacon, and Finch.

Among the Secretaries of States' staff and the Council Clerks, at the Signet and Privy Seal offices, and in the diplomatic service, positive royalists made a relatively weak showing, as against the active parliamentarians and the various kinds of neutrals, trimmers, etc. This non-commitment of the central executive to the King's cause is puzzling. Men who were serving or had spent much of their lives abroad may just have been out of positive sympathy with royal policy at home; and the ability to take a detached view of the issues sometimes coincided opportunely with sitting on the fence for reinsurance purposes. Foreigners too, even naturalized ones, may have tended to feel less directly involved, although some were as strongly committed as any native. Against the somewhat devious and erratic course steered by that bizarre character Sir Balthazar Gerbier must be set the sturdy convictions of G. R. Weckherlin.

The broadest contrast is between the royal household, and the law and revenue courts which had long ago, in Tout's famous phrase, 'gone out of court' and settled permanently in the capital. Unlike those of the other household departments, some of the Wardrobe staff were not peripatetic; and at least one of them, just too junior to be included in the 200, remained in service at Whitehall continuously from 1640 to 1660—and got away with it! But in general the staffs of all the other household departments were used to attending the King and Queen (or the royal children) on the summer progresses and on the Court's shorter journeys between the three or four main palaces: Whitehall, Greenwich, Hampton, Windsor. No radical step was involved in their leaving London at any time from January 1642 on; a number of them had been formally summoned to attend on the royal family before the end of that month. And even if York and Nottingham were further afield than a normal progress would have taken them, many had been with the King in the north of England in 1639 or 1640. The act of leaving Whitehall, even of leaving the London area, was not in itself anything revolutionary.

For the staffs of Exchequer, Common Pleas, and Chancery, and to a lesser extent those of King's Bench, the Wards, and the Duchy, it was a different matter. The law and revenue courts were sometimes adjourned out of London because of the plague, usually to Reading or somewhere at about that distance from London. But for many decades, and in some cases for centuries, these institutions had not perambulated with the King, and only severe plague epidemics had caused even temporary interruptions of their settled, long-established routine.

The King did not summon the officers of these departments to join him until after the war had begun, and this was probably a serious tactical mistake. Both his Secretaries attended him from the start, with the Signet Seal; but as can be seen from Nicholas's letters to Weckherlin in 1642 the Secretaries had not taken all their staff and their papers with them.[1] The Lord Privy Seal remained in London; the Great Seal, followed by the Lord Keeper, only reached the King in June 1642. Not until December were the Courts of Chancery, the Duchy of Lancaster, Wards, and Requests ordered to adjourn to Oxford for the following Hilary term (Jan.-Feb. 1643); the Receipt of Exchequer and the First Fruits and Tenths office were summoned there at the same time. But King's Bench, Common Pleas, and the Exchequer were simply ordered to adjourn for the first half of Hilary term, and to meet as usual, in Westminster, for the second half. This blunder may have arisen from false hopes about the outcome of the peace negotiations which were then pending. In February 1642/3 the King ordered all customs and other revenues to be paid at Oxford, and summoned the Auditors of the upper Exchequer to attend there. The next month he offered a free pardon to any officers, clerks, artificers, or workmen of the Ordnance who came to join him at Oxford. But only in November 1643 did he order the Judges of King's Bench and Common Pleas to adjourn their sittings to Oxford, for the rest of that Michaelmas and the whole of the following Hilary terms. Each of these letters or proclamations was followed by some kind of parliamentary riposte, ordering the officers in question to stay put. The breach became complete in the winter of 1643-4. Parliament then passed an ordinance depriving all office-holders who had joined or in any other way helped the King; Charles finally summoned the staffs of all the law courts and the holders of all other offices to join him; Parliament in turn forbade them to obey him on pain of deprivation; by the spring of 1644 the

[1] Berks. R.O., Trumbull MSS., XX, 60, 79.

King too was depriving those who had refused to join him, or had otherwise assisted Parliament.

A revolutionary crisis in mens' lives, like that of 1642-3, may interrupt and perhaps overthrow settled habits and traditions, but it is unlikely wholly to eradicate them. It was natural for the household officers to follow the King or the other members of the royal family; for them it was a conscious and deliberate act of disloyalty to turn a deaf ear to the King's exhortations, to disobey his orders, and to stay in the Parliament's quarters after the breach had become irreparable. For the members of the courts and departments settled at Westminster, with their branch offices scattered about the Holborn-Temple area and in the City, the positive, deliberate step was to move; physically speaking, it meant abandoning their posts, leaving behind most of their official papers, and in very many cases their own homes and private possessions. Many of the household officers were literally 'courtiers'; they lodged at Court, and when off duty they went away to their country estates. Although many officers of the law and revenue courts and the 'out of Court' departments were landowners, most of them had a London house; quite a number were truly Londoners, and had nowhere else to go. Men who were in a position to withdraw to the country perhaps had a better chance of preserving neutrality or of following a mild, passively royalist course than those who were forced to choose between London and Oxford.

By the time that the King did issue his formal summonses, it was too late. The convinced royalists had already rallied to him, perhaps more in their personal capacities than as the holders of particular offices: as for example some of those in the Exchequer. A few waverers trickled over during 1643, but most of them preferred to stay where they were in the capital, or to lie low in the provinces. It would have been easier for those who stayed in London to persuade a victorious King that they had been prevented from leaving the capital, than for those who had moved to Oxford to persuade a victorious Parliament that they had been prevented from staying. Such perhaps was the reasoning of Croke, Povey, Francis Phillipps (another senior Revenue Auditor), and several more.

This is not to imply that the Exchequer, any more than any other department, was solidly neutral and parliamentarian. The figures contradict this, as do the histories of the Fanshawe, Osborne, and Wardour families. In most cases it is only a slight proportionate preponderance one way or the other which has to be accounted for.

411

No court or department was 'solid', in the sense of being 100 per cent. or even 90 per cent. for King, for Parliament, or for neither.

The immediacy of the King's person, the more direct and literal sense in which they were his (or the Queen's or Prince's) servants, and their being accustomed to leaving Whitehall with the royal Court surely afford some explanation of why the balance of household officers tilted one way. And the reverse factors, being more remote from the sovereign, 'out of Court', and in less mobile departments, correspondingly help to explain the relative neutral and parliamentarian strength elsewhere in the central institutions.

This does not of course exclude there having been more men of constitutionalist and low church sympathies in the 'out of Court' departments, more believers in absolute monarchy, high Churchmen, and Romanists in the household. And to a limited extent there may also have been a social antithesis: lawyers and men of business experience (excluding monopolists) against courtiers, grantees, and other beneficiaries of the old order.

Councillors and Peers. The third group to be considered consists of the 54 peers and Privy Councillors who were alive in September 1642 and had held office or been in the Council before the end of 1640.

The smallness of this group means that it is often not worth comparing the actual and the expected proportions under the different headings of allegiance. But as far as this can profitably be done, the older men again inclined rather more than the rest towards neutralism, trimming, or inaction; the younger ones rather more to positive commitment one way or the other. Again there is a connexion between neutralism, trimming, and side-changing and entry to office, or the Council before 1628-9. The relation of allegiance to social status shows only one appreciable difference: those who inherited peerages were relatively more inclined to passive, or neutralist royalism, first-generation peers relatively more to neutralism, trimming, or side-changing than the members of this group at large. Nor does the location of their property tell us very much about the allegiance of councillors and office-holding peers, except that neutrals, trimmers, etc., were a little more likely than the others to have their main estates in doubtful or disputed territory. The Scottish-based ones were more likely to be royalists of one kind or another; those with large properties in Ireland more likely to be neutral or to trim. In general, the estates of peers were more likely to be scattered,

TABLE 50. AGE, DATE OF ENTRY TO OFFICE, SOCIAL STATUS, LOCATION OF PROPERTY, AND ALLEGIANCE (iii)

	R	NR	N & SC	N or P	all N	P	Total
Born 16th century . . .	23 (23·6)	5	11 (9·7)	1	17 (15·5)	4 (4·9)	44
Born 17th century . . .	6	1	1	–	2	2	10
Total	29	6	12	1	19	6	54
Percentage	53·7	11·1	22·2	1·85	35·2	11·1	–
Appts. before 1628-9 . .	20 (20·4)	3	11 (8·4)	1	15 (13·4)	3 (4·2)	38
Apptd. after 1628-9 . .	9	3	1	–	4	3	16
Lay peers by inheritance (incld. promotion)	11	5	3	–	8	3	22
Newly created peers .	11	–	7	1	8	2	21
Bishops	2	1	–	–	1	–	3
Knights	5	–	2	–	2	1	8
Estates in the King's qtrs. .	2·5	0·5	0·5	–	1	–	3·5
Doubtful and disputed .	13 (14·2)	2·5	8 (5·9)	–	10·5 (9·3)	3 (2·9)	26·5
Parlt.'s qtrs.	7·5 (6·4)	1	1	1	3	1·5	12
Ireland	0·5	–	1·5	–	1·5	0·5	2·5
Scotland	4·5	2	–	–	2	–	6·5
Unknown (possibly not yet inherited	1	–	1	–	1	1	3

and so rather less likely to lie in exclusively royalist or exclusively parliamentarian areas. Partly on this account peers may have been more likely to think in terms of the national outcome of the conflict, less of how it would go in particular parts of the country.

The place of peers and councillors in their own families provides another point of comparison with the medium-ranking group.

TABLE 51. PLACE IN THE FAMILY AND ALLEGIANCE (ii)

	R	NR	N & SC	N or P	all N	P	Total
First (incldg. first surviving) sons	19 (17·2)	5	4	–	9 (11·3)	4 (3·6)	32
Younger sons . . .	4 (7)	1	6 (2·9)	1	8 (4·6)	1 (1·4)	13
Unknown	6 (4·8)	–	2	–	2	1	9

Here too eldest sons were likelier to be active royalists than the younger and unknown ones; they were also likelier than the rest to be passive, or neutrally inclined royalists. In both respects the exact reverse is true, to a rather greater extent, of younger sons. And, as with the 200 medium-ranking commoner office-holders, no connexion can be seen between place in the family and active parliamentarianism.

The question of office as a grievance is somewhat more complicated in the case of this group. Superficially the allegiances of those who had been removed from office or Council membership and had retired (voluntarily or otherwise) are very similar to those of the group as a whole.

TABLE 52.   RETIREMENT AND DEPRIVATION, GRIEVANCE, AND COUNCIL MEMBERSHIP, AND ALLEGIANCE

	R	NR	N & SC	N or P	all N	P	Total
In the Council and or in office summer 1642	22	5	7 (8·4)	1	13	3	38
'Out' in 1642	7 (8·6)	1	5 (3·6)	–	6 (5·6)	3 (1·8)	16
Disobliged by the Crown, including passed over and temporarily 'out'	1 (9·1)	3	9 (3·8)	–	12 (6)	4 (1·9)	17
Privy Councillors only, as of October 1640 . . .	17 (16·6)	5 (3·4)	4 (6·9)	1 (·6)	10 (10·9)	4 (3·4)	31

But the first part of this table is in fact misleading. Three of the royalists were 'out' in 1642 because they had been attacked by Parliament (Laud, Finch, and Windebank), and two others had genuinely retired of their own free choice. A more meaningful comparison is obtained by taking all those who at any time had been seriously disobliged by the Crown in their capacity as office-holders or Privy Councillors. The 'In-out' or 'Grievance' hypothesis then appears to be overwhelmingly confirmed, and much more convincingly than with the 200 middling office-holders. But, as has been suggested earlier in this chapter, there are several cases (e.g. those of the Earl of Cork, Sir John Coke, Bishop Williams) where this hypothesis is only one of several possible explanations of allegiance in the Civil War. The general disquiet which Charles I's policy aroused among English Protestants with interests or estates in Ireland may have influenced the attitude of such apparently clear 'in-outers' as Lords Loftus and Mountnorris. And by the time that all other possible explanations have been eliminated, those left in this category are less impressive: Robert Carr, Earl of Somerset, sometime favourite of James I, had fallen from power and favour (and for a time been imprisoned for being an accessory to murder) as long ago as 1615; Lionel Cranfield, Earl of Middlesex, had been impeached, driven from office, and heavily punished in 1624, and was in his sixty-eighth year by 1642; Lord Herbert of Cherbury had also fallen from favour in 1624, but was later restored to the extent of receiving two titles, and a land grant, and being made a Councillor of War. Lord Stanhope had undoubtedly been evicted from the Post Office; but these four cases provide a fragile basis for any generalizations about deprivation or grievance as exclusive or determining factors in men's allegiance.

One perhaps less expected fact can be seen from the last line of the preceding table. Those who were members of the Privy Council on the eve of the Long Parliament's meeting at the beginning of November 1640 (and who were still alive in September 1642) were a little more likely to be passive or neutrally inclined royalists, and rather less likely to be neutrals, trimmers, etc., than the ex-Councillors and the peers holding lesser offices, who make up the rest of this group. But no other appreciable difference can be seen between the 1640 Councillors and the group as a whole. This may seem to contradict the findings, in the previous part of the table, about office and council membership as grievances; the probable explanation is that several of those with some cause for grievance of this nature were still Privy Councillors in November 1640.

Again, in so far as religious affiliations are known or can be inferred, these show a definite correlation with allegiance.

TABLE 53. RELIGION AND ALLEGIANCE (ii)

	R	all N	P	Total
Roman Catholic or high Anglican sympathies	7 (4·3)	1	–	8
Puritan and low church sympathies . .	–	6 (3·5)	4 (1·1)	10
Unclassified	22	12	2	36

Once more it is one thing to illustrate that this correlation existed, and quite another to understand the true relationship between religion and politics. As has been argued in the case of Sir Robert Harley, general hypotheses about this relationship can only be tested by detailed studies of individual cases. The quantitative connexions which have been established in this section must not be taken as proofs about the causes of allegiance.

With an emphatic proviso about the smallness of the total numbers involved, a division of this group according to their departments gives another standard of comparison with the previous one.

TABLE 54. ALLEGIANCE IN DIFFERENT BRANCHES OF THE GOVERNMENT (ii)

	R	NR	N & SC	N or P	all N	P	Total
Household depts. . . .	11·5 (9·7)	1	3	–	4 (6·3)	2·5 (2)	18
Legal	3	1	–	–	1	–	4
Privy Councillors without office	4	–	–	–	–	–	4
Court of Chivalry and Office of Arms	2	1	–	–	1	–	3
Finance	2	–	1	–	1	–	3
Scotland	2	1	1	–	2	–	4
Central executive and diplomatic	3·5 (5·4)	1	4 (2·2)	–	5 (3·5)	1·5 (1·1)	10
Ireland	–	–	2	–	2	1	3
Naval and military . . .	–	–	1	–	1	1	2
Misc. (Duchy, Wales, Privy Seal)	1	1	–	1	2	–	3

At this level the household departments were only very little more royalist than the government as a whole. The other royalist-weighted groups are the holders of legal office and the Privy Councillors 'without portfolio'. The central executive shows a bias away from active royalism and towards neutralism and trimming; this was also true in its middle ranks, except that there the bias was more towards active parliamentarianism. The apparent bias of Irish office-holders away from royalism is explicable, *inter alia*, by Strafford and Wandesford both being dead before 1642. In general, any contrast which may legitimately be drawn at the middle level of government between courtiers and administrators has little meaning nearer the top of the ladder.

ix OFFICE, ALLEGIANCE AND POLITICS

It may be well to remind ourselves that this book is about the administrative system, and more particularly the men who operated it. If it sheds any incidental light on the origins or nature of the Civil War, so much the better; but that is not its main purpose, and it is well to keep one's eye on the target. The previous section of this chapter is meant, on the contrary, to test out various hypotheses, in order to see what light the Civil War and the part taken in it by officials throw on the nature of the administrative system.

This process can be carried further. It is interesting to look on to 1649 and 1660, and to see how many of the King's servants from 1625-41, who were still alive, held office under the Republic and after the Restoration.

TABLE 55. SERVICE UNDER THE REPUBLIC AND AFTER THE RESTORATION

	Served under the Republic (1649-60)	Percentage in each group	Served after the Restoration	Percentage
All ranks, surnames A-C . . .	c. 22	20·2	c. 26	23·9
Medium-ranking commoners, surnames A-Z . . .	c. 36	18	c. 51	25·5
Peers and Privy Councillors . . .	4	7·4	8	14·8

Several of the passive or neutrally inclined parliamentarians, and a number even of the active ones, refused to recognize the authority of the Commonwealth in 1649, or to take the Engagement (the oath of fidelity to it); they thereupon either resigned or were forced from office. A few of those who were out of office under the Commonwealth may have returned under the Protectorate. But even allowing for those who had already died, the numbers from any of the three groups who held office at any time under the Republic are small. Absolutely there seem to be most from the revenue depart-

o 417

ments, and proportionately most from the courts of Chancery and Common Pleas, and the Alienations Office.

Almost all the surviving royalists recovered office in 1660-1, though not always the identical post which they had held before the troubles. But quite a sprinkling of the neutrals and trimmers, and even some of the active parliamentarians who were still alive, also kept or recovered office under the restored monarchy. Thanks to the general character of the Restoration (especially the role of Monck and the Presbyterians), there was not a complete purge of all those who had at any time accepted and served under the Republic. Like the Restoration land settlement, this was a cause of Cavalier disillusionment with Charles II, and of the future opposition to his government from his erstwhile most ardent supporters. However, those who failed to obtain the posts which they thought they ought to have been given in 1660-1 were not (with rare exceptions) survivors of the 1625-41 administration, but Cavaliers of the 1640's and 1650's who had not held office before the Civil War. This return of the pre-war men can be related to the return of the old system; a little more will be said about that in the concluding chapter.

As a source of information about the royal officials of the 1620's and 1630's, the evidence from 1642 and after emphasizes the importance of small individual differences, in temperament, circumstances, and outlook. And it should warn us against classifying these men solely according to their Civil War allegiances. If one excellent example of the active, 'entrepreneurial' type of office-holder is Sir Henry Croke of the Pipe, a neutral with parliamentarian leanings, another is George Mynne, who despite having been deprived of office by a prerogative court was an active royalist. If Sir Henry Compton, K.B., uncle of the Earl of Northampton, the rentier-like Custos Brevium of Common Pleas, was a royalist, Sir Edward Baeshe, the absentee Chamberlain of the Exchequer, was a neutral. Sir Robert Wolseley of the Patent Office, an active successful self-made official, was a royalist, while his colleague Sir Thomas Hampson of the Statute Office, who had succeeded to his position as his brother's reversioner, was a neutral or trimmer.

Nor, for instance, were the office-holding common lawyers mostly parliamentarians or neutrals and the civil lawyers mostly royalists. Indeed, of six Doctors of Civil Law who held medium-ranking office (including one who appears in the tables as a knight) only one was a positive royalist. Excluding judges, among those who had been called to the bar or studied the law for more than the conventional year or two, in the second group fourteen were royalists, nine neutrals or trimmers, and five parliamentarians.

Yet it would be a mistake to suppose that these various categories are totally unrelated. Among all the trained lawyers (common and civil) holding office in the law courts, and excluding the Crown law officers, there is a preponderance of neutrals and trimmers, and there are relatively few active royalists. Among those who may fairly be thought of as having been courtiers first and officials second, the royalists are easily predominant, even more so perhaps than they are among the holders of posts in the household (an overlapping but not identical category). The full-time careerists, whose whole position depended on their work as officials, seem to have been much more evenly divided. Granted the way in which the patronage system worked, absentees, and annuitary and part-time office-holders were more likely to be gentry with court connexions; the self-made careerists were correspondingly more likely to be products of the lesser gentry or of the urban middle class. To this very broad and generalized contrast between courtiers and civil servants, or as we may perhaps say between 'gentleman' and 'players', exceptions can be found, but they remain exceptions. That ardent Cavalier Edward Nicholas is as good an example of a conscientious administrative careerist as could be found; however, his ties with the Court and with the inner circle of Councillors had become even closer in the 1630's than they had been in the lifetime of his patron, Buckingham. By contrast the Court connexions of Sir Robert Pye, who had once had distinctly closer ties with royal and ruling circles than Nicholas, had perceptibly loosened under the personal government. Even Robert Henley, apparently very much of a full-time and self-made legal office-holder who became a passive or neutrally inclined royalist, seems to have been in the process, around 1640, of transforming himself into an absentee and a rentier; Samuel Wightwick, his *locum tenens* as Chief Clerk of King's Bench, was a passive if not active parliamentarian.

In the Exchequer, more of the officers who were actively involved in financial administration were neutrals or parliamentarians. These included the Auditor and the Deputy Chamberlains of the Receipt both Auditors of the Imprests, five out of seven Revenue Auditors, and the Surveyor of the Greenwax. On the King's side are found more of those who had ceased to play any significant part in organizing the revenue system and whose routine duties were largely performed by deputies and under-clerks: the King's and Lord Treasurer's Remembrancers, one of the Chamberlains, the Clerk of the Pells. Exceptions are provided by two out of four Tellers being actively and a third perhaps passively royalist, and by the other Chamberlain and the Clerk of the Pipe being neutral or passively parliamentarian.

If more was known about the religious beliefs and constitutional principles of more office-holders, it would obviously be easier to understand the line they took from 1642 on. Failing this, it can safely be said that their age, the date of their appointments, the location of their property, and whether they were first or younger sons all appear to be relevant considerations. Finally, bearing in mind the various types of office-holders and the striking differences in allegiance between the different branches of the central government, the most important political distinction among the King's servants is that between courtiers, using that term in its widest sense, and those without court connexions and influence. It can almost be said that some of the King's servants were beginning to be the public servants of the Crown while others were becoming more specifically the private servants of the sovereign. In its full modern sense this distinction was still far ahead; but in one sense it was already an issue, and on the long view it was partly what the Civil War itself was about.

It is less easy to see any direct connexion between the administrative system and the causes either of the peaceful revolution in 1640-1 or of the war which followed. If the central administration and all its members had stood firmly by the monarchy and backed all its policies continuously from 1637 or 1638 on, clearly the King's prospects of remaining in control of the situation would have been a good deal better than they were. The divisions inside the government, at all levels, to help to explain the ease with which 'Thorough' and then the whole edifice of semi-absolute monarchy were overthrown in 1640-1. It is equally certain, and no less obvious, that chronic inefficiency, especially in the use of the Crown's financial resources, reduced the government's capacity to meet its needs in 1639-40. At the same time a fundamental reform of the revenue and the spending departments, and of the methods of administration, in short a 'revolution in government', was far beyond the capacity of Charles I's régime. Had something like it been more vigorously and consistently attempted, the Crown might have been strengthened in some respects. But so many courtiers and other office-holders would have had to be disobliged and perhaps thoroughly alienated in the process that the Crown might easily have lost more than it gained on a short-term balance. So much can be affirmed without much doubt or controversy.

Turning from hypothesis to speculation, if the administrators had acted as a united body with common interests and a common outlook, they might have helped to bring King and Parliament together again in 1641-2 or to effect a compromise peace in 1643. However, they were not only disunited among themselves but they also lacked any constructive *via media* to offer to Pym or to King Charles. Nor is unity in itself always strength: the Gadarene swine were united in hurrying to the brink—and over it. Less even than the *noblesse de la robe* in France did the English office-holders form a coherent social class with common traditions, interests, and aspirations. But it does not necessarily follow that they therefore exercised a less constructive or less beneficial influence—or even a less powerful one. Their difficulties, and the divisions among them in the early 1640's may well have reflected with reasonable accuracy those of the English 'political nation' at large. Whatever may be the truth of this, these difficulties and divisions do not provide evidence for the existence of any one fundamental, 'first' cause of the Civil War, or for any monolithic explanation of its nature.

7

CONCLUSION

WE MUST NOW RETURN to the questions which were raised in the Introduction. How are the administrative system and the royal officials to be related to the political and social history of the time, to the general character of Charles I's government and to the upheaval which overthrew it? And what is the place of that epoch in the history of the English Civil Service, and of bureaucracy in general?

To try to answer these questions we must first look at them in less specialized terms than in the preceding chapters. First there is the more 'long run' chronological approach: this period must be set in the context of English administrative history over the centuries. Then there is the comparative approach: the administrative system in England, its nature together with its political and social significance, must be compared with that in some other European countries during the early modern age. Finally there is the more analytical, or perhaps one should say sociological, approach: the nature of bureaucracy needs to be considered and then the relevance of such a concept examined for the England of Charles I.

i CHRONOLOGICAL PERSPECTIVE:
THE COURSE OF ENGLISH ADMINISTRATIVE HISTORY

In monarchical societies central government usually begins as the personal household government of the ruler. Tout's classic distinction between institutions being 'in' or 'out of court' was framed with

English conditions specifically in mind. And, without careful study, it would be foolish to turn it into an all-embracing generalization, applicable for instance to the empires of the ancient world or of the Far East. But the distinction can plausibly be applied to virtually all the secular states of western Europe since the break up of the Roman Empire; it would be less easy to explain papal government along these lines.

This raises one of the fundamental problems of European administrative history. That is how far the institutions of England and other European states were alike simply because they arose in broadly similar circumstances and had to deal with broadly similar problems. And how far they were alike because they were modelled, consciously or unconsciously, on those of the Frankish Kingdom, the Carolingian and Ottonian Empires, and the Papacy, and so ultimately, in some slight measure, on Roman institutions. On the surface the evidence for the second interpretation is temptingly strong. But the working out of elaborate pedigrees for institutions can easily become a little unreal; it can become a game which, played for its own sake, is likely to be historically sterile. There are pitfalls too. Even in the *Chinese* Empire the great court officials responsible for different branches of the central government, and each with a subordinate hierarchy, bear some very vague and general resemblance to those of Rome, Byzantium, the Franks, the Carolingians, and the Angevins. At this point it is time to stop; institutional genealogy is getting out of hand!

But this does not mean that there was no imitation. Outside influences were important, especially from the eighth to eleventh centuries, when the conditions of life imposed broadly similar limitations on all European 'governments', and when men were rather easily impressed by what seemed to them more 'civilized' and therefore superior practices. This tended to become less true as medieval society grew more secure, wealthier, and more complex.

Such was certainly the case with English government, the continuous history of which begins with the Anglo-Saxon invasions. In the early centuries after the invasions it seems safe to infer the existence of 'pure' household government, of a time when no institutions had yet gone 'out of court'. Much the same was probably true of Normandy in the early days of the duchy. Although relatively more is known of late Old English, and immediately pre-Conquest Norman government, medieval historians still seem to be unsure about their precise nature; some of these ambiguities arise from the nature of the evidence, or the lack of it. Thus it is not clear which, if any, court officials of pre-Conquest England can fairly be regarded as the forerunners of later heads of non-household departments. It has been debated whether or not Edward the Confessor had a Chancellor, and whether or not the Norman Dukes had a Treasury. It is now thought that in England practice had got ahead of theory: Edward had an official who was in many respects like a Chancellor except in that he was not so called; and that he probably also had something that can fairly be called a Treasury. A tendency towards more elaborate central administration is already discernible well before 1066; it is difficult to estimate how sharp a break was caused by the Conquest, and idle to speculate what would otherwise have happened.[1]

The age of the Norman and Angevin Kings is generally agreed to have seen the great and really decisive expansion of central government. The twelfth century was *par excellence* the time of the Toutian process, when branches of the administration began to go 'out of court'. The Exchequer soon came to be physically and institutionally distinct from the single undifferentiated *Curia Regis*; the detachment of the Common Pleas followed more slowly, and was not definitely established until *Magna Carta*. These changes were paralleled by an immense increase in the keeping of written records; literacy thus

[1] *Note*. The references in the first part of this section are in no way meant to constitute a bibliography for English medieval administrative history; they merely indicate some of the works which I have found helpful. I am grateful to Dr. E. B. Fryde for suggesting some of them to me, and for other help on the medieval period.

On the Anglo-Saxon and Norman periods see L. M. Larson, *The King's Household in England before the Norman Conquest* (Minneapolis, 1904); Tout, *Chapters*, vol. I, chs. iii and iv, introductory ss.; C. H. Haskins, *Norman Institutions* (Cambridge, Mass., 1918); G. H. White, 'Financial Administration under Henry I', *Trans. Roy. Hist. Soc.*, 4th ser., VIII (1925), 56-78; G. H. White, 'The Household of the Norman Kings', *ibid.*, XXX (1948), 127-55; F. M. Stenton, *Anglo-Saxon England* (2nd edn., Oxford, 1947), pp. 406, 635-40; Stenton, *Latin Charters of the Anglo-Saxon Period* (Oxford, 1955), esp. pp. 11-12, 31-50, 53-4, 84-7, 89-91; V. H. Galbraith, *Studies in the Public Records* (1948), ch. II; F. E. Harmer, *Anglo-Saxon Writs* (Manchester, 1952), introduction, esp. pp. 1-6, 10-19, 24-45, 57-61, 92-3; G. Barraclough, 'The Anglo-Saxon Writ', *History*, n.s., XXXIX (1954), 193-215; S. B. Chrimes, *An Introduction to the Administrative History of Mediaeval England* (Oxford, 1952), ch. I.

became a primary requirement for almost all administrators. For this reason clerics, even if they were often only clerks in minor orders, came to play a still larger part in secular government than they had done earlier.

Although it is usually ascribed to the twelfth century, this expansion and transformation of government must have begun under William the Conqueror. Despite its pioneering use of writs and seals, and its having boasted the only 'national' taxation system in Europe, the Old English state could hardly have produced Domesday Book. Nor did this expansion of government slacken at the accession of John; notable increases in the keeping of written records can be dated to around the year 1200. Only in Henry III's reign can the Angevin administrative system be seen in its full maturity. In this context the term 'twelfth century' can therefore reasonably be extended to cover the 150 years or so, c. 1080-c. 1230. The profound changes during this period, including some which had got under way but were not complete by its close, can properly be described as an 'administrative revolution' or a 'revolution in government'.[1]

Following upon this revolution, during the years 1232-4 and 1258-64, and in a sense over the whole course of John's and Henry III's reigns a new pattern of conflict emerged in English politics. This pattern became classical in the sense that according to Tout it persisted without fundamental change for several centuries. Political conflict between the Crown and the baronage (or later between the Crown and other opposition forces, e.g. in the House of Commons) became inseparable, and at times indistinguishable, from conflict between two rival administrative systems, or at least between the protagonists of two conflicting views of what the administrative system should be. The Crown tended to rely, for what had ceased in practice to be merely the needs of the royal household, on the creation of new and adaptation of existing curial agencies, and on the King's personal servants. The magnates preferred to use the

---

[1] On the twelfth century see F. Pollock and F. W. Maitland, *A History of English Law* (Cambridge, 1898), chs. IV and VI; Holdsworth, *History*, vol. I, bk. I, ch. i, vol. II, bk. III, ch. ii; R. L. Poole, *The Exchequer in the Twelfth Century* (Oxford, 1911); Tout, *Chapters*, vol. I; Galbraith, *Studies*, ch. III; Chrimes, *Introduction*, chs. II-III; H. G. Richardson, *The Memoranda Roll for the first year of King John* (Pipe Roll Soc., n.s., XXI, 1943), esp. pp. xi-lix, lxxv-lxxxvii; C. T. Flower, *Introduction to the Curia Regis Rolls, 1199-1230* (Selden Soc., LXII, 1944), esp. pt. I, chs, I-V, pt. II, chs. III-VI, pt. III, ch. I.

King's Council as an agency of administrative supervision, and sought to control the established courts and departments by having congenial men in charge of them, or anyway men who would be more responsive to their pressures than the King's *familiares* were likely to be. This thesis undoubtedly sheds a great deal of light on thirteenth- and fourteenth-century history. But some of the most distinguished medieval historians since Tout have stressed that co-operation, not conflict, was the more normal relationship between King and barons.[1] The pure Toutian 'model' was first and most fully worked out as an explanation of Edward II's reign. And without serious qualifications it seems to involve a slight distortion of historical focus when applied to a considerable part of Henry III's, most of Edward I's and Edward III's, and perhaps the whole of Henry IV's and V's reigns. The model tends to over-emphasize times of conflict and sudden change, as against those of gradual evolution in the methods and machinery of government. This may seem a curious conclusion. And it may be due to a tendency, since Tout's death, to read between the lines of his work and put an unfair gloss on his findings. He would, one imagines, have been surprised and somewhat irked to be told that his was *too dialectical* a view of administrative history!

Whatever the truth of this, one qualification would certainly now be admitted. The pace and extent of the process by which institutions went 'out of court' did not vary constantly either with the power of the monarchy or with the personal authority of individual kings. If the Barons quarrelled with the King and got the best of it, they could control him more easily by subordinating his household to the great departments (notably Exchequer and Chancery) than by direct and constant supervision of his detailed domestic arrangements. Hence their emphasis on non-household government. But the reverse did not always follow. A strong King, on comparatively good terms with his magnates, might not need or want to emphasize the curial side of his government. He might do so for pragmatic reasons, such as the Wardrobe's superiority as an itinerant war ministry. In these conditions there might be personal or institutional differences between the household and the departments; but there was no

[1] See for example F. M. Powicke, *Henry III and the Lord Edward* (Oxford, 1947); for a rather more 'pro-baronial' view of administrative developments see B. Wilkinson, *Constitutional History of Medieval England, 1216-1399*, III (1958), esp. pp. 43-6, 210.

inevitable conflict between household and departmental government as such.

In administrative history the span of time from Henry III's reign to Richard II's saw the continuation and elaboration of several existing themes rather than the introduction of radically new ones. Despite the strongly marked 'administrative' character of parliament in its very early days, this period appears in retrospect less original than the one which preceded it. Chancery emerged as a distinct and separate department of government, as the Exchequer had done earlier; it also followed the Exchequer in going 'out of court', but much more slowly and gradually. King's Bench became distinct from the undifferentiated *curia regis*, as Common Pleas (originally called 'the common bench') had done earlier. It too was slower in ceasing altogether to itinerate with the King and his court, and in casting off its connexion with the household. The household itself became more specialized, with more offshoots and subdivisions. Three of its branches were particularly involved in the interaction of administration and politics. The Wardrobe, or 'Wardrobe of the Household', which was to become the Household below stairs, on occasions was little less than a war ministry with its own financial and secretarial branches. From the thirteenth to the sixteenth century, the Chamber was almost always of some consequence as a treasury and revenue department rivalling the Exchequer, and at times easily eclipsed it. The Privy Seal originated as a household secretariat to take the place of the already departmentalized Chancery. Unlike the Wardrobe and the Chamber, it too went out of court in its turn, being replaced there by the Signet Office and the King's Secretary; in the fourteenth century, for practical purposes the Privy Seal was used as the seal of the Council. Meanwhile the Council itself became a much more systematic and developed organ of government than it had been under earlier rulers. From being merely a gathering of the King's advisers, it developed into an institution capable of supervising the other branches of government and co-ordinating their work. A more important change, because it concerned the relations of government and society rather than changes *within* government, was the Crown's increasing financial dependence on parliamentary taxation and customs duties, instead of on the older hereditary and prerogative revenues. In the fifteenth century these newer revenues in turn became less and less adequate; hence, in part, the campaign under Edward IV and Henry VII to reinvigorate the old royal income, from land, feudal dues, and the profits of justice.[1]

From Edward III's reign on, the distinction between different types of officials often seems to have been more important, and to have caused more trouble, than rivalry between opposed sets of institutions. Except during the military campaigns of Henry V, the Chamber and Wardrobe do not seem to have been used again on any great scale as *extra*-household revenue and supply departments until the later fifteenth century. Even under Richard II, who took theoretical absolutism more seriously than any other medieval King, the clash was primarily between different ideas about government. It was also between different types of royal servants and advisers; and only on the secretarial side, at the seals, between curial and extra-curial administration.

In the history of English central institutions the century or so from *c.* 1350 to *c.* 1470 was marked by the predominance of the Exchequer, Chancery, and the Privy Seal. The first of these no doubt already had grave weaknesses by the end of the fourteenth century, but it seems only to have entered on serious decline in the course of Henry VI's reign. The second was in the process of giving way to the third, and even in some respects to the Signet, as the effective, and initiating secretariat. However, this was also the last period in which Common Pleas and King's Bench (itself only much more recently 'out of court') enjoyed undisputed primacy among the central law courts; in its legal capacity Chancery was growing in importance.

Historians continue to lament that much less is known about English central government in the fifteenth than in any of the three preceding centuries. This is partly due to the influence of Tout, and his own choice of 1399 as a stopping point, and partly unavoidable, due to poorer evidence, at any rate in the chronicle sources. In so far as it is simply due to fewer historians having worked systemati-

[1] On these fiscal changes see N. S. B. Gras, *The Early English Customs System* (Cambridge, Mass., 1918), chs. I-II; J. F. Willard, *Parliamentary Taxes on Personal Property 1290 to 1334* (Camb., Mass., 1934), introduction and chs. I, X-XII; E. Power, *The Wool Trade in English Medieval History* (1941), ch. IV; *The English Government at Work, 1327-1336*, ed. Willard, W. A. Morris, J. R. Strayer, W. H. Dunham (Camb., Mass., 1940-50), vol. II, ch. I, Strayer, 'Introduction', ch. IV, Mabel H. Mills, 'The Collectors of Customs'; S. K. Mitchell, *Taxation in Medieval England* (New Haven, 1951), esp. chs. I, III, IV, VIII; J. L. Kirby, 'The Issues of the Lancastrian Exchequer and Lord Cromwell's Estimates of 1433', *Bull. Inst. Hist. Res.*, XXIV (1951), 121-51.

cally on the record sources, this situation is on its way to being remedied. One very important development, about which surprisingly little has been written, is the laicization of government. This was a very lengthy process and one general to all western Christendom. In England its beginnings were made possible by the professionalization of the law, leading to the emergence of self-sufficient, non-ecclesiastical, law schools (the later Inns of Court and Chancery Inns).

The completeness of this change must not be exaggerated. There had been some laymen, perhaps usually in posts where literacy was not essential, in the household departments and even the Exchequer during the twelfth and thirteenth centuries. And literate lay officials had not been unknown in the twelfth, let alone the thirteenth century; none the less, the fourteenth century saw a marked extension of lay office-holding, mainly on the legal side of royal government. Already during Edward II's reign there were more laymen than clerics among the judges of the common law courts. For all three courts the numbers are laymen 28 or 29, clerics 24 or 25; for King's Bench and Common Pleas, without Exchequer, 16 or 17, and 11 or 12.[1] Before long the overwhelming majority were laymen. In the next century the same process can be seen in the Household itself. Under Henry V, the Cofferers, who had immediate charge of the accounts, were still clerks; in the course of the next three or four reigns laymen came to fill the post of Cofferer, as they had already done the more 'political' offices of Treasurer and Comptroller.[2] The same general change can be seen on the financial side. By 1490, according to Professor Richardson, the men in charge of collecting and administering Crown land revenues, 'either had studied law at the practical Inns of Court or were practising lawyers'.[3] By the mid-fifteenth century laicization was well under way in other branches of the central government. After the assumption of personal authority by

[1] Holdsworth, *History*, I (3rd edn.), 197, 232, 235-6, II (4th edn.), 311-18.

[2] Eileen de L. Fagan, 'Some Aspects of the King's Household in the Reign of Henry V', Summary of Thesis, *Bull. Inst. Hist. Res.*, XIV (1936-7), 194-6; Richardson, *Chamber Administration*, pp. 93 (and n. 28), 484; B. P. Wolffe, 'The Management of English Royal Estates under the Yorkist Kings', *Eng. Hist. Rev.*, LXXI (1956), 1-27; J. L. Kirby, 'The Rise of the Under-Treasurer of the Exchequer', *ibid.*, LXXII (1957), 666-77.

[3] *Chamber Administration*, p. 61 and n. 60, pp. 61-2.

Henry VI in 1437 almost all the Signet Clerks were laymen, although their chief, the King's Secretary, was still normally a clerk; indeed from 1402 to 1485 only two out of twenty-three successive secretaries were not. Another change was also in progress. Many clerks who served in the fifteenth-century royal secretariat had already served in the household of a lay or ecclesiastical magnate.[1] Employment under a lay magnate, minister of state, or senior office-holder was to become a more and more usual preliminary to entering the royal service. However, like laicization itself, this mode of entry to the King's service was coming in gradually, and unevenly in different branches of the administration. On the place of the 1530's in this process, Dr. Elton confirms and elaborates the suggestion made a few years earlier by Dr. Mathew. Underlying the many important institutional changes effected by Thomas Cromwell, he discerns 'one fundamental change, the change from a bureaucracy trained in the church or the king's household to a bureaucracy trained in a minister's household and then employed in the service of the state'. He goes on to emphasize, again in agreement with Mathew, that under the new system such officials remained dependent on the patronage of individual ministers, rather than on that of the King himself or of the Crown collectively, even after their entry to royal service.[2] But the most striking long-term contrast was surely between prior service as a clerk in some kind of ecclesiastical establishment, and as a layman in a lay household or estate office.

Whatever its exact connexion with changes in the patron-client mode of entry to office, laicization proceeded apace from the 1530's on. By the early seventeenth century clerics were unusual at the top, and except in ecclesiastical administration positively freakish lower down.

From its chronology, it is tempting to say that this was simply a result of the Reformation. 'Regular' clergy, that is all monks and friars belonging to orders, disappeared from England, and the number of 'secular' clergy in minor orders greatly diminished. Whatever the exact doctrinal position of its national church, and despite the survival of strong Catholic 'pockets' in parts of the midlands and the north, under Elizabeth I England became, in the

---

[1] J. Otway-Ruthven, *The King's Secretary and the Signet Office in the XV Century* (Cambridge, 1939), esp. chs. V, VI, and VIII, and Appendices.

[2] Elton, *Revolution in Government*, p. 308 (and n. referring to Mathew, *Social Structure*, p. 3 ff.).

cultural or social sense, a Protestant country. Yet the history of Catholic Europe—Spain, Portugal, France, Italy, Austria, etc.— does not suggest that the laicization of government would have been very much longer delayed even without Henry VIII, Cromwell, and the subsequent reformers. The nature of the connexion between laicization and the heritability of offices is still unclear; and it also remains an open question whether corruption and venality increased as a result of laymen, with wives and children to provide for, replacing clerks who only had nephews or other more distant relatives. But the emergence of an educated, or anyway literate laity, of a potential professional middle and upper-middle class, was a general west European phenomenon. Of course, it was interrelated with the religious upheavals of the sixteenth century, but this was far from being a simple case of cause and effect. In England indeed these administrative changes had begun even before the rise of Wyclif's 'morning star'.

Interesting as these problems are, they should not divert too much of our attention from the great institutional and fiscal reorganizations of the Tudor period: the rise of conciliar government, and the establishment of the new revenue courts. Historians of the fifteenth and sixteenth centuries may continue to debate whether or not Dr. Elton has over-emphasized the significance of the 1530's, but there can be no doubt about the importance of the changes in government during the longer time span, from Edward IV to Mary. By contrast, after the great Exchequer reorganization of the 1550's—and its postscript (the establishment of the imprest accounts with their own Auditors in the early 1560's), there was very little further change until the Long Parliament's introduction of government by committee in 1642-4.

But the system, if static, was not completely rigid. A few examples which illustrate this are worth reiterating. The Navy and Ordnance Offices became more important, although their structure and methods scarcely changed. The Household above stairs grew more elaborate, as well as more costly, especially when James I set up the Bedchamber as a separate department. On the executive side of government, the Secretaries of State and their personal staffs, and the Council and its Clerks dealt with an ever-increasing amount of the effective work of central co-ordination. And between 1537 and 1625 the Clerks of the Privy Council increased from one to nine or ten (four ordinary and five or six extraordinary). In the revenue system the most obvious developments were the Crown's growing dependence on the Customs, and the parallel extension of customs farming. But changes of potential importance were also taking place inside the Exchequer. The Auditor of the Receipt was closely involved in all the repeated attempts at financial reform from 1619 to 1641. He acted as the main link between the Exchequer and the Lord Treasurer, or Treasury Commissioners; and, apart from the increasingly archaic system of tallies, he provided more and more of the effective liaison between the Receipt and the various auditing officers in the upper Exchequer. Several new series of records, originating in the early part of Sir Robert Pye's tenure of the Auditorship, are evidence of attempts to provide better information about the Crown's general financial position at any given time.[1] The 'Balance' (of five-year averages of revenue and expenditure) produced at the end of 1635 was a fruit of this work; it was also indicative of Pye's close co-operation with the Revenue and Prest Auditors. The 'Treasury' did not need to have a bigger staff, indeed did not come into existence as a distinct department, partly just because relations with the Auditor were so close, and at least in the years 1619-24 and 1635-41 so cordial. Had this collaboration between Treasurer and Auditor been continued without interruption, it might possibly have led to the evolution of a Treasury less completely separate from the Exchequer than that which actually did emerge.

Scarcely any of these developments marked any radically new departure. They can all be thought of as having taken place within the framework of the Tudor state, and after the advent of a Civil Service composed of laymen.

On a long-term view the administrative changes which followed immediately after our period can easily be dismissed as an aberration from the main line of development in English government. On the surface the Civil Wars and Interregnum (1642-60) seem to have had little permanent effect in administration. On the contrary, the

[1] The Auditor's debenture books and order books from 1619, enrolment of Privy Seals from 1620, assignment books from 1622, declaration books from 1625, warrant books from 1626: see Giuseppo, *Guide*, I, 185-94.

Restoration can be said to have been more important in that it gave the 'old administrative system' a longer lease of life than it might otherwise have had. The soundness of this view will be considered a little later. First, what of the temporary changes? There were some striking institutional innovations, most notably in the system of committees under the Long Parliament and the Rump. In particular, the Exchequer of Audit was for practical purposes superseded by the Committee for taking the accounts of the Kingdom. There were in addition other less obvious, and perhaps less well known attempts to revise the conditions of entry and service and to alter the modes of payment.

First the question of payment. Those in charge of land sales were allowed to take poundage.[1] But since the object was to raise as much money as possible, this should not have had the same harmful effect as it did when permitted in the spending departments. When new posts were created, the tendency was for slightly more of them to carry fixed, and often quite sizeable, salaries.[2] Some attempt was made to curtail fee-taking, especially in the Navy and the Customs, and to exclude it from the new Excise administration.[3] The famous 'self-denying' ordinance of April 1645 actually included a clause aimed against fee-taking in *all* non-judicial and non-military offices. The only exceptions were offices held by those parliamentarian peers and M.P.s who had been confirmed in their places by the two Houses after being disabled by the King. While the political implications of this clause are far from clear, there can be no doubt about the 'tacking' which it involved. On to a bill disabling peers and M.P.s from holding civil or military office was grafted a clause implying that office-holders who were not members of either House should be paid by salaries and not in fees.[4] It was presumably the product of a committee appointed in the Commons the previous winter to survey the value of all offices in Parliament's gift, and to suggest in each case how much should be allocated to their holders and how much set aside for the state. Guizot, apparently the only historian except Cobbett to comment on this, saw it as a device to appease the public. But, like the anonymous plan discussed in Chapter 4

[1] *Acts and Ordinances of the Interregnum*, ed. C. H. Firth and R. S. Rait (1911), II, 185, 339-41, 437.

[2] *Ibid.*, II, 185, 609.

[3] *Ibid.*, I, 347, 1260.

[4] *Ibid.*, I, 664. See also *Commons Journals*, IV, 122.

of this book, it was also an attempt at administrative reform.[1] The same general idea was in the air again the following year; parliament was said to intend that all officers holding places of trust should 'account upon oath for the Profitts of their Place to the State, and bee allowed Stipends for the execution only'.[2]

Cases can be found where these aspirations were put into practice. In 1649 the Admiralty Commissioners' Clerk was given a stipend of £100 p.a., plus another £50 p.a. on condition that neither he nor his under-clerk took any fees.[3] The Lord Mayor and the two Sheriffs of London were forbidden from trafficking in subordinate offices, but their stipendiary allowances were raised to the princely heights of £2,500 and £1,800 each p.a. respectively.[4] Amongst other suggestions for administrative and legal reform, Hugh Peter, spokesman of the more radical Independents, suggested that practising lawyers as well as all law officers should be paid by the state, and should take no fees.[5] But this went beyond the limit of what was attempted.

The Levellers wanted a more effective and far-reaching 'place bill', or separation of powers, than that which was embodied in the self-denying ordinance. No officer drawing a salary, and no Receiver or Treasurer (that is, presumably, no one in receipt of poundage) should be eligible for parliament; nor should lawyers elected M.P.s continue in private practice.[6] On some administrative and legal questions there was only a narrow gap between the Levellers and the thoroughgoing Independents, like Hugh Peter and Henry Parker. It was the conservative Independents who used the issue of law reform in 1653 as one of the pretexts for ending the 'Barebones Parliament' and setting up the Protectorate.

[1] *Commons Journals*, III, 695, 699; Cobbett, *Parl. Hist.*, III, 308-9; F. Guizot, *History of the English Revolution* (Bogue edn., 1846), pp. 256-7. See also above Chapter 4, s. iv, pp. 234-6.

[2] *The Oxinden and Peyton Letters 1642-70*, ed. D. Gardiner (1937), p, 101, Henry Oxinden to his cousin, 15 January 1646-7. I am grateful to Mr. Christopher Hill for this and the next two refs.

[3] J. Hollond, *Two Discourses of the Navy*, ed. J. R. Tanner (Navy Rec. Soc., 1896), p. xix.

[4] R. R. Sharpe, *London and the Kingdom*, II (1894), 321.

[5] R. P. Stearns, *The Strenuous Puritan, Hugh Peter, 1598-1660* (Urbana, Ill., 1954), esp. pp. 309-10, 377, 382, 386-8.

[6] *The Leveller Tracts, 1647-1653*, ed. W. Haller and G. Davies (N.Y., 1944), pp. 321-2.

Under the Protectorate payment by fees was again accepted as natural and proper, but as under the monarchy an attempt was made to curtail fees, to limit their size and number. This can be seen in the ordinances restoring the Exchequer and reorganizing Chancery. One curious and perhaps unintentional surrender was made to departmental autonomy: revenue officers' salaries (i.e. their stipendiary Fees) were to be fixed by the Lord Treasurer and Chancellor of Exchequer, or by the Treasury Commissioners.[1] In general, salaries were fixed at well above the pre-war level. The Clerks, under-clerks, and other officers attendant on the Council of State together enjoyed allowances and payments totalling £6,000 a year. A Signet Clerk had been raised from nil to £150 a year, a Clerk of the Privy Seal from nil or £5 to £150, the four Tellers to £400 each, the Auditors of the Imprests to £500 each (but including their secretaries), the Auditor of the Receipt and the Clerk of the Parliament to £500 each.[2] The very much heavier burden of taxation borne by the country during the Interregnum, of which higher salaries for office-holders were a minor symptom, may have been partially counter-balanced by an appreciably lower burden of 'invisible' fee taxation.

However, even in 1650 the fees of some erstwhile Exchequer officials had been recognized as legitimate. Bailiffs and lords of manors and liberties which had recently been bought from the state were stated to owe so much, on each annual account, to the Foreign Apposer and to the Clerks of the Estreats and the Pipe.[3] So neither the Long Parliament, the Commonwealth, nor the Protectorate can be said—without careful qualification—to have been against fees as such. None the less, earnest and repeated attempts were made to regulate and restrict them, and in specific cases to replace them by larger stipendiary Fees (that is, salaries).

Some action, but not a great deal, seems to have been proposed and undertaken against life tenure, reversions, sale, and brokerage. There was the move, already referred to, against trafficking in City of London offices. The Chancery orders of 1654 also strictly forbade any kind of brokerage. Negative evidence can be very misleading. But it seems that offices were not sold on any significant scale under the Long Parliament or the Commonwealth, and only to a limited

[1] *Acts and Ordinances*, II, 918-21, 949-67, 1016-19.
[2] Dep. Kpr. Pub. Recds., *4th Rept.*, app. II, 190-7; *5th Rept.*, app. II, 252; *Cal. S.P. Dom.*, *1655*, pp. 369-70.
[3] *Acts and Ordinances*, II, 447-8.

extent under the Protectorate. As against this, the draft bill forbidding all sales of offices foundered along with its begetter—the Barebones Parliament.[1] It is of course arguable that even if it had been passed such a law would have been ineffective, like the act of Edward VI's reign, so long as payment in fees and other basic features of the system remained untouched. This is Dr. Swart's view.[2] Even so, there does seem to have been less traffic in offices from 1642 to 1660 than there was again after the Restoration. But here, as in other respects, the old order may have been creeping back from 1654 onwards.

The Barebones' bill left life tenure alone, but it did aim to stop the granting of reversions and the succession to offices of children and others who were incapable of executing them in person. The penalty for entering office contrary to these provisions was to be disablement from ever holding any place of profit under the Commonwealth.

There is therefore just enough evidence to suggest that some of the middle-class reformers during the Civil Wars and Interregnum had some of the same attitudes towards the administrative system as the protagonists of absolute monarchy. The vested interests of the predominantly gentry- and lawyer-staffed administration were perhaps equally at variance with the needs and aspirations of 'Thorough' and of a bourgeois-democratic republic. More than this it would be rash to say. No full study has been made of the reform movement in the 1640's and 50's. It is not even clear who was for, and who against the attack on fees in 1645, the measures suggested by Hugh Peter and others in 1651-2, the Barebones' bill in 1653. Nor is it clear how far the pre-war system was consciously being restored under the Protectorate. 1654-5 saw the reappearance of the Duchy of Lancaster court and its jurisdiction (subject of course to the restrictions in the 'Star Chamber' act of 1641) as well as of the Exchequer.[3] And the Protectorate entailed the re-establishment of a 'Household', albeit of a republican 'single person' and not of a crowned head. In 1655 this cost £64,000 a year, which was raised to £80,000 and then £100,000 in 1657 when the Lord Protector

---

[1] *The Somers Tracts*, ed. W. Scott, VI (1811), 177, 186-7. See also *Commons Journals*, VII, 283-4.

[2] Swart, *Sale of Offices*, esp. p. 113.

[3] *Acts and Ordinances*, II, 844-5; *Catalogue of the Thomason Tracts 1640-61* (1908), II, 101.

became more like a monarch under the revised constitution. Even so, it was absorbing a far smaller fraction of the total revenue than Charles I's Household before 1640.[1]

Whatever the extent of this restoration before the Restoration, the complete return of the 'old administrative system' certainly did not happen until 1660. Even then it was a restoration of the system and methods—and of the surviving men—but not of all the institutions from before the Civil War. Star Chamber, the Council in the North, the Court of Wards and Liveries, and (but for James II's brief experiment) the High Commission were seen in England no more. The restored Council in the Marches of Wales was only a pale shadow of its former self. Otherwise the institutional continuity was remarkable. The Household, the Chamber, and their respective offshoots were restored in their entirety; and the need to keep their cost down to a reasonable level at once became an urgent preoccupation of the King and his ministers. King's Bench was re-established under its old name; in Chancery and Common Pleas, at the Seals, and in the defence departments there had been changes, especially of personnel, but no complete interruptions. Even so, the central institutions were not simply being poured back into a rigid mould; and there were in fact to be considerable changes again here in the later Stuart period. The rise of the Treasury, the birth of the Board of Trade, the enlargement and subsequent division of the Secretaries of State's department, the appointment of new officers to regulate and oversee colonial revenue and administration, for the new tax revenues, and for the standing army—all this constituted a considerable achievement. Indeed, these changes almost deserve to rank alongside the early and mid-Tudor reconstructions.

While there was definitely more administrative change from 1660 to 1702 than from 1603 to 1640, a great deal did not change. Whatever had been the case during the Interregnum, after the Restoration offices under the Crown were often still treated much like other pieces of property, and most officers continued to rely for payment on fees, gratuities, and perquisites. There are, however, some signs that the Interregnum tradition of paying higher salaries was not wholly discarded, notably in the most important of the new revenue

[1] Dep. Kpr., *4th Rept.*, app. II, 198; *5th Rept.*, app. II, 250. It is not clear whether this was for all household expenses or only those below stairs; the £100,000 was to cover building repairs.

departments—the Excise, and in the Navy.[1] For some time longer all office-holders were still allowed to take part in parliamentary politics, and if they wished, oppose the Crown and their own superiors while enjoying relative security of tenure. The full distinction between political and non-political offices was slow to emerge and its growth is hard to trace accurately; it was scarcely discernible in the middle of Charles II's reign and it was well but far from definitively established by the second and third decades of the eighteenth century.

No sustained attempt was made to alter the 'old administrative system', until the age of 'economical reform', in the time of Burke and the younger Pitt. And, as several historians have shown, the reforms then initiated were at first tentative and limited; the great 'administrative revolution' was a very long drawn affair, and the old system took a very long time to die. Among the most decisive measures, before the reforms of 1853-5 and of 1870-1, were the Acts of 1817 and 1822, finally abolishing the fee system as it had existed down the centuries, and creating in effect a salaried public service.[2] The extraordinary longevity of the 'old administrative system' is surely to be explained along the lines indicated by Dr. David Mathew. It was the successive victories of oligarchy and constitutionalism in 1660, 1688-9, and 1714, and later the wars against France and the reaction against the French Revolution (1793-1815), which shored the system up and then enabled it to survive—even if uneasily—into the nineteenth century. From this viewpoint the Restoration is to be seen above all as an oligarchic victory over any incipient trends either towards 'enlightened absolutism' or towards middle class democracy.

The great formative periods in English administrative history are thus to be thought of as the twelfth century (or c. 1080-c. 1230), the Yorkist and early to mid-Tudor period (c. 1470-c. 1560), and finally the nineteenth century (or to be more exact c. 1780-1870). But if no

[1] The Auditor of the Excise was to receive £500 p.a. plus £200 for his clerks, and the co-Comptrollers £500 (*Cal. S.P. Dom.*, *1660-1*, pp. 522, 559); for the Navy see J. Ehrman, *The Navy in the War of William III, 1689-1697* (Cambridge, 1953), chs. VII and XIII.

[2] D. L. Keir, 'Economical Reform, 1779-1787', *Law Qtrly. Rev.*, L (1934), 368-85; E. W. Cohen, *The British Civil Service* (1941), chs. I-IV, pp. 19-71; A. S. Foord, 'The Waning of "The Influence of the Crown" ', *Eng. Hist. Rev.*, LXII (1947), 484-507; Binney, *Finance and Administration* esp. chs. II and VI.

more is said, this may produce a false emphasis. It implies an underestimate of developments from the thirteenth to fifteenth centuries, and under the later Stuarts, not to mention those since 1870. Also, and for our purposes this is more to the point, it implies that the events of 1640-60 can be written off as an aberration from the main stream of English history. This is patently false outside the field of administration. Within that field, it is however arguable that those events took effect in ways which are not at first sight obvious, or in every respect what might have been expected.

ii COMPARATIVE PERSPECTIVE: ENGLAND AND THE CONTINENT

At one time historians tended to say that sixteenth- and seventeenth-century England was so much a case apart from contemporary Europe that any comparisons were likely to be unreal or misleading. Contrasts might be drawn, yes: between the victory of absolutism on the continent and the rise of constitutional government in England. But this basic difference would have been held to invalidate detailed comparisons, for instance, between the English and French administrative systems. Now the pendulum has swung the other way. England under the Tudors and early Stuarts is often classified with the continental absolute monarchies. Of course, it is possible to strike some sort of mean; at least before 1640 there are great similarities but also important differences between, for example, Caroline England and the France of Richelieu and Louis XIII.[1] Sir George Clark, who certainly does not neglect social, legal, and constitutional divergences, has written of 'a normal European method of organizing the work of government' in the seventeenth century; 'the growth of bureaucracy—not its origin but its progress— was one of the characteristic seventeenth-century movements in most of the more thriving countries'. It is clear from the context that he does not except England from these generalizations.[2]

[1] Contrast the balanced appraisal in G. N. Clark, *The Seventeenth Century* (Oxford, 1931), ch. V, 'Comparative Constitutional History', with the closer identification made in F. Hartung and R. Mousnier, 'Quelques Problèmes concernant la Monarchie Absolue', Tenth International Congress of the Historical Sciences, *Relazioni* (Florence, 1955), IV, 3-55.

[2] *The Seventeenth Century*, pp. 83, 92-3.

Granted that comparisons of this kind can be illuminating, the best starting point is to compare England and France. The textbooks always remind us, and rightly so, that the English monarchy had virtually no local officials beyond unpaid justices of the peace and constables. If left unqualified, this is to overlook the customs staffs in the out-ports, the receiver-generals and lesser officials involved in the collection and management of Crown land revenues, the escheators and feodaries, the muster masters, and the clerks of the Crown and of the peace. None of these were unpaid in the sense that the J.P.s were, while few even of the central office-holders were fully salaried. But the general point is still sound. Numerically these officials, scattered over the whole of England and Wales, and totalling some hundreds, are to be compared with a total of certainly over 3,000, and probably over 4,000, in the one French province of Normandy in the 1630's.[1] Likewise at the centre, size provides the most obvious contrast. The population of France was probably three and a half to four times that of England and Wales, its land area at least three times as large. But even allowing for this, the two central administrations (although curiously enough not the two royal households) were utterly different in scale. The French establishment varied a good deal from time to time in different branches; but typically it included 4 Secretaries of State, 44 Masters of Requests, 300 notaries or under-secretaries, 180 judges of the supreme court in Paris (the *Parlement*), and 120 senior officers of the main auditing department (the *Chambre des Comptes*). Making full allowance for the difference in the size and population of the two countries, the French central government was proportionately as well as absolutely much larger.[2]

This may partly have been because France was a 'more governed' country than England. But that would be exceedingly difficult to demonstrate, and in the absence of criteria to measure 'governed-ness' probably no two historians would agree about it. Still, the French Crown did collect more as well as heavier taxes from its

[1] Mousnier, *Vénalité des Offices*, pp. 108-14.

[2] See P. Viollet, *Droit Public Histoire des Institutions Politiques et Administratives de la France, Le Roi et ses ministres* (Paris, 1912); M. Marion, *Dictionnaire des Institutions de la France au XVIIe et XVIIIe Siècles* (Paris, 1923); G. Pagès, 'L'Evolution des institutions administratives en France', *Rev. d'histoire moderne*, VII (1932); Mousnier, *Vénalité*, p. 408; R. Doucet, *Les Institutions de la France au XVIe Siècle* (Paris, 1948); G. Zeller, *Institutions de la France au XVIe Siècle* (Paris, 1948).

subjects; its judicial system was much more elaborate; so too was its military organization; and its interference with social and economic life was more detailed and far-reaching. In addition, the French Crown had a far greater and more direct financial interest in office-holding. This was partly because both existing and newly created offices were sold systematically to raise money. Then there was the annual payment (usually called the *Paulette*, but more accurately the *droit annuel*), due from officers in return for the rights of heritability and vendibility. Most important of all there were the heavy taxes and numerous forced loans, paid as a condition of enjoying official privileges and emoluments.

It has recently been suggested that Louis XIII and Richelieu largely financed their foreign policy and their wars out of the profits of the administrative system. These gains are very hard, perhaps impossible to calculate as a percentage of the total royal revenues of France. The complexity, and at the same time backwardness, of the financial system was such that neither then nor now could such a total be given; furthermore, the Crown's *gross* gains should include the office-holders' incomes in their capacity as Crown servants, and would be very different from its *net* gains from the system. This is not for a moment to deny that the French Crown's profits from office-holding were proportionately, as well as absolutely huge compared even with what was achieved under James I. In France the peak seems to have come in 1632-3, but the fullest information is available for 1639. That year marked the end of a 'plateau' when the yield from these sources had for several years been fairly steady, absolutely and as a proportion of the (calculable) total royal revenues. It was of course a year of very heavy military outlay. Of the Crown's *gross* expenditure 20 per cent. went on the remuneration of officers (excluding those in the fighting forces), and even this was only $\frac{3}{4}$ of what was owed them. Had they been paid in full, it would have absorbed no less than 62 per cent. of the normal receipts on the *ordinary* revenues, i.e. apart from what was raised to meet the extraordinary military expenditure. And even this takes no account of what the officers levied for themselves, direct from the subject; these perquisites and dues, as Professor Mousnier says, 'achevaient d'épuiser la matière contributive'. This is the obverse of his figures showing that for most of the 1620's and 1630's between 25 per cent. and 40 per cent. of the recorded royal revenues came from office-holding. The French Crown was in a sense caught in its own extraordinary system, of which it was truly both beneficiary and victim. Those who recommended the English King to emulate the French example presumably either could see only the benefits, or else were themselves interested parties.[1]

There was no English equivalent to the French *noblesse de la robe*. Whether the 'high robe' (that is the councillors and senior officers of the *parlements, chambres des comptes,* and other 'sovereign courts') should be classified with the nobility (which in France includes all the armigerous classes, and not merely the 'peerage' in our sense), or with the bourgeoisie depends on how these terms are being used. Technically, before the mid-seventeenth century membership of the high robe did not automatically confer even *ex officio* nobility; and when it did, three successive generations in the direct male line had to qualify in this way before such a family attained the same permanent noble status as the *noblesse de l'épée,* or *de la race.* Between the early seventeenth and the early eighteenth century a very substantial change seems to have taken place: by the period 1715-48 the high robe were much more nearly assimilated to the nobility of sword and birth. Under Louis XIII even the full councillors (though perhaps not the presidents) of the sovereign courts remained legally bourgeois; and in the last States-General before 1789 (that of 1614-15) such men sat as members of the *Third* Estate. However, if these class distinctions are considered less technically, more in terms of wealth, social outlook, and political attitude, the high robe even in the age of Louis XIII seem to be much nearer the nobility than they do to the bourgeoisie (merchants, retailers, and manufacturers in the towns, and the well-to-do upper peasantry). Many sons of robe families entered the royal army (a speedier route to technical nobility), or acquired fiefs (to be a tenant-in-chief of the King, or the possessor of a 'fief' was another mark of technical nobility). There was already a considerable amount of intermarriage between Robe and Sword, though apparently still much less than

[1] Menna Prestwich, 'The Making of Absolute Monarchy (1559-1683)', *France: Government and Society,* ed. J. M. Wallace-Hadrill and J. McManners (1957), 105-33, esp. pp. 120-1, 123; Mousnier, *Vénalité,* pp. 391-8, esp. p. 398, n. 187. In her otherwise admirably lucid summary of these pages in Professor Mousnier's work, Mrs. Prestwich does not seem to me to take sufficient account of this note, which makes it clear that the Crown's *net* gain would be a considerably smaller proportion of the gross turnover from office-holding than would appear from his figures or from the argument in the text.

there was to be in the eighteenth century. The high robe, like the great ministers of state and other senior royal officials (who also enjoyed *ex officio* nobility for life), and like the small élite of wealthy tax farmers, were far removed from the broad mass of the French bourgeoisie. This is borne out by the composition as well as the size of typical robe fortunes. In all the cases examined by Professor Mousnier where the evidence permitted of any conclusions, he found that in over half landed wealth comprised more than half the total fortune; in about a quarter of the cases land, office, and interest on loans and investments were of approximately equal value; in under a quarter of the cases did office comprise over half the total value of the fortune. In this respect, French office-holders were not so different from the English lawyer and office-holding gentry.

Apart from this question of its position, neither fish nor fowl, vis-à-vis the nobility and the bourgeoisie, for all its wealth, numbers, corporate pride, and undoubted importance the office-holding body in France was seriously weakened by two internal divisions. Horizontally there was a considerable divergence in outlook, corresponding to wide differences in wealth, status, and way of life between the greater and lesser officials. That is between the full members of the sovereign courts, and the top administrators (Masters of Requests, King's Secretaries, presidents of the *bureaux des finances*, etc.) and the host of lesser functionaries, whether in central or local institutions, whether employed in royal finance, the judiciary, the police, general secretarial duties, or public works. Several of the bargains between the Crown and the *noblesse de la robe* during the seventeenth century were in some degree struck at the expense of these lesser men. And when the sovereign courts did attempt to resist royal demands and to reform the constitution, in the first *Fronde* of 1648-9, they were not solidly supported in the lower echelons of the administration.

The other division was a vertical one. That is between the older institutions—mainly the sovereign courts (which though staffed with lawyers were of course concerned with finance and administration as well as with justice), and the newer ones—more closely centred on the King (for finance the *épargne* and *parties casuelles*; on the executive side the Secretaries of State, Masters of Requests, and increasingly from the 1630's the Intendants). The posts in this latter hierarchy (described by Sagnac as the *noblesse des hautes fonctions gouvernementales*) were non-heritable, and largely non-venal. But their separateness should not be exaggerated: this cream

443

of the royal bureaucracy was partly recruited from the robe class, while the holders of many top posts in the sovereign courts had themselves served a term on this side of the administration. Thus this division might simply be described as the equivalent of the English distinction between the older 'out-of-court' departments (Exchequer, Common Pleas, etc.), and the newer branches of the central government (Privy Council, Star Chamber, Secretaries of State, Navy, Ordnance, etc.). But in England the division was much less exact; there was no clear and firm line between posts which were and were not normally held by qualified lawyers, besides so many non-lawyers had some legal training and shared the outlook of their trained colleagues. In short, such a comparison is over-strained and untenable.

As has been suggested in earlier chapters, there were great variations in wealth, position, and outlook among English office-holders. But the divisions between greater and lesser, and between those in different branches of the administration were less marked, and less influential than among French officials. Just as the whole office-holding system was more important—fiscally, politically, and socially —in France, so too were the tensions which arose within it.

It is hard to say whether or not a comparison with England strengthens Professor Mousnier's final conclusion, that the French monarchy, 'with a King in principle absolute, was in practice during the sixteenth and the first half of the seventeenth century a monarchy tempered by the sale of offices'. By sale is meant here the whole system of office-holding, and the wide ramifications of office-holders' interests. Even so, taking into account the place of Parliament and the Common Law, and the political and social role of the English gentry, France was an absolute, England a limited monarchy.[1]

---

[1] Mousnier, *Vénalité*, esp. pp. 17, 58, 60-2, 438, 458, 493-4, 503-6, 515, 518, 532-3, 623; Mousnier, 'Les Offices de la Famille Normande D'Amfreville (1584-1656)', *Rev. Hist.*, vol. 183 (1938), 10-27; with these compare Mousnier, 'Recherches sur les Soulèvements Populaires en France avant la Fronde', *Rev. d'Hist. moderne et contemporaine*, V (1958), 81-113, esp. pp. 109-11, where the technically non-noble status of office-holders, including the high robe, is more sharply emphasized; P. Sagnac, *La formation de la société française moderne*, I, *1661-1715* (Paris, 1945), 35-9, 70-3, 106-16, 211-14; F. L. Ford, *Robe and Sword, The Regrouping of the French Aristocracy after Louis XIV* (Cambridge, Mass., 1953); E. H. Kossmann, *La Fronde* (Leyden, 1954). *XVIIe Siècle*, nos. 42-3 (1959), 'Serviteurs du Roi. Quelques aspects de la fonction publique dans la Société française du XVIIe siècle', appeared too late for me to make use of it.

It is a commonplace of our constitutional history that from the beginning the Knights of the Shire belonged to the Commons, along with the burgesses from the towns, and not to the Lords (the temporal peers and great ecclesiastics). This was both a cause and a manifestation of England's distinct constitutional development. Perhaps it should correspondingly be a commonplace of English administrative history that the position of the gentry, as well as the Crown's ambivalent attitude towards venality and inheritance, prevented the emergence of a distinct bureaucratic class. Instead, most members of the bureaucracy felt themselves rather to be gentlemen and landowners who happened, by merit or good fortune, also to be the King's servants.

The differences between the taxing powers of the English and French Crowns belongs to a comparison of constitutions rather than of administrative systems. But one comparison of fiscal *capacity* can fairly be made. For all his legion of officials, the French King could not have obtained reliable annual averages of all revenues and expenditures, net and gross, together with compact and fairly comprehensive statements of capital gains and losses and royal debts, such as were provided for Charles I. The English government did not of course have an annual 'budget', nor would they at that time have been able to grasp the idea of what this involved. But at least in 1635, 1637-8, and 1641 some of the raw materials were available on which to build a budget. Despite the figures which M. Mousnier and other French historians are able to cite, and the greater richness in many respects of the French archives, these materials do not seem to have been available for Louis XIII.

Another, more institutional contrast can be found in the structure and composition of the various courts, councils, and departments in the two countries. Due partly to venality, in France offices had been divided and subdivided, and an elaborate system devised of corporate duties and responsibilities. The 'college', or collegiate system of administration, as it became known, meant that relatively few important posts were held by single individuals. Superficially this is in marked contrast to the situation in England. Sir George Clark, in the passage already cited, suggests a possible parallel between the growth of administrative departments in France and the English system of putting a board or body of commissioners at the head of a department instead of a single 'great officer': e.g. the

Treasury, the Admiralty, the Board of Trade.[1] It seems reasonable to go further than this and to suggest at least a limited parallel between the collegiate system in France (and Gustavian Sweden) and the use of royal commissions in Stuart administration. This does not only apply at the top, where it perhaps reaches its apogee in William III's reign when even the Great and Privy Seals were largely 'in commission'; on this level Clarendon's opposition to the process and his preference for individual office-holders shows that the choice could be regarded as a political one. But at less exalted levels much the same thing had been happening repeatedly. Many of the Jacobean and Caroline royal commissions were in effect substitutes for the appointment of one man to a particular duty and position. In the various courts and councils, the collective nature of decisions, as of other duties, is obvious. So are the parallels with French and other foreign institutions and methods, e.g. with the system of conciliar government in Spain and the Spanish Empire. But this collective element was not limited to the spheres of justice and counsel. There was a considerable degree of collective administrative and financial responsibility among the eight or so members of the Board of Green-cloth. The same could be said of the four 'principal officers' of the Navy and Ordnance respectively.

Then there was the tendency to divide posts once held by single individuals. The most famous and obvious was the Secretaryship of State after Thomas Cromwell's tenure. Other instances are the Wardenship of the Mint and the Clerkship of the Wards. This is to be distinguished from the deliberate creation of multiple offices, e.g. the seven Revenue and two Prest Auditorships, where each individual had a clearly marked responsibility for a certain part of the departmental duties. The Revenue Auditors were only responsible for those accounts which they passed and signed individually, but the two Surveyors of the Greenwax and (as far as can be seen) the two co-Cofferers of 1625-30 were jointly responsible for the whole business of their respective offices. Closely related to this, but again distinguishable from it, was the deliberate use of one officer to duplicate the work of another, in order to keep a check on the former's honesty and efficiency; all 'comptrollers' were supposed to have originated in this way. In MS. treatises and other papers on the Exchequer the idea constantly recurs of the different officers acting as checks and balances on each other. The appointment of

---

[1] *The Seventeenth Century*, p. 92.

officers or clerks 'extraordinary' was another way of sharing out the work among more people, or of trying to satisfy more aspirants for office, without enlarging the permanent establishment.

At the political level there are striking parallels between 'conciliar government' in Tudor and early Stuart England, the French and Swedish colleges, the Spanish conciliar system, and even the structure and functions of the Privy Council in the Habsburg part of the Empire. All these monarchies can be thought of as responding in *broadly* similar ways to new problems of government, especially in Clark's view to the 'growing needs and . . . wider outlook' of the state, notably in economic matters.[1] It would also be possible to find parallels between the institutional reconstructions of the early and mid-Tudor period and the setting up of new financial bureaux and revenue systems in early sixteenth-century France. The setting up of the Swedish colleges, on the other hand, while strikingly similar in effect to the more gradual developments in France, seems much more the deliberate contrivance of a great King and minister, and to have no close parallel elsewhere. It is perhaps better thought of as the response of a monarchical system of government to problems confronting it at a much earlier stage of social and economic development, as more akin to developments in twelfth- and thirteenth-century England, than to those described by MM. Doucet and Zeller or by Professor Richardson and Dr. Elton. This is not to contradict Professor Michael Roberts's opinion that the reforms of Gustavus and Oxenstierna made Sweden about the best governed country in Europe; it is rather to suggest that the problems of government and society were not the same in Sweden as in seventeenth-century England or France. Just as some 'underdeveloped' countries today are trying to take a short-cut into the twentieth century, to telescope into decades or even years changes which have elsewhere been spread over centuries, so Sweden was trying to take a short-cut into the seventeenth century. And, as the sequel was to show, it was not the system of government but the whole economy and social structure which was—after a heroic attempt—to prove unequal to the task.

[1] *Ibid.*, p. 93; M. Roberts, *Gustavus Adolphus, A History of Sweden, 1611-32*, I (1953), ch. VI, esp. pp. 265-79; Doucet, *Institutions*, pt. II, ch. XVIII; Zeller, *Institutions*, pp. 111-46; Pagès, 'L'Evolution', *Rev. d'hist. mod.*, VII; R. B. Merriman, *Rise of the Spanish Empire*, IV, (N.Y. 1934), ch. 36, 'The Government of Spain under Philip II'; H. F. Schwarz, *The Imperial Privy Council in the seventeenth century* (Cambridge, Mass., 1943), esp. ch. II and supplement.

Detailed comparisons, to illustrate the similarities and the differences, could be made between English and Spanish administration, or to be more precise with the administration of either Aragon or Castile and their respective possessions. And the same could be done with England and the Austrian Habsburg dominions, or with England and Brandenburg-Prussia. By the mid-eighteenth century in several respects Prussian administration was markedly ahead of English; but it is not clear that this was so a hundred years earlier.[1]

The greater the differences between two societies in technology, economy, social structure, legal system, constitution, religion, culture, and so on, the more strained become analogies between their systems of government. Obviously, in terms of the lowest common denominator, up to a point the problems of government are the same everywhere, and up to a point equally the response to them is the same: all governments have something in common. The question is at what point problems and situations are so closely parallel that the comparative study of likenesses and differences becomes rewarding. The more alike in other respects two countries are, the more worthwhile it is likely to be to compare their institutions and the men inside them. For this reason a direct comparison is of limited significance except with France, although in some respects the most interesting one would be with the Netherlands. The obstacles to this are the almost total contrast in public institutions, and to a lesser extent the different balance of political influence between trade and land. The United Provinces were not only non-monarchical but also confederal; nor, despite the importance of London in national politics, is there any English equivalent to the social and political predominance of the business classes in two at least of the seven member states. Monarchy, national centralization, and the political and social preponderance of the landed classes were fundamental features of English life from 1603 to 1640; even during the Commonwealth and the Protectorate the differences are more marked than the similarities in any close comparison with the United Provinces.

The elements which have been described as making up the 'old administrative system' in England, can mostly be found on the continent, comprising something like an equivalent system. This is

[1] See W. L. Dorn, 'The Prussian Bureaucracy in the eighteenth century', *Pol. Sci. Qly.*, XLVI-II (1931-2); F. L. Carsten, 'The Great Elector and the Foundation of the Hohenzollern Despotism', *Eng. Hist. Rev.*, LXV (1950) esp. pp. 199-201; H. Rosenberg, *Bureaucracy, Aristocracy and Autocracy. The Prussian Experience 1660-1815* (Cambridge, Mass., 1958), chs. I-VII.

true at any rate of several other European states. To illustrate this, let us examine one such common element a little more closely.

The sale of offices was most prevalent in France, and next most in Spain and the Spanish Empire. It was less prevalent but still widespread in England, the United Provinces (especially Friesland), the parts of Italy not under Spanish rule, and some parts of Germany; it was distinctly less widespread in northern and eastern, and the rest of central Europe. The Dutch historian Dr. K. Swart suggests that, 'In societies with a primitive economy . . . sale of offices did not develop'. But considering the evidence advanced by Swart himself, as well as by other authorities, of sale in the Ottoman and other eastern empires, this raises doubts about the definition of a 'primitive economy'. Apart from this, in Dr. Swart's view the principal factors responsible for systematic sale were: one, 'a bureaucracy ruled by aristocratic principles'; two, 'remuneration by means of fees'; three, 'a flourishing of trade and commerce' together with 'a powerful middle class'; and four, 'an absolutist government which had no other means of meeting its financial emergencies than that of resorting to desperate expedients'. The third factor was partially lacking in Germany and Spain, the first and fourth in England and the Netherlands; all were present only in France.[1] On inspection it can be seen that some of these preconditions are extraneous to the administrative system, whereas others are simply different aspects of it. The first is an administrative feature but one not easily defined; the third and up to a point the fourth are part of the general historical context within which whatever administrative system existed would require to be set; the second is much more specific.

Payment of office-holders other than by salaries was another virtually European-wide phenomenon. It can in turn be related to the stage of development reached by the various national fiscal systems, and to the attitudes of the dominant social classes towards service under their respective Crowns and towards taxation. In many countries payment of officers in fees, gratuities, and perquisites went along with an extensive resort to revenue farming. This was less so in England, partly perhaps because apart from the Customs there were so few regular taxes to be farmed. Large-scale farming represented a tacit admission by the absolutist state, e.g. the French

[1] *Sale of Offices in the Seventeenth Century*, pp. 113-14, 117-18 and ch. VI, 'The Orient', pp. 97-111; see also H. A. R. Gibb and H. Bowen, *Islamic Society and the West*, vol. I, pt. i (1950), 178.

monarchy, that the revenues could not be fully collected, that the greater part of them would never reach the royal coffers—in cash or in credit instruments. An equivalent of the English system of defalcation flourished on a gigantic scale. Combined almost always with sharp practice and frequently with fraud by the farmers themselves, it meant a tremendous gap between the gross and net yield on taxes and other revenues. The aims of the English state were more modest, but whether particular revenues were constitutional or unparliamentary they were on the whole raised with relative success. The percentage of Ship Money collected and actually paid in before 1639 is incomparably higher than for example the net yield of the *Taille* or the *Gabelle* in France; if the mediocre year of 1639 is included, but the 'taxpayers' strike' of 1640 excluded, it is still probably somewhat higher.[1]

In its most extreme, one is tempted to say pathological form revenue farming is scarcely to be distinguished from farming the actual administration of a district to the person responsible for collecting the royal revenues in it. This can be seen in the Turkish Empire, in the oriental world generally, and in Sweden; even France did not fall far short of it. It is worth considering how near England came to anything similar. Take the case of a Receiver-General of Crown land revenues in a group of counties, such as Pym, 1613-38, or Wentworth in the 1620's. His own Fee, poundage, and portage were 'defalked' at source from what he collected, and he also took fees from the payers (bailiffs, farmers, etc.); for none of this did he need regular Exchequer authorization. A further proportion of his receipts were 'assigned' by tally, and were therefore paid direct to the treasurers or paymasters of spending departments, to individual officers and contractors, or to other royal creditors. For such payments he needed either a recurrent or a once for all ('dormant') authorization, and the tally itself, which the payee gave to him and which he then took up to the Exchequer of Audit to have his annual account passed. He was probably at least a year behind in paying in his net receipts and then in presenting his accounts, and he almost certainly used the cash balance for his own financial purposes. But for all this he was not strictly a farmer, and he had little autonomous authority in his counties. Looking at the situation in France, one is tempted to ask whether the English Crown was in all respects the weaker for having so few central officials in the localities.

[1] Miss M. D. Gordon, 'The Collection of Ship Money in the reign of Charles I', *Trans. Roy. Hist. Soc.*, 3rd ser., IV (1910), 141-62.

Treatment of offices like pieces of property, as reflected in the ways by which they were acquired and the terms on which they were held, varied considerably from one country to another. Dr. Swart emphasizes the aristocratic and clerical origins of the English attitude and the special, non-Roman, nature of English law. He does not of course imply by this that anything like the modern concept of 'public office' did exist elsewhere. Only a new view of the state and a new system of public finance, arising in the eighteenth and nineteenth centuries, could bring this concept into being. The difference in the early modern period, as he sees it, is that in France, and to a lesser degree in Spain, the treatment of offices as pieces of property was in part due to royal initiative. In England, by contrast, it was the more or less spontaneous product of the notions of 'liberties' or 'franchises' and of property rights generally, held by the upper classes at large, and formulated more precisely by the common lawyers. Professor Mousnier's study suggests, however, that the origins of venality in France were—if the antithesis is to be retained—as much feudal as royal. Moreover, the Anglo-Norman kings quite deliberately sold offices in the twelfth century, as did Henry VII at the beginning of the sixteenth. Dr. Swart's thesis thus requires some qualification, and it is perhaps unfair to him to make the contrast sound quite so sharp. Some contrast, in this field as elsewhere, there undoubtedly was during the sixteenth and seventeenth centuries; and it should provide another warning against glib equations of the English state under Elizabeth I and James I with the continental monarchies of Philip II or Henry IV.

One important point connected with office-holding and venality remains highly controversial. Dr. Swart contrasts the rabid *archomanie* in France and the serio-comic *empleomania* in Spain with the relative reluctance of the upper and middle classes in England to enter royal service. Or, if reluctance is too strong a word, he certainly implies comparative indifference and lack of eagerness, which is suggested by the absence of regular competitive bidding for offices. But it is one of the central arguments of Professor Trevor-Roper's paper on 'The Gentry' that there was, if not an equal, at least a comparable eagerness for office in Jacobean England, and a readiness to pay for it sufficient to push prices up steeply. Only someone who had worked as thoroughly on the source materials for France or Spain, or both, as on those for England could give an authoritative opinion. Failing anyone so qualified, it seems fair to say that, while Dr. Swart certainly over-emphasizes the contrast, none the less it is still there. It is impossible to read Professor Mousnier's *magnum opus* and then to turn to the English situation without being aware of it. On metropolitan Spain there is nothing comparable, though Dr. Swart's own chapter breaks new ground. It does however appear that the extent and intensity of the *empleomania* should not be exaggerated; in non-Castilian Spain there were strict and by no means ineffective limits on the Crown's power to create new offices. But in the Spanish-American empire Professor J. H. Parry has shown that venality was highly developed, perhaps even more than in Castile itself.[1]

One obvious contrast with Spain (as with France) concerns the sheer number of offices available. In the realms of the Kingdom of Castile alone there are estimated to have been 530 major posts; under the Castilian exchequer 60,000 subordinate places is thought to be an over-estimate—but even if one halves it, the figure is still striking enough! The Inquisition is said to have employed up to another 20,000 people, which makes the English ecclesiastical hierarchy, church courts, censorship, etc., look like very small beer.[2] Not that the numbers of its officials are the test of a government's effectiveness, but they are relevant in considering the competition for office among its subjects. Offices were not subdivided, posts did not multiply in Tudor and early Stuart England at a rate comparable with their increase in France or Spain. Of course there was an increase especially at the lower levels, among the under-clerks and servants' servants: a glance at the Household or the Six Clerks' office will satisfy one of that. And this increase was to some extent masked, or was less than it might otherwise have been, due to the use of patents and royal commissions as administrative instruments. It may further be argued that in the years *c.* 1612-28, to which the most striking cases of competitive bidding belong (except for the brief revival in 1639-43), the English Crown did come near to systematizing sale of offices as a regular form of revenue. Notwithstanding all this, the number of offices available—of all kinds at the centre, and of much direct *material* value in the localities—remained strictly

---

[1] J. H. Parry, *The Sale of Public Offices in the Spanish Indies under the Hapsburgs* (Berkeley, Cal., 1953); Swart, *Sale of Offices*, ch. II. I am grateful to Mr. J. H. Elliott for explaining to me the contrast between Castile and the other Spanish kingdoms.

[2] H. G. Koenigsberger, *The Government of Sicily under Philip II of Spain* (1951), Foreword by J. M. Batista i Roca, pp. 30-1.

limited. And perhaps the relative intensity of the competition for them, or anyway for some of them, in James and Charles I's reigns reflects precisely this. If the English Crown had increased the total number of offices available at a pace, and to a level, comparable with France and Spain, would this competition have been maintained?

After a point, the value of individual offices would surely have tended to fall. One also has to picture the English landowners, not to say lawyers and merchants, as being in a very bad way indeed to believe that the competition would have gone on indefinitely. Nor, finally, is it sensible to compare the eagerness for office in different countries such as England and Spain, or even England and France, without taking even fuller account of the striking differences in economy, social structure, and climate of opinion than of the considerable divergences in government policy.

It would therefore be going too far to say that English administration in the early seventeenth century was unique, and to leave it at that. But if one is to say that it was similar to French, and still more to any other continental administration, elaborate and numerous qualifications have to be made. Thus one ends up by saying little more than that there are both certain broad similarities and also certain very important differences. At a superficial level some of both of these are not difficult to describe; to explain adequately how and why all of them had come about would be to write a detailed comparative history of England and the continent over many centuries.

iii BUREAUCRACY

Whereas the very word bureaucracy was unknown in the England of Charles I, today it is used constantly in journalism and political discussion. But there is little sign that people know, still less that they agree, what the word means. The least controversial meaning is simply a large centralized hierarchy of civil servants, organized in departments, who carry on the work of government, mainly in the sense of administration as opposed to political decisions. The more familiar usage consists of this first one with a pejorative slant, a spoken or unspoken assumption that such a hierarchy of civil servants is a bad thing because its operations are inimical to freedom and enterprise: this meaning of bureaucracy spells controls, shortages, queues, form-filling, 'red tape', and petty tyranny. There is a third, rather more sophisticated usage, which depends on a more literal approach to the derivation of the word itself. According to this, bureaucracy means a hierarchy of officials who are so influential that they actually control, or have a predominant share in controlling policy as well as carrying on administration; on this view the bureaucrats themselves constitute the ruling power in the state, they *are* the ruling class.

Lexicographers, however, prefer the less controversial meaning. According to this, bureaucracy is (1) government by bureaux, that is by departments of public administration, and (2) the officials who staff these departments, referred to collectively or in the abstract. There is nothing about power or ruling classes, and a perjorative undertone only in some of the illustrative quotations.[1]

Political and social scientists offer a bewildering profusion of definitions. Some regard bureaucracy exclusively as a type of administration; others are pre-occupied with its wider connotations. For simplicity's sake these can be called the 'technical' and 'political' usages respectively, although in practice they are usually combined, or indeed confused, in the same definition.

The Italian political theorist Gaetano Mosca assumed that bureaucracy meant government by officials.

> In the bureaucratic state not all the executive functions need to be concentrated in the bureaucracy and exercised by it. . . . The main characteristic of this type of social organization lies . . . in the fact that . . . the central power conscripts a considerable portion of the social wealth by taxation and uses it first to maintain a military establishment and then to support a . . . number of public services. The greater the number of officials who perform public duties and receive their salaries from the central government or from its local agencies, the more bureaucratic a society becomes.[2]

The Austrian sociologist Michels was concerned with both the political and technical meanings. He seems to have assumed that bureaucracy was to do with the exercise of power, but he pictured bureaucrats as the agents by which the 'politically dominant class' exercised their control over the rest of society. Bureaucracy, that is, was to be thought of more as an instrument than as a force in its

[1] *Oxford English Dictionary.*

[2] *The Ruling Class (Elementi di Scienza Politica)*, trans. Hannah D. Kahn, ed. A. Livingston (copyright Mc-Graw-Hill Book Co., New York, 1939), p. 83.

own right. Michels discussed bureaucracy in the context of political parties. And, while bitterly regretting its political and cultural implications, he admitted that '. . . the oligarchical and bureaucratic tendency of party organization is a matter of practical and technical necessity.[1]'

The great German social theorist Max Weber came nearest, at least on the surface, to a strictly technical definition. Like Mosca's, his interpretation of bureaucracy is so wide that in practice it is almost equated with a phase or stage in the development of any government, irrespective of type. Its characteristics are fixed and officially agreed areas of operation, regulation, hierarchy, centralized control, written records, specialized office management, and full-time professionalism. If Weber's reflections on bureaucracy are considered as a whole, a good deal can be inferred about its connexion with political power and social structure. But his formal definition is concerned almost exclusively with the mode of administration and the type of administrators; there is nothing about power or about the petty tyrannies of officialdom.[2]

Present-day American sociologists and political scientists are in many respects the heirs and continuers of this European tradition. Professors Lasswell and Kaplan, for instance, define '*a* bureaucracy' as 'a hierarchy of considerable power and diversification, and low circulation'. They comment that 'the term as here defined is descriptive, not normative'. A bureaucracy is simply 'an impermeable and complex hierarchy'. On the other hand, 'bureaucracy' (without the indefinite article) 'is the form of rule in which the élite is composed of officials; the rulers are known, of course, as bureaucrats'; its self-perpetuating and specialist characteristics are also stressed.[3]

One of the most recent authorities stands on the borders of

[1] R. Michels, *Political Parties* (1915, repr. 1949), pt. II, ch. VII and extracts from Michels in *Reader in Bureaucracy*, ed. R. K. Merton and others (Glencoe, Ill., 1952), esp. pp. 88-91, 140-3.

[2] *From Max Weber: Essays in Sociology*, trans. and ed. H. H. Gerth and C. Wright Mills (1947), ch. VIII, pp. 196-244; also Weber, 'The Essentials of Bureaucratic Organization', *Reader*, pp. 18-27.

[3] H. D. Lasswell and A. Kaplan, *Power and Society. A Framework for Political Inquiry* (New Haven, 1950), pp. 205-6, 209-10; see also *Reader in Bureaucracy*, esp. pp. 27-33, 48-51, 114-35, 216-21, 360-1, 361-71 (pieces by C. J. Friedrich, A. W. Gouldner, R. Bendix, J. D. Kingsley, K. Mannheim, and R. K. Merton respectively); C. W. Mills, *White Collar, The American Middle Classes* (N.Y., 1951), esp. p. 78.

history and social science. In his immense study of *Oriental Despotism* the distinguished sinologist, Professor Wittfogel, emphasizes the dual role of bureaucrats, as constituting *a* ruling power in their own right, and as providing the agency through which the single will of the despot is executed. The despot is pictured as the ultimate source of power, but the officials also none the less 'wield' it and exercise great influence. Professor Wittfogel does not give a general definition, and he discusses Bureaucracy only in the context of 'hydraulic societies', or 'agro-managerial despotisms'. Even so, he clearly has in mind both a type of administration and a system of ruling, and his attitude is one of stern disapproval.[1]

The British contribution to this discussion is unimpressive by comparison. In view of the later attacks on him, it is interesting to find that Harold Laski went a long way towards an exclusively political and non-technical definition. He described bureaucracy as

the term usually applied to a system of government the control of which is so completely in the hands of officials that their power jeopardizes the liberties of ordinary citizens. The characteristics of such a régime are a passion for routine in administration, the sacrifice of flexibility to rule, delay in the making of decisions, and a refusal to embark upon experiment. In extreme cases the members of a Bureaucracy may become a hereditary caste, manipulating government to their own advantage.[2]

Here the idea of power being exercised, and the tone of disapproval have all but crowded out the technical definition in administrative terms.

Whatever their other differences, as for example on the meaning of bureaucracy, most political theorists and social scientists would agree that the state is a necessary part of modern life. And in the concept of the state they would include the machinery and personnel of central administration. Even those who are most trenchant in their attacks on the real or imagined excesses of the bureaucracy, such as its 'Parkinsonian' capacity to expand, would agree that *a* bureaucracy in the dictionary and Weber sense is indispensable. For better or worse, expert, professional, full-time administrators,

[1] K. Wittfogel, *Oriental Despotism* (1957), esp. pp. 305-7, 341, 345.
[2] *Encyclopaedia of the Social Sciences*, III (1930), 'Bureaucracy'; see also Ramsay Muir, *Peers and Bureaucrats* (1910), pp. 3-94. I owe this and the Michels' *Political Parties* references to Laski's article.

organized in hierarchical departments are part of the furniture of our world. And, whether or not they believe that excessive power is exercised by the existing bureaucrats, most such thinkers and commentators would agree that some power has to be wielded by someone. They would almost all assume that in any society policy must be formulated and decisions taken, that those actively involved in these processes are usually a very small numerical minority, and that (whatever constitutional conventions may say) the senior administrators are likely to be among them.

The Marxian theory of government and of the state stands in sharp contradiction to these assumptions. According to this, in all pre-socialist societies the state apparatus, including the central bureaucracy, is simply the instrument of the ruling class (up to this point the Michels view). And the ruling class is that which at any given time stands in the most favourable relation to the means of production, that is the property-*owning* class. In Leninist and post-Leninist terminology 'bureaucracy' carries a strong pejorative overtone. In a capitalist society it is simply the instrument of class rule by, of, and for the bourgeoisie. In a socialist society it refers exclusively to the misuse of their authority by public functionaries. Political leaders and theoreticians have admitted that it constitutes a serious problem under socialism, the transitional stage between capitalism and communism. But once the final stage of social evolution has been reached and the truly 'communist' society come into being, the state will begin to 'wither away'. In Engels's words, as quoted with approval by Lenin, at this stage 'the government of persons is replaced by the administration of things *and the direction of the process of production*' (my italics). This quotation is usually cut short at 'things', which makes it easier to attack. This is foolish, for there is a serious question at issue in its interpretation. On one view communist theory requires the belief that human society will so evolve that makers of policy and takers of decisions will cease to exist, or at least will cease to be distinguishable from other citizens; and that government will consist exclusively of administrative routine, with its officials (if any) metaphorically oiling and greasing a vast perpetual-motion engine. If this is what is meant, the non-Marxian student of history or government is likely to remain incredulous. The whole concept pre-supposes a change in human affairs so total that history can offer no evidence whatever of its likelihood.

P*   457

The Marxian theory of government can, however, be taken in a less extreme sense. Engels and Lenin may in fact have meant simply that the mechanical and impersonal aspects of government would increasingly preponderate over those involving direct personal relations. If so, then it is clear that this process has been proceeding for centuries, most markedly at the lower levels of administration among the lesser officials, and at a particularly rapid rate since the eighteenth-nineteenth centuries. And, for all that can be seen, it might well be further accelerated by the establishment of a communist world state. In a meaningful sense the operation of national insurance and the assessment and collection of income tax today are impersonal, concerned with the 'administration of things', whereas by contrast the incidence of a feudal right like wardship and even the levying of a tax such as a subsidy in the seventeenth century involved personal relationships to a greater extent; they were in short more a matter of the 'government of persons'. Indeed, this whole process is surely a part, though only a part, of what is normally meant by the bureaucratization of government. On this point there would seem to be a chance of finding common ground.

But the crux of the matter is whether or not *in any economic and social circumstances* the government of persons could be wholly replaced by the administration of things and the direction of the process of production. Part of the trouble is that these phrases are imprecise and can all too easily mean what their protagonists or opponents want them to mean. For example, in a politically unified world, with no foreign relations or defence (other than police) forces, the direction and control of the economy, taking this phrase in its widest sense, would constitute the main business of government. But, and here is the logical difficulty, it would still be the main business *of government*. And this means the political and administrative organization of *human* affairs. Furthermore, even the process of production involves people, that is human labour and its deployment. However expert and impersonal, or in one sense bureaucratic, administration becomes it is bound by definition to be concerned with human beings and not exclusively with 'things' or with the 'direction of a process'.

Ironically, perhaps, the most violent of all recent attacks on bureaucracy has come from the ex-communist leader, Milovan Djilas. He specifically and repeatedly identifies it with the tyranny of the new ruling class in communist countries, although he admits

458

the possibility of some later divergence between the industrial-political and the Communist party bureaucracy.[1]

So much for 'bureaucracy' in politics and social science. As might be expected, historians are a good deal less forthcoming, and therefore less overtly contradictory. In his important book, to which reference has already frequently been made, *The Tudor Revolution in Government*, Dr. G. R. Elton uses the adjective 'bureaucratic' rather than the noun 'bureaucracy'. Not all historians are prepared to accept his definitions, as he applies them to the contrast between English government before and after the 1530's. However, the *kind* of meaning which he intends is obviously to do with administrative methods, and a departmental hierarchy; it has little relation to the exercise of power by any class or group, and carries the very reverse of a pejorative undertone.[2] Dr. David Mathew, whose ideas on important points of historical interpretation coincide with Dr. Elton's, has written of 'the emergence of the bureaucratic class' and of 'the semblance of a nascent bureaucracy' in Caroline England. He defines 'the distinguishing marks of a bureaucratic society' as consisting of 'a system of graded preferment within an office constituted by the sovereign authority'. He goes on to speak of Venice as a society which had long been of this type and of the extension of this system in Tudor England.[3] His emphasis is therefore more on a particular kind of governmental hierarchy than on administrative methods; but in general his definition, like Dr. Elton's, is nearer to the philologists' and Weber's than to the hostile colloquial usage.

It would be a mistake to spend time trying to reconcile all these different meanings or to devise a better definition. It is only necessary to make clear how one is using the word in a given context. For historians (the same may not be true for political scientists) it is probably most sensible to think of 'bureaucracy' as referring to certain methods of administration. These must include, at a minimum, professionalism, regular hierarchy, division into departments, and heavy reliance on written records. Granted that bureaucracy, or a

---

[1] M. Djilas, *The New Class* (1957), esp. pp. 27, 35, 38-47, 60-1, 95-6.

[2] I am grateful to Dr. Elton for explaining to me in a letter his meaning of the terms 'household government' and 'national bureaucratic government'. Parts of his general thesis are criticized by Professor R. B. Wernham in his review of *The Tudor Revolution in Government*, in *Eng. Hist. Rev.*, LXXI (1956), 92-5.

[3] *Social Structure*, pp. 1, 3-4, and *passim*.

bureaucratic form of government, is found to exist in a given instance, this does not preclude us from asking questions about its alleged defects: routine, inflexibility, procrastination, extreme conservatism, and even petty tyranny. Nor are we thereby prevented from considering it in relation to the social structure of a particular country in a given epoch, and to the distribution of power in that society. Dr. Mathew, for instance, uses the phrase 'lions around the throne of oligarchy', and appears thereby to imply that in eighteenth-century England (or perhaps from the Restoration to the first Reform Act) the bureaucrats were in the last resort the instruments, indeed the creatures, of aristocratic government.

By these criteria, bureaucracy certainly existed in Caroline England. But this needs to be qualified in two important respects. First, the bureaucracy, or the bureaucratic government, was so small that it may thereby have failed to operate in the manner which this definition normally entails. The Privy Council and its clerical staff, the Secretaries of State and theirs were such factotums, ranging over such a multitude of questions, great and small, of such extraordinarily varied character, that this was no ordinary bureaucratic government as we know it: specialized, elaborate, and professional. Second, this bureaucracy had some other very un-modern characteristics, which serve to invalidate most analogies or comparisons with more recent bureaucracies. Many junior officials, although they were in the King's service, were appointed not by the King, or by the Crown in a more impersonal sense, but by senior officials (acting as individuals) councillors, or courtiers. Many subordinates in the central courts and departments, including some important personal assistants, were not in the King's service at all, but were the private employees of other officials. The granting of reversions, the tenure of offices for life, and the general tendency to regard positions under the Crown as property rights belonging to their holders further limited the Crown's freedom of appointment and promotion. These factors also limited its ability to regulate or abolish existing offices and to set up new ones. The ways in which officers were paid meant that financially they dealt direct with other office-holders and with members of the public; they were not effectively dependent on their own head of department, on the Exchequer (that is the King's financial advisers), or on the Crown itself. Only quite a small fraction of the office-holders were in practice full-time professional civil servants. Most were also landed gentlemen, practising lawyers, or (in a few cases) actively engaged in commerce. Nor did the thought of the age have any concept of 'civil servants' as an occupational classification, least of all as a class of people disqualified from taking part in politics. This was partly because the modern distinction, nowadays perhaps itself carried too far, between politics and administration was almost wholly absent.

Much of this would be true of most, if not all, pre-nineteenth-century bureaucracies. It would be easy, by employing too rigorous a definition, to conclude that, save in very rare and exceptional instances, bureaucracy had never existed before 1800. True, bureaucracy, as we know it, scarcely had existed, but to say on this account that it had not existed at all would be to show a shockingly parochial and unhistorical outlook.

With its elaborate and highly formalized procedure, the copiousness of its written records, the jealousies of its departmental divisions, its hierarchy, and its specialization, English central government had been thoroughly bureaucratic for a very long time. It is reasonable to date English bureaucracy from the 'administrative revolution' of the twelfth century. And even this is to regard Domesday Book, that stupendous bureaucratic achievement, as a flash in the pan. Another decisive shift, away from bureaucracy within the framework of household government and towards departmental 'out of court' bureaucracy, occurred in the Tudor period. All ages are 'ages of transition' but the tempo of change varies greatly from one age to another. This is as true in administration as in all other aspects of human life.

It remains to be considered how far the Caroline bureaucracy was bureaucratic in the sense meant by many social scientists and by almost all modern political commentators. That the officials themselves constituted *the* ruling class of early Stuart England need only be suggested to be seen to be ridiculous. Most of the middling and almost all the upper officials belonged to the armigerous landowning class; if there was *a* 'ruling class', this was it, and they formed part of it.

But they formed part of it with a difference. It is not necessary to interpret the Civil War as a conflict between the 'Ins' and 'Outs' to recognize that the interests and outlook of the office-holders were not in all respects identical with those of the 'mere' gentry, who did not hold office or reside in the capital; nor the interests and outlook of the 'mere' office-holders in turn identical with those of the office-holding landed gentry. One reason why the English central officials exercised less political influence than their French counterparts was because they were even further from constituting a definable, homogeneous class or social group. True, when the French bureaucracy did make its bid for national leadership, in the *Fronde*, it failed lamentably. Even so, the attempt was made, and some degree of internal solidarity mustered in making it. In England no such bid was made, and never could have been: the question did not arise.

So much for the Caroline bureaucracy as a ruling class, or as an influence within the ruling class. As an instrument of royal power, of would-be absolutism, its effectiveness is harder to estimate. Under the so-called 'eleven years tyranny', the personal government of Charles I, England was probably as 'well governed' as any country in Europe then could be without revolutionary social and political changes. To those at the receiving end central administration no doubt often appeared capricious and interfering; the financial needs alike of the Crown and of its servants were constantly felt. Yet within the limits set by its own requirements and by the general climate of opinion, the Crown was genuinely solicitous for the welfare of the people. By modern standards the rights and liberties of the subject were narrowly limited and ill defined. Yet there were safeguards against the abuse of executive power. For all that has recently been suggested to the contrary, even in the 1620's-30's an Englishman was better protected against arbitrary action by the Crown or its agents than were most of his European contemporaries of comparable wealth and social standing.

Government interference in business, in agriculture, trade, industry, building, and mining was a widespread grievance under Charles I. But it was a grievance against the policy of the Crown, especially its many fiscal expedients. Individual officials had to enforce the regulations and controls, some of which undoubtedly restricted economic enterprise. And some officials certainly behaved highhandedly, like 'jacks in office'. But there is very little, if any, evidence that the officials as such, the bureaucracy, were felt to be encroaching on the freedom of the people, stifling creative activity, or swathing the nation in red tape. The nearest one gets to such a feeling is in the tone of resentment adopted by some 'mere' gentry against the court and the government. There is Sir Anthony Weldon's complaint that the Messengers of the Chamber

> were countenanced in their abuse, and insultings over the Gentry (when in their Clutches): and to such a strange passe were disorders come unto [*sic*], that every Lacquey of these great Lords might give a Check-Mate to any Gentleman, yea, to any Country Nobleman, that was not in the Court favour.[1]

But Weldon had himself been expelled from office and from the Court in 1617; he comes in the category of embittered ex-office-holders, of gamekeepers turned poachers. As for the Messengers, there seem to be as many stories of their being insulted and even maltreated as of their behaving high-handedly or committing abuses.

Most of the complaints about royal officials relate to their exactions. The payment of officers in fees and gratuities constantly invited, and often almost compelled abuse. The Crown was at least aware of this, and in respect of fees did try to do something about it. Nor did all officers take, or attempt to take, excessive fees and gratuities. Most of them, we may infer, took what they felt was owing them, that is as much as they decently could; but only a minority were deliberate systematic extortioners.

It is impossible to tell how many instances there were of 'bureaucracy' in the bad sense. These are things of which written record is unlikely to have survived. Some kinds of officials were definitely unpopular, such as the Purveyors and the Saltpetremen. But this was usually because of the nature of their duties, which virtually compelled them to act high-handedly and interferingly. If retrospective evidence is allowed, the radical protest literature (pamphlets, etc.) of the 1640's certainly contains many demands for administrative, and more particularly for legal reforms. But apart from the question of fees, it does not contain a great deal in the way of attacks on officials as such. Exceptions must of course be made for the religious extremists who regarded all temporal government as the work of the beast, soon to be swept away, and for the Diggers, and perhaps some of the Levellers, who saw existing officials merely as instruments of class rule and perpetuators of social injustice. It would be unhistorical to expect to find the modern kind of grievances against bureaucracy, when in its modern form bureaucracy itself can scarcely be found.

[1] *The Court of King Charles*, being a continuation of *The Court and Character of King James* (1651), p. 207.

iv THE CIVIL SERVICE OF CHARLES I

To assess the place in history of Charles I's officials it is necessary to re-emphasize that they were still his servants, and not those of the Crown or the Public. True, some distinction can be drawn between the household staff and those holding positions in the law courts and the departments. But it is hard to know how much to make of this. As early as the thirteenth and fourteenth centuries there was some distinction between *familiares* and office-holders in the 'out-of-court' institutions. The great change, for the most part still to come, was in men's ideas about the state.

Fundamental changes in mental attitude, especially in people's tacit unspoken assumptions about the nature of God and man, of society and the world, are usually slow to take general effect. Such was the case with the change from the Ptolemaic to the Copernican and then to the Newtonian idea of the physical universe. But once they have come about, such changes are often remarkably complete. The new attitude seems so obvious, its premises so sure, that it is hard for people of later generations to think back and imagine the circumstances of a time when their own attitude was unknown, or was the prerogative of a few isolated individuals. In the early seventeenth century it was gradually becoming possible for men to think of loyalty to the state, to the 'common weal' or the public good, as something which might in certain circumstances be different from service to the King. Pym and the other parliamentarians in the Civil War claimed that they were not fighting against the King, but to rescue him from evil counsellors by whom he was being led astray. They either thought it impolitic, or else could not bring themselves, to deny the proposition that 'The King can do no wrong'. This reluctance to blame the King personally, to oppose him directly had a very different significance then from that which it was to acquire in the nineteenth and twentieth centuries. It reflected not the non-political role of the sovereign, but the religious basis of monarchy and the deep-seated contemporary horror of treason and rebellion. Even if Pym and his supporters in parliament did not subscribe to all this themselves, they certainly knew how powerful a hold it still had in the country at large. In 1642-3, even in 1644-5, republicanism was no more than 'a little cloud . . . like a man's hand'. And even in the years of victory, 1649-60, it failed to strike deep or widespread roots as a mental attitude among the people.

464

It is easy to repeat that all royal officials still were, and felt themselves to be the King's servants, much harder to estimate the actual degree of royal authority and control over them. How far was the King in fact master in his own house and his own government? The King and his ministers were aware of certain faults in the administrative system; so too were some of the officials themselves. And genuine attempts were made to remedy several of these faults. It would be completely wrong to picture the Caroline régime as drifting frivolously to disaster, blissfully unaware of its own shortcomings. Yet little was achieved. Why was this?

The King and his councillors were unaware of what appear to us as some of the most profound defects. They seem to have been unable to grasp that it is sometimes an economy to pay people more. It could be said that this was part of a wider failure to see the need to turn royal officials into salaried public servants. But this brings us back to the question of mental attitude. Salaried the officials might perhaps have been; public servants, before the Crown had itself been to a greater extent depersonalized and the King in some degree depoliticized, they hardly could be.

In other cases the Crown had some idea of what was needed, but lacked either the will or the authority to put such measures into effect. This was true of thoroughgoing economical reform in the household, and of the fee problem in the law and revenue courts.

There were also legal limits to what the Crown could do. In James I's reign responsible men had got up in the Commons and said that the fees of Exchequer officials were their 'freehold', and could not be touched without all property being threatened. Parliament, it is true, was not the same as the courts. But even the court cases brought against office-holders show the weaknesses in the Crown's position. In 1618-19 the Lord Treasurer had been dismissed for gross corruption, but his subordinate, the Auditor of the Receipt, had only been suspended, and had to be bullied and cajoled into resigning. The great Lionel Cranfield was easily removed from the Treasury and the Wards, but his mediocre brother Randall's tenure as Master of the Mint proved considerably harder to terminate. In the 1630's, for the four or five officers who were tried, found guilty of exactions, and deprived of their positions, there were several times as many who compounded, and kept their offices with substantially the same fees as before.

Officers who had committed venial rather than mortal crimes

could choose to bargain with the Crown, or in the last resort to stand their trial. Some did better, others worse, than those who submitted to the King's mercy, but at least there was room for manœuvre. Life tenure and the concept of office as a 'right' were the holders' main defences. But, of course, if an entire patent could be voided, or revoked on sound legal grounds, it availed an officer nothing that one of its clauses granted him tenure for life. Hence the importance of the decision given by the Judges of King's Bench in 1637, which seems to have widened the grounds on which a patent could be voided. It is not clear how far this judgment actually became an effective precedent.[1]

It is difficult to say exactly how much the King could touch officers' rights by issuing proclamations or by other executive orders. In theory he could not over-ride statute or go against the common law. In practice his ability to alter the law by pressure on the judges was one of the main constitutional issues of 1603-42. None of the three classic cases (Bate's in 1606, the 'Five Knights'' in 1627, and Hampden's in 1637) concerned office-holders' rights. But if the King could get the law altered concerning taxation, then clearly—with the judges' help—he could also get it changed as it related to office-holding. Moreover, apart from their privileges, officers' liabilities were involved when they allowed themselves to be the instruments of illegal action, for example in collecting unparliamentary taxes (Impositions after 1606; or, a clearer instance, Tonnage and Poundage after 1626). Some customs officers indeed discovered to their cost that royal proclamations and commissions under the Great Seal not only did not change the law but did not always protect those who broke it.

By statute the King in Parliament could alter any right or privilege of any office-holder. Legally there was no impediment to the statutory abolition of the Pipe and the Remembrancers' Offices, to the institution of a fee 'pool', and to the putting of all Crown servants onto fixed stipends. The limit here was set by political practicability, not by what was legally possible; ultimately it was determined by what was—given all the circumstances of the age—even thinkable.

If the Stuarts had been victorious, and if an absolute monarchy of the French type had been established in England, the modernization of English government would have taken place in an utterly

[1] See Chapter 3, s. iii, p. 125 (on the Searchership of Sandwich).

different political, legal, and social context. As it was, the gradual decline of royal power from the sixteenth to the nineteenth century to a large extent preceded the birth of the modern Civil Service. The outcome of the seventeenth-century constitutional conflict helped to determine the context within which the modern roles of both the Crown and the Civil Service have evolved. It may seem perverse to argue at one and the same time that his servants could not become 'public' officials while the King still ruled as well as reigned, and that an 'enlightened' absolutism might have initiated administrative reforms akin to those which were only fully achieved in the nineteenth century. There is force in this objection. But the answer to it may lie in suggesting some distinction between personal monarchy and absolutism. The governments of the eighteenth-century 'despots' were more bureaucratic, more departmentalized, than the government of Charles I. In this respect enlightened absolutism was a stage nearer to modern autocracy, where the ruler indisputably 'rules' but where the officials are no longer his personal or household servants.

In England the political victory of oligarchy appears to have had the effect of consolidating the 'old administrative system' and possibly of prolonging its existence. The eighteenth-century constitution and the unreformed Civil Service were in turn undermined by new forces. New demands were made on the state, and new standards expected from its servants, particularly from the 1780's on. Extra-parliamentary public opinion, above all the voice of the greatly expanded urban middle class, made itself increasingly heard. Finally the Crown became depersonalized; executive power passed from the monarch and his (or her) chosen advisers to a cabinet selected on a 'party' basis. The seeds of the nineteenth-century reforms in administration might have been sown by Strafford, or equally well by the Barebones Parliament. What had been prevented from coming about under the rule of King and oligarchy was later to accompany the establishment of the Crown's new position, the emergence of cabinet and parties, and the rise of public opinion.

All this is to assume that the social structure of the country and the balance of political power in it were decisive in determining the limits within which the administrative system developed. Such an assumption is not necessarily correct. Unless the underlying causes in history are believed to be exclusively of one kind (for instance economic and technological, or mental and spiritual), there is no logical reason why institutions of government and systems of office-holding should not have important economic, social, political, and even cultural influences. The question is how far, in practice, government (including of course the officials taking part in it) does exercise a major influence on how people live and think. And this includes the further question of how far such influence as it does appear to have represents anything more than an indirect effect of other non-administrative factors, which have—at a stage further back in the causal chain—helped to determine the system of government and the kind of people participating in it.

For England in the years 1625 to 1642 the conclusion is inescapable. It is surely beyond debate, that the growth of government and the rise of bureaucracy are major themes in modern history. But to contend that a particular phase in this process, or the political and social tensions which arose from it, provided the key to English seventeenth-century history would be to make oneself the victim of a sociological theory. And to maintain such a view would in the last resort be to go in the face of both the evidence and common sense.

The reader's as well as the author's own temperament and preferences will help to form our final picture of Charles I's Civil Service. We may think of Edward Nicholas, a worthy servant of 'Thorough', working tirelessly to administer the entire Ship Money project for a nominal stipend of only £200 a year, over and above all his routine work for the Admiralty Commissioners and odd jobs for the Privy Council. Or we may think of Sir Robert Pye together with the Prest and Revenue Auditors working overtime to provide the Treasury Commissioners with an unusually detailed statement of the Crown's financial position. On the other hand we may think of the Clerk of the Ordnance being found making a bonfire of departmental records in order to escape the scrutiny of an investigating commission. We may think of the officers of the Household systematically cheating the Crown for forty years by means of a transparent and shameless accounting device. Or we may think of those who waxed rich on the fruits of extortion from the public. Yet there must have been many more officials who fell between the extremes of laxity and conscientiousness. Many, perhaps most of them, must have worked moderately hard, with fair efficiency, sticking mainly to precedent and routine, with reasonable loyalty to the Crown, and profiting only modestly out of their positions. If such 'typical' civil servants of Charles I seem to have got buried in lists and tables, it is simply because evidence of a personal nature is so much likelier to have survived about those who were for one reason or another 'untypical'. But of their existence there can be no reasonable doubt.

In one respect typical and untypical are happily alike. The English language had reached that point in its development where almost anyone who wrote naturally—and not sycophantically or for conscious literary effect—wrote well. Even the most humdrum administrative details, the pettiest personal concerns, come alive in seventeenth-century English prose. If administrative history is sometimes said to be dull, this may sometimes be because the people involved in it were themselves dull. Whatever the truth of this for other epochs, no such extenuating plea can be entered here.

APPENDIX

POSTS IN THE CENTRAL GOVERNMENT

*Denotes those officers with whom we are mainly concerned in Chapters 3-6 of this book.

** Denotes that only the most important (administratively) in a group are in this category.

TABLE 56. THE CENTRAL EXECUTIVE

The King
*Privy Council
*Lord President of the Council (vacant 1631 on)
    *4 Council Clerks in ordinary, c. 6 Clerks extraordinary, their under-clerks (usually two each)
    *2 Keepers of the Council Chamber
    1 Keeper of the Chests and Records
    **c. 20 Sergeants-at-Arms (2 or 3 administratively more important than the rest, 1625-40)
    c. 40 Messengers of the Chamber
    *2 Clerks of the Cheque (paymasters for the Messengers)
*2 Secretaries of State (in charge of the Council's agenda, staff, etc., in Lord President's absence)
    *4 Clerks of the Signet
    *French Secretary
    *Latin Secretary
    *German Interpreter
    **4-8 personal secretaries and under-clerks
*c. 5 Ambassadors ⎫
*c. 16 Agents   ⎬(and their secretaries and household staffs)
*Lord Privy Seal (moribund 1625-8; relatively active 1628-42)
    *4 Masters of Requests
    *4 Clerks of the Privy Seal
    **deputy Clerks (?4)
*Lord Chancellor or Lord Keeper of the Great Seal
    Personal staff: 2 chief secretaries, 2 secretaries
    *Prothonotary
    *Clerk for engrossing patents
    4 under-clerks

470

TABLE 56—*continued*

*Examiner of letters patent
*Clerk of the Crown
 3 under-clerks
*Keeper of Wax *alias* Chafe Wax
*3 Clerks of Petty Bag
 under-clerks
*(9 Clerks of the enrolments; these Clerkships had come to be held
    by the Six Clerks of Chancery, who are included in the list of
    officers on the legal side of that court, and by the Clerks of the
    Petty Bag)
 8 deputies or under-clerks
*Riding Clerk (one of the Six Clerks)
*Writer of leases
 Sealer
*Usher
*Clerk or Keeper of the Hanaper (the 'treasury' of Chancery)
*Comptroller of the Hanaper (one of the Six Clerks)
*Attorney-General   } (Crown law officers; not Privy Councillors)
*Solicitor-General   }

TABLE 57. THE POSTS

*Postmaster General (a sinecurist 1625-37, the Secretaries of State *ex
    officio* 1637-42)
*his deputy, and *c.* 1630-7 the deputy's deputy (after 1637 simply the
    Postmaster)
*Foreign Postmaster or Master of the Foreign Posts (the same man as
    the (home) Postmaster 1637-40)
*Court Postmaster
    c. 50 local postmasters, or 'Posts' (in various towns and at the main
      stages)
    ?*c.* 50 Carriers (sometimes also called 'Posts'; there was not always
      a clear distinction between Posts and Carriers)

TABLE 58. THE HOUSEHOLD BELOW STAIRS

The Board of Greencloth
- *Lord Steward ⎫
- *Treasurer ⎬ The 'Whitestaves'
- *Comptroller ⎭
- *Cofferer
- *2 Clerks of Greencloth
- *2 Clerks Comptrollers
- *Master of the Household

The Hall, etc.
*Knight Marshal
7 Marshals of the Hall
6 Servers of the Hall
2 Surveyors of the Dresser
14 Surveyors of the Hall
4 of the Long Carts
1 Gilder
2 Wood bearers
1 Bellringer
8 Wine Porters
(46)

Woodyard
*1 Sgt.
*1 Clerk
2 Grooms
3 Yeomen
2 Pages
(9)

Ewery
*1 Sgt
3 Yeomen
1 Groom
1 Page
(6)

Boiling Hse
1 Yeoman
2 Grooms
(3)

Scalding Hse
2 Yeomen
2 Grooms
2 Pages
(6)

Laundry
1 Yeoman
1 Groom
5 Pages
(7)

Porters
*Sgt Porter
3 Yeomen
3 Grooms
(7)

Cart Takers
*2 Clerks
2 Yeomen
4 Grooms
(8)

Harbingers
*2 Gents
6 Yeomen
(8)

Cellar
*2 Sgts
*1 Gent
4 Yeomen Purveyors
1 Yeo of Bottles
1 Groom
2 Pages
(11)

Kitchen
*Chief Clk
*2nd Clk
*3rd Clk
4 Master Cooks
7 Yeomen
7 Grooms
10 Porters and Scourers
10 Children
(41)

Larder
*2 Sgts
*1 Clerk
*1 Gent
3 Yeomen
2 Grooms
2 Pages
(11)

Chandlery
*1 Sgt
2 Yeomen
1 Yeoman Purveyor
3 Grooms
1 Page
(8)

Compting House
*1 Sgt
2 Yeomen
1 Groom
2 Messgr
**3 Cofferer's Clerks
(9)

*Clerk of the Market

* **Confectionery**
1 Sgt
2 Yeomen
1 Groom
1 Page
(5)

Pastry
*1 Sgt
*1 Clerk
3 Yeomen
3 Grooms
3 Children
(11)

Almonry
1 Sub-Almoner
2 Yeomen
2 Grooms
(5)

Buttery
*1 Gent
3 Yeomen
2 Grooms
5 Yeomen Purveyors
2 Pages
(13)

Bakehouse
*2 Sgts
*1 Clerk
4 Yeomen
3 Grooms
3 Yeomen Purveyors
5 Others
(18)

Acatry
*2 Sgts
*1 Clerk
5 Yeomen Purveyors
3 Yeomen
2 Grooms
(13)

Spicery
*3 Clerks
1 Yeoman
1 Grocer
(5)

Scullery
*1 Sgt
*1 Clerk
3 Yeomen
2 Pewterers
2 Grooms
2 Pages
4 Children
(15)

Poultry
*1 Sgt
*1 Clerk
4 Yeomen Purveyors
1 Purveyor of Lambs
1 Yeoman
3 Grooms
(11)

Pitcher Hse
1 Yeoman
2 Grooms
1 Page
(4)

Wafery
1 Yeoman
1 Groom
(2)

Pantry
*1 Sgt
5 Yeomen
4 Grooms
2 Bread-bearers
(12)

Total approximately 305

TABLE 58—continued

Servants' servants (1637-8)

Compting Hse	5	Bakehouse	13	Woodyard	7	Confectionery	
Kitchen (for		Kitchen (for		Almonry	1	and Ewery	8
the Clerks)	13	the Cooks)	35	Porters	10	Pastry	15
Chandlery and		Pantry	9	Cellar	12	Buttery	11
Pitcher Hse	7	Larder	9	Wafery and		Poultry, Boiling	
Scullery	7	Stables	9	Laundry	3	Hse, and Scal-	
Guard (for the						ding Hse	12
Clerks)	10						

Total approximately 195

TABLE 59. THE CHAMBER AND ITS OFFSHOOTS

*Lord Chamberlain
*Vice-Chamberlain
Treasurer of Chamber (2 clerks)

Bedchamber	Privy Chamber	Chamber	Great Chamber
*Groom of the the Stole	*4 Gent Ushers	*6 Esqres of Body	*Gro Porter
2-4 Gents (unpaid)	*8 Grooms	*5 Cupbearers	14 Grooms
*5-7 Grooms	48 Gents in Ordy (12 on duty)	*5 Carvers	4 Pages
*4-5 Pages (12-17)	*King's Barber	*4 Sewers	5 Messengers
*Keeper of the Privy Purse	Confessors (26 at a time)	*4 Gent Ushers daily waiters	4 Yeomen Ushers
		*8 Gent Ushers quarter waiters (2 at a time)	*Knight Harbinger (29)

Miscellaneous

Chaplains, Chapel and Vestry staff (c. 54 at a time)
*6-8 Physicians
*4 Apothecaries
*5 Surgeons
Dentist
Clerk of Closet
*Surveyor of Dresser
3 Laundresses
Library Keeper
2 Limners
*Clock Keeper
Instrument maker
Coffer maker
2 Gun makers
Ratcatcher
Molecatcher
Matlayer
Sempstress
Embroiderer
2 Shoemakers
*Plumber
Perfumer
Spurrier
*Organ Keeper
Herbalist
*Goldsmith

2 Painters
2 Picture Keepers

Bowbearer
4 or 5 Officers of Bows
4 Officers of Bears, Bulls and Mastiffs (1*)
Cormorant Keeper
31 Falconers (1*)
c. 35 Huntsmen (2*)
15 Harriers (1*)
c. 45 Musicians (1*)
20 Sergeants-at-Arms
11 Footmen
42 Messengers (inc.: 2 Clerks*; also listed under Central Executive)
*Master of Barges
c. 44 Watermen

8 Sewers of Chamber
6 Gent Waiters (46)

The Band of Gentlemen Pensioners
*Captain
*4 other officers and clks.
50 Pensioners (25 on duty at a time)

The King's Guard
*Captain
**c. 9 other officers and clks
200 Yeomen (50 on duty at a time)

Robes
*Gent
*Clerk
Yeoman
3 Grooms
Page
Tailor
Brusher
(9)

Jewels
*Master
*Clerk
Yeoman
2 Grooms
2 Jewellers
(7)

Works
*Surveyor
*Comptroller
*Paymaster
*Clerk
Master Mason
Sgt Plumber
Master Carpenter
Purveyor
10-14 other Artificers and Craftsmen
Labourers (generally on temporary hire only)

Ceremonies
*Master
*Asst Master
Marshal
(3)

Removing Wardrobe	Revels etc.	Tents, etc.	Toils
*2 Clerks	*Master	*Master =	*Master
Yeoman	*Clerk =	*Clerk Comptroller	2 Yeomen
3 Grooms	Yeoman	*Clerk	(3)
2 Pages	Groom	2 Yeomen	
10 Clerks or Kprs of Standing Wrs	(4)	Groom	
(18)		(6)	

TABLE 60. THE STABLES

*Master of the Horse

*Avenor	*Clerk of Stable	*16 Equerries	1 Child Rider
*2 Clerks	8 Surveyors	46 Yeomen	2 Boys
of Avery	3 Marshal	97 Grooms	3 Keepers
* 4 Sgts	Farriers		1 Messenger

=186

*Master of the Queen's Horse

*1 Sgt	1 Surveyor	*4 Equerries	44 Grooms
21 Yeomen		5 Extra equerries	

= 77

Total =263

TABLE 61. THE QUEEN

*Lord Chamberlain
*Vice-Chamberlain
(Master of the Horse)
*Secretary and Master of Requests
Sergeant at Law
Counsellor at Law
*Clerk of Council; 2 Keepers of Council Chamber
Deputy attorneys in Exchequer and Common Pleas
*3 Gent Ushers of Privy Chamber
*2 Cupbearers
*2 Carvers
*2 Sewers
*4 Gent Ushers daily waiters
8 Grooms of Privy Chamber (*2 or 3)
*6 Gent Ushers quarter waiters
3 Servers of the Chamber
Clerk of the Closet
Apothecary
*Surgeon
4 Pages of the backstairs
4 Pages of the Chamber
7 Officers of the Robes (*2)
Clerk of the jewel coffers
6 Huntsmen
15 Musicians
24 Watermen

*High Steward of the Queen's revenues
*Chancellor and Keeper of Great Seal
*Treasurer and Paymaster; clerk
*Master of Game
*Surveyor-General
*Attorney-General
*Solicitor-General
*Auditor; clerk
Mistress of the Robes (wife of the Master of the Great Wardrobe)
Keeper of the sweet coffers
4 Maids of Honour
7 Chamberers
Laundress
Starcher
Sempstress
3 Laundry maids
5 Officers of Chapel and Alms
36 other pensioners (including some of her officers and some in other departments)
14 Kitchen
? Bakehouse, cellar, pantry, pastry
2 Harbingers
=c. 180 minimum (without Stable)

474

TABLE 62. THE ROYAL CHILDREN

Prince Charles

*Groom of the Stole and Gent of the Bedchamber (also the 'Governor')

Tutor

*4 Grooms of the Bedchamber
*2 Gent Ushers of Privy Chamber
*4 Grooms of Privy Chamber
*2 Cupbearers
*2 Carvers
*2 Sewers
*2 Gent Ushers daily waiters
*2 Gent Ushers quarter waiters
 2 Pages of the presence
 4 Grooms of the Great Chamber
 3 Officers of the Robes
*Physician
 Apothecary

*2 Surgeons
 Barber
 2 Pages of backstairs
 2 Officers of the vestry
 10 miscellaneous Chamber servants
*Paymaster and Clerk of Greencloth
*Clerk of the comptrollments
 66 or 67 other Household servants
*Master of the Horse (from 1639 only)
* Avenor
*2 Equerries
 c. 22 other Stable servants
*Attorney ⎫
*Solicitor ⎬ from (1638-9)
=c. 144

Duke of York

Governess (Tutor)
9 other Chamber servants

=10

Princess Mary

Governess
13 other Chamber servants
10 Household servants
6 Stable servants

=30

Princess Elizabeth

8 Chamber servants

=8

Princess Anne

10 Chamber servants

=10

TABLE 63. THE GREAT WARDROBE

*Master; who was also the accountant (an unusual arrangement)
*Clerk

*2 Under-Clerks
 Yeoman Cutter
 Carrier
 Robe Cutter
 15-20 Cutters
 13-15 Arras makers

 c. 10 Artificers
**9-10 Keepers of standing Wardrobes (some of whom were in effect quite important store keepers or head caretakers)
 Porter

Total c. 60

TABLE 64. THE COURT OF WARDS AND LIVERIES

*Master (head of the Court, usually a Privy Councillor)

*Receiver-General (treasurer, paymaster, and chief accountant)

*Surveyor (more concerned with the actual administration of wardships and the lands of those for whom the Crown itself acted as guardian)

*Attorney (principal law officer of the Court)

*2 Auditors (assistants to, and acting as a check on, the Receiver-General and other accountants)

*Clerk (general administrative assistant; in charge of the records of the Court; 2 co-Clerks in the 1620's and 1630's)

*Clerk of the Liveries (concerned with finance and management of livery, to some extent distinct from Wardship)

*Clerk Remembrancer (a new office instituted in our period)[1]

under-clerks

Ushers

Messengers

Porters

Feodaries (approximately one for each county; feodaries were officials of the Court functioning in the localities: an exception to the generalisation that the central government had no paid officers in the countryside)[2]

TABLE 65. THE DUCHY OF LANCASTER

*Chancellor (head of the legal and financial sides; usually a Privy Councillor)

*Receiver-General (treasurer, paymaster, and chief accountant; like the Receiver-General of the Wards he did not account to the Exchequer; he made out-payments both to it, and direct to the spending departments)

*2 Auditors, North and South of Trent (principal assistants to the Receiver-General, in charge of taking the accounts of local bailiffs, farmers, etc.)

*Attorney (principal law officer of the Court)

*Clerk of the Duchy Court (concerned with the judicial more than the financial side)

*2 Surveyors of Woods, North and South of Trent

Messengers, Porters

Chancellor's Secretaries

16-18 Receivers of revenues from Duchy properties grouped geographically (some were major landowners, others more comparable to the Feodaries)

[1] Bell, *Court of Wards*, p. 31.

[2] For other exceptions to this see below, Table 66.

TABLE 66. THE EXCHEQUER

(i) *Upper*

(Prest, augmentation-wise, and land revenue accounting)

*Lord Treasurer (or Commissioners)⎫
  secretaries (?2)   ⎪
*Chancellor of the Exchequer   ⎬ judges (common-law side Barons
  secretary   ⎪   only)
*Chief Baron   ⎪
*3 Puisne Barons   ⎭

*Cursitor Baron	(Ancient Course)
*2 Prest Auditors	*King's Remem-⎫
clerks (? 2-4)	brancer ⎪ also legal
*7 Revenue Auditors	*2 Secondaries ⎬ work,
clerks (? 7)	6 clerks ⎭ equity side
20 Receivers-General (in the	*Lord Treasurer's Rmbrcr
counties)	*2 Secondaries
*Receiver-General⎱ of Duchy	10 clerks
*2 Auditors ⎰ of Cornwall	*Clerk of the Pipe
	*Comptroller of the Pipe
(Miscellaneous acctg)	*2 Secondaries (senior one also=
*Remembrancer⎱ of First Fruits	Surveyor of Greenwax)
*Receiver ⎰ and Tenths	6 clerks or attorneys
3 clerks	*Foreign Apposer
*2 Receivers of recusant revenues	*Clerk of the Estreats
*2 Auditors of same	2 Clerks of the Parcels
	Clerk of the Nichills
(legal staff, common law side)	*2 Deputy Chamberlains
*Clerk of the Pleas	
4 clerks	*Receiver and Surveyor of Fines
(common law and equity)	2 Appraisers of forfeited goods
*Clerk of the Errors	
	*Surveyor-General of crown lands
*Chief Usher	*2 Surveyors of woods and forests
4 Ushers	20 Escheators (in the counties)
6 Messengers	
Marshal	=*c.* 104 plus 40 in the counties
Court Keeper	Total=*c.* 144
	*=46

Various revenue officers, not members of the Exchequer, but answerable
  to the Lord Treasurer:

*Receiver of Tobacco Licences	*Surveyor of Saltworks
*Receiver of Wine Licences	*Surveyor of Soapworks
*Aulnager and deputies	*Garbler of Madder

477

TABLE 66—*continued*

(ii) *Lower*

*Treasurer (or Commissioners)
 clerk
*Under Treasr (alias Chancellor)
*Auditor (or Writer of Tallies) — involved in all out-payments
*chief assistant
 clerks (?2-4)
*Clerk of the Pells[1]
 clerks (?2)
 — involved in cash in-payments

*4 Tellers — involved in cash out-payments only

*Tally Cutter
*2 under-chamberlains — involved in use of tallies instead of cash out-payments

*2 Chamberlains
*Usher
 4 Messengers
 ? Clerk of the Treasury (office obsolescent by seventeenth century)
 Total excluding overlaps with Upper Exchequer $= c.$ 23-5
 $ * =$ 13

 Total for whole Exchequer $= c.$ 170
  or excluding Receiver-Generals and Escheators $=$ 130
 $ * =$ 59

TABLE 67. CUSTOMS STAFF

*Surveyor-General
*2 co-Surveyors of London — (to supervise all other Customs officials, though not the Farmers; directly responsible to the Lord Treasurer)
*Surveyor of the out-ports

*3-4 Comptrollers for London — (to act as a check on the Collectors
 c. 18 Comptrollers for the out-ports and Customers)

*12-16 Collectors (in charge of different branches of the London customs,
 otherwise for specific types of customs revenue; in the 1630's some
 Farmers of the traditional customs were also Collectors of the New
 Impositions)
 c. 19 Customers (the equivalent of the Collectors in all out-ports, except
 apparently Bristol and Newcastle)
*Chief Searcher of London
 7 Under-Searchers of London

---

[1] Duties of the Clerk of the Pells included keeping a check on the
Auditor, who once referred to his colleague as 'my controller'.
This was the normal contemporary meaning of the word, though in
practice not all comptrollers did cross-check the accounts of the
treasurer or paymaster of their respective departments. (Hist. MSS.
Comm., *Cowper*, I, 229.)

TABLE 67—*continued*

c. 18 Searchers in the out-ports (possibly more, not receiving a Fee from the Crown)
Usher of the London customs house
c. 17=Waiters of the London customs house
2 co-Registrars of seized goods
5 other under-officers receiving Fees from the Crown at Bristol
other under-officers in the out-ports ⎫ (numbers can only be estimated;
and clerks there and in London ⎭ query minimum another 100)
Total=over 200
Total *c. 23

TABLE 68. THE ALIENATIONS OFFICE

*Clerk (duties unclear; possibly a sinecurist)
*Receiver (the paymaster and accountant)
*3 Deputies for Compositions (deputies for the Treasurer and Chancellor for the actual collection of the Alienations revenues)
3 clerks

TABLE 69. THE MINT

*2 Wardens (titular heads of the office, and its accountants with the Exchequer; possibly they became more active c. 1633-5 on, owing to the dispute about the Mastership: see Chapter 6 s. vi)
*Master (normally the effective head or chief executive; more or less in commission 1633-5; 2 co-Masters 1635-42)
*Comptroller (second in command, special duty being to check the probity of the Warden and accountants by internal auditing)
*Assay Master (general supervisor of the actual coinage operations; responsible for the gold and silver content of coins)
*2 Auditors (helped with accounts; in the mid-1630's one of them was also one of the two Prest Auditors in the Upper Exchequer)
*Teller (counted or weighed outgoing new coins and old ones coming in for re-coining)
*Surveyor of the Melting House
*Chief Graver (responsible for the execution of the design on the coins)
 clerks
 under-gravers
*Provost, or Chief Moneyer (of slightly more consequence than the others; in the later 1630's he seems to have acted the part of a modern shop-steward, standing up for the moneyers and other workmen against the senior officers)[1]
Moneyers (carried out the casting)
Porters
Messengers
workmen

[1] PC 2/48, pp. 406, 482, 502, 520 (1637).

TABLE 70. THE ORDNANCE OFFICE

*Master (titular head; sometimes a Privy Councillor; performed by Deputy *c.* 1630-33)

'*Principal officers*':

*Lieutenant (chief executive officer, *de facto* head of the office, also paymaster and treasurer; accounted to the Prest Auditors)

*Surveyor (responsible for the quality of all incoming supplies; the five principal officers were jointly responsible for their quantity and price)

*Clerk (dealt mainly with internal book-keeping, under the Lieutenant)

*Storekeeper (in charge of all supplies between receipt and issue)

*Clerk of the Deliveries (kept a record of issues, for which all five officers were jointly responsible, and had charge of the recovery of supplies and equipment after voyages and other expeditions)

Other officers:

*Master Gunner: Keeper of the Small Guns; Keeper of the Rich (i.e. decorated or ceremonial) Weapons

*Master's Clerk

9 clerks

**12-16 Artificers (some were important as manufacturers or merchants, and a few as 'Engineers')

20 Labourers

c. 100 Gunners (some were scattered in the royal forts and castles, a few available in the Tower, and the majority in theory *en disponibilité*, but in practice seldom to be found when wanted)

TABLE 71. THE ARMOURY

*Master (effective head, and accountant to the Prest Auditors)

*1-2 Surveyors (responsible for the state of the weapons)

*Clerk

2-3 other under-officers

12 Armourers, or more (skilled workmen of the self-employed type, perhaps hired on contract)

TABLE 72. THE NAVY (*sea-going officers excluded*)

*Lord High Admiral (one of the great officers of state and an *ex-officio* Privy Councillor; the Admiralty was in commission 1628-38)

*Lieutenant, or Vice-Admiral of England (unlike the Lieutenancy of the Ordnance, this had become a largely titular office by the 1620's and 1630's)

480

TABLE 72—*continued*

'*Principal officers*':

*Treasurer (accounted to the Prest Auditors; in practice the senior executive officer)

*Comptroller (kept a check on the Treasurer and on the other principal officers)

*Surveyor (responsible for the good condition of ships and all the tackle in them, especially masts, spars, and cordage)

*Victualler (in charge of all supplies of food and drink afloat. On a contract and *not* under the Treasurer; in a sense more like a 'Farmer', but salaried and holding by patent)

*Clerk, Clerk of the Acts, or Clerk of the Ships (in charge of the clerical side. Not yet the office which Pepys was to make it)

*2 Assistants, in the 1630's only (ranked with the Clerk as junior principal officers)

Others:

*2 Principal Storekeepers
*2 or 3 Master Shipwrights (or ship designers)
 4 Principal Masters of the Navy (professional master mariners available for advice in design, trials of new ships, etc.)
 under-clerks
 storekeepers in the various ports
 messengers

TABLE 73. THE TOWER OF LONDON; PRISONS AND HOSPITALS IN LONDON

*Lieutenant of the Tower (a position of trust and importance, ranking about with that of the Lieutenant of the Ordnance, but in times of external and domestic peace not an exacting one. The superior office of Constable of the Tower was filled only in 1640-2)

*Keeper of the Records (the bulk of the ancient records were housed in the Tower; most Chancery records were kept in the Rolls Chapel, Chancery Lane, on the site of the present Public Record Office)

*Upper or Over Jailer
 Chief Porter
 c. 41 Yeomen of the Tower (probably including jailors, but additional to the 200 Yeomen of the Guard)

*Warden of the Fleet Prison (at the east end of Fleet Street)
*Deputy Warden
*Keeper of the Gatehouse Prison (at the entrance to the Palace in Westminster)
*Marshal of the Marshalsea (on the South Bank)
*Keeper of the King's hospital in Westminster

TABLE 74. OFFICE OF ARMS AND COURT OF CHIVALRY

*The Earl Marshal (not strictly hereditary in the Howard family until 1672; generally exercised a rather remote headship of the Office of Arms, but occasionally asserted himself. By this time there was no permanent Lord High Constable, although Buckingham was once or twice said to have been toying with a plan to revive the office for himself. A temporary Lord High Constable was appointed specially for trials by arms, and a Lord High Steward for the trials of peers[1]

*Earl Marshal's Lieutenant (his deputy on the legal and heraldic sides)

*Garter King of Arms (the head of all the Heralds)

*Clarenceux King of Arms (head of the Heralds South of Trent)

*Norroy King of Arms (head of the Heralds North of Trent)

*7 Heralds: Richmond, Lancaster, Chester, Mowbray, Windsor, Somerset, York (assistants to the Kings)

**7-8 Pursuivants: Portcullis, Croix-Rouge, Rouge-Dragon, Blanchlion, Bluemantle, Rose Rouge, and one or two simply styled Pursuivants-at-Arms (assistants to the Heralds)

*Registrar of the Court of Chivalry (in effect clerk of the court)

*Constable's Lieutenant (acted legally for the Constable when one was appointed)

*King's Advocate (normally a civil lawyer of distinction)

Usher. Messenger

Proctors (equivalent to attorneys in other courts).[2]

TABLE 75. OFFICERS OF THE ORDER OF THE GARTER

*Chancellor
*Registrar
*Clerk

TABLE 76. KING'S BENCH

*Lord Chief Justice (senior to the Chief Justice of Common Pleas and the Chief Baron; sometimes a Privy Councillor)

*3 Puisne Justices

(*Crown Side*)

*2 Clerks of the Crown *alias* Coroners (2 co-Clerks in 1636; not necessarily divided; coroners in the sense of guardians of the pleas of the Crown)

---

[1] e.g. the Earl of Lindsey as Constable for Rea *vs.* Ramsay, 1631 (the King prevented this combat from taking place!); Lord Keeper Coventry as Steward for Rex *vs.* Castlehaven (on capital charges for sodomy and rape), 1631.

[2] G. D. Squibb, *The High Court of Chivalry* (Oxford, 1959), ch. X and app. II.

TABLE 76—*continued*

Secondary, or Deputy Coroner (secondary, as in the Exchequer, simply meaning chief assistant)
(*Plea Side*)
*Chief Clerk; 2 co-Clerks in the 1620's, and again in the 1640's
Secondary
*2 Custodes Brevium
*Marshal, or Keeper of the Marshalsea prison
Deputy Marshal
*Chirographer (engrosser of fines)
2-3 Filazers (filers of original writs)
Usher; lesser clerks, under-clerks, porters, etc.

    (*Note.* Not only had the number of Filazers shrunk from 13 to 2 or 3 since the mid-fifteenth century, but in the 1620's and 1630's some of the other minor posts may well have been combined, or held *in commendam* with more important ones. In 1740 according to Holdsworth, there was an officer called the Secondary or Master, on the Plea Side; in the 1630's the Chief Clerk himself was sometimes referred to as the Master.)

TABLE 77. PALACE COURT, ALIAS COURTS OF THE VERGE AND THE MARSHALSEA

Treasurer of the Household ⎫
Comptroller of the Household ⎬(all *ex officio*)
The Knight Marshal ⎭
*Steward of the Marshalsea
Coroner and Verger of the Household (seems to have been the only other officer)

TABLE 78. COMMON PLEAS

*Chief Justice (in theory the equal of the Chief Baron of the Exchequer, in practice more important)
*3 Puisne Justices
*Chief Prothonotary (occupied a position comparable to that of the Chief Clerk in King's Bench, but shared it with his two colleagues)
*2 Prothonotaries
*Custos Brevium (more important than his equivalent in King's Bench)
*2 Chirographers (in 1630's; normally a single post)
(*1) *c.* 12 Filazers (the senior Filazer seems to have enjoyed a superior status to the others)
*Exigenter (sent out writs ordering sheriffs to summon defendants)
*Clerk of Treasury of Common Pleas (presumably equivalent to the Clerk of the Hanaper in Chancery)

*2 Clerks of Pleas on Writs of Errors in Common Pleas and Exchequer, also known as Clerks of Errors (set up in 1625, extended to King's Bench in 1632)

Usher

*Keeper of Westminster Palace (also Warden of the Fleet Prison)

under-clerks (*c.* 6, assuming that the staff of the court was unchanged since the fifteenth century)

porters, etc.

TABLE 79. CHANCERY

*Lord Chancellor or Lord Keeper

*Master of the Rolls (second senior equity judge; legal adviser to the Crown; until 1636 also a Privy Councillor)

*12 Masters (the subsidiary equity judges)

*The Six clerks (also Clerks of the Enrolments; no case or other legal business could proceed without being allocated to one of the Six, who then saw it through the court; their role was comparable to that of the Chief Clerk of King's Bench or the Prothonotaries of Common Pleas. They had a staff of between 48 and 60 under clerks)

*Registrar (kept registers of all cases)

*Prothonotary (concerned with legal and administrative sides of the court's work)

*2 Registers of Affidavits

*Clerk of the Crown and 3 under clerks (also concerned with legal and administrative sides)

*Usher or Porter (a man of substance, like the Chief Usher of the Exchequer)

*1-2 Clerks of Subpoena Office and/or Writers of Subpoenas (unclear whether these are identical or not)

*2 Examiners; checked the docquets of case records

22 Cursitors; made out the ordinary, *de cursu*, writs

The following were neither engaged in the ordinary legal business of Chancery, nor in its work as a regular part of the Central Executive:

*Clerk of Presentations ⎱ concerned with the Lord Chancellor's duty of
*Clerk of Faculties ⎰ presenting parsons to Crown livings and granting ecclesiastical dispensations

*Clerk of custody of wardships and Post Mortems (his relations with the Court of Wards are not clear)

**2-4 Clerks of Rolls Chapel

*Writer of leases to the Great Seal

*Clerk of protection for losses

*Register of Bankrupts

*Clerk of denizations (in charge of the registration of aliens and their applications for naturalization)

*2 Auditors

TABLE 80. REQUESTS

*(Lord Privy Seal)
*4 Masters of Requests
*Registrar, or Clerk of the Court
 (presumably) Usher, Porters, under-clerks

TABLE 81. STAR CHAMBER

All Privy Councillors *ex officio* (numbered 28-42, 1625-40)
Lord Chief Justice of King's Bench
Chief Justice of Common Pleas
Attorney-General (always appeared for the Crown in major cases)
*1-2 Clerks of the Council in Star Chamber
*Deputy Clerk; 2-4 under-clerks
 (Registrar; possibly combined with Clerkship in 1630's)
Usher; Steward, Butler, and small kitchen staff.
2 Examiners for the King's causes
Clerk of Files and Warrants
Clerk of Affidavits
Clerk of Records

TABLE 82. EXCHEQUER CHAMBER

*Clerk
1-2 under-clerks
Keeper
Porter

TABLE 83. COUNCIL IN THE NORTH

*Secretary and Keeper of the Signet
*Attorney
*Clerk of the bills, proceedings, etc.
 Clerk of the Tickets
 Keeper of the bills of complaint, answers, etc.
 Secretary's clerk
 2 Clerks of the Seal (or Signet)
 Clerk of the Court, or Registrar
*Clerk of the King's letters
 2 Examiners
 There were also a Sergeant, a Pursuivant, attorneys, under-clerks,
   collectors of fines, porters and ushers

485

TABLE 84. COUNCIL IN THE MARCHES OF WALES

*Clerk of the Council (the principal executive officer, he was also Secretary and Clerk of the Signet; an absentee courtier throughout James's and Charles's reigns)
*Deputy Clerk, and probably 3-4 principal under-clerks
*Attorney
*Solicitor
*Remembrancer (kept a register of all cases, as a check on the Attorney)
*Examiners (in charge of all depositions by witnesses)
*Clerk of the billets (new since 1620's, perhaps also an offshoot originally from the Clerk's office)
*Clerk Receiver of Fines (*alias* Clerk of the Fines, perhaps also known as Auditor of Fines, unless this was a separate post)
Steward and Marshal of Ludlow Castle (head of the Lord President's household staff)
Porter and Gaol-keeper of Ludlow Castle
Sergeant at arms, pursuivants, under-clerks, attorneys, etc.

TABLE 85. THE HIGH COMMISSION

*Chief Registrar
*King's Advocate (equivalent of King's Attorney in other courts)
*2 Clerks of the Acts or co-Registrars
Usher, porter, etc.
Proctors (equivalent to attorneys in lay courts)

TABLE 86. ECCLESIASTICAL COURTS

(a) *The Court of Delegates* (jurisdiction over both Provinces)
   *Registrar
(b) *The Court of the Arches* (jurisdiction over Province of Canterbury)
   *Dean of the Arches
(c) *The Court of Audience*
   *Judge
(d) *Prerogative Court of Canterbury*
   *Judge (or commissary; in charge of wills and probate)
(e) *Court of the Archbishop's Vicar-General*
   *Vicar-General

TABLE 87. COURT OF ADMIRALTY

*Judge
*Registrar (also Registrar of the Court of Delegates, if it ever met, from *c.* 1631 to 1639)
Deputy Registrar
Proctor
Marshal
(presumably) other proctors or advocates, and under-clerks

APPENDIX

TABLE 88. THE STANNARIES

*The Lord Warden (in practice also Steward of the Duchy of Cornwall)
*The Vice-Warden (the effective judicial and executive officer)
  Stewards (in charge of district courts, subordinate to the Vice-Warden's court)
  (presumably) Clerk of the Court, and other under-officers

TABLE 89. PARLIAMENT

*The Gentleman Usher, Black Rod (technically a Chamber officer, he announced adjournments, and summoned the House to hear the King or Lord Keeper announce dissolutions)
*Clerk to the Parliaments (kept the Lords Journals, and was really the Clerk to the House of Lords)
*Assistant or Under-Clerk (kept the Commons Journals, and was really Clerk to the House of Commons)
  2 Sergeants-at-arms in ordinary (One was allocated to attend each House during sittings. In the Commons the Sergeant's duties were to bear the mace, to bring offending members of the public to the bar of the House, and to remove members who offended the House)

INDEX

Abbott, George, Archbishop of Canterbury, 345

Ability, and entry to office, 93-6, 275-7; and professional administrators, 282

Absentee office-holders, 279, 281, 374, 419

Absenteeism. *See* Deputies; Pluralism; Sinecures

Acquittances, or Constats, 36

Act, of Edward VI, against sale of offices, 190, 228, 229, 233; Star Chamber, of 1641, 47, 408, 436

Administration, definition of, 9-10, 12

Administrative, or economical reform, 61-3, 123, 195, 233-4, 434, 436, 438

Administrative System, 2, 6, 66, 68, 159, 237-9, 417, 420-2, 448, 464-6; economic importance of, 239-52; historic development of, 422-39, 461, 466-8; historical importance of, 467-468

Administrators, definition of, 9-10; professional, 279-82, 460-1

Admiral, Lord. *See* Lord Admiral; Buckingham; James, Duke of York; Northumberland

Admiral (or Vice-Admiral) of the Narrow Seas, 91, 102, 222, 232 (*see also* Mervyn)

Admiralty, Board of, 446

Court of, 52, 53-4, 137n., 151, 189; allegiance of officers of, 405; Judge of, 53, 353, (*see also* Marten); list of posts in, 486; total of fees in, 245

Commissioners, 22, 106, 123, 151, 232; Clerk of, 434; Secretary to, 133

Agents, or Residents, English abroad, 14, 25-6 (*see also* Augier; Browne, Richard; Carleton; de Vic; Gerbier; Hopton; Nethersole; Trumbull)

Aitoun or Aytoun, Sir Robert (the Queen's Sec.), 162

Alienations Office, 151, 222, 391, 408, allegiance of officers of, 405, 408, 418; Clerk of, 222; Commissioner of, 222; functions of, 40; investigation of fees in, 194; list of posts in, 479; total of fees in, 245

Alington, Sir Giles, 368

Allowances, paid to office-holders, 163, 166, 169, 171, 182

Alum, 288, 341

Ambassadors, English abroad, 14, 25-26, 320-1, 339n., 389-90 (*see also* Aston; Boswell; Crowe; Hopton; Leicester; Roe; Wyche)

Ancient Course. *See* Exchequer

Ancrum, Robert Carr, 1st Earl of (Keeper of the Privy Purse), 347, 385

Anglesey. *See* Villiers

Anglicans, holding office, 383-4, 404

Anglo-Catholics. *See* Arminians

Anglo-Norman Kings, 451

Anglo-Saxons, government of, 423-4

Anne of Denmark, 352

Annuities, paid to office-holders, 160, 161-5, 204-10; traffic in, 224

Anticipation, 67, 195-6

Antiquarians, as fee commissioners, 191, 194; holding office, 279

Appointment to Offices, 69-96, 159, 274-5, 277, 315, 334, 430, 433; rights of, 69-74, 96, 100-1, 460

Apsley, Sir Allen (lieut. of the Tower; Victualler of the Navy); mode of entry to office, 85; owed money by Crown, 75, 321; seeks reversion, 74-5

Archbishop. *See* Canterbury; *also* Abbott; Bancroft; Laud; York

Arches, Court of the, 52, 151; Dean of the, 52-3, 353 (*see also* Lambe; Marten)

Armiger. *See* Esquire

Lawyers, 326, 332, 429, 451 (*see also* Chancery; Civil; Common Lawyers) allegiance of, 418-19; as fee commissioners, 194; as fee payers, 202; as office-holders, 94-6, 240, 258, 276, 278-82, 412, 444; in relation to the administrative system, 251-2; total numbers and wealth of, 328-9
Leasehold. *See* Tenure of Offices
Leicester, Robert Dudley, Earl of, 147
Leicester, Robert Sidney, 2nd Earl of (Ambassador in Paris), 345; allegiance of, 365, 371; disappointed in 1640, 364; goes unpaid, 321
Leicestershire, 268; families connected with, 285-7
Lennox, James Stuart, 4th Duke of, also Earl of March and later Duke of Richmond (Lord Warden of the Cinque Ports), 350-1
Levellers, 434, 463
Ley, James, 1st Earl of Marlborough (Lord Treasurer), 320; ineffectiveness of, 39, 61; transfer and death of, 88-9
Life (and lives). *See* Tenure of Offices
Lincoln's Inn, 178, 273 (*see also* Inns of Court)
Lincolnshire, 268; families connected with, 86, 284, 285
Lindsey, Robert Bertie, 1st Earl of, formerly Lord B. of Eresby (Lord Great Chamberlain), 107
Livery, as a form of fiscal feudalism, 33, 407; as a form of payment of office-holders, 160, 172-3
Loans, expected by the Crown, 193, 200-1, 237, 239; made by Ric. Colchester, 295-8, Geo. Mynne, 120, 301-2, Edw. Nicholas, 317-18, Ro. Wolseley, 303-4; made to the Crown 165, 201, 307, 310, 348n., 380, Crown and Parliament, 312, 380
Loftus, Adam, 1st Viscount (Lord Chancellor of Ireland), 364, 371, 415
London (and Westminster), 67, 150-3, 267-71, 410-11; Bishop of (*see* Laud); Citizens of, 262, 263, 277; families connected with, 78, 86, 255, 312, 316, 396-7; Guildhall of, 337; (Livery) Companies of, 198, 255; Lord Mayor and Sheriffs of, 434
Londoners, 268, 270, 411

Long, Robert (Receiver of Recusant Revenues; Queen's Surveyor-General), 139, 321, 368
Lord Admiral, 21, 231 (*see also* Buckingham; Northumberland; Nottingham); Secretary to, 133 (*see also* Nicholas; Smith); value of office of, 211
Lord Chamberlain, 84 (*see also* Essex; Pembroke); diet of, 168; estimated income of, 206; powers and duties of, 21, 29-30; tenure of, 111
Lord Chancellor. *See* Great Seal, Lord Keeper of
Lord Deputy. *See* Ireland
Lord Great Chamberlain, 21, 107
Lord Lieutenant of Ireland. *See* Wentworth
Lord Lieutenants. *See* Officers, Local
Lord President of the Council, 17; powers and duties of, 14, 21; promotion to office of, 88-9, 110; tenure of, 111; value of office of, 211
Lord President of the North. *See* North
Lord President of Wales. *See* Wales
Lord Privy Seal, 235-6 (*see also* Manchester; Worcester); as head of Court of Requests, 47; movements of, in 1642, 410; powers and duties of, 14, 15, 21; relation of, to Household, 31, 169; tenure of, 111; value of office of, 211
Lord Steward, 128 (*see also* Pembroke) diet of, 168; estimated income of, 205; office of, at Buckingham's disposal, 345; powers and duties of, 21, 27, 30; tenure of, 111
Lord Treasurer, 11n., 61, 75, 84, 114, 116, 166, 235, 236, 307, 465 (*see also* Burghley; Cranfield; Juxon; Ley; Manchester; Salisbury; Suffolk; Weston); allegations against, 195-6; also Master of the Wards, 32; and Recusant Revenues, 139; capital and annual value of office of, 221; dismissal of, 365; entry to office of, 229, 231; in charge of Alienations, 40; income of, 203, 211; pension paid to, 161; powers and duties of, 15, 21, 37-9, 49, 161, 184, 312, 432, 435; promotion to office of, 111; secretaries of, 139, 339n.; temptation of, 180; tenure of, 111

Ordnance Office,—*contd.*
231, 290 (*see also* Carew; Newport; Vere); Master Gunner of, 254; officers of, 145, 153, 254, 346, 350, 410; offices in, 92, 123, 215; principal officers of, 169, 446; site of, 150; Surveyor of, 165, 208, 230, 290 (*see also* Bludder; Harris)

Osborne, family of, 284, 321, 411

Overbury, Sir Thomas, 83, 85

Oxford, 410-11 (*see also* Universities)

Oxfordshire, 268; familes connected with, 79-80, 294-300; proposed Knights in, 330

Packer, John (Clerk of the Privy Seal); a representative office-holder, 156-8; probable attitude in 1630's, 358

Palace Court, 45, 141; list of posts in, 483; officers of, 141

Palace of Whitehall, 151, 153, 409

Palatine, Elector and his brothers, 172, 341

Palatine, Electress. *See* Elizabeth, Queen of Bohemia

Palmer, Sir Henry, the elder, 102; the younger (Comptroller of the Navy), 102

Pardons, for offences in offices, 100, 199, 211, 304, 307, 362 (*see also* Compositions); offered by the King (1643), 410

Parishes (*see* Officers, Local), fees in, 194, 198

Parker, Henry, 434

Parkhurst, Robert (acting Clerk of the Hanaper), 120-1

Parkhurst, Sir William (co-Warden of the Mint), 372, 374-6

Parkinson, C. N., and Parkinson's Law, 129, 130n., 133, 137, 159

Parliament, 20, 57-9, 60, 337, 340-1, 427, 444, 465-6 (*see also* Act; House of Commons; House of Lords; M.P.s; Peers); of 1571, 183; of 1606, 185-6; of 1604-11, 187; of 1621, 188-91; of 1624, 1625, and 1626, 192-3; of 1625, 229; of 1626, 229; of 1629, 375; of the 1620's, 229, 293, 351-6; Addled (of 1614), 187; Barebones, or Little (of 1653), 434, 436, 467; Convention (of 1660),

212; Long (of 1640-53 and 1659-60), 66, 149, 213, 255, 293, 377, 379, 380, 383, 404, 421, 464, divisions of allegiance in, 393, 402-3, historians of, 384 (*see also* Brunton; Keeler; Pennington), measures of, affecting office-holders, 98, 145, 212, 225, 371, 386-7, 391-2, 407, 410-11, 431, 433-4, 435, speech in (1642), 381-2; Second Protectorate (of 1656-8), 391; Short (of 1640), 293; Clerk of, 435; list of staff of, 487

Parliament's Quarters, in the Civil War, 395-6, 399, 411, 413

Parliamentarians, in the Civil War, 464; office holders who were, 116, 319, 343-4, 363-71, 382, 384-6, 387, 393-421; passive or neutrally-inclined, 312, 380-1, 388, 393-421

Parry, J. H., 452

Patent, for a lighthouse, 247

Patents and Patentees (*see* Appointment; Commissions; Great Seal; Monopolies; Tenure), fees for, 178

Patrimony, and entry to office, 82-96, 156, 258, 265, 274

Patronage (or Clientage), and entry to office, 69-96, 156-7, 219, 258, 270, 274, 308-13, 360, 362, 390, 430

Paul, Sir George (Registrar of High Commission), 305-6

Peerage, 128, 260, 271n., 276, 340

Peers, 12, 20, 58-9, 178, 224, 240, 255, 265-266, 333, 368, 433 (*see also* House of Lords); allegiance of office-holding, 395, 401-2, 412-16; court, 77; creation of, 193, 332; numbers of, 323-5; of England and of Ireland and Scotland, 324; opposition leaders among (1640-1), 11; sons of, 261, 263-5; wealth of, 326-31

Pell, Sir Anthony, 180n.

Pell of Issue, 184

Pells, Clerk of (*see also* Wardour), allegiance of, 420; duties of, 37, 478n., estimated income of, 209; struggle of, with Auditor of Receipt, 183-4; succession in office of, 81

Pembroke, Philip Herbert, 4th Earl of and 1st Earl of Montgomery (Lord Chamberlain), 30; allegiance of, 365; appeal to. 84; as patron, 361, 381; material interests of, 349; opposition

Pembroke,—*contd.*
to Buckingham by, 61, 345; pluralist, 126; quarrel of, with Earl of Holland, 70; royal favourite, 92
Pembroke, William Herbert, 3rd Earl of (sometime Lord Chamberlain; Lord Steward), 30; opposition to Buckingham by, 61, 345; orders from, 128, 172; pluralist, 126
Pembrokeshire, 120, 395 (*see also* Wales)
Pennington, D. H., 393, 402-3
Pensioners. *See* Gentlemen
Pensions, granted by the Crown, 114, 160, 161-5, 204-10, 220, 349-50; non-existence of retirement, 165; traffic in, 224
Pepys, Samuel, 80, 150, 153, 154, 156, 158, 218
Percy family, 81 (*see also* Northumberland
Perquisites, payment of office-holders in, 160, 171-2, 449
Peter, Hugh, 434, 436
Petitions, 13-15, 236n., 303
Pett, Phineas (Master Shipwright), 149, 254
Petty, Sir William, 247-8
Phillipps, Francis (Revenue Auditor), 411
Pipe, Clerk of, 91, 131, 184, 187-8, 196-200, 217, 339, 420 (*see also* Croke; Rouse), annual and capital value of office of, 222, estimated income of, 208; Comptroller of, 184, 187, 316 (*see also* Vernon), estimated income of, 208; Secondaries of, 164, 187, 315-16 (*see also* Vernon); Secondary of, estimated income of First, 209; Office, 34, 37, 138-9, 435, 466, attorneys in, 56, fees in, 184, 191-2, 194-5, 196-200, under-clerks in, 188, 192, 194, 314-15
Pitt, Edward (Teller), 90, 388
Pitt, George (Usher of Chancery), 362
Pitt, John, 90
Pitt, Sir William, 90
Pleasure. *See* Tenure of Offices
Plebeian, rank of, 262-3
Pluralism among office-holders, 125-7, 132-6, 159, 165, 275
Policy, definition of, 10-11
Pooh Bah-ism, 133, 159

Poor, legacies for, 310, 313
Poor people as fee-payers, 202-3
Population, in seventeenth century, 322-3; different social classes, 323-331
Portage, 166-7, 450
Porter, Endymion (Groom of the Bedchamber), allegiance of, 385; allowed to enclose, 338; as Deputy Postmaster, 129-30, 369-70; Catholic sympathies of, 357; patrons of, 79; royal favourite, 132; usefulness of, 92
Portions, paid by office-holders, 310, 313, 316, 319; paid to office-holders, or their sons, 296, 303, 304, 306, 313, 316, 373
Portland. *See* Weston
Postmaster, 93, 103-4 (*see also* Burlamachi; de Quester; Frizell; Witherings)
Postmaster-General, 81, 129 (*see also* Secretaries of State; Stanhope)
Posts (or Post Office), 22, 62-3, 369-71, 415; list of posts in, 471
Posts (or letter-carriers), 14, 23
Poundage, 166-7, 433, 450
Povey, Justinian (Revenue Auditor; Auditor to the Queen), 390, 411
Prerogative, royal, 251, 340 (*see also* Charles I; Crown; King); Courts, 44, 47-51, 57, offices in, 95
Presbyterians, 418
Presents. *See* Gratuities
Presidents. *See* Lord President; North; Wales
Prests, 35 (*see also* Imprests, Auditors of)
Price Revolution, 175-6
Primogeniture, and office-holding, 259, 264-5, 271-2
Prince, the. *See* Charles; *see also* Charles I when Prince, and Henry
Princes. *See* Palatine
Prisons, royal, 174, 238 (*see also* Fleet; Gatehouse; Tower); fees in, 194, 198; list of posts in, 481
Privileges, legal, of office-holders, 173-174
Privy Chamber. *See* Chamber
Privy Council, 8, 49, 67-8, 95, 140-1, 148, 153, 154, 166, 234, 236, 431, 460; Clerks of, 103, 154, 362 (*see also* Becher; Boswell; Browne; Carleton; Jacob; Meautys; Nicholas Trumbull; Whitaker), allegiance of